MARKETING
From Scratch
THE INSIDE SKINNY
Third Edition

David Strutton
Kenneth Thompson

University of North Texas

Kendall Hunt
publishing company

Cover image © Shutterstock.com

All interior images not otherwise credited are courtesy of the authors.

Kendall Hunt
publishing company

www.kendallhunt.com
Send all inquiries to:
4050 Westmark Drive
Dubuque, IA 52004-1840

Copyright © 2019, 2020, 2021 by Dr. David Strutton and Dr. Kenneth Thompson

PAK ISBN: 978-1-7924-7339-5
Text ISBN: 978-1-7924-7340-1

Kendall Hunt Publishing Company has the exclusive rights to reproduce this work, to prepare derivative works from this work, to publicly distribute this work, to publicly perform this work and to publicly display this work.

All rights reserved. No part of this publication may be reproduced, stored in a retrieval system, or transmitted, in any form or by any means, electronic, mechanical, photocopying, recording, or otherwise, without the prior written permission of the copyright owner.

Published in the United States of America

DEDICATION

For Thressa, Ariadne, Dani, Stella, Emma, and Jude
—Dr. David Strutton

For Patricia
—Dr. Kenneth Thompson

ACKNOWLEDGMENTS

The authors thank Professors Aaron Schibik and Zachary Plunk for their material contributions to this text.

Prologue...vii

SECTION I Introducing Marketing Concepts, Issues, and Principles.........................1

    MODULE 1 Marketing Fundamentals 3

    MODULE 2 Marketing-Level Planning.. 57

    MODULE 3 Strategic-Level Planning 101

    MODULE 4 Segmentation, Targeting, and Positioning 137

SECTION II Framing Key Marketing Issues 179

    MODULE 5 The Environment 181

    MODULE 6 Research 209

    MODULE 7 Consumer Behavior... 237

    MODULE 8 Marketing Ethics and Social Responsibility..................... 289

SECTION III Managing Key Marketing Activities 341

    MODULE 9 Managing Products, Services, and the Product Life Cycle 343

    MODULE 10 Managing New Product Development 379

    MODULE 11 Managing Brands and Branding................................ 433

    MODULE 12 Managing Supply Chains and Logistics 465

    MODULE 13 Managing Pricing... 517

    MODULE 14 Managing Marketing Communication 571

    Glossary 653

PROLOGUE

Skinny . . .

The word skinny can mean thin or resembling skin. Okay. But neither dog hunts here.

Skinny also implies "naked" or "uncovered," as in the naked or full truth. That take on skinny preaches anywhere, but especially here. The stories told inside *The Inside Skinny* uncover many marketing truths that other books are loath to address for various reasons.

The word skinny may likewise be leveraged to transmit notions—the idea—that "inside information" is about to be revealed. This usage works here as well. Marketing knowledge and insights, of the insider-out sort, pervade *The Inside Skinny*.

Even so, here's the real "inside skinny" about marketing and marketing practice:

- ▶ Marketing is everything. Nothing happens and no one gets paid until someone sells something.
- ▶ Marketing is everywhere. Yes, marketing is legitimately omnipresent.
- ▶ Almost everyone is a marketer. Most people, but especially professionals, seek to vigorously promote themselves and their ideas, professionals generally strive not just to be listened to but also heard; they routinely scramble to elevate or sustain their influence or power—some professionals simply execute these tasks with greater grace and élan, and the differences in their skill sets and how effectively they execute those capabilities shows up most vividly in their promotions and paychecks. Think about ducks or even swans swimming on the pond. Each waterfowl is so beautiful, eloquent, and placid as it seemingly skims across the surface; but underneath, they are paddling—working—like you know what below. That's how many accomplished professionals seek to market and promote their value; winning the day without anyone seeing them sweat.
- ▶ Everybody is definitely a consumer; functioning as prospective or actual customers constantly seeking to take away the most "value" in every seller-buyer exchange, however that critical term "value" is defined, for themselves.

But that's not the entire "inside skinny" about marketing:

- ▶ Marketing also effects and affects everything and everyone.
- ▶ Everything good, bad, or indifferent that is happening anywhere inside domestic or global markets, societies and cultures emerge and thereafter sustain, expand, languish, or entirely disappear as a direct or indirect result of marketing.

And yes, here we write everything; we could be referencing physical phenomena such as sneakers or jeans and/or ideas such as climate change, #me-too, Pro-Life versus Pro-Choice, or Black Lives Matter that are routinely being marketed vigorously. Because if you've purchased the idea that climate change marketers have been selling—the notion that human activities are primarily powering climate change (too much fossil fuel consumption, too many cattle farting, too much methane, too little solar power) are primarily causing climate changes—what else that is not directly also marketing-related is causing the problems? After all, the idea that too much fossil fuel production and consumption exists is entirely marketing-related. As is too many cattle farting too much methane into the atmosphere because too many American consumers feel and think they are not eating unless they are consuming beef. Or what about too little solar power being produced or used; that's a marketing thing too.

As we wrote: *Marketing is everything.* Given this, surely now is a good time to learn more about the discipline, business function, and profession.

The wealth and welfare of nations and their consumer populations can radically improve, seemingly overnight, primarily due to marketing. Think China, a nation that evolved from a global afterthought to a "cannot-stop-thinking-about-the-nation" status during a historically short forty-year period.

Relatively harmonious and highly productive cultures emerge and sustain their successful status across time as a result of their good to great marketing strategies and practices. Think Australia, a nation that truly punches above its weight class on a global stage.

Legions of machines that don't just answer but ask questions can emerge, these miracles arose entirely as a consequence of extremely innovative and brutally efficient marketing competition. Which human-like marketing machine do you love the most? Alexa, Echo, or Siri? Or something else altogether?

Remarkable solutions that literally could be carried around in pockets; but solutions so alluring that they rarely leave consumers' hands. Nothing else but marketing is responsible for these solutions and for the myriad consumer problems that these technological solutions are creating. Hurt me, leave me, cheat on me—but please, please don't take my smartphone from me.

Tremendous wealth, by global standards, is now shared among high percentages of the citizens of most modern nations, all due to marketing-driven capitalism.[1] There has never been a better time or place in which to live than right now on Planet Earth. What, you thought there was nothing but a prevailing 24/7 crap storm swirling around out there around you and across the globe? As *Public Enemy* rapped *Don't Believe the Hype*. The media—each of whom themselves who are nothing more than marketers, every one—are merely competing against each other by broadcasting or posting stories

---

1. Capitalism disproportionally rewards winners, which means capitalism is harder on losers than winners. Even so, by global standards capitalistic economies produce far less onerous results for most citizens who are fortunate enough to live and work inside them. Opponents of capitalism, for example, might try out socialism, communism, or anarchy for five to ten years, and see how their experiences with the experience plays out. But inside today's capitalistic markets many people who occupy the vast middle often feel like comparative losers inside social networks where many peers repeatedly communicate selected and carefully curated highlights of their otherwise mundane lives. These social-networking processes often create perceived, as in merely imagined, problems. These feelings, however, feel like problems, nonetheless. The fact that marketers routinely inspire social comparisons that often end up making consumers "less-than-satisfied" with their current lots does little to promote the actual values of capitalism, either.

designed either to scare you, piss you off, or otherwise mess around with viewers' or hearers' emotions in order to get one more set of ears or eyeballs to pay attention to the media message for three to five seconds longer.

Get marketing wrong or use marketing under false pretenses to manipulate human minds into thinking non-productive thoughts, however, and everything everywhere spins awry. Previously generally compatible societies might even begin tearing their formerly unifying traditional sociocultural fabrics apart. Oh, please, wait . . . but there's no better way to phrase this, think the *United States,* right now. Seems like inside the current domestic political marketing climate many sellers (politicians) and buyers (voters) appear collectively determined to prove the truth of a 140-plus-year-old adage primarily attributed to *Mark Twain:* "It is easier to fool people than to convince them that they have been fooled."

Successful marketing efforts open doors that few would want to shut. Failed marketing efforts close doors that few, other than successful marketers, can reopen.

Ready to open up your professional and/or your organizational doors . . . to the prospect of unprecedented success? And then to jam the door stuck at open?

There's no point in not admitting that many people and organizations want and need to be better marketers. The workday will arise in most readers' professional lives, likely sooner than later, when they discover it is as or more important to effectively manage and market to those to whom they report than it is to effectively manage and market to people reporting to them. The success or failure of their future professional managerial efforts will consequently unfold based on how effectively or ineffectively readers market.

Just as there's no point denying that most humans or organizations covet more opportunities to exercise greater power and influence—always, supposedly for the right reasons. No reasonable way exists to deny the power of influence, or the influence of power. Or, for that matter, to deny that the phrase "to influence" is simply a kinder and gentler version of the phrase "to manipulate." Yet notions of manipulation itself are not universally onerous. The morality or immorality of manipulation depends on the motives driving the marketing influencer who is seeking to manipulate—no, we meant, "influence"—targeted others.

Real winners and losers emerge and sustain/elevate themselves as best as they can in the modern and highly competitive world that marketing has created. For better or worse the differences in terms of financial payoffs or happier lives that separate marketing winners from marketing losers grow by the day. Marketing knowledge is uniformly empowering. Meanwhile, consciously or unconsciously remaining ignorant about marketing practices—and about how best to do marketing to others as they do marketing to you—uniformly punishes the uninformed.[2] And whether marketers or customers end up winning or losing pivots almost entirely based on two factors. First, who is better or worse at telling and selling? And second, who is better or worse at choosing and consequently winning or losing?

---

2. Ignorance of any sort basically always represents a problem. As *Charles Darwin* wrote: "Ignorance more frequently builds confidence"—the wrong sort of self-assurance, by the way—"than does knowledge." Ignorance, in brief, is rarely blissful.

The Inside Skinny demonstrably illustrates how best to create and choose, and then tell and sell, marketing stories.

Principles . . .

Principles, marketing or otherwise, are foundational. Architects know that the larger and stronger the foundation, the stronger and taller the structure. The structure; okay, the book that is built out below houses all traditional and contemporary marketing ideas, issues, and principles. The lessons embedded inside *The Inside Skinny* can lead readers to a promised land where huge amounts of useful and appropriate marketing knowledge is currently housed. But the book will not pull them there. No, readers will have to push themselves to get this job done. But perhaps knowing that books are to smart people what the whetstone is to the knife, as *Tyrion Lannister* (yes, of course that Tyrion) said during *Game of Thorns*. Books sharpen everyone's mind. But only when they are read.

The Inside Skinny takes established marketing principles and recasts them in a new light by passing those principles through metaphorical marketing, environmental, and economic prisms to reveal various truths about key marketing success factors that have always existed inside them. During the seventeenth century *Sir Isaac Newton* did something similar when he passed white light through actual prisms to reveal colors that had been present all along inside the white light. *The Inside Skinny* provides accurate and timely information and reveals new insights and colors about foundational marketing principles and practices. At times, the book reveals various innovative marketing principles and practices that even many experienced and knowledgeable business decision-makers and consumers have not learned about . . . yet.

Advantage, readers; if they put in the effort necessary to exploit the opportunity to learn from this book. Yet many may seek shortcuts to the answers to pressing questions as they read this book. Those who choose this path of least resistance and less effort will literally and figuratively sell-themselves-short because they failed to learn enough to question this book's answers. Of course many readers will do this because the path of least resistance is the road most traveled because it's the easiest.

But to not read this book represents a mistake, one that many visit voluntary misfortunes on readers' present-day and future selves. (Missed opportunities to learn are a . . . .) During the nineteenth century *Frederick Douglass* discovered that reading proved the key to his personal freedom and rapid social/economic elevation from his former plight as a slave. Douglass wrote that he understood why his former masters deliberately withheld literacy from their slaves precisely because he understood that reading was so valuable, so life-giving, and conferred so many benefits to its practitioners.[3] There is so much to learn and apply to one's future or contemporary professional life among those who choose to read this or many other books deeply.

Yet many may refuse to follow this deep-read path—largely because they're unaccustomed to reading long-form text. For many people reading real books seems too much like work after having spent so much time peering into small rectangular screens while reading or sending texts and tweets.

Here's another skinny chunk of insider intelligence. Attempts to understand the text that follows by consuming *ESPN Sports Center*-like highlighted snippets of it probably will end poorly. *The Inside*

---

3. Robert L. Woodson and Joshua Mitchell, "How the Left Hijacked Civil Rights," *The Wall Street Journal* (January 16/17, 2021): A11.

Skinny unfolds in the same manner that, augh, math books unfold. Implying, readers must understand the initial principles and concepts presented in the first three Modules before they can master the illustrative applications that follow inside the other eleven Modules that follow.

So, go deep from the jump, by intensely learning and connecting the key foundational marketing concepts, principles, and issues introduced early on in order to understand the higher-order concepts, principles, and issues that must be learned later. Readers failing to connect later content with information that preceded it likely will get left behind as their performance falls-off. Context usually matters, and context certainly matters here. And unless readers establish proper marketing principle context early on, they may get conned by the text. Conned, as in missing out on key insights and failing to acquire key values, essentially wasting their time because they haven't learned what they should learn from any effective marketing foundations course.

Principles, being principles, never fundamentally change—accountants will always use balance sheets; for individual investors, the "Rule of 72" or "Dollar Cost Averaging" will always apply; for marketing managers, the marketing mix, and segmentation and targeting and positioning will always be BIG things. But marketing principles are constantly being shaped, refined, and rendered more or less important, useful, and relevant as those principles collide with dynamic technologies, environmental trends, customer tastes, competitive pressures, or international movements and events that are changing at the speed of baud. ("Baud" is discussed definitionally and practically below.)

The Inside Skinny was born from the idea that marketers need brisk yet inclusive guidelines—principles—through which they can grab sustainable marketing success. And everyone, at varying levels, is engaged in marketing, as explained below. For example, butchers and male or female prostitutes are two different types of marketers who are engaged in the selling of fresh meat, or what can pass as it—this, according to author *Alistair Horne*.[4] At varying times during the buying and selling cycles that butchers and prostitutes each attempt to manage they selectively display (promote) their products and willingly negotiate on prices and the terms of delivery by which those products may be purchased.

Most marketers need this book's stories and the solutions that those story-based lessons provide. Many marketers need *The Inside Skinny*'s solutions so much that they will suffer what could be described as "voluntary misfortunes" if they don't read it. Foremost among these voluntary misfortunes is the distressing fact that nonreaders would not become as successful as they otherwise could have been in business, marketing, and life. Indeed, the successful or unsuccessful execution of marketing principles, processes, and practices is inevitably linked to many life successes or life failures.

The way that most people who live and work in this world will end up not just surviving but actually thriving will entail their providing products or services and their problem-solving values to others that those others want, or actually do need, and are willing to pay for. Say or think what you want about *Steve Jobs*, and even the posthumous reviews of his personality and behavior were decidedly mixed, the man spent his professional life creating and marketing solutions that untold millions of people found useful, entertaining, and well worth paying lots for in order to own and use his products. Jobs spent

---

4. Alistair Horne, *The Fall of Paris* (London: Penguin Random House United Kingdom, 1965).

his professional life fundamentally making billions of people—people called customers—happier than they otherwise would have been had *Apple* and its values and solutions not existed, and he became a many-times-over billionaire as a result. *Aaron Sorkin*, Hollywood television and movie scriptwriter extraordinaire, is extremely wealthy because he has produced highly entertaining products that people really enjoy. And only a purely powerful marketer like *Howard Schultz* could convince so many to pay so much to consume so little of a former commodity. Of course, that's right, the former commodity but now specialty product is coffee.

The Inside Skinny tells fourteen discrete marketing stories. Each story is presented as a Module. Each Module peels back multiple facets of the same story; delivering lesser but still essential parts that coalesce logically inside the primary Module story. Each of the fourteen Module stories directly or indirectly describes one core marketing principle—be it product-related, research-related, promotion-related, supply chain-related, price-related, creativity-related, and so forth—that's not just nice to know but should also be mastered in order to create and sustain marketing success at organizational and professional marketing levels.

Most of the stories presented in *The Inside Skinny* are true. All of them should be believed. Neither preceding description was written in jest. The occasional marketing story that is told below is anecdotal, merely illustrative, as opposed to being embedded in empirical fact, or principled truth. Yet these sorts of stories could prove powerful too, because they exist to make or support important points.

Successful storytellers usually follow three rules.

First, effective storytellers make their audiences care about the story being told. Readers and hearers should care about the 14 stories that follow inside *The Inside Skinny* for three reasons. The first reason is because all audience members are already both marketers and consumers—as noted. The second reason is because every audience member should want, or need, to perform more effectively in each role they play—no one should ever stop striving to improve, least of all you mid-to-late sixty-something-year-old authors. The third reason is because this book vividly demonstrates the relevance of these stories to readers, as all good storytellers should do.

Second, successful storytellers eliminate the parts of their story that no one wants to hear or read, unless the boring elements that still remain actually and actively benefit hearers or readers of the story. "Boring," unfortunately, occasionally happens during the stories told below. But "surprising, interesting, and uniformly-useful" routinely happens there, as well. Or, at least that's the goal.

Third, effective storytellers made the important part or parts of their story appear interesting, quickly! We got this. Why tell stories in, of all things, a textbook? Boring, boring! The answer is because hearers or readers remember the beginnings, ends, and middles of stories better than they recall facts and figures. When told successfully, stories also represent the best way to earn empathy from targeted audiences—here, readers. Empathy, as in understanding how important marketing actually is to their present and future lives.

Honor these three simple storytelling rules, and while we cannot guarantee success, the likelihood that the full story of your professional and personal story will not just be revealed to but also remembered by your audience will rise materially.

Screenwriters *David Benoit* and *D. B. Weiss* wrote the following dialog for key character *Tyrion Lannister* (yes, him again) to utter during the final episode of *Games of Thrones*. Tyrion said: "Stories.

There's nothing in the world more powerful than a good story." Who are we, mere modern mortals who possess neither Meister- or dragon-like powers, to argue?

Need or want more evidence that attests to the power of a good story well-told? The first author's mother taught him as a young boy a biblical parable with an earthly story that had a heavenly meaning. We have not learned a better definition, yet, so let's go with Mom's description of a parable. Well, then, consider this. Jesus often taught from or answered questions based on parables—or stories.

Ever consider the possibility that business textbook authors secretly conspired long ago to ensure that the material they published rarely strayed too close to the realm of "mildly interesting" yet always remained two or more zip codes away from the "profoundly thought-provoking"? Perhaps you have thought about such matters, more likely you have not, but we most assuredly have pondered this possibility. *The Inside Skinny* consequently has purposely been written to be interesting, evocative, and at times provocative. So much so in fact that college students who often rarely seem to enjoy reading deep text may, by turn, actually experience enjoyment or annoyance with various portions of the content that follows. Even annoyance sounds great to us; its arrival definitely demonstrates one thing: readers were paying attention. The creation of enjoyment or annoyance among the recipients of most marketing messages represents major wins for messaging marketers—as explained below.

The Inside Skinny has also been designed to provide students with soft marketing skills. Soft skills, inside marketing settings (note, for the record, almost all public and private settings are marketing settings), are personal traits and interpersonal skills that both characterize and refine for better or worse one person's or marketer's relationship with other people best described as either customers or prospects. Inside any real-world marketplace, anyone's possession of soft marketing skills would clearly prove highly complementary to that person's hard skills, which refer to a person's knowledge and occupational skills.

And, oh yes, lest anyone forgot or somehow never realized it until now the ability to do marketing well is a highly marketable skill. This book has been designed to provide this specific ability and value as well.

By no means do we expect everyone to agree with everything written below. Books that challenge conventional wisdom or thinking; well, they sometimes impose interesting effects on people. Triggers may be alerted; aggressions aggressed; woke readers may get sleepy, sleepy folks may wake up. Who knows, safe shelters may be sought? This book occasionally may assail some certainties that readers possess. Sorry, but not overly so, because certainties can prove dangerous, especially in educational settings and among younger minds. Yet no sides are taken in *The Inside Skinny*, other than the side of an "inside-skinny" take on marketing truth.

If such outcomes result (i.e., alerts, aggresses, awaken-ness or non-sleepy-ness), all the better. As just noted, the reactions themselves imply that folks are paying attention, getting the point, even if they do not always agree with what they're reading. [Do you know how difficult it is to get and sustain people's attention these days? Actually, you probably do, given that you may be experiencing paying attention now!] But everyone reading *The Inside Skinny* will benefit from the reading, with or without agreeing with all the stories or their perspectives.

Denialism takes hold inside cultural, social, political, media, or educational environments whenever hearers, seers, or readers refuse to hear, see, or read other points of view. Denialism—of the points of views held by others who do not "think exactly like us"—is spreading deep and wide inside many contemporary domestic settings. But educational settings are meant to challenge the thinking of students; and to prepare students for business worlds in which they will be expected to defend or promote their positions. But educational materials, such as *The Inside Skinny*, are also meant to teach readers various sorts of critical-marketing-thinking-skills that will help them shape their worlds for the better. For the better, always? Yes, absolutely. Because if people are not constantly solving the problems of others then they cannot righteously lay claim to the honorable brand: MARKETER.

Note:

▶ Brands or brand-able entities are highlighted through the use of *italics* inside *The Inside Skinny*. Products, services, ideas, people, places, nations, politicians, institutions, organizations, and so forth, are all brand-able entities, objects, or ideas. Lots of italics consequently follow because marketing practices themselves routinely entail battles between brands. The occasional *Latin* phrase that appears inside economics, marketing, or other business or cultural contexts are also *italicized*.

SECTION 1

Introducing Marketing Concepts, Issues, and Principles

MODULE 1

Marketing Fundamentals

MARKETING IS...POWERFUL

How powerful is marketing?

Marketing is powerful enough to function like a magic potion that can create and sustain the successes of small, medium, or large organizations. Those organizations can be for-profit or not-for-profit business, institutional, governmental, or merely social in nature. But the potion works only if leaders inside those organizations master and act based on a combination of traditional and innovative marketing principles, processes, and practices. Marketing is similarly powerful enough to function like a magic potion that can create and sustain the successes of individual professionals. But again, only if those professionals master and act based on a combination of conventional and groundbreaking marketing principles, processes, and practices.

The magic potion that good to great marketing practices create and deliver can make small organizations or unknown professionals known. The smaller or lesser-known entities, be they organizations or individuals, then appear larger and better-known. Up to a point, inside most marketing contexts, becoming bigger and/or better-known is a desirable outcome.

Yet the same magic potion that good to great marketing practices create and deliver can make larger organizations or well-known professionals appear smaller and more personal. Larger or better-known entities then appear more accessible and relatable. Inside most marketing contexts, becoming more accessible and appearing or being relatable is generally another set of desirable outcomes.

The practice of marketing permits marketing professionals or organizations to locate and satisfy old or new customers. Or to create and satisfy new customers.

The practice of marketing then helps marketing professionals or organizations become or remain top-of-the-mind with new or old customers.

Marketing communications can operate like laser-targeted megaphones voicing and issuing friendly reminders; delighted-to-see-you greetings; kinder and gentler or in-your-face information; "come-back-to-see-us-again-soon" missives; absolutely pertinent, hilarious; or scare-you-to-death/piss-you-off messaging. Marketing communications often can even deliver two, three, or more of these key marketing communication outcomes at the same time!

Marketing practices can facilitate good outcomes. The values created through marketing efforts can solve problems. Marketing practices can facilitate bad outcomes. The values created by marketing activities can cause problems. The irony is that all four statements that began this paragraph are true—even though the first two statements clearly contradict the last pair. Marketing is often complicated. Marketing is sometimes paradoxical—the nature of paradoxes is discussed in greater detail below in this Module.

The word marketing is a gerund. Gerunds are verbal forms ending in "ing" that are used as nouns, but that convey the meaning of the verb. Okay, *The Inside Skinny's* first and last *English* lesson just ended. What gerund means right here, however, is that the word "marketing" also means "to market." This condition makes marketing an action word. Marketing is an activity that one person or a group of people does to another person or group. The "group" being referenced here usually would be corporations, some other organizational form, or collections of individuals otherwise known as consumers.

Readers' takeaway: Marketing is an action or an activity in which individuals or organizations should routinely engage or do—primarily to others.

WHAT IS MARKETING?

Three ways exist to define marketing. Actually, more than three definitions exist. But these three suffice given this book's purpose. Marketing is:

- The performance of business activities that direct the flow of goods and services from producers to consumers.
  - This is a good supply chain-based definition. The description definitely makes sense, because one of marketing's major functions is to create meaning from meaninglessness by bringing together diverse sets of customer demands with diverse sets of marketer supplies.
    - When one visits *Walmart* you might need dog food, gym socks, and windshield wipers. That's your demand, as a customer. Fortunately but not surprisingly—after all customers typically voluntarily visit *Walmart*—the mega retailer has got the supplies right there in the store for you.
- An organizational function and set of processes for creating, communicating, and delivering value to customers and for managing customer relationships in ways that benefit the organization and its stakeholders.
  - This is a better definition, more closely describing what actually happens inside successful marketing organizations.
- A *social* and *managerial process* through which *individuals* and *groups* obtain what they *need* or *want* by *creating* and *exchanging value* with others.
  - This is the best definition of marketing and is used throughout this book.

Nine individual words or phrases are highlighted above. The marketing implications associated with each highlighted word or phrase are introduced in the next section.

BREAKDOWN DEAD AHEAD: EXAMINING KEY ELEMENTS INSIDE THE BEST MARKETING DEFINITION

Marketing is a *social process*. The fact that marketing entails social processes means humans are always involved in marketing. All people are marketers, whether they realize or accept this fact, and most people engage in marketing, most of the time. Most folks want, often desperately, for others in their lives to listen/pay attention to them; to accept their ideas/recommendations; to be persuaded from their way of thinking to the "marketers" way of thinking/point-of-view.

Everyone, bar none, is likewise a consumer, all the time. No physical and intangible products exist around, on, or at times inside Americans right now that either they or a family member, spouse, friend, or employer did not acquire for them. Intangible products might include services, ideas, or various forms of information and knowledge.

These conditions further imply that normal and expected logical, rational, and profit- and cost-driven motives play out inside marketing processes. Typical goals, of course, include increasing profits or decreasing costs. Various other normal and expected irrational, biased, and emotional motives play out inside the same places.

Marketing is a ***managerial process***. This phrase implies that various strategies and tactics; goals and objectives; and resource advantages and constraints are always in play and should be considered by marketers. This phrase further implies that various external environmental and market-related threats, problems, challenges, and opportunities are always in play and also should be considered. The phrase managerial process finally implies that the relative presence or absence of strengths, weaknesses, or competencies also always play out as normal and expected parts of marketing processes for each and every individual or organizational marketer.

Marketing provides the ways and means through which ***individuals*** and ***groups*** obtain what they want or need. This condition, this fact, implies that consumers[1] as well as organizations are continuously engaged in marketing. Organizations themselves always function as marketers as well as customers because almost all organizations must buy something, often many somethings, before they can successfully market anything.

When consumers are involved in marketing as customers and organizations are involved as marketers, the process is described as B2C marketing. When one or more organizations are involved in marketing as customers and an organization is involved as a marketer, the process is called B2B marketing. The success of B2B marketers is generally driven by their ability to satisfy customer needs. The success of B2C marketers is generally driven by their ability to satisfy customer wants.

Needs, what are they? Needs exist inside human minds and bodies as states of felt deprivation. Needs reside inside the gap between where humans believe, feel, or perceive that they currently exist, and where they want to be. To lesser degrees, wants reside in this same place, or gap. What do humans do when they sense they are residing inside these gaps? They seek satisfactions, or solutions, often through any means available. Solutions, in turn, that either benefit or harm consumers in the short- or long-run.

Going forward, when readers read or see "need" they should think problem—or vice versa. Successful marketers correctly see themselves as need-satisfiers and problem-solvers, and thereafter plan and operate accordingly. Adversity—broadly described as problems—are part of nature and of everyone's existence. Real or imagined obstacles similarly arise inside everyone's or every organization's lives. When marketers are able to help consumers or organizations eliminate their adversity or

---

1. Everyone on earth consumes the values produced by marketers.

overcome their obstacles those consumers and organizations become stronger. So do those marketers' positions[2] inside individual consumer or collective organizational minds.

Marketers committed to earning and sustaining success relatedly should view themselves as both promise-makers and promise-keepers. Yet marketers should not make *Mary Poppins*-like promises. You know, the type of commitments that are easily made and easily broken. And to whom are said promises being made and kept? Yes, to customers and prospects.

Human needs arise naturally. Our needs never really go away, instead they remain more loyal to our human "natures" than the best family dogs. Implying, logically, marketers cannot and do not have to create needs. No, everyone—almost—instinctively experiences varying levels of desire to eat; to drink; to feel like they belong, fit in, or be deemed as cool or at least not invisible to others; to feel safe; and to encounter and/or sustain *agape, filial, erotic,* and/or *storge*[3] types of love in their lives. The list of naturally-arising human needs could have extended on—and on—essentially forever because shortly after any one need is satisfied others naturally arise to take its place.

The nature of human minds induce their owners into endless but often far from quiet vigils. Human minds naturally ponder, remember, or regret and experience preemptive or *post hoc* remorse for what once was or for what could be. Long sentence, yes, and one that's difficult to understand. What the sentence means, however, is this. Humans "create" their own problems (needs) with or without the intervention of marketers. Yet the fact that they do not have to create needs does not mean that marketers don't exploit their awareness of innately-arising human needs for personal or corporate gain—because marketers assuredly do exactly this. Often, marketing efforts to create customers' recognition of real or merely perceived problems may prove so persuasive that, over time, wants are transformed into needs.

This is exactly what happened with the artificial "need" for diamond rings that has long existed inside the *United States*. The desirability of, indeed the seeming social requirement for, diamond-studded engagement rings emerged artificially from a promotional ploy that was strategically created and executed to a fare-thee-well by the crafty *De Beers* diamond cartel around 1900. The popularity of diamond rings declined during and after *World War I* (1914–18) and failed further still during the circa 1930s *Great Depression*. In response, *De Beers* created a new marketing campaign in 1938. The rest is history-making marketing success. The gifting of diamond engagement rings now exists as an obligatory requirement for most couples who are planning to marry inside the U.S. In sum, what once was only a want has long since morphed into something that is very much experienced as a need.

Wants are the form into which needs transform as naturally-arising human needs are shaped by individual personality and culture.

Marketing is powerful. Yet culture is as powerful an influence. Culture is the most basic cause of human wants. People's native cultures, the ones into which they were born or raised, affect their perceptions, motivations, personalities, and emotional responses to myriad marketing and

---

2. The word and concept called "position" is extremely important inside marketing settings, and is discussed repeatedly throughout this and following modules. The meaning of "position" is defined below.

3. In the original Greek, *agape* refers to "spiritual love"; *philia*, to "affectionate love"; *eros*, to "sexual love"; and *storge*, to "family-oriented love."

non-marketing stimuli.[4] However, culture does not cause or create human needs. Needs remain constant regardless of decision-makers' cultural circumstances.

Marketing, meanwhile, is very much a part of every developed culture. Do marketing practices shape culture? The answer is yes. Makes sense, then, that marketing practices can also create or manipulate individual human wants as those same practices shape and reshape culture. And marketing often does exactly that.

Do *American* teenage boys get hungry? Do teenage boys raised in the *Pacific Ocean* island called *Bali* get hungry too? Readers know the answer, times two. That's because hunger needs arise naturally, particularly among teenaged males.

But are these respective segments of teenage boys likely to want the same solution (satisfaction) when the hunger problem (need) arises? Hardly. In truth, their respective cultural experiences have taught male American teenagers to *want* burgers, fries, maybe a little pizza, washed down with *Coke*, whenever they experience the hunger *need*.

What about the *Bali* boys? These young men are more inclined to *want* pork, beans, and fresh fruit juice when experiencing the same need. Why? Because their cultural experiences have taught them to "want" pork, beans, and fresh fruit juice when a hunger need arises naturally within their bodies and minds.

Turning to the highlighted definitional words **create** and **exchange**, exactly what is being created and exchanged? The answer is that **values** are created through customers' acquisition and use of products and exchanged from sellers to buyers. Values are anything, and we mean anything literally, that generates and/or delivers solutions. Marketing values are generally exchanged in return for something else having value. That something else of value, typically, is money.

But not always. Gratitude, for example, could function as a currency. Gratitude has a value that grateful partners can exchange with other partners to either acknowledge and/or signal their appreciation for something of value they gave to or made possible for the grateful partner.

An **exchange** and the **exchange process** entails a giving up and getting back of value. Simply stated, a get and a get is involved inside exchange. This premise holds true during all exchange processes. *Aristotle* acknowledged the importance of exchange, writing "They hold together through exchange."

How important is exchange to marketing? Exchange is the core concept of marketing. Absent exchange, there can be no marketing. This makes sense, because without exchange, no life would exist either. Think about the preceding in the context of how biological life is generated. Everything marketers do is done to create an exchange relationship between sellers and customers, if such relationships do not already exist; or is done to strengthen buyer-seller relationships, if such relationships already exist. Marketing, at many levels and in many ways, is not just business; it's also personal.

Exchanges are ubiquitous. When praying to a higher power, petitioners voluntarily enter an exchange relationship with the deity of their choice. Post-entry, prayerful petitioners often offer, or give up, promises and praise in the expectation they will receive, or get, certain values, in various blessed forms, in return. What else could these prayerful processes be but exchanges? Moreover, what are these prayer processes if not marketing?

---

4. Joseph Henrich, *The Weirdest People in the World* (London: Penguin Press, 2020).

Value is best defined as the difference, hopefully positive, between the benefits that are gotten and the costs that must be given up by customers before they can own and possibly use a product.

Value could also be described as the problem-solving ability of any particular branded product.

The value proposition of any brand is the sum total of all values associated with or delivered by that particular brand, or product.

Various ways exist to describe value. Air conditioning units, for example, have no value. The cool air that they generate, the benefits and solutions that emerge from air conditioners, those are the things about air conditioners that have value. Lawn fertilizer similarly has no value. Greener yards, the benefit or solution derived from using fertilizer, is the outcome that confers value.

A PIVOTAL POINT THAT SHOULD BE UNDERSTOOD

Marketers create, strategize, segment, target, differentiate, position, enter new or withdraw from old market segments, and ultimately win or lose based on their ability to develop and deliver more highly-differentiated benefits, value, and solutions to those same segments by managing exchange processes. This description applies entirely and absent any reservation to all sizes and types of marketers. The nature of market segments is discussed below.

Managing Customer Expectations

The value delivered by marketers can exceed customer expectations. The result is delighted customers.

The value delivered by marketers can correspond exactly with what customers expected. Good job, marketers kept their promises; that's not nothing. Satisfied customers may create special sorts of value in and of themselves. The type of value that proves extremely valuable to marketers themselves. That's because satisfied customers may tell others in their social network about the marketing sources—the brands—of their satisfaction. Of course, unsatisfied customers are similarly inclined to tell others about their sources of their dissatisfaction; in effect, those who are unhappy are much more likely "to spread the bad news" to others in their social network. This entire process may break bad or good for marketers. Either way, the process is still known as "word-of-mouth."

Or, the value delivered by marketers can fall short of customers' expectations. The marketer messed-up, it fell short, and for reasons described below, huge problems may emerge.

Under-Promising; Over-Delivering

Given the universal presence of this natural relationship between value, customer expectations, and resulting levels of customer satisfaction, marketers should often under-promise and over-deliver.

Under-promise, insofar as customers will then expect less. Then over-deliver, ensuring that customers get more than they expect. Consequently, not merely satisfied but absolutely delighted customers are produced.

Consider a marketing organization that previously was called *AvoMaster* (the marketer uses a different name today[5]). Among other products, *AvoMaster* prepared and marketed a pre-packaged avocado dish to grocery stores. The dish promised 6.25 ounces of cooked chicken breast meat along with healthy portions of rice and avocado. However, *AvoMaster* misrepresented one fact on their packaging, which, remember, promised 6.25 ounces of chicken. Meanwhile, each pre-packaged meal actually featured 6.75 ounces of chicken.

Many Americans ascribe ample value to their receipt of larger quantities of food. More-really-is-more for such customers, as it were. Okay, one might think, if *AvoMaster* really did deliver more chicken to customers why would the marketer not just state this, outright offering that exact promise, on its packaging label? The answer is that *AvoMaster* strategically under-promised and over-delivered. And yes, the tactic worked, because more customers ended up delighted, even if they could not quite put their finger on why they were so satisfied. As often happens, in this situation, the "what is delighting me" proves more impactful on customers' levels of satisfaction than the "why am I feeling delighted?" Meaning that the "why" ultimately matters very little to most customers.

---

5. Name cannot be revealed due to confidentially agreement.

MODULE 1.1

Sustainable Success Requires...

Want to be more persuasive? More influential? Seeking to become or remain a professional and personal brand that others pay attention to, gravitate toward, and respect? Finally, do you aspire to great professional success?

Most readers answering truthfully are likely answering yes to all four questions. Well, accept our congratulations or condolences.

Why would we congratulate or console you? Because for better or worse you're already thinking like a marketer. And given that you're already cloaked yourself inside marketing skin, why not learn how to do marketing better? Yet most professionals are missing the full command and mastery over marketing practices that they should possess and from which they would surely benefit. Most professionals have yet to master marketing's power.

KEYS TO MARKETING SUCCESS

Success inside most professional endeavors—including marketing—is predicated on the ability and willingness to do many big little things well. Yet three major baselines exist on which marketing success can be established and sustained.

Success Baseline 1

Marketing success is:

> ▶ ... Predicated on standing out rather than fitting in.

While matching your outfit to your job is important, adding offbeat element—say, red tennis shoes—to traditional ensembles can make people appear more competent because they seem unique. The appearance, if not the fact of greater competence, that's a pure play win for any professional marketer. Don't strive to be like the haystack. Be like the needle inside the haystack.

If marketers seek to stand out they similarly might envision twerking, for example, especially if they were the younger, 2012–2013 vintage, version of *Miley Cyrus*[6] and her brand as a professional entertainer. She vigorously and vividly twerked with *Robin Thicke* during the 2013 MTV Award Show and, with the viral assistance of the internet, instantly shredded her prior *Disney Girl* brand image. More germane, here, is that Ms. Cyrus became the highest-earning female performer in the world during the next calendar year. That's what standing out, strategically, can do for professional careers[7]—and for all other marketing entities.

But if the marketer is a politically left-leaning comedian, as most comedians are, they might decide to stand out from comedian competitors by targeting illegal immigrants rather than *Donald Trump* or other conservatives as foils for their jokes. Are comedians marketers? Surely, because comedians continuously attempt to sell the humor in—which is the value of—their jokes. Comedians' jokes "solve problems" by making hearers or seers laugh and temporarily making them feel better about themselves (yes, I'm better than him or her) or the world (if things are that funny then things cannot be that bad). Yes, comedians are marketers and jokes are their products so long as their jokes provide any sort of solutions. Or are we joking, strategically standing out, or both?

What if the marketer is *Netflix*, which creates new content (i.e., television shows or movies or documentaries) as products, that eventually will be shown on internet-enabled screens? Lots of new content is being developed for these small screens.[8] *Netflix* alone developed about 900 original series and films, each of which are both products and brands, for the small screen during 2020. In the face of so much competition, shows must work much harder to stand out, merely being extremely sexy or exceptionally violent is not enough anymore, these products usually also have to be a little strange or shocking. Take the formerly popular television series called *Veep,* developed by *HBO*. Every single character on the show is a crazed political stereotype. Black and white politicians, political consultants or donors, marketing researcher, gays, lesbians, hangers-on and groupies, and so forth: every character is outlandish and outrageously incorrect in ways that hilariously stand out from a wrath of so-called competitors.

One might likewise think and act more like *Kanye West*, who never would have become *Kanye!,* marketing entrepreneur-extraordinaire, absent his predilection for strategically standing out from other rappers or black activists. Once upon a time not so long ago, by publically and repeatedly

---

6. Brands and brand management are instrumental to sustainable marketing success. To underscore this point, and to emphasize the extent to which "marketing is everywhere and affects everything," *branded* products; services; for-profit and not-for-profit organizations, including institutions and leagues; political parties/causes and trends; or people, including celebrities or politicians are highlighted by *italics*. What this use of *italics* reveals about the degree to which essentially the entire world now exists is a heavily-*branded* place is remarkable.

7. Professional positions differ from regular jobs in that for better or worse professionals' inner mental and emotional lives are tightly connected to their work. When people perform inside professional positions they are rarely not working, again for better or worse, because "the job" is typically rattling around inside their minds. By contrast, most people who have regular jobs only work inside factories, offices, or while logged-on. Students should accept that it's acceptable to pursue either professional positions or regular jobs based on any degree they earn while also understanding that almost any professional position that is actively pursued and secured will prove markedly more challenging, rewarding, and pressure-packing than almost any regular job they could execute. As long as their regular job did not entail hunting snakes or swimming with sharks.

8. Sophie Gilbert, "The Revolution Will be Televised," *The Atlantic* (June 2019): 42–47.

professing his admiration and liking, again, for then *President Donald Trump*. Talk about cutting against the grain.

Most successful marketers and marketing organizations have long understood the value of standing out rather than fitting in, sometimes even among their prospects or customers. Since around 1940 various cigarette marketers—*R.J. Reynolds, Philip Morris, Brown & Williamson*, and their fellow marketing conspirators—have targeted their marketing efforts toward teenagers based on the age-old marketing premise that selling customers once and thereafter servicing them forever, or in the case of cigarettes addicting them forever to your brand (forever might come rather quickly for smokers), always entails a good basic strategy. Specifically, cigarette marketers first have always appealed to teenagers' desires to appear more mature; in this regard, to stand out favorably from their apparently less mature friends. And second, cigarette marketers have long subtly appealed to teenagers' naturally arising desire to rebel against what their parents, even when those parents smoke themselves, would want them to do.

Cigarette manufacturers, like every other marketing organization, do more than make, distribute, promote, and sell products or services themselves. Cigarette manufacturers are customers, as well. Imagine there was a famous and highly respected *Madison Avenue*[9] advertising agency that utterly and highly publicly rejected the very idea of working for a tobacco firm during a time when more than 50 percent of *American* consumers smoked. An advertising agency that violated a broadly accepted advertising industry norm in a highly visible way at the time when other major *Madison Avenue* firms would willingly have cut each other's throats to obtain a slice of that delicious tobacco-dollar pie. Suppose that firm did this during the late 1960s to virtue-signal to the rest of corporate advertising purchasing marketplace how honest, upright, and moral its brand and its work was, six decades before corporate virtue-signaling became a thing? Such a firm clearly would be seeking marketing success based on a decision to exercise its prerogative to stand-out rather than fit-in.

Success Baseline 2

Marketing success is:

▶ ... Predicated on making new-things-known and old-things-appear-new.

Jesus Christ is history's greatest marketer. Two thousand-plus years after his death he still boasts more than 2,000,000,000 followers. Far more fans than all *Kardashians* combined currently enjoy. The number slightly exceeds *Buddha's* or *Mohammed's* followers, as well.

Jesus, as marketer, stood out from other prophetic marketers of his time by refusing to fit in. He stood out in his ability to develop and continuously narrow-cast[10] good news about new products, which arrived in the form of ideas that solved important customer problems. What problems did this

---

9. *Madison Avenue* is a well-branded phrase that has long been used to identity and designate the top thirty or so huge advertising agencies that collectively comprise "*Big Advertising*" inside the *United States*.
10. Back then, no television programming, newspapers, or social networking sites existed to make "new-things-known."

particular marketer, and his unique ideas as products, solve? The problem, and eternal question, that was solved because the question was answered is what happens to humans after they die.

Jesus, as marketer, was likewise able to stand out through his ability to make old-things-appear-new. Among the old-things made to appear-new by Jesus was the ancient *Jewish Law*. Even during *Jesus's* time on earth, the Law was some 1,100-1,500 years old.

Success Baseline 3

Marketing success is:

> ▶ . . . Driven by the development and delivery of new stuff.

Human beings absolutely love "the new." How much? So much so that some furniture aficionados actually crave new antiques—an oxymoron if there ever was one.[11]

For most humans all manner of "new stuff" genuinely sometimes functions like shiny objects. The new often acts like lures that initially attract and subsequently quickly ensnare people . . . first demanding and thereafter commanding these folks' attention. Sometimes "the new" morphs into items or experiences that humans cannot-happily-live-without, until they acquire these new shiny objects—and have had them for a while. Then with the passage of time, sometimes slowly but often quickly, something funny inevitably happens. The funny something that inevitably materializes is the new shiny object did not confer lasting happiness, after all.

"Want" is a common *English* word. The term emerged from the *Hebrew* word for lack. Poor folks want to be rich. Rich folks want to be famous—or the President or richer still. The point is that most people, some of the time, generally want something that they currently do not possess because they perceive that they lack or actually are missing something that appears valuable to them—often just in that moment. This want rule applies no matter how much the human actually already has. The *French* philosopher, mathematician, and scientist *Rene Descartes* apparently was right when he wrote, and we paraphrase: "We are only truly happy when daydreaming about some future event that will make us happy." You may who know *Descartes* was even if you not know him if you have ever heard or read the statement "I think therefore I am." He is the source.

No one should be shocked by these descriptions. Not when happiness, for most all humans, is merely a moment in time before they need something else new, again, to make them happy, again. Most of us human folk would surely be better off if we could live in accord with the adage "happiness is not having what you want but wanting what you have." But fortunately for B2C marketers, most consumers will find that this laudable standard, even when it is actively pursued, is exceedingly difficult to meet.

The opposite of happiness is discontentment. Happy people are satisfied. Happy people feel as if they need nothing more other than what they already have, in this moment. This particular condition

---

11. An oxymoron arises when two incongruent (incompatible) thoughts are bundled together. One example of an oxymoron is that during the 2020 COVID-19 crisis *Nevada* churches were shut down, due to concerns about crowding. Meanwhile, the state's teeming with customers' casinos were allowed to remain open. Another oxymoron is the fact that the further northward one drives inside the state of *Florida* the more deeply one enters the cultural South.

actually represents bad news for marketers. Consequently, marketers often set about purposefully creating discontentment. Many categories of marketers have clearly mastered the task.

Beyond question, modern marketing, with all its technological underpinnings and weapons and ways of insinuating both its negativity and its promised solutions into our lives, simultaneously adds to and subtracts from overall consumer happiness. Indeed, marketing practice simultaneously adds to and subtracts from America's collective inventory happiness in predictable and increasingly understood patterns—as will become ever more evident as you read through certain modules inside *The Inside Skinny*.

About now is anyone else examining their own past? And thinking/experiencing feelings about that new car, outfit, boyfriend/girlfriend, or husband/wife that was going to make you feel happy forever? But your erstwhile solution, sadly, ended up falling short. Even if you are not thinking and feeling these things, marketers are! And because these professional "players" understand these conditions, marketers are manipulating too many consumers to purchase stuff those individuals don't need and cannot afford. And are manipulating American customers in far more situations and in far more subtle ways than most consumers can easily conceive.

EFFECTIVELY MANAGING TIME AND RELATIONSHIPS

People, being only human, often think too little about identifying the right time to do certain things. Things such as marrying; switching positions or professions; investing financially, educationally, emotionally, or temporally in some future prospect; or consciously growing one's own fungible talents. This reticence to think can prove problematic; the timing of such decisions or life affairs definitely matters.

Timing. First things first. Doing tasks and assignments in the right order; the order in which activities are pursued and completed also matter. Few to no cowboys or cowgirls in history have ever successfully pulled up their tight jeans before they pulled on their boots.

Or more esoterically, consider that most men, when asked, respond that they spotted their future wife or current dating partner first in the bar or the banquet. Yet an equally plausible truth is that she may have spent more than a little time planning such that he would encounter her best version when they meet. Who is the predator; who is the prey; and who is the planner in this particular exchange setting?

Data suggest people should spend a minimum of one year together before marrying. Turns out that deciding who to marry is the most important life decision for most folks. Data suggest professionals should switch positions every three years if their goal is to maximize income. Long-term data suggest the best time to invest is always *right* now. Anyone sensing why the three of the most exciting words that any wise marketer could ever possibly hear are: The data say/suggest!

Basically, living in the moment sans much forethought or planning makes little sense most of the time. People make better plans when they imagine future versions of themselves or their organizations. Planners, along with all decision-makers, should make decisions today as if they were looking back from the future upon the consequences emanating from choices they made today. The associated relationships are locked in. Decisions generate behaviors generate consequences. Consequences that turn out well or poorly for decision-makers.

This whole process is karma-like in nature. The word karma derives from *Buddhism* and *Hindu* teachings about reincarnation. Karmic teachings hold that people's actions in their current lives, good or bad, determine what their fate will be in future existences. But of course, what determines people's actions? Yes, their decisions. When the word karma is deployed in English—for example, as certain media mavens opined it was *Donald Trump's* bad karma to get COVID-19 back in 2020—karma speaks to a fuzzier concept that people's destinies stems from how they live their lives. But hey, that's nothing but decision-making, again. Or put differently and in a more familiar context, one reaps what one sows. Karma is not inherently vindictive. It does presuppose a vengeful god doling out people's just desserts. Karma is not retaliatory. Karma does not punish. Karma captures the absolutely neutral consequences that anyone's actions always generate. Karma is consequence. Nothing more or less. No need exists to over-mystify things.

No need exists to over-mystify decision-making either, although many people clearly do just that. The only things that usually happen inside even profoundly important decision-making contexts is determining "what," "when," and "how to do something." Integrate timelines for beginning and ending these decision-making processes, and anyone can transform himself or herself into a better decision-maker.

Prior to making any important decision intelligent marketers or sharp-minded consumers should consider might be lost or gained if they make the right or wrong choice. Thoughtful marketers might follow *Suzy Welch's 10-10-10 Rule*. Here's how the *10-10-10 Rule* works:

- ▶ When marketers, or anyone, are about to make decisions that appear or actually are important to them, they should ask . . . how will they feel about the consequences that their choice presumably will generate 10 minutes from now, 10 months from now, and 10 years from now. Decision-making is often overly biased by immediate pain or stress that decision-makers are experiencing or by the promise of immediate pleasure or release from stress that decision-makers are seeking. But all decision-makers can frame these short-term pain or pleasure consequences inside more revealing long-term perspectives by asking the three questions embedded in the 10-10-10 Rule. And those decision-makers would usually screw up much less as a consequence . . .

Seven Simple Principles: Following Them Enhances Prospects for Personal Marketing Success

Your prospects for future personal and professional success will unquestionably turn for the better to the extent that you understand, engage with others, and make decisions based upon the following seven principles:

- ▶ Principle 1: Accept that regardless of what you do professionally, you are a marketer who must effectively create and manage relationships in order to succeed.
- ▶ Principle 2: Accept that successful marketing efforts often require that you first make people know, like, trust, and respect your personal or professional brand.

Right now you might be thinking, yeah, I got this. And you probably do because almost everyone wants to be liked, trusted, and respected. But indulge us for a moment and learn something useful about how often our instincts about how to impress others are wrong.

One often flawed approach entails futile attempts to balance self-promotion with humility by engaging in humble bragging. Humble bragging could entail, for example, telling a prospective business partner that somehow I keep "getting asked to lead all the most innovative projects at my company." Never assume that such a communication approach represents a good way to convey to others that you are accomplished but not arrogant. Instead, your prospective partner's exposure to your humble bragging efforts usually makes the target like and respect you less, because they are quite likely to rightfully or wrongly perceive that you are scheming and that your words are insincere.

A better approach right here would entail mentioning one or two things you're proud of and delivering the message directly, simply, and un-apologetically.

The nature of human nature at its most natural is reveled and underscored through three additional simple decision-making principles. Consequently:

- Principle 3: When marketers meet someone, they should say thanks for making time for me.
- Principle 4: When marketers meet others they ask them about themselves, and when asking extend beyond banalities such as "How are you?"
- Principle 5: When marketers meet someone they should endeavor to make them laugh—unless this suggestion is beyond their bandwidth (sometimes it is) or inappropriate given the context (meeting a stranger at a funeral). Do so quickly. No long windups are necessary and in fact are inappropriate. Comedy or humor provides ephemeral moments of escape in an overly stressed, overworked world. Few downsides here, the ability to cause laughing and engage in mutual laughter almost always proves useful—with some presumably obvious exceptions.

Marketing efforts do not stop being serious when customers or prospects laugh any more than great jokes stop being funny when someone dies—this, despite the funeral reference just made. Humor is real; humor works. But is humor serious or funny? Don't ask us, ask one particular ethnic culture, and its membership is likely to respond that humor cuts both ways. The culture being referenced is that of the *Irish*. The *Irish* are widely recognized by those who really understand the culture to treat serious things as jokes and jokes as serious things. That's a fascinating intersection of seemingly divergent ideas, and as you eventually will read about how often intersections of previously divergent ideas can often prove fascinatingly valuable and highly creative marketing tools themselves.

- Principle 6: When meeting people marketers should ask those folks about their problems. Marketers should then dedicate themselves resolutely to listening carefully to the responses. Marketers should listen intently as if they assumed the person to whom they are listening knows something that they don't; because more often that one might suspect their assumption will be correct and they will consequently reap the benefits from an opportunity to learn something valuable from them.

Here, marketers should ask real questions. Marketers should make genuine inquiries of their relational exchange partners rather than a shallow "What's new?" or "How's it going?" Marketers should ask the kind of questions designed to stimulate insightful responses, not reactions of shock, annoyance, perplexity, or anger, from recipients.

More discussion follows about the extent to which listening represents a welcome present to all customers or prospects who are given the gift of listening from marketers. But for now, words offered by *George Elliot*, a male pen name for a female writer, should prove sufficient. Ms. Elliot wrote that "Blessed is the man who, having nothing to say, abstains from giving us worldly evidence of this fact."[12]

Saying less than what is necessary themselves and allowing the other to talk is usually a wise choice for marketers. If and when the folks want more information, they will ask you. Meanwhile, the questions asked should guide the directions you pursue or issues that you cover in your response. And tell us true, in their hearts who doesn't really enjoy the opportunity to talk about themselves or their organizations and the problems and challenges that either entity is confronting? That's right, the answer is very few indeed.

> ▶ Principle 7: The last step that marketers committed to success should follow when meeting new people is to help them solve their problems. Because, when marketers develop and ultimately present the gift of a solution to customers the ultimate entity or person being helped is the marketer and his/her organization itself.

Steps 1–7, described as principles above, are not tricks. The only trick is understanding and accepting that no tricks or shortcuts to personal marketing success exist. Instead, there are just lots of human beings—the few rich, the somewhat greater numbers of people living at the end of their rope, and the many more folks living out their lives in-between—all wanting and hoping that individual marketers and marketing organizations will treat them better than dirt.

Individual marketers and marketing organizations alike exist as branded entities. That's why individual marketers should think, act, work, live, play, and remain resolutely aware that these no-trick, success tricks represent a ready path toward enhanced prospects for greater marketing success.

---

12. Gordon S. Haight, *George Eliot: A Biography* (New York: Oxford University Press, 1968), 523.

MODULE 1.2

How Customer Minds Actually Work

The ideal strategic marketing mind should integrate thoughts about past, present, and future conditions and the wins or losses that were, are being, or could be experienced there. The where of the "there," of course, is the past, present, or future.

Strategic marketers should also evaluate the prospect that odd, unexpected factors will rise up in ways that affect and possibly interfere with their plans.

Meanwhile many customers, especially those purchasing inside the B2C marketing category, are not strategic at all. In effect, these sorts of nonthinking customers, who are better described as consumers, give marketers unfair advantages.

Feelings of nostalgia, for example, deepen consumers' sense of life's meanings and regrets. Their nostalgia consequently causes consumers to "feel" as if they should do something now, because time is passing. Such feelings could hardly be described as strategic.

Marketers, meanwhile, can easily foster feelings of nostalgia among targeted consumers. For example, contemporary marketers often use songs, images, or movies/television programing taken from the 1960s, '70s, or '80s era to stir up aging baby boomers' emotions, and make them more susceptible to marketing manipulation. Or perhaps contemporary marketers are able to exploit songs or images from these eras for their own manipulative purposes because the tunes were written before most good music died.

Or, for example, did you know that those who are most likely to run marathons or cheat on spouses for the first time during ages ending in nine—as in twenty-nine, thirty-nine, or forty-nine years of age? Human beings are apparently inclined to envision their lives playing out as decade-long books. And books whose respective chapters merit, if not demand, big endings. Nor can many folks avoid allowing impending age milestones to goose their yearning for more meaning in their lives. Imagine you're a marketer who actually is selling something that genuinely does add meaning to people's lives. Hey, this could happen! Any guesses regarding what specific age cohorts such marketers should target?

But smarter consumers should try thinking and being more strategic then, because they'll end up becoming better consumers. Of course, even "better consumers" sometimes struggle to win in situations where winning entails customers taking away more value from the exchange than marketers garner, or vice versa. Take the one-sided contest that has been waged across the decades between flyers and the domestic airline industry. The business model and profit structure of the domestic airline industry is apparently built on torturing customers—smaller seats, overcrowded planes during pre-COVID-19 times—and then forcing them to pay extra to have the torturous experiences eliminated. And there's not much that even the most strategic consumers can do to win this particular fight about securing more value from the airlines that the airlines are squeezing from them, other than choosing to drive rather than fly.

Human Minds Operate at Three Levels

The human mind is naturally and therefore intrinsically wired to operate at three levels:

- I will; I won't; or I want.

The last level, "I want," is the one that matters most to marketers. The "I want" level is where marketers take and often make their kill shots.

Meanwhile, according to *Proverbs*, four things on Planet Earth are never satisfied. They are:

- Leeches; they keep on sucking for more, more, more; essentially until they explode.
- Empty graves—always crying out for more, despite the fact that humanity has been filling up graves, feeding them, for approximately 100,000 years.
- Barren wombs—no further comment appropriate or safe during a *#me-too* era.
- Fire; the bigger fires get, the more matter they desire to consume, and consume rapaciously as the flames continue to grow, until all oxygen or matter is exhausted.

But the preceding passage wasn't really concerned about leeches, fires, or empty graves. Instead the words metaphorically conflated certain known natural facts with facts about another creature that is similarly never satisfied, at least not for long. Yes, the creature is the human race.

Were we allotted only one brief phrase to describe the typical consumer mindset, that phrase would be: a little bit more. Okay, we also could have written: not enough yet. These notions of wanting "more, more, almost always just a little more" are clearly exemplified in many consumers' extravagant natures. Most humans are rarely fully satisfied, for long. Fact is, most humans, no matter how much they have, want more.

Human minds and spirits are apparently wired to want. After all, what is happiness? One insightful answer: Happiness is a moment in time before we need something else new again to create more happiness.[13] Too many customers, addicted or not, live and consume in a world where too much is still never quite enough.

Oscar Wilde was an *Irish* playwright and poet, and a world-class wit who indirectly addressed this topic. Mr. Wilde wrote that there are two tragedies in life, "One is not getting what one wants. The other is getting it." Please read between the lines here. Once you do, you'll hopefully realize that the authentic tragedy being referenced by Wilde is that once satisfied, humanity's nature is to quickly

---

13. David Strutton and Kenneth Thompson, *Marketing from Scratch: The Principles You Really Need to Know,* 2nd ed. (Dubuque: Kendall-Hunt, 2016).

want something more, and usually something new, again, to make us happy again. This is a great world in which to be a marketer.

Understanding the Understated Role That Happiness Plays Inside Marketing

This thing, this phenomenon, that we call human happiness typically is more about anticipation than reality. Most humans are little more than big, feeling-empty-even-if-we're-not, holes yearning almost continuously be filled up, again and again. And since all humans are also consumers; well, the point should be clear. Tough personal question to follow: Have you ever found yourself in a situation where you were more in love with the prospective future idea of someone being in your life than the actual someone (him or herself) actually being in your life? If you've answered yes, then you may already understand what is meant by the statement that happiness is often more about anticipation of an event or gift than the actual arrival of the event or gift.

Americans are culturally attuned to pursue happiness. Hey, the phrase is featured early on inside the *United States of America's Declaration of Independence*. And, like good little citizens, most of us do actively pursue happiness. Often, arguably, a bit too fervently. That's okay. The right to pursue happiness is any American citizen's unalienable right. Notwithstanding the fact that real happiness emergences as the product—the consequence—of having moral purposes, dignity, self-control, and deep relationships with other people present in their lives, many Americans passionately pursue happiness through economic and consumption means.

No surprise to follow: Many humans often want the wrong things. Getting personal: Are you seeking and wanting, right now, to fill up your emptiness—not to mention to gift yourself with relief from reading this book? The solution wouldn't entail a small but hugely alluring electronic screen, would it?

Two related thoughts follow. The second thought is actually important inside strategic marketing contexts. First, when they cannot obtain what they want, wise consumers understand they should want what they get. Then second, insofar as marketers routinely manage prospective or actual customers' expectations, consumers should presumably manage their own expectations about what is reasonable to have, hold, and attain, possession-wise.

By the way, in an ironic, unexpected, but generally highly-effective strategic marketing twist, marketers often manage customer expectations first by tamping them down, keeping those expectations reasonable, and then exceeding those customers' expectations in terms of the actual value that their brands deliver, as already discussed above. What's more, additional discussion of this important marketing tactic follows in another module.

A Paradox

Paradoxes exist whenever two opposing arguments hold an equal claim on truth. Here's a paradox: Most American consumers have less than they want. Yet nearly all Americans have more than they need, to the degree that products most American consumers will view as bare necessities would be viewed as nearly unimaginable or certainly unattainable as luxuries by most of Earth's citizens.

Indeed, the set of most American consumers includes most homeless Americans. This sector, despite their unenviable plights still usually muster enough resources to acquire cigarettes and cell phone service. No criticisms are being offered or implied. If you have ever spent much time around the homeless you will realize these statements simply represent observable facts.

Here's another paradox, one that resides at the intersection between two facts: The first fact is that air conditioning keeps people cool and actually saves lives. Air conditioning is a broadly marketed product. The product delivers benefits that in turn confer value (i.e., cool air) while solving problems emanating from the presence of too much heat. Wonderful stuff. But . . . the second fact is that air conditioning is one of the largest contributors to CO2 emissions, and thus to the possibility of global warming. That is, if indeed global warming as opposed to natural climate change is real and not merely a marketer-inspired construct. Climatic scientists, public interest groups, and politicians alike routinely seek to market their own ideas, which is only natural when their marketing efforts generate valued returns for those marketers. Global warming is one of the ideas and products that these three professional groups routinely market.

If you're green, or environmentally conscious, but also overheated, try resolving this paradoxical problem during any August pretty much anywhere inside Texas.

This paradox is as irreconcilable as the one that arises when liberal politicians market the ideas[14] that they support guaranteed higher wages for lower income or social class-based constituencies and that they also support free and open immigration—and that you should vote for them despite that fact that simultaneously achieving each outcome is fiscally and practically impossible. One point being, never let irresolvable paradoxes get in the way of good marketing stories when precisely-defined and highly-segmented groups of potential voters are being targeted. Worth nothing, low income-based and social class-based constituencies are two entirely different market segments.

But marketing facts should matter too. Free and open immigration always decreases wages for workers already in the country, particularly lower income employees. Nations cannot have open immigration and a full-blown social welfare state each at the same time. The idea is paradoxical to its core.

We're not using this example to raise anyone's ire, by the way. The example is used to cast light on two common marketing ploys. Ploy one, over-hyping. Ploy two, over-promising. Simple, really. And simply wrong too, especially from a long-term marketing perspective.

Hedonic Treadmills

Many American consumers live on hedonic[15] treadmills. That is, residing inside continuously swirling loops where they're temporarily satisfied with whatever new thing they wanted and obtained but then suddenly or slowly find themselves lustfully moving forward toward wanting something else that is new—all in never-ending loops. The next thing consumers know, they own thirty-five pairs of

---

14. As discussed below, ideas are routinely marketed as products that will deliver value and purportedly solve problems if they're enacted. Even when supposedly valuable ideas—see above—create more problems than could not possibly be solved.

15. Hedonic, or hedonism, relates to humans' natural pursuit of pleasurable sensations or feelings.

shoes—and want more because none of what they have seems to work with the new outfit they have acquired. These conditions are usually great for individual marketers. These conditions are often bad for consumers and for large swaths of society.

Any guesses about how well these circumstances play out for the American economy? You're right. Rather well. Modern American consumer behavior seems to operate on almost *Pavlovian-like* instincts. Marketers ring an advertising or promotional "bell," and consumers "mindlessly-lust" after something new. Those delightful dings or other alluring sounds that phones make aren't associated with incoming messages by accident.

Consumers—notable chunks of them, for sure—are classically responding to acquisition and consumption cultural stimuli that has taught them one of the surest measures of and ways to acquire love, happiness, and self-worth are the objects they purchase or give. And many domestic consumers can never have enough goods or services, or give enough to others, to satisfy the intense craving for more stuff, and for higher levels of consumption-induced status. In a society in which most all of most everyone's needs are met, everyone rich and poor must be kept feeling perpetually deprived—and in turn increasingly perpetually bound up in debt—to keep these Pavlovian-like responses[16] going. But, as noted, the broader economy benefits greatly from these exact processes, and there is tremendous value in that.

This collection of facts and implications come together in ways that suggest successful marketing outcomes should be relatively easy to secure. Successful marketing depends upon first identifying, and then giving, people what they want . . . .

MARKETING ORGANIZATIONS ARE . . .

Question: What's a marketing organization?

Best answer: Every organization is a marketing organization.

Yes, churches, temples, mosques; they simultaneously qualify as both marketing organizations and products insofar as each entity competes vigorously for souls and for resources, usually financial but perhaps just their attention, from the human bodies that house those souls—and the entire process often actually does solve human problems.

The claim has just been made that churches, temples, or mosques function as marketing organizations, products, and solutions. Let's take a deeper dive into the assertion. People of faith began demanding more religious freedom as soon as COVID-19-driven lockdowns began in March 2020. In the media, in the courts, and in the streets, many churches immediately declared that opening or keeping their doors open was good for American consumers.

---

16. Pavlovian responses refer to the pairing of conditioned and unconditioned stimuli and to the creation of learned responses through processes described as classical conditioning. (Or, more elementally, one might consider dogs, bells, foods, and salivating responses when considering so-called Pavlovian responses.) The word "Pavlovian" refers to a famous *Russian* psychiatrist named Ivan Pavlov. Dr. Pavlov elicited predictable responses from laboratory animals by pairing conditioned and unconditioned stimuli. So yes, consumers are being compared to dogs. And rightfully so. Because marketers can and do manipulate many consumers into making certain predictable responses, especially by using internet-based technology.

The data suggests they were right. Emotional well-being absolutely tanked across the board during the year of mayhem that 2020 was. Except for one consumer segment: people who regularly attended church in person. According to a new *Gallup* self-assessment survey, Americans' perceptions of their own emotional well-being declined to its lowest level in more than two decades, with the number of those who reported positive emotional or mental well-being down 9 percent from 2019. While the degree of changes in mental health varied among different groups, quality of life perceptions fail among every demographic—men, women, liberals, conservatives, whites, non-whites, rich, poor, married, and unmarried—except for devout religious people. And that's a problem. Remarkably, faithful churchgoers were the only people who reported *improvements* in their emotional health between 2019 and 2020. Among consumers reporting weekly participation in religious services, 46 percent reported their mental health as "excellent." That was a 4 percent bump from 2019.[17]

Schools, nonprofit organizations, or hospitals, they're all marketers too. Each organization just referenced wants citizens to learn, give, or get healthy there, in their specific institution—and not somewhere else.

Charter schools, as opposed to public schools, exist because many parents believe they do a better job of solving their children's educational problems than public schools. That's marketing—giving people additional choices, changing existing products into superior products.

The four primary US military branches each compete vigorously with each other to secure finite governmental resources or qualified recruits in a pool where less than half of the eighteen-to-twenty-five-year-old domestic population meets physical, moral, or intelligence standards. Securing funding from the government, recruiting worthy recruits, each activity entails marketing too.

Perhaps a better opening question inside this section would have entailed asking readers to name a successful organization that does not also engage successfully in marketing.

The answer, again, is that every organization engages in marketing. Some organizations simply do marketing better than their counterparts. And the differences between organizations that do marketing well and those that fail to do marketing well is clear to most clear thinkers. The *United States Postal Service* (USPS) engages in marketing. So do politicians or governmental branches themselves. For a while now, however, few to none of these entities has executed marketing well. Put differently, their respective brands have certainly lost much of their former power.

Any argument that politicians are nothing less or more than marketers can be easily defended because politics itself is nothing more or less than marketing. Politics combines the art of the supposedly possible with the art of persuasion. This description applies to all politics, all the time. Moreover, the two primary domestic political parties, *Democrats* and *Republicans* alike, absolutely conduct their business affairs as competing marketing organizations, and the individual politicians who politick under either *Donkey* or *Elephant* branding identities absolutely exist and operate as human products. Politicians are human products charged with the marketing goal of promoting and selling their own ideas' value.

The most successful political marketers excel at building and burnishing the value and influence of their professional brands. Successful political marketers achieve these ends by adjusting their presentations of self and messaging to fit whatever is trending up in the moment among their targeted

---

17. Kylee Zempel, "New Mental Health Survey Shows Church is Essential," *The Federalist* (December 10, 2020).

voting audiences. This is reality. Few informed American citizen-voters would assert that many current politicians are anchored to certain bedrock political principles.

If politicians are always marketers does that mean that voters are always consumers in a routine sort of B2C context? The answer is yes, absolutely. Voters always choose the politician brands whose ideas they most want to associate with and/or the political brand that voters believe will best-solve their specific problems. Voters purchase the brand with their votes. Voters similarly choose the politician brand that they perceive will do the best job of solving their problems.

Realistically, the solving of voters' problems could also be recast as choosing one political brand for purposes of ensuring that the other political brand is not elected to create new problems, in accordance with voters' perceptions. Lesser-of-two-evils, and all that!

Best question of all: Can you name a successful organization whose success is not largely grounded in marketing?

Answer: Now we've gone and done it. We've asked readers to do the impossible. Because every successful organization is also a successful marketer. Except maybe, and just maybe, for the *United States Federal Reserve*, which is better known by its popular branding name, the *Fed*. Oops, perhaps the *Fed* is a marketing organization after all. Or, at least *The Fed* is an organization that practices branding.

The Revealing Roles of Holes

What do *Home Depot* customers actually acquire when purchasing a ¼-inch drill bit either online or in a brick-and-mortar store? Do customers acquire a brand, a machine, a tool, a chunk of steel or piece of metal made from something harder still? Well, yes, customers actually are purchasing all these things, and even more. But the key value, which is also the real solution, that customers are actually acquiring, or purchasing, is a ¼-inch hole.

Why would customers want or need to purchase a ¼-inch hole? The answer is because those customers are experiencing or anticipating problems for which the ideal solutions begin with a ¼-inch hole. Two implications follow:

- *Home Depot*, a retailer that functions as the marketing inside this customer decision making example, is actually marketing a hole. Hopefully, the best possible and most valuable hole to those customers who need such a hole.
- All customers who purchase any branded product base their decision on their perceptions that this particular drill bit brand, and it alone, will do a better job of solving their problems/satisfy their needs than any other alternative brand from the same product category that they could have purchased would have done.

Marketers consequently should always view themselves as values-providers, need-satisfiers, and problem-solvers. Marketers then should position the values, the need-satisfying benefits, and problem-solving capacities delivered by their products as the best available inside the product categories in which their product competes. The best sports utility vehicle brand inside the SUV product category. The best brand of jeans inside the jeans product category. Or the best brand of bottled drinking water inside the bottled drinking water product category.

Being perceived by targeted segments of customers as authentic problem-solvers or genuine need-satisfiers represents a true no-lose value proposition[18] for any marketer that is good enough or fortunate enough to earn the branding distinction.

Here's why: How easily can you envision situations in your life where problems never seem to go away? You can probably envision such a set of circumstances pretty easily because after all, "Life is hard." The good news, of course, is that at least life is short—too soon to make such a joke?

Yes, life does appear to be full of problems. Don't believe us: Just ask any middle-school student. Yet among any older and naturally more experienced consumer crews this seemingly perpetual onslaught of problems likely arises because humans keep changing their definitions of what constitutes problems. This process might be described as concept-creep. Or perhaps better described as consumer problem-creep?

But what is happening can be probably better understood as moving-our-own-goalposts. This intrinsically human tendency ends up frustrating people. After all, how can individuals know they're making progress toward solving problems when they keep redefining what is required to solve those problems? All in all, however, these innately-arising processes create situations, markets, and indeed an entire world in which marketers ought to succeed rather easily.

Another Path Toward Marketing Success

Another basic three-step path toward marketing success is thus revealed.

- ▶ First, create real or imagined problems in the minds of others.
- ▶ Second, create real or imagined solutions to those problems.
- ▶ Third, deliver those solutions to those customers who actually are or who perhaps merely perceive they are experiencing those problems.

Every corporation marketing inside the global pharmaceutical sector, for example, succeeds based on its ability to prevent health-care problems or to solve such problems after they have emerged.

For now, every corporation marketing inside the global oil and gas sector succeeds based on its ability to solve or to prevent energy-related problems.

Every lawyer or law partnership marketing its values and solutions inside the domestic legal sector succeeds based on, well, again the point is clear. Indeed, law partnerships operating inside the legal sector often effectively stir up genuine or perceived problems themselves. Not coincidentally, this exact marketing tactic represents another surefire route toward marketing success, particularly in those situations where your legal firm is perceived—or positioned—as the alternative that is uniquely qualified to solve the problem. "Are you suffering or do you know anyone who is suffering from asbestos-related mesothelioma?" This is not a sick joke; law firms exist who exclusively prosecute such cases. Anyone need a *Legal Hammer* because of an at-work injury? Well there is a *Houston*-based *Texas Hammer Law Firm* out there.

---

18. The simplest way to define the phrase "value proposition" is that the concept simultaneously represents and captures the grand total of any brand's problem-solving capacity. Value propositions can feature both emotional (feeling-based) and rational (practical problem-solving) components. Value propositions also integrate elements of the "give and get" concept. That is, the exchange concept. Value propositions can be genuine or merely perceived.

MODULE 1.3

Know What...?

WHAT'S A "PRODUCT"?

Products may be broadly defined as anything that can be offered to individuals, market segments, or entire markets for customers' attention, acquisition, use, or consumption that might also satisfy individuals', segments', or entire markets' wants/needs—or solve their problems. Products might also be appropriately described as anything that can solve customer problems and profit marketers/marketing organizations in the process.

Products can be tangible or intangible in nature. Tangible products are called products. Intangible products are called services.

Tangible products may feature and boast intangible service dimensions. Automobiles, which are surely tangible products (just feel those plastic bumpers), also feature intangible warranties or GPS-based navigational services.

Intangible products feature and boast tangible dimensions. Legal services, surely intangible, are delivered inside clearly tangible physical surroundings and are often literally contained inside tangible documents.

Consumers and organizations often buy either tangible or intangible products to secure access to the problems either solves. But consumers, in particular, also often purchase effectively branded products or services such as *Coach* or *Apple* in order to receive the social, cultural, or personal values that products embody and say about the folks consuming them.

The same product can mean and/or pronounce so many different things to so many different people inside so many different situations.

Take the deadly but humble cigarette. No, seriously, take them away. Surely no one, probably not even smokers, in their hearts, truly wants cigarettes around. But here they remain, nonetheless. Likely they remain because of various values and solutions that cigarettes, as products, provide.

Smoking. Naughty yes, but smoking surely must feel nice to those indulging in it in the moment. Every cigarette smoked serves a purpose—butts provide signals, medication, stimulation, or sedatives. Cigarettes function as playthings, accessories, objects of fetish. Cigarettes provide something to help pass time, to enhance. Cigarettes offer smokers a communication tool that signals either come hither or stay away. The stupid cigarette functions as a product that, ironically enough, actually stimulates reflection and meditation among users. Perhaps the greatest economic values generated by this product as customers consume it are stained teeth and rank breath which generates marketing demand for teeth whiteners and mouthwash or diminished to eventually expired lung capacities which itself generates for heavily marketed health-care services and products. Economic values in turn inspire legions of increasingly more sophisticated and expensive medical treatments—or products.

Who knows, perhaps the three-headed strategic marketing alliance that features well-trained and highly-paid medical, pharmaceutical, and insurance service marketing professionals, at its core, secretly applauds the tobacco marketing industry. Goodness knows, not all the new business opportunities generated by this cult of smokers have died out yet. And as apologists for the whole unholy industry might argue, people are going to die from something.

WHAT'S A "MARKET"?

Markets consist of all actual or potential customers for products or services. Markets are heterogeneous in nature. The word heterogeneous, in this context, means consist *of* dissimilar or diverse constituents. More plainly stated, the people or organizations inside markets, the human or corporate entities that constitute B2C or B2B markets, are rather diverse.

Multiple markets exist. Even for commodity products such as corn. There are, for example, human food, cattle, or chicken feed corn markets. There is a corn-based ethanol, a type of fuel, markets. And trust us, you don't want us to go on, because many other corn-based markets exist.

There are various markets for transportation services. Trucks, trains, ships, airlines, pipelines, buses, and any form of automobile or truck or sports utility vehicle which provide transportation services represent different transportation services markets.

Markets for ideas also certainly exist. The idea that abortion is a right versus the idea that abortion is murder has been vigorously and sometimes viciously marketed inside the political marketplace for at least six continuous decades. Ideas arguing out the marketing case for man-made or merely naturally arising causes for climate changes are similarly marketed as vigorously and almost as viciously.

WHAT'S "MARKET SHARE"?

Market share is the ratio between the firm's sales volume and the entire industry sales volume (i.e., an organization's share of products sold throughout the market in which the marketing firm competes). Marketing organizations generally pursue, as strategic goals, either greater market share or maintenance of their current market share. Retaining current market share often proves difficult when firms face increasing competitive pressures, changing customer tastes or economic positions, or seek or are forced to raise their own prices.

Imagine a global marketplace in which 1,000 pair of athletic shoes were sold annually. Inside this world market imagine that *Nike* sold 250 pairs of shoes; *Converse* sold 250 pairs; *Adidas* sold 240 pairs; and laggard *Reebok* sold only ten pairs of sneakers. Inside this world *Nike* and *Converse* would each enjoy a 25 percent market share, *Adidas* a 24 percent market share, while *Reebok* is badly losing the market share race after clocking in with a merely 1 percent share. That's how simple market share is, and how simply market share can be calculated.

WHAT'S A "MARKET SEGMENT"?

Market segments are relatively homogeneous,[19] smaller submarkets existing inside much larger and more heterogeneous markets. Homogeneous, here, means that the people, organizations, or institutions who comprise market segments share certain key characteristics in common. The fact that these characteristics are shared makes it more likely that the consumers or prospective consumers inside B2C marketing situations or organizations/institutions inside B2B marketing situations who comprise particular market segments will respond in the same generally positive or generally negative nature to the value or values that are created and delivered through a particular marketing mix.

The description offered in the immediately previous sentence underscores why each market segment that any marketing organization targeted should be pursued by one and only one unique and hopefully uniquely desirable marketing mix. The key word in the preceding sentence is "one."

WHAT'S THE "MARKETING MIX"?

The marketing mix is a tool that firms manage with the intent of creating hopefully differentiating value for the branded products that they make and market.

When products are marketed, organizations typically have four ingredients to "mix." The four ingredients, generally better known as the 4Ps, are the product, price, promotion, and place.[20] Place is the term used within the 4Ps to designate and capture the various distribution or supply chain activities that successful marketers must execute successfully.

However, when services are being marketed organizations or professionals must mix and manage seven ingredients. The seven ingredients, or 7Ps, are again: Product, Price, Promotion, and Place,

---

19. If the word heterogeneous means "diverse or different," and it does, then yes, homogeneous means "similar or the same."

20. The 4Ps of marketing should not be confused with the 4Ps of stakeholder capitalism. Stakeholder capitalization prescribes that corporations are not just responsible to shareholders—that's traditional capitalism—but also to communities, marginalized minorities, or society in general. The 4Ps of stakeholder capitalism are the Principle of Governance, the Principle of Planet, the Principle of People, and the Principle of Prosperity. Meanwhile, stakeholder capitalism is nearly indistinguishable from sustainable capitalism. Sustainable capitalism promotes the belief that an individual or organization can or should ultimately thrive unless wider society also flourishes. Stakeholder capitalism further holds that sometimes enough wealth, gathered inside one person's or small group's hands, is enough. These are two beliefs or principles that nearly everyone can get behind, unless you're the one or part of the few ones who are thriving or hoarding the wealth. That's where bad old-fashioned human greed and self-interestedness kicks in.

comprised of distribution or supply chain management processes. Plus, anew: People, Processes, and Physical Surroundings.

People create and deliver services. Processes provide the means through which services are created and delivered. Physical surroundings include and reflect the settings or environments in which services are created and delivered.

On the surface, the marketing mix does not appear overly complicated. And truth be written, the traditional marketing mix is not all that complex. There are, after all, only four elements.

But ruminate on the following facts. Only seven music notes exist. There are, however, many ways to mix and match these notes. For example, a recent story about the *iPod* noted that more than 19,000,000 songs are available for download. All generated from mixing and matching, and adding and subtracting, only seven musical notes!

Similar characterizations and descriptions apply to both the 4Ps and 7Ps. Whenever marketers change any aspect of any of the four or seven marketing mix ingredients, an entirely new marketing mix generates entirely new and different values. And perhaps they created a new song, as well, insofar as songwriters, singers, musicians, and directors exist and absolutely operate as marketers themselves. Along the same vein, new or old songs themselves exist as products, themselves. A point and a fact that makes perfect sense whenever one agrees that given songs have value because they have the capacity for solving our problems when we feel, say, bored (distract me!), lonely (my music is my friend!), sad (lift me up!), happy (and want to express our joys, get on your feet!), and so forth.

WHAT'S "MARKET SEGMENTATION"?

Market segmentation is a process through which broader, larger, more heterogeneous markets are divided into narrower, smaller, more homogeneous market segments. These smaller sub-units, or segments, feature related or similar characteristics. These markets could be consumer or organizational in nature.

Various bases or criteria are employed to segment broader markets into narrower market segments. When entire markets have been divided into smaller subsets consisting of customers or prospective potential customers characterized by similar preferences; demands; tastes; attitudes and beliefs; demographic characteristics; lifestyles; wants, needs, or problems; and/or so from the process is called market segmentation. Once market segmentation has occurred and market segments have been created, marketers find it easier to target and position their hopefully unique and uniquely desirable marketing mix values to the segments they have targeted. The fact that the membership of segments share much in common implies the segment's constituents are more likely to respond positively or negatively to particular marketing mixes, and to the distinct sets of values that those marketing mixes create. Remember, values deliver benefits and solutions.

To illustrate, contemplate two well-known market segments that are characterized and differentiated by their respective memberships' wildly divergent beliefs and attitudes. Two segments most readers presumably already know exist. One segment has self-branded as *Pro-Life*. The other self-brands as *Pro-Choice*. The first segment believes, passionately, that its ideas protect human life. The second believes, passionately, that its ideas protect human rights. Each segment is motivated by a unique set of attitudes, perceptions, and assumptions about which specific all or nothing actions/non-actions (abort a baby/sustain a baby's life) are compassionate, decent, and moral/immoral.

Please keep this well-known progressive principle in mind as you ponder this real-world description of these two highly discrete market segments. The principle is this: the degree to which any society is civilized, moral, and socially responsible usually can be judged by evaluating two criterion. First, by how a society treats its prisoners as well as the number of people it imprisons. Second, by how a society treats helpless and defenseless people who live inside it. Can anyone describe babies as anything other than helpless and defenseless people?

WHAT'S "TARGETING"?

The term targeting, also called market targeting, suffuses throughout this book. Segmentation, targeting, and positioning efforts—which are each ongoing processes—should fit together like perfect gloves slipping onto well-matched hands. And inside successful marketing organizations, a tally that includes all successful organizations, the three marketing activities do fit together in this fashion. Targeting, or market targeting, entails strategically identifying—selecting—the precise segment or segments that marketers will target through their marketing mixes. Marketing organizations should strategically develop unique-and-uniquely-desirable marketing mixes for each segment they choose to target.

Indeed, the marketing world is unique. Unique insofar as the world of marketing freely and concurrently offers buyers and sellers the feeling that they are right, or winning, and that the other side to the exchange is wrong, or losing. The fact is that if things did not feel right to both buying and selling participants inside these marketer/customer exchange relationships neither side would participate.

Repeating, every marketing exchange features buyers and sellers. Yet inside most marketing exchange relationships, either buyers or sellers are actually right and the other is wrong. One side is "right," or winning, because it takes away greater value from the exchange. The other side therefore is necessarily "wrong," or losing, because it takes away less value from the exchange. That's because the value taken away from sellers was less than the value of the amount buyers gave up to obtain the objects of transaction involved in the exchange. Or because the value given up by sellers exceeded the value of the amount buyers gave up to obtain the objects being exchanged. Logically, two sides competing for the same scarce dollars inside buyer-seller exchanges cannot both win. Not so, however, in these magical worlds of feelings and perceptions about value that marketers create.

Marketers consequently face situations in which success is not so much based upon being skillful enough to finesse customers into doing what satisfies the marketer's best interests, as it is based upon being skillful in conceiving or creating values that satisfy the best interests (i.e., wants, needs, problems) embedded inside targeted customer segments. Customers are inherently self-interested. For that matter, so is all humanity. So, whenever and wherever marketers covet their own success, they should go beyond simply fishing where the fish are; they should also fish in places (i.e., targeting the right segments) where the specific fish being targeted are more likely to bite on the specific bait (value) marketers are strategically creating/delivering through their marketing mixes.

WHAT'S A "MARKET POSITION" AND "POSITIONING"?

A market position is an image and set of benefits, or problem-solving values, that is associated with branded products. Positions are created and reside inside the collective mind of targeted customers relative to the positioning images that competing organizations and their branded products have created for themselves.

As already noted repeatedly, even at this early point: Life is full of problems. No one should think that bad things might happen. Everyone should know that bad things will happen. Just wait a while. And when the bad—the problem—inevitably arises some marketing organization's brand should be there, well-positioned inside your brain as first choice to eliminate the bad or solve the problem.

The act of positioning entails executing the necessary strategic steps to ensure that the marketing organization's market mix offering generates and delivers clear, distinct, and desirable perceived benefits and solutions inside targeted segments' collective minds relative to the positioning benefits (and perceived solutions) that competitors have sought to create for themselves and their brand. Positions are created through for-profit or not-for-profit organizations' thoughtful management of their marketing mixes.

Once positions are established, they should be continuously managed. Would you purchase a highly desirable house and never do routine maintenance on it? Or not expend the energy or money necessary to replace outdated or broken house fixtures? The answers, presumably, are no. That is why positions should be routinely managed.

When successfully achieved, positioning relates to . . . the place a brand occupies within customers' or prospects' minds—or within the collective mind of an entire targeted market segment. To illustrate, reflect on *Coke, 7-Up,* or *Dr. Pepper*; each name represents a well-known and well-positioned soda brand. You know the brands; you can readily envision their respective flavors, sensations each generates in your mouth, or see one brand's product's distinctive color inside the eye of your mind. Each branded product is good, tasty, and bad for consumers, right?

But most American consumers also perceive each branded product as being different, one from the other, along various attributes. Meanwhile, *Coke's, 7-Up's* and *Dr. Pepper's* brand managers each strategize ways to position their brand as the one choice perceived as different from and better than the other two brands along various discernible (to consumer) attributes. When executing marketing mix strategies, marketers should attempt to create uniquely desirable positions—places inside consumers' minds—for their brands.[21] The phrase "different from and better than" is key to understanding the essence of what a "market position" and "the act of positioning" actually are. The phrase "different from and better than" is also key to understanding the essence of differentiation. The "point of intersection" between the marketing terms "positioning" and "differentiation" that was just described is not coincidental.

---

21. Jack Trout and Al Reis, *Positioning: The Battle for Your Mind* (New York: McGraw-Hill, 1981).

WHAT'S "DIFFERENTIATION"?

P.T. Barnum wrote: "No one ever made a difference by being like everyone else."[22] We write: No marketing organization ever made a difference, or for that matter became and remained successful, by selling products that were just like the products other organizations are selling.

Acts of differentiation entail strategic attempts to create the perception or the reality that one brand is different from and better than alternative branded solutions. Where is this perception or reality created? In that truly most important of all marketing places; that is, inside targeted customers' collective minds.[23] At many levels, and in many ways, most of what marketers do directly or indirectly relates to the pursuit, growth, or retention of differentiation. Differentiation is important!

Differentiation is inextricably connected with *positioning*. When firms successfully achieve differentiation for their brand or brands, they have also successfully achieved positioning. When organizations successfully position their brand or brands they have also successfully differentiated.

Brand differentiation is a process that attempts to establish and exploit differences in the perceived or actual values that are created and delivered by two or more competing brands. The goal of these differentiation processes is to make one brand appear more attractive than other competing alternatives by contrasting and emphasizing its unique qualities versus those competing brands. Successful differentiation creates competitive advantages[24] for differentiating marketers. This is because customers usually view well-differentiated products as unique and/or superior. Differentiation is created through the strategic management of marketing mixes. The development of superior strategies and the subsequently superior execution of those strategies will almost inevitably create better—as in stronger and more determinant—differentiation.

The ability of any organization or individual to differentiate and position successfully generally also follows from their possession of relative or absolute core competencies. Core competencies can be derived from various sources. A partial list of the sources from which core competencies can be developed includes any marketing organization's talent, financial resources, technological skills, experience, patent, brand power, brand loyalty, or first-to-market or top-of-mind, as in evoked set-related, advantages.

While Differentiation Is Natural, Marketers Still Must Promote It

Human beings automatically differentiate between people based on whether they are tall, short, fat, skinny, old or young; and based on their skin color or hair color; and based on whether they are wearing formal or informal clothing, boots or running shoes; and based on whether their facial countenances are smiling or glowering. And that's just for starters. These distinguishing features emit

---

22. F. R. Shapiro, *The Yale Book of Quotations* (New Haven: Yale University Press, 2006).

23. The phrases "customers' collective mind" or the "collective mind of the segment" are other ways to describe segments themselves.

24. A competitive advantage is a condition, asset, circumstance, or core competency that places marketing organizations and their brands in favorable market positions relative to competing marketing organizations. One core purpose of any marketing strategy is to create competitive advantages, hopefully advantages that prove sustainable.

a signal to perceivers that inform them whether the person bearing feature X, Y, or Z is friend or foe; someone we know or have never met; someone we should welcome, even if a stranger; or someone we should seemingly instinctively bow up against or run from.

The process of differentiation is only natural, in brief. All humans rely on these conscious or unconscious acts of separation and segregation, which is not a "bad word" when used inside this context. Human beings consequently differentiate, all the time.

So should marketers and marketing organizations. In fact, every strategic and not necessarily so strategic decision that marketers make should be done with the direct or indirect goal in mind of establishing key points of difference in the minds, eyes, ears, and perceptions of targeted customer segments, if favorable differentiation does not exist. Or strengthening key points of difference in the minds, eyes, ears, and perceptions of targeted customer segments, if favorable differentiation already does exist.

WHAT ARE PERCEPTIONS?

Perceptions are the "imagined realities" of human beings. Perceptions develop inevitably as individuals experience and attempt to make sense of stimuli that continuously surrounds them or that flashes in and out of their worlds. Perceptions function like lenses inside eyeglasses. Sometimes, to change our perceptions, we must change our glasses; our points of viewing, so to speak. This is a task that is likely to prove easier to describe in writing about than to achieve in reality. Changing our perceptions is exceedingly difficult. The primary reason is because as people age they usefully become more of what they already are while growing less tolerant of the prospect of change. This is why, but not the only reason, why marketers usually should not attempt to change people's minds.

The creation of perceptions entails an active, continuous process. Were they honest, many people would have to agree that their perceptions about the same people or the same ideas shifts dependent on how hungry, tired, or pissed off they are. This is in part why customers' perceptions are often faulty; essentially misconstrued. Meaning-creation—envisioning this brand, person, or idea as good or bad—occurs during these perception-creating processes. Over time, perceptions arise that shape, influence, and actively bias customer decision-making.

Have you seen the movie *Toy Story*? Yes, we are aware that four episodes now exist inside the *Toy Story* franchise and product portfolio, but to make the point let's stick to the original. Likely most readers have seen *Toy Story 1*. However, the fact remains beyond any possible pushback is that no pair or group of viewers have seen the same movie. That's because all customers' perceptions shaped their interpretation of the product they made sense of as they experienced it.

Can and do marketers shape customer perceptions? You bet. Can marketers shape customer perceptions for better and for worse? You bet, again.

The Role Perceptions Play Inside Decision-Making

Four steps unfold inside every consumer decision-making process. The same four steps likewise occur inside any strategic marketing decision-making process. First, decision-makers perceive, as in attempt to make sense of, situations. Second, deciders deliberate, as in evaluate or weigh out, possible courses of action that are available in these situations. Third, deciders calculate which choice, from a menu of possible actions, will best serve their interests because, in their perceptions, the choice will do a better job of solving their problems. Fourth, on the basis of these calculations decision-makers then decide which action to pursue.

Experts have long assumed that step three was most important. More recently, however, experts are increasingly realizing that first step, the perceptual step, is most important. At first glimpse, it appears that perceiving what a situation entails is a straightforward procedure. All one has to do is look around and see what's happening, right? But the step that appears simplest is actually the most complex. That is because most perceptions take place absent decision-makers being consciously aware that these sense-making processes are unfolding.

Experts apparently were initially wrong because they operated based on two faulty assumptions. The first erroneous assumption is that human beings primarily engage in rational calculations. That would be a "hard no." The second faulty assumption is that decision-makers always attempt to maximize their own self-interests. Wrong again, a lot of the time, as it turns out.

Assumptions, especially the poorly grounded variety, often prove disastrous. Often, in fact, it's not what professionals don't know that hurts them—or leads their reasoning astray. Instead, what professionals, experts, think they know for certain gets them in trouble. Which represents another reason to question one's reflexive tendency to believe in the value of professional experts. After all, the *Salem Witches* were burnt to death based on the decision of a panel of men who mostly had graduated from *Harvard College* (now *University*). How much more expert could this set of gentlemen have been in their time?

Marketers should always watch their assumptions. Especially assumptions about what customers are actually perceiving. As inscribed at the *Temple of Apollo* at *Delphi*, in *Greece* (today, an absolutely spectacular tourist site), "surety brings ruin." (The other two famously and universally useful inscriptions embedded there above entrances to the temple are "nothing in excess" and "know yourself.")

WHAT ARE "BRANDS"?

Brands are names, signs, symbols, designs, colors, or some combination of these and other dimensions that identify and distinguish or differentiate the marketer of a product/service from other organizations marketing the same product inside the same product category. The color of a branded product, for example, may not seem like such a big deal to many consumers. But colors, and they alone, can make material differences for legions of other consumers. Tens of millions of middle-aged and older men understand what the color blue means to them and their sexual partners. For them, the color blue connotes Vitamin V—or *Viagra*. *Viagra*, as a name and brand, is marketer-generated. The prefix "Vi" is intended to subtly insinuate VIgor or VItality. Meanwhile, the color "*Carolina Blue*" gear does not sell well inside Texas. No worries, "burnt orange" or "Mean Green" gear has never leapt off the shelves of *North Carolina* sporting goods stores. Branding success rarely happens accidentally.

To further illustrate the difference between brands and the product categories in which brands reside and compete, consider battery-powered (or cordless) electric drills. This particular type of drill represents a unique product category. Electric drills that feature a plug-in cord would represent another product category. As would, if anyone used them anymore, hand-powered drills. Now consider the words, listed alphabetically, *Bosch, Bostich, Craftsman, Dewalt, Festool, Hitachi, Husky, Kobalt, Makita, Milwaukee, Porter Cable, Powermatic, Rigid, Rikon, Ryobi, Skil*, or *Stanley*. These are seventeen of the world's best-known power tool brands, and marketing organizations. Yet how many of these brand names would easily and quickly leap into your mind, into your evoked set, if you experienced a problem that required not just a drill bit but also a drill itself to solve? In your first author's case, only four of the brands. (Much more information about the "evoked set" and the basis for its extreme importance follows.)

Brands can also be described as psychological constructs that capture all meanings, images, sensations, and experiences that targeted customers or prospective customers associate with products offered by specific for-profit and not-for-profit marketing organizations. Brands are powerful. Brands are pervasive.

The time-telling devices known as watches can merely function as a show of hands, or perhaps as a show of digits. But well-branded watches can also function as pieces of art; as signals or reflections of traditions, wealth, taste, or status; as signals of culture; as sources of emotion; as objects of desire; as storehouses of beauty; as denizens of design. These days, when many consumers wear a watch, do they really care whether it tells time accurately, or tells time at all? There are smartphones for that. Or do those consumers care more about what the well-branded watch tells about them?

People are brand-able; as are products, services, places, and ideas. Each entity exists as both a brand and product, because each might potentially create value and solve problems.

WHAT'S INNOVATION OR AN INNOVATION?

The word innovation, as a process, or innovation, as a product, captures two sides of the same coin.

Innovation, as process, produces something new and useful. This description means that the word innovation functions as a verb.

Innovation, as product, is something that is both new and useful. This description means that the word innovation functions as a noun.

The process of innovation and the product as innovation, either variation, consequently provides superior solutions to customers who buy them.

Beyond this, inside either of its varieties, innovation is just a $10 word for using new ideas to improve anything; for example, a product, process, or how we learn. The concept innovation, however, should not be confused with the concept called invention, for reasons that are explained below.

Creativity is the key to successful innovation. Creativity is similarly the key to myriad other desirable marketing outcomes.

WHAT'S CREATIVITY?

Creativity, described, entails the ability to see or think about the same things, as stimuli, that everyone else is seeing or thinking about and yet deriving, or creating something that is new, different, better, and most importantly, able to deliver greater value than other solutions, or products, that currently exist. Typically, creative types create superior ideas that lead to superior new products—and solutions.

Creativity entails creating new ideas or information bytes, primarily inside the minds of creative individuals, and then establishing previously unconnected intersections between those new "data points." If you're sensing the processes described above appear similar to deep thinking, we'd agree!

HOW DOES TECHNOLOGY IMPACT MARKETING?

Silly question, this. A better question would have entailed asking in what ways does technology not shape marketing practice? As *Sophocles* wrote millennia ago, "Nothing vast ever enters the world of mortals without issuing a curse"—and we would add, blessings, as well.

Recent technological changes have materially impacted how:

- Marketers connect with customers;
- Customers connect with marketers;
- Consumers connect with each other;
- Firms collect information from customers;
- Marketing organizations deliver products and services to customers; and how . . .
- . . . Marketing organizations create and sustain strategic-level and tactical-level competitive advantages.

What do the preceding six descriptive phrases mean?

The first description means that during a relatively short period *Amazon* morphed from its former exclusive position as an online marketer of books to the world's largest seller of everything without ever opening a single physical store.

The second description means that increasing numbers of *Walmart's* or *Kroger's* customers never enter their stores anymore, either, because opportunities exist for customers to text, email, phone, or link-in their food and other goods orders and have them physically delivered to one's car or home.

The third descriptive phrase means that new movies opening weekend's sales once were and someday again will be ignited or extinguished by positive or negative customer WOM or e-WOM about the film. (Big *Hollywood* features once and may again open on Fridays; these words were written during March 2021, when physical theaters were still mostly shuttered.)

The fourth phrase means that *Facebook's* biggest source of revenue and profits is information; information, that is, about you as one of the social networking giant's billions of customers.

The fifth description means that drones and driverless delivery trucks will soon be fixtures inside many consumers' lives.

The final description means that once upon a time gaming companies such as *GameStop* could temporarily and hilariously ("hilariously" as in "ridiculously") boast upon stock valuations that exceeded the total stock value of *Delta Airlines*.

Technology is already a huge deal for all marketers. Technology is poised to become a bigger deal, still. For example, a 2018 *Internet Trends* report issued by *Axios.com* reported that half the world's population, or about 3.6 billion people, now enjoy access to the internet. Reflect upon the implications of this trend while considering the degree to which routine participation on the internet magnifies people's natural predispositions.

Technology is a one-way street, it is always moving forward. The task of managing technology effectively has proven an insurmountable challenge for some companies, while providing huge opportunities for others. Many failed; many succeeded; creative destruction and its consequences is real.[25] But what could one reasonably expect? When hard times or severe challenges arrive, hard solutions are required.

Within the *First World* many consumers have already implanted technology into their bodies. They did so through their fingers. Some consumers hold these technologies in their hands, nearly constantly, and from that vantage point the technologies control and direct most of these consumers' lives.

Technology has taken over many consumers' lives. In other news water is still wet. But has technology given consumers equivalent value in return? The purpose of digital technology should be to enrich human interaction. Has it? The thing about marketing technology, and all technology is marketing technology, is that technology has made the world of information much more dominant while making consumers' worlds much smaller—how many square inches does the average smartphone face contain? And there is a material—and likely still expanding—loss in that.

Have consumers sworn allegiance to a dwarf world, or to a giant world? And if you're a consumer reading this content now (trick statement; all readers are consumers) keep the following statements top-of-your-mind. As you peer anxiously, longingly, expectedly, hopefully, lovingly (consumers do love/hate their phones, right) or most likely anxiously into that little screen, remember, there's a thousand or more software engineers and developers on the screen's other side. The primary, if not sole, purpose of many of these engineers is to destroy whatever resistance to the screen users can muster or retain—turning them into addicts. In short, many consumers have lost control of their relationship with technology because technology has become better at controlling them than they are at controlling it.

Social media often function like nicotine. Their exposure to a little of either legal substance often can hook more susceptible, perhaps weaker-willed, users for a lifetime. These hooking processes, generating highly addictive outcomes, naturally are rigged by design. These factors, among others,

---

25. Creative destruction is an important economic and marketing concept. The concept describes what happens as new ideas, products, organizations, or technologies are developed and introduced inside existing markets. What happens, fundamentally, is that new product entities and their solutions are created and become widely disseminated while old product entities and solutions are destroyed or displaced. Hence, a continuous strategic need arises to engage in new product development as a prerequisite for sustainable marketing success.

are why marketing routinely kicks ass and takes names in the technology-driven war being waged continuously for customers' hearts, minds, attention, and wallets.

Video game developers purposefully design games in ways that make them difficult for players to stop. Games are designed to touch the pleasure centers of human brains in ways similar to how gambling or drinking/drugging activities addict many users. The game *Fortnite* was introduced during 2017. The new game amassed more than 125,000,000 users during its first year in the global marketplace. *Fortnite* encourages players to socialize, acting as hot social networks that replaced and superseded the role that malls and other teenager haunts had formally played. The *Wall Street Journal* reports the average American aged thirteen or over spent 7.8 hours playing video games during 2019, and is probably underreporting the actual numbers. Marketing researchers understand that once consumers understand they have or had a problem, or that too much gaming is generally frowned upon by "society" they usually underreport their usage. Another way to state the same point; consumer gamers often lie about how much they play because they know much of older society frowns upon the activity.

Is Big Tech BAAD?

BAAD to Worse: We already know TECH is a four-letter word. But exactly how BAAD are tech giants such as *Amazon, Google*,[26] or *Facebook*? *Apple* or *Microsoft* should not similarly be deemed bad or BAAD. Not when *Apple* [or rather, its key *Chinese* supply chain partner *Foxcomm*] still actually makes products that consumers want to buy, even in the face of fierce global competition. Or for as long as Microsoft solves real problems, as opposed to often creating artificial tribulations.

Oh yes, back to BAAD. What does BAAD, the acronym, actually mean? Too Big. Too Anticompetitive. Too Addictive. And too Destructive to Democracy and/or humanity's emotional and psychological well-being. Doesn't matter whether you agree TECH is BAAD. What matters is that readers ponder whether bad technology exists, and then make their own choices based on the insights that result.

How large and BAAD is *Big Tech*? Well, at a recent church service that one author attended the minister was introduced, walked to the podium, and then requested of his congregants: "Pull out your Bibles, and turn them on," before reading the scripture that provided the basis for his sermon. While the preacher had cracked a joke, was he really joking?

Use of the acronym BAAD is not meant to imply that *Big Tech* and its leadership are inherently evil. Not unless you think that the clearly capitalistic goal of making a lot of money for oneself by creating and marketing a value that so many consumers obviously wanted so badly is evil. Which we don't happen to believe. After all, no one could have imagined that *Facebook* "likes," or lack of *Facebook* "likes," would cast millions of teens and millennials into bouts with depression. Such consequences were surely unintentional even as they are also surely real.

---

26. *Google* changed its name to *Alphabet* during 2015. *Alphabet* was created as a holding company split into two divisions. One division houses *Google*, which still primarily relies on search advertising for profits. The other houses "other future bets." The future bets division features various new projects such as driverless cars. But since people remain more familiar with *Google* than *Alphabet*, the more familiar brand name "*Google*" is used throughout.

Tech addiction is another real deal thing that is clearly capable of wreaking substantial emotional or psychological damage upon addicted consumers. In the day, when people got dumped they felt terrible. But Old School dumpees were not forced to simultaneously endure continuous e-exposure to dozens of other "friends" who are seemingly experiencing wonderful times. (Not to mention, quite possibly, exposure to happy images of the dumper.) After all, few users *Instagram* the boring parts of their lives. One might argue that excessive participation in social media diminishes the human aspects of human lives. Fact is, we just did.

Overstating the allure and addictiveness of the web is impossible. With one click, users can conjure forth the whole world in pixels on small portable screens. Once software engineers mastered the technology beneath the web, thousands of apps were developed and marketed that allow young and old consumers alike to do virtually anything—texting, image sharing, self-monitoring. Cell phones are innovations that were originally designed to allow users to make phone calls anywhere. That was it. But marketing progress and innovations are what they are, natural and necessary things.

Like rust, innovative marketing progress never sleeps. Thank you, *Neil Young*. And these in their beginnings, reasonably simple technologies have since evolved to where they now permit consumers to hold the magic of the web in their hands and to go deeper, deeper, deeper into the magical bonds provided by the internet. Now, like *The Sorcerer's Apprentice*, *First World* markets are discovering to their chagrin how uncontrollably malignant their web addictions to the magic have become for many consumers.

How malignant? Slightly more than one-third of current college students profess problems with depression. One argument as to why is related to the fact that the human brain likely was not designed to accommodate the volume of inner-self-directedness that screens generate in their lives. This deluge of inner-self-directness often devolves into an ordeal that in turn foments incredible amounts of anxiety because this much self-centeredness is neither natural nor normal. People who spend too much time inside their own minds might secure profound introspection and insights and evolve into brilliant intellectuals. Or not.

The evidence on this front is clear beyond question. Many people who spend too much time locked inside their own psyches are often heading down a dark and depressing tunnel. Whether they're adolescent girls or boys staring at photoshopped images of "perfectly-figured" women or men, college students measuring themselves constantly against better prepared or innately more intelligent college student peers, or young men in a state of rage about perceived or actual discrimination—something has got to give. To many consumers of social networking technology the stakes online "appear"—are perceived—as impossibly and inhumanely high, and impossible to negotiate down to tolerant levels of serious and planned periods of no e-connections. Lives lived too much online have been exposed as destructive and dehumanizing alt-realities.

One might argue, persuasively, that a couple of decades of overexposure to an internet world and its easily obtained yet generally unearned diversions/delights have rendered too many social networking addicts mentally, emotionally, morally, physically, or intellectually underprepared whenever real-world challenges rise up in their lives. Of course, one might be wrong to argue this, as well.

Any combination of the overly-critical and overly-certain has often proved the bane of many professed prognosticators. In fact, this nasty intersection of too-critical and too-certain has led many folks who are attempting to explain the present or predict the future off career cliffs.

Meanwhile *Google* may be breaking-bad in another way. *Google's* longstanding brand slogan was *Don't be Evil. Alphabet*, more recently, inverted this positioning statement, suggesting the corporation exists to *Do Good Things. Google's* and *Alphabet's* founding mission statements each reflect their leaders' professed desire to make all information universally and freely available. But apparently, someone at *Google* forgot this promise and has fallen off-mission. During late 2018 the search firm announced that its new customized *Chinese* search app that's configured to preclude access to any sources of information that *China's* government felt might undermine their authoritarian rule. For now, *Chinese* users will have access to information about *Tiananmen Square, George Orwell's "Animal Farm," Wikipedia,* or the *New York Times,* to tag but a few among dozens of well-branded events, works of art, or information sources. *Alphabet* apparently decided that the potential value associated with regaining access to a market that features 1.4 billion+ potential sets of eyeballs is the value of *Google's* founding mission and branding principles. *Google* was originally kicked out of *China* during 2010.

Then there is *Twitter. Twitter* generally prevents consumers from thinking deeply. Excessive *Twitter* usage degrades consumer intelligence; the facts are in and available, all around, for anyone who is watching to see! The acts of tweeting and consuming tweets often accentuates the negative or weaker sides of the human natures of those human beings who use and read the e-channel as a mode of communication.

And why would this diminution of human intelligence not arise? Social media generally, but particularly *Twitter*, miraculously distil concentrated versions of full-life hostilities into mere handfuls of characters. *Twitter* also destroys consumers' sense of proportionality by making most problems seemingly appear as if they were the same size—which obviously is untrue.

Whether a *Hollywood* celebrity wore the wrong color to the *Oscars* and consequently appeared "un-woke" may be a fact, a story, even a "problem" to some. But the *Twitter* issue itself is not as significant as the problem that would arise were the *Iranian Navy* to sink a *British* supertanker inside the *Straits of Hormuz. Twitter* noise, however, makes such disparate problems appear same-sized. The use of social networking incurs opportunity costs. The addictive-by-design nature of social media typically prevents or precludes consumers from engaging in other more intellectually or practically valuable activities, such as getting up, walking around, and losing oneself in nature or thought.

Nothing much is new here. A time in which innovators generated nothing but good and beneficial ideas and products has never existed. And never will . . . *Payday loans*, prostitution or old-school pornography, supposed pharmaceutical solutions that actually create other, non-electronic forms of deadly addiction, for example; similar categories of morally questionable products have always proliferated. Marketers playing "create-an-addiction" games create dangerous paths on which their brand or product loyalists travel.

Addiction genes reside inside consumers. Yet addictions themselves are fickle creatives. For many addictive consumer types, one "hit" of the product proves too many while one hundred "hits" never proves enough.

Addiction is one side of one BAAD story. There is another side to a technology story that has nothing to do with bad or BAAD. Another take is that technology, particularly the robotic sort, is ultimately destined to play a net-positive role thanks to the relentless ways that it replaces humans who can only say or do repetitive things. Of course, those whose values might be replaced likely also includes narrow-minded thinkers.

WHAT'S THE "MARKETING CONCEPT"?

The marketing concept is a business philosophy that puts customers, and the tasks of identifying and satisfying their wants and needs, first. First, that is, as long as the marketing professionals or organizations also profit from the processes executed to solve those customer problems.

The philosophy known as the marketing concept is grounded in an understanding that most strategic-level goals are best achieved by correctly identifying and defining customers' problems and then solving those problems by delivering values and solutions perceived as superior to the values and solutions offered by competitors.

This philosophy prescribes that everyone working inside any organization should view themselves as a marketer.

The marketing concept also admonishes all employees to learn that nothing happens and no one gets paid until and unless some marketer sells something and another customer entity buys the something. No one gets paid, that is, at least in the long run after the venture capital has been exhausted, as so many dot.bomb marketers learned to their great chagrin across the decades. These buying or customer entities could be consumer-oriented (B2C) or organizational-oriented (B2B) or governmental-oriented (B2G) in nature. Don't short sell the importance of B2G marketing to either the government or the market sectors. The marketing sector and the various solutions it provides as necessary to the operational functionality of the government and the dollars it spends to acquire those solutions are to the economic functionality of the marketing sector.

The potentially haughty term "philosophy" has been freely tossed around inside this marketing concept discussion. Yet this textbook is not designed to teach anyone about philosophy or philosophies, except for the marketing concept, which is an important business philosophy. That is, with one other exception, Module 8, which discusses the topics of ethics and social responsibility, and introduces an important ethical philosophy called enlightened self-interests.

There is, however, one broadly useful fact that readers should understand about the nature of philosophies. The fact is this: philosophical principles are not like taxi cabs; instead, they are like buses. No one who believes in a particular philosophical principal—such as the marketing concept—can direct it. Just like no one who rides on buses can direct them (yes, one can direct cabs). People who believe in any philosophical principle must travel wherever the philosophical principle leads them. The marketing concept is a business philosophy and one that every organization, organizational leader, and organizational member should follow. This means that those same marketers should pursue only those opportunities that the marketing concept dictates are best suited for them to "chase." Logically enough, discussions about opportunities and the best sorts of opportunities to pursue follow inside ensuing Modules.

WHAT'S THE "INSIDE-BASEBALL" GAME THAT MARKETERS SOMETIMES PLAY?

"Life is hard," or so suggests the opening line of *Scot Peck's* best-seller *The Road Less Traveled*. And indeed, many American consumers know that their lives are difficult. Yet by all objective global measures, life is anything but difficult for all but a few American consumers. And revealing aside:

Most Americans who complain about life in America have never traveled widely outside the *United States.* Yet were such perspective-challenged travelers to visit most any foreign locale where American tourists are nowhere to be seen, they usually would quickly realize how good they have it. At the very least, they would realize how much stuff they have!

Marketing plays no small strategic role in making life inside *America* appear harder than is actually the case for many consumers. Primarily by making many Americans feel as if they actually need things and experiences that they only want, often creating desires for goods or experiences that consumers surely do not need, especially in excessive quantities. Simple or complicated goods and activities involved with excessive consumption of healthy-body-snatching fast-food, cigarettes, or alcohol; resource-snatching oversized automobiles; or spirit- and often emotion-snatching pornography, e-games or social networking, or gambling.

No worries, however, because marketers have ready-made, customized solutions, in the form of products, available to solve the problems that arise from the unsatisfied wants that the consumption of such items actually created. Notably, here we are referencing the exact problems that marketers themselves often played a material role in creating. Accident, coincidence, or designed and highly desired strategic marketing outcome? If successful marketers are masters of the need-satisfaction creation business, and this absolutely is the case, most successful marketers are also absolutely masters of the problem-creation game.

Marshall Field (1834–1906), the name of both the man and the famous *Chicago*-based department store that Mr. Field founded and still bears his name, summarized the core principle of the marketing concept. Mr. Field said: "Give the lady what she wants."

WHAT'S THE RELATIONSHIP BETWEEN ECONOMICS AND MARKETING?

This book is about marketing rather than economics. Even so, economics is the mother—or father, if you prefer—of marketing. As such, economics and economic concepts pop up more than occasionally throughout this book.

There are key differences, however, that distinguish marketing and economics. Economics is about choice, and making choices. Marketing is about exchange; and creating, sustaining, and strengthening exchanges.

Economics, at its core, addresses choice-related decision-making executed at both individual and organizational levels. And usually the exact point where marketing thought and practice begins and becomes important is the exact point at which economic thought and practice can no longer accurately predict or effectively explain supposedly-rational human decision-making. Every marketing issue, principle, guideline, assertion, or solution discussed below also directly or indirectly relates to economics and economic decision-making.

Every conscious action we make as humans results from an economic choice (what's in this behavior for me?) as our brains engage in continuous ciphering about whether it's better right now to eat or decline, to fight or flee, to study or to get high. Our economics brains are continuously asking: If I decide on this choice and engage in this behavior, what's in it for me? Decisions generate behaviors

>>> behaviors generate consequences >>> consequences generate good or bad outcomes for you, or me. Everyone would do well to learn and remember this truism.

Buying a way-too-expensive but looks-so-good-on-me outfit will, for example, "waste" finite dollars. (Meanwhile, everybody's dollars, even those banked by billionaires, are limited.) But those extra dollars spent may get individual consumers through the gate with the guy or gal they want so badly to reach for so many different reasons; help folks land that big job on the other coast after the third interview; or simply earn an opportunity for consumers to finally, albeit temporarily, feel better about themselves. This last possible value relates to consumers' self-concepts, as discussed in depth inside the seventh Module.

Life choices are deeply connected with economic-based decisions, which concurrently means that life and its choices are all about marketing. Because right at the point where traditional economics theory and the economics discipline's rational- and utility-based decision-making formulas can no longer accurately predict, explain, or justify human choices is right where marketing theory kicks in as a discipline and a practice that can more accurately predict, explain, and justify human choices. Marketing researchers usually predict human behaviors more accurately than economic researchers because marketing accounts for the irrational and highly subjective decision-making criteria on which many humans base many of even their most important decisions. Marketing practice, unlike traditional economics theory, addresses the fact that choices that are perceived as irrational by some may appear completely irrational to other decision-makers, and vice versa.

Somehow believing that economic and marketing decisions and the resulting human behaviors and consequences that those decisions create can be separated from everything else happening inside *First World* markets is typically overly simplistic, naïve, and wrong. The vast majority of economic disparities that exist at micro or macro levels inside America are driven not by racism, sexism, or any other form of...ism. These disparities instead are usually driven by poor individual decision-making.

WHAT'S DE-MARKETING?

Last and probably least practiced, a marketing activity known as de-marketing actually exists. De-marketing basically entails using advertising or other promotional efforts in an attempt to lower demand for products that are in short supply or for products, such as cigarettes or alcohol, that often injure users.

De-marketing messages are often designed to infuse viewers, hearers, or even readers with the fear of God. Here, however, that fear of God relates to the "bad things" that may happen to users who smoke cigarettes, drink excessive amounts of alcohol-related products, or consume various illegal drugs. Yet de-marketing efforts are also regularly communicated through kinder and gentler advertising messages, or initiated about products that when consumed in any reasonable quantity approaching reasonable are actually healthy. For example, the wait staff, particularly inside high-end restaurants, often actually "sell" the value of a fish dish by making the case that this specific meal does not taste or smell "fishy."

NOT ALWAYS EXCITING, BUT ALWAYS IMPORTANT . . .

The preceding discussion was, at times, tedious. Yet this recitation of unadorned marketing facts was necessary. Your understanding of the previous concepts and principles should function as building blocks on which future marketing successes can be built. Or, if you fail to learn them, won't be built.

For what it's worth, the preceding paragraph purposefully finessed readers' thinking by using a negatively-framed marketing story. Additional details about the highly persuasive nature of negatively-framed marketing messages follows during Module 14.

MODULE 1.4

Other Fundamental Marketing Insights

WHAT ELSE... DO SUCCESSFUL MARKETERS KNOW?

The concepts, definitions, and principles introduced above are intended to function as building blocks upon which much of the rest of the knowledge and skill sets that readers should glean from *The Inside Skinny* are based. Still, one more set of foundational ideas and issues exist that are best learned now. Successful marketers also usually know, understand, and act based on the following ten fundamental marketing insights.

Fundamental Marketing Insight 1

Successful marketers know that the lessons embedded in the marketing concept apply to many aspects of life. Not coincidentally, the marketing concept especially applies to the parts of their lives that are authentically important to most human beings. The parts of their lives, for example, related to the attitudes, aptitudes, and behaviors that generally accelerate professional success or to the avoidance of attitudes, aptitudes, and behaviors that often hasten professional failure.

Fundamental Marketing Insight 2

Successful marketers know that their personal communication skills really matter. Foremost among those personal communication skills are say: listening, listening, listening, writing, writing, writing, and speaking, and then listening some more—and no misprints are present earlier in this sentence. All actual or aspiring marketers should habituate themselves to not be inattentive to what others have to say and, to the extent possible, get and remain inside the minds of speakers in brief, to display empathy. Listening is and always will be a critical key marketing skill set. Critical, that is, to marketing success. Listening is an asset that should be cultivated and then leveraged.

Marketers should listen to understand the person with whom they are communicating. Marketers should not listen to determine whether someone or the information the other is giving is right or wrong. The determination of right or wrong—or of agreement or disagreement—can be made later.

Marketers should pursue genuine-listening. The hyphenated-phrase implies marketers should not think about what they plan to say next as they listen to customers, prospects, or supply chain partners. Again, marketers should simply listen.

Do you want to demonstrate genuine respect or love for particular people? Of course you do; after all, you like them—or more important still inside marketing contexts, you want them to like you.

Then listen to them. Listen intently; listen uncritically; listen without interrupting your mind's ability to understand what it is hearing by preparing or mentally rehearsing what you are going to say next.

Listen to learn. Learn about what? Usually, marketers should listen intently to better understand the "pain points" of speakers. Why? Because those marketers can then better understand what prospects or customers need and how they can help those prospects or customers solve their problems.

At least one additional huge value accrues to any marketer who learns how to listen. The simple act of listening to them can loosen prospective or actual customers' tongues—most people love to talk about themselves and their own or their organization's problems. The simple act of listening, then, allows marketers to gain insights into the true nature of prospects' and customers' problems, and to gain their confidence and respect.

Will following these easily described but difficult to execute active-listening processes actually help marketers solve customer problems? And help marketers satisfy customer needs, as well? The answer to each question is, yes, absolutely.

Consider the Golden Rule. The Golden Rule suggests we should "Do unto others as you would have them do unto you." Presumably, most readers already knew the Golden Rule. But inside marketing contexts, a Platinum Rule should also apply. This rule suggests we should "Do unto others as they would have you do unto them."

In other words, this updated version of the Golden Rule suggests marketers should:

- Slow down,
- Pay attention to, and . . .
- Learn from customers' own words.

Marketers should always strive to learn more about customers' wants, needs, problems; about their most pressing pain points, revisiting a phrase mentioned above. Marketers then should respond in ways that create and deliver values and signal to customers and prospects that not only have they been listening, but that they also understand.

Slowing down, ironically, often proves the fastest way to get to where most marketers want to go.

All the while, the value and importance of writing and speaking properly should not be ignored, even as the value and importance of listening skills are praised. After all, many internally- and externally-focused marketing communications entail some combination of writing and speaking. Consider the following guidelines:

- When writing or speaking, short words are best.
- Older short words better still. As are short sentences…
- And questions. Or answers.

When writing or speaking, never permit verbs to wander far from their subjects. Brevity has its rewards and its challenges. Up to the test? Not if you don't think and edit before you speak or write. The need to get to the basic important facts as quickly as possible remains a constant imperative. As does the need to avoid word salads. Think about it. (Then reap your rewards.)

When writing- or speaking-in-marketing use clear prose, unfussy metaphors, and quick quips. Marketing communicators (writers and speakers) can create intersections between quick quips and unfussy metaphors. For example, the *Greek* philosopher *Aristotle* logically asserted that no two things can occupy the same space at the same time. Was his the first theory to explain inner city or college campus parking? The two statements exemplify the point.

Speaking well is critical. When asked to identify the best investment that young people can make, *Warren Buffet* replied: "Imagine working on one skill that—once improved—will raise your value by 50 percent. That skill is public speaking."[27] *Warren Buffet* is the founder of *Berkshire-Hathaway,* a marketing and financial guru, and has at various times been the richest man on earth.

Fundamental Marketing Insight 3

Successful marketers know that marketing and/or interpersonal brand impressions—first, last, and in-between—truly matter; but especially those first impressions. Suggesting that people or brands never get second chances to make good first impressions is far from cliché. How could the suggestion be cliché? The point made always remains true.[28] In fact, most clichés, and for that matter, most stereotypes, only evolve into the status of cliché or stereotype because they are embedded in fact.[29]

And most everybody already realizes the high value of good first impressions whether or not they have actually actively considered the point.

What about you? Do you ever consciously dress to accentuate or to camouflage? The answer does not matter. Either way—dressing to accentuate or dressing to camouflage—you're usually dressing to impress a targeted market segment (perhaps a segment of one) in some way, shape, or form. And yes, of course, people often dress with neither communication goal in mind.

---

27. Carmine Gallo, "Billionaire Warren Buffet Says This One Skill Will Boost Your Career Value by 50 Percent" (2017), *Inc.com.*

28. David Strutton and Terrence L. Holmes, "Managing Buyer-Seller Relationships One Impression at a Time," *Business Horizons* (November/December 2002): 67–78.

29. A few thoughts on clichés and their usage appear appropriate here, primarily because marketers, like every other adult, are routinely judged based on what they say or write. Less intelligent or poorly informed people tend to write or speak using clichés because they have nothing more original to write or say. (Please note that less intelligent or poorly informed people are often distinct groups.) That's not good, and is a major reason why the ability to think and to act creatively is so important to the success of most professionals. Fortunately, various methods through which marketing and other types of professionals can become more creative thinkers and doers—and writers and speakers—are shared during Module 10.

Some simple and easily executable advice about how to manage the impressions one is making on key others follows.

- ▶ First, marketers should identify the impression or impressions they are attempting to convey. Once marketers understand the exact impressions they are trying to convey to targeted groups or individuals they should be better at delivering them, particularly across time. These targeted segments or individuals might include customers or clients, prospective customers or clients, their direct bosses or other higher-ups, and even professional or personal peers.

Impression management "activities" that might be marshalled and initiated by marketers could include the color of their hair; the shoes or skirts or pants that marketers choose to wear; the ink that marketers choose to acquire and display or not display or to never acquire at all; the manner in which marketers speak and the words marketers use (code switching is a real thing—look it up), in addition to too many other forms of strategically-issued verbal and nonverbal communication cues to reasonably list here.

- ▶ Second, after marshalling and actually initiating impression management activities intended to project the desired impressions to the right targets, marketers seeking to manage impressions should gauge and track the responses being elicited among those targeted others.
- ▶ Third, marketers should adjust accordingly based on their evaluation of what is or is not working.

People who are blessed with effective self-monitoring skills are often masters of reading other people's reactions. For that matter, so are great poker players. People with good self-monitoring skills are usually also good at managing the impressions others form about them.

How exactly do people read other people's reactions to what they are saying or doing? Essentially, by reading the faces of those others. Human faces function like ever-changing, living color billboards that signals their owners' intentions and attitudes. Other people's faces therefore contain most of the clues that marketers should examine when attempting to monitor the mental states and emotional reactions of others. Much of what can be known about the mental state of others can be learned from their faces before they even speak. The human face is the most basic indicator of emotions and attitudes. Faces can be read to determine whether their bearers' intentions—whether one's relational partner plans to buy or not buy; plans to speak truthfully or deceitfully; plans to fully disclose or keep hidden key chunks of information and facts. (More reasons still why wearing masks in public during the COVID-19 crisis proved so challenging.)

Fundamental Marketing Insight 4

Successful marketers know that almost everything anyone does—anywhere and everywhere in their lives—has direct or indirect marketing implications.

Fundamental Marketing Insight 5

Successful marketers know that everyone never represents an acceptable marketing segment or target market.

Fundamental Marketing Insight 6

Successful marketers understand that knowledge functions as the most basic source of competitive advantage. Successful marketers further understand how important their ownership of and willingness to leverage competitive advantages actually is to their own or to their organization's marketing success.

Most women reading this now are likely strong; most men reading the same words now are likely beautiful. Or vice versa; what else could one safely write in today's environment?[30] But the power and beauty of youth, regardless of which gender these naturally-arising physical assets attach themselves to, inevitably fades. However, one asset inevitably grows in power as human beings age. The asset is their knowledge.

Successful marketers know or learn that the pool of relevant knowledge floats around inside a dynamic universe—and what is most valuable to know or to learn is not the current body of knowledge, but the leading edge of what is known and understood inside any particular discipline, field, or business sector.

Successful marketers learn how to learn, because the marketing world is extremely dynamic. Successful marketers further learn what learning approach works best for them. Successful marketers, finally, are willing learners.

Fundamental Marketing Insight 7

Successful marketers know that change is inevitable. They likewise understand and accept that change rarely if ever arrives in straight, predictable, or comforting lines. Finally, successful marketers accept that they must deal with change, manage change, and lead change, across time; if they plan to become or remain successful.

Perhaps the biggest, though not the only, challenge to sustainable marketing success entails developing the personal and organizational willingness to prepare continuously for change—especially when things are apparently working well. This is probably due to two factors. First, change will be resisted—either directly or indirectly—by someone; usually, several somebodies. And second, because change does not always represent progress; a statement that is true beyond question. Yet change is always necessary for progress inside to occur for any individual marketing person or organization.

---

30. Everyone has heard about political correctness, right? But if you haven't, you may better understand "political correctness" as an inability to speak truthfully about the obvious that often arises inside many contemporary corporate or educational contexts. More recently, some cultural observers increasingly suggest that woke, or being woke, imposes similar sorts of effects. One thing is certain, as this book was being written woke was having its moment. One thing that remains certain and uncertain: for how long will that moment last?

People who are genuinely motivated to succeed should consistently accept the inevitability of change, stay ahead of change, and do their best to lead change. And, once possessed of this predisposition, their best likely will be quite good.

No one can predict the future, not even their own. But everyone enjoys opportunities to create futures more to their liking. One key to creating more desirable futures in which to live, work, and play entails accepting and leading change.

Accepting change or changing itself, however, is difficult for most human beings. The phrase "most humans" includes both consumers as customers and marketers as managers and planners. But failing to initiate change inside existing plans in situations where circumstances clearly demand that some measure of transformation occur may leave institutions' worst impulses unchallenged or their ideal goals either unstated or unsupported.

Meanwhile, changes are difficult for most people to accept or initiate because as they age, people usually become more deeply immersed in and committed to whatever they already are year after year as they age. This human tendency makes the notion of tolerating much less initiating change harder to accept. The phrase "[becoming] more of . . . whatever we already are" as we age could entail becoming more rabid fans, quieter introverts, or more deeply addicted addicts. Once these "who-we-are" attitudes ossify inside minds, attitudes and minds alike become even more difficult for marketers to change. Ossified—as in hardened or fossilized—to the point where if our minds were buildings, they would feature ten floors of basement and one floor of rise.

Of course, sometimes people actually do change their minds. But voters, who are consumers, rarely change their attitudes about what branded human political product they're going to purchase through their votes or donations just because marketers tried to force them to change. And not only would such consumers not easily change their minds, they usually would be easily (and these days greatly) offended by marketers' attempts to tell them to change. In such situations, marketers are not able to show them the light without convincing consumers that their previous attitudes were wrong. Not . . . likely to . . . happen.

Marketers should generally accept the premise that their differentiation and positioning efforts, no matter how well-intended, created, or executed, will usually fail to change customers' minds. So, what's the solution? Actually, there are two solutions. First, target a new segment using the same, more-appealing-to-them, marketing mix. Or second, target the same market segment with a revised, now-more-appealing-to-them marketing mix. The ever pressing need that marketers constantly confront to successfully execute segmentation and targeting processes should now be more apparent.

Fundamental Marketing Insight 8

Successful marketers know that they must become or remain customer-focused and heavily committed to marketing. Such professionals or organizations, in effect, make promises. More importantly, each entity keeps promises it makes.

Fundamental Marketing Insight 9

Successful marketers know that the individual marketers or organizations that deliver the most value throughout their life spans and across various contexts almost always win. Organizations have life cycles too.

Fundamental Marketing Insight 10

Successful marketers know and accept that marketing is a part of their lives, for better and for worse. Successful marketers realize they are either marketing or being marketing to, all the time. Given these universal conditions, why not learn how to be more successful as both marketer and consumer?

MODULE 1.5

A Messy Illustration about Modern Marketing's Scope, Nature, and Impact

The chicken industry is messy, well, actually no small portion of it actually is chicken ****, which itself is routinely converted into fertilizer. But man, is the chicken industry profitable. Still mostly consumed in wealthy countries, pork and beef sales have remained mostly constant since 1990. Chicken consumption has grown by 70 percent.

Humans gobble so much chicken that the bird now accounts from 23 billion of the 30 billion land animals now living on farms. The total mass of farmed chicken exceeds the total weight of all other birds in the world. Stores selling cooked or uncooked chicken, whole or in parts, abound. The reasons why are obvious. Chicken is an inexpensive, tasty, and well-marketed product. The retail price of one pound of American-produced poultry has fallen $1.71 to $1.92 since 1960, adjusted for inflation. The price of beef similarly fell, but only by $1.17 per pound to $5.80.

Chicken loyalists can thank selective breeding. Chicken marketers launched "Chicken of Tomorrow" competitions for farmers in the 1940s. The aim, as described by publications of the time, was to produce "one bird big enough for the whole family—a chicken with breast meat so thick you could carve it into steaks, with drumsticks that contain a minimum of bone buried in layers of juicy dark meat, all costing less rather than more." This sounds like a new product developer's dream, to us. The breeding competitions produced something along the lines of modern broiler chicken.

Since then chickens themselves, as well as the chicken marketing industrial sector, have each continuously grown. Chickens that were the selected breed in 1957, 1978, and 2015 were compared. At fifty-six days old the three birds had average weights of .9 kilograms, 1.8 kilograms, and 4.2 kilograms. Economies of scale matter and work big-time, implying that inside this context raising one big bird is more efficient than raising two smaller options. Today farmers need only 1.8 kilogram of feed to raise 1 kilogram of chicken, down from 2.5 kilograms in 1985. One kilogram equals 2.2 pounds.

The intense use of antibiotics means farmers no long worry as much about their product's health. Before World War II farmers kept hens for their eggs and would eventually sell their meat once those chickens grew less efficient on the egg production front. This approach made sense because supply chain and economic efficiencies matter greatly. But modern antibiotic prophylactics, produced by a huge domestic pharmaceutical marketing sector, permitted poultry marketers to cram more chickens into smaller spaces where they walked less and consequently needed less feed. Yes, this process was and remains hellish for chickens. But the process proved a boom for the entire chicken supply chain, including retailers, and a blessing for individual chicken eaters inside America. Chicken consumption also grew because of rising cultural concerns about people ingesting too much saturated fat as they chomped down beef and pork, which led to heart disease or more colon cancer.

But it's not only fussy Western eaters who increasingly favor chicken. Rising incomes mean that demand for the meat is rising even faster in poorer countries. Chickens consequently are now the world's most widely traded meat. Economically, chickens are, in effect, the opposite of cars. They are produced whole. But their value is maximized once they are broken up. Global regional differences exist, however, implying, at net, that segmentation, targeting, and positioning always matter too. Westerners, for example, prefer lean white chicken meat; many *Asians* and *Africans* prefer darker meat, which includes legs and thighs. These preferences are reflected in local prices. American breasts are 88 percent more expensive than legs; in Indonesia breasts are 12 percent less expensive. Differences in the price of chicken feet are starker. The notion of eating talons is abhorrent to many Westerners, but feet figure prominently in many *Cantonese* recipes. China now imports 300,000 tons of "*Phoenix Claws*" annually. Hmm, *Phoenix Claws*, a creative marketer and brander was clearly at work here.

The fact that different countries specialize in different kinds of production also boosts trade. The *United States* and *Brazil*, the world's two largest chicken exporters, are poultry powerhouses that produce huge quantities of chicken feed, the primary cost in poultry production. *Thailand* and *China*, by contrast, dominate the processed-meat market, probably because success in each nation requires inexpensive, skilled labor. *Russia* and *Ukraine*, once net importers of chicken, have become net exporters as their grain sectors have grown. Are you sensing how marketing touches everything everywhere?

Marketers that sell or want to sell their chicken abroad face risks. Chicken has proven a flashpoint in trade negotiations. *China* imposed tariffs on *Yankee* birds in 2010 and then banned all imports in 2015, shortly after the arrival of avian flu. Who knows whether the ban will be lifted, much to the angst of American farmers, who would love to be paid more for the 20 billion chicken feet they produce each year at a rate of two *Phoenix Claws* per chicken! But for now, these feet mostly become large animal feed that passes through ever more efficient American agricultural supply chains.

The *European Union* similarly banned the import of chlorinated American chicken in 1997; owing to concerns that the wash allows lower hygiene standards in farms. Arguments about chicken also proved a big stumbling block in negotiations for the *Transatlantic Trade and Investment Partnership*, a now-failed trade deal. Some Brits fear that leaving the *European Union* will eventually void any trade deal signed with America requiring them to accept imports of such chicken.

Although the chicken boom has been good for consumers, animals' rights advocates worry that the meat industry cost-cutting measures have come at the birds' expense. The size of modern chickens is the core source of problems, in the views of many. Broilers feature breast muscles that are too big for their bones to support, leading to lameness. Chickens have become so unresponsive to humans that they appear Zombie-like. Their muscles and fat have each expanded to the extent that modern birds cannot physically mount each other for sex. This, in turns, means they have to be starved to get in the mood while hunger pangs them out of the mood. Due to these and other factors more consumers are willing to pay more for meat raised under better conditions. Sales of free-range and organic chickens, which has outdoors access, have taken flight. In *The Netherlands*, there has a backlash against plofkip—the *Dutch* word for "exploded chickens." Sales of free-range eggs have surpassed caged alternatives in the same nation.

Concerns about the health of livestock have led the *European Union* to pass the world's strictest regulations. Farmers, as responsive and rational marketers, logically are increasingly interested in improving the quality of life for their birds. But yes, these industrialized poultry lives never last long and always end with a sharp point.

One final point is this, the first, Module: You do realize we are just discussing chickens. Right? How much more complicated would these supply chain and marketing descriptions prove were we discussing something important, like, say, perfume, vodka, or smartphones? The answer is much more complicated still. For better or for worse, this is a "marketing world," and we're just living in it.

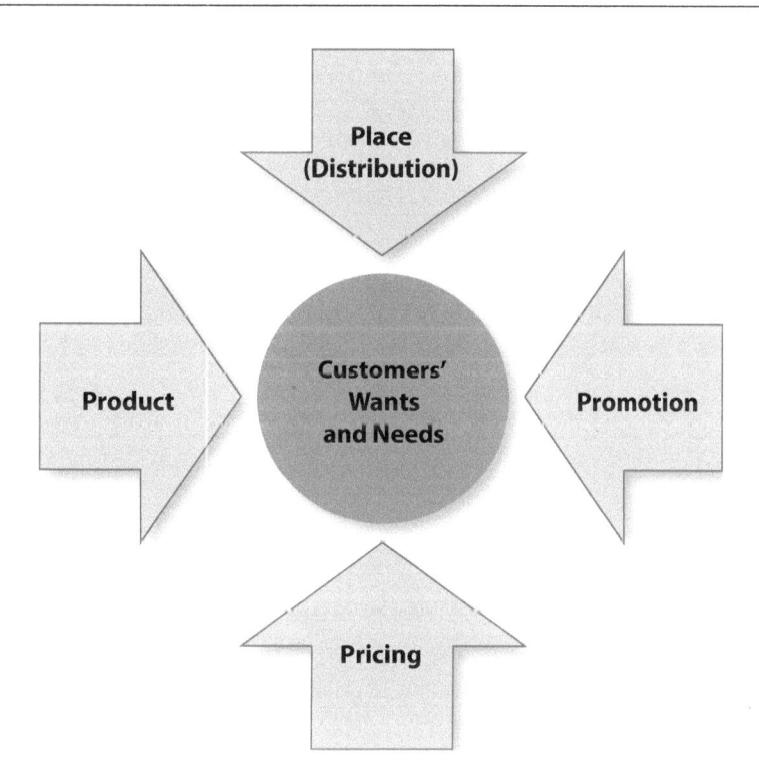

FIGURE 1.1
The Marketing Mix is the specific combination of interrelated and interdependent marketing activities employed by organizations to meet objectives.

FIGURE 1.2
The Marketing Mix

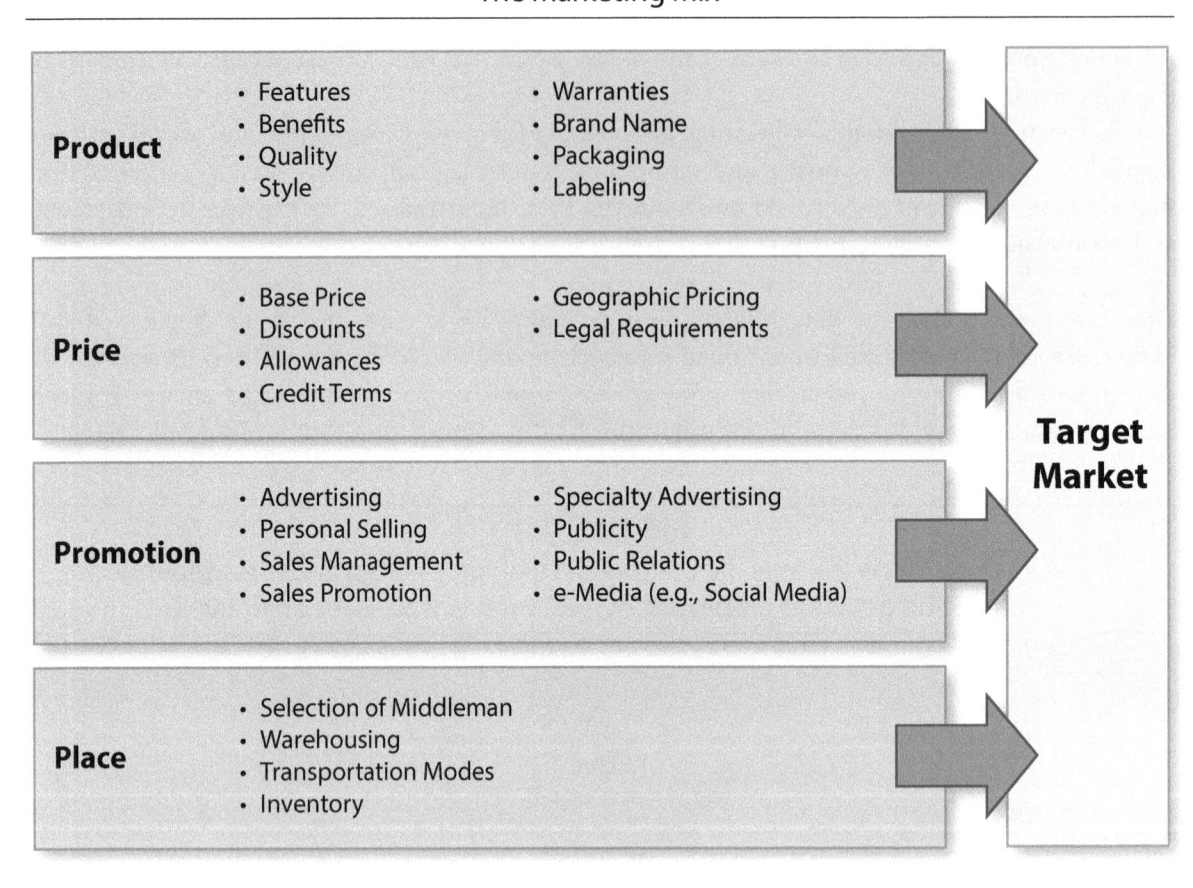

Product
- Features
- Benefits
- Quality
- Style
- Warranties
- Brand Name
- Packaging
- Labeling

Price
- Base Price
- Discounts
- Allowances
- Credit Terms
- Geographic Pricing
- Legal Requirements

Promotion
- Advertising
- Personal Selling
- Sales Management
- Sales Promotion
- Specialty Advertising
- Publicity
- Public Relations
- e-Media (e.g., Social Media)

Place
- Selection of Middleman
- Warehousing
- Transportation Modes
- Inventory

→ **Target Market**

MODULE 2

Marketing-Level Planning

MODULE 2.0

Nine + One
Strategic Marketing Laws

Principles tell people what works. Principles exist to solve or to prevent problems. The decision to follow principles is generally a good idea. The decision to learn more about the principles present inside any important and relevant discipline—such as marketing—is always a good idea.

Principles never become principles unless they have been proven to work across time and contexts or marketplaces. Otherwise, they never earn the esteemed label, principle. The fact that principles work is why accounting, operations management, IT, economics-finance, logistical and supply chain, managerial, and marketing principles are taught inside most business schools. Being all business, business schools logically focus on their discipline's core principles.

Principles typically explain and illustrate how decision-makers can best use certain time-test tactics inside specific disciplines, such as marketing, and in the process elevate those decision-makers' prospects for success as they attempt to manage marketing, supply chain, financial, operational, or technological activities. Meanwhile, time-tested tactics, and not just of the marketing sort, are typically grounded in principles.

Laws, by contrast, tell decision-makers what they can and cannot do—or should or should not do. Laws keep people in-bounds. Think of the child bumpers alongside bowling alley lanes; they function to keep kids' bowling balls outside the gutters.

Laws also permit decision-makers to discriminate between right and wrong choices—or between better and worse choices. Especially inside marketing contexts, where surprisingly few completely black or white decisions exist to be made. Often few to none one best absolutely will-work-every-time choices exist to be found or executed inside strategic decision-making marketing context situations. Things rarely if ever tie-off neatly at the ends of marketing decision-making columns, certainly not in the same manner numbers precisely tie-off inside accounting or financial spreadsheets.

Roman philosopher *Cicero* wrote, "The more laws, the less justice." Riffing slightly on this insight, the more laws or principles, the less likely it is that any marketer will follow all of them. The following set of marketing laws or principles is consequently limited to Nine + One. By the way, the + One is the most important of these ten marketing principles as well as one of the two or three laws or principles that will prove most difficult to execute successfully. The + One is the most important law or principle because the exact same marketing organizations that have executed this law or principle successfully usually are the same firms whose brand names reside high up, if not at the top, inside most B2B or B2C customers' evoked sets.

MARKETING PLANNING LAW 1

"The Law of Leadership" suggests marketers should be first-to-market, in order to have a chance to remain first, in the mind.

These days most young Americans don't know much about history—here we merely write the sad truth. But more than a few citizens still know that *Charles Lindbergh* was the first person to fly an airplane solo across the *Atlantic Ocean*. He completed the journey in 1927, the same year *Babe Ruth* hit sixty home runs; apparently 1927 was a good year for record-breaking performances. Lindbergh, who died in 1972, remains famous today, largely because he was first-to-market.

But how many people, products, ideas, places, brands, innovations, solutions, and so forth, can be first? The answer, logically, is one. Consequently, additional principles/laws that virtually assure marketing success are needed. Fortunately, they exist.

MARKETING PLANNING LAW 2

"The Law of Category" suggests that if you or your organization, product, idea, and solution cannot be first-to-market or first-to-mind, then you or your organization, product, idea, or solution should strive to be first-in-a-category.

The law of category further suggests that if your brand cannot be first-to-market, then you should establish a category in which your brand can be first. Question: Who was the second person to fly an airplane solo across the *Atlantic Ocean*? The answer is Bert Hinkle, and his second-place finish, though interesting, hardly registers on any historical stage excepting one assumes with Mr. Hinkle's ancestors. Because he was second, and because no one cares about second place. You know the old story, which is nothing if not true, unless you are the lead dog the view never changes.

Okay, so who was the third person to fly solo across the Atlantic? You're right, you probably guessed it; the answer is *Amelia Earhart*. Ms. Earhart was first in a gender-based category. Does her brand still resonate today? Check, it does, and therein resides evidence supporting the second principle.

The first law underscores the claim that "the early bird catches the worm." The second law points toward the fact that, yes, but . . . "the second mouse gets the cheese." However, what if you're not interested in being early and catching worms or being a fast-follower and getting your cheese on?

Yes, there's yet another marketing law or principle for you to pursue, as well—see Marketing Planning Law 3. A law whose value supersedes, as in replaces, the values associated with the first and second marketing laws. Which is hugely beneficial, because only one firm, product, or brand can be first inside any market or market segment and because no guarantee is in place that any firm or product or brand can create a new category.

MARKETING PLANNING LAW 3

"The Law of the Mind" suggests that if your organization and its brands cannot be first-to-market or first-to-a-category, then you and your organization should do whatever is ethical and possible to become first and remain on top in the collective mind of whatever market segment your organization is targeting.

Who was the first woman to compete in an *Indianapolis 500* formula automobile race?

The answer to that question is not the recently retired mega-successful human brand, *Monster.com* celebrity endorser, and notably non-first-place-race in an American Indy style race car winner *Danica Patrick*,[1] famous though she remains. The answer instead is *Janet Guthrie*. We agree, who? What happened? Ms. Guthrie was clearly first in her category. Should that alone be enough? No, because just as clearly, Guthrie did not earn or retain her first place or top-of-the-mind "poll-position" in the collective mind of the marketplace. Such failure is a big deal for brands that never ascended to first place, a roster that by default features most brands.

While we're playing this top-of-the-mind name game, what's the brand name of the first machine introduced into the then-new personal computer product category? The answer is not *Dell, IBM, Apple, HP, Gateway, Mac,* nor any other name from within the list of usual suspects. The answer instead is *ALT-AIR 8800*. The brand name rolls right off the tongue, right? Well, no, this was hardly the case because the *ALT-AIR* brand rolled right into and then out again from the market's collective mind. If indeed the ill-fated brand ever ascended to that esteemed position. Again, we see how being first-to-market or being first-in-a-category failed to prove sufficient, because a brand never achieved the status of being first-in-the-market's-mind.

An evoked set exists as the limited, usually three to five, group or set of brands that comes to mind first[2] when problems that brands from known product categories[3] can solve arise inside customers' lives. Marketers need their brands to be included inside the evoked sets of the segments that they target. Post-entry, the likelihood that decision-makers will select their brand increases substantially. The prospects for success of any individual brand pivots materially (for better or worse) on the degree to which the brand enters or fails to enter individual consumers' or entire market segments' evoked sets.

Once brands enter and embed inside evoked sets, they automatically reside at or near the top of metaphorical ladders inside human minds. This "residence" is important. After all, no one buys

---

1. Ms. Patrick never won a domestic *NASCAR* or *INDY* Car-style race; she did win the *Indy 300* race in *Japan* during 2007.
2. Coming-to-mind-first is also known as top-of-the-mind-awareness. Marketers engage in all manner of promotion-related marketing mix activities in the hopes of earning or sustaining top-of-the-mind-awareness for their brands.
3. Vodka product categories, or jeans, perfume, purse, vacation destination, or automotive product categories exist.

anything without first knowing the thing exists. Promotional efforts, as ingredients inside marketing mixes, are typically used to execute these brand-into-mind-insertion processes. Other sorts of positioning efforts are also pursued to introduce brands, along with their presumably differentiated values, inside the "collective" minds of targeted consumer segments.

For example, college students might perceive they are experiencing personal problems for which the best solution is to drink more beer. If *Iron City's* brand of beer does not reside inside these college students' evoked sets when these sorts of personal problems arise, *Iron City* is out of luck. Essentially, because the *Iron City* brand was never in the game.

Getting inside customers' evoked sets, locking your organization's or own professional brand inside their minds is a big part of the marketing game. And quoting *Omar*, an epic bad guy/good guy character from the paradigm-shifting cable series *The Wire* who eventually took down another bad guy/good guy character named *Stringer Bell*: "The game is out there. It's play or be played." And the games that marketers play in order to insinuate their brands high up inside customers' evoked sets grow fiercer by the day as globalization processes and new product development initiatives grow unabated and the competitive pressures placed on virtually all marketers consequently expand.

Fortunately, at least for marketers, some types of human problems don't ever go away—and are nearly universal, as well. The need to feel as if one "fits in"; the need to not feel lonely or rejected, for example; these states of felt-deprivation arise naturally and routinely among most people. What's just been described is obviously too bad and quite sad for many consumers. Yet this nearly omnipresent and highly pressing need "to-fit-in" is absolutely wonderful for marketers selling products and solutions that promise blissfulness, forgetfulness, or diversions to consumers. This is not a joke.

What follows is not a joke, either. But have you noticed how much social media and alcohol, including beer, have in common? Indeed, social media and alcohol are highly similar insofar as both marketing products are simultaneously the actual cause of and supposed solution for many problems.

MARKETING PLANNING LAW 4

"The Law of Perception" is grounded in the fact that marketing competitions are often waged and won or lost based on perceptions. Competitions between, say, *Coke* and *Pepsi*; *McDonald's* and *Burger King*; or *Apple* and *Samsung* might easily come to mind as useful examples. Perceptions, you recall, are best understood as imagined realities.

William Shakespeare summarized the value that well-managed customer perceptions can offer marketers. *The Bard,* the playwright's most famous branding identity, wrote: "There is nothing either good or bad, but thinking and perceiving that makes it so."

Aaron Sorkin recently wrote; "Often, the appearance of reality may be more important than reality itself." Sorkin is a superstar-level television and movie writer and producer, if you don't know his name you know his work.

Victor Nabokov said, related to the same topic, "Reality is one of the few words that means nothing without quotation marks." The author of the book called *Lolita* was sardonically explaining how subjective and relative, from perceiver to perceiver, perceptions actually are.

This brusque turn toward the literary was made to underscore the fact that when any two customers perceive the same stimuli they are often only coincidentally or accidentally seeing and experiencing the same thing. Customers only see what they perceive—nothing more or less. And all the while, for better and for worse, marketers occupy wonderful platforms from which to manipulate what customers see and perceive.

An irony is that marketing managers might logically also be described as marketing manipulators. However, all that most marketers are manipulating are elements of their marketing mix. In some situations when the word "manipulator" appears readers should have thoughts about the word "exploiter," as in exploiter of actual or prospective customers. But note, however, that the operative phrase was "in some situations." In some situations, marketers do actively exploit customers by manipulating them, and primarily by manipulating customers' perceptions. But this statement does not apply universally.

For example, most marketing promotional activities entail manipulation at some level. But especially advertising. Advertisers can and do finesse customers. Primarily because successful advertisers understand the customer's need to feel unique at the same time those same customers need to feel that they fit in with others. The best ads often deliver these exact values—feeling unique while also feeling as if one belongs to a desirable group—to targeted segments. Look around; someone may be playing you.

Social media, meanwhile, not just enables but actually facilitates individual encounters with things, especially news, that confirm their biases and weed out contravening facts. Yes, *Facebook, Google,* and *Twitter*, as well-branded marketers, do exactly this.

Why are the products and brands known as *Facebook* or *Twitter* so popular? To no small degree the answer relates directly to the capacity that each media platform gives its users to broadcast and to market their rage—as if the free and open distribution of anger embodied real solutions to complex problems. The recent introduction of social media further heightened the emotions of an already fraught society. *Facebook* and *Twitter* have never created content; products that have value. No, that supply chain function and marketing task is outsourced to their customers. Those customers, who also ended up being content creators, in turn, quickly learned that making more extreme statements attracts more attention for them. Inside social media consumer-to-consumer communications, the traditional rewards of supposedly righteous anger—primarily, acknowledgment and acceptance of our own unhappiness, along with feelings that the expression of our anger allows us to resolve our complaints—are not only eliminated but actually expanded as they are replaced by new incentives. (When you read the word "incentives," as you will again, think values and rewards.) Incentives such as the opportunity to earn more retweets, likes, followers, and social influence. Such incentives frequently and materially elevate the frequently challenged self-concepts of users, who addictively leverage this opportunity to ascend from zero to hero in that most important of places. Yes, their minds. The targets of *Facebook*- and *Twitter*-delivered rage bombs usually are strangers less inclined to hear out angry people than to blast back, using both barrels.

This cycle is simultaneously vicious and addictive for users. Yet this cycle is virtuous and profitable for social media marketers. And unfortunately, the happiness of many American consumers, their sense of equanimity, and national cohesiveness itself continue to circle the drain.

Best to believe that most masterful marketers have also mastered the task of manipulating people's perceptions. Because in believing this you would be right. Marketers' ability to sway customers' perceptions, in the meantime, is poised to grow exponentially. After all, virtual reality, by definition, creates substantial customer uncertainty about what is real or unreal.

MARKETING PLANNING LAW 5

"The Law of Focus" (AKA, "The Law of Ownership") is grounded in the extreme differentiating and positioning value that results from owning something. Owning what, where? Here the answer generally entails owning well-positioned words or phrases inside customers' or segments' collective minds.

The *National Football League (NFL)* once was so powerful that its brand actually owned a day of the week during each fall and winter season. The day was Sunday. In other marketing competitions, which brands own the word for coffee, the colors brown or green, MP3 players, or overnight (shipping) . . . inside the collective mind of each product category's respective target market? The answers, respectively, are *Starbucks* or is it now *Dunkin; UPS* (brown) or the *University of North Texas* or the *pro-environmental movement* (green); MP3 players (*iPod*), overnight (*FedEx*) *X-box, Kleenex, Band-Aid, Google, Facebook, YouTube,* or *Tweet* illustrate other older or current examples of brands that own words in the minds of respective markets. As does the owner of the word mayhem, *Allstate Insurance*, which is an excellent word for an insurance company to own inside its targeted market's mind. Guess *Allstate* got tired of being known for their "good hands," that is, as the "good hands" people.

To succeed, brands must "own something," or so said *Sara Blakely*. At the time she uttered these words, *Ms. Blakely* was the wealthiest American woman who had made her fortune entirely on her own. Blakely, founder and owner of *Spanx*, said, "I keep saying this to the team. We've got to own something. If we own butts, and then launch out from there, that's ok. You don't want to limit yourself to butts in consumers' mind, but you do not want to try to become everything to all people too quickly."

Ownership—acquiring and controlling it—is stunningly important to marketing success. People care about what they own; they take care of it. While it has happened, few people ever wash rented cars.

MARKETING PLANNING LAW 6

"The Law of Attributes," also called the "Law of the Opposite," is grounded in three related facts. First, all products have attributes. Second, all marketers succeed or fail based on their ability or inability to create and sustain genuine or perceived differentiation for their product. Third, all prospective customers make decisions about which alternative to purchase, generally from brands that constitute their evoked sets, based on their positive or negative evaluations of the competing products' attributes.

Having made these assertions, let's now recall that only those brands that are present, that have acquired residence, inside decision-makers evoked sets are evaluated. Consumers inevitably engage in these processes. But usually absent conscious awareness that they're doing this.

Product attributes are often called product features. Any distinction that may exist between the usage of the phrases product attributes or product features is immaterial. Features and/or attributes each create and/or deliver product value. The value of products is reflected in their perceived or actual ability to solve customer problems.

All marketers should identify, develop, and then emphasize an opposing/opposite attribute that negates or surpasses any competitor's attributes. Any creative marketer should be capable of doing this. All successful ones are. To illustrate, if your competitors' toothpaste brand emphasizes the brand-able attribute of Best Cavity Fighter as its key point of differentiation, then your firm's toothpaste brand might emphasize the attribute of Best Teeth Whitener as its point of differentiation. Your competitor might respond by emphasizing, for differentiating purposes, its brand's ability to deliver Fresher Breath. To which your corporation might react by accentuating its toothpaste brand's higher Kiss-ability Quotient, and so on. Better target this newly positioned brand at smarter people who know what quotient means—and this too is no joke. These positioning and repositioning processes unfold as games, actually marketing battles that are waged, won, or lost based on which brand does differentiation better-longer.

MARKETING PLANNING LAW 7

"The Law of Concentration" implies that marketers should strategically concentrate their strengths and then target these advantages, these core competencies, against their competitors' comparative weaknesses.

In American football, or in actual high school, college, or *Olympic*-style wrestling, the-low-man, the one best able to concentrate—leverage—his strengths against opponents' comparative weaknesses inevitably wins. The underlying premise is simple. The lower body is typically stronger and always better grounded than the upper body. This exact physical principle also prevails and plays out inside marketing competitions.

The honey badger is an infamously single-minded mammal. Through bee stings, snakebites, and various other degradations, afflictions, nuisances, and obstacles, the beast never stops killing and eating. That's because as the magazine *National Geographic* wrote, "Honey badger don't give a shit." Honey badgers concentrate on their core purposes (killing, eating, reproducing), and across time have developed and refined certain core competencies—strengths—that permit them to kill and eat well. More marketers would be more successful were they to become more single-minded in their attempts to develop, concentrate, and leverage their strengths.

Times will arise in marketing settings when it is entirely appropriate and indeed strategic to slide honey badger sorts of beast-mode. It is similarly true, however, that in marketing settings virtually any individual or organization can achieve everything they could possibly want in this world by simply concentrating on helping enough other people get what they want (i.e., focusing on solving their problems first).[4] Beast-mode, concentration-wise, is not uniformly bad, however. The good or bad of many acts depends upon the purposes for which one is initiating and executing them.

---

4. This statement is grounded in The [Philosophical] Theory of Enlightened Self-Interests. The theory is fully discussed during Module 8 and was briefly referenced earlier.

MARKETING PLANNING LAW 8

We turn now to the marketing "Law of Candor," but before doing so the word "candor" itself should be defined. Candor is a quality that motivates those who possess it to speak openly and honestly about things, including decisions, outcomes, or consequences that often speak poorly about the speaker.

The marketing Law of Candor suggests that people who have made mistakes of volition or omission should, when called out or exposed, take ownership of the facts. Candid marketers do not obfuscate, obscure, or hedge the truth. Candid marketers instead take ownership, assume responsibility, and tell the truth when something goes wrong, subject to the presence of two conditions. The first condition: you or your organization really is in the wrong. The second condition: you and/or your organization actually care about your long-term branding reputation.

Tiger Woods did not act honestly when things went wrong, public relations-wise, all those years ago; *David Letterman* did. Both men existed and continue to exist both as humans, brands, and products, and the fact that both men were caught cheating, big time, on their wives a number of years ago was brought to the public's eye at almost exactly the same time. One further fact is that Woods did not take ownership of his transgressions injured his branding power to the point where, more than one decade later, it has never fully recovered. Letterman, by contrast, quickly took highly public ownership of his marital transgressions when he was rightly accused of fundamentally doing the same thing. (He confessed his misdeeds on his show on the night of the day his cheating came to light.) Letterman's brand power suffered little, if at all.

In the depths of the mid-2000s *Gulf Oil Spill*, *British Petroleum* did not take quick responsibility for what had gone wrong. Not coincidentally, the marketer has since re-branded itself as *BP*. By contrast, *Johnson & Johnson*, the consumer-goods and pharmaceutical giant did respond instantly in the midst of the horrific consequences that arose when *Tylenol*, its mega successful pain-relief brand, was secretly laced with cyanide and six users famously died. But the fault really wasn't on the marketer; *Johnson & Johnson* and its deceased customers were victims of 1980s-era *domestic terrorism*. Many years later *BP* still struggles to recapture its magic branding dust; *Tylenol's* brand equity was restored less than three months after *Johnson & Johnson* re-stored a new version of *Tylenol*, a new product that featured as a new attribute tamper-proof packaging, to retailer shelves.[5, 6]

Huge value can be mined from stellar reputations. *Proverbs* suggests, "A good name is to be chosen over great riches, and loving favor rather than silver or gold." A wise insight, surely, but good names—highly-respected branded or personal reputations—frequently also lead to great corporate or individual professional wealth, especially in marketing contexts.

---

5. In response to this product tampering disaster, *Johnson & Johnson* instantly removed *Tylenol* from all retailer shelves. When the cyanide-based poisoning incident occurred, *Tylenol* enjoyed about an 80 percent market share in the over-the-counter analgesics market sector. *Johnson & Johnson* kept *Tylenol* out of stores for several months. Then the marketer strategically reintroduced the brand with a tamper-proof packaging feature. Tamper-proof packaging was the first of its kind; an innovation at the time. *Tylenol* not only recaptured all of its former market share, the brand actually captured about 10 percent more market share, eventually securing nearly 90 percent.

6. Racheal Bell, "The Tylenol Terrorist," *Crime Library*, True TV (2006).

Correspondingly, the possession of great wealth, or even ordinary wealth, changes everything in financially well-off consumers' lives. Wealthy people typically enjoy more options about how to spend their time or money. Because others know the rich might donate money or help them, people often come up and tell them how great they are, how what they said was wise or wonderful or fantastic, or how wonderful they look.

Meanwhile, the possession of great financial resources, genuine treasures, cannot purchase happiness. Educator *John Stuart Mills* wrote that, "Happiness is a by-product of pursuing some other worthy goal." Mills apparently understood that happiness often seemingly appears out of nowhere as a reward for people who were not actively seeking it.

Mills' lesson similarly applies to brands and to the values embedded in brands' reputations. When marketers pursue and achieve the right sorts of marketing goals, desirable branding outcomes seemingly arise as natural consequences. A conscious choice to honor the Law of Candor should generate, as by-products, more respected brands.

The ability and willingness to create and sustain relationships with prospective customers, actual customers, or other targets such as supply chain partners, employees, or investors is absolutely key to the initial development and eventual maintenance of marketing success. Few if any other activities that marketing organizations or individuals could ever execute would create new or strengthen existing relationships more effectively than simply treating others with openness and honesty. Candor is another key to marketing success, especially over the long run. Candor is critical because walking in the truth contributes directly to both the emergence and maintenance of a stellar branding reputation. Moreover, think about how much stress-free mind-space is freed-up among candid marketing leaders and managers who no longer have to remember to whom, and in exactly what manner, they lied.

MARKETING PLANNING LAW 9

"The Law of Unpredictability" reminds us about a fact that most smart people already understood: Making predictions is difficult, especially when the predictions are about the future. Yet humans are still wont to make them. This purportedly wry statement is actually no joke at all, because successful marketers are supposed to make accurate predictions today about future human behaviors. Yikes. Maybe that's why *The Doors* sang, "the future is uncertain and the end is always near" in the brand's song *Roadhouse Blues*. Maybe this is why the *Bible* is about one-third prophesy.

The only things marketers can know with comparative certainty are historical in nature. The only thing marketers know for sure about the future is that they're making predictions based on incomplete or inaccurate information that is often obtained from biased and/or less than rational sources.

What is known with greater certainty is that marketers don't win future bets by being in love with the current state of their own ideas and refusing to let their ideas grow and evolve organically across time. Marketers will more likely succeed by relentlessly re-calibrating their beliefs and predictions about the future in ways that more accurately capture actual rather than desired or imagined market or environmental conditions.

Thinking about choices—the process of decision-making—in this manner inculcates profound attitudinal shifts. Shifts that entail movements away from binary, entirely right-or-wrong thinking and toward more probabilistic approaches. Moving toward decision-making contexts in which marketers have no choice but to accept the existence of and consequently select from shades of gray.

Re-framing decision-making process in this manner clarifies. The more marketers recognize they're betting on their beliefs, which are always biased, the more likely they are to accurately temper their predictions, their decisions, their statements, and their senses (judgments) about the right or wrong paths to follow. These marketers also would more likely revise their beliefs when new non-supportive information arrives. No harm, no foul, or false accusations in play here: Everyone's beliefs are biased.

MARKETING PLANNING LAW + ONE:

This + One Marketing Planning Law is best written, albeit awkwardly, as:

> ▶ "Creating Solutions to Problems Customers Did Not Realize They Had, Yet . . ."

This + One Law means and implies that ultimately, the best way for marketers to achieve mega-levels of success is to create new value that solves new problems that the world, or at least the membership of targeted market segments did not realize it had yet. What ultimately happens is that B2C and B2B customers alike are made happier because those customers either feel or actually do become more successful as a result of their deciding to consume the new value that solves their "new problem."

Why does essentially everyone in the world "need" a smartphone today when no one in the world knew they "wanted" a smartphone or perceived that they would have major problems inside their lives without one a scant fifteen or so years ago? The twofold answer to this question is first because *Apple* understands the existence and power of this + One Marketing Law. And second, *Apple* executed the "Law of Creating Solutions to Problems that Customers Did Not Realize They Had, Yet" in a remarkably effective and now-sustained fashion.

Complete this far from simple mission, and then any marketer's next task is to convince the world that it has the problem that the solution the marketer just created "was made to solve." Stated more accurately, marketers do not need to convince the entire world. Instead, the marketer only has to convince the market segment being targeted by the marketer who created the problem that it, the segment, has the problem. Voila, once targeted segments begin believing they're experiencing "the problem," guess who has the solution? That's right, the marketer provocateur; the singular marketer who was innovative enough to create both the solution and the problem.

What types of customer problems? Actually, the problem type does not matter. What matters instead is that the problem is perceived by targeted customers and positioned to targeted customers as one that only this particular marketer's brand can solve. This particular brand, and it alone, purportedly suffices to provide a solution, because the presence and existence of the new brand and its solution is the reason why the problem arose in the first place. Read the preceding two statements carefully. Each is written exactly as intended. At times, marketers develop and promote solutions to problems that did not or do not genuinely exist. Yet by managing their strategic positioning efforts marketers are actually purposefully creating perceptions among targeted customers that these problems DO exist. At net, the best way for marketers to succeed big-time often entails creating new problems and their supposed solutions, and then selling the existence of the problems to targeted customers.

Some ideas presented in this or in most other books are comparatively trivial in nature. The idea being introduced and explained is empathically not trivial. Readers should process this law accordingly.

The core idea promoted herein can be summarized and illustrated as follows. Successful marketers generally understand how to act like arsonists, by creating problems, while also generally functioning as firefighters, by solving problems, pretty much within the same breath.

Marketers who excel at creating problems surely also believe those problems should have human-created solutions, and that they are just the humans to solve them!

Did the notion of politicians, as problem-creating human marketers that they themselves purported to be best equipped to solve, pop up in anyone else's mind? Want to solve most "political problems"? Then remove the media and the politicians. Solutions to political problems, if the problems indeed are authentic (often a debatable point), would often immediately come to mind; the problem-solvers then would enjoy the opportunity to think more freely, clearly, and fairly.

Apple again. The original *iPod* was an immediate and huge success. The following marketing principle, or law, explains why. *Apple's iPod* was the first widely-known MP3-type product that offered consumers the-then unique ability to carry huge selections of hand-picked and curated music around with them, and actually play the tunes, pretty much all the time. Prior to *iPod's* market introduction, consumers around the world had no idea they needed to carry on their person hundreds of precisely categorized songs with them on a 24/7/365 basis. Pre-*iPod*, people were all already listening to their music, and were satisfied with the media delivering their favorite music during preceding decades. But once the new solution was available, and was shown to be easy to use, many consumers quickly realized they had a problem if they did not have the solution. The rest is *Apple* history. *Apple* history? Sure. Since 2008, *Apple* has owned the world. We're just living in it.

Or, study the following data, taken from *Time Magazine* (2010): "24% of 3200 college students sampled in a recent survey took psychiatric medication in 2008, compared with 11% of college students in 1997." The most recent evidence suggests the student number right now is closer to 33 percent. The statistic further reinforces historical principles discussed below.

What do you think happened? Did, during a twelve-year-period, domestic college students become about 110 percent more likely to suffer from psychiatric problems? Or, is it more likely that once *Big Pharma*[7] became extremely proficient at marketing anti-depressant medications purportedly

---

7. *Big Pharma*, or the world's ten largest pharmaceutical marketers. From highest to lowest revenue, that would be *Johnson & Johnson, Novartis (Switzerland), Pfizer, Roche Holding AG (Switzerland), Bayer (Germany, Merck & Co., Sanofi S.A. (France), GlaxoSmithKline (UK), AstraZeneca (Sweden),* and *Apple.* Is this reference to *Apple* offered in jest? Yes, sort of. But not really. The truth is that *Apple's* products simultaneously stimulate/sedate, educate/stupefy, and solve/create psychological problems among tens of millions of users.

providing pharmaceutical-based solutions more depression-related problems somehow "magically" became "more apparent" during the years 1999–2008?[8]

The evidence is ample and difficult to dispute. Once supposed pharmaceutical solutions to psychiatric problems existed, more and more psychiatric problems were diagnosed or otherwise suspected to exist. And, as you likely suspect, far more than 24 percent of US university students regularly take prescribed psychiatric-related mediation(s) today, as discussed during the next paragraph. Marketing never sleeps, after all. Call us cynical, but is it possible that *Big Pharma* and *Big Medical*, being marketers and solution-providers to their cores, implicitly or explicitly realized that far more profits could be secured by each sector if and when more consumer depression-related problems were diagnosed? Sure, this is possible. Indeed, this is likely what happened.

This story, disturbing as it is, does not end there because between 2009 and 2017, an additional 52 percent increase in the onset of depression among high school students has been reported. Why? Was it more screen time, another phenomenon and purported solution brought to the world, ironically, at unreasonable prices, by marketing? Perhaps. More family breakups? This surely did not help. But likely, most of this additional "growth in [authentic or merely perceived] depression" emerged as a result of *Big Pharma* marketers continuously flexing their muscles in the service of their desire to create the perception among high school-aged kids, and those older, that they had a problem—and Pharma had a solution.

The *Big Pharma* corporations and their psychiatric/psychological medical partners are nothing if not persistent, especially when the task involves creating new consumers problems that need to be solved. This newly invented emotional malady is called burnout syndrome. Burnout syndrome arises at work when employees get bored, stressed, or fatigued. Yeah, right, sounds like a normal day at the office to us—and no doubt to most people who work inside professional office settings. But if marketers can persuade enough people that they are suffering from this problem the same pharmaceutical corporations or psychological practitioners can likely also master the task of convincing the same employee/consumers that marketers also have a solution for the "problem." (See disclaimer).[9]

This marketing principle applies to nations too. This makes sense because nations are products—and absolutely elect to brand themselves as such. *Russia*, for example, is rightfully infamous for creating problems and then sitting down at the table with the afflicted parties for purposes of negotiating, brokering, and selling—all marketing functions—its solutions. Those *Russia*-created problems have arisen, most recently, inside *Crimea*, *Syria*, and *United States Presidential Elections*. *Russia's* proposed

---

8. "College Students Exhibiting More Severe Mental Illness, Study Finds," *American Psychological Association* (August 12, 2010).

9. The associated text, which remains fundamentally true, was written before Corona-19 and its dire consequences appeared on anyone's radar. During 2020 and 2021 depression rates among young people—often as young as elementary-school-aged people—utterly blew up. The primary cause of the depression pandemic that arose during this period was the forced isolation and boredom visited against their will upon legions of young people as schools shut down, remote teaching and non-learning learning proliferated, and students themselves grew more isolated . . . feeling truly alone. "Social needs" are real; see Module 7. Once their social needs were no longer satisfied, depression problems soared among young consumer segments. This relationship was entirely predictable. In fact, the 2021 data showed that young people were ten times more likely to die from depression than from COVID-19 during 2020. COVID-19 was such a freakish event: so far the only disease in history where the healthy were quarantined along with the sick.

solutions often entail less than candid promises to not cause more problems if the victim of the initial problem that *Russia* created agrees to bow down to the offending nation's, as a marketer, proposal. *Russia*, like many other successful marketers, benefits from functioning as both arsonist and fireman.

John Swartzwelder is a-should-be-famous person about whom readers likely know nothing. Mr. Swartzwelder should be famous because he wrote fifty-nine episodes for *The Simpsons*. One of the wittiest and revealing lines he ever wrote for *The Simpsons* illustrates exactly how an array of marketers function both as fire-starters (problem-creators) and firefighters (presumed problem-solvers) at various junctions inside lives as they consume one particular product. Said *Homer Simpson*, in the midst of a manic barroom, as he delivered a toast: "To alcohol! The cause of, and the solution to, all of life's problems."

How many tens of thousands of large and small marketing organizations have profited and continue to profit immensely from selling alcohol? How many thousands of large and small marketing organizations have profited and continue to profit immensely from peddling "cures" (solutions) for the negative consequences that trail excessive alcohol consumption like trash in the wake of huge ships?

Or, sadly, the "creating solutions to problems . . . that do not yet exist" principle may have been unethically applied inside the domestic health care sector. Writing in *The Atlantic Magazine*, Ferris Jabr suggests that most consumers have no need whatsoever to visit the dentist every six months, despite what the dentistry industry's marketing endeavors to have you believe. Jabr further writes that consumers might postpone having micro cavities filled because they often heal on their own or avoid having any root canal work done before getting a second opinion. The article goes on to describe the profession "as much less scientific—and for more prone to gratuitous procedures"—than most customers assume.[10]

SHOULD AND DO THESE MARKETING LAWS/PRINCIPLES ALWAYS APPLY?

The answer to the question embedded inside the header is a clear and easily defensible "no." Serious marketers or those who aspire to one day function as serious marketers should learn these nine + one marketing laws and understand why they exist. Then, if and when marketing conditions and contexts merit it, they can be broken. Like many laws or principles, there are times and places where these admonitions will not apply or will fail to capture or direct marketing decisions to the best possible approach.

---

10. F. Jabr, "The Trouble with Dentistry," *The Atlantic* (May 2019): 75–83.

MODULE 2.1

Developing/Executing Strategic Plans at Marketing Levels

LEVEL I AND LEVEL II PLANNING

Strategic business planning can and should be conducted at two levels.

First, planning should be executed at the corporate level. At the corporate level the strategic goal of organizations is to meet and beat competition in ways that ensure those organizations' survival and long-term success.[11] Strategic planning is conducted at an overall organizational level for accounting, financial management, information technology/operations management, human relationship, and marketing/supply chain functional areas.

Second, planning processes can be executed at each functional level. Functions, again, that include the marketing/supply chain management level. Fundamentally, the job of marketing strategists is to create customer demand. By contrast, the fundamental job of supply chain managers is to fulfill, or satisfy, customer/partner demand.

Nothing happens inside any organization until someone, marketers, sells something. Nor can anything be sold by any organization until someone and something provides marketers the means to sell the typically branded product. The "someone" is usually supply chain managers. The "something" is always supply chain management processes.

---

11. The preceding statements are all true and useful. But what are strategic goals themselves? Or goals as orders, for example? Yes, goals actually are orders issued from higher-ups inside organizations. But strategic goals also exist as aspirations; marketing planners' hopes that what they have directed to happen ultimately comes to pass.

Module 2.1 is designed to address strategic business planning at the marketing-functional level. The two-headed goal of marketing strategists is to:

- Manage their "marketing mixes" in ways that create differentiating value and uniquely desirable positions for their brands . . .
- . . . As their organization targets specific market segments.

The marketing mix is the primary tool that any organization can wield to create value for and capture value from customers. The supply chain management function exists as one of the 4Ps that collectively make-up marketing mixes when tangible products such as *Hanes* underwear are being marketed. The supply chain management function relatedly exists as one of the 7Ps that collectively constitute marketing mixes when intangible services such as *Match.com* or *Ourtime.com* dating services are marketed. Inside either the 4Ps or the 7Ps supply chain management planning processes and actual marketing activities are classified within the Place "P."

FIRST, THINK INSIDE-OUT AND THEN OUTSIDE-IN

Marketing strategists first should think inside-out. Why? Because planning processes, like automobiles, are best driven from the inside-out, not the other way around. But situations arise in which marketing planners should also think outside-in. In fact, such situations routinely arise.

To think outside-in, planners should step outside of and then look back into their organizations. At that point managers should ask and honestly answer the following questions:

- What customer needs does our organization satisfy now?
- What customer needs could we satisfy now? In the future?
- What is the gap between the needs we could satisfy in the future and the needs that we satisfy now? How do we bridge the gap?
- What competitive advantages[12] do we currently enjoy?
- What competitive advantages should we emphasize as we develop and execute our marketing mix?
- What old competencies[13] should we de-emphasize?
- What new competencies should we create?

---

12. Competitive advantages are defined as strong points of differentiation and positioning advantage that firms either possess or seek to create by developing and executing their marketing strategies. Ideally, competitive advantages are sustainable.

13. Competencies, often described as core competencies, are resources that marketing organizations possess or marketing activities that organizations can perform particularly well. Core competencies generally exist as resources and activities upon which lasting differentiation and successful positions can be established. The sources of core competencies might include an organization's possession of branding advantages; design advantages; more efficient supply chain management processes leading to lower costs and/or higher product performance; technological advantages; or closer relationships, which lead to greater intimacy with and greater loyalty from customers. This list could be extended.

The outside-in planning process appears easy, is absolutely logical, and is apparently difficult to master. Outside-in-strategizing is difficult to execute because humans are cognitively wired to envision managing change-related tasks as activities that should be done from the inside-out.

When engaging in outside-in thinking strategic decision-makers are forced to deliberately change their points-of-view. When planning, looking at business life or just plain life from both-sides-now always makes sense. First, because people don't see strategic trends, opportunities, or threats as they are; people see these things as they are. Second, because human beings' points-of-view; as they seek to understand and make-sense-of stimuli, are intrinsically dependent upon their points-of-viewing. Contemporary *Israelis* and *Palestinians* experience the same environmental stimuli. However, the two citizen (and consumer) segments differ radically in their interpretations of these stimuli, because their points-of-view are typically so radically different.

We believe that the best way to understand complex systems such as marketing organizations and their problems, challenges, or environmental opportunities or threats is to examine those systems from an outsiders' point-of-view. For example, planners could adopt the perspective of outsiders who seek to acquire or destroy them. Marketing planners clearly could benefit, for example, from evaluating their companies through the eyes of corporate raiders. What this means is that marketing planners could empathically place themselves strategically inside their competitors' brains if not their shoes, and then decide what they as planners could do to ensure that the pirates win. Then those marketing planners should pursue an opposite tact to elevate the prospects that their organization wins.

SECOND, THINK ABOUT WHAT SHOULD BE THOUGHT ABOUT

Marketing strategists should think about, then identify, and eventually prioritize what they should be thinking about.

Before planning, marketing managers should evaluate how best to:

- Position or re-position their brands, as necessary—Marketing planners may need to create new and useful and therefore innovative ideas leading to new products that satisfy either new or existing customers' demands and problems more effectively.
- Pinpoint key external environmental changes and challenges—Planners should detect opportunities and threats as early as possible, ideally way before competitors, as market conditions, environmental factors, and customer preferences shift and evolve. Planners should keep-their-collective-head-on-swivels. Observations and investigations should be done either to keep organizations on the offensive or to pre-plan defensive measures. Cultures, for example, change constantly, in predictable yet unknowable ways. Exactly when do cultures change? Who knows? At what point in American cultural history did it become verboten for drugstores to sell cigarettes out in the open while condoms began being openly displayed? The one thing known for certain right here is that marketers should constantly pay attention to their environments.

- ▶ Lead their firm's internal social system to new and more desirable places—Successful planning entails putting the right people together; ensuring these right people interact through the right sorts of behaviors; and making certain that the right information—insights that facilitate better decision-making faster—is available for them to deliberate as they prepare to make presumably strategic decisions.
- ▶ Mold productive teams. The primary challenge that arises when attempting to mold productive teams follows from the need to get competent, high-ego people to work together smoothly.
- ▶ Establish goals. Ideally, marketing managers will identify and prioritize desired outcomes that balance what organizations can become with what is realistic but still challenging for those organizations to achieve.
- ▶ Address social and environmental forces by anticipating, clearly identifying, and ultimately responding to all manner of external pressures that organizations cannot control but should manage, mitigate, or exploit to the extent possible. Such pressures inevitably influence the future outcomes that organizations should plan to achieve.
- ▶ Establish sharp priorities (and perhaps even introduce "catfish" into their organization's internal environments).

The initial part of the two-step process by which sharper organizational priorities can be established is relatively easy to manage. Define the path forward by establishing goals. Then align resources, actions, and the organization's human resource energies (the Talent portion of the "3P's") in ways designed to achieve the goals. The second part is more esoteric and requires a longer explanation—particularly our "what-the-heck" reference to "catfish." This follows.

During a time when no reasonably-priced *Trader Joes Wild Salmon* brand existed, consumers living near the northeastern *Atlantic Coast* region ate a lot of codfish. They ate cod in a similar fashion and for similar reasons that salmon is popular and deemed healthy today. Consumers around the country eventually wanted a piece of the action, especially after efficient rail shipping services began to proliferate throughout America (that's the supply chain, by the way).

So, enterprising marketers who had their fingers on the pulse of this environmental trend began loading live codfish on trains inside aquariums. But post-arrival, the still-alive and therefore fresh but inactive, bored, and depressed cods failed to deliver the textures or taste that coastal fans of codfish had come to expect. The solution, because successful marketers who also plan to continue their success specialize in developing and providing solutions, was to insert catfish, natural predators of codfish, in the same aquariums. The now active and more engaged codfish suddenly tasted much better post-arrival from their train trips.

To keep sharp and fresh in their planning most professionals need catfish in their lives. The presence of catfish keeps marketers on their toes; keeps them sharp as opposed to lazy. What's your catfish? If you don't know and/or don't have one or two, it's time to identify them.

MODULE 2.2

Overview

A three-step process should be pursued when strategic marketing plans are developed and executed.

STEP 1: ANALYZE MARKETING OPPORTUNITIES

Organizations must pick and choose the right marketing opportunities. Primarily because no single organization, product, or brand can be all things to all people. Consequently, strategists should pick and choose their shots.

Marketing opportunities exist whenever and wherever unsatisfied or less-than-fully-satisfied customers or prospects exist. Satisfied people don't buy much of anything—other than the obvious need that exists to purchase necessities or staple goods.[14] This is why one crucial marketing task often involves making customers perceive that they are unsatisfied—before offering these unhappy souls actual or merely perceptually satisfying solutions.

Making customers feel unsatisfied is rather easy to do. The *Rolling Stones*, after all, wrote and performed a famous song suggesting *"You Can't Always Get What You Want."* Nothing has changed during the intervening fifty years since this song (or new product) was first written, including the fact that most consumers still don't realize that they cannot always get what they want. Many, though not all, of those consumers consequently continuously feel miserable.

Some marketers have mastered methods through which they create false wants and needs—creating whims inside customer minds that only their brand and the solutions it promises to deliver can satisfy them. *Apple, Prada,* or *Mercedes* come to mind. The *United States* generally lacks reliable or extensive public transportation systems. Therefore, most Americans need a reliable automobile. At the same time, most Americans would also want a *Mercedes*, or some similarly prestigious brand, as

---

14. Staple goods are inventoried items that are core to one's business or are core to the performance or conduct of consumers' or customers' normal business or personal activities. For example, hooks and fishing line are staple goods for any tackle shop. Meanwhile, hooks and fishing line also represent staple goods for any consumer who enjoys fishing—unless s/he exclusively uses nets or traps to solve his/her fish-catching "problems."

well, to provide a solution to their transportation problems. But the fact remains that most Americans do not actually "need" such a high-priced and/or prestigious solution; instead they merely "want" it.

These three brands have masterfully managed their marketing mix in ways that have made the particular values they are selling appear compelling to the world—at times seemingly irresistibly compelling, even at high prices. And neither of these three brands are being criticized here. Instead, *Apple, Prada,* or *Mercedes* are being held up as laudable examples of how to do marketing right.

Marketing opportunities also exist wherever customers' or prospective customers' problems or needs have not been solved or satisfied. We see again why successful marketers embrace the principle that they operate in the need-satisfaction/problem-solving business. Marketers, at net, should view themselves as problem-solvers and need-satisfiers, as well as promise-makers and promise-keepers.

Finally, marketing opportunities exist wherever firms are creative enough to develop solutions to problems that prospective customers did not yet realize they had; likely because the supposed problems themselves are not actually real.

A lot of marketers also function as problem-creators. However, all marketers should view themselves as such—as problem creators. This is because when individual marketing professionals and their organizations are able to use promotional and/or new product development efforts to "create" particular sorts of problems and position those "problems" or "shortfalls" inside the minds of customers or prospective customers; that is, the types of troubles that those marketers and them alone are uniquely qualified and positioned to solve, the problem-creating marketers can increase their branding power, market share, prices (usually), and of course their revenues and profits. Creating perceptions among consumers, for example, they are NOT thin enough, healthy enough, wealthy enough, popular enough, blemish-free enough, and on and on. Point in fact, the list of human wants that can be stimulated through creative marketing efforts is essentially endless. But if those prospective and targeted customers are smart enough to make the right decisions by purchasing the products, no, the solutions that a given marketer's brand offers to their problems, then they can finally be happy. Or so the associated problem-creating marketer or marketing organization would gently or vigorously promise to the customers it is targeting.

STEP 2: SELECT TARGET MARKETS

Target markets are groups or a group of customers or prospective customers that marketing organizations are best prepared to pursue, serve, and satisfy.

Marketing organizations should select (or target) the segment or segments whose needs (or problems) they are best able to satisfy (or solve). Marketers satisfy needs or solve problems through the genuine or merely perceived values that their marketing mixes create and deliver. Marketers exist to satisfy customers' needs. Marketers exist to solve customers' problems. When readers see the word "need," they should think "problem." When readers see the word "problem," they should think "need." (Yes, these exact points have been previously made. However, this purposeful repetition should signal how these four points actually are.)

After these targeting (or selecting) processes are complete, marketing organizations should create unique marketing mixes, each capable of creating and delivering uniquely desirable values, for each segment that they plan to target. When targeting new segments, marketers often need to develop unique and uniquely desirable new marketing mixes. When targeting new-to-the-world segments that they have created through innovative new product development, marketers already have hopefully created a uniquely desirable new marketing mix.

STEP 3: DEVELOP/EXECUTE MARKETING MIXES

As a logical and informative way to understand marketing mixes and how they operate, first, think meatloaf. Next, think about marketing mixes themselves. Finally, think about how these two concepts—meatloaf and the marketing mix—are connected.

When thinking meatloaf, ignore the *Bat Outa Hell* actor/singer named *Meatloaf* who also starred in the late 1970s cult classic movie called *The Rocky Horror Picture Show*. No, consider the sorts of meatloaves that American consumers have eaten, literally consuming them, for generations. The sort of dish that you or some family member has mixed together on various occasions based on various recipes, and then cooked and served (delivered in the marketing mix vernacular) to you and your family, and then you and your crew literally ate it up.

Now reflect upon three additional related issues. First, various recipes exist that can be used to cook/create desirable and relatively healthy or unhealthy meatloaves. Second, every time chefs change any ingredient in meatloaf recipes, entirely new meatloaves are created. Third, some meatloaves that emerge from these new recipes will prove more appealing, attractive, and valuable to certain types of consumers. Yet those same consumer types, or segments, may utterly reject other meatloaf products that emerge. All of which is utterly logical and predictable. After all, as noted, few to no products can be all things to all people.

The connection between meatloaf and the marketing tool called the marketing mix works like this: Any time marketers change any element (ingredient) inside their marketing mix (recipe) a new marketing mix, one that delivers different sorts of values, has been created. Each segment targeted by any organization in turn will either seek out, ignore, and/or be turned off/turned on by different sorts of branded marketing mix value. This is why marketing organizations are continuously changing and upgrading their marketing mixes and the values that those mixes create and deliver. Or, at least, this is why marketers should continuously refine their marketing mixes and the values each delivers. The goal is to pursue every reasonable measure to ensure that one and only one set of marketing mix values aligns with the core values that the members of each targeted marketing segment value are most likely to desire and embrace.

The doll named *Barbie*, for example, recently received a full makeover. For the first time since she was introduced to American girls during 1959, *Mattel* expanded the line of iconic toys to include three new body types—curvy, tall, and petite. Young customers could also customize *Barbie's* hair style, color, and texture, along with her skin color, for the first time. These changes in *Mattel's* original marketing mix[15] were belatedly initiated to accommodate and address the fact that the domestic

---

15. *Barbie*, the doll, illustrates the product portion—or ingredient—of the "4Ps" for *Mattel's* marketing mix.

population is far heavier and more racially diverse than it was during the era when *Barbie* was first introduced.[16]

Marketing mixes, as well as targeted market segments and preferred positioning choices, should evolve across time and market context. And being real, *Mattel* had no strategic choice but to change *Barbie*. The toy currently exists as a cultural relic that likely is approaching the end of its Product Life Cycle (see Module 9). Barbie is a vestige of the past that is no longer compatible with the cultural *zeitgeist*.[17]

Targeting (Pursuing) Multiple Segments

Marketing firms usually target multiple market segments. Think about *Applebee's*, the restaurant chain, for example. *Applebee's* clearly recognizes large segments of consumers exist who would like to eat out occasionally but who are unable or unwilling to spend a lot of money while doing so. Does *Applebee's* have a marketing mix for them? Sure it does; the marketing mix value proposition is called *Applebee's Two-for-$20* or *Two-for-$25* two-course or three-course meal deals.

Obviously, another type of consumer segment exists that wants to dine out but is calorie/health-conscious—and knows that restaurant meals on average are far fattier and more calorically-challenged than those they could prepare at home. *Applebee's* acknowledges this fact and this segment too and has prepared customized marketing mix offerings for the consumers who comprise this segment. The restaurant features several items on its regular menu as healthier choices.

Finally, there is most of the American population. Huge segments of consumers exist who want to dine out, drink-all-they-want, and consume all-the-fat and have all-the-fun, all-the-time—and from the looks of things does not appear overly concerned about calorie content. Oh yeah, does *Applebee's* ever have a marketing mix offering for them. *Applebee's*, after all, positions its brand as *The Neighborhood Bar* and offers as many big burger and fries or chicken-fried-steak options, along with whatever alcoholic beverages any consumer would reasonably or not so reasonably want to drink while they're eating all that fat. *Neighborhood Bar* imagery is part of *Applebee's* positioning and branding promise.

Repeating ourselves, marketers should develop a unique and uniquely desirable marketing mix for each segment they target. *Applebee's* does exactly this. This implies, as well, that marketers such as *Applebee's* hopefully develop a strongly differentiated value proposition and position inside the collective mind of each targeted segment. This makes perfect strategic sense. It's never good to stand for nothing. Stand for nothing and organizations or for that matter individual people will likely fall for anything. In the meantime, customers are unlikely to fall—as in love—for the marketer's brand.

---

16. Because the point illustrates key marketing principles, note that *Barbie* was originally developed based on a "love doll" model and targeted toward *German* men during the early 1950s. The specific marketing principles illustrated through this lurid example are new product development, re-targeting, and re-positioning.

17. *Zeitgeist*, ironically, is a *German* word that literally means spirit of the times in "spirit (geist) of the times (zeit)" in the *English* language. The word *zeitgeist* is also frequently used in the contemporary *English* language.

Positioning by Managing Marketing Mixes

By now you hopefully realize that marketing organizations should attempt to establish desirable *positions* by successfully managing their marketing mixes. *7-Up, Classic Coke,* and/or *Dr. Pepper* all compete inside the soft drink product category and market sector. Each brand competes effectively.

For instance, when you read, see, or hear the word, *7-Up,* as a brand name, does a particular set of images enter your mind? The answer, almost certainly, is yes. This is because the soft drink product known as *7-Up,* or rather its brand managers, have successfully positioned *7-Up's* key traits, characteristics, and values in your mind. Similarly, when you read, see, or hear about the *Classic Coke* or *Dr. Pepper* soft drink brands, similar sorts of perceptual processes likely unfold inside your mind. Right? Those "perceptual processes that likely unfold" inside consumers' minds include a mixture of feelings, thoughts, associations, images, and the like.

What about the automobile product category? Think about the *Dodge, Ram,* and *Prius* brands. Can you tell these three automobile brands apart, without actually seeing any of the physical products, inside your mind? Could you similarly explain with a reasonable degree of accuracy exactly what each brand promises to customers with respect to the benefits, solutions, and values it will deliver to customers, should they purchase the *Dodge, Ram,* or *Prius* brand? Maybe you can, maybe you cannot, and the answer largely depends on whether you are a truck guy or gal, or a greenie. But among the tens of millions of American consumers who do care about their trucks and/or care about trucks in general—or who care passionately about the environment—well, on average those folks would have little to no trouble precisely explaining the values that each brand promises.

Marketing positions entail unique bundles of perceived values, attributes, solutions, even warm or hostile thoughts. These unique perceptual bundles are created, and hopefully take up residence—if the positions are positive—inside the collective minds of targeted customer segments. Marketers create these perceptual bundles. This is another way of saying marketers create positions.

The word position, from marketers' perspective, can be described in at least three different ways. First, positions can be described as sets of images (i.e., mental representations) that customers develop about characteristics associated with branded products. Second, positions can be described as collective sets of perceptions that targeted market segments develop and retain about brands' abilities to satisfy their needs or solve their problems. Third, positions could be described as how particular brands measure up against—are perceived as more or less desirable than—competing branded products from the same product category. Certain automotive brands, smartphone brands, or blue jeans brands are perceived as more or less desirable than other competing auto, smartphone, or blue jeans brands.

Winning brands are perceived as more desirable based on the positions that their product managers, brand managers, or marketing managers have established for them. Brands should be positioned inside targeted market segment's communal mind such that the brand is perceived as "the one" that delivers unique and uniquely desirable value. Successful differentiation leads to successful positioning. Successful positioning leads to sustainable competitive advantages.

MODULE 2.3

SWOT Analyses, Missions, Goals

The identification of opportunities or threats represents a reasonable first step in most strategic marketing planning processes. Opportunity and threat identification typically begins with SWOT analyses.

STEP I: SWOT ANALYSES

The word "SWOT" is an acronym. The "S" and the "W" stand for Strengths and Weaknesses. The "O" and the "T" indicate Opportunities and Threats.

Strengths/Weaknesses

Strengths and weaknesses exist inside marketing organizations themselves. Organizational strengths or weaknesses follow from any marketing organization's advantages or limitations relative to the strengths and weaknesses (advantages or limitations) possessed by their primary marketing competitors. Marketing organizations should leverage their strengths; ethically exploiting them. Relatedly, strategic marketers should do everything possible, strategically speaking, to either strengthen their organization's weaknesses or mitigate the effects of their organizations' weaknesses.

Assume that your organization is a professional football team; that you coach it; and that your team's strength is its ground—or running—game. In brief, your team specializes in "ground and pound." There is good news: the relative weakness of next Sunday's opponent is stopping the run. The preferred strategy is clear. Run the ball down an opponent's throat until and unless that competitor initiates strategic responses designed to strengthen or mitigate (lessen) its defensive weaknesses. (Your team presumably would then switch up its strategy and then start flinging the ball around more often.)

Similar principles apply inside business competitions. One marketing organization might derive strategic advantage from technological strengths or reputational advantages that it has earned and now enjoys. This marketer might choose to emphasize and exploit these advantages when differentiating and creating positional advantages against competitors. And competitors such as *Nike* price accordingly (think higher, or premium prices). *Nike* is logically, strategically, and ethically—because no consumers are forced to pay more to purchase *Nike* branded shoes—exploiting its strategic strength in order to win its marketing competitions. As the brand's name implies it should; after all, *Nike* is the name of the ancient *Greek* name for the god of victory.

However, other marketers might possess and strategically leverage their possession of cost-based advantages as they seek to differentiate and establish desirable positions for their brands. Supply chain efficiencies that have been strategically cultivated can facilitate cost-based advantages. Marketers that enjoy cost-based advantages may spend less treasure when making products or when pushing those products downstream toward end-user markets. *Walmart's* cost-based advantages allow the retailer to charge lower prices across a broad range of product categories but still earn acceptable profits. When offering lower priced products *Walmart* is exploiting strengths that the retailer strategically created. Not surprisingly, *Walmart* has also earned great reputational advantage,[18] tremendous customer intimacy, among tens of millions of Americans who appreciate the fact that *Walmart* offers lower prices along vast assortments of product categories. This consumer support is clear; they vote with their wallets.

Opportunities/Threats

Opportunities and threats exist outside . . . of marketing organizations. Opportunities or threats would exist even if marketers did not exist.

Opportunities and threats are typically related to environmental trends, customer trends, competitor trends, regulatory trends, economic trends, and so forth, that the marketing entity is confronting.

Opportunities or threats consist of trends that are moving in favor of or moving against the best strategic interests of marketing organizations. Trends moving in favor of organizations are called opportunities. Trends moving against the best interests of organizations are deemed threats.

At times, the same uncontrollable environment trend may function either as an opportunity or threat inside the same firm. Radically higher domestic fuel prices, for example, represent an opportunity for Toyota's *Prius* gas-sipping hybrid car brand. This same surge toward higher fuel prices, however, represents a threat for Toyota's *Tundra* gas-guzzling truck brand.

---

18. Facts are facts and consequently are stubborn, as in stiff-necked, things. Facts should not be ignored. The fact is that *Walmart* has inspired legions of critics, as well. Mammoth-sized tradeoffs exist between the values being generated and those being destroyed whenever Walmart comes to or stays in a market. But back to those facts. Fact 1: By managing its supply chain partnerships so effectively well *Walmart* has saved billions of dollars for millions of domestic consumers for decades. Fact 2: For decades, *Walmart* has also destroyed thousands of smaller domestic retailers who have a snowball's chance in . . . of leveraging *Walmart*-sized economies of scale. The fact that *Walmart* logically purchases less expensive foreign-made goods to retail domestically also rankles many Americans. What's present here is part paradox, because each set of conflicting facts presented is true, and part wicked-problem. A paradox that creates wicked-problems inside the minds of many consumers and public policy analysts that unlikely will be resolved during any reader's lifetime.

STEP 2: DEVELOP A NEW OR REFINE AN EXISTING MISSION

A reasonable second step in any strategic marketing planning process entails (a) examining the firm's current mission; (b) creating a new mission for the firm, if one does not currently exist; or (c) refining the firm's current mission. If firms' internal strengths or weaknesses have evolved or devolved, or if the external opportunities or threats facing marketing organizations have radically changed, the time to refine the mission has likely arrived.

The goals that marketers develop through the strategic planning process should always align with their organizations' mission statements. This is the primary reason why substantial attention or renewed attention should be paid to any marketers near or at the beginning of the planning process.

The American author *Mark Twain* said the two most important days in people's lives are the day on which they were born and the day on which they figure out the reason why. If they already exist inside a given marketing organization, mission or vision statements exist to explain and answer the "reason why question" to engaged employers; missions are designed to answer "why does this firm exist." If they do not exist in the same place, mission or vision statements must be developed to explain, among other things, the reasons why a firm exists.

James Thurber was another renowned American author and humorist. He wrote, and suggested, everyone should learn what s/he is running toward, running away from, and why. That these two famous thinkers and doers thought and expressed the same core sentiments about the importance of having a mission, without, to our knowledge, cribbing from one another, should directly underscore to readers exactly how important it is for them, and any organizations they lead, to have the right mission in place.

Success inside marketing, or for that matter inside life, often comes after professionals let go of or ignore the small things that bother them in order to remain resolutely focused on the bigger things that they need to do and the outcomes that they absolutely must achieve. Such professionals, in brief, understand the profound strategic differences that distinguish "nice to haves" from "must haves" or that separate "nice to do's" from "must do's." Nice to haves or dos are luxuries. Must-haves or dos are necessities.

In brief, strategic planners should develop or refine the mission, remember the mission, and resolutely remain on mission.

A Mission Is . . .

Any organization's mission equals that organization's current vision equals that organization's future direction. Mission statements are that important. Mission statements designate opportunities that marketing organizations should or should not pursue. The importance of missions, which are equivalent to self-directing visions, has been recognized for millennia. *Proverbs* 29:18 states "where there is no visions people perish." Please substitute the word "organizations" for the word "people" inside the preceding proverb. There, now you understand more completely just how important missions actually are.

Mission statements, correspondingly, might frame organizational futures (as well as employees' collective futures) as places where nasty pasts indeed can become the past—as in gone—as organizations develop more desirable futures for themselves and their customers by following the guidelines (i.e., pathways), laid out inside mission statements. Mission statements should encourage employees and direct (focus) their future efforts while simultaneously constraining their efforts to certain tasks.

Missions should state that our organization can pursue this particular opportunity. Or emphasize that our organization should not pursue another opportunity. These concepts are not that difficult to understand. Our firm, for instance, can sell various types of fast-food. But our organization should not sell any form of haute cuisine. Or so our firm's mission statement should prescribe—or dictate.

The best mission statements are neither too broad nor too narrow. If missions are stated too broadly marketing organizations miss opportunities to achieve or sustain focus. If missions are stated too narrowly marketers miss opportunities that otherwise should have been taken into account, and possibly pursued and exploited.

Mission statements, in general, should describe:

- Who and what organizations currently are;
- The ideals, competencies, and solutions that organizations and their employees presumably should value; and
- What organizations are now and what they should become in the future...

Missions as well as the marketing goals that missions "facilitate" and "approve" should always be forward-looking. This means missions and goals are each future-oriented. Experienced and presumably expert duck hunters or fighter pilots never shoot behind their targets. They shoot toward where ducks or enemy planes are flying.

The core mission of any US university is to:

- Retail, or teach, and distribute knowledge,
- Warehouse, or store, as in warehouse, knowledge,
- Produce, or create, knowledge across disciplinary fields.

That's it ... this is all any university ever does or should do. All that engagement/bickering with legislatures or interest groups, competing for funds and sports victories, or construction of buildings, while each marketing-related, still remains mere ancillary efforts in comparison to these three core mission points.

But yes, myriad different ways exist for universities to retail, warehouse, and produce knowledge. That's why each such institution has a unique mission or vision statement.

The next example of a mission gave an organization direction and motivated it to initially achieve (albeit temporarily) most of its strategic goals. Trigger Alert, however, the organization is ISIS. The mission statement of ISIS follows:

▶ "The mission of ISIS is to inhabit places of chaos, and to then stimulate additional chaos, all driven by the goal of making non-Moslems hate all Moslems in order to stimulate a caliphate, a holy war, a jihad, as a result."

Perhaps your organization and the purpose of its mission will one day be as focused as the mission of ISIS once was, and to lesser degrees still remains. But presumably your organizational mission will never feature such evil intent at its core.

The best mission statements focus on satisfying customer needs. This makes sense. The reason why any firm exists, the core purpose of any firm . . . is to create satisfied customers at the end of each exchange transaction. Organizations and their missions consequently should focus on identifying and satisfying customer wants and needs at a profit. Sounds like the marketing concept, right?

The best mission statements also indicate or identify and facilitate distinctive core competencies that organizations either already possesses or could develop—and eventually leverage to their strategic advantage. Core competencies, as you have learned, entail something that given marketers do exceptionally well or something that they possess, particularly in comparison to close competitors. Marketers should create strategies that allow them to earn, sustain, and grow their core competencies.

In turn, their possession of, and willingness to leverage, distinctive core competencies can allow organizations that successfully develop and execute their strategic marketing plans to become or be perceived as one of the following:

▶ Low-cost provider in the market sector or product category which the marketer competes (i.e., *Walmart*, *Southwest Airlines*, most fast-food brands). Offering, simply, the lowest prices among all firms competing in the same sector (or product category);

▶ Technological leader (i.e., *Apple*, *Amazon*, *Google*, *Facebook*, *Nike*, *Prada*, etc.) amongst all marketing organizations competing in the same sector or product category; or, as the . . .

▶ Marketing organizations that achieve greater customer-intimacy inside market sectors or product categories in which organizations compete have built or sustained closer relationships with customers. Along the way, such firms typically create a sensibility or set of feelings shared among customers that these organizations, or more specifically their brands, really understand and cares about customers like them (i.e., *Apple*, again; *Nike*, again).

The Only Three Ways to Differentiate and to Position

The pursuit of either cost leadership, technological leadership, or greater customer intimacy leadership represents the three, and only three, ways for marketing organizations to successfully differentiate and position the value of their brands. Myriad ways, however, exist to develop, promote, and leverage either cost-, technological-, or customer-intimacy-leadership. The numbers of ways to create any core competency is limited only by the creativity of the marketing organization and its marketing planners and other marketing employees.

STEP 3: DEVELOP SMART GOALS (AND OBJECTIVES)

Once opportunities and/or threats have been identified, and the mission has been reviewed, revised, and is understood, smart goal-setting can begin. The acronym SMART, used inside strategic marketing planning contexts, implies that any organization's marketing goals and objectives should be:

- Specific; implying that the precision and clarity of goals matters greatly.
- Measurable; because what gets measured is what gets down.
- Actionable; implying that the means through which the goal or goals can be achieved should be identifiable and doable.
- Realistic, but motivating. Similar to missions themselves, goals should stretch and challenge the humans who populate marketing organizations but not be deemed impossible to achieve by the people who work inside them.
- Time-Sensitive; implying that timelines against which goals should be achieved must be in place.

SMART goals also stretch and motivate the marketers who are charged with achieving them. In fact, smart goals sometimes might also be characterized as stretch goals. Stretch goals are the sort that realistically would prove difficult to achieve. Meaning, at net, marketing managers that have achieved about 80 percent or so of the specific stretch goals are still doing a good job. The problem with an over-emphasis of stretch goals is that marketing managers would usually prove astute enough to figure out how to play this mind game. A takeaway, then, is that while the occasional implementation of stretch goals is probably useful, their routine use is not.

Marketing strategists should never establish goals until after the planners have established a new mission statement or understand and accept the parameters and constraints of their existing mission statement. This is because any organization's goals must be compatible with that same organization's mission.

Marketing goals can be stated broadly and qualitatively. Mere words, so long as they are attached to timelines, can be used to state goals. The fast-food marketer *Wendy's* corporate goal, stated, is to:

- "Build lasting relationships with our customers by enhancing the value of their consumption experiences so as to increase their visit frequency and loyalty, thus building sales and profits through superior service and products."

Wendy's corporate goal covers the most relevant fast-food marketing bases and provides a useful example.

Marketing objectives should be stated quantitatively. Numbers, percentages, and words, along with timelines, should be employed. For example, 20 percent market share by end of March 2023; 50 percent brand name recognition by December 31, 2023; a 40 percent growth in revenues, or 12 percent reduction in costs of transportation, by a certain date.

Goals should come first; before objectives. Marketers should pursue minimal numbers of goals. Each goal, however, should feature several associated objectives. As marketers achieve their objectives they should be making and tracking progress toward achieving their goals. Metrics, also called measurements or benchmarks, including timelines, should be established for both goals and objectives.

The use of metrics permits and facilitates measurement of marketers' progress or lack of progress toward their strategically designated goals and objectives.

The rod and staff used by good shepherds as they manage their sheep are not wielded as weapons to inspire fear among sheep—even though the same rods and staffs might occasionally be used in offensive or defensive manners against predators. Instead, shepherds use their rod and staff in love and in ways that provide both direction and protection to the sheep for whom they are responsible. Similar descriptions and purposes apply to metrics and how managers ideally should use them as they evaluate the employees who are their responsibility. Managers should employ metrics to protect (by identifying "issues" before they become "problems") and to direct (this is where you really need to go) employees who report to them.

Inside strategic settings those activities and outcomes that are not measured are rarely treasured. The inverse is also true. Inside strategic settings professionals, marketing or otherwise, almost always perform to their metrics; especially when they are rewarded or punished for achieving or failing to achieve their objectives and goals. Another equally rhythmic way to make the same point is to write:

- Subordinates are almost always more inclined to do what their managers inspect as opposed to what their managers expect. If you as their manager can control a marketing unit's expectations through the metrics you impose upon them, you cannot entirely control the group's success, but you can push their success further down the road.

Either way, the strategic activation of managerial inspections should complement the imposition of strategic managerial expectations in the form of either goals or objectives.

In the end managerial commitment to prevent bad or undesirable subordinate behavior is measured by managers' will to discipline it. Meanwhile, managerial commitment to inspire good or desirable subordinate behavior is measured by managers' will to reward it.

Organizations must grow. In most contemporary marketing environments (which are extremely competitive), marketing organizations that are not moving forward are usually falling behind. Strategic marketing goals, as well as their associated objectives, consequently should almost always be growth-oriented.

MODULE 2.4

Achieving Growth

Even if you don't know what emus are you probably do know about ostriches. So now, please envision an image of birds less handsome than but otherwise similar to ostriches. There, you pretty much have got the emu and its "look" down. If you cannot envision a kangaroo; well, you don't get out much, do you? Each animal is native to one country; the one nation in the entire world that is also an entire continent; talk about a differentiable branding opportunity. That's right, emus and kangaroos share an Australian heritage.

Each animal shares two additional characteristics in common. First, neither emus nor kangaroos can take a single step backward. Stepping back is anatomically impossible for each. Second, each animal is prominently positioned on *Australia's Code of Arms*; the nation's cherished branding emblem.

Do you suppose this branded product placement occurred by accident? You know better. By making this strategic branding choice, *Australia* has subtly signaled to the world and to its own citizen/consumer population that it's not taking any steps back, either. Not coincidentally, this geographically-large but sparsely-populated nation punches far above its weight on global stages. Geographically, *Australia* is approximately the same size as the 48 contiguous *US States*. But population-wise, the "down-under" nation only features about 29 million citizens. *Australia* has the third lowest national population density in the entire world.

However, *Australia* wields extreme market and branding power in large part because of the nation's unyielding growth strategy and ongoing strategic commitment to move forward continuously. And *Australia's* decision to prominently position emus and kangaroos, resolutely-only-going-forward-beasts that each is, underscores how much emphasis the nation places on the need to continuously grow through marketing and other means. The *Australian* nation is winning, big-time, on global stages because Aussies are writing their own story based on their tenacious execution of carefully crafted strategies that include, among other elements, the ugly emu and cherubic kangaroo.

Australia further signals its branding power by closely associating its national brand with sharks. These lords of the sea incongruously die by, of all things, drowning if they don't swim forward continuously. Similar to how even the most powerful marketing organizations can inexplicably die if they fail to move forward relentlessly toward desirable destinations that have been designated by strategic goals and plans. For an example, merely think about what has recently happened to a formerly great marketing organization first branded as *General Electric* that currently goes by the banner *GE*.

Not ironically and likely not coincidentally, a well-branded shark species that goes by the name *Great White* is already closely associated with *Australia's Great Barrier Reef*.

Marketing success is usually based more on addition rather than subtraction, even though strategic subtraction often proves important.[19] This principle is fundamental.

Three primary ways exist through which marketing organizations can achieve growth, or addition. The first approach entails successfully targeting new segments. Another tactic involves successfully developing new and/or more appealing value by revising existing or developing new marketing mixes. The third method entails simultaneously pursuing the two prior tactics in tandem. (This topic is discussed more fully in the following section.)

If we may generalize, marketers usually should strive for more than stable growth. Stable growth is essentially a C-level grade—blah—that resides between successful "A's" and unsuccessful "F's." Marketers relatedly should strive for growth that follows from solid to inspirational marketing planning and efficient execution of marketing activities. Marketers should never aspire to grow based merely on *Field of Dreams* "build it and they will come" types of reasoning. Marketing organizations should ground their growth prospects and plans in the premise that they will grow based on the development of something new (a product and its solution) that is also more useful, different, and/or better than other products (and their solutions) that currently exist in terms of its ability to deliver superior values and solutions. That's because in the highly competitive real world markets in which most marketers operate and compete, if they built it and no one comes their firm dies.

THE PRODUCT-MARKET EXPANSION GRID

As noted, three fundamental ways exist through which to achieve marketing growth. First, by successfully targeting new market segments. Second, by successfully developing new products, values, and solutions while also managing and possibly changing other ingredients in the marketing mix. Third, by successfully engaging in a combination—a mixing and a matching—of these two core marketing activities.

The Product-Market Expansion grid consists of a four-cell matrix. A description of the four cells that constitute the matrix follows:

- ▶ Market penetration growth strategies—Here, marketers change one or more elements in their marketing mix but keep the product inside the marketing mix the same. Typically, the elements being changed inside an existing marketing mix is promotion, price, or both.

---

19. Subtraction, as in lowering costs, can also similarly facilitate marketing success. Cost savings are routinely earned by marketing organizations that manage their supply chain relationships more efficiently.

Marketers initiate these tactical changes to their existing marketing mixes in an attempt to sell more of an existing product to the same target market. *Arm & Hammer Baking Soda*, for example, developed and then used different promotional messaging both to explain and demonstrate how the same-ole-same-ole baking soda could be used to solve numerous other household problems having nothing to do with baking. The marketer executed this strategy decades ago. The decision was a brilliant strategic response to an environmental threat that had arose. The environment threat in question was that fewer women were baking as higher numbers of women began working outside their homes. Market penetration strategies can be executed by using coupons, lower prices, or new promotional campaigns that underscore new uses for old products.

- Market development growth strategies—here, marketers identify new market segments to pursue. They pursue these new target markets by using existing products and the same marketing mix. Video game marketers pursued this when they began targeteding existing games toward female gamers. The sales of *Estee Lauder's* premium priced products took off after the cosmetics marketer began selling them extensively throughout airports. Notably, this growth in sales occurred during the same period when generated brand revenues at the same time were crashing and burning inside domestic department stores.

- Product development growth strategies—here, firms develop entirely new or tweak existing products that are subsequently targeted toward current market segments. *Apple* essentially has pursued a product development strategy since it first introduced *iPhones* in 2007. How many new generations of *iPhones* have been born since then?

- Diversification growth strategies—here, marketers develop new products and target the new products toward new target segments. The diversification tactic combines the market development and product development growth strategies. Video game marketers were pursuing diversification strategies when they first began developing new, more relationally—rather than violence-oriented games, and targeting the new video game products toward female gamers.

Module 2.5

Leveraging the Marketing Mix as a Growth Tool

The marketing mix is not a marketing growth tool. The marketing mix is the one and only marketing growth tool. Consequently, this traditional product-related marketing mix tool receives highly-detailed attention. The marketing mix, as you hopefully recall, consists of the "4Ps" when products are being marketed. The marketing mix consists of "7Ps" when services are being marketed.

PRODUCT

Products are best described as anything that any customer or prospect believes has value that can also profit a marketer. Products and services exist on a continuum. Many tangible products possess a substantial service dimension. Many, if not most, intangible services feature a physical dimension.

PRICE

Price, defined simply, is the amount of value that any customer must give up to get or obtain a product. Please note the implied reference both to exchanges themselves and to the values "gotten and given" (exchanged) inside "exchanges." Pricing should be strategically managed in ways to both create and capture value for the marketing entities that develop and manage the pricing plan, as discussed below.

PROMOTION

Promotions, collectively, are the communication arm—or weapon/tool—that marketers or marketing organizations can wield to deliver their particular stories to targeted subsets of broader markets.

Promotion is also the communication dimension—element or ingredient—inside any marketing mix. Basic communication goals that marketers generally aspire to achieve by managing their promotional mix elements include:

- Issuing reminders to prospects and customers;
- Conveying information to targeted prospects and customers;
- Achieving persuasion among targeted prospects and customers;
- Delivering incentives to targeted prospects and customers;[20] and/or ...
- ... Building stronger or establishing new interpersonal or professional relationships with B2C, B2B, or B2G customers. The importance of developing new or strengthening existing buyer-seller relationships cannot be oversold. The following underscores why: Relationships are the sources for our greatest joys (pleasures) or our greatest sorrows (pain). Why would things differ inside the relationships that exist or could exist between buyers (customers) and sellers (marketers)?

Each of these five communication goals are generally targeted toward highly refined target segments.

A Promotional Mix Inside the Promotional Ingredient Marketing Mix

The promotional element (the promotional "P") inside the marketing mix features a promotional mix all its own. The promotional mix elements traditionally include:

- Advertising, personal selling, sales promotion, publicity/public relations, and direct marketing.

There's more to the promotion mix than that, however. Designs, brands, colors, product shapes, the use of spokespersons, and so forth, these communication elements are also used to confer and/or deliver specific marketing messages. Taking the time to develop and implement the right story and to develop marketing messages that feature the right mix of words, images, or perhaps music, matters.

As does the development and delivery of a generally accurate mix of words and images. Marketers, for example, might decide to call a cat a fish. But they would do so in vain because the feline still will not scratch, meow, or breathe underwater.

---

20. An incentive is something, truly anything, that motivates targeted individuals or organizations to make decisions and/or to perform actions that the incentivizing agent desires to have them perform. Inside this setting the incentivizing agent would typically be a marketer. The need to strategically design effectively incentivizing marketing mixes is a critical marketing activity. Incentives are usually developed as parts of products or services themselves; communicated and therefore delivered from promotions; or reflected, as in manifested, inside prices and pricing strategies. Each of these practices is discussed more fully below because while incentives are merely footnoted here they and their use becomes very important below.

PLACE (SUPPLY CHAIN MANAGEMENT)

Place, or supply chain management activities, entail the processes and inter- and intra-organizational relationships through which products, including services, move from their source points to whatever venues [either brick-and-mortar retailers or e-tailers (i.e., online retailers)] that customers use to obtain the generally branded products or services that those B2C or B2B customers perceive will best satisfy their needs—or, as readers should know, solve their problems. An overarching goal that generally exists and indeed predominates inside supply chains entails providing whatever levels of service customers require at the lowest possible costs to the firm. Here, the use of the word "require" means whatever prospects or customers reasonably demand or want.

Inside supply chains, multiple organizations typically enter into partnering relationships with one another. Inside these supply chain relationships, partnering firms essentially sell to and buy from each other. Selling firms function as marketers; buying firms function as customers. However, once those products and services are sold and bought inside these supply chain relationships, the formerly customer firms pivot, and begin marketing (or selling) to the next buying organization. The next buying organization exists downstream in the supply chain each shares.

The various supply chain activities are involved in these "selling and buying" processes which always flow downstream. Supply channels generally flow downstream from "sourcing points" to the end points where final customers, who could be either consumers or organizations, exist.

The general purpose of these partnering relationships is for two, three, or more firms to each achieve greater efficiency[21] and lower costs by collaboratively cooperating with one another than any individual supply chain partner organization could achieve by working alone—and consequently having to do everything for itself by itself. When firms choose to participate and partner inside supply chains, they usually do so in order to secure greater opportunity to focus diligently on the one or two things they do best. In doing so, each partnering organization presumably exploits its core competencies and honors the Law of Concentration.

Firms partnering with other firms inside supply chains then enjoy the opportunity to become more like *In-and-Out Burger, Apple,* or the *U.S. Army*, for example. That is, these marketers then could become highly focused on and committed to developing and executing their marketing strategies based on a handful of core competencies. Does the *U.S. Army* manufacture its weapons or uniforms?

---

21. What does efficiency mean? Let's see. Everyone surely can agree that jet airliners should be designed and built to fly as efficiently as possible. Which raises the question of how much should, say, a *Boeing 777* plane weigh? Given that we are neither physicists nor aeronautical engineers the probability of your authors actually knowing the precisely right answer is remarkably low, unless we *Google* the question. But wait a minute, turns out we actually do know the right answer. *Boeing 777s* should weigh exactly as much as they need to fly safely and "at specification" (as imposed by various regulatory oversight organizations), but not an ounce more—that's how efficiency rolls. Why do we know that answer is right? Because that weight total, whatever it happens to be, is the most efficient amount. By the way, we did look up the weight number. Empty *Boeing 777s* weight 297,300 pounds. But this fact is relatively unimportant, because empty passenger planes have never been flown. Flying empty *Triple-7s* is not only impossible [no fuel, no pilots; no lift, no thrust], it's also grossly inefficient [no passengers, no cargo; no revenues, no profits]. Do you see, once again, how nearly every human endeavor touches directly or indirectly upon marketing and marketing practices?

No, because the Army's supply chain partners perform these activities, executing these manufacturing functions, for soldiers and their leadership. Should the Army make its own ammunition? After all, quality then would be assured. The answer, again, is certainly not; the Army instead should focus on developing plans that sharpen its core competencies while allowing ammunition manufacturers to focus on and exploit their own core competencies.

Does *Apple* actually build the various products it sells as part of the *Apple* parent brand? The answer is no. *Apple* builds nothing itself. Nor does *Apple* ever ship any products or components across the *Pacific Ocean* to *China* or from *China*, either. Never has; almost surely never will. *Apple* focuses on what it does best and outsources the rest; thereby permitting the shippers and transporters who do transport Apple products across oceans and around the world to focus on what they do best.

Firms participating and partnering inside supply chains outsource the performance to other firms of marketing functions that must be performed when and if other firms can perform the functions better. Many different marketing functions are typically outsourced (i.e., warehousing, shipping, order processing, manufacturing, promoting, to name several).

The Term "Supply Chains" Is Hardly Random

Supply chains are called supply "chains" for a reason. Marketing organizations are linked together in chain-like fashion inside supply chains. These supply chains generally rise up efficiently or fall down ineffectively, together, again because the marketing organizations that partner inside them are linked together through an element called flows. (Flows are fully discussed during the Supply Chain Module.)

All the while, though, it is easier for one deficient partner organization to drag down other corporations mutually sharing supply chain membership off a cliff than it is for one super-successful firm to pull up all other supply chain players from low, dark places. This should not surprise. After all; chains are only as strong as their weakest link. Implying, absent much subtly, we should all be careful about whom we date, marry, or elect to partner with inside "supply" chains.

Module 2.6

Efficiently Allocating Resources

THE THREE T'S (3Ts)

This book uses the acronym "3T" as a proxy for the term, resources. By name, the 3Ts are "time," "talent," and "treasure." All organizations always possess finite qualities of each "T"; just like all humans. Questions related to how best to allocate these limited resources consequently always arise as key strategic marketing issues during planning processes. These resource allocation questions always must be answered.

Time is finite in nature. And clearly so, in fact. In other news, life is actually short. Choices therefore truly matter. Especially decisions relating to how people choose to allocate their own finite inventories of time, talent, and treasure. What's more, the more bad choices we make earlier in life, the more limited our choices usually become down the not too distant roads into our respective futures.

Every professional only has a limited number of productive hours available during an entire career. That is 168 hours per week; forty-eight to fifty working weeks a year; forty to forty-five professional years out of a lifetime; the numbers appear about right. Time may prove a vicious enemy of professionals who take it for granted. Those individuals who waste too much time because they put no plan in place.

Or expressed differently. Even when one has lived to be eighty-two years and seven weeks old one has only been on earth for 30,000 days. That's not a lot. No point in wasting many of those days. Wasted time can never be reclaimed. Time mulligans—do-overs—can never actually exist. After all, time only moves forward.

But as always, life balances should remain in play. "Sure wish I had spent more time in the office" is a phrase rarely seen on tombstones. Okay, no one has ever seen it yet.

Talent is the least finite—or stated differently but the same, most expansive—resource among the 3T's. This is certainly true on an individual by individual basis. Within reason, when people feed their minds the right ingredients and then focus their efforts, their talents expand.

As for any of us as readers and learners, why not commit to work as hard as possible on one thing that is absolutely critical to corporate or your individual success during a reasonable time frame, and see what happens? The chances are that what happens will prove good—and desirable.

Then there is treasure—money. What institution or individual ever had more money in its coffers than the contemporary US government? Presumably, no such entity has ever existed. But what is the deficit total today? We don't know either, but the deficit's absolute heft, girth, and height speaks directly to the fact that all marketing organizations, such as the *Federal Government*, should allocate their finite resources carefully.

Economist *Milton Friedman* once offered telling commentary about the US government and its apparent inability to manage limited resources efficiently. Specifically, *Dr. Friedman* wrote that "If the United States government were in charge of the *Sahara Desert* America would quickly run out of sand." Hmmm. History, as well as the present times, make it difficult to argue against that argument. Too few assets coupled with too much mission creep multiplied by special interests plus paying off your supporters usually delivers undesirable outcomes.

Whenever strategic decision-makers only have finite resources at their command they should allocate those resource to where the most need or biggest opportunity for return exists. In other words, strategic managers need to allocate their resources in one or the other direction, all the time, because resources are always limited (finite).

THE BOSTON CONSULTING GROUP (GROWTH SHARE, PRODUCT PORTFOLIO MATRIX)

The *Boston Consulting Group (BCG)* Growth Share, Product Portfolio Panning matrix exists to marketing managers to identify the best or worst brands inside their firms' product portfolios[22] in which to invest their limited resources.

The four-cell *BCG* matrix features two dimensions, just like any other two-by-two matrix.

The dimensions are, first, a given brand's relative market share. Relative market share is measured along the horizontal (running side-to-side or east-and-west) axis.

The second dimension is inside the growth rate of the market in which the brand competes. Growth rate is measured along the vertical (running up-and-down or north-and-south) axis.

Whenever two dimensions intersect inside matrices, four cells or categories are created. The four categories that are revealed inside the BCG Matrix are named "Star," "Cash Cow," "Dog," and "Question Mark?" The category in which a particular brand is classified (as in "categorized") provides

---

22. Product portfolios consist of the entire set of products that any organization markets. The product portfolios inside any organization may feature different product categories or different product lines, and definitely will feature different products.

strategic insights about how many or few resources organizations should allocate toward marketing that particular brand.

Descriptions of what each category means follows:

- Brands that are classified and designated as "Dogs" have only earned low market shares inside low-growth markets.
- Brands that are classified and designated as Question Marks? compete inside high-growth market but have earned, to date, low market shares inside those expanding markets.
- Brands that are classified and designated as "Cash Cows" enjoy high market shares inside low-growth markets.
- Brands that are classified and designated as "Stars" enjoy high market shares inside high-growth markets.

Using the BCG Matrix

Dogs: Dogs may breakeven, neither earning nor consuming much cash. But dogs are generally viewed as cash traps because businesses have money invested in them, even as these spent resources yielded little to no value in return. Dogs are prime candidates for divestiture. Divestiture means selling off, eliminating, an asset; also known as kicking the asset to the curb. Products, ideally, are assets to the firms that market them.

Question Marks?: Those brands classified as Question Marks? enjoy high growth prospects, because the market in which they compete is growing, but low market shares. Question Marks? will consume a lot of cash but may generate little to no profit in return. In the end many Question Marks?, who are also known as "Problem-Children," lose money. However, since the brands compete inside growing marketers, they might be transformed into Stars. Managers usually should invest more in Question Marks? when brands enjoy growth potential or sell/drop them if they do not.

Cash Cows: Cash Cows are market share leaders, generating more cash than they consume. These brands typically feature low growth prospects because they compete in slow or no growth markets (i.e., the soft drink or fast-food industries). Cash cows provide the treasure required to convert Question Marks? into market leaders; to cover administrative costs, fund marketing research, and/or new product development; to service corporate debt; and to pay dividends to shareholders. Marketers generally should invest in Cash Cows to the degree that proves necessary to maintain current profitability levels and should milk gains in a steady and moderate manner.

Stars: Brands that possess the highest market share and generate the most cash are called Stars. Monopoly and first-to-market brands frequently gain stardom. However, due to their high growth rates, Stars consume substantial amounts of cash; they must be fed, resource-wise. This generally results in an approximately equivalent amount of money—treasure—coming in and going out. Many Stars eventually become Cash Cows when they sustain their success until market growth rates decline. This, ultimately, is a strategic marketing goal. Marketers should invest in Star brands.

Once marketing managers understand where each brand that is arrayed inside their product portfolios fits inside this four cell matrix, they can evaluate individual brand's value to the firm more objectively—and how much or how little of their finite resources should be invested in supporting marketing efforts initiated on behalf of the brand.

Four basic investment (or allocating scarce 3T resources) strategies exist:

- **Build**—Here, firms increase their investment in the brand in an attempt to grow its market share. For example, Question Marks? ideally can be grown into Stars. Ultimately, given the passage of time and the fact market growth rarely if ever continues forever, the former Star brand may earn the status of Cash Cow.
- **Hold**—Hold happens when firms have no more to choose to invest in a brand, but decide to hang tight investment-wise inside the same quadrant. Then, as *The Beatles* sang, *Let It Be*. At least for a while . . .
- **Harvest**—When marketers harvest they reduce their investment in and extract maximum cash flows from the brands. Each activity is intended to increase the marketing organization's overall profitability. Cash Cows are prime targets for harvesting strategies.
- **Divest**—When marketers divest themselves of brands, they remove some or all of the amount of money that previously was allocated to the marketing of the product. Dogs, naturally, are routinely divested from the product portfolios of marketing organizations.

The four basic resource allocation tactics appear to be both logical and strategic. And the allocation tactics are, except for one problem. The problem associated with using the *BCG* product portfolio planning matrix is that the process works by determining the cell into which any brand should be placed based on past data.

Looking backward into the past is often useful. After all, *Winston Churchill* suggested, "The further one can see back into the past the further ahead one can see in the future." That's because folks who strategically look backward secure often actionable historical understandings and insight. Winston knew a lot, and he was right in uttering these words too.

But looking backward is not as useful when strategists are deciding how to expend finite resources in the future. Modern markets are extremely volatile, in both the present and likely in the future. Inside actual marketplaces the past is often not prologue, despite the cliché that suggests otherwise, when the subject entails questions about how best to spend or allocate limited resources in the future.

FIGURE 2.1
Summary: Elements of Strategic and Marketing Plans

Elements of Plans	Description
Contents	Table
Executive Summary	Concise overview of the plan.
SWOT • Industry and Competition Analysis • Environmental Analysis • Marketing Program Analysis • Market and Customer Analysis • Critical Resources Analysis • Demand Analysis	A description of past, present, and future conditions in each area as they impact the profitability of the marketing effort. The analysis in these areas taken together comprises the Market Opportunity Analysis.
Summary of Market Opportunities and Threats	Based on the situation analysis. Summarizes the major market opportunities presented to the firm. Also summarized are the major threats to the firm that may require a change in marketing strategy.
Marketing Objectives	Identification of the goals the firm wishes to achieve by serving the selected market(s). Includes financial and non-financial.
Marketing Strategic Focus	A concise description of the strategic focus the firm intends to employ to achieve its marketing objectives.
Target Market(s) and Market Position	Identification of the customer groups the firm intends to serve. Identification of the desired image for the firm and its products relative to competitors.
Marketing Action Programs • Product/Service Plan • Promotion Plan • Pricing Plan • Distribution Plan	A detailed presentation of the specific objectives, strategies, and tactical activities in each area of the marketing mix required to implement the overall marketing strategy.
Budget and Financial Analysis	Detailed breakdown of the costs associated with each action program and additional financial analysis such as break-even analysis, cash flow statements, incremental analysis, and cannibalization analysis.
Monitoring and Control Program • Monitoring Procedures • Information Sources • Contingency Plans	Detailed description of the methods and sources of information that will be used to monitor progress on the plan and allow for corrective action in the event of problems.
Appendices	Supporting materials as required.

FIGURE 2.2
The Product-Market Expansion Grid

	MARKETS	
PRODUCTS	Old/Existing	New
Old/Existing	Market penetration	Market development
New	Product development	Diversification

FIGURE 2.3
Boston Consulting Group's Growth-Share

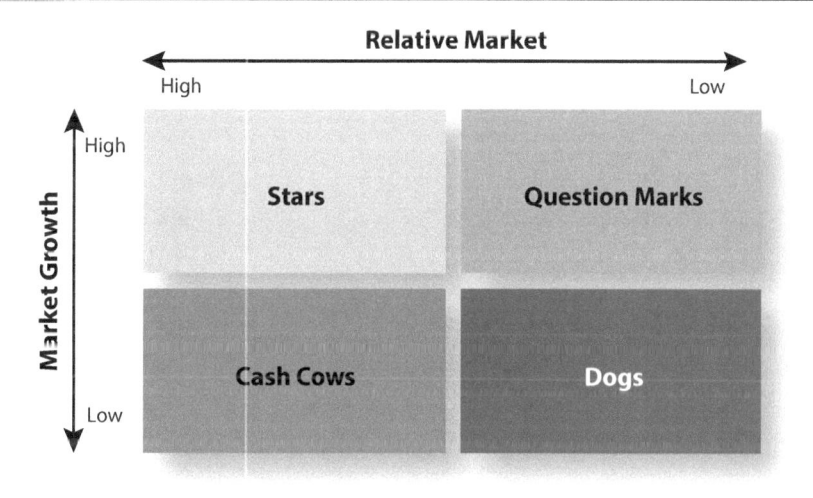

	Relative Market	
	High	Low
Market Growth High	Stars	Question Marks
Low	Cash Cows	Dogs

EXHIBIT 2.4
The Components of a SWOT Analysis

	Advantages	Disadvantages
Internal	**Strengths** Special expertise Personnel Access to resources Technological advantages Brand insistence Unique offering	**Weaknesses** Lack of resources Financial weakness Technological disadvantages Brand weaknesses Undifferentiated product offering
External	**Opportunities** New markets New technologies Legislative rulings Technological advantages Brand insistence Unique offering	**Threats** Environmental trends Legislative rulings Lack of access to critical resources Technological change Changing consumer trends Unique offering

MODULE 3

Strategic-Level Planning

MODULE 3.0

Marketing Strategy Is . . .

Module 2 discussed tactical planning processes that should be considered and executed at the marketing-functional level. Module 3 discusses planning processes that should be considered and executed at more strategic levels inside marketing organizations.

This Module by Module breakout into more tactical-level planning processes versus more strategic-level planning processes was intentional. As such the breakout and separation of Module 2's marketing-level content from Module 3's corporate-level content was a strategic choice made by the authors.

Readers should also understand one additional context-establishing point. The separate sets of content that are present inside Modules 2 and Modules 3 also could have been presented as one beastly-long marketing planning discussion. The authors opted to not pursue this operation. Going beast-mode in terms of this strategic presentation would have made students' execution of their "learning strategies" far more difficult. Knowing this now, however, students should not be surprised to learn that they occasionally will encounter the same broad issues and subjects addressed in Module 2 and Module 3.

STRATEGY IS . . . GROUNDED IN MYRIAD SOURCES

Please . . . pull out three large pots. Then half-fill each with water. Bring all three pots to boil. Now, insert one carrot, one egg, and a spoonful of coffee into one and one container. Finally, let each element cook inside its respective pot for seven minutes.

What will happen? The water in one pot changes a formerly hard carrot into soft mush. The water in the second pot transforms a formerly soft egg into hardened matter. The coffee, however, changes the formerly clear water into another element in the third container.

In this story, strategy is the coffee—the agent of change. The environment, including the marketplace, are the pots and their water—the elements and the places in which everything happens and changes. Marketers should be the coffee. And strategic marketers do metaphorically see themselves as the coffee in our scenario—even though coffee does not literally enter the picture. That's because strategic marketers function as agents, perpetrators, and leaders of change, even inside contexts where initiating change is difficult. Of course, initiating change proves difficult across most contexts.

Marketers, indeed all businesspeople, well, actually everyone, should plan, or strategize, because they are vulnerable. Every professional should also plan, or strategize, because they are shrewd.

The modern *English* word strategy is rooted in an ancient *Greek* word that signified military commander. Little surprise here. About 29 percent of modern *English* words feature an ancient *Greek* heritage.

This conflation of the modern *English* word "strategy" with the ancient *Greek* word for "military commander" is logical. Military commanders and marketing strategists each have always limited, or finite, resources under their control.

Each group fights or competes based on and constrained by known missions. Sometimes those known missions prove motivating. Military commanders and marketing strategists each derive their goals, objectives, and strategies based on their understanding and interpretation of their respective missions.

Military and marketing managers each seek to capture, control, and/or defend terrain. Military commanders strive to capture, control, or defend space situated on land, in the air, or on the sea. Soup-to-nuts, what marketing strategists actually concern themselves with at the most basic level possible is capturing, controlling, or defending space inside human minds. Essentially, the eight inches or so between adult humans' left and right ears.

Military and/or marketing strategies are similar in that each seeks to take away more value from a situation than the original balance of power between the assortment of competitors or enemies suggested was possible.

Military and/or marketing strategies both also entail the art and science of creating and executing power; power that in turn will benefit one's organization, one's customers, one's investors, and/or oneself.

Military and/or marketing strategies likewise both entail leading and/or managing change. A daunting task and challenge, this.

Not Just Accommodating but Managing Change

Change is rarely linear. This assertion remains true regardless of whether the changes are unfolding under harsh warlike conditions or emerging as normal and expected cultural, economic, or scientific transitions and progress. The pathways that changes follow often appear meandering, unfocused, and aimless. That is, unless the changes that are unfolding are initially engineered and eventually steered by thoughtful and mission-driven strategic goals.

Strategic planners are and should be the source of both these missions and these mission-driven goals. Planners should stay on top of changes and lead changes whenever possible.

Truly strategic planners should never be products of their environment. Because that outcome implies planners never had, or lost, control. Instead, strive; planners should strive to make environments a product of their strategy—to the extent this outcome can be achieved.

Any marketing organization or individual marketing professional can either lead change or be changed-by-change. But when strategists permit themselves or their organization to be changed by change the resulting dynamics—themselves changes!—often play out in ways that organizations and their strategists end up enduring rather than enjoying. Ask yourself: Would you rather find yourself in front of a bus trying to stop it or at the vehicle's rear trying to help push it forward? Especially when the bus is already in motion. A lot of the time, there is no point in fighting change. Almost all of the time, by contrast, many more points are available to be earned or scored by leading change.

As noted, change does not always represent progress. But change is always necessary for progress to occur. Consequently, people and organizations typically should accept change and, to the extent possible, lead changes.

Do professionals or organizations routinely accept change? Are you kidding? Yet changes keep happening. Do you realize there was a time when *The History Channel* broadcast history shows and *MTV* played music?

MARKETING STRATEGY IS . . . GROUNDED FUNDAMENTALLY IN DECISIONS, DECISIONS

Why do people choose one rather than another alternative in situations where decision-makers possess the power, resources, and opportunity to choose any alternative they want? The answer relates to deciders' perceptions of value, right? The answer is that decision-makers inevitably choose those alternatives that they perceive will deliver the most value to them.

But does everyone perceive the same values the same way? Unsurprisingly, the answer is no. This is the primary reason why marketers need to, should, engage in market segmentation and target marketing; AKA targeting. Marketers should engage, first, in segmentation and thereafter in targeting in order to identify, develop, and deliver specifically designed marketing mixes that are precisely customized and positioned to satisfy the needs of select customers or prospective customers. Those select—or targeted—customers or prospective customers presumably exist inside segments.

Defining and Managing Products

Remember how products were broadly defined and described during Modules 1 and 2. These broad definitions and descriptions were purposeful. Products were described there as . . . anything that individual marketers or marketing corporations can offer to consumers (B2B) or organizations (B2B), to segments or to entire markets . . . for their attention, acquisition, use or consumption . . . that might also satisfy those individuals' or organizations', segments', or entire markets' wants/needs—and solve their problems. Based on this definition, tangible products, intangible services, people, places, and ideas each exist and function as products.

Laptops or baseball hats, bats, and balls are tangible products, as are any and all of the underwear or outerwear garments that clothe us.

Any list of intangible products might include the provision of haircuts or hair coloring, airline travel, the provision of medical, legal, or accounting solutions, or even dating services such as, say, *Match.com, BlackPeopleMeet.com,* or *OurTime.com.* Educational lectures exist as services that deliver value, solve problems, and thus function as products, as do religious services such as sermons, baptisms, or wedding/funeral ceremonies. Each service exists as a product because each "service" solves problems by providing necessary values to "customers."

People, as human brands and products, could entail politicians, celebrities, or business professionals.

Places can be deemed products too. Some places are even deemed as sacred products. For example, once widespread perceptions spread across the collective minds of markets that a place has been visited by miraculous or transcendent events (*Israel's Temple Mount* or *France's Lourdes*), they are often marketed as products. Take locations characterized and imbued by the undeniable prior presence of great nobility or sacrifice *(D-Day's Omaha Beach)* or settings that have been eternally marked, branded, by the blood of martyrs or the brutal suffering of innocents (the *Auschwitz* concentration camp); such sites are treated as products. More prosaically, however, places are marketed as products because wily marketers have strategically promoted, branded, and successfully positioned selected places as products. *New Orleans (The Big Easy); New York City (The Big Apple);* or *Las Vegas (What Happens There, Stays There)* easily come to mind because each city and site is positioned and branded as a highly desirable place for certain targeted segments, or audiences, to visit. The obviously qualified phrase "certain targeted audiences" is because neither *Las Vegas, New Orleans* nor *New York City* is perceived by everyone as an appealing place to visit.

Finally, ideas (i.e., theories, propositions, or laws) are every bit the marketable products that more tangible goods are. Abortion is a "health care" service that is simultaneously marketed and de-marketed, though not by the same marketers and marketing organizations. Yet abortion also exists as a marketed and de-marketed idea. Do you support *Pro-Life* or *Women's Rights* as an idea? Don't answer; responses are not germane to this discussion. What instead is germane is that decision-makers deciding/not deciding to support abortion inside their minds or as the process plays out a product inside their lives entails the "purchase" or "non-purchase" of an idea—and a product.

What follow are three facts well worth reinforcing again, right now.

- ▶ Fact 1: Whatever is a product can be branded.
- ▶ Fact 2: Whatever product is branded can be differentiated.
- ▶ Fact 3: Whatever product has been successfully differentiated has also been successfully positioned, or *vice versa*.

Defining Market Segments (Again)

Remember how market segments were defined? That's right, as relatively homogeneous and smaller submarkets, or segments, existing inside more heterogeneous and much larger markets.

Inside B2C or B2B marketing contexts the people (consumers) or the organizations that constitute market segments share certain key characteristics in common. The fact that these shared characteristics exist within a specific segment implies that the consumer or organizational constituents who comprise targeted B2B or B2C segments are more likely to respond in similar fashions to the sorts of unique and uniquely desirable values that should be created and delivered through specific marketing mixes. These "similar responses" "within segments" generally would play out as positive or negative reactions to the same marketing messages or to the same sets of product values as messages and/or values are delivered through marketing mixes.

The following point will be made time and again in various ways and through various methods during the remainder of this book. But why not learn the point now? Marketing organizations should develop a unique and uniquely appealing marketing mix for each segment that they choose to target.

MARKETING STRATEGY IS...USEFUL

The process of strategizing—of developing business and/or marketing strategies—is useful. The processes of strategizing and creating plans:

- Forces organizations to engage in systematic, forward-looking planning.
- Forces planners to prioritize their goals.
- Leads to more efficient utilization of always finite sets of resources that organizations have at their disposal. Decisions related to how best to efficiently allocate scarce resources are never not crucial—or strategic in nature. Marketers should marshal their resources prudently. That way, marketers are less likely to find themselves in the ridiculous place where they can neither defend new nor secure old market share.
- Helps organizations respond more quickly to opportunities and threats as either or both trends arise inside organization's internal or external environments.
- Establishes clear performance metrics, or benchmarks, against which progress or the lack of progress toward mission-driven goals can be assessed.
- Increases the likelihood any organization is focusing on the right things and doing the right things right. This statement is far from cliché. "Right ways" to do "wrong things right" simply cannot exist. The very idea is illogical.
- Provides safe harbors in which possibility-thinking can occur. In situations where possibility-thinking is not merely allowed but actively encouraged, the prospect of creating and evaluating new ideas and new approaches is enhanced. That's innovativeness, played out inside a planning process.

MARKETING STRATEGY IS...QUIRKY (AT TIMES)

When the subject turns to business rivalries and planning, organizations or people should choose who they hate carefully. Because who they hate—and consequently choose to compete most vigorously against—can make them great. Do this, and if an organization ends up delivering values that prove superior to the values created and delivered by its bitter rival, the first organization stands an excellent chance of winning big itself.

Big-Time Sports

Reflect on the *University of North Carolina* and *Duke University*. These two outstanding research and teaching institutions are located only eight miles from one another. Now, if you did not already do so (such is the power of owning a word), think about college basketball. During the last forty-two *NCAA* basketball seasons these teams have each won five national championships. The fact that ten of the last forty-two titles that were awarded were won by one of these two teams when more than 200 teams play *Division 1 College Basketball* underscores the fact that marketing organizations should choose their rivals carefully.

Targeting the right opposition, and keeping these competitors or enemies targeted continuously, forces planning entities to continuously clarify and sharpen their game. Essentially everyone works more fervently against their enemies than they cooperate with their friends. To act in this manner, yes, is human nature. So, choose to ascribed as an enemy or competitor carefully. This is not to say anyone should ever ignore or abuse their business or personal friends. These allies should also be selected carefully.[1]

Big-Time Electricity Legends

To further illustrate the same point ("who you hate can make you great"), think about *Nicoli Tesla*, whose last name today is purposefully used somewhere else by someone else for his own edgy branding purposes; about Tesla's mentor *Thomas Edison* (yes, the man credited with creating the electric light bulb); and finally about the product we know as electricity. In the original *AC/DC* (alternating current vs. direct current) electricity showdown, *Edison* and the corporation he founded, *Edison General Electric*, and *Tesla* and his firm, launched a brutal strategic marketing and promotional campaign over whose electric current was better that played out across decades. The marketing and promotional campaign was brutal largely because *Tesla* and *Edison* were not only fierce business rivals. In this case, they also hated each other.

The reasons why the two men hated one another are immaterial here. But two notable victims of the collateral damage did materialize. The first was a rogue former circus elephant who was named, or branded, as *Topsy*. The elephant was purposefully executed for the "crime" of killing his trainer through the application of alternating current. The second was a convicted and condemned prisoner, executed by electrocution over a brutal eight-minute-long farewell. The competing and publicly-held executions were held to publicly demonstrate the value of alternating current as opposed to direct current. The human execution "service process" fared especially poorly. Extremely so. Edison and his crew had to electrocute the man twice in order to kill him.

A real marketing and humanitarian mess; a genuine public relations disaster. According to *George Westinghouse*, a supply chain partner of *Tesla*, "To execute him more mercifully they should have used an ax, instead."

---

1. Not for nothing did the chaplain inside the maximum security *George Beto Prison,* located near *Palestine, Texas,* tell the first author shortly after he entered prison for the first time. "Show me your friends and I will show you your future." The chaplain presumably shared this thought because he understood their friends may create more problems for many people than their enemies. Not that planners can ever afford to ignore their enemies—their competitors. Smart man, this chaplain, who also shared the sentiment that "Friends multiply your pleasures and divide your pain." Quell your fears, however. The first author was visiting *The Beto Unit* as a *Kairos Prison Minister.* In other words, visiting and attempting to create value as a marketer for his targeted audience: *The Men In White.* (Prisoners inside this maximum-security prison were always all dressed entirely in white; had close-cropped hair; and bore scant physical resemblance to the prisoners routinely depicted in movies. There was a lot of ink, however; including, yes, some teardrops.)

One clear-cut winner, however, arose from this hate-on-hate blood contest. Yes, again the victors were American consumers. Far more Americans received superior electric currents at lower prices quicker than would have happened had the feud not existed.

Big-Time Technology "Giants"; Yes, Redundant

Or, finally, reflect on *Bill Gates v. Steve Jobs*. The well-known fact that Gates, co-founder of *Microsoft*, and Jobs, co-founder of *Apple*, disliked each other so intensely that they jointly created a global marketplace in which their companies competed fiercely for several decades. Who won? Check the financial and fame-based data. Both won.

Who else won? Society, the global economy, the world—due to the life-altering and paradigm-shifting products that *Microsoft* and *Apple* developed and marketed. For the happy but still sad record, Messieurs Jobs and Gates genuinely made nice with each other several months before Steve's premature passing in 2011.

Yet this line of strategic reasoning (i.e., what or who you hate can make you great) is not nearly as dark as many may suspect it is. In sports rivalries, the competitor your team "hates" the most is likely also the competitor that your team respects the most. So, there is that. And this sport-related adage also likely applies inside most other non-sporting contexts that house business competitions. Marketing competitions are unfolding everywhere, whether you realized this fact until now or not.

MARKETING STRATEGY IS . . . BROUGHT TO LIGHT IN UNEXPECTED PLACES

What does *Ole St. Nick* have to say about strategic success? No, not that St. Nick. The St. Nick in question rarely laughs, at least in public, and he's never ho ho ho-ing. Turns out this St. Nick is *Nick Saban*; mega-successful coach of the *National Football League* farm team playing college football in *Tuscaloosa, Alabama*—at the *University of Alabama*.

St. Nick once was asked to describe how he turned the corner, because Coach Saban was not always mega-successful, and how he became not consistently but unbelievably successful. Saban shared the following thoughts:

- "The key to success is not looking at the future or the past but just the game in hand and breaking down to just the fundamentals what will prove necessary to succeed in this particular game.
- The best way to be consistently successful is to focus on the process and not the outcome.
- Once a process is in place; continually refine and improve the process.
- Follow the process all the time.
- Don't get wrapped up in near-term results. Play the long game."

Then recruit the best high school football players in the country to play for your team year after year after year. That also creates and sustains success in this particular marketing competition.

MODULE 3.1

How Strategies Should Work

To prepare for success in the future, study the present. To understand the present, examine the past. With one hand the past pushes planners back. The past drives planners back because, as the Southern Gothic (his branding identity) novelist *William Faulkner* wrote: "The past is never dead."

Yet with the other hand the past moves strategists forward. The past should not just be tapped but actively used to move planners forward. But only when strategists take time to listen and attend to its lessons.

Therefore, strategic planning processes should . . .

- ▶ Entail a look into the past. Everything has happened before and is recorded inside historical records for us to learn from. There really is nothing new under the sun. Contemplative, after-the-fact investigations consequently should be conducted to discern what organizations did right or wrong—back then, in the past. Marketing organizations or individual marketing professionals generally should keep doing or expand what they have done well in the past, so long as the market remains receptive to the marketing mix values that were being generated. Relatedly, strategic-minded individuals or corporations should eliminate or lessen what they did wrong or what worked out less than ideally in the past. Planners and the organizations they lead may or may not want to extend their organization's past into its future; the past may have been horrific or terrific. Strategically-speaking, however, such strategic thinkers and their organizations should give themselves the opportunity.

- ▶ Entail a look around the present. The purpose here is to identify best opportunities to pursue or worst threats to avoid or mitigate. The present genuinely does represent an appealing gift for truly strategic planners. That's because the present time is exactly where marketing planners can identify the best opportunities to pursue and/or the worst threats to mitigate or avoid. Forever successful in what is still admittedly an unknown future is composed of innumerable well-chosen "now's"—or present times. No one can truly and accurately predict their futures. But everyone can create futures more to their liking if and when they make good to great strategic decisions inside "the present" that today offers.

- Entail a look, the best possible, into a still unknowable future. Predictions, difficult though they are to accurately make, given that they are issued about unknowable futures, still must be made before the best possible goals can be identified.

- The preceding three bulleted statements invite consideration of a famous *Irish Proverb*. The proverb suggests, "May you have the Foresight to know where you are going; the Hindsight to know where you have been; and the Insight to know when you have gone too far." One might presume that following this admonition would work out well for one's life; one might rest even more assured that the proverbial counsel would prove useful to planners.

Strategists who choose consciously to honor these basic planning principles will, at the least, discover that they must struggle more to fail. Yes, you read that right.

If persons or organizations don't ask where they are, they can never know where they've been. Fixed points in the past, present, and future must exist or be developed against which planners can benchmark.

Strategists Should . . .

- Understand that planning requires preparation, but that planning creates preparation. The importance, the value, of preparation would be difficult to overstate. *Abraham Lincoln* purportedly said: "Give me six hours to cut down a large tree and I will spend the first four sharpening the ax." Now would Lincoln, branded by marketers even inside his own lifespan as *Honest Abe,* lie to you? The whole truth is that he probably would have, everyone appears to emit at least "white lies" every now and then; but that would ruin the story.

- Move quickly, based on their wisdom, which can be grown based on anyone's willingness to prepare, and grounded in actionable knowledge.

- Move patiently, again based on their wisdom or based on the actionable insights emerging from the preparation that went into planning.

Moving Fast . . . But

Today's business world is one in which the fast eat the slow for breakfast. This is why the exact strengths and activities that once made organizations great can also kill them, longer term, unless the proper strategic initiatives are taken, as needed, to keep organizations agile.

Today's marketplace, the one into which new organizations are born and in which they must compete, survive and possibly thrive or die is also a setting where organizational culture eats organizational strategy for breakfast. The presence of the right organizational cultures and values can tip the scales in favor of victory when losses appeared inevitable. The presence of the right mission or vision, by themselves, would rarely prove sufficient to ensure that the right organizational cultures and values arrive or can be sustained. But absent the directions and restraints imposed by strong missions or visions the right organizational cultural values almost certainly will not emerge.

Yes, we just implied that organizational culture contributes more than organizational strategy to marketing success, despite the attention being paid to strategy during this book's first three Modules. But that's another story for future *Management, from Scratch*, books to tell.

One outcome is likely, however. Marketing entities that move too fast often get eaten by more patient, better prepared, and more opportunistic marketers. Consequently, strategists should also . . . think aggressively or assertively like people of action while acting patiently like people of thought. But is it better to lean more heavily toward action or patience?

Trick question, this. It is better, indeed usually best, to demonstrate a thoughtfully strategic balance toward achieving or maintaining a balance between these two opposing perspectives. The ability to achieve balance in both thought and deed is important—and usually represents a worthy pursuit inside strategic marketing settings.

A Balancing Act

The need to achieve a thoughtful strategic balance is present in the pursuit of goals that split the difference between what an organization ideally could become with what is realistic for the same organization to become.

The need to achieve a thoughtful strategic balance is present inside the unrelenting need that many contemporary firms confront to balance their long-term goals with their short-term demands.

The need to achieve strategic balance is present within the imperative that marketing organizations confront to marry their internal pursuit of profitability with their publicly promoted initiatives to be socially responsible. Earning reputations for being a socially responsible may often prove a necessary precursor to developing or preserving desirable positions or brand identities inside competitive B2C or B2B markets. Yet earning profits is always a necessary precursor to the continuing existence of any marketing organization—and yes, this rule even applies to so-called not-for-profit organizations.

The need to achieve strategic balance arises inside planning scenarios where marketing organizations seek to secure sweet-spot market positions wherein those firms' brands seek to gain or sustain recognition as products that deliver the highest reasonable quality at the lowest reasonable prices.

Now that the ongoing need to achieve balance has been extensively vetted and explained, consider two additional planning principles that "strategic" strategists should always consider. First, strategic planners should understand that ditches—traps into which they might fall—exist on either side of almost all roads. Second, planners should understand that in many instances either side of the road might lead to disaster or success.

Planners should seek balance, in all things. The preceding statement represents another admonition that is more easily written than achieved. Pursuing "too much, too soon" can prove as tragic a strategic failure as pursuing "too little, too late." Moderation, a balanced perspective, is rarely not a good idea.

Except in those rare situations—and they do exist—where people have shown too much moderation in exercising moderation itself, and end up not doing much of anything, ever.

Think about the Right Stuff

Few junctures exist inside professional lives in which the opportunities or threats that they choose to think about as well as how they to choose to think about them won't make material differences to those professional's future success or failure. Our present-day selves should always be nice to—or at least considerate of—our future selves when deciding whether to work or play; study or get drunk; exercise or lay around.

Back to the regularly scheduled program, genuinely strategic planners should:

- ▶ Accept that when planning the hardest thing to do often entails determining which bridges to cross and which bridges to burn. Determining which bridges to cross is akin to identifying the right opportunities to pursue. Determining which bridges to burn is analogous to selecting the right opportunities to ignore or quit. One thing is certain: No organization has enough juice—sufficient resources—to pursue all possible opportunities.
- ▶ Understand that they may encounter their destiny[2] on roads that they purposefully took to avoid a potentially fateful opportunity or threat—and to know what to do if this happens. Knowing what to do when destiny raises its beautiful or hideous head follows from having contingency plans in place—and from being sufficiently well-informed to move quickly but with patience when opportunity or threat arises.
- ▶ Accept as honorable facts the degree to which marketers should never fight fair fights and need to plan so well that fair fights never arise for them.

The preceding point about not fighting fair does not sound nice, does it? But as long as one fights ethically, honoring the rules of whatever competition is playing out, why would anyone want to fight a fair fight? Why would anyone want to compete against competitors or enemies that might actually win and destroy them?

Know your foe. Build your plan. Marshal your resources. Manage your time. Only then, consider acting. Or not acting. Yes, that sounds *Yoda*-like. But decisions to not act can result from good planning too.

Great planning personas clearly understand the potential benefits embedded inside good crises.

Playing (Strategic) Games as Crises Arrive

Crises are called crises because they involve situations featuring problems or questions for which no self-evidently good solutions or answers exist—at least in the short-run. If easy solutions or answers existed in such settings, the situation could not rightfully or logically be characterized as a crisis.

---

2. Destinies can be good or bad, right?

A well-known saying summarizes the value of a good crisis. The saying suggests "A crisis is a terrible thing to waste." Problems or opportunities that appear too expensive or too challenging to even attempt to address during normal climates often morph into necessities—must-dos—during crises, and then the requisite resources plus the will are somehow magically found.

The arrival of crises often represent great opportunities not just to plan for change, but to also actually initiate change. The written *Chinese* language uses symbols rather than letters to depict words. The *Chinese* language uses two intersecting brushstrokes to denote the word crisis. One brushstroke represents danger. The other stroke represents opportunity. Depicting the components of crisis and what crises actually represent in this manner is useful. The arrival of crises represents both opportunities and threats to individuals who are sufficiently well-balanced and strategic to view them, crises, as such.

The arrival of crises might prove valuable for other strategic reasons. *Littlefinger*, an infamous and eventually rightfully-executed character inside the *HBO* show's *Game of Thrones*' product portfolio of characters, once suggested that "chaos"—disorder of the sort that crises might engender—"is not a pit but a ladder." True enough. But chaos only unfolds as opportunity to those marketing managers who are strategic enough to recognize crises as the opportunities that most actually are. Yet planners should learn and thereafter never forget that the threat or actual arrival of crises can fuel productive choices every bit to the degree that that event can fuel destructive choices.

History informs anyone who knows anything about the past that anarchy, risk, and instability often lurk on the other side of chaos. But the presence of chaos is also a place where marketers can uncover myriad opportunities for their firms to respond creatively and consequently grow and strengthen their brand positions relative to competitors.

Planning is tough. Even though not planning, and ultimately not having a plan, is tougher still. Do you have a plan for your professional life, for your career? Should you?

There are additional challenges, however. Executing presumably good plans even moderately well is also extremely difficult. The presence of entropy is one of the primary reasons why the preceding statement is never not true.

Entropy is a natural condition that exists inside all organizations and organized systems. The concept of entropy correctly explains how and why things inexorably fall apart unless purposefully preventative intervention is imposed by some outside force. Developing anticipatory radar-like skills of the sort that may prove necessary to detect emerging crises before they blow up into full-blown disasters will never eliminate entropy,[3] because such anticipatory radar-like skills are impossible to fully develop.

But the presence of some form of crisis detection-device will mitigate (lessen) entropy's negative effects, make planning easier, and place success more within most planners' grasp. Execution of strategic planning processes themselves will, at the least, make it easier for planners to anticipate the arrival of many crises before they fully arrive. And remember, as *Littlefinger* suggested, the arrival of

---

3. Entropy—defined as lack of order or predictability; a gradual decline into disorder. Entropy typically reigns supreme inside markets and indeed all manner of environments. Entropy means, in brief, things fall apart—and do so naturally. Unless, of course, someone initiates strategic measures to keep things in order.

crises may represent a "ladder-up" for the few who are prepared and willing to react quickly to the threat or presence of chaos. For what its worth (a lot), marketing research simultaneously exists as a crisis-detection and an opportunity-detection device.

STRATEGISTS SHOULD ALSO . . .

Strategists similarly should learn and would consistently benefit from following twelve nearly-universal strategic planning principles. These principles follow.

Strategic Success Principle 1: Planners should pursue logical solutions.

When it first began growing from its *Seattle* origins and expanding throughout the entire country, *Starbucks* strategically located new stores, whenever possible, near dry cleaner and video stores. Why, you may be thinking? The answer is completely logical and derived from the fact that dry cleaner and video store customers had to visit each establishment twice. Please note, at the time, such stores were hugely popular; dry cleaning stores, of course, still are. *Starbucks* consequently enjoyed two shots at consumers' coffee business when its stores occupied these physical positions.

Strategic Success Principle 2: Planners usually should pursue the simplest possible solutions.

Occam's razor[4] suggests the best solution to any pressing and complicated problem, when planners are analyzing and drawing inferences from data, is always the simplest explanation that accounts for all the data. By the way, the need to plan is always a pressing problem. The razor further indicates that strategic problem-solvers/decision-makers should understand that, *ceteris paribus*,[5] the simplest explanation, process, or solution is always the best.

---

4. William of Occam was the thirteenth-century English philosopher and theologian who created this Law of Parsimony. More about Occam and his razor follows.

5. *Ceteris paribus* is a *Latin* phrase and frequently used economic concept that means "other things equal," "all other things being equal," "other things held constant," or "all else unchanged." Sounds exactly how the world does not work, right? Yet the existence of *ceteris paribus* is important to any researcher seeking to experimentally investigate causal relationships between two or more stimuli. The reason why is because inside experimental research designs, all other possible casual factors must be held constant. That's nice, and the presence of this condition is what makes experimentation even possible. Think about the associated implications, however. Do conditions ever remain inside the real world or real markets? The answers are "no" and "no" and this is why the question of generalizability must always be answered successfully when firms conduct experiments or other statistical analyses as part of their marketing research efforts. Generalizability, in turn, is defined as a measure of how applicable the merely sampled results of any market research study are to the entire population that is being investigated—or researched.

Strategic Success Principle 3: Planners should always account for the role played by technology.

Technology, which changes constantly, also constantly changes everything else. Technology changes how customers connect with marketers; how marketers connect with customers; and how customers connect with customers.

Technological changes have permitted modern-day consumers to acquire the sorts of far-flung freedoms that the marketers of new convertible automobiles used to promise to their then more gullible customers. Freedom in terms of how customers pay for new products (*PayPal*); freedom in terms of how customers acquire new products (what entity could sell and deliver bottles of shampoo as efficiently as *Amazon*); or freedom in terms of how customers communicate either with marketers or with other customers about products (*Twitter* and *Twitter*, yes repeated purposefully).

Technology, it's a one-way street. And technology is a broad thoroughfare, at that, and one that's always moving forward into the future.

Strategic Success Principle 4: Planners should accept, account for, and adjust to the fact that some factors affecting their plans are uncontrollable.

No matter how diligently marketing strategists plan or how much they wish circumstances differed, human minds cannot be controlled. Occasionally manipulated, yes, but not controlled. Minds can be sufficiently incentivized that people are led to water, but not enough to make them think. But customer minds cannot be controlled; at least not the deeply held attitudes that are embedded within them. Yes, this is a good thing. The planning takeaway, however, is that this fact of marketing life underscores the need to engage persistently in segmentation and market targeting (target marketing).

Marketers generally should not try to change people's minds. Attempting to change minds as an overarching marketing strategy would usually lead to failure if not outright disaster. Marketers should rarely try to change customers' minds for the same reason that people should rarely try to fix others; say, their spouses. Why? Because people have to want to change their own minds or to fix their own problems—or changes will not happen. After all, how many psychologists does it take to change a light bulb? The answer, surprisingly, is only one. But the light bulb really has to want to change.

Instead of trying to change B2C or B2B customers' hearts or minds, marketers should develop stories and products and values and solutions that preemptively align with the things and thoughts that the customers who constitute market segments are already doing, thinking, feeling, wanting, or needing. Marketers, of course, create these stories and products and values and solutions by strategically managing their marketing mix.

Strategic marketers should not spend excessive time thinking or worrying about factors they cannot control. Instead, planners allocate more time toward thinking and doing something about factors they can control or influence. Strategic marketers, however, should never ignore uncontrollable factors. Such factors, which routinely arise in the form of favorable or unfavorable environmental trends, must likely contain various opportunities or threats.

Strategic Success Principle 5: Planners should understand that Gold Rules.

When planning, marketing strategists should dance close either to the revenue or cost line, or both. If the finished strategy is not designed to elevate sales or tamp down costs, or achieve both outcomes, change and improve the plan. If strategies neither grow revenue nor cut costs, or achieve both ends simultaneously, what's the point?

Don't confuse the marketing planning principle that this book describes as "Gold Rules" with the idea known as the Golden Rule—"do unto others as they would have you do unto them," as written in *Luke*. Nor should marketing planners confuse the principle that Gold Rules with the updated Platinum Rule—"do unto others as they would want you to do unto to them" . . . which is another great marketing rule—but not one that applies here, either.

Strategic Success Principle 6: Planners should manage two types of risks.

The first type of risk that marketing strategists almost always encounter entails "Sinking-the-Boat." The prospect of sinking-the-boat involves risks of ruining organizations by . . . making overly huge strategic bets, and losing.

The second risk type that marketing strategists routinely confront entails "Missing-the-Boat." The prospect of missing-the-boat involves allowing great strategic opportunities to walk right by . . . including opportunities to act boldly when others cower timidly or equivocate.

Another core planning issue exists that is related to risk. Planners should always account for the presence of risk. The issue in question when risk is being considered is called the Waterline Principle.

To understand how the Waterline Principle works, imagine you are on a ship. Now imagine that any strategic decision you make that breaks-bad will blow a hole in your ship. If the failed plan blows a hole in the ship's infrastructure above the waterline, where the ship won't immediately or perhaps will never take on water, the hole can be patched. Everyone then can learn what not to do, next time and sail on toward presumably better days. But if a failed plan blows a hole in the ship below its waterline, a deluge of water will pour in, and may pull the ship below the surface. When holes are too big, ships sink fast, with no chance of a second chance to learn from mistakes that were made.

Making big strategic bets is clearly acceptable. No guts, no glory; as prospective or actual "heroes" are wont to think or say. Risk and returns actually do rise and fall together. Stretch goals inevitably should raise expectations, while remaining within reach or almost within reach. No strategic planner has ever substantially benefitted from meeting low expectations. Good to great strategies are often surprisingly audacious.

But good to great marketing strategies also should be tactically plausible. As inferred, goals, no matter how much they stretch, should be achievable.

Audacity is not just bravery, or guts. Audacity also entails the art or science of knowing how and when to not be overly audacious. Yes, the issue of and the need for balance was just introduced again.

The takeaway from the Waterline Principle is that marketing planners generally should avoid making bets big enough to blow holes below waterlines, if things were to go wrong. All or nothing sorts of less than well-calculated strategic thinking, betting practices, more often lead to nothing than to something.

However, this mindset is not the only take on how best to confront and manage risks. Really successful people or companies become really successful because they recognized that the use of normal channels or same old same old ideas as means to acquire or achieve something of value represent "mindless-traps" into which uncreative people who lack initiative and are unwilling to accept risks routinely fall. What's another way to spell mediocrity? That's right, A.V.E.R.A.G.E.

A closing thought on this topic; although the thought could have been slid anywhere inside this discussion because the insight it reveals will only rarely not apply: Scared money don't make much money.

All the while, however, successful strategists never become or remain successful unless they learn to manage the risks, costs, and predicted returns present inside every significant decision. Unless, that is, they learn enough to become smart enough to not be dumb enough to fall routinely into the "all or nothing" mode of decision-making.

Strategic Success Principle 7: Planners should distinguish between challenges associated with managing uncertainty as opposed to challenges associated with managing risk.

Material differences distinguish risk from uncertainty. Risk is challenging, but manageable. Manageable because reasonable estimates of probability of certain known outcomes happening can be estimated based on available data whenever risks arise and are being assessed.

Uncertainty, on the other hand, is tough, a real… Think about real-world interpersonal relationships and how they often play out—badly. People will often choose unhappiness over uncertainty by clinging to relationships that they clearly know are terrible. Think, sadly, about obviously emotionally or physically abusive romantic or marital relationships—yes, these are exchange relationships too. The human propensity to select known unhappiness over unknown uncertainty simultaneously underscores and manifests how psychologically challenging conditions of future uncertainty prove to be for most decision-makers most of the time.

This exact condition also underscores how tough it is to manage uncertainty.

If asked, most strategically minded managers would prefer to receive known bad news now than to continue to experience uncertainty. Managers can plan to accommodate, or make the best, of known bad news. No such opportunity exists in conditions where unknown uncertainties prevail.

When risk exists, reasonable assessments of the probability that certain known events will happen/arise are also present. In strategic situations involving risk, the entire set of likely outcomes is also known. What remains unknown are exact probabilities of those outcomes actually occurring. Such situations are not pleasant, but they are manageable. This is another reason why marketing research is so important. Marketing research usually generates fact-based insights regarding the probability that certain managed (by marketers) or unmanaged outcomes will happen. That these insights exist is pivotally important. Such marketing research insights might be accurately compared to present-day peeks into what is more or less likely to happen in the future—if me or my organization engages in certain strategic activities. And such insights are hugely important. Rare is the person who plays chess effectively while blindfolded.

By contrast, when uncertainty exists, not only is what might happen next unclear; the probabilities of these unknown things happening are not known, either. Two unknown-unknowns are in play. Not cool. Indeed, the situation is scary and dangerous. Under such uncertain conditions planning and any material actions are often understandably shut down.

Uncertainty is always more difficult to plan for and to manage than risk. When planning, uncertainties should be avoided when impossible. When this is not possible, uncertainty should be mitigated to the extent possible.

Calculated risks are known risks pursued for the sake of real potential gains inside conditions where the entire range of possible outcomes is known and reasonably accurate probability assessments of each outcome actually happening can be calculated. By contrast, taking risks for the sake of risk under conditions of uncertainty is nuts.

However, another perspective should be considered when the subject entails whether or not to take risks. A side that argues it might prove more gratifying to enter the closing phases of one's professional life wishing "I hadn't" rather than wishing "I had" taken that chance. Yes, this argument leans into emotional-based reasoning. But the argument still makes a reasonable case for risk-taking.

Strategic Success Principle 8: Planners should accept that some strategic marketing problems are truly-wicked. Wicked to the point where no-one-best-solution to the challenge or difficulty could ever truly exist.

Wicked problems abound inside many professions. Wicked problems of the sorts that create seemingly irreconcilable paradoxes. Scientists and policymakers are each card-carrying members of the marketing profession. How and why? Primarily because scientists and/or policymakers each want nothing more fervently than to have their ideas about how best to solve vexing problems that arise within their professional market spheres to become the chosen ones. The acceptance or rejection of these ideas among members of their professional peers group—their colleagues—pivots to shocking degrees on how well or poorly these scientific or policymaker professionals have previously positioned their individual professional brands and resulting ideas as being not just different but better than other scientists' or policymakers' brands and ideas.

Consider two seemingly irreconcilable marketing issues, bundled into one global problem. The first marketing issue is that air conditioning keeps people cool and actually saves lives. The second marketing issue is that air conditioning is one of the largest contributors to global warming (which is only a problem if one believes global warming marketers who loudly proclaim that global warming is killing people [we don't]). All of which is true only if the marketed idea of global warming as a human-made creation is real rather than a marketer-inspired fabrication about naturally-occurring climate changes. (More marketing.) But remember all along, scientists are marketers. Scientists routinely create and market their own ideas about how best to understand and solve problems. Try resolving this wicked air conditioning-global warming problem inside Texas during any of the state's five summer months.

Now please consider three additional and yet surprisingly interconnected issues. The third issue is that cow farts contribute more to global warming than do air conditioning emissions.[6] The fourth marketing issue is that far more people, not just more American consumers around the world want to eat beef and now possess the financial means to do so. Beef production, on per-pound-produced-basis, consumes ungodly amounts of fresh water,[7] another finite resource. Yet another profoundly wicked problem is arising for another future marketer to solve.

No worries, however. Marketing's got the world's back. Artificial meat[8] is here—just visit *Burger King*. Another solution that's undoubtedly poised to create, at minimum, a fifth issue and problem. A problem related to how to convince more American consumers that they should eat the stuff. No worries. Marketing's "got" this problem in hand, as well. After all, marketers succeed best when concurrently operating inside problem-creating and problem-solving worlds.

Broader and less controversial examples of where and how other truly-wicked strategic problems exist include the need that business and marketing strategists confront to:

- Balance any organization's long-term goals with the short-term demands that its decision-makers, those exact planners, would also inevitably and simultaneously always confront.
- Find completely unclaimed market place; generally by discovering an unmet customer want or need where little to no competition already exists and then trying to satisfy their want or need by solving their problem.
- Balance the desire to develop and market higher quality products or services while holding down costs.
- Protect profits inside increasingly commoditized and globalized markets.
- Balance an organization's and its investors' desire for profits or dividends with a corporation's need to be socially responsible—and thereby enhance or sustain its branding power.
- Create and sustain branding power.
- Manage diverse views and/or goals while strategizing inside any organization.

Two marketing terms and concepts were introduced in the final two bullet-pointed statements. The first concept is "branding power." The second concept is "diversity." The meaning and implications of each concept follow.

Branding power is discussed inside many modules that follow. Power, generally, entails any "actors" ability to direct or influence another's behavior or the course of events themselves. Attach

---

6. Cow farts create more environmental damage than do CO2 emissions from automobiles, as well.
7. Reliable sources agree that approximately 2,500 gallons of water are required to raise one pound of beef.
8. *Impossible Foods* and *Beyond Meat* are two leading artificial meat brands that emerged during the early 2020s.

the word "power" as a suffix to the word "brand" and the ensuing phrase efficiently summarizes the core meaning of the terms "brand- or branding-power." Brand- or branding-power arises inside marketplace in certain situations where the power of brands imbues them with the ability to direct or to influence future behaviors of actual or prospective consumers and consumer segments. "These brands possess" "those abilities" because they have earned the power. The sources of any brand's power are hardly absolute. But such sources exist as forces that virtually all organizations who market brands should covet and seek to create through the development and execution of effective strategies.

Now, turning toward diversity, the prevailing sentiment these days is that diversity is good—and appropriate. Especially given the fact that the presence of diverse views inherently elevates creativity inside most moderately-sized and well-managed groups. But the presence of diversity is difficult to manage. Why? Because yes, while it's true that opposites attract; opposites eventually typically repulse. When managing diverse points of view, strategic planners should keep a degree of tension in place between collaboration and competition. Following this path will keep organizations and the people planning the futures of those organizations awake, and more open and amenable to appropriate change. One approach entails developing seemingly contradictory goals (i.e., simultaneously seeking to lower costs and improve quality) in order to spur enormous efforts and create insights as planners struggle for a while—but not forever—to reconcile the irreconcilable.

Strategic Success Principle 9: Planners should accept that often no one best solution exists. Instead sometimes there are only tradeoffs between bad and worse options.

Strategic solutions developed inside marketing contexts are likely to prove neither completely right nor completely wrong. That's because the types of problems that marketing strategists attempt to solve are rarely framed in black and white. Instead, shades of gray prevail.

The primary reason why these gray outcomes routinely arise inside marketing planning contexts is because strategists' as well as customers' perceptions of which option represents the most logical, rational, or valuable alternative often radically differ. Yes, surely, most professionals are logical and rational inside their own minds. But are such professionals logical and rational in the same ways? Readers already know the answer, which is no, not everyone who is logical and rational is logical and rational in the same manner. And therein lies much of the problem.

Marketing decision-makers should avoid the bigotry of binary choices. Often, no one completely right or wrong strategic decision exists because most marketing strategies deal directly or indirectly with human behaviors—and how wobbly, how transient, how subject to change are our human behaviors dependent on whether it's raining or we're hungry?

Marketing strategists instead should accept tradeoffs and that less than entirely perfect decisions and outcomes are often as good as it gets, because perfection realistically rarely exists. Strategists should honor or at least recognize the thoughts of *Voltaire*, who argued we humans should never let the perfect be the enemy of the good. The life of marketing strategists and marketing managers plays out inside the grays much of the time—pretty much the totality of what either group knows for certain is that each must continue to grow their revenues (sales), profits, and/or market share.[9] To assume otherwise is naïve, wrong, and a guarantor of stress. A recipe for regret. Meanwhile, most, though not all, regrets are a waste of time. Regrets are the past wreaking havoc on our present and future happiness.

Marketing decision-makers should likewise avoid the dangers associated with splitting. Splitting is a psychological defense mechanism through which decision-makers unconsciously frame ideas, alternatives, or choices in all or nothing terms—for example, my options are all good or all bad. The term was originated and its meaning fleshed out in the 1930s and 40s by a psychoanalyst named *Melanie Klein*.

The splitting concept describes how any thoughts and feelings that are, for whatever reason, deemed intolerable are split off from decision-makers' conscious awareness. The consequences that are generated lead to partial, completely incomplete views of (or "takes" on) all of the elements and range of possible outcomes that logically should be considered inside strategic decision-making contexts.

To see any alternative decision as pure risk, decision-makers must split off the parts of it that feature any semblance of upside. The presence of splitting severely distorts reality. The presence of splitting makes it more difficult for decision-makers to develop viable solutions to problems. The presence of splitting generally exacerbates problems over time. If they do not receive due and fair attention, problems inevitably will get worse, things increasingly will fall apart; parts decay, entropy exists. *Neil Young* was right: Rust never sleeps.

The best way to eliminate splitting or to mitigate its negative impacts in situations where some measure of splitting is unavoidable is to be aware that the phenomenon and its negative affects exist. Identifying threats before they fully arise is almost always a strategic course of action. Such threats clearly include the dangers associated with the bigotry of binary choices or splitting. Because then full- rather than half-measures to defeat or avoid them can be formulated on a context by context basis.

Strategic Success Principle 10: Planners should watch their assumptions and avoid making many, if any at all.

Occasions regularly arise when it is not what decision-makers don't know but rather what planners thought they knew for certain that usually hurts them. Especially in the midst of preparing plans. Yet everyone knows what happens when they assume too much, don't they? Assumptions are not necessarily the mother of all screw-ups. But following the wrong assumptions have surely parented many outcomes that the involved decision-makers would have preferred not happen.

A nineteenth-century humorist named *Josh Billings* neatly summarized this logic: "It's not what people know that causes them trouble. It's what they know that ain't so."

---

9. And hopefully, marketing strategists and managers alike realize that the prospect of concurrently growing revenues, profits, and market share is essentially nil. Readers should realize this too.

Strategic Success Principle 11: Planners should not just accept but embrace the importance of relationships; embed this truth inside their planner hearts and planner heads; and plan and act as if every ounce of their future professional and personal success depends upon this principle, because it does.

The ability to earn and create customer relationships, sustain existing customer relationships, and then strengthen them; essentially, this is the whole marketing game.

Why? Because customers never owe anything to marketers. Nothing. Instead, marketers always confront the strategic obligation to make, market, and deliver solutions that customers perceive, inside their "imagined-realities," are worth giving up their hard-earned money to obtain . . . through exchange processes. Otherwise, customers will not feel right about exchanges—and either will not enter or remain in said exchanges. Such customers will not feel like, as in perceive, that they're winning. Winning in terms of how much value they are getting in relation to how much value they're giving up to "get the give." Remember our definition of exchange as a "get and a give"?

Strategic Success Principle 12: Planners should accept no need exists to panic, as in never ever—at least not in public.

Marketing failure is rarely fatal. One can always get another job or start another marketing venture.

However, marketing success is never final, either. Some known or unknown competitors are always creating something new and presumably useful and valuable. Meanwhile, existing customers are inevitably growing more bored with the same ole same ole. Each premise applies to all manner of non-marketing successes and failures as well. Prosperity, success, these outcomes are fragile and tenuous in nature.

Marketing success is tenuous indeed. *Detroit* was the richest large American city on a per capita basis in 1954. Less than forty years later *Detroit* was the poorest large, albeit rapidly shrinking even at the time, American city. Remember: Cities, states, or regions exist and are marketed as products too. And as the values being generated or taken away by cities as places and products change, the value and appeal of the product itself—here, *Detroit*—can radically increase or decline. Hence its former citizens got out of Dodge as quickly as possible, and very few consumers voluntarily elected to move into the failed product that *Detroit* had become. But is *Detroit's* failure fatal, or permanent? Please see above.

Discerning strategists might secure a useful sort of calming perspective from acknowledging these two truths.

MODULE 3.2

History Suggests . . .

The historical record is clear. *Homo sapiens*[10] who do not remember their past mistakes are doomed to repeat them. Historical logic further underscores the fact that wise people similarly enjoy the opportunity to learn from the successes of the past. And then, post-learning, those same wise folks enjoy the opportunity to engage in the same or similar processes and/or activities that facilitated those past successes. Ample reason exists to remain wary, however, because . . . *news flash* . . . things change. Said changes, in turn, might routinely invalidate the future utility of contemporary marketing tactics that once worked in the past.

An essential axiom of military strategy is that success seldom succeeds twice. Written more expansively but hopefully also more revealingly: A supposedly new marketing strategy featuring few to no material (meaningful) changes that has been developed in response to always changing environmental opportunities and threats[11] is quite unlikely to work again. Enemies or competitors have brains and plans of their own and, assuming either has survived to fight or compete again, will learn both from their failures and your successes. Those military enemies or marketing competitors vow, in effect, that they will never let the same bast----s beat us using the same plans again.

Even so, we encourage you to learn from the following historical quotes. These quotes collectively explain and illustrate several underlying causal factors that clearly have contributed to various historical failures or successes. Please also consider what scientist *Carl Sagan* wrote about the value that can result from understanding the past: "You must know the past to understand the present and predict the future."

Marketing strategists can never know the future with certainty. Nor can any other genre of strategist or planner. The preceding statement will never not be true despite any promises made about marketing researchers' "purportedly-powerful probability-based prognostications."

Too many unknown competitive, technological, or economic factors exist, or other unexpected environmental events arise, to achieve more than relative accuracy when strategists attempt to predict

---

10. Homo sapiens is a *Latin* phrase that means "wise man."
11. Far more about environmental opportunities and threats will be discussed during Module 5.

the future. However, strategic marketers can understand past events with greater certainty. And draw actionable planning insights regarding how best to go forward from that certainty.

That's why we're looking back to history right now to derive serious important and always relevant planning lessons from what we can learn there.

HISTORICAL PLANNING LESSONS

Historical Planning Lesson 1: "Failing to plan is like planning to fail"—former *UCLA* basketball coach *John Wooden*.

The implication: Rather than controlling events, those decision-makers and marketers who fail to plan will find themselves controlled by them. Trust us, you don't want events to control us. Want to fail? Then don't plan.

Coach *John Wooden* was quite the quote machine. He is also known for having said "be nice to those you are passing on the way up, because you'll likely encounter those same people on your way back down" and "move quickly but with patience." This latter phrase may appear oxymoronic, upon first reading. It is not, because planning creates preparation and consequently generates useful insights, making it more plausible that individuals or organizations indeed could move quicker, but patiently.

Historical Planning Lesson 2: "Plans are nothing, but planning is everything"—former US President and *World War II* General *Dwight D. Eisenhower*.

The implication: No plan ever works out exactly as planned. This fact is well-known. As is the fact that no plan ever survives the first smoke of battle. Bad stuff happens, unexpectedly. People panic. Enemies—or competitors—fail to respond as anticipated.

Yet if planners already realize that none of their plans will ever go perfectly right the reality of the resulting confusion or slander will prove less disturbing and consequently easier to recover from. Contingencies should always be in place to adapt and respond to unexpected situational outcomes as they arise. The mere act of engaging in planning processes and this activity alone creates preparation that makes it more likely that these adaptive—or contingent—processes can be successfully executed. That's because the planners themselves will already possess most if not all of the necessary information in place to contingently and rapidly adapt their original plans.

Had *Ike*, General Eisenhower's brand name, been more creative and less focused on saving the world from *Nazi* tyranny, he might have stated his case differently. Something similar to better to have a gun (plan) and not need it . . . than it is to not have a gun (plan) and need it.

Another contingency planning point is clear-cut: "Make sure everyone knows the plan so it's easy to change." This is a 1967-era Israeli tank commander's acknowledgment of the unavoidable effects of the smoke of battle during the *Six Day Israeli–Arab War*—and how best to manage them. Sounds easy, but think for a minute about human nature and you'll quickly discern how often this is not the case.

Yet if getting everyone to know and buy into the plan were easy, a longstanding *U.S. Navy* axiom that opines "There's always some son of a bitch who never gets the word" would not exist. Successful strategic leaders understand that often they will need to pound, pound, pound an understanding of their plans inside subordinates' heads, and reward them when they follow and penalize subordinates if they don't.

Historical Planning Lesson 3: "A good plan, violently executed today, is better than a perfect plan next week"— World War II Army General *George Patton*.

The implication: Don't wait for a perfect plan to be developed or to arrive before acting. Marketing professionals who opt for this course of non-action action inevitably will be waiting a long time. No perfect plan will ever exist.

In the interim, environmental opportunity after opportunity may pass by and remain ignored. Alternatively, environmental threat after threat may arise and effectively be ignored. Indeed, inside planning contexts, the maxim "nothing suffices but perfection" may be expressed more succinctly as "impending paralysis." Marketers should generally avoid pursuing planning perfection.

Traditional planning experts suggest marketing organizations should establish BHAGs (i.e., Big Hairy Audacious Goals) and do what is necessary and morally acceptable to achieve them. This makes sense. The most successful marketing plans often have been audacious. Big bold plans, however, should always also remain tactically plausible. The value of balance is reinforced, again.[12]

But another planning approach exists. An approach perhaps best exemplified by the strategy *Dr. Martin Luther King* used to elevate the new *Civil Rights Movement* to top-of-the-mind levels in America's collective mind as a young man during 1955–56. Remarkably, *Dr. King* was only twenty-five years old at the time. His marketing strategy instead entailed being opportunistic. Acting opportunistically, in this context, means identifying opportunities before anyone else does, but also being willing and able to strike first by delivering differentiating value after opportunities have been discovered.

The classic sociocultural example of King acting opportunistically entails *Rosa Parks's* bus-related protest; which triggered a 1955–56 *Montgomery, Alabama*, bus boycott; and a national media furor

---

12. Do BHAPs (Big Hairy Audacious [Marketing] Problems) also exist? Naturally, and absolutely. How about the very real problem of deciding whether to kill more American consumers from disease by opening up the economy, again, despite threat of COVID-19 at the end of May 2020, or perhaps kill even more domestic consumers still by shutting down the economy in response to COVID-19. Shutting down the economy and creating an economic depression (lost jobs, huge upticks in consumer depression, suicides, partner and child abuse) and an absence of face-to-face health care including for surgical procedures for non-CV related problems killed consumers too. Which was the least worst problem to solve? Tough question to answer, right? Planning is rarely easy.

that was strategically generated by *Dr. King* on behalf of *Civil Rights* gains throughout the United States. All this happened, and quickly, during a pre-internet, 24/7/365 media world. The arc of *Civil Rights* history quickly changed for the better as a result.

Opportunism may lack the panache of grand strategies and strategic thinking. So what? Being ready, willing, and able to pull the trigger on opportunities as soon as they arrive and are identified often represents the best strategic alternative.

There are a few more things to understand about the nature of opportunism, however. First, the "willingness to act opportunistically" and plain ole "human intuition" are closely related. And second, while intuition—and/or opportunism—can point decision-makers toward the right direction(s) to pursue opportunism or intuition alone rarely lead to the right solution. No, even when the right directions are identified strategic marketers still must develop a plan to exploit their directional success.

Life is short. Everyone dies. That means, the time for action is often right now.

Procter & Gamble Co. certainly understood and acted based on this premise during 2020.[13] *Procter & Gamble*, better known by the brand *P&G*, is a giant consumer goods marketer. *P&G* traditionally has conducted meticulous marketing research and developed intensely hierarchal (top-down) marketing plans before introducing new products to market. Indeed, the supply chain behemoth was traditionally known for these classic strategic tactics.

During February 2020 (what gigantic environmental threat was blowing up at this exact time?), a new disinfectant spray called *Microban 24* that could kill 99+ percent of cold and flu viruses hit the market. Sales boomed immediately after the new product was available on real and virtual shelves. In response to concerns driven by COVID-19, panicked shoppers snatched any virus-killing cleaners off the shelves as supplies of *Lysol* or *Clorox* drained to zero.

Okay, no real surprises there. Of course, the COVID-19 pandemic precipitated a surge in sales of cleansing products. What else would any thinking marketer expect to have happened? *Microban* revenues eventually exceeded $250,000,000 during 2020—a rare recent new "new product" hit for old-school *P&G*.

Two outcomes proved surprising, however. First, the degree to which *P&G* had acted opportunistically. The B2C giant set out to launch *Microban 24* through a skinny planning team that consisted, in its entirety, of five employees. The product was released without relying on legions of marketing researchers and research test subjects (consumer focus groups) generating marketing intelligence that subsequently guided every strategic decision. The product was released with lightning speed as *P&G* exploited an environmental threat and converted into a corporate opportunity. *P&G's* state-of-the-art production facilities did not even produce the new product. The actual production of *Microban 24* was outsourced in a strategic fashion to a series of supply chain partners.

The rapid-fire introduction of this blue spray bottle signaled how radically *P&G* had revamped the management of its strategic planning and new product development processes. A complex near top-to-bottom managerial planning structure that often put brand managers and regional marketing

---

13. Sharon Terlep, "How P & G Cleaned House before Covid-19," *The Wall Street Journal* (November 14, 2020): B1–B3.

directors in fierce conflict with each other had previously existed. But in this case, centralized new product development and strategic planning teams that previously had decided, in unilateral and slow-played fashions, which new product ideas were approved and how the resulting new products were marketed were, if not entirely eliminated, stripped of much of their previous power. As noted, *P&G* got its opportunistic-on. As had *Dr. Martin Luther King* decades before.

"Life is what happens while you're busy making other plans."

Or so *John Lennon* wrote and sang inside his 1980 song called *Beautiful Boy*. Substitute the phrase "opportunities are passing by" for the phrase "life is what happens." There, the key selling point being marketed about the need for marketers, at times, to plan and act more opportunistically has just been reinforced.

Historical Planning Lesson 4: "When absolute superiority is not attainable, one may be produced at decisive points by making skillful use of the resources you have"—*Prussian Field Marshall Claus von Clausewitz*.

Three implications follow from this strategic military declaration. The first implication rightly suggests that marketers should "attack" their competitors or enemies at their weakest point.

The second implication is that, when attacking, organizations should concentrate on executing and leveraging the values associated with what they do best.

The third implication is that planning organizations should develop and execute measures that ensure their always limited resources are used efficiently. A fourth implication actually follows from the third: Planners should always respect the precious nature of their own or their organization's 3Ts.

The 3Ts of planning are time, treasure (money), and (human) talent, as previously stated. These are the only three types of resources that any individual or organization ever has available. Of the three, talent is usually the most indispensable, most valuable, and most resilient asset. The most important dimension of any talent-based resource that could possibly be mustered by any marketing organization derives from the creativity of its human resources. The power of creativity, just like creativity itself, is infinitely scalable—particularly inside problem-solving contexts. Their own professional and personal creativity can be grown by and within anyone reading this now—see Module 10.

Even so, one might logically ask which "T" is most important? The answer is easy: The resource that firms have the least of is the most important "T," because those firms must determine—strategize about—how to acquire more of it. The value associated with pursuing and achieving balance again rears its head.

Strategic marketing organizations that seek to consciously hew closely to *Clausewitz's* lesson as they develop and execute plans could parrot *In-N-Out Burger*. *In-N-Out Burger*, launched in mega-health-conscious *SoCal* (a recently-coined brand identity for Southern California), sells only burgers, fries, and shakes. But *In-N-Out Burger* makes extraordinarily good burgers, fries, and shakes, and consequently grew into a mega-success.

Organizations honoring this planning lesson might choose to emulate the four U.S. Armed Forces branches. Listed alphabetically, these are the *U.S. Air Force, Army,* the *Marine Corps,* and the *Navy.* Each of these four marketing organizations[14] concentrate almost exclusively on doing what it does best. The *Army*, for example, does land-based warfare best. Consequently, waging land-based warfare is the skill set, or core competency, that the *Army* seeks to strengthen and leverage—all the time. The *Navy* concentrates on water-borne warfare. The *Air Force*, yes, focuses on airborne warfare. Fortunately for the cause of freedom everywhere, the *Marines Corps* is uniquely qualified to fight effectively on land, the sea, and in the air—and has even been known to pronounce these competencies and points of differentiation in its branding messages. Organizations and/or people should similarly focus on what they do better or could do better than other organizations or people.

The importance of focus—the willingness and ability to execute with laser-like focus—is difficult to overstate. *Dr. Isaac Newton*, the history-shifting and paradigm-breaking *English* mathematician, physicist, and theologian once was asked "How do you gather your insights and knowledge?" *Newton* replied simply yet completely: "I take the time to focus and concentrate."[15]

Quiz time, which is actual tantamount to thinking time. Can value ever be gleaned from a decision to resolve problems by ignoring them, say, as politicians are wont to do? The surprising answer is yes, probably, but only under conditions where the problem you are electing to ignore is not worth focusing upon.

Takeaway: Don't just focus. While focusing is nice, that alone is not enough. Strategists should also focus on doing the right things, right.

Historical Planning Lesson 5: "If you don't know where you are going, any road will get you there"—Anonymous source.

Again, three strategic implications follow from this assertion.

First, create or possess a plan; then refine the plan if necessary—and refining will prove necessary. Professionals should always plan their work; work their plan; and adjust their plan as conditions, but most particularly, opportunities and threats, change.

Second, develop only one, two, or three goals as part of that plan.

Turning back toward the four U.S. Armed Services. Collectively, the *Marines, Army, Navy,* and *Air Force* have traditionally shared two and only two strategic goals. Goal 1: Keep the peace. Goal 2:

---

14. The *U.S. Air Force, Army, Marine Corps,* and *Navy* are each marketing organizations and powerful brands. Powerful organizations too. Each military brand cultivates its own unique positioning image—and advantage. Each armed service seeks to recruit the best employees and to play the largest role in ensuing conflicts. Each competes vigorously with other military branches for limited government-issued resources.

15. Isaac Newton, *Isaac Newton's Papers and Letters on Natural Philosophy and Related Documents,* eds. I. B. Cohen and R. E. Schofield (Cambridge: Harvard University Press, 1958).

If peace is not possible, and war ensues, win the war. Every objective laid out by any of the armed services should directly or indirectly contribute to the achievement of either the first or second goal. Objectives are always subordinate to goals, and consequently servants to goals, as well.

Three, put the right measurements or metrics in place as a means of measuring progress, or lack of progress, toward achieving those goals. The right measurements are crucial to planning success because people perform to their metrics. Employees are likewise more likely to perform to their metrics when superiors reward them for achieving goals or hold back rewards when they don't. Keep in mind that even when particular data points about people's performance cannot be counted, the task of evaluating their performance usually still matters greatly. Better still, consider how *Dr. Albert Einstein* framed these measurement and evaluative processes. The physics genius said: "Not everything that matters can be counted, nor does everything that is counted matter."

When managing measuring processes, two questions should always be asked. First, is the firm measuring the right things right? Second, is the firm measuring any of the wrong things? Then stop! As noted, there is never a right way to do the wrong thing.[16]

Want to ensure that the people who report to you are doing their best work, especially when you have given them a project to complete by an agreed-upon date? Then ask those subordinates two additional questions as they are about to hand-in; okay, email via an attachment, their assignment. First, is this your best work? Second, are you sure you've checked through this enough? Once those people reporting to you begin to anticipate the questions they will be asked, and presumably realize the only good answer is "yes," times two, the first round of work they submit should improve materially.

Measuring performance improves performance. But measurement is not enough. A value must be placed on the performance being measured. The question of what return a specific marketing initiative will earn in exchange for its investment of time, people, or money against a specific mission-driven objective or priority should also be answered.

Three concluding thoughts about metrics and measuring performance follow. First, marketing managers should almost always establish high expectations for their reports based on the success benchmarks that they have established. No one ever lived up to low expectations, as stated above.

Second, marketing managers should be aware that the Good-Heart Principle exists, and then make accommodations for its presence. The Good-Heart Principle suggests managers must be judicious about the measurements that they instill inside their units. This is because reports, employees, may employ unusual means to hit their benchmarks. Veterans Administration Hospitals are evaluated based on waiting times for patients once they reach, or get inside, emergency rooms. Veterans Administration Hospitals have actually kept patients inside ambulances and NOT allow them to enter ERs until the ERs have emptied out and the waiting time is drastically shortened. Talk about triage.

Third, while this book was not written to show or tell management or strictly strategic stories, all managers should also understand they'll be made or broken by their subordinates. Most people are extremely human, and act and respond accordingly. The interior modern professional workplace is as much an ongoing drama scene as it is a game of strategic chess. This is where the notion of being nice and fair to people you're passing on your way up comes into play.

---

16. Warren Bennis, *Leaders: Strategies for Taking Charge* (New York: Harper Business, 1985).

Historical Planning Lesson 6: The man who chases two rabbits catches neither—Chinese Proverb.

The implication: Focus, focus, and focus on what you or your organization does best. Marketers, regardless of their ilk, typically should focus on developing and exploiting a narrow range—two or three at most—of core competencies. *Ben Franklin*, yes America's famously bespectacled *Founding Father*, is famous for having said, "Be a jack of all trades but master of one." Any chance ole Ben knew something about the value of focus? There's a high likelihood that he did. Ben knew something about pretty much everything during his time.

Ben Franklin likely appreciated the power of being focused, as in being unified around one goal or small set of goals during any particular period of time. In any endeavor, the side that is divided is usually losing or eventually will lose. Divided as in focusing on too many different goal-driven activities or terms of disagreement. Or divided due to dissension. Perhaps that is why Mr. Franklin purportedly said, after being one of fifty-six signatories to the *American Declaration of Independence*: [Now] "We must all hang together or we shall all hang separately."

By following these two mind-concentrating lessons,[17] a corporation might consciously choose to be more like *Apple*. *Apple* does branding great. *Apple* executes design at world class levels. And make no mistake about it, *Apple* steals, adapts, purchases, or creates the best new ideas that lead to desirable new customer solutions in the form of new products. And that's it . . . *Apple* does not make a single product it markets. Nor does *Apple* ship or warehouse any of the product it sells. These production, shipping, or warehousing functions are outsourced to one or more of *Apple's* supply chain partners. But what *Apple* does do, and concentrates on doing extremely well clearly, is more than enough.

There's more. When focusing on catching only one rabbit at a time, marketers would do well to focus intently ensuring that the right rabbit is chased. The *American Revolution* was based on one marketed idea that was introduced to the world market in 1776. One can argue that the *American Revolution* succeeded because it strategically pursued only one rabbit; that being liberty. The *French Revolution* was based on two marketed ideas that were introduced to the world in 1789. The second revolution failed—and did so quickly and heinously—because its creators attempted to simultaneously capture two incompatible rabbits. The two rabbits were a new regime (product) featuring both liberty and patriotic state power. The *Russian Revolution* (launched, 1917; collapsed, 1989) grew dysfunctional and eventually sociopathic because it chose to chase the wrong rabbit, patriotic state power.

Ideas, which are products, foment revolutions; every single time. The evolution of any revolution can never be separated from the ideas of the marketers who instigated the revolt. Knowing what you know now, how else could one describe revolutionary leaders but as marketers?

---

17. Most thoughtful minds would agree that the prospect of death as a consequence of a failed revolution would usually concentrate the mind.

Historical Planning Lesson 7: "Chance favors the prepared mind"—French scientist *Dr. Louis Pasteur*, the man who brought the world *pasteurized* milk.

Two strategic implications follow: First, prepare—by planning, early. Second, leverage the preparation that planning processes provide. Then, when opportunities or threats appear, the organization is either absolutely ready or readier than less prepared friends or foes.

Historical Planning Lesson 8: Dig wells before you are thirsty—another *Chinese* Proverb.

The implication: Don't wait until it is too late to plan to muster the necessary resources or to establish the appropriate goals. Instead, plan ahead. Similar to how living day-to-day for any one of us isn't so much living as it is surviving, not planning forward ahead well into the future pretty much ensures that surviving is all that non-planning firms will muster.

Quiz time: When is the best time to plant a tree? Answer: Twenty years ago. Second question: When is the second best time to plant a tree? Answer: Today.

Austria and *Italy* jointly decided to build a track over the high and steep *Alps Mountains* that separate *Vienna, Austria* from *Venice, Italy*—the distance is not as far as you likely think—and did so between 1848 and 1854. Or long before train engines powerful enough to make the climb existed. Then, when requisite-sized engines chugged onto the scene a couple of decades later frozen *Viennese* citizens were able to travel to relatively sunnier *Venice* all the quicker, as were *Viennese* sausages.

Historical Planning Lesson 9: "Luck is where opportunity and preparation meet." Anonymous.

The implication: Many people who appear lucky in fact may have been well-prepared; ready to succeed when the right opportunity to succeed arose.

Take *Olympic* swimmer *Michael Phelps*, for example. Mr. Phelps is a hard-working, fish-like man, if there ever was one. Like all other world-class swimmers, Phelps's human physique genuinely is similar to the typical fish's physique. He has really long feet and really big hands (two sets of flippers); along with short legs and a long torso (fishlike again), especially for a man 6'4" tall. So, beyond question, Phelps was born with the genetic predisposition (the opportunity) to swim like a fish. The takeaway, however, is that Michael began training seriously at age eight. Let's call that what it is. The preparation that often proves indispensable before certain lucky souls, well, get lucky. And in the end, Mr. Phelps was lucky, or was he great enough, to win twenty-something *Gold Medals* because opportunity and preparation happily intersected inside him.

One may make one's own luck inside many marketing contexts through dogged perseverance and the willingness to take measured risks in pursuit of worthy goals. Then one can put one's good fortune to good work to produce more value by solving newer or bigger, or newer bigger, problems.

Historical Planning Lesson 10: "We don't have a strategy, yet."—former *US President Barack Obama*.

Two marketing implications: One, create a strategy. Two, even when one has no strategy, no need exists to broadcast this deficit to competitors or enemies.

Mr. Obama was responding to a *CNN* reporter's August 29, 2014, question when he issued this utterance. The reporter was asking how the *United States* was going to respond to the ISIS threat in *Syria*. That is, responding to the threat of an enemy force (a marketing organization?) that Mr. Obama had previously branded as the *Al-Qaeda Junior Varsity Team*. Upon hearing this, ISIS broke big, bad, and bold in *Syria*, burning this; blowing up that; and killing, torturing, and beheading thousands. Could have been coincidence, but . . .

During the remainder of the *Obama Administration*, the *United States* never stopped or slowed down ISIS's reign of terror in *Syria*. But the then incoming *President Donald Trump*, during early 2017, ended this reign. Because the man had a plan and executed it decisively. The strategy began with a bang. Specifically, stage one of the plan entailed dropping one *GBU-43/Massive Ordnance Air Blast (MOAB)* bomb, a marketed product, on an underground ISIS headquarters, killing hundreds and effectively decapitating ISIS's leadership in an instant. Through this and other strategic air responses the ISIS threat in Syria slowly and then precipitously declined in strength.

MOAB is the US military's most powerful non-nuclear weapon. The product is better known by its branding acronym: *Mother of All Bombs.* Like many great brand names, the branded *MOAB* acronym effectively describes the bomb product's unique problem-solving capabilities.

Not coincidentally, this unusual branding signature has its roots in history. Another infamous human brand, *Saddam Hussein*, the now long-executed dictator of *Iraq*, once promised he would unleash the "*Mother Of All Wars*" if the *United States* attacked *Iraq*. The *United States* did attack, *Saddam* never unleashed. The war lasted exactly one hundred hours before *Iraq* surrendered.

Historical Planning Lesson 11: "If you don't have a competitive advantage, don't compete."—*GE CEO Jack Welch*.

Three implications emerge from this historical lesson: First, establish the right goals. Second, ground one or more of these goals in the perpetually related needs to achieve differentiation and earn positioning advantage. Three, properly measure outcomes and then reward progress/punish failure to progress toward achieving these goals. Organizations and/or people navigating based on these three guidelines are likely to revel in the results that accrue.

Jack Welch assumed the CEO role at an organization then known as *General Electric* at a dire time in its history (1979). Long story summarized, the corporation was doing poorly in the marketplace. In response to the crisis, Mr. Welch created ten Strategic Business Units (SBUs) inside the firm, and then summarily told each SBU leader to find, to create, a way to differentiate based on a competitive advantage. Welch then went on to admonish each leader of each SBU that he (*General Electric's* senior management at the time were all men) was expected to earn a first or second place market share inside the particular market segments being targeted by the SBU by a date certain—or else recraft their resumes as a precursor to working elsewhere. SBUs are defined as the smallest business units inside any organization for which independent planning can be done and for which sets of independent resources exist.

Differentiation is critical to any professional's, to any brand's, and/or to any organization's success. That is, favorable types, or points, of differentiation. (No one should seek out negative differentiation, despite statements such as there is no such thing as negative publicity. Of course some publicity is highly injurious to professional and corporate brands—just ask *O. J. Simpson, Lance Armstrong, United Airlines, Uber,* or *British Petroleum*, which actually changed its brand name in response to bad publicity and is now known more simply as *BP*.)

The statement "differentiate or die" is not hyperbole. The adage, which is absolutely useful and appropriate, did not arrive accidentally. One idea to learn, know, and retain about differentiation is that almost anything can be differentiated if the differentiating actor is sufficiently creative.

Take salt, for example. Salt is constituted of sodium and chloride. Salt is one of the most abundant minerals on earth. Salt is remarkably homogenous.

Salt is also a product; it surely brings many values to the table. Salt savors cooked food. Preserves fresh or newly killed food. Restores human health—consider the saline solutions that has or will run through pretty much every readers' veins. Salt has even been used as money. Salt was valuable enough during an earlier era that ancient *Roman* soldiers were occasionally paid in salt rather than monetary coins. Their monthly pay was called "salarium." "Sal" was and is *Latin* for salt. The *Latin* root remains in the *French* word "salaire," and from these *Latin-French* origins migrated to the English "salary." Ha, now the cultural phrase "s/he is not worth his salt" makes sense. The negative implication was that the shirker was not creating enough value, was taking away more in pay than s/he was producing. My goodness, maybe the whole world really is about creating value, solving problems, and acts of marketing themselves.

Even so, given how plentiful salt is today and how homogenous the simple mineral compound has always been, salt must be difficult to differentiate.

Salt, we dare write, is just salt. No, actually we dare not utter those words, at least not around *Morton's Salt*. In 1914, *Morton's Salt* first began successfully promoting and differentiating its salt as the product that poured when it rained on a big-time and apparently ever-lasting scale. *Morton's Salt* created these laudable outcomes for its brand by prominently placing their then-new positioning statement—*When It Rains, It Pours*—on the side of the innovative container. The innovation was simple but new and useful. The container featured a metal pouring spout. This was the innovation. The famous container, still used today, also featured a little girl with an umbrella and raindrops showering upon a blue background. She's still around too.

The rest is differentiation history. The lesson and takeaway is that when organizations are sufficiently creative and committed to earning differentiation, differentiation can be achieved. Even when highly homogeneous, presumably un-differentiable products are being marketed, positioning is possible.

MODULE 3.3

A Philosophical Close

This Module's final take on strategic-level planning pivots around one word: "essentialism."[18]

Effective strategic planning, inside marketing or any other relevant business context, requires more than just doing things right. Effective strategic planning also requires that the right things be done right. Essentialism isn't solely about getting more tasks done in less time, although the concept focuses on timing and argues that closure, finishing what you start, is also relevant and useful.

Essentialism instead is about getting only the right things done.

So how should essentialism play out inside strategic marketing planning contexts? Essentialism could play out in the form of planners focusing intensely on only the utterly necessary and completely dispensing the trivial. For example, developing a mission and curating from it a handful of affiliated goals. The resulting goal-driven actions thus are treated as utterly necessary—and therefore essential.

Focusing on these two essentials should ensure, to the extent possible, that resources are not spread too thin but instead that just enough "T's" are invested to feed the few goals that decision-makers have deemed essential, and consequently worthy of pursuit. Prima *Russian* ballet dancer *Anna Pavlova* made the following argument: "To follow, without halt, one aim. There is the secret to success." Except in this discussion we'll grant planners the grace to pursue two or three aims, because successful marketers generally must successfully execute two or three goals in a simultaneous fashion.

Essentialism likewise would entail deciding to not tolerate so little risk that the prospect of generating bountiful long-run returns becomes a non-starter while concurrently deciding to not pursue so much risk that future prospects for long-term success or even survival might be blown to oblivion should the big strategic bet not pay off.

We don't know exactly where the right risk-return-ratio or ideal resource allocation model begins or ends inside any strategic plan. No other purported or actual planning experts know, either. But the fact of knowing that the concept known as essentialism exists and should be accounted for inside strategic planning, and the knowing alone, should generate material value across the long-run. We further know that over the long-run focusing on finding essentiality and achieving balance

---

18. Greg McKeown, *Essentialism: The Disciplined Pursuit of Less* (New York: Currency, 2020).

as decision-makers generate and execute their plans will more often generate more value for their organizations than any other planning philosophy that we could have advocated would generate.

The long-run, or the place that begins tomorrow where everyone plans to succeed and presumably live-in during their future, was emphasized above. However, we'll modulate this emphasis with the caveat that planners generally should not focus on planning for "too-long" a "long-run." Because, as economist *John Maynard Keynes* correctly asserted "in the long-run we'll all be dead." The long-deceased Professor *Keynes* was surely right about this particular point. The proof literally lies—interred—all around us.

MODULE 4

Segmentation, Targeting, and Positioning

MODULE 4.0

Win or Lose?

Blocking, tackling, and scheming (strategic game plans) matter greatly inside American football. Blocking, targeting, and scheming are American football principles. Teams that block, tackle, and scheme better than their opponents almost always win.

Marketing similarly features blocking-, targeting-, and scheming-like principles. These three strategic marketing principles are called segmentation, targeting, and positioning. When marketing organizations execute these three activities effectively the executing firms will find it difficult to lose. When marketing thinkers (strategists) and doers (managers) execute one or more of the three basic marketing activities poorly their associated organizations will almost inevitably lose. Worth noting, the same marketer or group of marketers can and usually does function both as thinkers and doers.

What Thressa Said

After her husband recently said he almost enjoys small-group interactions more than large-group social experiences, Thressa Strutton replied: That's because "a lot of humans are not instinctively herd-like or herd-seeking creatures. Unlike horses, cattle or dogs who instinctively create, join and follow herds. That's presumably because horses, cattle or even dogs are far less likely than humans to prey on their own species. Cattle or horses never prey on each other (horses do tussle with one another to establish or maintain alpha dominance) the only times dogs would actually eat one another would involve *Walking Dead*-like post-apocalyptic situations." Thressa, former horse breeder and rancher that she was but forever horse and dog lover that she remains, well, the lady was right.

Human beings? Well, take a peek backward down any historical avenue and discover the degree to which plain ole human folks often fail to herd well. But when humans share common attitudes or opinions, implying that they also generally like or dislike the same things or ideas, those consumers are much more likely to herd together into what marketers could call market segments.

Or, for that matter, when humans share similar ages; zip codes; university, college, or sports team allegiances, think hordes of rabid football or basketball fans; educational attainments; political orientations; skin hues (ethnicities); and/or religious orientations; those consumers are much more likely to herd together into market segments. Groups, that is, who generally share certain attitudes, opinions, beliefs, and preferences for or against certain brands and products.

Yet in some ways, every consumer is already like every other person on earth. Most people think they're not like everyone else. They are wrong, however. Every human shares certain key needs and problems with every other human being.

But, of course, in some ways each consumer is also unique. Humans don't all share the same needs or experience the same problems.

Finally, in some ways all consumers are like many other consumers who share their cultural identity, gender category, ethnic identity, social class memberships, attitudes, beliefs, preferred lifestyles, age, love for a team or brand, and so forth. All consumers are like many other consumers who share, in other words, many or all of the human traits and characteristics listed two paragraphs up.

All of which implies, before marketers can succeed, they must segment well. The act of segmenting fundamentally entails grouping—or herding—consumers or firms that share certain characteristics together into an entity called a "segment." Details about how these herding, grouping, and/or segmentation processes are managed are provided below.

When striving to market successfully, marketers should not simply fish wherever fish swim. No, marketers should get more strategic whenever possible by fishing exactly where the specific types of fish that they are seeking to catch, targeting, are more likely to bite on those marketers' particular sorts of bait are swimming. That is to say, marketers should fish—or target—where the types of consumers found in a particular body of water (market segment) are more likely to bite on the specific type of problem-solving value that marketers currently deliver or one day could deliver through their marketing mixes.

This implies, before marketers can succeed, they must target segments effectively and then position their brands' values effectively within the targeted segment or segments. The more actionable marketing research knowledge that marketers possess about the segments they target, the more likely it becomes that those marketers can reach their targeted segments successfully. Which represents a good start but hardly the whole ballgame. Because strategic marketers understand that they also should reach these targeted segments with an appealing combination of product-delivered problem-solving values and marketing messages that prove meaningful, persuasive, and ideally determinant to the B2B or B2C customers who comprise the targeted segments as those customers make decisions about which brand to purchase from among any number of known brands inside a particular product category. You just read one of the two or three longest sentences in the book. Longest, and most complicated, in fact. So please read it again. The content inside this sentence is extremely important.

One more time, as we repeat so you will remember, the marketing mix functions as an adaptable tool that marketing organizations or individual marketers use to create and deliver appealing combinations of appealing values along with meaningful and persuasive marketing messages. And, again one more time, the marketing mix functions as the adaptable tool that marketing organizations use to create both differentiation and unique and uniquely desirable positions for their brand or brands.

Despite the best efforts of marketing researchers, those individuals investigations into consumers' favorite books, TV shows, movies, or music rarely provide deep insights into those individuals' psychological makeup. But consumers' favored product brand choices often point the way toward the market segments in which they most belong. Smart B2C marketers, which means strategic marketers, understand that knowing the movie or book that consumers favor reveal insights that can be used to predict consumers' tastes, habits, and ultimately their wants and needs. Strategic marketers is another way of writing smart marketers.

Watch out. Someone is following and targeting you. Two useful facts follow.

- One, you may not care about marketing but marketers very much care about you.
- Two, marketers are out to get you, but typically out to get you in ways that help you solve your problems, satisfy your needs, and—net-net—make you happier. Yes, we did write "typically," and yes, typically surely does not mean always.

Make what you will of these two complementary facts. But a third related fact will also always remain in play: Your knowledge of these facts' existence and how you should respond to the knowing will be colored by whether you currently occupy the role of consumer or marketer.[1] Nothing is new here. Human beings' points-of-view—their perceptions—have always been heavily influenced by their points-of-view.

---

1. Everyone, often during genuinely crucial times in their lives, performs as a marketer. Just as everyone, throughout their lives, performs as a consumer. Knowing these facts now, is there any reason to not learn how to perform more effectively inside either role?

MODULE 4.1

Segmentation

Acts of successful market segmentation requires acts of successful division. During segmentation processes marketers divide larger groups of potential customers—at times, entire markets[2]—into smaller segments of customers who are more likely to purchase or use whatever product is being marketed. Essentially, when they engage in segmentation processes marketers divide more heterogonous, larger markets into more homogenous and smaller groups. In the process marketers convert and transform larger masses of less-alike consumers into smaller collections of more-alike consumers.

These descriptions apply to all marketing organizations that decide to engage in market segmentation. There are at least three reasons why all marketing entities should segment. First, no single marketer can successfully appeal to all B2B or B2C customers at the same time. Yes, pretty much everyone would enjoy owning and driving a *Ferrari*. But with starting prices circling $345,000+, few folks can afford the brand.

Second, many marketers must judiciously select the customers with whom they attempt to create lasting relationships, particularly as marketing organizations partner with B2B customers inside supply chains. Some B2C customers or B2B customer-partners aren't worth the high expenditures that would prove necessary to secure or maintain a relationship with them. Certain customer relationships simply aren't worth the pain to maintain. Customers do get fired. Founded in 1837, *P&G* is among the world's largest detergent, hygienic, and food and beverage products marketers. Roughly twenty years ago *P&G* summarily terminated dozens of relationships with smaller grocers and other stores. The reason was because the costs of doing business with smaller customers, given the lower quantities they purchased, cut too deeply into *P&G*'s distribution-based economies-of-scale[3] (EOS) and thus into *P&G*'s profit margins.

---

2. Markets, as defined and described earlier, entail entire sets of potential/actual purchasers and/or users of products who also can actually afford those products. Everyone, as in we'll target "everyone," rarely if ever constitutes an acceptable description for markets.

3. Inside supply chain or other strategic marketing contexts, the term economies-of-scale refers to the reduced costs on a *per unit* basis that arise from the opportunity to produce, promote, or deliver larger *total* quantities of products.

Third, contemporary marketers must be choosy about whom they target. This is primarily because no such thing as mass markets[4] exist anymore. Repeating a familiar refrain, technological evolution is largely responsible for this change. Not long ago during a pre-internet age, most Americans got their news or grabbed their entertainment through a handful of media. No longer. Inside contemporary markets marketers seeking to reach huge amounts of consumers with a single message can use the *Super Bowl* . . . and that's about it. But another factor is driving this trend. The domestic population continuously grows more diverse, literally on a daily basis. The divergent sociocultural values that accompany diversity are persistently making markets less homogenous and consequently less interested in or less likely to "like" the same products, services, brands, or messages.

Criteria Used to Create Market Segments

No one single best base or criterion exists from which larger markets can be segmented into smaller, more similar, more actionable segments. Successful marketers consequently use different segmentation variables, alone and in combination, first to learn how best to understand a market and then and only then to divide larger, more diverse markets into smaller, more homogeneous segments.

Using Geography (to Segment)

The national, state, regional, city, or even zip codes-based neighborhood residences of consumers can be used to segment them. Marketers may elect to focus on only one geographic area, or emphasize one or two areas more than other geographic regions. *NFL* marketers, for example, don't sell much *Dallas Cowboys* branded gear in *North Carolina*. Nor is much *Charlotte Panthers* branded gear sold in *Texas*.

Geographic location matters greatly. Is the *Dearborn, Michigan*-based outerwear manufacturer *Carhartt*, who primarily markets heavy outdoor menswear, likely to sell more winter coats in *Houston, Texas*, or in *St. Paul, Minnesota*? You know the answer, of course. But this does not mean that *Carhartt* completely ignores the Houston-area? Certainly not, the manufacturer markets throughout the region. But this does mean *Carhartt's* bread-and-butter, segmentation-and-targeting-wise, entails intensively pursuing customers who are living in or around cold weather cities such as *Chicago, Cleveland*, or *St. Paul*.

Geographical location influences consumers' attitudes, preferred lifestyle choices, and behaviors. Geography influences automobile choices; more foreign cars are sold in Pacific Coast California than in land-locked and union-bound Ohio, where *Buy American* is more than just a branding identifier and credo. Far more surfboards are sold in *Santa Barbara, California*, than in *Galveston, Texas*, even though each city is located right-by ocean or gulf waves. A surfing culture pervades Cali. In Texas, not so much.

Denton, Texas, is a wonderful place to live. *Denton* is also a far-from-wonderful place to own a bike for non-suicidal riders. The roads are rough-on, as in dangerous-for, bikes and their driver. The aforementioned *Santa Barbara*, by contrast, has built wide and safe bike lanes on all city streets plus

---

4. Mass markets, defined, are large but relatively homogenous groups of potential/actual customers for given products.

the weather never gets too hot or too cold. Any guesses as to which geographic site represents a better place to market bicycles and/or bike repair shops?

Geographic location can matter greatly right down to a micro-level, as in the right or wrong side of streets or roads. Being located on the proper, as opposed to the wrong side, of the street may prove critical to the long-term success of restaurants that specialize in serving breakfast (offering easier points of entrance or exit to the bulk of workers as they drive in the morning to their employment locations), or of restaurants that specialize in serving dinner (offering easier ways in or out to those same workers as the bulk of them travel back from their workplaces to their houses or apartments).

Using Demographics (to Segment)

Age, gender, family-related measures, occupation, income, religion, and ethnicity are the demographic metrics that B2C marketers most frequently use when they segment.

The *Greek* origins of the *English* word demographics make sense as soon as you read them. "Demos" meant "people." "Graphics" meant "arithmetic measurement." People-measurements, the word demo-graphics makes perfect sense. One reason why this particular segmentation base is used so frequently follows from its ease of measure.

In addition, knowing that an individual is seventy-two years old, features a *European American* ethnic origin, is male, and lives in the rural South lends great insight into what he is likely to want or to reject outright as a marketing choice. For example, as he chooses political candidates inside voting booths.

Demographics are destiny. These three words, which did not originate here, represent more than clever or alliterative phrasing. The preceding environmental discussion emphasized that it is not so much environment trends that marketing strategies should study and exploit/avoid. Instead, the leading edges of, say, environmental demographic trends is what marketers should scan, research, and understand. The *Hispanic* population, for example, is trending up inside the *United States*. Already the second largest ethnic-based demographic category, *Hispanic Americans* remain the fasting-growing domestic market segment. *Hispanic Americans* are more/less likely to purchase certain brands/products than are *European Americans* or *Asian Americans*. If a marketer is already successfully targeting *Hispanic Americans*, it occupies a sweet spot. Said marketer also occupies a spot that fortuitously is well-positioned to quickly grow sweeter still. The prevailing demographic trends redound to that marketer's best interests. Why? Because demographics are destiny.

Demographic trends often represent the leading edges of sociocultural evolution. But this is probably not the case with respect to the marketing and consumption of tattoos. The fastest growing demographic, in terms of getting tattoos, is married, white, suburban women. Wow, that's edgy, equal parts badass and soccer mom.

Tatts have long since become so trendy that it's no longer considered taboo to get tattoos. Rebellious left the tattoo station a decade or so ago. Married, suburban, white women have only rarely been leading harbingers of cool. After all, there was that "soccer mom voter" thing about ten years ago.

Some decent free advice follows; that is, if you plan to pursue a professional criminal career: Don't get tattooed anywhere where judges can see the ink, at least in Texas; where judges still mostly lean conservative.

Trends come and go. And environmental trends often exhaust themselves and play-out like depleted gold or silver mines. When the trends do end, as in if consumers slowly and then suddenly grow tired of all the ink (same ole same ole gets so boring), boom times will arrive for tatt-removing servicers. That's an impending trend and prospective opportunity that some sector of marketers should own as their friend.

Age

For what types of products does age work as a segmentation criteria? Did pharmaceutical products just rise to the top of your mind? Yes, that works. A hugely disproportionate amount of health-care consumption and expenditures emanate from older people, especially during the last three to five years of their life.

How about diapers? Do diapers seem a product category for which age would function as a logical segmentation base? Clearly, yes. Although not always entirely in the ways that one might initially assume. For example, about 31 percent of diapers current sold domestically are targeted at and used by adults.

Interesting thing about age. The aging process undoubtedly affects consumers and their decision-making processes throughout their entire life cycle. So much so that actions or prohibitions that once were viewed as punishments during our youths (not getting to attend a party) morph into desired goals as we age into adulthood (not having to attend another party). Yes, age, or the broad age categories to which consumers belong, can radically impact their choices.

For example, consumers get older every day. Yet some birthdays carry more weight than others. Researchers have discovered that at the start of a new decade of life (thirties, fifties, and seventies) consumers often search actively for new sources of meaning in their lives. Often this search entails pursuing new challenges or seeking experiences that break their normal lifestyle patterns, such as having an extramarital affair (not a recommended consumption choice). Or visiting heretofore exotic unvisited locales. Or, jumping out of perfectly functional airplanes or boats.

Strategic marketers take heed and pay attention by targeting such consumption opportunities toward individually identified consumers as they approach these pivotal benchmark birthdays in their lives.

Gender (Sex)

For what types of products does age work as a segmentation criteria? The answer is lots of types. More often than not, marketers of products as disparate as weapons, movies, books, music, or toys create segments based on the gender that targeted consumers share. Smaller guns, for example, to fit into women's purses. Or promoting ultra-violent movies or head-banging music, to attract young males.

As for toys, despite even then decades-long feminist pushback, a 2012 *New York Times* article wrote that gender-based targeted advertising is more pronounced now than it was during 1995. The underlying strategic rationale is logical. Toy marketers practically understand that when they divide markets into narrow demographic segments, they can then market more slightly-different versions of the same toy to different segments. Nostalgia often motivates parents but especially grandparents to give the types of toys they fondly recall from their childhood. Many parents argue, again logically and often based on observation, that boys and girls typically like different toys, either because the parents appreciate the high social costs that sometimes still gravitate toward boys who enter pink zones or because of their own desire for traditional gender conformity.

Adopt one side or the other of this impending argument if you wish, but the example that follows clearly illustrates an absolute gender-based consumer difference. The example also clearly features practically-significant "consumer behavior-related" decision-making implications. When men meet potential new female romantic partners, their bros usually ask, "What does she look like?" When woman meet potential new male romantic partners, their female friends (apparently, no female equivalent to bro exists) typically ask, "What does he do?" Think these intrinsic-gender-bound differences are routinely reflected in each genders' consumer behavior? You should, because they are.

Sex differences definitely exist, even as we progress through the third decade of the twenty-first century. There is no point in denying this genuine—rather than imagined—reality. For example, younger men often marry younger women thinking that their spouses will never change. Younger women often marry younger men thinking they can change them. Funny how each gender can think so different yet each be wrong each time. Another marketing-related thought about marriage: When mates enter marriage the new deal appears ideal yet the exchange process often transmogrifies into an ordeal and consequently drives one or both exchange partners toward seeking a new deal, again. Well well, as established during Module 1, exchange is the core concept in marketing. So does this condition mean marketing is a core component inside marriage? We think the answer is yes.

Like a jolt from the future, a 1982 *Enjoli* perfume ad proclaimed loudly, proudly, and famously that, "Because I am woman . . . I can bring home the bacon and fry it up in a pan." The ad offered more than a nod and wink to an at-the-time truly-finding-its-footing "women's liberation" movement. The advertising message also heralded women's emergence as forces to be reckoned with in the workplace. In the intervening decades *American* women have not only made huge strides in pay and equal opportunity, they also control more than 50 percent of personal wealth inside the *United States*. Yet, according to the *Wall Street Journal*, women are still behind the times when it comes to taking control of their big-picture, long-term financial decisions. Whether this gap exists due to a lack of time, interest, or overall financial knowledge remains uncertain. What is known with clarity is that this gap is accompanied by seriously-important marketing segmentation implications because it prevails across women of all ages, income, and educational levels.[5]

For example, that these differences exist at all suggests that financial services marketers (investment houses, insurance service providers, wealth managers) should engage in more gender-based differentiation, should target women differently, and should position their financial services values and solutions differently when pursuing women as customers. Because this book is not driven by financial services marketing or gender studies, we'll develop no more precise recommendations than those three. But the persistence of this gender difference speaks powerfully of the prospective power associated with gender-based segmentation as many (albeit not all) marketing strategies are being developed and executed.

---

5. Sarah Max, "What's Holding Women Back?" *The Wall Street Journal* (December 15, 2020): S1–S2.

This discussion about "gender differences" between men and women assumes the existence of a binary gendered world in which many woke consumers obviously feel they can no longer comfortably reside. So why knowingly wander into the jaws of this controversial environmental trend? The answer is because any consumer's or organization's degree of relative "wokenesss" logically might also function as a segmentation criteria. Woke, as opposed to asleep, consumers will almost certainly be turned on/turned off by differing brands and brand values. Meanwhile, those specific "turn-offs" or "turn-ons" are surely relevant to all manner of marketing segmentation efforts that currently are or one day might play-out inside B2C markets.

Segmentation criteria are everywhere, as you can see. Just like marketing operates and exercises its non-random bursts of persuasion and influence everywhere across the world.

Family Life Cycle Stage

The most basic family life cycle stages are single; married; never-married or divorced; never married with children; married with children; married with no children living at home; and widowed. At what life cycle stage is a family most likely to buy a refrigerator, or the new home to go with it? A mini-van? A crib? A college education? A fabulous vacation? This list can extend seemingly forever, and the "right time" to purchase any of these products is heavily family life cycle stage dependent. These two facts underscore how frequently family life cycle stage influences consumer behavior.

The best-known of these family life cycle stages, probably because the stage proves so alluring to marketers and consumers alike, are the fabulous DINKs. DINKS is an acronym: <u>D</u>ouble-<u>I</u>ncome, <u>N</u>o-<u>K</u>ids [living at home]. DINKs often have real money, particularly of the discretionary sort. That expensive sports car you've been pining for, dear husband, go for it babe. The bucket list luxurious three-week getaway to *Italy's Tuscan* or *Lake Como* regions that you waited years for, dear spouse, well sweetheart, pack some comfortable shoes too. Because as fate would have it *Medieval Italian* cobblestones and modern *Badgley Mischka* high heels are wildly incompatible with one another.

Children have displaced dads, moms, or parents generally as lords or ladies of the realm inside many contemporary households. The rise of two-income households has upended traditional power dynamics. Years ago the father's role as sole breadwinner gave him primary decision-making power. Usually, this is no longer the case as most moms work outside the home. When these factors are coupled with the fact that the average number of children is falling rapidly individual kids now enjoy a big natural bump in decision-making and buying power. The drop in average family size, in particular, has reduced competition between kids themselves for resources from their parents at the same time those families themselves have more resources to allocate.

Occupation

When the subject turns toward the use of job status as a potential segmentation criterion, think apparel. Will their occupational status as blue collar, white collar, or professional workers likely affect their apparel choices? Or the brands and types of automobiles they drive or alcohol they drink? All the answers, beyond question, are yes.

Religious Affiliation and Level Religiosity

The fastest growing religious affiliation for years inside the *United States* has been "nones." *Millennials*, in particular, have stopped attending religious services and have increasingly traded in organized faith for political agitation in a change that may or may not deliver a life full of meaning and substance to the switchers. Their call, after all, this is America; citizens have the freedom to make their own choices.

Nones are respondents who answered researchers' questions about their religious affiliation by clicking "None." This does not matter, however, to marketers who use an individual's religious affiliation or the absence of such in his or her life as a segmentation base—because such consumers' NONE status says so much that segmenting B2C marketers might find useful about what these individuals value or fail to value in their lives. Consumers' connections or absence of connections with religion influences their beliefs, rituals, values, and sense of self as well as the sort of communities with which they are most likely to identify or reject. Yes, the absence or presence of religious connections can materially affect consumers' product choices.

Let's use food as an example—and pluck some low-hanging fruit. Kosher foods, for example, these come to mind. Or for that matter, so do pork products, whose consumption is proscribed by various religions. Indeed, most religions impose certain moral standards along with expected codes of behaviors on their membership.

Ethnicity or Race

Ethnic-based segmentation bases matter and are widely employed. For example, college-educated *African American* women[6] annually purchase more books than any other market segment. This trend may suggest publishers either should publish more books targeted specially toward black women. Or, a strategic analysis of this environmental/marketplace trend may suggest that book marketers should publish more books that appeal more to other ethnically-based gender segments.

Based on their marketing research based insights, marketers also know that *African American* women spend substantially more on hair care products or services than any other ethnic group inside the *United States*. This is true particularly about hair care dollars spent as a share of the spending consumer's household income. The supply chain for straight black hair as a product, for example, extends all the way from *America* to *India* and then from *India* back to *America* again, according to the *Chris Rock* documentary called, *Good Hair*. Brands such as *Mixed Chicks Straightening, Argan Smooth Silk Press*, or *Giovanni Straight Fast* abound. *This-Is-Where-Black-People-Meet.com,* an online dating primarily targeting an African American clientele, have used ethnic membership as a segmentation criterion for decades.

Ethnicity, ethnic identity, and ethnic membership—be it *African American, Asian American, Indo American, Hispanic American, Native American,* or *European American*—matters greatly to marketers as they segment, because the ethnicities with which consumers most identify often impact how, what, and why they buy. The opportunity to use ethic identity as a segmentation base has proven beneficial

---

6. "College-educated African American women" represents an educational-level-based, ethnic-based, and gender-based market segment.

to various organization's marketing efforts seemingly forever. The nation, however, would likely benefit from reaching a point where no one felt the need to hyphenate X–American so much. But as long as these ethnic identifiers also remain a key segmentation device for political marketers, this is unlikely to happen.

Using Psychographics (to Segment)

Psychographic segmentation activities involve dividing consumers into segments based on their social class status, preferred lifestyle choices as measured through a combination of their activities, interests, and opinions (i.e., their AIOs, and their personality characteristics).[7]

How do psychographics work? During a recent Presidential election, the candidates' respective marketing campaigns understood that people who ate at *Red Lobster*, shopped at *Burlington Coat Factory*, liked *George Clooney*, usually stayed up late, watched *NBC,* and listened to jazz were much more likely to vote for candidate *Obama*. *Democrats* targeted, messaged, and positioned their brands' values accordingly. Yet people who drank *Sam Adams* beer, paid for groceries by credit cards, ate at *Olive Garden*, watched *Fox,* read political blogs daily, and closely followed college football were much more likely to vote for candidate *Romney*. *Republicans* targeted and positioned their political stories accordingly.

The process can be explained simply, although the processes through which psychographics are used to segment markets are not necessarily simple themselves. But for now, an unpretentious explanation suffices, lifestyle choices that consumers make influence consumer product choices that consumers make. The premise here is related to the fact that the social classes to which consumers belong or aspire to belong also influence the product choices consumers make.

Using Behaviors (to Segment)

Behavioral segmentation activities entail dividing consumers into discrete segments based on their level of knowledge about branded products, their attitudes toward branded products, or their usage rates with respect to given branded products—or some combination of these three factors.

Using Purchase Occasion (to Segment)

The occasion for which or in which a purchased product or service might be given or used exercises a large influence on what consumers buy. Take wine, for example. Do you think consumers might purchase one branded bottle of wine when acquiring the product simply to get a comfortable buzz-on but buy another wine brand if the same product was being gifted to a friend? Think a consumer

---

7. Readers will learn more below about how marketers can strategically develop personalities for their brands over time. Marketers often win their positioning and differentiating competitions by aligning the created personality traits of their brands with targeted market segments that either currently share or would one day like to share particular personality traits in common with the brand!

might buy still a third brand were he purchasing wine for a dinner party at his home for his boss and her spouse? We think he would, as should you. Consumers would almost certainly choose different brands of wine based on the occasion for which they were acquiring the wine.

That's how occasion-based segmentation works. Marketers can use their awareness of the reason why a particular brand was being purchased to adjust the value proposition that they seek to develop for the brand. Marketers could even, and indeed should, use the occasion for which a given branded product is acquired as a basis for creating a more desirable market position for the brand. "When you care enough to send the very best"—the *Hallmark* greeting cards' positioning slogan—speaks directly about the "importance of the occasion" for which a particular branded greeting card is being purchased. The occasion-based phrase also speaks directly about the "importance of the person" for whom the gift card is being purchased. Finally, the occasion-based advertising slogan speaks directly about the quality and suitability of the gift—here, a greeting card—that has been purchased.

Using the Primary Benefit Sought by Consumers (to Segment)

Benefit-based segmentation is based on differences in the specific benefits that various consumer segments are seeking from a product when contemplating whether to purchase a brand from a known product category. Consumers, for example, might purchase a watch so they can know the time; so they could know the time, while scuba diving underwater; so they can metaphorically shout out to the world, "Hey, look at me and how much I have and social status I enjoy"; or to honor/acknowledge a child or grandchild's graduation.

Is there reason to suspect the differing consumer types that flesh out these four segments will purchase the same watch? No, there is not. That's because four discrete sets of benefits, values, and solutions-sought are embedded inside each purchasing context. The four distinct types of customer solution-sought naturally would be delivered through four discrete and targeted marketing mixes. Each marketing mix should be uniquely designed to deliver and promote one and only one of the aforementioned benefits to each targeted segment.

Another interesting insight is coming to light about watches as timepieces during an era when nearly everyone checks the time on their phone. According to *Applenews* and *The Wall Street Journal*, men around the world continue to wear broken watches. But they only wear watches that boast luxury branding status. While aesthetics materially influence these decisions (i.e., continuing to wear watches as jewelry rather than timepieces), classically-branded watches also embody one of the few simple luxuries left in the world. Classic watch brands also offer males an opportunity to subtly distinguish themselves as more powerful and/or successful inside modern workplaces.

Using "User Status" (to Segment)

When employed as a segmentation criteria, user status requires that marketers classify customers into unique segments based on their usage behaviors. Consumers, for example, might be classified as heavy users, medium users, light users, first-time users, or "never used the product before" segments.

Marketers are much more likely to target heavier users or first-time users with uniquely designed marketing mixes.

Of course, marketers would often like to convert many of their customers into heavier-user-status categories. A classic strategy for getting customers to consume more of a specific brand within a popular product category was first used during the 1920s and for decades after by *Dr. Pepper*. The slogan, positioning statement, and encouragement for drinking greater quantities of *Dr. Pepper* was: "*Dr. Pepper* at 10, 2, and 4 o'clock."

This brand of *Dr. Pepper* would be the real full-bodied version, featuring all the caffeine, all the sugar, all the taste; a product that guaranteed to either get or keep you going. Believe it or not, the positioning plea was research-based. During the 1920s scientists had recently confirmed that drinking more caffeine and sugar actually gave people more energy. Go figure, who knew? This little historical insight speaks directly to why 10, 2, and 4 were the times and numbers used (i.e., 10:00 a.m., high noon, and two in the afternoon) are just when lots of people doing either physically- or intellectually-challenging work could use that pick-me-up.

A well-known managerial/marketing principle often enters the picture when marketers segment based on user status. The rule of thumb is called the 80-20 Rule. The 80-20 Rule is also known as the Pareto Principle. The Pareto Principle is named after Italian economist *Vilfredo Pareto*. He noted, in 1906, that 80 percent of the land in Italy was owned by about 20 percent of the population. Pareto further developed what would later be branded as his principle by observing that 20 percent of the pea pods in his garden contained 80 percent of the peas!

When applied inside marketing settings, the 80-20 Rule suggests approximately 80 percent of profits emanate from 20 percent of customers; 80 percent of product sales from 20 percent of products present in a product line (marketing organizations generally sell multiple products); 80 percent of sales are generated by 20 percent of advertising (a larger question that often arises about advertising and its effectiveness is, which 20 percent?); 80 percent of complaints emanate from 20 percent of customers; or that 80 percent of sales from 20 percent of the sales team.

These percentages represent approximate rather than exact numbers. The Pareto Principle plays out across various internet settings. Inside the *Twitter* world, for example, about 10 percent of users generate more than 80 percent of the tweets. This 10 percent sends-out an average about 750 tweets a month. Most users don't send any tweets ever. Comparatively high percentages of these tweets are anything but pleasant in nature. As noted above, it seems as if *Twitter* is a communication tool that is somehow able to magically concentrate human anger. Who knows, founder Jack Dorsey might win a future *Nobel Peace Prize* were he to voluntarily eliminate *Twitter* today.

The Pareto Principle itself suggests that marketers should segment markets into five roughly 20 percent increments, based primarily on customers' usage rate, and then concentrate much of their marketing mix emphasis on the top 20 percent heaviest users. This exact segmentation, targeting, and positioning strategy is employed by most of the fast-food industry. The Pareto Principle likewise informs marketers as they strategize about where to allocate the lion's share of their marketing efforts and resources. For example, the Pareto Principle also suggests 20 percent of inputs usually create about 80 percent of outputs; 20 percent of efforts typically create about 80 percent of results; and 20 percent of causes typically generate about 80 percent of consequences.

Even pre-COVID-19, only 12 percent of American consumers were visiting the cinema to see movies on a frequent basis. Frequent was defined as once or more a month. These loyal customers account for more than 50 percent of annual ticket sales, however. While not precisely illustrating the 80-20 Rule, the trend underscores the premise. Marketers should allocate more efforts toward getting a bigger chunk of this 12 percent to attend much more than once a month. This group, which is already more inclined to visit, then should prove more receptive to these movie marketer's messages.

Larger, more heterogeneous markets can logically be classified into smaller, more homogeneous segments based on customers' loyalty status. This segmentation approach is based on customers' loyalty or the absence of customers' loyalty to branded stores, to airlines, hotel, and/or rental car service providers, or to well-branded products themselves. Loyalty-based segmentation generally focuses the most attention on customers who demonstrate the most loyalty to and/or are most frequent purchasers/users of a brand. This focus of more attention would generally assume the form of dispensing additional incentives to customers who display greater loyalty. Firms often reward customers for their loyalty by creating marketing mix values designed to deliver unique values that keep these customers happy. Happy, as in delighted. Happy, as in not only having their value expectations met, but in also having those expectations greatly exceeded.

Segmentation Bases Are a Buffett; Marketer, Take Your Pick

Effective marketers rarely limit their segmentation methods to only one or two options. But if marketers only had two bases or criteria on which to segment, their best choices would usually entail using two or three demographic variables in combination with one or two key psychographic measures.

Creating Attractive Segments

Effective, viable, and consequently potentially attractive market segments should be:

- Measurable—The size, purchasing power, and customer profiles associated with attractive market segments are usually measurable. These measurements are typically executed through marketing research. Key questions that would need to be asked and answered when firms are assessing the measurability criterion are:
    - How large is the segment, now?
    - How likely is the segment to grow larger in the future? Future growth prospects are critical to segment attractiveness.
- Accessible—Attractive segments should exist within the effective and efficient reach of the marketing organization and its marketing mix efforts. The "accessibility" issues and questions that typically would come into play here are:
    - First, can our organization reasonably reach the market with its current distribution and promotional efforts, or with distribution and promotional efforts we could develop?

- Second, would any decision we made to execute either of these two marketing mix elements (i.e., either the distribution or promotion functions) cost too much for our firm to execute?

▶ Substantial—The question to be asked as substantially is evaluated entails whether the segments are large or substantial enough to be profitable now or eventually would be large enough at some future point to make our targeting efforts worthwhile?

▶ Differentiable—Attractive market segment should respond in identifiably different ways than other market segments to the marketing organization's marketing mix efforts. Otherwise the segment is not attractive.

▶ Actionable—The organization should be able to design marketing mix programs that will prove attractive to segment membership. Otherwise the segment is not attractive.

- When evaluating the action ability of segments, a concept called structural attractiveness often comes into play. Structural attractiveness relates to the presence or absence of powerful competitors and of potential/actual substitute products. Along each dimension, fewer is clearly better.

When marketers choose which segments to target, they also choose the firms against which they will complete. This is a notable statement, so please note it.

This fact creates scenarios in which the goal of earning and sustaining marketing success, or of actually thriving as marketer, sometimes may prove more about staying in your own lane than one might suspect. Part of the evaluation of action-ability process might entail strategically deciding to not swerve unnecessarily into someone else's lane—or segment. Presumably, other firms already possess the resource base and inclination to crush your foray into their segment. Or resource-rich firms who might retaliate by pursuing segments where your firm currently enjoys a powerful position and therefore force your organization to reallocate finite resources for defensive purposes.

The action-ability of a segment is also related to the degree to which it would prove necessary to engage contractually with powerful supply chain suppliers or vendors that may or may not be available in the market in order to reach the targeted audience. When suppliers or vendors are overly powerful, relative to your organizations' power, either might then seek to exercise excessive control over what your organizations does, strategy-wise.

The action-ability of any given market segment likewise can be assessed by evaluating how well does, or could, a firm's current or future mission, goals, objectives, and resource allocation decisions align with what would be required, value-proposition-wise, to pursue the segment effectively.

One two-part bottom-line question should always arise when firms are evaluating the attractiveness of a given segment. The question is:

▶ Does our marketing organization already possess the capabilities and/or resources to effectively satisfy and serve this segment?

▶ Or, could our organization efficiently acquire the capabilities and/or resources that would prove necessary to satisfy and serve this segment successfully?

MODULE 4.2

Market Segment Targeting

The age of shotgun marketing is dead. Not so long ago domestic marketers who had the resources could indiscriminately toss out their promotional messages into the broader marketplace without bothering much about targeting anyone, and sufficient numbers of consumers would catch or be hit by the messages. Basically, marketers could blast away with both barrels. Back in those days, marketers who had created new and useful products (i.e., innovations) and had just a decent message could succeed absent much segmentation and targeting.

Today, marketers generally must target consumers with laser-like, technology-enhanced precision and efficiency in order to succeed—and would also require a more than merely decent promotional messages. This laser-like targeting is necessary to succeed inside globalized markets that feature so many different high quality products from which consumers can choose, and inside technologically-enhanced markets where more consumers are better informed about these choices than at any point in history. More consumers are better informed because technology gives those who are willing to put in the effort the opportunity to learn more.

Data mining, as part of now-normal marketing research processes, has made this sort of more precisely refined targeting possible. Information captured by behemoths such as *Amazon, Google, Instagram,* and *Facebook,* usually with consumers' tacit permission, has facilitated myriad data-mining opportunities.

Targeted sets of consumer profiles that are based on the Big Five personality traits (as discussed below) now can be easily built out by analyzing consumers' Likes and Dislikes on *Facebook* posts, and by machine-coding of what consumers have written or read on Twitter. The Big Five consumer personality traits that marketers usually covet, because they can easily exploit them are the openness, conscientiousness, agreeableness, extroversion, and narcissism of consumers.

User Tweets can be mapped to determine how often and when consumers are serene, alert, depressed, tense, or elated. Okay, that's nice—or scary—but so what? The answer to the always relevant "so what?" question is that possessing these and other sorts of insights about individual consumers makes it easier for marketers to target individual consumers and ensure that they receive the right message at the right time. "Right," that is, from the perspective of marketers. Then, for example, marketers can deliver the "right product-story" at "the right time" to lift up consumers' spirits or emotions if they are depressed. Alternatively, marketers' strategic delivery of "the right product-story" at "the right time" might permit consumers to go full-narcissist if they're feeling less adulation than they believe, in their own minds, that they so clearly deserve. Joke, or not joke? Answer, definitely not a joke. The new targeting scheme is impressive, terrifying, and true.[8]

The *Linked-In* profiles of professionals can be data mined to capture the number, executive level, and geographic concentration of their connections. Until recently, such rigorous analysis was reserved exclusively for the most valuable consumers or the most dangerous citizens—individuals about whom knowing the absolute right information or making the absolutely right targeting decision was worth the high cost. No longer.

What's happening is that *Google, Facebook,* and other *Big Tech* firms are continuously creating binary breadcrumbs to keep track of consumers and their shopping desires and their shopping behaviors as well as other wants as they track consumers to and from their homes. *Hansel & Gretel* fairy-tale breadcrumb-like effects writ real inside an Internet Age? Actually, yes, or something close to it. And yes, the learning and societal consequences are often truly pernicious. Many consumers who already know what is actually happening, how they are being tracked like prey, hate the process. Some of these consumers knowingly embrace the exploitative process. The majority of those in the know meekly shrug their shoulders. For them, that's "new" life in the big city—and they're right!

Among many perceptive social networking technology critics, *Big Tech* is becoming the new *Wall Street*. These critics are also aware that the children of *Silicon Valley* execs are often prevented, by their own parents, from using the same technological "solutions" that their own marketing organizations have created. Now you are aware too.

TARGET MARKETING

Assume that a large number of attractive market segments has been identified. In fact, so many segments have been tagged that it's irrational to assume that any given marketer could successfully pursue and service each of them. Few to no firms have enough resources, including time, talent, treasure, available to pull off this marketing play.

The following story is true. Once upon a time, after devices today's young people finding himself in a casino, one author overheard a self-described dieting woman who was lingering lustfully over a dessert bar say . . . "So many calories, so little time." Presumably, this woman recognized that she could not/should not possibly eat everything on the buffet that she wanted to consume. Nor, for that matter, can any marketing organization successfully pursue every fish that it would like to eat, oops, target. In fact, marketers should not even try.

---

8. *Facebook, Instagram,* and *Twitter* are conducting living social experiments on a global stage. Those experiments, in turn, are generating goodness-only-knows what sorts of consequences among the users of these brands. These consequences are primarily playing out and wreaking havoc among younger users. That's because at this stage in the evolution of the internet younger consumers have never encountered natural human—primarily face-to-face—relationships inside a non-socially connected world. *Facebook, Instagram,* and *Twitter* are executing sociological and anthropological experiments of a sort that no University Research Review Board would approve, because these experiments are clearly hurting many of the test subjects—something that review boards would not permit to happen.

No one can eat, or should try to eat, everything they want. Not enough time, money, or discretionary pounds exist to support such decisions. Nor should marketers . . . in a metaphorical sense . . . try to pursue (eat) every opportunity they detect. Marketers can neither efficiently nor successfully pursue and satisfy every possible customer.

Dearborn, Michigan, is located directly south of the contiguous city of *Detroit*. *Ford Motor Co.* is headquartered in *Dearborn*. Founder *Henry Ford's* old family farm was located right outside *Dearborn*—and not wanting to run the farm for the rest of his life he decided to build engines for this still-new innovation called the automobile in 1903. The rest is automotive, and marketing, history.

Today, *Dearborn's* population features the highest percentage of *Muslims* of any *American* city. This happened because Mr. Ford, a known racist, did not want to hire *African Americans* to work in his factories. So instead, he began importing *Middle Eastern* workers (primarily *Syrians, Jordanians,* and *Palestinians*) by the thousands during the late 1940s. To increase the marketing value proposition associated with moving from warm *Middle Eastern* to freezing *Michigan* climates, Henry Ford even built a huge mosque for *Dearborn's* new residents before any of them arrived.

Contemporary *Dearborn* features two *Walmart* superstores. As consumers enter the front doors on the grocery sides of either store and turn right, the first thing they encounter are two fifty-five-gallon-sized barrels of fresh dates. The strategic merchandising choices that *Walmart* management has made in their *Dearborn* store locations exemplify the logic of target marketing and marketing mix management.

Target marketing entails first identifying and thereafter attempting to satisfy the needs (solve the problems) of a targeted segment of prospective or actual customers. Consumers from the *Middle East* (a geographic segmentation base) or who grew up in *Middle Eastern*-dominated cultures (a cultural segmentation base) are culturally-inured to love eating dates. So would most other readers if they ever enjoyed fresh dates.

Marketing mix management entails strategically changing—literally mixing and matching the four or seven in order to create new and more appealing values—the product mix, or pricing, promotional or distribution elements inside any organization's marketing mix. Walmart offers this specific product mix on a strictly localized basis. Consumers won't find date-based marketing mixes on *Mackinaw Island* or on *Nine Mile Road* (yes, *Marshall Mathers III* reference here). Few to no other *Walmart* stores located anywhere inside America, but outside the greater *Detroit* region, feature barrels of fresh dates arrayed as the first marketing mix impression that customers encounter as they enter stores.

Marketing mix management entails strategically mixing and matching the four elements (when marketing products) or seven elements (when marketing services) associated with the marketing mix in order to create new and more appealing values. Each new and presumably more appealing set of values, in turn, is then targeted at a specifically identified and hopefully well-defined target segment.

Target marketing entails evaluating the various segments that have been identified in order to determine which ones are more or less attractive and then deciding which segments to pursue. Target marketing is where many marketers end up making or losing profits. Marketers should target the market segments that are most likely to respond favorably to the values offered by the existing marketing mix. Or, marketers should target market segments that are most likely to respond favorably to the new values that revised marketing mixes that marketers could create would deliver.

Since World War I (1914–18) combatants' survivability and their prospects for success have largely depended on their ability to deliver more targeted killing power at longer ranges and with greater precision than their enemy. Marketing competitions unfold as milder forms of war, but war nonetheless.

In marketing, battles are waged and won or lost primarily based on which brands secure more favorable perceptual spaces inside the collective mind of targeted market segments. (More favorable perceptual spaces could also be described as uniquely desirable market positions.) Survival as well as success in these marketing competitions depends on firms' ability to achieve similar outcomes. That is, those firms' ability to deliver more precisely targeted and concentrated value propositions to the segments they target than their competitors can deliver to the same target segments.

TARGET MARKETING—FOUR LEVELS EXIST

Level 1: Target-Broadly

Here, marketers market as if no segments exist. This targeting tactic is called undifferentiated or mass marketing.

When marketers target-broadly their organizations view the world as if only one market segment, which obviously would encompass the entire market, existed in the world. The same marketer then would deliver one marketing mix to this world. Undifferentiated target marketing treats all potential buyers as one homogeneous group. The overarching theme that is in play here is to focus on what is common or similar across customers (i.e., concentrate on delivering values that all customers presumably need . . . specific values, benefits, and solutions).

Rather than producing different marketing mixes aimed at different segments, undifferentiated target marketing attempts to reach all potential buyers using one targeting strategy. Undifferentiated marketing treats all segments and members of a B2C or B2B population the same. The targeting strategy used here is to use one approach that aims to appeal to as many B2C or B2B customers as possible. Undifferentiated targeting approaches are more appropriate when little real differentiation exists across competitor products.

Where little real differentiation exists and no perceptual differences can be created and there are no alternative products (brands), firms end up marketing commodities. When commodity-like markets exist, competing successfully on the basis of values other than lower price or extremely reliable availability and service becomes difficult. Steel, petroleum, cotton, wheat, and pork bellies are generally viewed as commodity products. Their markets, not surprisingly, are viewed as commodity markets. But not always. Pork bellies exist as the originating source for bacon or sausage or ham, and here one might note how various well-positioned brands of bacon or sausage definitely do not exist as commodities but as well-positioned brands that command greater higher or lower prices and market shares. *Jimmy Dean Sausage*, anyone?

When possible, marketers should not allow branded products to be transformed into commodities[9] inside customer minds. Sometimes, however, such outcomes are impossible to prevent.

Level 2: Target-Narrowly

This tactic is better known as concentrated or niche market targeting. When concentrated or niched targeting is used marketing organizations target large shares of narrowly defined segments. Success requires fine-tuning of the marketing mix. Product, price, promotional, or distribution value offerings are carefully managed, mixed, and massaged in order to satisfy the special needs and solve unique problems that predominate within precisely defined segments.

Firms that market smoking cessation employ concentrated targeting. First, because these marketers target only smokers. But second, because these marketers actually are only targeting those smokers seeking to quit. Brands such as *Chantix, Zyban,* or *Nicoderm* are each targeted toward a minority of a minority segment, if you will, since only slightly less than 20 percent of American consumers actually smoke.[10] When targeting consumers as part of niched segments, marketers pursue tightly defined groups who might accurately be described as the fervent few.

Panera Bread has carved out a cozy and lucrative niche market segment for its brand through narrow targeting. A *Panera* niche that effectively bypassed fast-food brands such as *Burger King* or *KFC*,[11] along with fast-casual food brand chains such as *Applebee's* or *Olive Garden*. *Panera* blended the pace of the fast-food giants with the more sophisticated menus of the later sit-down restaurants and tossed in a dash of aspiration.

Rather than marketing burgers and fries, *Panera* originally achieved success and kept its fans happy and loyal by offering slightly upscale but highly-distinctive lunch options such as roast turkey and caramelized kale paninis, vegetarian summer corn chowder, and agave lemonade. *Panera* currently owns a substantial portion of a niched consumer segment who, in that moment, "desires sophisticated food fast." *Panera* will undoubtedly continue to innovate in a strategic attempt to sustain this appealing competitive advantage.

Sirius radio executes its business model as a niched radio station. The once-innovative marketer targets consumers who are willing to pay to not have to listen to advertising as they listen to music or talking heads opine on various topics. Additional discussion about the more narrowly-focused *Sirius* options inside the niched *Sirius* product portfolio platform follows when the micro-targeting topic is introduced.

---

9. Commodities are competing products from the same broad product category that essentially are interchangeable with and indistinguishable from each other. The bottom line about commodities is that in most people's perceptions one belly of hog; one bale of hay or of cotton; or one barrel of oil is pretty much like any other belly, bale, or barrel.

10. As more fully discussed during Module 6, many actual smokers are probably lying about their habit. Why? Because smokers are often treated or feel like social pariahs. Smokers are thus often unwilling to admit publicly that they smoke.

11. *KFC*, the brand name, features more than a little history. *KFC* was once called *Kentucky Fried Chicken*. But shortly after the word "fried" no longer resonated favorably inside many domestic subcultural quarters, "Kentucky," "Fried" and, most surprisingly, "Chicken" went away as brand-identifiers.

Level 3: Target-Extremely-Narrowly

This targeting approach is better known as micro-targeting. Again, only one segment is targeted. But this once merely niched segment is now extremely narrowly defined and targeted. The difference between niche-targeting and micro-targeting is a matter of degree. Each targeting approach requires marketers to specifically tailor products and marketing mix programs to suit the tastes, meet the needs, and solve the problems of highly specialized B2B or B2C customers. Marketers who micro-target, however, pursue even more refined customer targets by developed extremely refined marketing mixes.

Lockheed Martin makes and markets military planes, and the various accouterments necessary to keep military airpower ready to fly—and fight or protect. *Lockheed Martin's* marketing plans are grounded in an extremely focused targeting strategy. The firm sells products to one major customer, the four *United States* Military Service Branches. Of course, as noted, the domestic military services include four separate branches: the *Air Force, Army, Marine Corps*, and *Navy*. Billions of resources are invested in identifying and then satisfying the air power-related needs of the *Air Force, Army, Marine Corps,* and *Navy*.

As you might image, the air-related needs of these four brands differ materially. That these differences exist and pronounced is logical, natural, and to be expected. After all, the warfare-waging problems that the four armed services branches routinely confront also radically differ.

Because it operates in a radically different domain from most competitors, *Outlaw Country* uses an extremely narrow targeting approach. *Outlaw Country* is a radio station featured on the product portfolio of stations offered by *Sirius Radio*. *Sirius Radio's* product portfolio entails the entire list of musical genres [products] offered under the *Sirius* branding label. *Outlaw Country,* for example, positions its brand and musical portfolio as a place designed for consumers willing to pay to listen to great old country artists like *Country & Western* music branding legends such as *Buck Owens* or *Carl Perkins* who no longer scored much airplay on country radio stations, who are also willing to pay to not listen to commercials. The branding tagline and positioning statement for *Outlaw Country* is "No Fences, No Badges, No Commercials." These six words comprise the entire promotional message that *Outlaw Country* marketing managers use as the *Sirius* corporation seeks to differentiate this specific brand.

Queer Gym, a small workout facility located just outside *Boston*, exclusively targets the LGBTQ, but most specifically, the Trans community, as members. Quoting from the marketing organization's website: "At the Queer Gym, there are no mirrors, no creepers, no mansplaining, no body shaming. Just a supportive community of folXs with diverse backgrounds and goals werking out and having fun together." The spellings are correct; they are also intentional. *Queer Gym's* positioning approach and value proposition epitomizes micro-targeting.

The present and the future of marketing has shifted away from past broader targeting practices where larger quantities of fewer products were sold toward market scenarios in which smaller amounts of many different products are sold. Marketing practices in general have evolved toward targeting larger numbers of highly customized, or niche(d), market segment interests. These strategic changes have been facilitated by the laser-like electronic targeting abilities that internet-based and internet-enabled "consumer tracking" devices enable. You may recall the electronic breadcrumbs reference. Another factor driving this shift in marketing orientation derives from the fact that so many different product and brand options are now available on the internet from which customers can choose.

The net of these trends are that brands and marketers' promotional efforts are increasingly being targeted in more narrowly focused and more accurate ways. *Amazon, Facebook,* and *Google* allow marketers to track and target customers with the accuracy of *Star Wars*-like *Death Stars*. Think of essentially obscure bands from any musical genre who are still able to command just enough loyal customers to keep their sales going and their band brands alive. Entrepreneurially-minded marketers[12] clearly should contemplate playing small-ball as they execute targeting strategies—being satisfied with hitting singles or accepting walks rather than swinging from the heels trying for long balls, or home runs, all the time. Playing small ball, for now, as a means to sustain and eventually to grow the size of their customer base.

Targeting really can get micro—and precise. *Scott Walker*, a recent governor of *Wisconsin*, opposed a tax hike on gasoline. So, the governor, or more likely his marketing handlers, created advertisements that ran only on screens at gas pumps as citizens were filling up.

Thanks to audience fragmentation, a breaking-apart, inside the entertainment industry, oligopolistic[13] distribution methods no longer exist among television or movie distributors. Today it's far easier to cater to audiences of die-hards than to successfully broadcast or to engage in mass marketing. This exact tactical premise plays well on *Broadway*, where it's easier to service niche audiences for *Angels in America* than to produce new products (*Broadway* shows) that hold broad appeal throughout age, gender, and ethnic demographic categories. Occasionally *Broadway* benefits from breakout hits that began targeting a niche audience—the musical *Hamilton* fits this description. Such crossover hits are increasingly rare, however. More typically, *Broadway* producers focus either on attracting niche audiences or developing blockbuster children's shows such as *The Lion King* or *SpongeBob SquarePants*. Two great things about marketing Broadway shows targeted directly at kids: First, kids don't buy the tickets so they don't care about the premium prices that are charged. Second, kids rarely attend shows by themselves. Okay, actually this never happens. Implying that when *Broadway* sells one or two tickets to kids, producers are guaranteed to sell one or two more to grown-ups.

Level 4: Differentiated-Targeting

Differentiated targeting, as a marketing strategy, entails pursuing multiple segments at the same time. This is called differentiated or segmented target marketing. Uniquely designed and consequently differentiated market mixes are then targeted toward each segment the marketer elects to pursue. Each

---

12. Entrepreneurship entails the activity of establishing a business or businesses, taking on the associated financial risks, and doing these things with the hopes of earning market share and profits foremost in one's mind.

13. Oligopolistic markets and their natures are more fully discussed during Module 13. But for now suffice to say the term oligopoly describes market conditions in which a handful of large competitors dominate market shares inside the market's various product categories. Product categories such as smartphones, airliners, or social networking services are typically marketed by firms that are themselves competing inside oligopolistic markets.

set of 4Ps or 7Ps should be strategically mixed such that it delivers unique—and uniquely desirable—value to the consumer or organizational members of targeted segments.

The strategic decision to use this targeting approach greatly increases the costs of marketing. Of course, when the strategy succeeds, revenues tremendously increase. This makes sense. Absent the promise and prospect of earning higher profits, why engage in differentiated targeting?

Dallas-based *Brinker International*, a marketing conglomerate that introduced *Chili's*, *On the Border*, *Maggio's*, and *Macaroni Grill* branding alternatives to the restaurant marketplace, employs the differentiated targeting marketing approach. In turn, each restaurant brand offers various healthy, better-tasting-fattier, less-expensive, or more-expensive food choices to targeted market segments. The exact nature of the marketing mixes that this *Brinker International* family of restaurants uses to differentiate and position their value propositions as representing unique-and-uniquely-desirable value-laden choices depends upon the wants, needs, problems, and other characteristics associated with each segment that is targeted.

In their own ways *General Motors*, *Toyota*, and *Nissan*, automotive brands and marketers all, employ exactly the same strategy. This targeting strategy has been around a while. *General Motors*, for instance, launched a highly publicized way of segmenting the domestic consumer marketplace during the 1920s. *General Motors*, which typically now uses the abbreviated brand *GM*, also arrayed its various auto brands into precisely calibrated, from lower to higher, price hierarchies. *GM* boasted five branding slogans and positioning statements. Five discrete market segments resulted. The branding slogans/positioning statements were:

- "*Chevrolet* for the *hoi polloi* [literally, the general populace or masses].
- *Pontiac* for the poor but proud.
- *Oldsmobile* for the comfortable but discrete.
- *Buick* for the striving.
- *Cadillac* for the rich. A car for every purse and purpose."

Fortune Magazine wrote at the time . . . "This was a sort of price-sorting. But customers themselves did the sorting [segmentation and targeting] based on prices they were willing and able to pay."

We write now, holy cow. Can you imagine writing such blunt advertising copy to today's consumers? For "the masses"; for "the poor but striving"; or "for the rich." Cries of discrimination and elitism would surely ensue from various quarters. This communication approach likely would not work today, but it surely did back then.

However, this sort of message would attract a lot of attention. And sometimes the pursuit of customer attention in and of itself represents a worthy advertising, communication, and marketing goal.

Which Targeting Strategies Make the Most Sense When?

When marketing resources are limited the concentrated—or niche—targeting approach generally makes the most sense. Undifferentiated marketing—actually involving no targeting efforts—is more logical when variability among competitors' products is low. As noted, such conditions may arise when marketers are producing and marketing steel or wheat, commodities each.

A product's stage in its life cycle (the Product Life Cycle is discussed fully in Module 9) should also be considered as marketing managers are choosing their targeting strategy. If firms are marketing new-to-the-world products or so-called disruptive innovations (discussed fully in Module 10), pursuing an entire market through undifferentiated targeting strategies is logical. That's because in these situations marketers are creating entirely new markets as they introduce new products. That's because the new product is "it," as in the one and only alternative that exists and competes inside any marketplace at the exact point it is introduced.

These new markets consequently exist as entities over which those marketers can claim ownership.[14] Yet any marketers' actual ownership of markets always proves temporary in those situations where the new product introduction proves successful. Successful new products always attract new competitors. Those new market entrants seek to imitate and emulate the original marketer's success by introducing their own "new and improved" versions of the original new product.

For older or more-established products that have entered mature stages of their Product Life Cycles, differentiated targeted approaches, in which multiple target segments are pursued, generally make more sense. When sufficient resources exist, marketers should almost always engage in differentiated target marketing strategies.

---

14. To some degree, people always own what they create. Excepting, one supposes, children that they bear.

MODULE 4.3

Positioning

Any brand's positioning power is equivalent to that brand's value proposition. Value propositions capture and reflect the sum of potential and actual values that positioned products offer to prospects or customers. The total value proposition associated with wedding dresses, automobiles, homes, or vacation destinations, for example, are extremely complex in nature. Complex because wedding dresses, automobile, homes, or vacation destinations each can deliver numerous different types of values, benefits, and solutions to the individuals or families who own and use them. Yes, one can own a vacation destination, albeit temporarily, and we're not even referencing time-shares.

When marketers deem one, two, three, or more segments as target-worthy, their next goal should entail the creation of a unique,[15] and uniquely desirable, position in the minds of the customers/prospects that comprise each of the respective targeted segments. Say, a restaurant might target three different segments. Those three segments, by turn, primarily seek healthier food choices, lower-priced options, or the opportunity to enjoy a really good time along with their food as their determinant value. Determinant as in "decisive" or difference-making.

How do marketers achieve such positioning? Yes, by managing their marketing mixes. Specifically, by choosing:

- ▶ The values—the benefits and the solutions—that these marketers strategically build into their products.
- ▶ The stories that these marketers communicate and emphasize about their products in their promotional efforts.

---

15. Unique means "(the) one and only," or "nothing else like it exists." Unfortunately, *English* speakers or writers routinely misuse the word. Unique cannot be qualified. An idea, product, or message is either unique or not unique. An item or idea cannot be somewhat, extremely, or a little unique—there's no middle ground. In this regard the meaning of the word "unique" can be conflated with the meaning of the word "pregnant." A woman either is or is not pregnant. No in-betweens, no modifiers need be applied to the words unique or pregnant. The legitimate ability to claim that a new product or a new product idea is unique is highly desirable inside marketing contexts. That is, unless the new idea or product is uniquely bad or evil.

- To the extent possible, marketers should manage what others (primarily, current customers) say about their products as those independent messengers engage in word of mouth (WOM) or electronic-word of mouth (e-WOM).
  - The best way for any marketer or marketing organization to manage what others say about their products is to create solutions that don't just meet and satisfy but hopefully greatly exceed the expectations of their customers.
    - At that point, while nothing is assured, the likelihood that only positive WOM or e-WOM will originate from customers is greatly enhanced.
- How to strategically price their products in ways that simultaneously create and capture value.
  - The various means by which marketers can price products in ways that concurrently create and capture value is explained in the Pricing Module.
- Where and how to market at traditional retail or technology-age e-tailing levels as well as how to move products forward toward customers from whatever points inside their supply chains products were sourced, assembled, and/or produced to the points inside their supply chains where final customers exist.

Each element inside the traditional marketing mix was just referenced. This is not coincidence.

There are two reasons why marketers should always position based on the benefits, values, and solutions that their brands actually or purportedly deliver.

The first reason is that marketing organizations should engage in positioning in order to achieve or sustain differentiation.

The second reason why marketers should position is to earn or maintain sustainable competitive advantages (SCAs). SCAs exist as assets that marketers should strategically pursue. SCAs also exist as assets that marketers should seek to strategically exploit, once they have been developed.

Specifically, SCAs should be exploited by marketers who seek to offer and sustain higher prices. SCAs likewise should be exploited by marketers who seek to profitably offer lower prices. Finally, SCAs should be exploited by marketers who seek to avoid or blunt erosions in profitability or market share that result from new competitive pressures that ramp up across time whenever marketers strategically elect to price at either premium or discounted levels. However, these new competitive pressures are much more likely to arise when marketers elect to price at premium levels.

The ability of marketing organizations to develop an SCA or SCAs is generally based on marketers' branding advantages, their resource advantages, or on their possession of and ability and willingness to exploit a core competency.

Core competencies, in turn, are based on marketing organizations' possession of technological leadership, customer intimacy or cost leadership advantages, or on marketing organizations' possession of some combination of two or three of these differentiating values. Core competencies represent any activity—something that generates value—that marketers do different and better than their competitors. Meanwhile, that "something"—which also functions as an asset—that marketers possess also "gifts" them with the ability to deliver more appealing values (or solutions) to targeted segments. Marketers who own core competencies should leverage them, taking advantage of the core competency, to earn sustainable competitive advantages. Marketers absolutely should leverage core competencies when their competitors don't possess the same capability (say, a branding- or resource- or technology-based advantage) themselves or don't execute the particular capability effectively.

Two Positions on Positioning

From customers' perspectives, positioning entails the way a branded product is defined by consumers on important attributes. Yet a market position might also be viewed as the place a brand occupies inside consumers' minds; especially relative to the places occupied by other competing brands.

Marketers logically should seek to create and manage appealing and differentiating value propositions[16] that ultimately permit their brands to occupy more desirable mind-places or positions than the mind-places or positions occupied by competing brands. Marketers should strategize accordingly. These more desirable mind-places would typically reside higher up inside consumers' evoked sets; sitting on the top-of-the-mind rungs of those metaphorical ladders inside B2C consumers or B2B customers minds that were discussed earlier. Those metaphorical ladders, as you may recall, were emblematic of consumers' "evoked sets." The competitions being waged and won or lost by marketers at this point pivots on whether the values that targeted customers perceive are associated with the *Cadillac* versus *Mercedes* versus *Lexus* brands—or for that matter, between the *Lincoln*, *Infinity*, or *Hyundai* brands—that pop-up-first inside their minds whenever consumers recognize that problems have emerged in their personal or professional lives that potentially could be solved by choosing and purchasing an automobile from any of these brand families.

Marketing competitions are not battles between products or brands. Marketing competitions instead are battles between customer perceptions about those products or brands that are waged inside B2C consumers' or B2B customers' minds. Marketing competitions also entail battles for "preferred space" inside customers' minds. That preferred space is generally higher up inside customers' evoked sets. Again, we are referencing the concepts known as "top-of-the-mind" or "top-of-the-mind-awareness."

From a marketer's perspective, positioning is an activity that entails implanting brands' unique benefits and their differentiating value inside the minds of customers. All marketing efforts, all the ways in which marketers strategically manage and maneuver their marketing mixes, should be executed with the goal of developing unique-and-uniquely-desirable positions for their brands in mind. Going forward, marketers first should strategize and eventually execute in ways intended to lock down these positions inside the collective mind of targeted market segments.

Customers will position brands inside their own minds regardless of whether marketers attempt to create mindful positions for customers. Customers will position brands rightly or wrong, or for better or for worse from marketers' points of view. Marketers, however, should control this process. In brief, marketers should "do positioning" to customers before customers "do positioning" to them.

---

16. Yes, value propositions are established through efficient and effective management of the marketing mix.

When positioning, marketers seek to differentiate their brands by building perceptions inside targeted market segments' collective minds that valued sets of desirable benefits, values, and ultimately solutions will be delivered by the brand being positioned. These uniquely desirable sets or collections of bundled benefits should be developed and delivered through firms' marketing mixes. This is, by now, a familiar theme. These sets or collections of bundled benefits should be designed to appeal directly to the wants, needs, and/or problems that dominate, or are perceived as most important, inside specifically targeted market segments. These sets or collections of bundled benefits should coalesce in ways that make the brand appear cooler, more desirable, not just different but also better and perhaps, in the end, worth acquiring even at often higher prices.

First, think *Apple, Prada,* or *Gillette.* Now, congratulate each brand. Because each has achieved the exact sort of desirable positioning outcomes described above inside its consumer technology, fashion, or shaving product categories and markets.

Executing Positioning Strategies

When positioning, the basic communication goal is to differentiate brands by associating unique bundles of benefits with each brand. The emphasis here is again on the word "unique." These unique bundles of benefits should be structured (designed), promoted (communicated), and priced inside value propositions that are strategically designed and mixed to appeal to substantial portions of customers within a targeted segment.

These bundles of benefits, values, and solutions can be merely perceptual in nature. For example, drinking *Red Bull* has never actually given wings to anyone. A perceptual bundle of benefits might stimulate a felt sensation among individual members of targeted market segments that "wearing this brand will make me more popular" in situations where that perceived reality never materializes as fact.

These bundles of benefits might also be absolutely genuine and authentic in nature. For example, *Tylenol* actually does relieve pain. *Turbo Tax* actually does make income tax preparation easier and/or saves money in those situations where individual consumers' tax preparations would require the professional services of a certified public accountant. In each case the perceived as well as promised bundles of benefits are real.

To develop successful positions, strategic marketers should execute three steps. First, marketers must identify and should actually be capable of delivering a set of possibly sustainable competitive advantages. These SCAs will deliver greater value—superior benefits and solutions—to targeted customer segments than competitors can deliver to the same segments. Makes sense. Marketers that deliver greater value (i.e., either perceived or genuine) will win.

Second, marketers should choose the right competitive advantages to promote and position or deliver to targeted customers. The B2C or B2B decision-makers who constitute differing target segments should be attracted to the brand and actually influenced to purchase it by different value propositions. Each of these different value propositions represents a different solution to customers.

Third, marketers should select specific positioning strategies for each of their brands and then allocate the resources necessary to create and maintain each position.

Whenever possible, the positions that marketers pursue for their branded products be based on determinant differences. Determinant differences are the Gold Standard, if you will. When used in a positioning context the word "determinant" means the branding difference is important to customers as they make their brand choices. However, for determinant differences to exist and be used as a basis for successful positioning, actual or perceptual differences must exist between brands. Again, the brand difference must be important to customers as they decide which brand to purchase. Otherwise the difference cannot be described as determinant.

Southwest Airlines has successfully hung its determinant brand positioning advantage on the idea and promise that passenger Bags Fly Free on its airplanes. The same positioning strategy has been used for around nineteen straight years—that's sustainable. The first reason that the branding tagline Bags Fly Free proved determinant as a positioning statement is that no other major airline can make this claim. So, the difference was real. The second reason is that having the opportunity to not pay for suitcases when they fly is important to most customers as they are deciding whether to fly on one versus another domestic airline brand because, thank goodness, there are still different branding alternatives available.

Differentiating and Positioning Brands

Brands can be positioned and differentiated based on special features, attributes, and ultimately solutions that marketers strategically associate with the branded product.

Many automobile brands are positioned in exactly this manner. For example, if you have kids, love them, and don't want to injure your kids in a car wreck, which brand is best-positioned to satisfy your particular needs? The answer is actually two brands: *Volvo* and *Subaru*. Each brand has successfully positioned itself as the safest auto choice for decades.

And indeed, each auto marketer has specifically designated its vehicles to be the safest. Neither *Volvo* nor *Subaru* have issued empty or false promotional promises. Each marketer instead has hung its positioning reputation on an authentic safety hook. Safety, unsurprisingly, is a big deal to a large segment of consumers. As explained in greater detail during Module 7, safety is usually designated as the second most important basic human need.

In a full-on ironic twist, individual brands housed within the three separate cigarette, e-cigarette, and vaping product categories have each positioned themselves as safer alternatives in both the past and present. Traditional cigarettes brands (*Marlboro*) first began using this positioning strategy in the 1960s, by attaching filters and then promoting their filtered brands as light or ultra-lights. Light was code-speak for "you'll then inhale less tar or nicotine," which was recognized even back then as being bad for them. New ultra-light alternatives were then developed and positioned as being safer still.

Notice how the words safe or safer themselves were never used. Consumers rarely get turned on by or remain loyal to product categories in which one brand knowingly promotes itself as safer than other brands in the product category. During the last six or so years an e-cig brand called *Jewell* has strategically promoted its product as the "smoking alternative." The missing prefix to "smoking alternative," of course, was "safer." But safer—and safety—is surely implied.

All the while, for six or so decades cigarette and e-cigarette marketers have almost exclusively targeted younger people through overt and covert promotional methods and messages. Cigarette and e-cigarette marketers targeted younger people, generally those aged between twelve-to-eighteen-year-olds, largely because forty-something adults are rarely stupid, naïve, or rebellious enough to wake up one morning and happily declare: "Yes, finally. The day has arrived when I can begin consuming an insidious, infantilizing (could the constant sucking be otherwise described?) and highly addictive product that if used as directed for a sufficient number of years could harm my health or outright kill me. Now, at last, the important people around me in my social circle will finally start seeing me as the superbad and cool guy or gal that I really am!"

Positioning Based on Services

Brands can be positioned based on services that marketers strategically associate with them.

Hyundai, the now hugely popular *South Korean* automobile marketer, first entered the American marketplace in 1986. *Hyundai* marketed one brand of car, the *Elantra*. And the market . . . did . . . not . . . care. Crickets . . . was the only response not heard. By 1986 American consumers had long since grown way-cool with the ideas of buying car brands made by *German* or *Japanese* marketers, or with purchasing refrigerators or electronics from other *South Korean* firms. But automobiles made there? No thanks.

Then, in 1996, *Hyundai* become the first brand in the world to attach and promise a 100,000-mile, bumper-to-bumper warranty service to its automotive products. Every other brand that eventually made the same or a similar promise was a second, third, or fourth, and so forth, market-follower. The *South Korean* firm secured, and has kept, the high marketing ground, by Being First to Market—honoring the first Marketing Law introduced during Module 1. *Hyundai* succeeded by standing out from rather than fitting in with the rest of the automobile marketing crowd.

Hyundai learned from its being-first success lesson, and quickly discovered another opportunity to exploit what it had learned. During 2007/8, at the bottom of America's *Great Recession*, the creative marketer made and kept a startling promise to American consumers. The positioning promise was that if you bought a *Hyundai*, and lost your job, you could bring the car back, your loan would be forgiven, and your full measure of money returned. No questions asked, only unearned grace provided. Yes, Hyundai was first-to-market, again, with a value/solution that really meant something to nervous or outright fearful consumers.

General Motors and other domestic and international automotive marketers made the same promise to American consumers a couple of weeks later. These belatedly-issued promises left American critics logically questioning whether these other auto marketers actually cared about the American car-buying public. Or were they just belatedly offering this solution because *Hyundai's* first-to-market strategic action forced them to? The non-responses made by American consumers at the time toward automotive brands not named *Hyundai* provided all the insights needed to answer the question. *GM* was actually targeted for ridicule by some late-night TV jokesters. That's not the type of standing-out rather than fitting-in success criterion that we introduced earlier.

Meanwhile, *Hyundai's* happy result was that the *South Korean* marketer has finished top-four or higher out of all global automotive brands in the US automotive market share during each ensuing year between then and now, and has occasionally earned the highest market share.

Positioning Based on Channels

Brands can be positioned based on the distribution channels (and in this case, the retailing brands) that marketers use to distribute and promote them.

Imagine your marketing organization designs women's apparel. Visualize further that your marketing organization recently inked an exclusive contract wherein *Walmart* will sell its new blouse in all its stores. Congratulations. This is a huge deal. *Walmart* confers access to 160,000,000+ potential customers inside America alone. But what does the retailer say about the brands that it merchandises and retails? Maybe the retailer's brand lowers perceptions about the quality or cache your blouse's brand? Does *Walmart* affect your brand's position? You know the answer.

Visualize the same situation. Except now the blouse brand that your organization has designed will be exclusively promoted and sold by *Nordstrom's*. Again, congratulations. This is also a wonderful accomplishment. Now what does the retailer's brand say about your product? Something different, right? Do you see the point about how its distribution can affect a brand's position?

Positioning Based on People

Brands can be positioned based on people, including celebrities, who are associated in various ways, shapes, or forms with them.

The type of people who use the product, are seen with the product, or endorse the product speak volumes about whether the product is hot, as in cool, in this moment or so-last-week. As you will learn during ensuing Module discussions, social groups, reference groups, and opinion-leaders can all play material roles in influencing the brand and product choices that consumers make. Do you think, for example, that the female stars who show up at the *Oscars* or the *Grammies* each year decked-out-to-the-nines in the finest dress, shoe, haircare, and bling brands paid for any of these items themselves? No, hardly. Indeed, marketers behind the various brands may actually pay the celebrities to wear their gear or use their services. Because certain high-fashion, luxury brands often strategically seek to secure affiliation and association with the hottest human fashion brands of the moment.

Meanwhile, contemporary marketers realize they must tread carefully when dancing-with-the-[using]-stars as direct or indirect brand endorsers. Basically, because celebrities have ways of messing up or otherwise going-off-the-boil. During the 1980s and 90s the first names of the four most prominent celebrity brand-endorsers were Bill, Mike, Michael, and Michael, again. *Bill Cosby's* long run as a leading celebrity endorser actually extended into the 2010s; functioning as spokesperson for brands as disparate as *Jello, Coke, Texas Instruments,* and the *US Census* and he lifted the image and power of each brand. But allegations that he had serially raped women after roofing them surfaced and Mr. Cosby's endorser career brusquely ended. Former *World Heavyweight Boxing Champion Mike*

Tyson's high-end endorsement career[17] came and went quickly. But Tyson and his endorser allure burned fiercely for a few years before *Diet Coke, BMW, and Kodak*, again, realized that having their brand affiliated with a spousal abuser and a convicted rapist was a non-starter. Renowned singer/dancer/performer *Michael Jackson's* endorsement career actually did catch fire; his hair, during a video shot for an infamous *Pepsi* commercial. But not surprisingly, unsuccessfully prosecuted allegations of pedophilia ultimately proved a bad look for the high dozen mega-consumer brands he once endorsed. *Michael Jordan's Nike, Hanes,* and *Oscar Mayer* brand associations continue to soar high—particularly for a fifty-something man. But then again, he's *Air Jordan*.

There you have it. A representative sampling of formerly golden celebrities gone-bad as endorsers. Marketers slowly and then more quickly realized that using celebrities as positioning spokespersons is riskier and more expensive than using manufactured celebrities. Success story one might include *Subway's* use of Jared as manufactured celebrity spokesperson. After all, nothing could go wrong with pulling an ordinary Joe from the crowd to rep . . . oh, wait a minute. But manufactured celebrities such as the *Can-You-Hear-Me-Now* man, for *Verizon;* the cool *Apple Dude* who continuously bested the *IBM* nerd; or *Flo,* with *Progressive Insurance* often do work out well. Even so, marketers are increasingly using cartoon characters or animals as positioning devices because they rarely get arrested or accused of illicit or immoral behaviors.

Positioning Based on Images

Brands can be positioned based on images that marketers strategically construct for them.

Marketing managers for the sports utility vehicle brands such as *Jeep, Land Rover,* or *Ram* have carefully cultivated branded images that have effectively served the physical products bearing their brands. Each brand features a personality that practically shouts rugged, outdoorsy, adventurous, and strength combined with attractiveness, and/or prestige—as well as, not coincidentally, "I can also afford to be seen driving and getting out of this ride!" These branding appeals and positioning values often prove highly appealing to consumers who perceive their actual or aspirational personalities, or their self-concepts, as rugged, outdoorsy, adventuresome, strong, and attractive, and/or a social status winner. Meaning, these positioning traits proved irresistible to certain well-defined lifestyle- and personality-based consumer segments.

But, of course, automobile brand personalities are hardly all-rugged-all-the-time. Essentially unchanged in its design and shape since 1948, *Volkswagen's* Beetle remains a brand about which people, including former owners, speak with heartfelt emotions, as if they were talking about old friends. The oversized BUG-eyes, as part of the brand design, helped. But the *VW* brand was never overly prideful; never exuded haughtiness; never issued irredeemable promises. As VW made promises the brand never forgot its genuinely humble origins (*Adolf Hitler*, yes, him, designated the vehicle as the

---

17. Former boxing champion *Mike Tyson* endorsed *Bitcoin* a few years back. Who knows, perhaps the endorser's reliability speaks volumes about the *Bitcoin* brand itself. Moreover, as Tyson once said: "Everyone has got a plan until you punch him in the mouth." *Tyson's* famous quote underscores the necessity to have contingency plans in place, because plans rarely work out as planned—as discussed during Module 3. *Tyson's* branding identity once was and still remains. *Iron Mike*.

"people's car" during the 1930s), and always remained easily serviceable, dependable, and ready to help. Sadly, the classic *VW* Beetle brand halted production during 2019.[18]

Positioning Based on Symbols

Brands can be positioned based on symbols that are strategically affiliated with or attached to them.

You got this. You know that five intersecting rings means, *Olympics!* You get that the *swoosh* symbol means, *Nike!* You understand that *Golden Arches,* means *McDonald's.* What readers undoubtedly also recall is a *Creepy King* meant to lure in kids. But what the marketer's use of the *Creepy King* really underscores is that *Burger King* made an incomprehensible positioning choice. Pedophile-like positioning spokespersons generally fail to attract the attention of kids or their parents in ways that any marketer would desire.

Hyundai's positioning symbol is, according to the South Korean automobile marketer, "More than a symbol. It's the way we do business." Take a moment to envision the rightward-tilting, interlocking H brand logo that's affixed on each Hyundai vehicle. Yet, that positioning vision is probably locked inside most readers' minds. *Hyundai* claims that the Hyundai brand logo may look like the first letter of the automaker's name, but that it also symbolizes two people—the company and customer—shaking hands. Nowadays, even with the value and social acceptability of handshakes declining, the brand's promise to customers remains intact, in the form of a 10-year/100,000-mile warranty on each and every *Hyundai* vehicle that is sold, as just mentioned.

Or, consider the *Christian* brand of religion, for example. Which, like all religious organizations routinely engaged in marketing to secure new customers; keep existing customers loyal; and secure the attention, beliefs, and yes, frankly, sources of funds from existing patrons. For *Christian* believers the cross and the empty tomb each function as symbols of hope because they each symbolize the promises of resurrection and salvation for those [customers] who believe in this focal *Christian* idea and the ideals associated with it.

There's something that actual or aspiring marketers should understand whenever they seek to use symbols as positioning/differentiating devices. The something is this: Few to no symbols could ever exist that would represent, attract, or satisfy everyone. The need to engage successfully in both segmentation and targeting activities as necessary precursors to successful positioning and sustainable marketing success is further underscored.

Positioning Based on Animals and Cartoons

Brands can be positioned based on animals and cartoon characters that are strategically affiliated with or attached to the brand.

Marketers use surprisingly high numbers of animals and cartoon characters to position their brands. Animals or characters that, by turns, might appear appealing, fearsome, lovable, cute, powerful, wise, trustworthy, and so forth. Each italicized word, in its own way, signifies a different

---

18. "Volks," in German, means people. "Wagen," in German, was a synonym for car.

type of position-able value. The list of examples is long: Clydesdales, for *Anheuser-Busch*; cats (along with *Sara McLachlan*; oh, those kitty eyes!) used to position the *Society for the Protection of Cruelty to Animals*; *Smokey the Bear*, to position forestry safety as important; *Tony the Tiger*, spokes-tiger for *Frosted Flakes*; the *Gecko*, the lovable lizard who serves as spokes-reptile on behalf of *GEICO*; *Snoopy*, trusted and beloved spokes-dog for the otherwise big-ole, mean-ole *Northwestern Mutual Insurance Co*; *Elves-in-a-tree*, working away for *Keebler's*; to tag but a few.

And on the plus side remember that these sorts of celebrities don't expect to get paid, although *Clydesdales* do eat a lot, and rarely get into trouble by getting drunk in public; wrecking their cars; and/or saying or doing really stupid, or worse, stuff.

Positioning Based on Unique Selling Propositions

Brands can be positioned based on unique selling propositions (USPs) (i.e., dominant value propositions), that are strategically associated with the brand because the USP holds great appeal to targeted consumer segments.

Unique selling propositions are factors that differentiate one brand from other competing brands. Within targeted segments an existing recognition or merely the perception that particular brands are the lowest cost, highest quality, or first ever of their kind inside their respective product categories would function as USPs. USPs exist when one brand is perceived to have what competitor brands from within the same product category don't have. The positioning advantages leap off the page.

Avis, the rental car agency brand, used to use, "*We're number two, we try harder,*" as its positioning slogan. *South Africa*-based diamond marketer, *De Beers*, far and away the world's largest diamond marketer, accurately proclaims as its positioning statement that "*Diamonds are forever*"—even though love often is not. *M&M's* brand claims at its positioning statement that the multicolored pieces of candy "*Melts in your mouth, not in your hands.*" Yum. *Domino's Pizza* used to promise "*Fresh, hot pizza in 20 minutes or less or it's free.*" Of course, the brand that now only goes by the name *Domino's* had to stop that USP because it lead to too many lawsuits as delivery drivers careened around with little regard for safety. *FedEx* made its original positioning bones and hook by suggesting, "*When it absolutely, positively has to be there overnight*"—*FedEx* is the only rational choice.

The passage of time has long demonstrated that all six of the brand positioning value propositions that were just reported positioning value propositions were based on a compelling Big Idea.

Writing about the intersection between big ideas and positioning brings to mind one of the huge ideas that presumably everyone in the world would readily purchase. The idea in question entails defeating cancer; or as author David Strutton and his family used to sometimes shout during dinner about his battle with leukemia, "We're Kicking Cancer's Ass."

Which brings to the top of one author's mind Houston-based *M.D. Anderson* and its current positioning statement. The statement is grounded in one epically large idea: *Making Cancer History.* Get the double entrendre? How profoundly meaningful and wonderful would it be, to so many consumers, for an institution to "make history" by rendering cancer a remnant of a historical past? What a great "big idea." What an awesome positioning statement on which to hang the branding hook of one of the ten federally-designated *Cancer Research Centers* that market solutions to cancer-related problems inside the United States.

Positioning Based on Features, Attributes, and Benefits (FAB)

Brands can be positioned based on individual or multiple brand Features-Attributes-Benefits (FAB) that deliver an appealing mix of values and solutions.

This is the strategy used by most marketing organizations; even as those firms also emphasize one or more of the positioning tactics described above. Marketers should carefully select, for emphasis, only those differences (key features, attributes or benefits associated with their branded product) that are worth worth promoting, because the differences are important to the membership of the segment(s) being targeted. Product-, promotional-, and/or pricing-differences on which firms would typically differentiate/position their brands should be:

- Truly important, as in determinant, to customers and prospects as they make decisions.
- Truly distinctive, or viewed as genuinely different by customers and prospects.
- Truly superior, as in genuinely better, to alternative brands offered by competitors.
- Easily communicable, which means a brand's important and/or superior benefits can be presented and explained to targeted segments in ways that customers will attend to, understand, and believe.
- Difficult for competitors to copy or match, especially in the short-term.
- Affordable, at least to customers being targeted in the firm's primary targeted segment or segments. Notably, affordable need not mean inexpensive.

Value-Based Positioning Strategies, Broadly Framed

Organizations, products, or brands can be positioned to targeted market segments by promising they'll offer/provide:

- More value for more price,
- Less value for much less price,
- More value for less price, and easily-claimed but difficult to truthfully execute positioning value-proposition, or
- ... The same value for less price.

The final positioning value-proposition, same value for less price, is most frequently used. *Creator*, a *San Francisco*-based purveyor of hamburgers, claims to deliver burgers worth $18.00 at *San Francisco* restaurant prices for only $6.00, again, at *San Francisco* prices. *Creator* further promises the delivery of quality found at upmarket restaurants at fast-food prices. The foundation behind this positioning claim is that its *chef-de-cuisine* is a bot named *Flippy*.

Creator's burger bot is a multi-armed unit occupying a nine-square-foot or so physical space. Customers send their orders to *Flippy* by tablet or text. Flippy then customizes everything from how well-done the burger is to the various accoutrements—cheese, type of cheese, onions, tomatoes, the works—flopped on top of patties. Because it customizes burger product options, *Flippy* also functions as a customer-targeting machine. *Flippy* grinds meat; sizes out and forms patties; griddles them by initiating processes governed by heat sensors; chops tomatoes, which reportedly is the toughest process of all; dices onions; and grates assigned types of cheese; slices, butters, and toasts buns; assembles these finished materials into finished products, somehow finding the time to dispense sauces and seasoning; and then, absent any human touch, bags the whole affair for pickup.

Yes, this marvelous machine testifies as much to the power of technology cut loose inside strategically creative marketer brains as it does to the power of positioning. But the point about successful positioning based on the same for less is nonetheless made.

Positioning Is Differentiation; Differentiation Is Positioning

In the end positioning always comes down to differentiation. And only three strategic approaches, which ideally ultimately create core competencies, exist through which brands can be differentiated and positioned.

One core competency, as discussed, is customer intimacy. Customer intimacy is relationship-based. When customer intimacy has been strategically created customers simply feel closer to, experience a tighter affinity with the brand. Customers may feel as if the brand was made for them. Customers may rightly or wrongly sense that this particular brand gets them—and understands as well as anticipates their every need. *Nike, Apple, Facebook, Amazon*, and *Google* have strategically created high levels of intimacy with targeted customer segments—although *Facebook's* intimacy with its customers is increasingly being eroded.

A second core competency is technological leadership. Here, firms are perceived to deliver the best possible technological solutions to customers. Best possible is usually based on a given firm's earned technological advantages. *Nike, Apple, Facebook, Amazon*, and *Google* each stake their market positions on technological leadership. No accident that these brands also reside among the world's most highly valued, in terms of their stock valuations, marketers.

The third core competency is cost leadership. Cost leadership is price-based. Cost-based advantages derive from marketers' resource advantages; business modeling/strategic-expertise; economies-of-scale; or technological expertise. The presence of cost-based advantages permit marketers to charge lower-than-market-average prices and grow their market share. The presence of cost-based advantages alternatively permits the same marketers to charge market-average prices and reap much higher-than-average profits. *Walmart, Southwest Airlines, Dollar Store*, and yes, again, *Facebook, Amazon*, and *Google* are each winning positioning competitions inside their product category markets based on cost-leadership advantages. *Facebook* and *Google* famously don't charge B2C customers anything to consume their services. However, those users—and their information—are the products that *Facebook, Google*, and other marketers sell to B2B customers, as discussed. *Apple CEO Tim Cook* nailed the identity of the value being sold when he recently said that "if the service is free then you are the product."

Marketers can rarely achieve more than two of these core competency-based differentiation strategies at one time. There's one critical catch, however. The catch is that achieving success along all three dimensions is practically impossible. This is because the costs—resources [the 3Ts]—required to achieve success along either the technological leader's or customer intimacy values are so high that the costs generally preclude firms from choosing to price at anything less than premium levels. But when firms concurrently deliver two of these values to the market (*Apple* did and does deliver greater technological advantage and customer intimacy; *Home Deport* once did this as well, but eventually largely lost one core competency-based advantage; customer intimacy), they will be extremely successful.

The fact is that whenever firms achieve differentiation on only one of these three values and deliver market averages on the other two competencies they will likely be successful. However, such one-trick-pony firms are unlikely to secure success on grand scales. Finally, if firms achieve advantage across all three core competencies, they will rule the marketing world—at least temporarily. Hence, we keep referencing *Google, Facebook,* and *Amazon*—three of the *Big Tech's Big Five*. Because currently this is their marketing world to rule. We regular folks are just living in it. As written earlier, technology changes everything, including almost everything about marketing.

MODULE 4.4

How Segmentation, Targeting, and Positioning Tactics Work

The *Democrat National Party* is a marketing organization that sells people; we call them politicians, and their ideas as products. Those politicians brand themselves as *Democrats* and generally position their ideas as progressive.[19] These branded political products attempt to differentiate their value propositions and problem-solving prowess by advocating the presumed power of their ideas. The primary *Democratic National Party branding* symbol is a donkey.

The *Republican National Party* is a marketing organization that sells people, yes, those politicians, and their ideas as products. Those politicians brand themselves as *Republicans*, and generally position their ideas as conservative. These branded political products attempt to differentiate their value propositions and problem-solving prowess by advocating the presumed power of their ideas. The primary *Republican National Party branding* symbol is an elephant.

Each marketing organization routinely engages in segmentation, targeting, and positioning strategies. Each organization engages in these three interrelated marketing activities each and every day in everything it does, says, writes, and probably thinks. Politicians operating inside either marketing organization continuously subdivide, or segment, the entire market of potential and actual voters based on their age, race, economic status, sexual orientation, and educational attainment. Along with the gender of actual or potential voters, because male and female consumers generally vote somewhat differently because males and females often perceive the value of certain issues (ideas and their values) differently. (Even so, we fully agree that a great many women vote exactly like a great many men, and vice versa. Here broad generalities rather than specific absolutes are being described.)

What does the typical *Democratic/Republican* voter look like, ethnically- and gender-wise? What does the average *Democratic/Republican* voter contemplate, attitudinally or belief-wise? What do the two collections of voters generally drive, automobile-wise? What do they usually own, product-wise;

---

19. For myriad reasons, the term "liberal" has apparently been viewed as an unappealing word for decades. Perceived as a word that casts off negative connotations, even among *Democrats*, who now strongly prefer labeling themselves as progressives. As for *Republicans*, they're always happy to affix the still generally negative branding identity liberal to the *Democrat Party's* donkey's tail.

or aspire to do during their spare time, as would be reflected in their AIOs or lifestyle choices? Where are average *Democrats/Republicans* more likely to live, geographically? Is it inside suburbs, cities, or rural areas, or inside red states or blue states? These deceptively simple questions matter, as do their answers. And by answering them accurately any marketing expert could profile two highly divergent market segments of B2C consumers (voters!) along demographic, attitudinal, psychographic, or geographic dimensions. These are essentially the research questions that most B2C marketers must ask and answer before they can segment, target, and position their value propositions successfully. By the way: If the generally college-educated readers don't know the answers to these frankly easy-to-answer questions they should step outside, look around, and begin reading long articles and books too complex to be comfortably consumed on five-inch screens.

Which consumer/voter segments do *Democrats/Republicans* target? Broadly stated, *Democrats* target consumer market segments whose dominant values, beliefs and attitudes would brand them as progressive—though not exclusively so. Broadly stated, *Republicans* target consumer market segments whose dominant values, beliefs, and attitudes would brand them as conservative—again, though not exclusively so.

Anyone who has even casually observed domestic politics during the last twenty-five or so years understands the degree to which *Democrats* and *Republicans*—or generally liberal and conservative thinkers—have conclusively demonstrated they cannot come together to solve problems. This condition, ironically, represents a marketing problem. Because the chief purpose of any marketer, and politicians who function both as products and as marketers, is to solve customer problems.

The primary reason why the marketing party branded *Republican* and the marketing party branded *Democrat* hate on each other so much—and have proven insufficient to the task of surmounting this problem—is because each marketing organization sincerely and virulently disagrees about the best solutions for several core political problems. For instance, problems related primarily to the role and size of government, which in turn generally relate to tax-related ideas or products. Or problems about the role that God should play inside people's or nation's life, which generally play out inside of combined abortion rights and sexual orientation rights ideas or products that left- and right-thinking politicians are marketing. Finally, problems associated with the metaphorical role that guns should play in American society also generally play out as combined free speech and personal human rights ideas, or products. Three "G's", if you will: Government, God, Guns. It's likewise amazing how often political disputes comes down to questions about whose "births" and whose "rights."

The following points are summarized simply and absent any bias. The political marketers whose leaders and constituencies use an elephant as their brand identity believe the rich should pay less, as a percentage of their incomes, in taxes. The political marketers who brand-identify using a donkey believe the opposite. *Republican* marketers generally believe government should be smaller and provide less help for people; that people should be free to help themselves. *Republicans* tell voting segments that they trust them to spend their own money wisely. *Democrats* generally seek a larger government, requiring higher taxes, which ultimately provides more assistance to people. *Democrats* advocate to their targeted segments: Give us more of your money and trust us to use it wisely as we help you. *Republicans* believe governmental regulations should be weaker, freeing up business and capitalistic spirits; *Democrats* believe the opposite. *Republicans* believe baby's rights supersede mother's rights; *Democrats* believe the opposite.

These genuine differences are reflected in the highly divergent positioning statements that each political party promotes, and in the messages about the two value propositions that the two political brands convey through their promotional or communication efforts.

How else does each political marketing party position and differentiate its brand and value proposition to the market segments each targets? In their messaging, *Democrats* position *Republicans* as evil. *Republicans*, by contrast, position *Democrats* as stupid, at worst; as misguided and malicious, at best. Each competitor currently positions its values based more on what the other side is, and on what its brand is not, as opposed to positioning based on special attributes, benefits, values, and solutions uniquely associated with either the *Democrat* or *Republican* brand. Exceptions exist. But not as many as one would hope. Not in partisan political markets where only your brand's team and point-of-view merits the presumption of innocence.

These attitudinal differences are genuine. They are not contrived. These branding differences are material, absolutely large, and meaningful enough to drive the promotional stories upon which each political marketing party hangs its core ideas and values. And indeed, these differences are reflected in the promotional and positional messaging efforts of the Republican and Democratic brands.

Each political marketing entity only shares one idea in common. At this historical juncture each marketing brand—*donkeys* and *elephants*—appears willing to sell its soul to secure more votes. Domestic political marketing has pretty much devolved to this point.

Need proof? Look around. Ironically, marketing is likely responsible for this devolution as well. If there were no [marketing] media, and therefore no *MSNBC/CNN/Facebook* versus *Fox News* customer bases to "play to" not on a daily but rather an hourly basis, politicians probably could sit down together and derive reasonable solutions to a remarkable array of problems within a few days.

FIGURE 4.1
Relationship between product-markets, market segments, and niches.

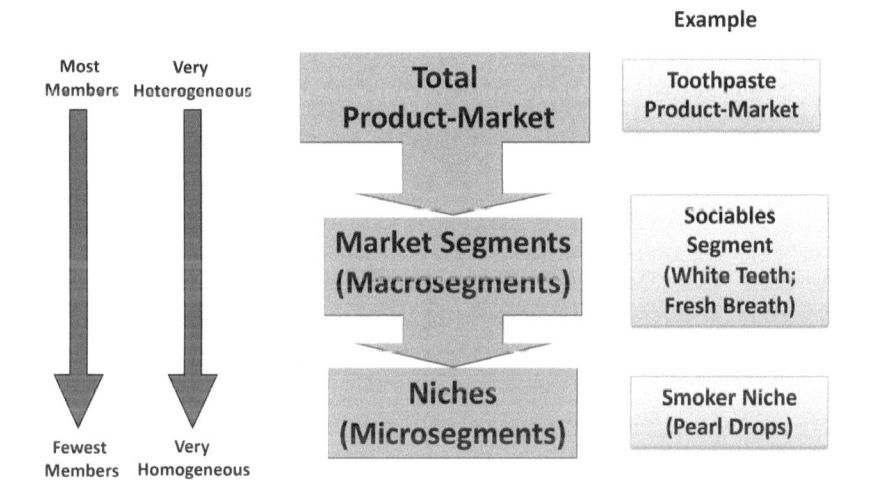

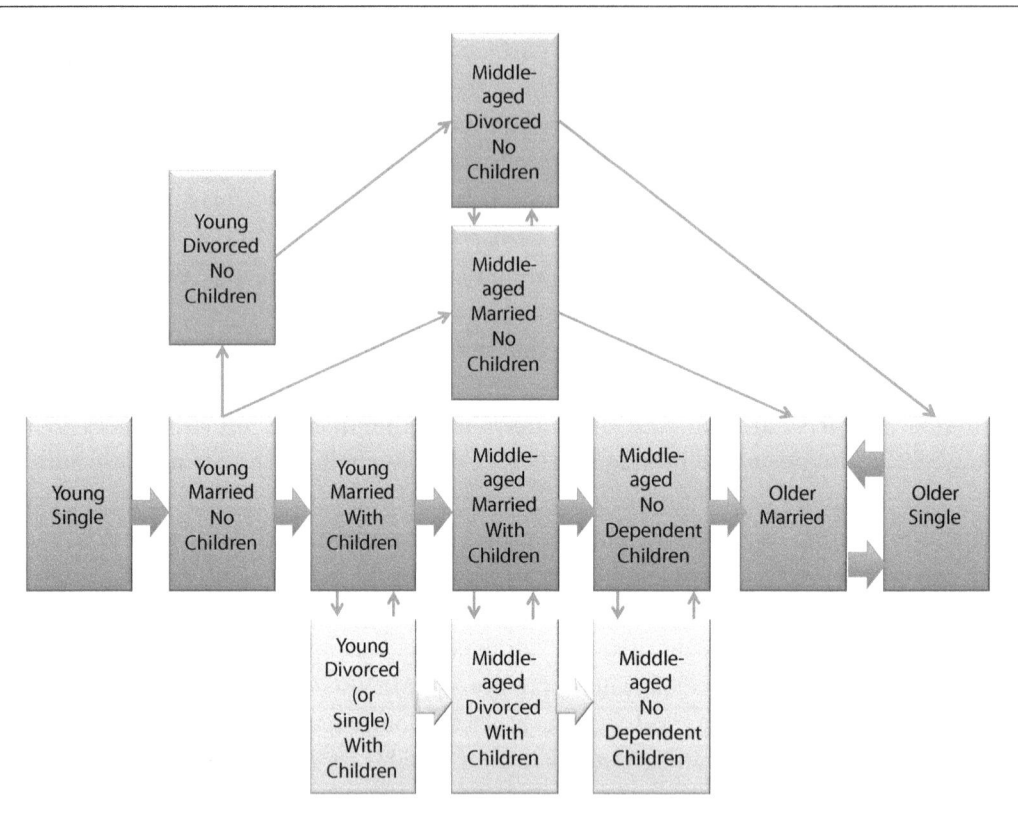

178 Section I Introducing New Marketing Concepts, Issues, and Principles

FIGURE 4.2
The Family Life Cycle

FIGURE 4.3
Market Targeting: Selecting Market Segments—Four Broad Choices

Undifferentiated	**Concentrated**
One generic marketing program for all segments combined	A focused marketing program for a single segment
Differentiated	**Micro Targeting**
Multiple programs for a number of different segments	Treat each customer as unique with a dedicated marketing mix

SECTION II

Framing Key Marketing Issues

MODULE 5

The Environment

MODULE 5.0

Answering Seven "What's" and One "Why" Questions

ONE HUGE ENVIRONMENTAL TREND

Obesity. For one reason, obesity is simultaneously a major crisis and an environmental threat inside the United States. The reason is that extreme corpulence makes almost everything and everybody that it touches worse off.

The domestic health-care system? Everything costs more because obese consumers drive up health-care prices for everyone else. Costs rise, because heavier consumers proportionally consume so much more health care than do their fitter counterparts. Market prices as well as supply and demand within markets are always marketing and economic issues.

The coronavirus crisis? The virus became much deadlier because obesity functions as a co-morbidity[1] factor that accelerates the risk of COVID-19. Economic growth was radically dampened as marketing media fomented fears and worse. The economy is always a marketing issue. One additional COVID-19-related marketing observation. Novelist *Neil Gaiman* once wrote "Fear is a wonderful thing, in small doses." A little bit of rational fear helped consumers keep their masks on, while in public. A wonderful thing. A little bit too much irrational fear, as was routinely stoked by collaborating media and politicians (some will disagree with this view, which is okay), helped keep large parts of the *American* economy tamped down. Not a wonderful thing.

Professional employment prospects? These too are lowered for notably heavy candidates. All because discriminating in favor of or against prospective job candidates based on their weight is the last form of "acceptable" (but never spoken out-loud) discrimination that pervades throughout American workplaces. (Workplace hiring decisions are always marketing decisions. Why? Because *ceteris paribus* organizations always hire the candidate who they perceive represents the best solution because he or she will generate the greatest value for the hiring organization.) No, obesity-based hiring discrimination is neither legal nor morally acceptable, but this particular bias nonetheless functions

---
1. Morbidity means "the condition of being diseased." Co-morbidity, then, implies one disease is combined with another.

as far and away the most prevalent form of discrimination in play in the professional workplace. Even overweight people themselves discriminate against hiring other overweight people when slimmer alternatives are available. The preceding two statements are not opinions, by the way, but grounded social science facts—subject to Googling if one wishes.

Domestic military recruiting? Indeed, this marketing function is affected given that fewer and fewer recent high school graduates meet the standard military training requirements for military service. The recruitment of potential soldiers, sailors, airmen, or marines by the U.S. Armed Services is very much a marketing activity. Each military branch fights vigorously with its brothers' branches to land the best human capital to fill out its rank and file.

Marketing itself? Does the surfeit of weight affect marketing practice, just as domestic obesity is affected by marketing practice? Absolutely, because myriad marketers understand how much easier it is to sell foodstuffs that make people fatter rather than fitter, and strategically exploit their awareness. Just like smart marketers understand it is easier to turn an aquarium into fish stew than to turn fish stew into an aquarium. Things—people's bodies—systems—entire environments . . . fall apart, due to entropy, unless those things are carefully managed.

Little West Virginia

In 2000, 23.9 percent of West Virginian citizens were obese. The rate made little *West Virginia*, by one measure, the biggest state in the United States. About 20 years later, in 2019, 23.8 percent of Coloradans were obese. This figure made much larger *Colorado*, by this weighty metric, the smallest state in the *United States*. With the exception of a handful of lower-population but heavier-weight nations such as *Tonga, Samoa,* and *Kuwait,* the *United States* is the world's "largest" country. Forty-two-percent of the *American* citizenry is obese, according to recent environmental statistics.[2]

So what? The so-what is that this one seemingly simple but actually strikingly impactful environmental metric—the average body weight of domestic consumers—has been transformed at an astounding pace during the last twenty-something years. Impactful how? First, because the aforementioned disease and disability that both accompany and stimulate obesity have contributed to materially higher health-care costs and to materially lower life expectancies. Second, because these heavy trends have contributed to a now $72 billion marketing dietary industry that sells both ideas (strategies and tactics) and products dedicated both to making millions of *American* consumers feel bad about their weight and to helping them shed it. It matters not, apparently, whether much of this industry's supposed solutions are actual scams. Scams? Really. Yes, and absolutely. Because if the marketing sector's supposed dietary solutions—solutions, that is, that extend beyond eating and drinking less and exercising more—were not scams one can only suppose there would be many tens of millions fewer too-big-for-their-own good Americans hanging out.

What is happening here, in sum, is one major environmental trend (growing obesity); one mega-environment threat (to *American* citizens); and one massive environment opportunity (for health-care marketers of all stripes and sorts). And hang on, because there's more: This entire array of dynamic environmental effects actually results, albeit unintentionally, from three specific marketing efforts.

---

2. Barry Eastwick, *Just Eat* (New York: Penguin Random House, 2021).

The first effort entails the marketing and subsequent proliferation of "processed-to-within-an-inch of their formerly natural lives" foods.

The second effort entails a dramatic growth in "bet-you-cannot-eat-all-this-in-one-setting" portions. These values are primarily targeted toward consumer segments whose membership is only too willing to man-up or woman-up to the challenge.

The third marketing effort entails the development of "they came, they saw, they conquered" (yes, echoing *Julius Caesar's veni, vidi, vici*) our hearts, souls, and brains hand-held technology devices. The presence and proliferation of these devices have kept millions of consumers vigorously thumbing-away while sitting around languidly for hours, if not days. This makes sense, of course, because why would anyone want to walk around outside enjoying nature when much more interesting stuff than nature could be imported into domiciles as information that marketing algorithms have customized just for "me" blazes by at addictive speeds on my 5.5 (on average) square-inch screens?

Yes, But What About Real Hogs?

Meanwhile and yes, ironically, as *American* consumers on average have grown fatter American hogs, on average, have grown leaner. Hogs got leaner across an approximately twenty-year time frame because hogs were placed on lower-fat diets as almost the entire pork industry responded to macro-environmental trends that generally encompassed consumer and public policy concerns about the need to eat healthier (read, less fatty) foods. So far, sounds good. Right? Well, not really, because numerous expensive and inexpensive restaurants that formerly had specialized in serving tasty pork-based dishes slowly, then quickly discovered that their dishes were less tasty. Their customers began recognizing this shortfall, as well. In brief, neither buyers nor sellers were happy. But restaurants themselves began complaining to the pork-producing industry, essentially asking them for more of the old-style fatty pork.

The rest is porcine history. These at first sporadic restaurant consumer complaints soon grew into a deluge and the pork industry stood up, took note, and responded strategically by breeding higher fat percentages per pound of meat back into their hog population. These farmers happily re-customized these back-to-the-future products in exchange for long-term and exclusive agreements to supply said pound of pork annually to these restaurants. Such is the product life cycle—or the seesaw—that marketers sometimes ride as they customize their products to satisfy customers' changing wants, needs, and in this instance, tastes.

Product customization is no longer something done only inside automotive, jeans, laptop, cosmetics, or eyeglass marketing sectors. Product customization, initiated in response to dynamic environments trends or customer preferences, is a foody-thing, as well. Yep, re-sculpting the bodies and BMI of real pigs.

Unending Environmental Trends—and Marketing Consequences

As you just read, external environmental trends are always at work in various and often unexpected ways. The effects of environmental trends may be obvious or may remain obscure. Such effects also might benefit, prove benign, or absolutely undermine any marketer's current and future success prospects. Indeed, the same environmental trend might prove both beneficial or benign and damaging or malignant to the same marketing organization or to different marketing sectors.

During 2020 *California*—itself the world's fifth largest economy, behind *Germany* but ahead of *India*—passed regulations that will ban the purchase of new gas-powered automobiles in the state by 2035. Oil and gas marketers such as *ExxonMobil* and *British Petroleum* shuddered in response to the environmental threat, as did their share prices. By contrast, the hearts of *Faraday Future*, *Byton Technology*, and *Fisker Inc.*, electric car marketers all, must have leapt in joy upon learning about this fabulous environmental opportunity. Two radically different strategic marketing reactions to the same environmental trend, of course.

You tell us; is the following environmental trend line good or bad for marketers? Another way of asking this same question would be: Does the following environmental trend line represent an opportunity or a threat to marketers?

The year 2019 was the first annum in which average Americans spent more time on their mobile devices than watching television screens. A marketing research agency called *EMarketer*, as reported in *MarketWatch.com*, determined that Americans spent three hours and forty-three minutes a day on mobile devices during 2019 as compared to three hours and thirty-five minutes watching TV screens. In total, the average American consumer spent more than seven hours daily staring into screens.

Notably, as often happens, this discussion stacks one environmental trend upon a new trend upon yet another trend.

For instance, the US birthrate fell 2 percent from the previous year during 2019. This was the fourth straight year of decline (*NPR.com*). The decline was attributed primarily to economic insecurity among people of reproductive age, and their fears or concerns—your choice—about the costs and career disruption of raising kids. The American birth rate, as this book was written (2021), is now the lowest in thirty-two years. At 1.7 children per woman, the birthrate is less than the human replacement rate. As every demographer knows, and now you know as well, the replacement rate for humans resides between 2.1 to 2.2 babies per woman. Rise above that figure, and population numbers organically grow. Fall below, and populations shrink.

Should marketers care about this ongoing birth dearth? The answer depends on what products and values those marketers are selling—and this statement is no joke. Should America as either a nation or a culture care? The answer is unequivocally yes, for reasons extending beyond this focus of this discussion. Worth pointing out, however, is the fact that most *European* nations long ago entered a condition that demographers describe as a demographic winter. *European* birthrates have fallen below replacement rates. *Europe*, generally, is now reaping cold economic whirlwinds as a consequence.

Then the bottom really fell out of the global baby market during 2020. This even worse version of the birth dearth proved anything but a bundle of joy for domestic and international organizations that make and market baby products. In response, most of those firms, being strategic to their cores, developed new product lines and shifted their targeting focus to other consumer segments and thus to other sets of customer problems that they could solve.

Marketing strategists should always account for these trends as they develop planned responses. Another way of expressing the same point is that marketers should always care about environmental trends.

Take *Reckitt Benckiser Group PLC*, for example. The marketing organization has expanded its nutritional product category to include a new focus on elderly consumers' health. *Reckitt*, primarily known in nutritional marketplaces for the milk supplement *Sustagen,* was responding to environmental trends suggesting that fewer *Chinese* and *American* births would dampen baby-feeding sales during 2021 and beyond. This was a big deal given that combined *Chinese* and *American* births captured slightly more than half of the global baby formula market. With *American* and *Chinese* birthrates hitting all-time lows, *Reckitt's, Nestle SA,* and *Danone SA* all felt the pressure.

There is one possible strategic marketing upside to this environment trend: When fewer children are born, their parents typically spend more money on the ones they have. The industry has responded strategically by creating pricier baby food options. *Nestle*, a Switzerland-based corporation that is best known in the broader "baby & child" product category for *Gerber's*, first launched a premium priced milk powder brand called *Belsol* in the *Chinese* marketplace. Shortly thereafter, a new infant formula was launched that was created to solve or avoid problems that typically arise during the first 1,000 days of babies' lives. The product stair-steps the delivery of desirable supplements at just the right period during those 1,000 days, or so *Nestle* claims. (No reasons exist to doubt *Nestles'* claims.)

P&G was previously introduced and described as a consumer good giant. Giant implies a big footprint, and for *P&G* that footprint includes the baby care sector. The *Cincinnati, Ohio*-based firm has similarly been rocked by the decline in birthrates. In response, *P&G* has developed more sophisticated products that can justify higher prices—as is usually the case with all sorts of new products. More elaborate diapers are now available that use tape or feature pants-like fits on those baby bottoms.

Then there is *Irving, Texas*-based *Kimberly-Clark*, best-known in the baby marketplace category for its *Huggies* brand of diapers. The corporation recently introduced a new diapers product line. Cleverly branded as *New Delivery*, the diapers are constructed from plant-based materials and cost about five times more than less expensive diaper brands. But for well-heeled parents seeking to get their green-on[3] as they outfit their more scarce new arrivals, the more environmentally-conscious alternative may prove just the ticket.[4]

It's informative and indeed educational to understand how vigorously, quickly, and effectively this specific marketer sector—call it the "baby care" market—responded to one admittedly non-trivial environmental trend; otherwise known as the birth-dearth. No one should be surprised, however, because tiny babies have always been big business.

WHAT'S AN "ENVIRONMENT"?

Environments consist of the surroundings in which people, animals, plants, or organization live or operate—and in which those persons, animals, plants, or organizations strive to survive or hopefully thrive. External environments can be global, regional (i.e., *North American*), national (i.e., the *United States*), statewide (i.e., *Texas*), local (i.e., the *DFW Metroplex*), or indigenous (i.e., *Denton*) in nature.

---

3. As discussed elsewhere, the color "green" might variously describe one's affinity for frogs (*Kermit*), for the *University of North Texas* (*Mean Green*), or for the environment (buy Green). The color "green" functions as a brand identifier that signals a given consumer's preference for pro-environmental activities and products.

4. Saabira Chaudhuri, "Birth Drop is No Bundle of Joy," *Wall Street Journal* (November 17, 2020): B4.

All marketing firms operate inside Macro-Environments (also called External Environments). Macro-Environments primarily consist of demographic, economic, natural, technological, and/or cultural environments. Macro-environmental factors generally harbor both threats and opportunities for marketing organizations.

Environments also exist inside all successful marketing organizations; and remember, all successful organizations are successful marketers. These are called internal environments. Internal environments are also called Micro-Environments. Micro-Environments consist of organizations' (a) customer relationships; (b) relationships with suppliers and other marketing intermediaries who collectively comprise supply chains; (c) competitors; and (d) myriad other relationships with various publics (i.e., stockholders, public interest groups who may or may not support what the firm is doing or plans to do, customers, etc.). Marketing organizations can legally and logically should create relationships with each micro-environmental public except competitors. Marketing organizations must manage these relationships effectively before they can create and deliver any sort of perceived or tangible value, much less truly differentiating values.

WHAT ENVIRONMENTAL FORM IS MOST MANAGEABLE: THE MICRO OR THE MACRO?

Neither micro- nor macro-environmental factors are controllable. But micro-environments are clearly more manageable, particularly when marketers strategically plan for, establish, and strive to manage key relationships.

WHAT'S AN "ENVIRONMENTAL TREND"?

Environmental trends are patterns of gradual or more rapid change unfolding along an environmental dimension. Environmental dimensions include, for example, the economy, society, culture, demographics, technological, governmental/regularity factors, and so forth. The following two statements, each written recently in *The Economist,* capture and reflect relevant environmental trends:

> ▶ "Kids these days just want to live in their own fucking little worlds in their own bedrooms watching *Netflix* and becoming obese. [In the meantime] There has been a huge increase in social pressure to become a good parent."—*The Economist,* 2016

That these two evocative assertions capture two important sociocultural demographic trends is not in question. What's worth questioning, however, is whether a given environmental trend represents an opportunity or threat; and for what sorts of marketer? The question is worth answering, and must be answered, especially as marketing organizations prepare and execute their strategic plans. That's because each environmental trend will play out favorably or badly for various B2C or B2B marketing organizations. Play out favorably, or unfavorably, in terms of creating environmental threats or opportunities for various B2C or B2B marketers.

Back to the topic of environmental trends themselves. A sadly fascinating demographic trend—one that's sort of like watching a slow-motion but clearly destructive tidal wave—is rabidly playing inside contemporary American society and, therefore, inside domestic consumer marketplaces. The trend: Today's teenagers are more connected to each other but at the same time also lonelier than any preceding teen-aged person in history. Why?

A large part of the trend evolves out of the lost human-on-human connections underscored in the trend introduced above by *The Economist*. For the first, but not for the last, time we see how one environmental trend triggers other environmental trends inside environmental contexts. Today's American teens are lonelier than any teen generation in history primarily because too many young people today take away value from playing e-games or engaging in social networking that they used to obtain from face-to-face exchanges with other teens inside real work physical settings. What sorts of human values are mostly being lost? Actual wins and losses, actual human opportunities for competition or cooperation, genuine human sources of excitement, and actual hugs, handshakes, and kisses, to note just a few of the important human values that are being increasingly lost.

WHAT'S AN "ENVIRONMENTAL OPPORTUNITY"?

Environmental opportunities are environmental trends that are breaking-favorably for marketers because they, the trends, enhance the success prospects of marketing organizations' current or future strategic marketing plans. Opportunities are similarly present in existing or emerging trends in the environment that support or promote the best interests of the firm. Whenever doing so is ethical, opportunities should be exploited.

WHAT'S AN "ENVIRONMENTAL THREAT"?

Environmental threats are trends that are breaking-badly for marketers. Breaking-badly because the existence of the trend degrades the success prospects of marketers' current strategic marketing plans or future strategic marketing plans that those marketers could develop.

Environmental threats should be identified because marketers need to take strategic actions to avoid them or mitigate their negative impact. Avoiding threats means getting out of harm's way. Mitigating threats entails first understanding them and then developing plans to alleviate, or ease, the harm that threats otherwise would visit on their heads.

For example, profound environmental shifts, trends, are unfolding among the US population regarding what the living seek from funerals for their dead. Not long ago when Americans died funeral directors (nothing if not preternaturally-comforting marketers) could reasonably expect to sell $2,999 to $11,999 caskets, $1,999 to $3,999 burial vaults, and expensive embalming and cosmetics treatment services to bereaved families, among other various "necessary" and unnecessary services and items. All at ridiculously marked-up prices that make the living spin-in-their-beds, because the living have no financial option but to struggle how to figure out how to pay for all that stuff. But now, the combined acceptance of cremation, increasing desires among either the deceased or survivors (or both parties) for green burials (no embalmment, less expensive biodegradable caskets), and the fact that more funeral service-related information is more readily available online is visiting huge threats upon these purveyors of the traditional American way of death. No longer will as many gullible or ill-informed domestic consumers not know that they can refuse unnecessary services or feel too embarrassed to question or negotiate prices.

Environmental Threats Often Seemingly Arise Out of Thin Air

COVID-19 likely came to your mind, carried as the virus is by the air, as you read this header. However, the ensuing decisions, behaviors, and consequences that resulted as almost all strategic marketers responded to the environmental threats imposed by the arrival of COVID-19 were anything but predictable. For example, the 2020–21 COVID-19 pandemic radically altered a norm that had long governed most automotive purchases inside America: finding your new ride on the lot and driving it home that same day. For months automobile dealer stocks—their inventories—ran about 25 percent thinner than normal, a hangover effect from two months of pandemic-related faculty closures during the spring of 2020. The shortfall left many anxious buyers with no other choice but to order their preferred brands and wait a few weeks. The whole affair ran counter to most domestic car shoppers' traditional desires to achieve instant gratification, and to dealers' longstanding expectations that they would happily send customers' home in a new car on the very day they bought it.

Okay, but material upsides also emerged from this radical environmental shift. Automotive sector leaders discovered that stocking fewer cars, particularly among periods of pent-up high demand, lifted profits for manufacturers and dealers alike. Now these two sets of supply chain partners—car manufacturers and independent or dealer-owned automotive dealerships—are apparently leaning more permanently into the idea of carrying fewer vehicles on the lots. This change, inspired as it was by an environmental threat, will likely mark a long-term shift in how autos have long been sold inside the United States.

For decades *American* auto dealerships kept endless rows of vehicles outside their stores in enough colors and variations so that buyers could find what they wanted when they wanted it during pretty much any physical visit they took. Reducing those inventory storehouses of sheet metal and plastic drove more customers toward their only other option, pre-ordering cars online and then waiting weeks for their arrival, which have long been common practice inside *European* markets. These changes had and will continue to have serious implications for the absolute value of dealer-owned real estate and for how automobile marketers manage their factories.

The benefits of leaner dealership inventories on car lots have been an unexpected byproduct of the pandemic. Automakers strained mightily to boost output after the Spring, 2020 shutdown. This task was made more difficult by an unexpected surge in consumer demand for new cars. A sellers' market emerged, wherein automotive marketers were to avoid discounts as prices for new vehicles ratcheted upward toward record highs. The inventory crunch gave production and marketing priority to their most popular and profitable models and feature combinations, and lowered supply chain management costs in the process. Meanwhile, dealers saved money by holding (and paying manufacturers) for less inventory, and cars sold faster at higher prices, as noted. The typical vehicle spent 25 percent fewer days parked in dealership inventories during this period, as compared to the previous two-year period. The previously referenced shift toward online marketing and purchasing processing lowered dealership costs, as well.[5]

The primary takeaway: all these marketing managerial changes followed from logical and strategic responses to a single, albeit singularly powerful, environmental threat.

---

5. N. Naughton and M. Collas, "Dealers Seek Gain From Smaller Car Lots," *Wall Street Journal* (2020): B1–B3.

At other times, however, environmental threats have literally arisen from thin air. The thin air in the following example is helium. A global shortage of helium once deflated revenues at *Party City*, according to *CNN.com*. Helium is the second most abundant element in *The Milky Way*. However, on Earth, supplies are dwindling. Most helium is extracted in tiny amounts from natural gas wells that are drilled by fracking marketers. While helium is pocketed throughout the Earth's thin outer crust, the element is notoriously hard to capture because it floats up, up, and away (i.e., like helium balloons).

Which brings us back to *Party City*. Helium balloons were *Party City's* best-selling product, and a primary reason why consumers walked through the store's doors as opposed to buying party supplies through *Amazon*. The recent helium shortage has raised balloon prices; balloon sales quickly deflated. An inverse relationship between price and demand usually applies. In response, *Party City* shuttered forty-five stores during 2019 to boost overall corporate profitability. As helium supplies drifted down, helium prices took off. And as helium prices rose inside B2B supply chains, *Party City* had no other strategic option other than to raise prices at retail levels. Rather than paying what they view as excessively higher prices, even party-hearty consumers increasingly opted out of balloons altogether.

Environmental threats routinely arise from a line-up of usual suspects. But technology is typically foremost among this list. But the specific environmental threat (and, as it turns out, opportunity as well) introduced below plays out at more important levels than those typically posed by *Facebook*- or *Instagram*-like technological trends.

Human heartbeat monitoring technology has advanced to the point where very early pregnancy stage heartbeat monitoring and/or sonograms are nearly universally available and reasonably priced. One predictable marketing consequence is that far more pregnant women are now taking advantage of the opportunity to have sonograms conducted. A second unexpected marketing consequence, emanating directly from the first, is that value of one of *Planned Parenthood's* core promotional approaches has been dramatically undermined. Until recently, one of the abortion marketer's (and, yes, Planned Parenthood markets and provides more than just abortion services to its customers) core value propositions and selling points pivoted around the idea that the customer "problem being solved" is a fetus rather than a human being. Post-sonogram-peek, the "this is only a fetus" promotional pitch becomes harder for any marketer to successfully sell.

This technologically-driven trend could potentially affect the lives of millions of current or future US citizens. A fact carrying no water here. What carries weight, however, is that this trend imposes material threats to the marketing success of *Planned Parenthood* and other marketers that promote and provide abortion services. And yes, of course, as just noted, *Planned Parenthood* markets more than just abortion services. Like most large-scale marketers, *Planned Parenthood* offers more than one product in its portfolio of marketed solutions. Of course, this trend won't negatively impact the effectiveness with which *Planned Parenthood* can market other health-care solutions to women. Environmental trends are like that. The same trend can dramatically threaten the prospects and performance for one strategic business unit inside given firms, while rendering other SBUs inside the same firms either better off or unaffected.

Again, such environmental trends and opportunities would exist even if *Party City* or *Planned Parenthood* or the entire domestic or foreign automotive marketing sector did not exist.

CAN THE SAME ENVIRONMENTAL TREND PLAY OUT AS BOTH OPPORTUNITY AND THREAT?

The indisputably correct answer to this question is, "yes."

As just referenced, the COVID-19 pandemic emerged and played out during the 2020–21 period as one of the most powerful environmental trends in anyone's living memory. This specific environmental trend, which played out as a threat, immediately soured the prospects for the fast-food industry's biggest recent strategic bet: breakfast. Mornings went from rising star status to the point where the meal is now the slowest time of the day, an unfortunate dog offering, for fast-food restaurants. This, after breakfast had emerged continuously as the fast-food marketing sector's leading strategic means of growing revenues during the preceding decade or so.

During the COVID-19 era many Americans consumers who formerly had grabbed a quick, often as in drive-by form, breakfast on their way to work no longer leave home to work. The problem that fast-food breakfast purveyors confronted during the crisis and its consequential and possibly long-tailed aftermath was then they redesigned their product portfolios—their morning menus—to cater to consumers on the go. Well, many of the former go, go, go gang have stopped . . . going anywhere but to their home office computers.

But as just noted, crises that foreshadow threats to certain marketers or entire marketing sectors (the fast-food industry, for example) often represent opportunities to other marketers and sectors (here, prepackaged food). Packaged breakfast items, such as cereal or coffee, surged during the 2020–2021 time frame. Surged to the degree that according to the *Wall Street Journal*,[6] *Kraft Heinz Co*. President Carlos Abrams-Rivera suggested: "We are in a position to own breakfast." Wow, remember our prior discussion about how much marketers stand to gain from owning words in the collective minds of markets. Among other logical breakfast-oriented brands, *Kraft-Heinz* markets *Oscar Mayer* bacon, *Maxwell House* coffee, and *Philadelphia Brand* cream cheese.

The arrival of environmental crises themselves can be twisted into and treated as either opportunities or threats. As such, crises definitely facilitate the development of more innovations or to the broader and faster acceptance of innovations, either as ideas inside marketing organizations themselves or in the form of new products that have been introduced to the marketplace.

Witness, for example, the development of the proliferation of *Zoom* use among professionals, families, and formerly in-person social gatherings. Or witness, more evocatively, the rapid albeit temporary arrival of drive-through strip clubs. Despite the pandemic, innovative strip club owners found ways to lure customers back in and keep their bartenders, servers, and entertainers employed. Enter the drive-through strip club, where you can order a burger and beer from your car, while performers dance with masks on behind a barricade. At least a couple such joints temporarily operated inside the United States during the COVID-19 crisis. The set of such creative clubs includes *Portland, Oregon's, Lucky Devil Lounge* or *Houston's Vivid Gentlemen's Club*, which each temporarily provided such mobile services. And no, neither of your authors visited such places. Instead this news was discovered inside the hipster magazine *Fast Company*'s website.

---

6. Julie Wernau, "Fast Food's Morning Bet Goes Bust," *Wall Street Journal* (November 8, 2020): B3.

The Spirit of These Times

The English word zeitgeist in its original *German* form literally means spirit (see the connection between the *German* geist, for "ghost," and zeit, for time). Few words or phrases captured the environmental zeitgeist that prevailed throughout US culture during 2020 and 2021 than "doom scrolling." Anyone, a roster that probably includes all readers, who has recently spent time online knows what the word doom-scrolling means even if they have never heard of doom-scrolling.

The *Wall Street Journal*[7] reports that doom-scrolling refers to "spending excessive amounts of time on devices poring over grim news." Unfortunately, the word and the environmental zeitgeist appear likely to have staying power. However, as discussed during Module 9 when the Product Life Cycle concept is more fully introduced, nothing in this world lasts forever. And if you don't believe us, consider the famous ring that *King Solomon* purportedly had that possessed the power to make happy people sad and sad people happy. His otherwise unadorned brass ring featured one simple inscription carved inside its circle. The inscription read "This too shall pass."

WHAT "ENVIRONMENTAL DIMENSIONS" ARE MOST IMPORTANT?

A list of the environmental dimensions that almost certainly are most important follows. The absolutely most important individual dimension or dimensions, however, would vary on a marketing firm by marketing firm basis. Listed below in alphabetical order, the top nine environmental dimension are:

- ▶ Competitive trends: The competition, defined, are rivals, adversaries, or antagonists whose actions prevent or inhibit any particular marketing entity from achieving its strategic goals.
- ▶ Cultural and subcultural trends: Culture, defined, is the collective customs, attitudes, and beliefs, arts, social institutions, norms, values, and acknowledged achievements that characterize particular social groups, regions, or nations. Collective customs are reflected in attitudes and beliefs that cultures or generational cohorts within subcultures share. Environmental trend-wise, what matters most to most marketers are customs, attitudes and beliefs, and values that are shared among the membership of cultures or subcultures.
- ▶ Customer or prospective customer trends. Customer and prospective customer trends relate primarily to changes in targeted segments' customer attitudes, likes/dislikes, and preferred lifestyles. The topic of consumer lifestyles is discussed in extensive detail during Module 7.
- ▶ Demographic trends. Demographics, demography, and demographic trends each represent extremely important topics in most marketing contexts. The seemingly clichéd phrase "demography is destiny"[8] did not become classically important to marketers without due

---

7. Ben Zimmer, 2020 "The New High-Tech Way to Slide Into Despair," *Wall Street Journal* (December 12, 2020): C3.

8. The phrase "demographics are destiny" may appear trite, perhaps cliché-like. It is neither, however. The phrase instead is four-square-solid, well worth knowing. If they get and stay ahead of demographic trends it would prove difficult for marketers to lose. If marketers ignore and/or fall behind demographic trends it will prove difficult for them to win.

cause. Demographic trends are usually the most useful criterion[9] that marketers can employ as they engage in marketing segmentation.

- Economic trends: An economy, defined, entails the wealth and resources of a country or region, pertaining primarily to marketing systems through which products and services are produced, promoted, distributed, and priced—and ultimately, hopefully, sold.

- Regulations and laws: Defined, regulations and laws entail rules that particular governmental institutions impose and that others are supposed to recognize as regulators or governors of their behaviors. These rules exist as everyday factors that change over time but constantly confront, and either constrain or benefit, various sorts of marketers. Some marketing sectors—industries—are more likely than others to be impacted by changing regulations and laws. Laws/regulations protect and affect competition and competitive practices. They affect marketing mix activities. Laws/regulations affect customer behavior and how marketers are supposed to treat customers. The environment or consumers themselves, in ways that affect the marketing plans and practices inside particular industries and for particular firms, are protected by laws and regulations.

- Societal trends: Society, defined, is any group of people living together in a more or less ordered community; generally ordered divisions also exist inside societies.

- Supply chain intermediaries—and partners: Supply chain intermediaries and partners include upstream suppliers (i.e., source firms) and downstream intermediaries (i.e., retailers) for marketing organizations. Any marketing firms' supply chain intermediaries may include retailers, warehouses, shippers, or other downstream [toward the end use customers] partners. These supply chain processes, which are hugely important, are extensively discussed in Module 13.

- Technological trends: Technology, defined, entails applying practical knowledge to solve human and other sorts of problems.

Singling Out the Importance of Subcultures

Subcultures are usually more important than cultures to marketers. The primary reason is because subcultures exist and can be "used" as ready-made sources of potentially attractive, or for that matter definitely unattractive, don't even think about marketing to them, subcultures.

Generation Z, or *Gen Z*, is a generationally-based subculture. *Gen Z* is roughly defined as the American generation born between 1997 and about 2012–14. (Demographers, demographic experts, have never uniformly agreed upon an exact annual end birth date year for the Generation.) The generational cohort, market segment, and/or subculture contains around 68 million domestic consumers. The next generational cohort up from Gen Z, age-wise, are the *Millennials*. The *Millennials*, demographers generally agree, are born between 1981 and 1996 (meaning members of the generation were aged twenty-five to forty during 2021).

---

9. A criterion is a measurement or benchmark.

Denim was anointed long ago as the "people's fabric." Across the decades the implicit designation as the "people's fabric" has spurred and sustained high sales volume within a product category that houses so many powerful brands (*Levi's, Wrangler, Diesel, Lee, Pepe, True Religion, Calvin Klein*, etc.). But certain formerly sales-enhancing values long associated with denim may be fraying around the cuffs, and for that matter, wearers' thighs. While certain denim-heads have heralded the demise of the skinny jean for several years, the fit continues to top jeans brands' best-seller lists, remaining one of the most popular styles for women worldwide. But younger generations of women are refusing to fit in. What is being discussed is an environmental sub-cultural phenomenon, by the way.

Gen Z opinion leaders and social influencers recently started an organic movement to dethrone skinny jeans. The environmental, cultural, and demographic trend is playing out on the cohort's favorite virtual battleground: social media. Uncounted legions of *Generation Z* users on *Instagram* and *TikTok* posted video clips during 2020 insisting that skinny jeans are canceled and that *Millennials*—who apparently are the style's biggest fans—should stop wearing them if they want to appear *Younger*. Some Z-warriors went so far as to insist that all others should throw away their skinnies, cut them up, or even set them on fire. Each sentiment and behavior ironically could run completely counter to two other cultural values purportedly held dear by the *Generation Z* cohort, which also is lauded and often lauds itself by virtue-signaling its commitment both to sustainability and to anti-bullying.

Some hard-ball consumer attitudes are playing out here, for sure, but these *Generation Z* cultural fashion and style critics may be on to something. A retail market intelligence (marketing research) platform that goes by the brand name *Edited* confirms that distinct shifts to looser clothing styles are underway across the women's bottoms and tops board. Sales of men's relaxed and straight fits were 15 percent year-over-year. Sales of women's wide-leg, straight, and paper-bag styles were up 97 percent, 69 percent, and 24 percent, respectively, again, year-over-year (2020 versus 2019). While *Generation Z* is loudly pronouncing its aversion toward skinny, *Millennials* largely remained steadfast in showing their love for apparel silhouettes that hugged their bodies. A generational split in cultural values may have appeared. Indeed, for every prospective *Generation Z* customer that trolls consumers who are wearing skinny jeans on social media, apparently there's a millennial-aged consumer who is resolutely dedicated toward holding the line and defending the skinny.[10]

WHAT'S "ENVIRONMENTAL SCANNING"?

Environmental scanning is akin to heady quarterbacks or point guards looking down the football field or basketball court as they constantly process what is happening right now, this instant, and then quickly determining where the best opportunities to pursue will reside in the future. Sometimes those futures arrive almost immediately. At other times these now more manageable futures arrive further down the road, perhaps during the next series, in the next half, or even in the midst of the next game against the same competitor. Environmental scanning is similarly what enables truly proficient ice hockey players to skate not to where the puck is right now, but to where it will be in the (admittedly near) future. A parallel description naturally applies to soccer players and soccer balls.

---

10. "If Gen Z Cancels Jeans, Will Others Follow?," *Sourcing Journal* (February 9, 2021).

Defined technically, environmental scanning entails observing, researching, and interpreting various, almost inevitably uncontrollable environment trends that might impact an organization.

Defined more practically, environmental scanning is a strategic process that entails continuously monitoring the relevant external and internal environments of firms. The purpose of environmental monitoring is to identify trends that pose opportunities or threats for strategic organizations. These trends either enhance or degrade marketers' prospects for survival and future success. Positive trends enhance marketers' success prospects. Negative trends degrade them.

Environmental trends themselves need not be profound—except, perhaps to lovers of *Sex and the City* and the shoe-obsessed character *Carrie Bradshaw*. But here goes, anyway. Women's high heels are apparently losing a little of their fashion allure. OMG, first skinny jeans and now this! The *Washington Post* recently reported that sales of high heel shoes recently declined by 12 percent (this decline arose before the COVID-19 event made professional work attire a thing of the past for many). Women's sneaker sales, however, rose by 37 percent. At the time market research analysts suggested that three environmental trends are contributing to this fourth environmental trend. First, more causal workplaces. Second, more Americans working from home. Third, more Americans walking to work.

Fashion being highly fashionable (i.e., and therefore being utterly dynamic in nature), this trend might easily stride off in a new direction any year now. Of course, because fashion is often merely fashionable, when apparent changes arise, much may appear to have happened even when nothing important has changed. Fashion, mere fashion, often functions as a remarkably insightful environmental barometer because fashion usually combines elements taken from now-known environmental pasts with still-evolving environmental presents.

WHAT'S THE RELATIONSHIP BETWEEN "GLACIERS AND MARKETING PRACTICE"?

Before answering, let's all get on the same page and note that glaciers are persistent though not permanent bodies of dense ice moving under their own weight and reshaping their surroundings as they move. They form when the accumulation of snow exceeds the melting of snow, often across centuries. Glaciers grow or shrink across time, depending upon the prevailing climatic conditions that surround them. Glaciers should not be confused or conflated with icebergs. Icebergs are used in a similar analogical (used as an analogy) in the Ethics and Social Responsibility Module (Module 8).

Oh yes, back to the relationship question: Do glaciers impact their surrounding environments? You know the answer, right? Especially if you have seen America's *Great Lakes*, these giant water-filled holes in the earth created by the last great retreat of *North American* glaciers.

Do their surrounding environments impact glaciers? Again, you know the answer, right? Whether or not you believe in *global warming*, you still presumably know that glaciers are retreating around the world as a result of generally rising global environmental temperatures.

Do marketing practices and firms impact their surrounding environments? Yes, older people like your authors cannot believe what passes for acceptable entertainment—note the far more prevalent use of F-bombs, SOBs, and Sht—on prime-time television these days.

Do their surrounding environments impact marketing practices and firms? Yes, older people like your authors cannot believe what passes for acceptable entertainment on television these days.

The answers to all four questions is YES. Consequently, the relationship abiding between marketers' sector and their surrounding environments is analogous to the relationships prevailing between glaciers and their surrounding environment.

Marketers should continuously scan their external environments in a strategic attempt to identify opportunities and threats before competitors discover them. They should just look around, carefully and continuously. The resulting insights (i.e., environmental knowledge) presumably should assist those firms in their strategic and marketing planning as well as their execution of those plans. The products developed and the branding values established by such firms then should enjoy a better chance of being First-to-Market, marketing law one; First-in-a-Category, marketing law two; or First-in-the-Mind, marketing law three.

Environmental scanning should play a crucial role in marketing planning. Environmental scanning processes should be used to generate useful market information that can be transformed by strategic planners into actionable marketing knowledge/insights. Marketing managers execute environmental scanning by conducting marketing research and carefully paying constant attention to relevant environmental events and trends that continuously unfold around them. Reading books and newspapers, even online, helps too—this is a serious comment.

WHY ENGAGE IN ENVIRONMENTAL SCANNING?

The best answer relates to the reason the famous 1930s *Great Depression*-era bank robber *Willie Sutton* gave when he was asked by newspaper reporters why he robbed banks. Mr. Sutton's famous and indisputably logical reply: "Because that's where the money is."

But more reasons than Willie's words exist to engage in environmental scanning. Things, various environmental factors, constantly change. Changes don't always represent progress. But changes are always necessary before progress can occur. (Yes, you have read this before.) And they, changes, are currently occurring at record rates—practically at the speed of baud.[11]

Too often organizations largely consist of nothing more or less than people who feel threatened by the threat or reality of change. This common condition likely arises because humans can more easily envision things quickly getting worse than quickly getting better.

Customers themselves almost always love the new, however, so long as "the new" is not too new, for reasons explained below. Most customers are certainly attracted to "the new." The new is a glittering lure, after all. *Winston Churchill* once asserted that, "One can do whatever one wants if the [new] thing takes people by surprise."[12] In writing these words the great leader argued in support of the value of "the new," "the shocking," and "the unexpected." He proposed further that one almost always gets away doing whatever he or she wants as long as the thing being done truly takes people by surprise.

---

11. Baud is the measure used to track the speed at which information travels across the internet.
12. Rick Atkinson, *The Day of Battle* (New York: Picador, 2007): 4.

Marketing merit is embedded inside *Churchill's* arguments. Especially if and when individuals' or organizations' marketing missions feature the related goals of persuading and/or influencing targeted others.

Sometimes, marketing or military planners and doers should do the unexpected. Even, and perhaps especially, when doing the unexpected is difficult. This reason is because what they are doing will then, by definition, really be unexpected. Such unanticipated strategies or tactics consequently often catch competitors, opponents, or enemies by surprise. The values of first mover, as in first-to-market, advantages then become available for the taking.

Despite these affirming arguments about the value of change the fact remains that most customers, or for that matter marketing planners, feel threatened or put off either by the prospect or the arrival of too much change. Especially when said changes relate to products they already habitually and/or routinely consume.

What's really happening, typically, is that humans simultaneously crave and fear the new. We all know fear, don't we? That's right, fear is the negative emotion that functions like darkrooms in which older consumers develop their negatives. We know, however, that the preceding makes no sense if you don't know that prior to smartphones most photographs were developed through negatives on film. But marketing evolution—new product development—make film negatives largely a thing of the past.

Need proof about humanity's simultaneous longing for but anxiety about the new? Even the faces that most humans deem most attractive, it turns out, are those perceived as most average. Average-sized noses, eyes, chins, and so forth. These human condition make new songs, movies, or books that concurrently are fresh and familiar the sweet sport for entertainment marketers. Relatedly, among fashion marketers, new items that are edgy without appearing crazy-edgy are more likely to succeed. In brief, new products that are "strange" but that don't feel like "strangers."

The "need" for new products to feel simultaneously "fresh and familiar" is likely a primary reason why automobile marketers dramatically change their cars' or trucks' appearances, performance metrics, features, or functionality from one new model year to the next only about once every ten years or so. The fact that an oppressive expenditure of always finite time, talent, and treasure is also necessary to radically re-engineer and then re-design radically new vehicles is also absolutely in play. This combination of factors likewise surely has its say in tamping down the emergence of profoundly new automobile models on a year-by-year basis. But, you know what? Either way, it's all marketing.

The power of this "fresh but familiar" imperative is also likely why the sedans, trucks, or SUVs produced by various automotive marketers today actually look strikingly similar to each other. Our suspicion is that non-automotive aficionados often (but obviously not always) have difficulty telling the make and model of various automobiles—think *Toyota, Nissan, Hyundai, Honda*, for example—apart without first examining the branding symbol affixed to the front or rear of the ride. This condition was not always true, by the way. Automobiles and trucks slowly then suddenly began looking more the same than different as the world first began rapidly shrinking, marketing- and supply-chain wise, during the 1990s.

MORE ENVIRONMENTAL CHANGES; AND OPPORTUNITIES AND THREATS

As is often the case, fine lines can arise that must be managed. Or is it that bridges can pop up that must be crossed or blown up? When developing new products, marketers usually should avoid marketing items or ideas that are too foreign for one segment to understand or too familiar for another segment to care about. Alternatively, new product developers could negate such problems simply by targeting market segments more carefully and effectively.

Yet strategic marketing organizations that plan their work and work their plans have far less reason to feel threatened by change. To the contrary, marketers seeking sustainable marketing success should realize treat resides inside every ThREAT for those who are strategic, smart, and brave enough to find the delight inside managed change.

A great many environmental changes and trends eventually may prove to be marketing opportunities, in disguise. On the other hand, the same environmental changes ultimately may prove to be marketing threats, in disguise. Trends that represent nightmarish threats for some firms may represent gold-plated opportunities for others. In large part, the outcome (i.e., whether environmental trends represent marketing opportunities or threats), depends on the marketers involved and how well-prepared those organizations or individuals are to confront environmental changes.

Marketers generally should continuously scan their environments to keep abreast of, account for, and possibly change their plans to exploit opportunities or avoid/mitigate the threats as either is detected. Such marketers hopefully would discover these environmental opportunities and environmental threats first, and thus respond strategically to them more quickly than their competitors. The method of discovery usually entails marketing research (Module 6).

Environmental threats can emerge from unexpected quarters and in unexpected forms.

Is the *National Football League* (the *NFL)* a service, an entertaining distraction, or an intangible product delivering values that others willingly pay for? The answer is yes, yes, and yes. The *NFL* provides entertainment services and solutions that are valued by some.

Yet the *NFL* as a successful service is experiencing some extreme heat and with the heat, a material decline in its former popularity. In large part because the *NFL*, in its efforts to reposition, rebrand, and redesign the product that is football, and in the process make football the safest violent sport.

Other causes underlying the slump in *NFL* viewership during the 2019–2021 seasons have probably been overdetermined: For one, regular season games tilted toward the bad and therefore boring. The 24/7 *Trump* show on networks has siphoned viewers. Big name stars have retired or been injured. *Colin Kapernick's* initial 2017 anti-flag protests alienated many fans, as did the piggybacking protests issued during the 2017 season by many of his brethren. This alienation was especially pronounced among two segments. First, those already inclined to believe football should be banned. Second, the league's still largely white fan base that tilts rightward toward patriotism.

But the deepest problem and environmental threat to the league's continued popularity isn't emerging from professional football itself. The sport remains a well-branded product. The most-pressing emergent and continuing threat instead is the intersection between the broadcast TV business model that supplies most of its revenue and technologies that have created numerous opportunities for passionate and less passionate fans to consume the service. On-demand services such as *Netflix, Amazon,* and *HBO* also compete with the *NFL* in ways that plain old live television never could: Their shows can be paused and games watched only when they are interesting.

The eternal consumer trade-off question—What do I want to do with my free time?—is being beneficially transformed for fans who regret, post-game, spending nearly four hours watching eleven minutes of action and around one hundred minutes of commercials. Technology offers freedom from this assault on, or abuse of, viewers/customers' always finite time.

It turns out that smartphone screens offer perfectly serviceable communication channels through which to consume roughly ninety seconds of game highlights and not walk away feeling like a sport they love has abused their time. The movement of fans toward fantasy football—once a new but now a well-established and popular product—has fast-forwarded this customer trend. Millions of professional football fan now could care less about a particular team as opposed to caring passionately about how a group of players they selected "to root for" are performing on any given Sunday. (Talk about declines in brand loyalty, which we actually will do, in depth, during Module 11.) According to the *Samford University Sports Business Report*, 70 percent of smartphone owners use the gadgets for sports consumption. No, the *NFL* need not panic. There will still be audiences for full televised games, commercials and all, until those generations of fans get old and actually die off.

When audiences are fragmenting, programing that could pull in large audiences (even if those audiences are shrinking) can still command a high price for its advertising platform. For marketers seeking media homes on which to platform their brand messages targeted primarily at young men, the *NFL* still represents a major media platform. The *NFL* operates as a giant content-producing machine. Professional football as a heavily marketed product provides a constant flow of sports-fan soap opera that sustains dozens of other businesses, including social networking influencers who spend their time bashing or elevating the league. Powerful though it remains, however, the *NFL* is increasingly failing to capture most of the revenue generated by its brand.

Or, consider what is happening inside *Philadelphia*. *Philly*, as locals from the city and region brand it, is both a city and a place long labeled and culturally ridiculed as "*The City of Brotherly Love.*" Sales of sugary soda dropped 38 percent in *Philly* during 2018 after *Philadelphia* imposed a 1.5 cents per ounce tax on the product during 2017 in a ham-handed effort to increase city tax revenues and cut citizen's calorie counts. But sales in neighboring cities increased almost as much as they dropped inside Philly.

Never underestimate a *Nanny State's* desire to impose regulations on consumers' behaviors. Nor should anyone short-sell consumers' willingness to expend extra efforts to overcome negative regulatory effects. Water is hidebound determined to seek out and eventually find the path of least resistance toward the lowest possible location. Many Philadelphians were equally determined to find ways to drink less expensive soda; to find their own path of least resistance. Net neutral sales levels emerged for soda purveyors such as *Coca-Cola, Pepsi-Co,* and the like. Yet things could have turned out much worse. And if the government increasingly imposes its will inside the fast-food and soda worlds, eventually they probably will turn down.

Module 5.1

Key Environmental Trends: A Sampler

Brief stories about several relevant environmental trends follow. As do explanations of the marketing implications associated with each trend. The sole unifying principle known for certain about the following list is that the first five items on the list might differ materially if a similar list were composed three years from now. The sixth trend introduced below appears constant; locked-in.

But for now, there is value in knowing that these trends exist. Value is similarly associated with asking whether these trends, considered individually, represent threats or opportunities; to which sorts of marketing organizations or sectors each represents an opportunity or threat; and why.

Environmental Trend 1: More than one-third of American consumers are obese, slightly more than another third of domestic consumers are overweight but not obese, and, even though this trend is now the norm, being overweight is still not deemed a desirable trait when viewed through most sociocultural lenses. Specifically, *TIME* magazine recently reported that well more than two-thirds of American consumers were overweight or obese.

Is this environmental trend a threat or opportunity, to what types of marketing firms, and why? As you ponder this three-part question you might consider restaurants, gyms, the pharmaceutical industry, the apparel industry, the counseling industry, and on and on . . ..

Environmental Trend 2: Right now, slightly less than half of American adults—a record low—are married. And the median age at first marriage has never been higher for brides (26.5 years) and grooms (28.7)—according to a *Pew Research Center* analysis of the *United States*. These trends have continued unabated—fewer Americans being married, while hitching up at older ages—each year since 2012.

Is this environmental trend a threat or opportunity, to what types of marketing firms, and why? Hint: Envision, perhaps, wedding planners, bakeries, or destination-wedding-site marketers, while not excluding real estate, day care, or refrigerator marketers.

Environmental Trend 3: The percentage of people inside the *United States* who regularly attend a church, mosque, synagogue, or temple is lower than at any point in domestic history and dropping further year by year. Nones—as in "no" religious affiliation is the fastest growing demographic. *Millennials*, in particular, have largely stopped attending religious services and are often exchanging organized faith for greater political agitation. This particular consumer behavior choice is pretty much guaranteed to not deliver greater happiness or peace of mind, or lives chock full of meaningful service. Or not. We'll leave that choice up to you.

Is this environmental trend a threat or opportunity, to what types of marketing firms, and why? Hint: You might think churches and/or golf courses as you respond.

Environmental Trend 4: Between 2000 and 2018 global apparel production more than doubled. During the same period, the average number of times a garment was worn before it was disposed declined by 36 percent in the United States. In *China*, the same percentage was 70 percent.

Is this trend a threat or opportunity, to what types of marketing firms, and why? The consequences associated with this trend are a bit tougher to divine but we would still like to know what *Chinese* symbols mean fast fashion[13] in *Mandarin*.

Apparel is a fascinating product category. Adults, regardless of gender, consciously dress to reveal, conceal, camouflage, accentuate, distract, appeal, or fit-in with/stand-out-from the crowd. What did we write earlier about how many different values a given product can produce dependent primarily on how the item is actually promoted and positioned?

Environmental Trend 5: As discussed, baby-making is experiencing a deep decline inside most developed or so-called *First-World* nations. Domestic marketers of diapers and bottles are feeling the pinch. As are marketers of bubble bath and nursing pads. As also noted earlier, about 31 percent of diapers sold in the *United States* are the adult version. The negative and positive effects of this trend reverberate on and on throughout the entire economy. For example, entire states and cities exist in which sales of adult diapers soon will surpass sales of baby diapers. *Kimberly-Clark*, marketer of *Huggies* brand diapers (nappies, in *Euro*-speak) recently announced it was pulling out of most of *Europe*. The reason is low fertility rates. Worth noting, these low fertility rates are the consequence of other environmental trends that will not be discussed here.

Is this environmental trend a threat or opportunity, to what types of marketing firms, and why?

Environmental Trend 6: This particular trend is an unexpected but empirically verified environmental movement that is materially influencing consumer decision-making and consequently their behaviors and produce choices. This trend also arrives at exactly the same time each calendar year. The highly predictable trend in question is the arrival of the fall season.

---

13. Fast fashion is the term that apparel (clothing and accessory) marketers use to describe inexpensive designs that move quickly from catwalks to stores to address new trends and to satisfy constantly changing consumer wants. This innovative fashion tactic disrupted longstanding traditions whereby new fashion lines were introduced seasonally. Today, fast fashion retailers may introduce new clothing items multiple times during one month to remain "on-trend." The introduction of fast fashion, as a new product development tactic, has radically changed the supply chains for apparel items.

Fall, the season, is actually the real time for making *New Year's Resolutions*; yes, another branded idea! Fall is also the time to get married; 39 percent of weddings occur during this season. Gym memberships soar during September. They are, in fact, 32 percent higher in September than January. Consumers' attention shifts to new topics during the fall season; time spent browsing coupons, educational opportunities, or career options soar during September. Department store and specialty store makeup sales rise 30 percent in September. Grocery store revenues surge as people commit to cook themselves and plan out their meals driven by the goal to get or stay healthier or fitter. Changes in temperatures inspire many to clean out garages and closets and get better organized.

Is this environmental trend a threat or opportunity, to what types of marketing firms, and why?

OWN TRENDS WHEN THEY'RE YOUR FRIENDS

Are you sensing how environmental trends can affect consumers' behavior in predictable, less predictable, and, at times, unknowable ways? And are you now understanding better how and why marketers should make it planning job number one to own-the-trend, when-the-trend-is-their-friend?

Levi Strauss & Co. honored this principle in 1986 by strategically introducing a new sort of men's pants in response to its recognition of an emergent trend in the US marketplace. The men's pants were branded by the now-famous name *Dockers*. Literally bottom line, on men's bottoms at least, *Dockers* strategically split the difference between too-causal and too-dressy, insofar as this appealing intersection related to men's pants.

What trend did *Levi Strauss* coopt as its friend? Managerial researchers of the time had recently discovered and began arguing that workplace productivity materially increased when professional workers could dress more causally. To this point in time male professionals typically labored while clothed in suits and ties. Shortly after these productivity findings were revealed a cultural idea called *Casual Fridays* was born. And as casual Fridays grew more popular *Dockers* arrived right on its heels—and thighs and bottoms.

The rest is men's-pants history. *Dockers* has dominated market share in a casual pants market sector that it alone created ever since. *Dockers*, the brand and its mother company, *Levi Strauss,* won. And to a large degree *Dockers* continues to win, based on the fact the brand honored the Law of Category. If you cannot be-first-to-market, because obviously men's pants existed before *Dockers*, create a category in which you can be first. That's exactly the marketing strategy that *Levi Strauss* developed and followed.

MODULE 5.2

Changes; One Thing Leads to Another

"Ch . . . ch . . . ch . . . *Changes*," as rocker *David Bowie* sang during the 1970s.

The only constant in life, business, marketing, warfare, politics, culture, life, and so forth. Indeed, according to ancient *Greek* philosopher *Heraclitus*, "The only constant is change."

And then came *Elvis*. Who, according to the famous American composer *Leonard Bernstein*, was the greatest American sociocultural-consumption force during the twentieth century. *Elvis* introduced a black rock-blues musical beat to white everything—including music, language patterns and words, dance moves, and clothing styles. In response, a new social revolution emerged that streamed directly from the 1950s to the 1960s. The 1960s, in turn, proved a decade that changed everything else for better and for worse in an unrelenting musical crescendo that continues to this day.

But then, during 2018, *Rap* and *Hip-Hop*, as a musical genre and brand, began selling more albums than any other musical form. What sorts of changes do you think this still-evolving cultural trend will introduce? And do you believe those changes will break better or worse for marketers, and why?

"EVERYONE SHOULD WEAR SUNSCREEN"

As weird as the video *Everyone Should Wear Sunscreen* may initially appear, few readers will regret watching it. (*YouTube* the video all the way through, perhaps a couple of times.) The video is short, funny, and useful. No one will regret watching. A point arrives late in the video where the narrator intones, with extreme seriousness, presumably because he knows he's right and offering great advice: "Do . . . Not . . . Read . . . Beauty . . . Magazines, They . . . Will . . . Only . . . Make . . . You . . . Feel . . . Ugly."

The section's explanation of how and why one thing leads to another—that is, how one environmental trend leads to another and still other trends, with each possibly producing resounding strategic marketing implications—follows from the specific video admonition. But before we go there, consider one additional question.

- ▶ If you are an American-born woman, has your perspective about the appropriateness of your body weight been distorted by marketers and their practices?

Readers should not actually answer this question, because the following discussion indirectly answers it for them.

Meanwhile[14]—

- ▶ The average American woman is 5'5" tall and weighs 163 pounds.
- ▶ The average American female model is 5'11" tall and weighs 117 pounds.
- ▶ Most fashion models are thinner than 98 percent of American women.
- ▶ Four out of five American women say they're dissatisfied with the way they look.
- ▶ On any given day, almost half of the women in the United States are dieting.

That this is interesting information is granted. But what really matters in the context of this environmental scanning discussion is that:

- ▶ The average 5'10" tall American man weighs 197 pounds. Yes, he's statistically overweight on a body mass index metric, as well; but is likely far less concerned about that condition.
- ▶ He is also far less than likely than she to graduate from college, for what that's worth.

The fact that average American males are far less likely than their average American female counterparts to graduate from college represents an environmental trend that is worth a tremendous amount. And this is where this story about the current American cultural environment really takes wings. Yes, but, what does this story have to do with the relationship between environmental scanning, revealed environmental trends, and strategic marketing planning?

The failure of contemporary men to complete college at rates similar to modern women is playing out as a still-rising unbalanced sex ratio that increasingly is influencing consumer behavior decision-making—and the general marketing environment. Consumer behavior decision-making has been fundamentally influenced by this trend because comparatively fewer numbers of marriageable men are available to get hitched to comparatively larger numbers of marriageable women.

The presence of this imbalanced ratio, first, makes financially successful and secure or otherwise attractive men more cad-like and less reliable as dating or marital prospects. The presence of this imbalanced ratio, second, makes women more likely to place less faith in men and invest more heavily in themselves. Marketing opportunities and threats consequently abound for firms and products that primarily target women—or men. Each environmental opportunity or threat emerges directly from this one environmental trend.

Many American men have lost serious economic ground, making them less marriageable. Yes, most of these men have lost serious economic ground largely due to their comparative lack of education. College-educated women, by contrast, live in social worlds where the proportions of marriageable men to marriageable women are more equivalent, because the men that these college-educated women

---

14. Sourced from the aforementioned *The Economist;* a prestigious *British* business and economics publication. So are the male statistics that follow.

encounter in their meat markets typically enjoy more stable and higher incomes and typically embrace more egalitarian views of child care and housework. Why care about this? Not simply because as marriage goes also go notions and principles of what constitutes the right size and role of government and the structure of families themselves. Myriad marketing threats and opportunities arise, yet again.

Being married settles down most men. When men fail to marry, they are more likely to fail to settle down too. Yes, marketing-related opportunities and threats each arise as a consequence. Women routinely avoid marrying men who make less money than them or who hail from or currently occupy a lower socioeconomic status. Men, not so much. They'll chase pretty; we're just reporting nature here . . . The *Welsh* culture (from *Wales*, along with *England, Scotland,* and *Ireland*, one of the four major national subsets that comprise *Great Britain*) has a Medieval-era saying that applies to these contemporary marketing processes: "Trech wyneb teg da gwaddol." Translated, into *English*, "Better a fair face than a fair dowry."

These environmental assertions are not propaganda. They're social scientific, cultural, and economic facts. Facts that often cause socioeconomic problems, because traditional nuclear family units exist as building blocks for lists of desirable outcomes too lengthy to express here.

Marriage has become more aspirational than a realistic option for many people populating the lower social classes. For now, however, marriage still remains an expected and realistic outcome, a reasonable aspirational goal, only inside the lives of economically better-off upper or middle social class consumers.

Then there is the fascinating point of inflection at which the medium age of first childbirth became lower than the medium age of first marriage. This environmental trend also merits consideration. When this sort of trend emerges you know the norms, values, and beliefs about what is acceptable or unacceptable in society have also changed. The society in which any firm competes as a marketer is part of that marketer's environment. Environmental threats or opportunities again are in play for various marketing organizations.

The net effect of this single environmental trend (i.e., American men graduating from college at materially lower rates than domestic women) is that marriage is openly retreating. During 2000, married twenty-five-to-thirty-four-year-olds outnumbered their unmarried counterparts by 55 to 34 percent. By 2016, this ratio had flipped. Young Americans have become wary of marriage. One purely marketing-related reason derives from the fact that sex has become increasingly inexpensive for men. Compared to the past, the latest social science findings suggest that many contemporary women expect little in return from sex. Little in terms of time, attention, commitment, or fidelity from their erstwhile partners. Men, in turn, are logically and self-interestedly less inclined to provide these goods or values in exchange for sexual pleasure—not with internet sex (a cultural, societal, and technological trend) also easily available as a viable, ever-compliant alternative [another environmental trend]). Video porn stars, even the amateur variety, never say "no." Marketers have created "markets" in which virtual women often represent product substitutes for the real thing for many men—by solving/satisfying their innately-driven needs for sexual release.

These environmental trends are bolstered by women's increasing economic independence as their educational accomplishments continue to outstrip men's accomplishments by wider and wider margins while the risk of pregnancy declined. *The Pill* was and remains, first and foremost, a marketing solution to a universal human problem [need]. The problem, of course, was unwanted pregnancies. So we circle back again to where we began. The social and personal costs that once were potentially or actually associated with having or not having regular human sex inside or outside the bounds of marriage have radically diminished—changed! Yes, yes, yes; environmental opportunities and threats for marketers abound.

All this has left, as well as made, too many unmarried—unmoored—American men too aimless, too addicted, too angry, and too alone. Ironically, this problem is not that difficult to resolve, not from marketers' perspectives. Myriad marketers are only too happy to provide video-gaming, video gambling, great TV and *YouTube* entertainment choices, internet porn, and pharmaceutical "solutions" that are so addictive, so alluring, that many American men forget all those other problems for hours if not days at a time.[15]

Yes, here we are obviously referencing opiates. But hey, that's marketing, too—this is a purposefully evocative statement that unfortunately is also 100 percent accurate.

---

15. Beth Macy, *Dopesick: Dealers, Doctors, and the Drug Company that Addicted America* (New York: Harper Collins, 2018).

FIGURE 5.1
Macroenvironments can dramatically affect the firm's operations.

TABLE 5.1
Major Legislative Actions Affecting US Businesses

Legislative Action	Description
1890 Sherman Antitrust Act	Prohibits the formation of monopolies and other actions that effectively restrain trade and interfere with competition in markets.
1906 Food and Drug Act	Formed the Federal Drug Administration and gave it the power to regulate the sale of adulterated food products and poisonous patent medicines. Set requirements for accurately labeling such products. Outlawed the sale of products that were unsafe or ineffective.
1914 Clayton Act	Enhanced the Sherman Antitrust Act by setting more stringent prohibitions against price discrimination, exclusive dealing, and the use of tying contracts.
1914 Federal Trade Commission Act	Established the Federal Trade Commission (FTC), which oversees interactions between businesses, to ensure fairness. Authorized to issue "cease and desist" orders to curb unfair trade practices related to advertising and pricing.
1936 Robinson-Patman Act	Supplements the Clayton Act to strengthen prohibitions against price discrimination. Allows FTC to restrict the use of certain discounts and allowances unless they are offered on a proportionate basis to buyers.
1938 Wheeler-Lea Act	Empowered the FTC to regulate the advertising of food and drugs. Declared all misleading, unfair, or deceptive practices to be illegal, regardless of injury to competition. Primarily intended to apply to false and misleading advertising.
1946 Lanham Trademark Act	Protects brand names, trademarks, and service marks.
1966 Fair Packaging and Labeling Act	Dictates how consumer product packages are to be labeled with respect to contents and producer.
1972 Consumer Product Safety Act	Established the Consumer Products Safety Commission, which is tasked with setting and enforcing safety standards for consumer products.
1991 Americans With Disabilities Act	Established that it is illegal for organizations to discriminate against anyone with disabilities with respect to public transportation, accommodations, and telecommunications.

MODULE 6

Research

MODULE 6.0

From Raw Insights to Strategic Actions

From the point where the nearly 206-mile-wide *Amazon River* enters the *Atlantic Ocean* it extends generally westward for 3,977 miles through *South America* up toward its *Peruvian Andes Mountains*-based source. The river flows continuously and powerfully like earth's mightiest supply chain. Small wonder indeed that the prescient, ambitious, and willing-to-play-the-long-game entrepreneur *Jeff Bezos* branded his start-up venture, *Amazon*. *Amazon*, the internet giant, began as an online bookstore based in Bellevue, *Washington*, during 1994.

The *Amazon River* flows through untouched rain-forested regions for thousands of miles. Because highly porous limestone proliferates underneath these rain forests, river water routinely, albeit slowly, leaches through the stone and travels deep underneath the earth. Hundreds of huge underground pools have formed miles below the rivers' surface. Across thousands of years tiny sightless transparent fish somehow migrated to and evolved inside these pools. These fish have never experienced the sun or the surface. No human has ever seen these fish but scientists somehow know they exist.

These blindly ignorant fish care more about the topic of marketing research than most undergraduate students. This state of affairs is truly unfortunate; because marketing research is an important topic that all businesspeople should not just care about but understand. Just like marketing research itself is an important activity that all senior and mid-level marketing managers should pursue. Those managers should understand certain core concepts about how to execute marketing research because the process generates environmental, competitive, and customer insights and ultimately the types of strategic and tactical knowledge that inform both the development and the execution of the planning and marketing mix management processes introduced above.

THE SOURCE OF …

Readers may recall a sentence that asked, "Where do all these insights about environmental trends originate?" The answer was marketing research. Marketing research-based information and insights are fundamentally important because marketers cannot become successful or remain successful unless they can make accurate current bets about future human behaviors. Indeed, marketers who know the future even a little better than their competitors and are willing to plan and execute their segmentation, targeting, and positioning efforts based on what they know typically would have a hard time losing. Of course, the preceding statement must be accompanied by a disclaimer: No individual marketer could ever fully know the future.

When marketing research initiatives are successfully executed new and presumably more accurate insights into futures are generated. These "future insights" are the core values—or solutions—that marketing research efforts produce.

TOUGH SLEDDING, NONETHELESS

No reason exists to get ahead of our skis, however. Because even when marketing research is successfully conducted, organizational or individuals' futures remain far from completely knowable. Making accurate predictions is a notoriously difficult task. Especially when those predictions are about the future.

Future human behaviors are especially tough to predict. Largely because the same choices that appear utterly rational to one group of decision-makers might strike another group of decision-makers as completely irrational. B2C and B2B customers alike generally believe what they are going to believe—and, often, even compelling contravening facts will not stop them. Marketing researchers have likewise long understood that what people say they want to do or buy and what they actually end up doing or buying are often markedly different things. These sorts of consumer misrepresentations—often, their outright lies—should always be accounted for by experts as they conduct marketing research.

CONVERTING INFORMATION INTO KNOWLEDGE

The marketing research process initially generates information. But hopefully, those same marketing research processes eventually produce specific informational insights that can be transformed into actionable knowledge. Actionable marketing knowledge, the sort that can be employed as strategic plans are developed, executed, and typically revised, represents the "magic potion" that effective marketing research efforts can generate.

The right sort of knowledge can be leveraged by strategic marketing planners to earn sustainable competitive advantages. As noted, three fundamental core competencies exist through which SCAs and the sort of determinant[1] differentiation that promotes sustainable and desirable market positions

---

1. The word determinant has come up before. But the term merits further consideration now that the word determinant will continue to arise again and again. "Determinant" is that important. While applied inside marketing "determinant" means a branding "difference" itself is "important" to customers as they make their choices from among a number of brands competing inside the same product category. For determinant differences to exist, two conditions must exist. First, actual or perceptual differences must exist between one or more that distinguish one from the other(s). Second, these brand differences must be important to customers as they decide—determine—which brand to purchase. The need to create and sustain determinant differences will never not be important.

can be achieved. As you by now should absolutely understand, marketers can achieve differentiation by creating:

- Customer-Intimacy—To achieve customer-intimacy marketing organizations must know more about their prospects and customers than their competitors know about their prospects and customers. Marketing research can create their knowledge.
- Technological-Leadership—To earn technological advantages firms should know more about what customers want or need in the technological realm, and then, once armed with this knowledge, actually develop the capability to deliver exactly what customers want or need, technologically-speaking. Marketing research can produce those insights.
- Cost-Based Advantages—To achieve cost-based advantages, organizations must either possess resource-based advantages, technological-based advantages (sometimes the sources of technological advantages are patent protected), supply chain partnership-based advantages, or economy of scale based-advantages (EOS) that allow those firms to lower their associated costs of doing business. Supply chain-based advantages, in particular, derive from EOS-based advantages that two or more firms can reap when they partner efficiently with each other. When leveraging EOS cost-based advantages, firms may elect to lower their prices in order to gain market share advantages. Or, the same marketers may opt to price at levels that approximate their competitors' prices and as a consequence reap much higher profit margins than their competitors can secure. Two trade-offs are typically in play. First, higher prices generally decrease or at least threaten the market share "owned" by firms that have raised prices. However, those marketers' profit margins increase. Second, lower prices generally permit firms to more easily protect market share. But the profitability of those marketers decreases. Marketing research should remain in play and have a say as all of these processes play out.

WHY WINNERS WIN

Marketing organizations that acquire superior environmental knowledge from successful marketing research efforts, that possess superior or merely adequate resources, and that act strategically while remaining grounded in an appropriate balance of action and thought usually win their marketing competitions. A formula worth remembering and applying when possible at organizational and individual levels:

- Better marketing information/knowledge = better marketing decision-making = better marketing performance.

Ancient historical military, political, and business precedents exist to support this exact point. For example, in his circa 500 BC book, *The Art of War*, Sun Tzu wrote that military leaders should:

- Know Themselves—In marketing planning contexts, this would entail knowing your organization and its strengths and weaknesses; . . . and even if this is all you know, you will win some of the time.[2]

- Know Their Enemy—In marketing contexts, this would entail knowing your competitors' strengths and weaknesses; . . . and again, if this is all you know, you will win some of the time.

- Know Their Terrain—In marketing contexts, this would entail knowing your organization's external environment and opportunities, threats, and unsatisfied customer needs embedded therein. . . . And, again, if this is all you know, you will win some of the time.

As far as increasing the prospect of winning all the time goes, the marketing solution is simple. Acquire all three relevant sets of knowledge; yes, by successfully executing marketing research, and then you or your firm will discover that losing proves more difficult. The ability and willingness to collect the proper information about your marketing organization (related to its strengths and weaknesses), your firm's enemies (competitors' strengths and weaknesses), and the terrain in which your marketing organization must compete (surrounding market and environment conditions) is indisputably a source of pure military or marketing power. Principles that once applied and still apply to strategic military leaders surely still apply to strategic marketing leaders as well.

Writing approximately 2,500 years after *Sun Tzu*, the famous *American* marketer *PT Barnum* echoed these first two points. Mr. Barnum wrote: "Possession of a perfect knowledge of your business and customer is an absolute necessity in order to insure success."[3] The advice appears timeless and universally appropriate and speaks directly to the prospective power of marketing research-based information, insights, and knowledge.

Sometimes people can win by losing. This is true of weight, for instance. Sometimes people can win by quitting. This is true of bad habits. But few to no people have ever won, benefitted, from ignoring, missing, or losing out on opportunities to secure additional accurate and relevant information about themselves, their enemies, and their relevant surroundings.

INFORMATION IS POWER

What is the number one sign of heart disease inside the *United States*? Easy answer here. That's right, the answer is death.

The takeaway, of course, is that it pays for consumers to know and to understand what is happening around as well as inside themselves. Pays off big-time by extending those consumers' lifespans, an outcome that most consumers covet. Sounds like not just practicing marketers, but everybody, should

---

2. The following information-share is purely coincidental and was partially shared above. That does not detract from the significance and irony of the point. During approximately the same historical time frame in which *Sun Tzu* wrote *The Art of War* (which emphasized *"Knowing Yourself"*) a famous maxim was inscribed over one entrance to the *Temple of Apollo* in the city of *Delphi* in the nation of *Greece*. The words, stated completely, were: "Know thyself." Only one point is certain: *Sun Tzu* and the denizens of *Delphi* did not know each other. Yet each reached the same profound conclusion at about the same time.

3. F. R. Shapiro, *The Yale Book of Quotations* (New Haven: Yale University Press, 2006).

prepare, plan, and pursue whatever measures are necessary and appropriate to ensure that the proper information is always close at hand when the related insights are needed to make decisions about how to exploit opportunities or avoid/mitigate threats. Realistically, however, information rarely becomes a source of power, practical utility, and success—or for that matter, a source of life or death information—unless it is converted into actionable knowledge.

This is why, for example, politicians consistently focus group-test different ways of discussing issues or staking-out various positions before adding one or another idea[4] to their stump speeches or talking points. All presidents, or rather their marketing communication team [including speech writers], do this before they deliver new speeches. *Democrat* and *Republican* marketers focus-group almost every word or idea they say before communicating them publicly through marketing promotions to different targeted customer voter segments.

Democrat and *Republican* politicians have traditionally said different things to different groups, or voter segments, depending on the specific like and dislikes; attitudes and biases; wants, needs, and most pressing (perceived or actual) problems that characterize those voting segments. (This is harder to do during an era where every utterance is videoed.) These strategic behaviors represent nothing more or less than targeting their marketing mixes to specific target segments (audiences). Politics is marketing, involving the art of marketing the possible and new political ideas.

Yet strategic marketing planners and doers typically don't actually need more information. Instead, they generally need better information; the sort that can be converted into actionable strategic or tactical knowledge.

One may logically conclude, then, that marketing information is important. Yet despite the widespread recognition of this fact, marketing strategists often lack either the right sort of marketing research information or have too much of the wrong sort of information. They lack the proper type of knowledge to make the sorts of quick decisions required to succeed inside today's highly-competitive and hyper-dynamic globalized markets.

Focus Groups, as a Source of Information

Marketing focus groups usually consist of small groups of deliberately selected people who participate in planned question-prompted discussions. Small groups, here, means from nine to twelve focus group participants. Focus group memberships should be handpicked to ensure that the constituency accurately "represents" the larger "population" being researched. Focus group discussions are designed and executed to secure consumer perceptions about particular topics or area of interest in non-threatening and receptive environments.

Focus groups are purposefully small. Their smaller sizes facilitate shared focus group experiences that permit customer attitudes and opinions first to be revealed and shared more easily, and ultimately allowed to build-out one upon another as one new insight or idea after another is uncovered and then builds upon another and another—as the process continues in an organic fashion. Focus groups are designed and managed in ways that allow members of targeted segments to interact and influence

---

4. Ideas are the primary products (i.e., values and solutions) marketed by politicians. Yet politicians also market their own personae and personalities as products, dependent on whatever branded version of themselves they are acting out during a particular event or on a particular day as they speak with different targeted audiences of customers—okay, constituents and/or voters. Everything is marketing, after all, echoing a point previously made.

each other during their mutual—or shared—discussion and consideration of ideas and perspectives. The focus group process materially differs from personal interviews, which consist of one-on-one engagements in which one marketing researcher asks a series of planned questions to one respondent at a time.

RESEARCH-GENERATED KNOWLEDGE

No surprise here, but it turns out that knowledge rather than information is the true operant[5] resource for marketers, especially when marketers already sufficiently possess sufficient quantities of talent and treasure. When marketers possess useful and actionable knowledge the strategic insights that they can glean from it should guide marketing strategists as they create, execute, and eventually revise plans. The phrase "eventually revise their plans" follows from the fact that no plan ever works out exactly as planned.

Marketing knowledge likewise operates as the foundation for competitive advantage [at individual or organization levels] and for economic growth at micro [individual organizations] or macro [entire economy/market] levels.

Marketing research efforts can generate two types of knowledge.

First, descriptive knowledge is produced. This means the insights generated through marketing research describe changing trends—say, changing customer likes or dislikes; or economic surges and declines. Such trends might represent either environmental threats or opportunities for the marketing organization conducting the research. Descriptive knowledge essentially diagnoses and explains what is going right or wrong, and why.

Second, prescriptive knowledge is produced. Prescriptive knowledge informs marketers about what they should do, basically by providing prescriptive insights that identify and suggest logical next strategic steps that should either be considered or actually pursued. Answers to questions such as what marketers should do, say, to solve customer problems more effectively; to secure superior gains and benefits from environmental opportunities; or to avoid disastrous losses from environmental threats are often revealed through prescriptive insights.

Descriptive—or diagnostic—information must come first . . . always. No marketing decision-maker can reasonably or righteously be expected to develop, make, or offer prescriptive recommendations until they have developed diagnostic insights.

MARKETING INFORMATION SYSTEMS (MIS)

Most strategic firms implement marketing information systems or MIS. The implementation of an MIS is usually conducted to address the near-universal need that marketers confront to secure better, not more, information. "Better information" could be described or defined as the sort that can be transformed into descriptive and prescriptive knowledge. But inside marketing circles "better information" can be described and spelt differently: more dollars.

---

5. Operant, the word, means effective, functional, or tending to produce useful results.

Marketing information systems first determine and then acquire exactly the sort of information that marketers need to properly develop and execute strategic marketing plans. Well-designed MIS develop only the exact information actually needed to secure the best strategic solutions. Well-designed MIS also deliver the right type of research knowledge to marketing decision-makers in the right form and at the right time. The right form of knowledge is that which is both understandable and actionable. Rightly timed knowledge is that which exactly when the insights are needed to inform actual marketing decision-making. The net outcome, again . . . is better marketing decisions. Well-designed MIS likewise balance the information that would be nice to have with the information that decision-makers must have and can afford to attain.

Raw information might be secured through internal business sources; external marketing intelligence sources; or through primary and secondary marketing research activities of the sort described in greater detail below.

The entire set of viable strategic marketing alternatives to marketers is always constrained by the finite nature of those marketers' 3Ts. The "entire set of viable strategic marketing alternatives" should be reflected in the two or three strategic goals that marketers should or should not—or can or cannot—reasonably pursue.

The missions of marketing organizations also play a role in determining which alternatives are more or less viable—or appropriate.

As noted, any organization's strategic goals must be consistent with its mission.

Consider These Trade-Offs

Trade-offs always arise between the value-adding benefits associated with having an extra chunk of marketing research information available versus the costs associated with acquiring benefit/value. The benefits, or value, secured from the marketing research product minus the costs associated with acquiring the product equals the benefits, or value, of the knowledge. Broader and clearer insights can emerge from deep dives into small details. This statement is true and will forever remain so.

But marketing strategists should not automatically assume the extra costs associated with obtaining extra information is always worth the cost of obtaining it. As always, those extra costs draw down from the finite quantities of organizational time, talent, and/or treasure that are available but that alternatively could have been allocated toward other objectives and tasks.

Beware of These Biases

Marketing researchers, marketing planners, and marketing doers should always remain aware of automation bias. And commit themselves to fall victim to it, because automation bias can prove pernicious. When working with technology, experts, including marketing strategists, often experience complacency about the myriad technological tools that they routinely use. This complacency leads decision-makers to assume, automatically, that everything is operating or being operated as it should—and is producing reliable, valid, and useful environmental, customer, or competitor insights. Confident that their machines will work flawlessly and handle any problem that crops up, attention drifts, mistakes happen—and are often detected too far down the road to do much good.

Automation bias occurs when experts place too much faith in the accuracy of information provided by machines, and have been lured into a false sense of security. This trust becomes so strong that they ignore or discount the value of other sources of research-based marketing information, including their eyes and ears. Not a good idea. Automation bias will likely degrade marketing research performance. Automation bias engenders unforced errors related to omission and/or commission.

REAL-WORLD ILLUSTRATION

Subaru is a *Japanese* automobile marketer. During 2005, as a result of marketing research, *Subaru* unexpectedly learned that its 4-wheel drive brand enjoyed great acceptance within the American lesbian community. This information arrived as a delightful surprise—*Subaru* had never specifically targeted this market segment.

Seeing and seizing upon a strategic environmental opportunity, *Subaru* quickly began to specifically target the lesbian automobile buyer segment by re-positioning its 4-wheel drive SBU brand. A two-pronged targeting and repositioning strategy was initiated. First, *Subaru* began sliding insider jokes into its advertisement's promotional stories. Specifically, *Subaru* used dog-whistle phrases in their advertisements. Essentially the marketer was using subtle positioning phrases or words that mostly only *LGBTQ* community memberships would have understood or even noticed during this "non-woke," still often closeted, era. Second, the Japanese automobile marketer hired *Martina Navratilova*[6] as a celebrity spokesperson and brand endorser.

Dog whistle marketing messaging entails using coded words that have one meaning or perhaps no meaning for the general population but feature other far more impactful meanings for members of targeted audiences. Those targeted segments are often minority or woke populations. In the current cultural vernacular the word "woke" means being alert—possibly overly alert at times—to the presence of perceived or actual societal injustices.

The knowledge and prescriptive insights that emerged from marketing research allowed *Subaru* to manage a renewed marketing mix in ways that permitted the 4 wheel drive brand to earn a more desirable market position, a state of determinant differentiation, and ample competitive advantages that proved sustainable inside the lesbian target market.

A cultural adage suggests "people never see the same river twice." This particular chunk of conventional wisdom is accompanied by the additional benefit of being true and useful. People never see the same river twice because all streams constantly change.

Marketers such as *Subaru* likely realized this and surely continue to understand that they must constantly monitor and track these constantly changing rivers driven by the goal to lead and stay current with their changes. Marketing research is required, and should be used, to continuously monitor such environmental trends.

---

6. Martina (she typically went by her first name), at the time, had only recently retired as the world's greatest female tennis player but had long since positioned herself favorably as a cultural folk hero by outing and branding herself as a proud lesbian. Ms. Navratilova quickly acquired near-iconic status in certain demographic strata based on her willingness to stand-up and to stand-out by willingly making her public proclamation. Ms. Navratilova outed herself decades before outing oneself was no longer a newsworthy event. Standing-out rather than fitting-in often proves critical to marketing success—as has already been shown.

MODULE 6.1

The Marketing Research Process

Former Presidential advisor *Ben Rhodes* wrote that President *Barack Obama* used to tell him that the primary role of the President—as Marketer-in-Chief—"was to tell the best possible story about who we are as a country."[7] Makes sense, because whoever tells the best story usually wins, across many contexts. Appealing narratives—the best stories—can exert the sort of powerful gravitational pull that winds up bending "facts" in the directions of the brands that tell them.

This premise applies as much to traditional marketers as it does to politicians, lawyers, or as non-traditional marketers. But then again, the premise should apply because politicians, lawyers, and novelists are not only products themselves, they are also routinely engaged in marketing activities (often marketing themselves as human [professional] brands, of course). The branding narratives or stories that brands tell really matter. Including your own brand. The strategies that marketers develop and execute leading up to and justifying the story matter too. Compelling brand narratives never emerge whole cloth from nothing. The strategies that marketers develop and execute after the brand's first stories are told, and hopefully eventually become well-known, matter greatly as well.

The difference for most traditional marketers, however, is that as they construct and tell their stories they must take data-based facts as they exist rather than inventing facts in the ways that political, legal, or novel-writing marketers often appear to do. Marketers should develop and execute their branding strategies and the stories those strategies produce based on factual knowledge, the sort presumably gleaned from strategic marketing research efforts.

MARKETING RESEARCH IS DESCRIPTIVE

Marketing research processes are analytical, fact-based (empirical), and data-driven. Or should be. The marketing research process involves collecting and analyzing information relevant to a specific marketing problem or opportunity/threat facing the marketer that is conducting the research. Marketers and marketing researchers should never attempt to identify solutions to problems or create

---

7. Ben Rhodes, "America's Story Must Win Out," *TIME Magazine* (July 7, 2018): 35.

strategies to exploit opportunities until after the underlying causal factors that are creating problems or opportunities/threats are comparatively well-understood. Note the use of the word "comparative." Marketers and marketing researchers often encounter situations where they could not possibly completely understand the full nature of the underlying causes of problems, opportunities, or threats that they or their organizations are confronting.

Insights generated through marketing research links customers/prospects to marketers through information that has been collected and analyzed. Information that ideally proves transformable into operant knowledge. This information is typically used to identify and define marketing problems or opportunities/threats. Once those problems and opportunities/threats are identified and defined the resulting knowledge is then used to generate, refine, and evaluate marketing mix activities. This knowledge is used to improve marketing as a functional process inside any organization that engages in marketing research.

Marketing Research Uses Secondary and/or Primary Data

Marketing research can be executed using either secondary or primary data. Data is analyst-speak for information. Secondary information is information that already exists because it was previously collected for other purposes. Perhaps the secondary data was gathered through accounting or sales-tracking metrics.

Secondary data, for example, could include in-bound pricing and out-bound pricing information collected by *U-Haul* or *Ryder* as either organization rents trucks to customers who are moving household items from one location to another. Out-bound pricing as in the premium prices that high state income tax and real estate cost states such as *New York* or *Illinois* charge to consumers moving to no property tax and lower real estate cost states such as *Florida* or *Texas*. The prices charged to customers moving out of the two blue states into either of the two red states during 2020–21 were around ten times higher than the prices charged to people moving from the blue states to either of the red states. That's because northbound demand was so much lower while the supply of trucks remained the same. These factoids illustrate the power of supply and demand and the effect that either economic factor exercises on pricing levels. But this discussion is about marketing research. When researching where a national brand such as *Planet Fitness* should open up its next franchise, a decision to borrow or just read about secondary data collected by *U-Haul* would surely make sense as *Planet Fitness* or any other expanding franchising system generally benefits from tracking population trends—and going to where larger numbers of consumers are going.

Turning toward another deeper take on the marketing strategy executed by *Planet Fitness*. The national exercise and fitness franchising giant likely examined other sources of secondary data while crafting its targeting and positioning strategies. The positioning statement of *Planet Fitness* is simple, elegant, powerful, effective, and was clearly carefully chosen and crafted. The *Planet Fitness* positioning statement is: "You Belong!" The statement and every other promotional message associated with it is targeted toward the growing numbers of heavier American consumers—as discussed during Module 5—who usually would prefer to be lighter and fitter and who are willing to work to get there but who often feel uncomfortable not only joining but actually routinely exercising inside other nationally franchised gyms such as *LA Fitness*.

For better or for worse, and by contrast, *LA Fitness* "clubs" are recognized, positioned, as a local "meet (meat) markets" in most of their 750+ US locations. The core brand identity of *LA Fitness* gyms is they exist as sort of a tangible *Match.com* site with heavy weights, sexy ladies, and studly dudes (yes, we know women can be dudes too) strutting about displaying often enhanced versions of what their maker endowed to them. Please don't shoot the messengers, the previous sentence accurately summarizes the primary targeting and positioning strategies that *LA Fitness* pursues and employs effectively.

Secondary information is much easier to collect than primary information. That's nice. But the downside is that secondary data often only tangentially addresses the actual problems that marketing research processes are intended to address. Internet databases and internet data sources, as sources of secondary information, are becoming more important inside marketing research processes. Indeed, easy access to the behaviors of consumers on social networking sites—thank you *Facebook* or *Google*—is replacing the need for certain sorts of classic marketing research. But everything that marketing planners possibly might need is rarely available online. Consequently, the need to conduct primary research often arises.

Primary information is new or original information. Primary information never exists before the research processes used to generate it were conducted. As a reminder, primary information is developed, collected, refined, and analyzed by marketing researchers in order to identify or address particular marketing problems or opportunities. Secondary information costs far less to collect than primary information. Information or data collection processes themselves require substantial expertise. Relatedly, primary information is far more likely to yield insights that actually solve problems or identify new opportunities.

Marketing Research Depends on Data-Gathering and Data-Analytic Expertise

Marketing researchers must possess the data-gathering expertise to design the right methods for collecting the right sort of information. Marketing researchers also must possess the data analytics types of expertise that will prove necessary to analyze and draw prescriptive recommendations from either the secondary or primary data that they have analyzed. The marketing research process manages and implements data collection and analytical efforts. Then marketing researchers summarize and communicate these findings and the implications and insights associated with them to key decision-makers inside the organization that has conducted the marketing research.

Despite these detailed findings of marketing research processes, marketing researchers would do well first to remember and then to leverage, when possible, information available from one other source. *Steve Jobs* best described this source when he said, "Your most unhappy customers are your best sources of learning (marketing information)." *Jobs* went on: "Especially given that these days your unhappy customers don't just moan; they go online and actively complain before potentially millions of eyes." Researchers and various other marketers should always tap into negative customer views, opinions, and/or experiences as another useful means to secure valuable marketing knowledge.

MARKETING RESEARCH IS DIAGNOSTIC AND PRESCRIPTIVE: IT DESCRIBES AND PRESCRIBES

Marketing research is usually conducted for two primary purposes. The two purposes are related to one another. The first purpose is to diagnose and describe marketing problems or environmental opportunities or threats more accurately. When this happens, propositional knowledge has been developed.

The second purpose of marketing research is to develop effective prescriptive inferences regarding how marketing organizations should strategically address problems or opportunities through informed management of their marketing mixes—after those problems or opportunities have been defined and refined through marketing research activities. When this happens, prescriptive knowledge has been created. Marketing research should lead to prescriptive recommendations related to the goals and segmentation, targeting, and marketing mix management activities that strategic marketing organizations are doing now and will be executing in the future.

These two purposes combine in ways that make marketing research processes similar to what happens when people make appointments with doctors in order to secure treatments for health-care problems. Typically, when consumers visit doctors' offices, nurses or doctors ask questions and/or subject patients to tests in order to diagnose their problem and its causes—basically trying to clearly distinguish the symptoms of a patient's problem (a raging fever) from the core cause of the problem itself (a bad bacterial infection). Accurately identifying the causes rather than the symptoms of either medical or marketing problems often takes time, patience, introspection, expertise, and a slew of asked and answered questions.

These medical marketers are developing diagnostic and propositional knowledge. Doctors then use the new diagnostic information (knowledge) about the current problem to make prescriptions, to tell patients what they should do (exercise more, lose weight), take (pills), or experience (surgery) to solve the problem. Doctors dispense prescriptive counsel, based on the descriptive or diagnostic knowledge they already possessed and have developed through their interactions with you, the customer—and patient.

Prescriptive Research Is Based on Statistically Based (Probability-Based) Assessments

Prescriptive marketing research knowledge is typically generated through statistical analysis. Their use of statistics implies that marketing researchers must collect information, usually in raw data form, from representative consumer or organizational samples. Representative samples, and sampled information drawn from them, supposedly accurately represent (or capture) the attitudes, opinions, preferences, or behaviors of an entire population of interest. A population of interest might include every American who has ever purchased any sort of classical music. A representative sample is best understood as a small quantity of something (say, a carefully selected group of people) that accurately reflects the larger entity (say, the entire population of interest). Stated differently, representative samples exist when small numbers of people accurately reflect the entire membership of larger populations.

Various research questions are asked to representative samples. Or, various marketing research experiments are conducted on representative samples. In a class featuring 300 students, in which half the students are male and half are female, a representative sample might include eight students: four males, four females.

Still, any marketer who puts excessive stock on probability-based inferences drawn from even supposedly representative samples should often pull back on the reins a bit. Ever heard the adage about a murder defendant's life being in the hands of twelve people who were not smart or motivated enough to get out of jury duty? Well, all readers have heard it now.

Now consider that for the time being, most political polls are comprised primarily of responses from consumers not smart enough or insufficiently motivated to screen their calls. Tell us how representative these samples are? We hope you realize the answer is not very.

Marketing research processes are typically driven by statistical analyses, purposefully repeating a point made earlier. But statistical analyses themselves permit massive amounts of information, or again, raw data, to be compressed into a few meaningful numbers. Ideally, greater efficiency, more accurate predictions (probability-based assessments), and less uncertainty (again, based on probability-based assessments) is generated as a consequence. Therein lies both the value and primary purpose of statistical analysis.

Statistics and probabilities are profoundly important. But statistics and probabilities are not nearly as complicated as many suspect. For example, if you survive your sixties the probability that you'll survive through your seventies profoundly increases. But you fail to make it through your sixties the probability—the likelihood—that you'll survive your seventies diminishes to 0 percent. There, that statistic and that probability were not so difficult to understand, were they?

Statistical Analyses: Simplifying Things

Statistical analyses and probability assessments themselves essentially boil down to developing, managing, and deducing (drawing forth) key strategic insights from a few meaningful numbers. The few meaningful numbers that are typically generated through statistical analysis include the mean, mode, and median, along with the variance—which is also known as range—present in the entire set of numerical responses.

The mean is the average. To generate a mean all relevant numbers are added up and divided by the number of numbers to create a mean. The median is the middle value in the list of numbers.

To find the median, numbers are listed numerically from smallest to largest.

The mode is the number or response that occurs most frequently. If no number in the list is repeated, then no mode exists in the list.

The variance or range of a sample of responses is determined by the difference between the largest and smallest values present inside the entire data set.

The now-deceased comedian *George Carlin* once was a huge celebrity with more than half a brain. George once joked: "Think how stupid the average person is." (That's the mean!) "Then realize that half of all the rest are stupider than that." (In this example the mean is also the medium.) That's exactly how these two key statistical measures work and illustrates how that even statistics can prove funny.

Which should surprise no serious thinkers who typically understand that if one tortures numbers or statistics enough they will confess anything.

Probability assessments allow marketing researchers and strategic planners to make more reasonable decisions in marketing contexts featuring imperfect information and substantial uncertainty. Probability assessments also permit marketing researchers and strategic planners to quantify, measure, and assess the level of risk embedded inside in given strategic marketing decisions. Probability assessments also make it possible for marketing researchers to eliminate much of the uncertainty that marketing planners otherwise would have to manage. This outcome is extremely desirable. Remember uncertainty's nasty nature?

FOUR INFORMATION-DRIVEN MARKETING RESEARCH ACTIVITIES

The marketing research process features four basic activities. First, information-identification activities. Second, information-collection or information-gathering activities. Third, there are information-analytical activities. Fourth, the marketing research process features information-reporting activities. This fourth and final activity entails converting information into understandable and actionable knowledge and typically culminates with the written and oral presentation of key findings to senior level decision-makers inside the marketing organization.

Marketing Research Information Identification

During information-identification activities, marketing researchers ask specific questions. This assortment of questions can only be asked after researchers have created and identified the right questions to ask. These questions are asked in order to gather information that presumably can resolve problems [problems that presumably have been properly defined] or properly address environmental opportunities or threats.

One important question that routinely arises at this point in the research process is "Why?" Specifically, why did this particular problem [or environmental opportunity/threat] arise? "Why" questions should be asked to separate problem symptoms from authentic problem causes. Researchers should keep on asking "Why did this problem arise?" until they conclude that the "why" question can no longer be reasonably answered. When this happens, researchers have arrived at core causes of problems. Marketing research, when properly executed, exposes the roots, or the core causes, of problems.

Marketing researchers should almost always investigate the core causes of problems, rather than their symptoms. When solving problems, researchers should not confuse problems' symptoms with their actual causes. When dealing with actual human illness, for example, excessive body temperatures generally represent symptoms of a problem. Wherein viral infections, in the same context, represent the actual causes of problems.

The cause of a problem, once understood and mitigated or eliminated, can also be the cure insofar as the threatening cause itself can sometimes be removed or avoided. At this point it is no cliché to write: Problems well-defined are problems half-solved. Nor is it ever hyperbolic to suggest that poorly-defined problems can never be fully solved. These are important considerations, insofar as anyone can be absolutely right about the problem and undeniably wrong about the problem's solution. But the probability of developing the wrong solution declines precipitously if and when one gets the problem right. Therein lies another major value associated with the use of marketing research.

Marketing Research Information Gathering/Collecting

Research information that is gathered or collected cannot be converted into actionable knowledge unless it is current and accurate. Information accuracy, in turn, relates to two statistical properties. Information must be reliable and valid before it is deemed accurate.

Reliable information is collected from questions or measurements that are free from systematic or statistical error. An absence of systematic error implies that the respondents, the people who are sampled and answer questions, actually understand what the questions are asking.

Valid information is secured from questions measuring exactly what they're supposed to measure. Valid questions capture no more and no less information than what they purportedly measure.

Marketers cannot develop valid information unless they have first developed reliable measures, or questions.

While these "accuracy" metrics are useful, research information itself remains far from perfectly accurate. The fact that differences exist between what marketers can measure and what those same marketers want or need to know routinely arises as a matter of course. Nothing new to see here, so to speak. That's marketing life, which unfolds in unpredictable gray-shaded worlds.

In the end, information is like mushrooms. There's good information. There's toxic information. There is information that will make you see visions.

Then again, there is also reliable and valid information that helps marketers see the future—not perfectly, but at least with greater clarity. And that's exactly the sort of information that marketing researchers should seek. The ability of strategic managers to distinguish the real from the imaginary and the possible from the impossible increases in lockstep with increases in the reliability and validity of any information gathered through marketing research efforts.

Analyzing Marketing Research Information

Then, during the third set of research activities, marketing researchers statistically analyze information that they have collected. This analysis is conducted to develop strategic, knowledge-based inferences—prescriptive insights—based on problems, threats, or opportunities that have been identified. Strategic inferences, which are based on prescriptive knowledge, are generally developed about one or more of the following issues:

- ▶ Which market segments exist? This marketing research addresses segmentation problems or opportunities.

- Which market segments should this organization target? This research question addresses targeting problems or opportunities.
- How should this organization promote its products? This question addresses communication and promotion problems or opportunities.
- What communication channels or media and what stories should our firm use to communicate key messages to targeted customers/prospects? This question addresses communications and targeting problems or opportunities.
- Where and how should this organization distribute its products? This question addresses distribution, place, or supply chain management-related problems or opportunities.
- What, if any, new products should this organization develop? This question addresses new product development problems or opportunities.
- What aspects, if any, of our existing product portfolio should be changed? This question addresses marketing mix, positioning, and new product development problems or opportunities.
- What current product features/attributes/benefits should be changed, emphasized, or de-emphasized? This question addresses new product development, marketing mix, and positioning problems or opportunities.
- Is this organization positioning effectively? What, if anything, should be changed about the firm's current positioning strategy? This question addresses positioning problems or opportunities.
- At what pricing levels should this organization offer each product in its product portfolio? This question addresses pricing problems or opportunities.
- What unmet or less-than-fully-satisfied wants/needs exist among targeted marketing segments or among segments that our firm could target? This question addresses marketing mix and positioning problems or opportunities.
- Which wants/needs might this organization satisfy better than its competitors? This question addresses marketing mix and positioning problems or opportunities.
- Is this organization satisfying/not satisfying existing customers? This question addresses customer relationship management, segmentation, targeting, or positioning problems or opportunities.
- Is the firm's branding campaign working? This question addresses branding, promotional and targeting problems or opportunities.
- Who are this organization's current competitors? Who are its likely future competitors? What are our primary competitor's strengths and weaknesses? This question addresses strategic planning problems or opportunities.

MODULE 6.2

What Do Marketing Research Analysts Investigate?

Marketing research is conducted to create situations where managers can make better—more fully-informed—bets about the future. "Better bets" and being "more fully informed" go hand in hand. Yes, the same basic point was introduced earlier inside this module but the point being resold here is such a big deal that the idea is repeated twice. (Inside Module 14, you will actually read about the extent to which great communication value is associated with repeating key points up to three times.[8]) Organizations or individuals who can predict the future merely a bit better than their competitors rarely lose. When properly conducted, marketing research facilitates additional and more accurate insights into futures that nonetheless remain far from completely knowable.

This is basic reason why during Old-School Days when the print media still published stock market price quotes, yesterday's newspaper was worthless. But tomorrow's *Wall Street Journal*, received today, and while the stock markets were all still open—that would prove priceless.

Marketing research generally seeks to determine empirical, or fact-based, answers to the following questions:

- ▶ How should markets be segmented?
- ▶ Which segments should be targeted?
- ▶ Which marketing mixes are most likely to succeed? Remember, a different marketing mix, yielding different customer values and solutions, should be developed for each market segment targeted.
- ▶ Which type of product is most likely to be purchased?
- ▶ What price are customers most willing to pay?
- ▶ What positioning story does our current brand transmit? What future positioning messages could our current or future brands transmit?

---

8. The "Three-Hit Rule" is being referenced here.

- ▶ What promotional story will message recipients most likely attend to, like, remember, or be persuaded/motivated by?

But that's not all. Additional marketing issues, ideas, and problems that are typically addressed through marketing research include but are not limited to research related to:

- ▶ Cool-Hunting—Making observations and predictions regarding changes in new or existing cultural trends that will lead to new hot, as in "cool," opportunities.
- ▶ Customer Satisfaction—With our firm's or our competitors' products.
- ▶ Concept-Testing—To determine whether customers tend to like or be inclined to purchase a product based on the new concept or idea.
- ▶ Price Elasticity—To determine how changes in our pricing impact demand for given brands or branded product lines.
- ▶ Test-Markets—Involving small-scale launches of new products.
- ▶ On-Line Panels—Assessing consumer behavior issues and responses to the marketer's current marketing mix or to a marketing mix that could be strategically developed.
- ▶ Positioning—How does the market see the researching marketer's brand relative to other competing or non-competing brands?
- ▶ Brand Equity and Brand Names—each topic is discussed more fully during Module 11.

Finally, marketing researchers generally seek information that can be converted into knowledge and eventually actionable insights related to questions regarding:

- ▶ Competitors—Specifically, what competitors are doing now or likely will do in the future with regard to their marketing strategies (i.e., pricing, distribution, and promotion) as well as new product development.
- ▶ Customers—Specifically, what customers like or dislike, prefer, and desire along their attitudes and unmet wants and needs. The reasons underlying those traits or characteristics are investigated as well. Answering how, how much, when, where, what, and why questions to the extent that answering these questions is possible.
- ▶ Relevant Environmental Trends—Information about what's happening, trend-wise inside the marketplace; primarily information about our strategic friends, namely opportunities and threats.

The marketing research-engendered presence of these sorts of information and knowledge, along with the strategic marketing insights each generates, inevitably facilitate superior plans and greater success.

Module 6.3

Old-School Takes: The Ways Things Once Were

Consumer researchers are experiencing some notably crazy times. The evidence is mounting and increasingly confirming how bad most consumers are at decision-making. The evidence is clear: Many consumers lean heavily toward making impressionable, emotional, and irrational decisions.[9] The passions, hearts, or perhaps the libidos of consumers are obviously sometimes "forcing" them to make choices that their reasons, logic, and heads would never accept—and damn the consequences. Consumers often end up purchasing products or services they don't need, cannot afford, at arbitrary prices; paying with credit card money that they don't have, often for silly if not downright stupid reasons.

Marketers, particularly those well-versed with the latest research, are well aware of these less than rational consumer tendencies and often strategically exploit those tendencies. Retailers of all stripes know that if they play soothing music, "suckers" hang around longer and buy more. Marketers of various types know that if they can make targeted customers happy, they buy more on that basis alone. Would you like a glass of cheap wine while you shop for our overpriced baubles? That'll cheer you up! Consumers actually often believe that price designates the value of products, rather than the other way around—that is, the actual or perceived value of products designating their prices. The value-price relationship should be driven by this "value-driving-prices" proposition.

It's true: Bad decisions often lead to good stories. But the fact is that bad decision-makers had better have good future stories around to substitute for other values that they would have already lost. Our minds—the source-points for all good or bad decisions—can be great assets. Or liabilities. Our choice . . .

Bad decisions, or decision-making, is hardly limited only to consumers. Periods of local, regional, or national market expansion, such as the one the United States experienced between 2016 and 2020, rarely die of old age. Instead, expansions are usually murdered; destroyed by bad fiscal, regulatory, or public policy decisions made and instituted at local, regional, or national levels. Perhaps even bad decisions made in response to the arrival or unexpected environmental threats, such as COVID-19.

Viennese, as in Austrian, psychologist Dr. *Sigmund Freud* contended, more than one hundred years ago, that humans are governed by irrational unconscious urges. Yes, many of his theories have since

---
9. Peter Noel Murray, "How Emotions Influence What We Buy," *Psychology Today* (2014).

been disproven. Yes, cigars usually are just cigars rather than phallic symbols. And no, extremely few men want to have sex with their mothers; his so-called *Oedipal complex*. But even though Sigmund is the one who started human behavioral research, he is not the *Austrian* citizen referenced below.

No, that honor goes to Dr. *Ernest Dichter*, another Viennese psychologist. In his 1960 book, *The Strategy of Desire,* Dichter wrote, "You would be amazed to find how often we mislead ourselves, regardless of how smart we think we are, when we attempt to explain why we are behaving the way we do." Dichter argued, correctly as ensuing decades of research have shown, that consumers' decisions are driven by subliminal[10] whims, desires, and fears, but especially their fears! In this book, he explained, "What people actually spend their money on in most instances are psychological differences [in how they perceive] illusory brand images." Once marketers realized the extent to which B2B decision-making was an emotional minefield, the strategic ones were able to leverage huge success out of their fields of knowledge.

Decades ago, the marketing researcher famously rehabilitated the slumping fortunes of current brand-name organizations such as *DuPont, Procter & Gamble, General Mills, Exxon,* and *Chrysler.* His genuinely manipulative marketing (primarily promotional) strategies radically transformed how hundreds of products were marketed, ranging from cake mixes to cars. He fathered the focus group, a marketing research tool discussed earlier inside this module. Dichter was also first to understand and exploit the power of WOM.

Dichter also pioneered motivation research. During an era inundated with more naïve and less well-informed consumers, his marketing methods killed. So much so that in 1957, *Vance Packard's* book, *The Hidden Persuaders,* described American consumers as "the most manipulated people outside *The Iron Curtain*." What would Mr. Packard have to say today, sixty-plus years on?

To develop actionable marketing research insights into what really motivated consumers' choices, Dichter thought it necessary to get people to discuss their everyday habits and thoughts at length. Rather than subjecting people to lengthy questionnaires that are still often used today, he preferred deep, psychoanalytic approaches with fewer participants. "Let people talk long enough," Dichter proposed, "and you can read between the lines to find out what he really means." Finding out what consumers really meant as well as what really motivated them was a godsend to marketers.

When products are scarce or perceived as such and consumers are consequently happy to buy whatever they get, marketers have little need to understand what makes consumers tick, what turns people off or on, if you will. But during times of prosperity, as typically prevail throughout the *United States,*[11] and supply outstrips demand as countless practically indistinguishable goods are competing for B2C segments' mind-share, marketers must rely on branding, positioning, and promotions to distinguish the value of their brands. The marketing insights he provided were tailor-made for his time and used to flesh out and direct the strategic marketing communication efforts of his client firms.

---

10. Subliminal is equivalent to subconscious, or below the threshold of human awareness.

11. Taking COVID-19 and its consequences out of the picture, these are the good ole days; don't watch so much TV or spend so much time online if you believe otherwise—if you are thinking that these are not the "good ole days." Remember TV and many websites or newspapers or radio networks exist mutually as part of a great-dissatisfaction-creating-complex. Which makes them, beyond question, marketers insofar as they attempt to create at least perceptions of problems and then set about solving them.

DICHTER MINED MINDS

What makes one brand of bath soap sexy? Or makes one brand of soap more interesting than competing soap brands? Notably, "interesting" alone may prove sufficient to move the marketing needle when people are purchasing bath soap.

Dichter launched his American research career by helping Ivory sell soap. Contemporary researchers at the time might have asked shoppers, "Why do you use this brand of soap?" Or asked, more provocatively, "Why don't you purchase this brand of soap?" He disdained this genre of questioning, opting instead to pursue open-ended questions inside in-depth interviews. Somewhat like therapy ("Tell me how do you feel about that"), with Dichter mining the responses to extricate hidden or unconscious consumer motives. This being the 1950s and 60s, the expressed thoughts offered by consumers were far more discrete and demure than is often the case today. But Dichter discovered that bathing afforded rare moments of personal indulgence, particularly before romantic outings—said one bold female, "You never can tell."

Dichter rightly or wrongly ascribed an erotic element to bathing, writing "one of the few occasions when puritanical Americans (in comparison to Europeans at the time) are able to caress themselves is while applying soap?" As to why American consumers choose one and not another brand, Dichter suggested the determinant factor was not the brand's price, smell, look, or feel, but all these things plus the personality—in his native Germanic tongue (*Austrians* speak *German*), the gestalt of the brand.

To understand what the word and concept known as gestalt really means, imagine a circle featuring only ink points. All that exists is a series of dots; lots of holes in-between. But when exposed to those dots people attempt to create a whole by filling in the blank spots inside the circle. That's the *Gestalt*.

These insights represented huge breakthroughs for marketing research. Dichter, the father of modern marketing research, was first to propose that brands have images, even souls, and that brands are not always purchased for the practical functional solutions they provide but for the values and meaning that the brands appear to embody. This was huge. Researchers have since established that possessions of consumers often function as extensions of their own personalities—either what they are or what they aspire to be. He further discovered that brands function as mirrors that reflect consumers' own desired image for themselves. Dichter basically admonished that marketers should figure out the personality of their brand, because they will better understand how to market the brand.

Branded soaps could be young or old, sexy or staid. The researcher dubbed *Ivory* a "somber, utilitarian, thoroughly cleansing tool." The brand *Camay*, by contrast, was deemed a "seductress." Sort of clean and dirty at the same time. These research insights contributed to *Ivory* positioning statements that proclaimed: "Be smart and get a fresh start with Ivory" and "Wash your troubles away." Each positioning statement (branding slogan) proved successful.

Please remain mindful of the time in which Dichter lived, worked, and created—a time that ended six, seven, eight, or more decades ago. Several innovative research ideas that he proposed at the time now appear antiquated, self-evident, and/or outright sexist today. That's because the prevailing cultural and societal norms have changed so radically during the intervening decades. But his then-new and still-useful ideas were certainly not sexist or self-evident back in his day.

The hit research ideas—like politicians, this marketer's ideas were his products—that permanently placed Dichter in the marketing pantheon related to *Chrysler*. *Chrysler* was having a devil of a time selling its relatively new line of *Plymouth* automobiles. Dichter headed to Detroit, conducted extensive interviews with more than 200 potential car buyers, and concluded the main problem laid in *Chrysler's* advertising. Ad messages boasted these new 1939 *Plymouths* were "different from any other car you've ever tried." This claim apparently triggered unconscious fear-responses among many prospects, for whom familiarity with brand meant safety—and the desire for safety is a basic human need.

Convertibles represented only about 2 percent of automobiles sold during 1939. Yet responses from this same sample revealed that most men, particularly middle-ages ones, wanted one. When Dichter advised *Chrysler* to place convertibles near dealership windows as bait, more men indeed were lured in. But when they returned to actually make purchases, they typically arrived with their wives (this being the 1930s) and choose sensible hard-top sedans. *Plymouth's* product line offered both.

The marketing researcher concluded that convertibles represented youth, freedom, and secret wishes for a mistress, each of which are wistful or visceral temptations. The researcher recommended *Chrysler* reposition its convertible advertising—and honoring the role spouses play in final decisions, began placing advertising inside women's magazines. This was/is a media selection decision. The new advertising campaign emphasized that it only took "a few minutes" to feel comfortable with the new *Plymouth*. Convertible sales blew up, seemingly overnight.

Dichter, however, made his real marketing research bones on, of all places, the domestic baking front. The researcher proposed that baking represents an expression of femininity. So, when women pull cake or bread out of the oven "in a sense it was like giving birth." Thus, *General Mills'* new cake mix, one requiring that cooks only add water, was initially a flop because it threatened women's femininity. Thanks to the innovative marketing researcher nearly all such mixes have been reconfigured such that cooks are required to add an egg, symbol of fertility, to the mix. He went on to encourage domestic marketers to impress on women the importance of cooking as a means of demonstrating love to their families. Marketing manipulation, anyone?

Some other ideas and recommendations offered by Dichter remain a bit far out to discuss during a *#me-too era*. But in bringing this discussion home, worth nothing are the facts that Dichter correctly surmised that inside *America's New World*, as opposed to *Europe's Old World*, ostentatious displays of brands became a substitute for nobility or an aristocratic family tree. He recognized, before anyone, that consumers seek out brands that correspond with the group with which they want to associate. He correctly concluded that branded objects, services, or destinations have special meanings. Meanings related to sex, insecurity, or desires for prestige. Dichter learned, through research, that many consumers feel guilty after purchasing self-indulgent products, recommending that marketers sell things such as expensive cigars, wines, automobiles, destinations, and so forth as rewards for the deserving. Many of these insights retrospectively appear old-school today, because these understandings were the bleeding edge of the cutting edge of marketing research in their time.

MODULE 6.4

New School Takes: The Ways Things Are Today

Google tracks consumers who access its services through their own mobile devices—hunting them down, targeting them to within one-square-foot of their actual locations by triangulating latitudinal and longitudinal coordinates. GPS, folks. *Google* is simultaneously continuously selling these consumer locations to advertisers. These marketers, in turn, instantly deliver customized ad messages about stores, shops, or restaurants situated nearby those consumers' actual locales. The advertising payments it earns from sharing this locale information with advertisers is a primary source of *Google* revenues. After all, when consumers use *Google's* nominally-free marketing services, they're actually paying by sharing their personal information. Personal research information that *Google* shares with other marketers. Consequently, when consumers use *Google's* marketing services *Google* actually converts them into marketable products. This is how research often works today.

The *Google* business model is being described, appropriately, as surveillance capitalism. Surveillance capitalism is an evocative phrase used to describe a loosely regulated battlefield that has captured more personal information than any military force in history. An *Orwellian* future is increasingly becoming an *Orwellian* present. For those who missed the *Cliff Notes* version of *1984*, *George Orwell's* 1949 novel called *1984* was set in the then-future date of 1984 and portrayed a global marketplace plagued by perpetual war; omnipresent propaganda, or was it *fake news;* and 24/7 *Big Government*, *Big Brother-like* surveillance. Say or think what you want but *Orwell* apparently got the *Big Government* part right.

Google, of course, delivers famously free internet-based search-related (or is it research?) services to consumer users. So how does Google get paid? For customer information and the customer attention that the giant marketer provides. *Google's* entire business model is based on getting and keeping customers' attention. Changing what customers do, influencing how customers think. *Google* sells predictive certainty to marketers seeking to engage in the targeting of prospective or current customer segments—which should include all marketers.

This means that *Google* must collect tons of data. Surveillance capitalism driven by the ability to track where everyone is going on- and offline. In ways that make advertising as successful as possible. Technology has created a new-to-the-world market and new-to-the-world modes of marketing research. A place that has never previously existed that trades exclusively in human futures. Just like there are markets that trade pork belly or oil futures, which are each commodities, of course. Surveillance capitalism is the factor that made internet firms the richest organizations in history.

Google watches, tracks, and measures—researches!—everything that consumers do online. *Google* measures what consumers look at and for how long. *Google* knows when consumers are lonely or depressed, when they are looking at photos of exes. *Google* measures whether individual consumers are introverted or extroverted, neurotic or rock solid; *Google* tracks and sells information related to consumers' basic and specific personality types. All this data, again more than in history, are poured into marketing research systems that feature almost no human interaction and then insights are squeezed out on the other end in the ability to make better predictions about what we are going to do, who we are, and what we want to become through consumption. Models are built that predict actions and the company that has the best predictive, or targeting, models wins. All the videos we have watched, clicks we have liked, all gets fed in again and again to build better models. Once you have the model, where you will go next or what videos you will watch can be predicted; what kinds of emotions tend to trigger you . . . . But they will squeeze in a sneaker ad, for just the right brand, before all this starts or ends.

Web-based video marketers are typically driven by three major marketing objectives. One, user engagement, to drive up usage and keep their customers scrolling, Two, the growth objective, to keep consumers coming back and to invite as many of their friends as possible and for those friends to invite more new friends still—primary, secondary, tertiary. Three, there is an advertising objective, ensuring that while all this is happening web-based and video marketing are optimizing the receipt of money from advertisers. Each objective is powered and guided by research data-based algorithms that determine exactly what content to show these e-marketers and how to keep those numbers going up. Then *Facebook* sells Diana's attention for 3.62 cents per impression, or exposure to an ad that has been picked out for—targeted exactly at—her.

Facebook has created a world in which online connection (the human need for social relations, see *Abraham Maslow's* Hierarchy of Needs: Module 7) has become primary and yet in that world anytime two people connect it's financed only through a sneaky third party who is paying real money to manipulate those two people. An entire global generation of humans has been created who have been raised within a context where the very meaning of interpersonal communication is utterly impersonal and manipulated in nature; where the very meaning of culture is manipulation. Deceit and sneakiness is at the absolute center of everything that this generation does. As the famous science fiction writer *Arthur Clarke* (author of *2001, A Space Odyssey,* published in 1951) wrote, "Any sufficiently advanced technology is indistinguishable from magic." These are magical times, readers, and sometimes the marketing magician is moral and sometimes s/he/it is not.

Technologists have used what they learned from research to build addictive features and benefits into their products and into the supposed solutions those products offer to users. Persuasive technology is modified to an extreme with the perpetual goal of modifying someone's behavior. *Big Tech* seeks to incentivize its product users to do this or that specific action and to "do it" with their finger(s).

How infantilizing are these processes, when you think literally about them. The whole process is like motivating babies to suck on their thumbs by incentivizing them instead of watching babies engage naturally in this behavior. Every time product users refresh, something new pops up.

Psychologists call this planned electronic process a positive intermittent reward—or reinforcement. But the suckers—okay, the product users—don't know when they are going to get the reward or how much they will like it, so they keep pushing e-buttons.

This entire process operates exactly like slot machines laid out inside huge casino hotels. *Big Tech* is planting unconscious habits deep inside not our brains but our brain stems, which are far more primitive and absolutely instinctual in nature. Users are being programmed absent awareness. You see that phone sitting over there and you know that just by reaching out and touching the device a reward just might be delivered to you. These are not accidents. These behaviors are produced through intentional design techniques. Another marketing trick is photo-tagging, as in receipt of an email that says you have just been photo-tagged. So naturally, you will open the email or text message. Gotcha!

EXHIBIT 6.1
Basic Steps in Marketing Research Process

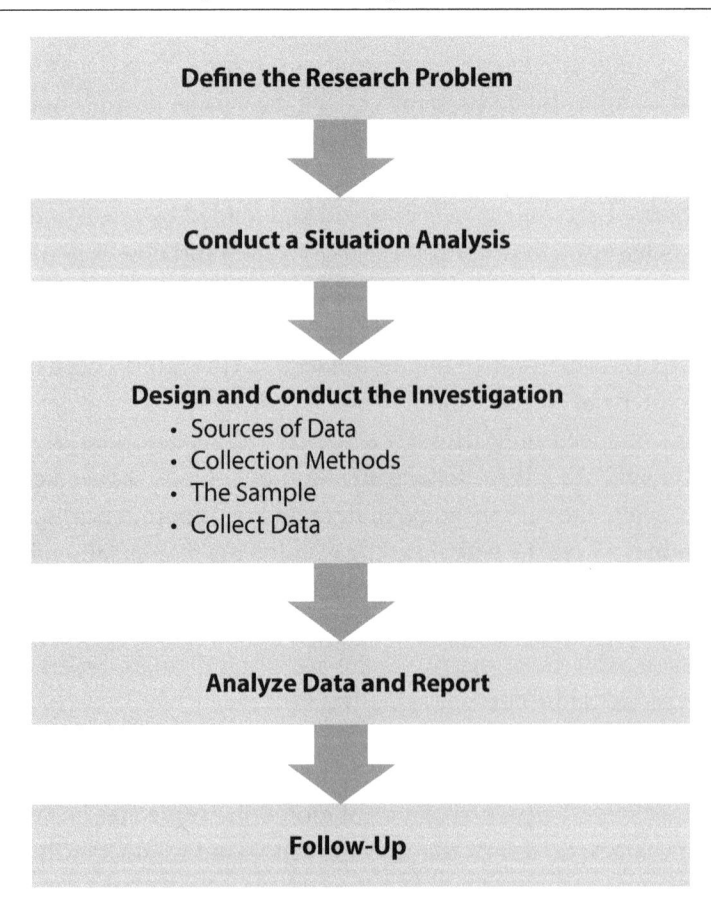

Define the Research Problem

⬇

Conduct a Situation Analysis

⬇

Design and Conduct the Investigation
- Sources of Data
- Collection Methods
- The Sample
- Collect Data

⬇

Analyze Data and Report

⬇

Follow-Up

TABLE 6.1
Select Sources of Online Secondary Data

Name	URL	Description
USA.gov	www.usa.gov	Portal to all publically available government websites, including those maintained by the SEC, Census Bureau, CIA.
Securities and Exchange Commission	www.sec.gov	The SEC provides a wealth of information on its website, which includes access to the EDGAR database of disclosure documents such as 10Ks and other filings.
US Census Bureau	www.census.gov	Site contains a wide range of census data on the US population, businesses, government agencies. Also provides access to key economic indicators. The site is searchable via usa.gov.
Google	www.google.com	Google has a number of popular search engines for general web searches, searches of academic literature (Google Scholar), image searches, and newspaper searches.
Dunn & Bradstreet Business Reports	www.dnb.com	D&B is a premier source of commercial information and prognostication on businesses and business conditions.
Fuld and Company	www.fuld.com	Compendium of competitive intelligence tools and techniques used by companies worldwide. This site is a must for firm's interested in staying on top of their competitors.
Hoovers Online	www.hoovers.com	Proprietary information on about 18,500 companies and 600 industries. Furnishes access to additional information on nearly 13 million companies from leading providers such as Dun & Bradstreet.
Proquest	www.proquest.com	A multidisciplinary database that searches all ProQuest databases for which a library has a subscription.
Ebsco Host	www.ebscohost.com	EBSCOhost Provides access to various EBSCO databases which can all be searched simultaneously. Available from most university libraries.
Wall Street Journal Online	http://online.wsj.com/home-page	Extensive data on markets, companies, products, environments, trends. A must for all serious business professionals. Subscription required.

MODULE 7

Consumer Behavior

MODULE 7.0

Even Ostensibly Simple Decisions Can Prove Absolutely Complicated

As both a discipline[1] and a set of strategic activities, marketing is intimately involved in the art and science of "buy-ology." Thanks again, Thressa Strutton, for introducing this deceptively simple idea into this book. After all, how complicated can seemingly simple consumer purchasing decisions be? The answer, however, is extremely complicated, a response that at this point likely surprises no one.

Here's one example of how one seemingly simple consumer buy-ological decision might actually play out. Suppose you book a Monday night train or Tuesday morning flight to get from *Milan, Italy,* to *Paris, France,* for a business meeting that your marketing organization is paying for. Being an experienced traveler, you realize that inside *Europe* both modes of travel are remarkably efficient and relatively inexpensive. Assume further that you're a confident traveler. Should be a relatively simple consumer decision to make. Let's begin.

First, why consider taking a night train at all? Why not fly, drive, or conjure forth your favorite genie for a magic-carpet ride, preferably with an aisle seat? Most travelers would likely weigh out three factors, or reasons, why they might take a sleeper train.

The first buy-ology is logistical. Say you work at the *Milan Stock Exchange.* You have a face-to-face meeting scheduled for Tuesday in central *Paris,* at noon. Air or rail? Air means an early Tuesday morning start, beginning with a taxi to *Milan's Linate Airport* followed by a 07:25 a.m. *Alitalia* flight departure. Eighty-five euros (about ninety-nine dollars) in coach; but, hey, someone else is paying, and the idea of being divided from the proletariat by a nylon curtain still gives you a weird sense of superiority, so a business seat it is. Now somebody is in for three hundred and ten euros.

Traveling by rail, by contrast, involves dining at home, then catching the 11:00 p.m. train on Monday night, from *Milan's* central train station. Again, having your own space, a sleeping compartment to

---

1. There are, for example, also Accounting, Financial, Managerial, or Decision Science disciplines. A discipline is a body of accepted knowledge, ideas, principles, and processes. There is also a Marketing Discipline, for example, and you are studying it right now.

yourself, will be expensive, at two hundred and seventy euros. You're male, and if you don't mind sharing with another man, however, the price plummets to eighty-three euros. A steal. Unfortunately, you *do* mind, since that other man, in your shuddering imagination, might be a gabby insomniac with complex gastric issues and feather-light fingers, a possible pickpocket—or worse.

The plane and the train roughly align in terms of cost alone. The same premise applies for arrival times: 09:40 at *Paris*-based the *Orly Sud Airport,* or thirteen minutes earlier at the *Gare de Lyon Train Terminal* inside central *Paris.* And there's the rub, and a difference, and perhaps a determinant difference at that. Almost all *European* night trains deliver their passengers right into the cores of cities. Whereas all in-bound *European* planes deposit passengers, at best, on the outer rims of the cities that the trains serve. A cab ride into *Paris* from *Orly-Sud* (or, more irritating still, from *Charles de Gaulle Airport*), during rush hour, is the antithesis of fun, and rather expensive, but you may not fancy the relatively grubby schlep by public transport to downtown. Alight from the night train, though, and you will find *le Tout-Paris* ready to greet you. Being in no hurry, you amble along the platform to breakfast in a restaurant so royally gilded on its walls and ceiling the yolk of your poached egg will bask in the reflected glow.

A second possible buy-ology related reason to travel by night train is *flygskam.* The word means "flight shame" in *Swedish. Flygskam* gives name to the guilt that gnaws—or might gnaw—on your vitals when you realize that, by flying from anywhere to anywhere else, say, for a skull-jolting weekend on the dance floor, a dalliance on the beach, or a business meeting, you will hasten the bleaching out of *Australia's Great Barrier Reef.* (You know, by adding to the global carbon inventory.) However, if consumers can spread the shame, say by forcing celebrities to charter their own yachts in a fit of conscience, so much the better. The vice of flying, thus exposed, has spawned a reciprocal *European* virtue: *tågskryt, Swedish* for "train brag," as practiced by woke *Europeans* who not only swap the skies for railroads but, having made the sacrifice, visit Instagram or TikTok to demonstrate their virtue for, well, their virtual friends.

The science is solid. If our *Milanese* broker flies to *Paris* (about four hundred miles), he will release one hundred kilograms of carbon dioxide into the atmosphere. Not personally, of course, unless he ate a second helping of osso buco at home the night before. But then again, the plane will fly anyway—with or without him. That's not counting the carbon footprint he leaves behind as he taxi rides to *Linate Airport* at one end and from *Orly-Sud* to his downtown *Paris* business rendezvous at the other, probably traveling both times in fuming snarls of traffic. Should he go overnight by train, the journey will be more circuitous, and maybe thirty miles longer, but the CO_2 output will be under four kilos. That's a material difference, and it's genuinely hard to spot a downside, unless it's the annoying halo of ethical self-satisfaction hovering over a traveler's head.

Will *flygskam* have any lasting effect on commercial enterprise? The signs are (or were, before the advent of COVID-19) distinctly promising that it will. A new *Nightjet* train from *Vienna, Austria,* to *Brussels, Belgium,* established by *Austrian Federal Railways*, or Ö.B.B., has been widely lauded as an eco-friendly travel option to the *European Union* capital and made its maiden run during January 2020. A serious journey, at just over fourteen hours. Ö.B.B. estimates that the rest of its night network has already saved the world twelve thousand short-haul flights a year: a delicious irony, given how greedily the budget airlines have eaten into train travel in recent decades. Further rail innovations lay just down the track, not least new sleeper services from *Vienna* and *Munich, Germany,* to *Amsterdam,* capital of *The Netherlands* that began during December 2020. One can but hope that such enviable schemes, intended to address the climate crisis, will not be stopped in their tracks by the rival environmental threat through which we currently sweat.

A third buy-ology type of reason that our intrepid traveler might choose a sleeper train is no more practical but potentially tastier than an apple. It's certainly more alluring. At stake, you might say, on any train is the prospect of hidden and perhaps even "forbidden" adventure. Although it is unlikely, as you clatter through the night, that any opportunities for more prurient adventures will befall you, the possibility that they *might* remain ever present, just out of sight past the next curve of the track. To remain awake to that possibility, even as we're meant to be sleeping, is the prospect of pleasure that beckons consumers back, year after year, to this beguiling locomotion. No wonder trains and movies—marketed products both—make such cozy bedfellows—so pleasant that trains zipping through the darkness, with windows illuminated, actually *look* like filmstrips. Plots, laid down on rails, dash ever onward; anticipation and myriad possibilities flow freely like steam. We slipped that one past the editor. As noted, a final and perhaps the best or worst buy-ology type of reason for any single consumer to decide to take the night train.

Turns out, this seemingly simple consumer choice turns out to be anything but simple to actually make.

OUR TIME; OUR CHOICES; OUR RESPONSIBILITIES

American as well as international consumers' consumption choices—be they simple or complex such as the one recounted above—often generate behaviors and outcomes that create better or worse future consequences for them. Those future consequences are those consumers' current responsibility as they, for example, decide whether to travel by plane or train or purchase a *Toyota Tundra* or *Dodge Ram* pick-up truck. Readers generally have been sufficiently exposed to pop psychological principles to know how reasonable it is to connect our own personal poor choices to our present-day problems. Change is the essence of life; similar to how exchange resides at the core of marketing. Or similar to how marketing is impossible without exchange.

American consumers, in particular, should accept that they are responsible for many of the bad consumption outcomes that happen to them. Offering only sympathy, especially for themselves is misplaced kindness. Oh, I feel so sorry . . . for myself; better take another "hit" . . . these sorts of choices never has and never will cut it.

Consumers should likewise accept that they alone are ultimately responsible for generating most of their own more promising futures. Healthier, wealthier, happier lives, in no particular order, might be yours if you make the right consumption choices, and not just because these three desirable outcomes are intrinsically interrelated. Consumers should realize they are also the primary authors and creators of those future outcomes too.

Who knows, perhaps a great place to start creating a healthier, wealthier, and happier life might entail choosing to more vigorously consume educational services that would generate greater genuine value to them if said educational consumers—and education is very much a marketed product—simply dug in and paid attention. Of course, many consumers of educational services already do exactly this. But many other consumers who purchase and use educational services voluntarily decide to consume less of a highly-valued product that they or their parents have paid dearly for—by, say, not showing up for class on time or at all, or by never really deeply reading the assigned books or articles. Or, by taking online versions of courses while paying online helpers such as *Quizlet* to complete the courses for them.

What's next (i.e., what should I buy next, in order to improve), is a question all mindful consumers should keep scrolling near the tops of their brains. Yet too many American consumers pass through their lives relatively unaware they're surrounded by recognized and unrecognizable factors that manipulate the consumption decisions they make. Consumers, however, can learn to make better decisions—including superior consumer behavior choices—by ramping up their understanding of:

▶ The known and unknown forces that impact and influence their choices.
▶ How the consumption choices/decisions they make impact their physical, emotional, and economic well-being.
▶ How they and other consumers use choices to express and create their own identities.

The ability and the willingness to acquire targeted understanding is often a prerequisite for positive change. This is especially true when discussing any repetitive pattern of behavior that is obviously not serving us well. *Socrates* was right when he said, "The unexamined life is not worth living." That more consumers do not take his advice testifies to the hard work that conscious self-examination implies.

The reasons why consumers choose to purchase the products they buy or use are often obscure. Most consumers, when asked, imagine that their behaviors are usually the products of conscious choice. However, most consumers are wrong.

The vibe pursued here is not so much a 1960/70s-era rockers "*The Who*" "*Won't Get Fooled Again-*like" take. Instead, insights about how to make best possible consumption decisions given where consumers are in their life cycles have been and will be presented.

In the interim, if merely expensive *Ford Super D F-450 Platinum* trucks or a wildly overpriced *The Eye of the Dragon* brand of vodka actually are the choices that capture consumers' dearest hopes and make their dreams come true then the correctness and consequences of those choices remain those consumers and them alone to manage. After all, the *United States* is "home of the free." This freedom, which is embedded in a cultural value and is reflected in the idea of consumer sovereignty, underscores the fact that domestic markets operate as places in which consumers usually always have complete autonomy to choose what they will, so long as those consumer choices do not hurt anyone else. All adult Americans, unless incarcerated, have available the option to treat every moment like its either Saturday night (get out, party, have fun) or Monday morning (get up and go to work or school)—until the butcher's bill comes due. The only thing certain is that the bill will arrive, and that decision-makers will be happy to or regret having to pay it.

THE WAY THINGS ARE

The *United States* needs capitalism and relatively free markets to create wealth, sustainable wealth, for its citizenry. The *United States*, in turn, also needs sustainable wealth-generation if only to pay the various federal and state governmental institutions that issue transfer payments to many citizens and to keep these government "marketing" entities themselves going and growing. After all, any marketing institution that is not continuously growing is actually falling behind.

Contemporary *American* capitalism is defined not by a producer mentality but by a consumer mindset. Year in and out across decades, about 70–73 percent of the domestic Gross Domestic Product (the well-known GDP) is driven by consumer decisions and purchases. Stated more specifically, the health and wealth of the entire domestic economy is based on favorable consumer expectations. That's because favorable consumer expectations motivates additional consumption which attracts additional B2B investment, stimulates greater quantities of increasingly more efficient marketing production (due to the emergence and continued development of economies-of-scale), which in turn further increases consumer consumption—and grows the economy by perpetuating a virtuous cycle.

But at the same time *American* economic prosperity in some ways continues to be an economic mirage, purchased with credit cards. Many and indeed perhaps the majority of consumers continuously buy more and more stuff they cannot afford and don't actually need. Consequently, the domestic marketplace features paradoxical conditions in which masses of consumers engage in behaviors that harm them individually, but that are good for the nation's economy as whole. How ironic.

Incentives Play an Important Role

The consumer decision-making world is simple, deceptively so, on the surface. Rational people respond to incentives.[2,3] That's it. But rational consumers don't all respond in the same way to the same incentives, nor does any reason exist to believe consumers should or ever would all respond in the same way to incentives. This is another reason why marketers should engage in segmentation and precisely target those segments they are best able to serve and satisfy.

Incentives do not always arrive, fully-formed, in monetary terms. Consumers, for instance, buy products in order to realize their aspirations—that's the foundation of many marketers' success. The

---

2. Incentives, further described, could include any factor or stimuli that motivates or encourages people to do something. Agreeing to not charge homeowners who use less than a pre-agreed amount of water during a drought is an incentive.

3. The use of incentives can generate unintended consequences. The original version of the *Affordable Health Care Act* was first provided to consumers in 2011. The incentives provided by the product to people who made just enough money to qualify for governmental health-care subsidies consequently dis-incentivized many to not work harder/longer in order to make more money. Because, if they made more money, their governmental subsidies disappeared. Were these consumer decisions logical or irrational? Pick your poison. Politics offers menus—*product portfolios*—of ideas, ideals, and branded political professionals (politicians) from which to choose. Not coincidentally, political ideas, ideals, and professionals each exist as products, traveling across a topic on which we have already tread. More recently, similar dis-incentivizing outcomes arose with respect to COVID-19 relief checks being issued to displaced workers, many of whom did not want to go back to work as the post-COVID-19 economy sprang back to life, because they would have to take a pay cut.

promise that many successful consumer brands make is to help customers become what they want to become. Wouldn't you look great stepping out of that *Escalade*? All eyes in the room would surely pivot toward you were you wearing those *Jimmy Choo*'s.

LinkedIn, as both marketing brand and product, offers a different sort of "incentivizing promise" to consumers. The marketing promise originally made and the solution still offered by *LinkedIn* is that working or prospective professionals could more safely navigate the dangerously dynamic rapids of the new employment economy by building a craft—a boat, if you will—comprised of cyber-connections. This creative idea made and continues to make sense in an employment marketplace in which many professional workers understandably are no more loyal to their employers than their employers are to them. Each person's professional social network, arguably, operates either as a guarantor of employment or an insurance policy against unemployment. Do you see the two marketing solutions that are present inside the value offered through each marketing promise? That is, if these promises made about the value of personal professional network are honored.

Regardless of their form, incentives are usually designed to directly elevate the self-interests of targeted recipients. This quality, and benefit, ensures that incentives are one drink that few consumers ever refuse. Herein lies the basic source of the appreciable power of incentives. How pervasive and powerful are incentives? Given that peer pressure alone can incentivize decision-makers into making good or bad decisions, incentives appear extremely pervasive and powerful.

Here's an ironic twist, however. In order for excessively progressive (liberal) governmental policies to prevail or sustain their success [were they to prevail], the highly motivating power of incentives must be ignored or eliminated. Why would and why should anyone work or study harder than others work or study in order to further their future self-interests—and future family welfare—if in the end everyone secures the same financial reward or grade anyway? We don't know the answer either, because without the presence and promise of incentivizing rewards there is no reason to work hard.

Consumer Decision-Making Is Complicated Indeed

Consumers also purchase products or services or support ideas in order to keep up with or stay ahead of others. Those others typically reside inside those consumers' social circle or inside social circles to which individual consumers long to belong. (Call these aspirational social circles.) These social circles, in turn, could involve genuine human-to-human relationships or play out entirely online.

When doing or buying one brand becomes more costly than doing or buying another brand from the same product category, which something do you believe most consumers are going to do or buy—if they are rational? Becomes more costly, that is, in terms of money or time spent; inconvenience or stress endured; perceived or actual risks that must be dealt with; or self-worth or prestige that is lost or gained. When the choice to do something or buy a brand becomes easier, less expensive, or more beneficial in any way consumers would generally choose to do more of the something or buy the brand—if they are rational, right?

But in weighing their choices, consumers also bear in mind the overall constraints pressing on them, not only the physical costs, benefits, and consequences associated with particular choices. But only if decision-makers are rational.

Consumers also evaluate the future consequences of their present choices. Or at least they should, if they are rational. Indeed, when facing important decisions decision-makers should project themselves into the future and envision themselves looking back from that future vantage point toward the present (the "right now") while examining the good or bad consequences that ensued from made decisions. After all, decisions always generate behaviors that always generate consequences.

But as previously inferred who is rational, all the time, in their behavior as consumers? The answer is that very few to no people always act rationally. This is why understanding the factors that motivate consumer behavior decisions is never a slam dunk, not even among the best marketing researchers.

Minds induce their human owners into endless vigils that are rarely quiet. Our minds are characterized by endless interactive struggles and episodes where we ponder, remember, regret, or experience remorse—and unrequited desires. Humans consequently constantly "create" problems inside their own minds with or without the intervention of marketers. Marketers need only understand the nature of those problems and the identities of those customers (conduct research, then plan, and eventually segment properly); reach out effectively to those potential or actual customers (conduct research, then plan, and eventually target properly); and then develop/deliver sets of values that would prove necessary to successfully solve those customers (conduct research, then plan, and eventually position effectively) in order to succeed.

This process sounds simple. The process just described should make sense because it is strategic and reflects the key marketing principals and activities introduced during Modules 2–6. But then the kicker, the fly-in-the-ointment arrives; in the form of the following question:

▶ Yes, but . . . who knows what actually and accurately motivates anybody or their decision at any point in time?

Unstated, Even Unknown, Factors Motivate Human Decisions

John F. Kennedy was inaugurated as President of the United States (a professional marketing role that today is broadly branded through use of the branding identifier—and acronym—*POTUS*) in 1961. During his inauguration address *President Kennedy* famously challenged American citizens "to reach the moon before the decade is out." Well, landing a man (women were not deemed astronaut-worthy at the time) on the moon before 1970 appeared like a worthy and unifying goal at the time—and *America* hit the mark during July 1969! But what true underlying factor motivated *JFK* (Kennedy's branding acronym, as noted earlier) or his advisory council to make the choice to challenge *America* in this manner?

One school of thought exists suggesting that President Kennedy laid down this challenge to America because the *United States* was getting badly beat in space-based scientific firsts by a communist foe who had bigger missiles.[4] *Russia* had bigger and more powerful missiles than the United States because the communist nation had erroneously projected ten years earlier that a nuclear warhead package would weigh about 6,000 pounds. American scientists and its military leaders knew better, understanding that a 2,000-pound nuclear payload would suffice. America's smaller *Redstone*

---

4. Remember the differentiating and positioning value associated with being "first to market"?

and *Jupiter* missiles were engineered accordingly. America ended up with smaller/less space-worthy missiles.

The "so what?" takeaway from this story is at the time (a) the global marketing struggle over whose ideology (*American* capitalism versus *Russian* communism/socialism) was superior and which brand of governance would prevail was truly blowing and going, and (b) America's smaller missiles simply weren't cutting it, brand reputation-wise. Kennedy and his advisors consequently directed, and motivated, America toward the moon as a gambit to develop larger *Apollo* branded missiles.

Four additional takeaways are evident. First, size actually did matter here. Second, marketing matters, all the time. Three, marketing is everywhere and affects everything. And fourth, the branding image of the *United States* as a truly powerful and inspiring nation that stood second to none on global—or was it a universe-sized—stage was materially elevated for decades after this first-to-market (i.e., first to the moon) victory.

MODULE 7.1

Fishing Stories—and Definitions

Consumer behavior (hereafter, CB) refers to the buying behavior of final consumers. CB also references the factors that influence final consumers' buying behaviors. Final consumers, themselves, are individuals and consumer households that buy products or services for their personal consumption.

Marketers study CB, as they should. Marketing research is the best tool through which to study CB.

Marketers should study CB in the same ways and for the same reasons that fishermen study fish. Why do fishermen study fish? Usually, in order to understand how best to catch them. Marketers absolutely attempt to catch consumers.

However, marketers should also study CB for the same reasons that ichthyologists[5] study fish. In other words, study their behaviors in order to understand fish/consumers better. Then, either marketers (fish scientists) can serve consumers' or fishes' needs better in order to help consumers (fish) solve their problems more effectively.

When researching consumers' behaviors, marketing organizations should answer the following questions about consumers and their behaviors:

▶ What, where, how, and how much consumers buy, as well as when they buy. Marketers then should answer a why question, specifically why consumers buy what they decide to buy.

The first five questions are essentially the same basic questions that newspaper reporters must answer as they write news articles. Once these marketing research questions are answered in the best possible fashion, the resulting insights—which hopefully actually include actionable strategic knowledge—should be used to develop and execute marketing strategies. The first five questions are also relatively easy to answer.

---

5. Ichthyologists are scientists who study the habitats, behaviors, and other factors that influence the reproduction and well-being of fish and other sea creatures. The primary reason why ichthyologists study fish and sea creatures is to help them.

Facebook, for example, continuously assesses consumer metrics that have become standard marketing value-adds across the entire *Amazon, Google, Twitter, Snapchat* spectrum. Such as tracking the e-pathways consumers take across sites and apps; discerning and developing an understanding of what is clicked, and when and where clicks occur; as well as how frequently users search for information about or actually purchase particular brands, product categories, names, or keywords. Just think, *Facebook* once was a novelty—a procrastination pit—rather than an omnipresent threat to consumers' or countries' freedoms. Well, at least *Facebook* achieved in its initial marketing mission of "making the world more open and connected."

By contrast, however, the sixth question—why?—is exceedingly difficult to answer. Why is "why" so difficult to answer? One explanation is because the reasons why consumers do anything are locked inside their respective minds; inside their so-called "black boxes." Most people know what airliners' black boxes are. In crashes where no one survives, planes' indestructible black boxes explain why after big, often inexplicable problems, such as crashes, have occurred. They can even be recovered inside ocean depths because black boxes ping location signals for years.

Black boxes, for humans, are their minds. Who knows what's truly happening inside human brains, at any moment? Who knows what's truly motivating consumers at any point in time, especially when decision-makers are trying to solve truly vexing problems?

A second reason why "why" questions prove difficult to answer is that what makes sense as a reason to buy/not buy anything in one consumer's mind often appears absolutely irrational or illogical to other consumers. Humans differ one from the other. Sometimes they differ radically. Successful marketers consequently must engage nearly continuously in segmentation, targeting, and positioning processes. Marketers should generally group together consumers who would answer the same "why," the same way.

A third reason why "why" questions are so difficult to answer is that consumers habitually lie about their true attitudes, intentions, or behaviors. During the 2016 presidential marketing campaign, remarkably higher numbers of people actually voted for President *Trump* than reported to marketing researchers (pollsters) that they intended to vote for him. Why? Largely because they did not want to implicitly be accused, inside researchers' minds, as being branded as deplorable racists, sexist, nationalists; insert your favorite pejorative "ism" here, as this book parrots *Hillary Clinton's* famous 2016 description of potential *Donald Trump* voters as "deplorables." But hey, political marketers expect voters and potential voters to lie to them, and statistically account for this fact. Obviously, however, these researchers failed to account for the extent to which voting consumers were lying to them. Why did so many consumers lie and keep their lie to themselves? Because of the rancor and acrimony that characterized the market at the time, divisions that have worsened since then. Many consumers "rationally" did not want others to know who they planned to vote for, because they did not want to be criticized or worse.

Marketers should always try to answer "why" despite the difficulties that they will usually encounter. The primary reason why the preceding statement is true is because those customers who answer "why" in a similar fashion represent a natural market segment.

Many contemporary experts do not agree with the motivational ideas that *Ernest Dichter* originally developed, as discussed during Module 6. Another school of experts exists that suggests every non-instinctual thing that happens inside human minds is either biologically or culturally determined. Many human activities and responses actually are instinctually pre-programmed inside the "reptilian" portion of our brains. What happens, as consumers decide what to choose or not choose, often results from complex, varied, multidirectional, cascading interactions among their genes and their environments. At other times, those same what to do/not do responses are governed by comparative simple brain processes. [6]

Researchers, including marketers, are beginning to understand the full intricacies of what unfolds inside the black box processes of consumers. However, researchers will likely never fully understand these quite-human, well-hidden, carefully guarded, and often apparently illogical processes.

---

6. Human brains feature three primary parts. The term "reptilian brain" is often used today to describe the ancestral brain that unconsciously regulates humanity's vital functions (breathing, heart rate, blood pressure); humanity's naturally-arising needs (eating, drinking, reproducing); and humanity's primitive behavioral responses (fear, hate, fight-or-flight responses). At net, the reptilian brain governs human feeding, fleeing, fighting, and . . . reproducing responses. Fish, birds, amphibians, and reptiles are governed by the same brain. The second human brain part governs emotions and judgments. The third regulates learning, imagination, language, and perceptual attributions. Marketers routinely develop products and promotional messages—elements of the marketing mix—that are specifically designed to appeal, often at the same time, to one or more of these human brain parts.

MODULE 7.2

Controllable Marketing Stimuli

Various stimuli influence consumers' behavioral choices. Marketers cannot control most of these stimuli. Yet the uncontrollable nature of such stimuli does not imply that strategic marketers can afford to ignore them.

Certain stimuli, however, can be controlled to varying degrees by marketers. The 4Ps are controllable marketing stimuli, for example. The marketing mix exists as a strategic tool that marketers can design—mix and match—in order to deliver hopefully substantially differentiable value to targeted segments of consumers. The marketing mix can also be used to create more desirable market positions for specific brands.

The marketing mix consists of product, price, promotion, and place, for products. The 4Ps, in brief.

For services, three additional Ps—people, processes, and physical surroundings—can be managed strategically. The 7Ps, in other words.

These controllable marketing stimuli may shape consumer perceptions about marketing brands and organizations. Remember the Law of Perceptions? That was the law suggesting that marketing is not so much a battle of products or brands as a battle of perceptions about the value of brands that are competing against each other inside the same product category. This battle unfolds in consumers' minds. Perceptions, of course, exist as imagined realities. Imagined [consumer] realities that marketers can and do shape.

Controllable marketing stimuli enter consumer decision-makers' black boxes as inputs. Certain outputs—consumer responses—eventually result. These responses include consumer decisions about:

- ▶ Product choices or making no choice at all—what or what not to buy, along with why? This is a what-to-buy question. Notably, when consumers make no choice at all, they have still made a choice. Relatedly, giving consumers more choices is usually not better for business. Two famous fruit jam studies gave consumers six choices and twenty-four choices of jam, respectively. Consumers were far more likely to choose to buy and to buy more when only six choices were available to choose from. The number and presentation of the options that consumers are given can impact what they choose, whether they choose, and how satisfied they are with their choices.

- Brand choices—another what-to-buy question.
- Dealer/store choice; e- or traditional purchase choices—a where-to-buy question.
- Purchase timing—a when-to-buy question.
- Purchase amount—a how-much-to-buy question.
- Pay attention to or ignore what marketers say.
- Like or dislike anything marketers are saying and selling.
- Evangelize[7] to others about the great or horrible experience they had with the product, firm, store, or brand. Modern evangelizing is a consumer-initiated communication process that entails either WOM or e-WOM. Word of mouth (WOM), regardless of whether it's delivered through traditional or electronic channels, often proves to be one of marketers' best friends or worst enemies.

Managing the Nexus between Stimuli and Responses in Our Lives

Human lives will play out for better or worse based on how well or poorly individuals respond to marketing and non-marketing stimuli as either set of potentially motivating factors arise. Consumers who learn to manage these how-will-I-respond-to-stimuli-processes effectively usually enjoy more successful lives. The decisions and choices that humans make in response to stimuli as they are exposed to the stimuli always generate better or worse consequences. When bundled across time, those consequences eventually generate more or less desirable futures for decision-makers.

In many ways, and for many reasons, life is what happens between the stimulus and response.[8] And the ways in which people respond to stimuli as they arise/arrive make huge positive or negative differences across the arc of their lifetimes. Consumers, for example, who fail to take care of themselves physically, spiritually, or educationally while they are younger often sadly discover that the consequences of these earlier decisions catch up with them later.

An alternative take on this whole consumer and how they live their lives perspective follows. Readers would be cheated if we did not raise up this take for your attention. This perspective itself certainly argues against the importance and need for planning. The promised take: "Life is what happens while you're busy making plans." The modern proverb was made famous by ex-*Beatle John Lennon* in a product he created and released in 1980. But the phrase actually originated with American writer and cartoonist *Allen Saunders* in 1957. The product developed by *Lennon* was a song called *Beautiful Boy*, a lovely tune and evocative set of lyrics written about his son, Sean.

---

7. In its original *Greek* usage the word "evangelize" meant "to spread good or bad news." This meant, further, that an evangelical was a person who spread good or bad news about any topic or idea.

8. When discussed inside consumers' decision-making contexts "stimulus-" and "response-" processes entail actions or choices that are performed or made as responses to stimuli with or without conscious thought. A "stimulus" entails anything that incites, rouses, or provokes and consequently motivates consumers to take an action, think, experience emotions, or respond in any other way. A "response" is, well, you know what a response is. Every single consumers' life will turn out far better or far worse for them based on how effectively they manage the gap between their exposure to a stimulus and their response to the same stimulus.

MODULE 7.3

Uncontrollable Stimuli

Consumers' behavior is also influenced by stimuli over which marketers exercise zero to little control.

These uncontrollable stimuli include various factors, forces, and events that are present in the economic, technological, political, cultural, or social lives of consumers. These sets of uncontrollable stimuli further include personal factors such as consumers' demographic characteristics, attitudes and beliefs, family life cycle stage, psychological/physiological needs/motives, and preferred lifestyles.[9] The preferred lifestyles of consumers are primarily measured by the activities, interests, and opinions of consumers, or their AIOs. AIOs collectively capture what consumers prefer to do, activity-wise, and prefer to think about, in terms of the interests and opinions, during their free time.

Each uncontrollable stimuli may directly or indirectly shape how consumers perceive and react to marketing stimuli as those stimuli enter consumers' black boxes as inputs. The fact that marketers cannot control these factors does not imply that marketers can avoid to ignore them. Marketers who ignore the impact of these uncontrollable stimuli on consumer decision-making and their resulting behaviors do so at their own peril.

Marketers typically should use marketing research insights collected about some or all of these personal consumer characteristics to classify individual consumers into specific market segments. Then those marketers can engage more effectively in market segmentation. Market segmentation then should be followed by strategic decisions to target particular segments through specifically positioned marketing mixes.

Some marketing segments will inevitably prove more attractive than others to specific marketers. Attractive segments could be characterized as those more likely to respond favorably to a marketer's current marketing mix. Alternatively, attractive segments could be characterized as customer groups that are more likely to respond favorably to a new marketing mix that marketers could strategically develop in order to generate and deliver new values—or solutions. Other segments will prove less attractive to specific marketers. Presumably, these segments should not be targeted.

The set of uncontrollable stimuli that influence CB can be classified into four broad categories. The categories are cultural, social, personal, and psychological stimuli.

---

9. Lifestyle measures choices are also commonly described as "psychographics."

CATEGORY I: CULTURAL STIMULI

Culture is the most basic cause of a person's wants and behaviors. Culture is not the most basic cause of people's needs. Needs remain constant and consistent regardless of cultural circumstance.

Culture, defined, is the entire set or collection of values, ideas, or attitudes shared among or learned from the members of a group. Any large group can and does have a culture; its membership also represents and shares a culture. *Cheesehead* consumers (fans) who root for the *Green Bay Packers* football team simultaneously represent and share certain cultural ideas, beliefs, values, likes or dislikes, and so forth in common.

Culture is learned from consumers' family, friends, teachers, and their exposure to nearly any media message, among other contributing factors.

Culture is lens-like. Think THICK eyeglasses through which you see/attempt to make sense of what is happening around you. The marketing world throws and sometimes actually targets all manner of marketing stimuli at us. And consumers can never make sense of those stimuli (fully understand them) or determine whether the stimuli are good or bad or right or wrong inside their own minds until after those consumers have filtered the stimuli through their cultural lens.

Envision a stimuli, if you will. The stimuli might arrive in the form of an event, advertisement, person, place (a city, a country), or idea that you're experiencing. Do you perceive the stimuli as acceptable or unacceptable?

Their cultural membership exercises large effects on what consumers embrace or reject. Fans of the *Chicago Bears NFL team*, for example, are unlikely to gladly accept *Cheeseheads;* the branding label that die-hard *Green Bay Packer* fans cling to so gleefully. How unlikely? About as statistically likely to happen as is the probability of getting struck by lightening on 365 consecutive days.

Culture is also glacier-like. This means, first, that cultural factors influence marketing practice. Meaning, further, that marketing practice shapes cultural factors.

Cultural changes occur at glacial paces as ideas and values are passed forward from generation to the next. But change does arise, and indeed arises more quickly inside subcultures than broader national or regional cultures themselves. More discussion about subcultures follows.

Cultures, additionally, are ocean-like. All cultures. Consumers live inside cultures like sea creatures immersed in the midst of these oceans; without realizing they're immersed. Again, all consumers. Their cultural or subcultural memberships normalize and homogenize consumers, making them more alike without the conscious realization of the cultural creatures themselves. These normalizing and homogenizing enculturation processes unfold without consumers feeling or knowing that they are happening. Just like fish live out their lives without knowing or feeling they are immersed in water.

Consumers first create cultures. Then, over time, as their creations grow in influence, consumers' cultures recreate them.

Cultures or subcultures are also self-perpetuating. Upon a vast global stage, certain cultures have rightfully earned reputations for their abilities to nurture their grievances; tend them with loving care; and indeed to elevate the importance of these grievances to the point where the resulting hatred is passed forward from generation to generation across hundreds of years. Forget not, forgive not; some cultures elevate the value of hate and conflict. If you know anything about global cultures, you will understand the deeper implications associated with the two preceding statements.

Subcultures

Subcultures are similarly important to marketers; likely more so than cultures themselves. In fact, subcultural membership played a huge role in who voted for who during the last three presidential elections. These same membership classifications undoubtedly will play similar roles during upcoming election cycles. Humans are tribal. Subcultures are often tribal too. Ethnic identify, for example, usually shapes if not outright dictates cultural or subcultural membership. A close knit *Asian American* subculture exists inside the US; in the same manner that powerful *African* or *Hispanic American* subcultures abide inside the same place. Ethnic identity, however, is not the only driver of subcultural membership. Many generally younger *European Americans* identify strongly with *African American* subculture; rap or hip-hop anyone?

The presence of subcultural differences inside one country or cultural differences across two or more countries can cause consumers belonging to those subcultures to perceive, process, interpret, and/or make sense of the same information—the same marketing stimuli—differently. These differences are meaningful for marketers who understand what differences exist and who are willing to exploit their knowledge.

Biology versus Culture

Biology enables. Culture forbids. Biology willingly tolerates a wide range of possibilities. Culture commands its members to pursue some possibilities and forbids them to pursue other possibilities. Biology, for instance, enables men or women to enjoy sex with either men or women. Some *Middle Eastern* and *African* cultures, however, legally forbid men having sex with men or women with women.

Individual consumers, however, experience no "hard and fast" obligation to honor what their cultural or subcultural membership suggest they should or should not do. Even so, lots of millennial and younger consumers have lots of tats. Presumably in part because that's what the subcultures they most identify with suggests they should do. Or perhaps it's because millennial or younger consumers are more likely to feel or experience emotions through their eyes and think through their emotions. (Oh, that's not fair; younger consumers have always often felt through their eyes and thought through their emotions. Doing so is part of being young.)

Twitter and/or *Facebook* and *Instagram* exercise powerful known and unknown influences. Millennial eyes matter greatly because images—visual cues—are disproportionately important to the segment. Feeling-based thinking dominates among millennials because emotions often prevail over logic among the cultural subset. Do these descriptions characterize all millennials? Of course not, far from it. Generalizations, not universally applicable details, are being offered. No good, bad, or indifferent traits or tendencies have ever characterized all members of any culture.

People hailing from different cultures experience great difficulty understanding each other's ideas even inside situations where those ideas are accurately translated. This problem arises even when each party understands the other's language. For example, liberty is a hallowed *American* word. But when the *English* word liberty is translated into its *Chinese* counterpart, the written characters mean "The idea of self-will." Self-will, in the *Mandarin Chinese* culture, connotes selfishness, or every person for him or herself. Another example: democracy, the word, originates in the ancient *Greek* language. In the *Greek*, democracy meant "ideas of the people." In the current domestic cultural idiom, democracy therefore represents a process. This essence is lost inside the contemporary *Chinese* idiom and culture.

Cultures and Subcultures Operate as Natural Segmentation Criteria

The cultural or subcultural memberships to which consumers belong (and with which they most identify) function as a natural criterion[10] from which marketers can create attractive market segments. Individual consumers' cultural category membership is a key factor that marketers should research and understand as they develop, target, and deliver promotional stories.

Understanding the parts of culture that are relevant to the consumers they are targeting or wish to target is important to all organizations' marketing success. As important, however, is an understanding of the most relevant and pressing trends and movements inside cultures. Cultural trends contain, in whole or parts, environmental opportunities or threats to marketers. Such as, for example, the newly emergent opportunity to use pretty much whatever formerly forbidden word you want in a bid to capture the American reading public's waning attention.

The back page (i.e., the magazine media's most expensive advertising space) of a distinctively non-flashy national publication called *The Week* recently featured a full-page advertisement. Nothing unusual about that. What was new and is germane here, however, was that this advertisement was kicked off, in 32-size FONT type, by a positioning header stating: "This tastes like sht! Blah!" The advertisement was promoting *The Original Oatly Oat Milk*. Neither democracy nor cultural decency is threatened by the *Oatly* brand's use of the word; oh crap, we almost just did it ourselves. But the magazine's, advertiser's, and our usage of the word underscores how rapidly cultural trends evolve and how marketers apparently sense they are strategically-compelled to change their marketing mix execution in response to the trends.

Even now, certain quintessentially *American* cultural values remain critical both to what it means to be an American citizen (as might be played out through consumption choices) and to marketing organizations selling certain brands to US citizens. *Jeep*, the automobile brand, has long symbolized the *American* freedom and desire that exists to go anywhere or do anything as long as no one else or no "property" is injured in the process. Not coincidentally, those round, horse-like *Jeep* eyes (headlights)

---

10. The word criterion, as used above, is a synonym for metric or measurement.

symbolize *America's Wild West*. SUVs, in general, are big, powerful, aggressive-looking or aggressive in fact—core American cultural values, all. Then there is *Merrill Lynch*, the investment house. *Merrill Lynch* has always used a bull running ahead of and standing apart from the herd as its unique brand identifier. This breed-apart-from-the-herd imagery symbolizes and captures, in one iconic image, rugged-individualism, another core cultural value. Don't merely run with the bulls, run ahead of the bulls. And yes, *The Bull* is a *Wall Street* branding emblem that symbolizes a rising stock market; better invest now!, as *Wall Street's* financial marketers collect their fees regardless of whether your investments yield acceptable returns.

CATEGORY 2: SOCIAL STIMULI

Like culture, various social factors function as natural criteria from which potentially fruitful market segments can be created and effective marketing mixes can be prepared for those consumer groupings that are targeted.

Social Class

Social class functions as a measurement that can be used to develop successful market segments. Social classes exist as relatively enduring and ordered divisions inside the American population. Generally, six social classes are thought to exist inside *America*. The six are labeled the upper-upper, lower-upper, upper-middle, low-middle, lower-upper, and lower-lower social classes. The consumer membership inside each social class category is relatively homogenous in nature. Consumers residing within particular social classes share relatively similar values, interests, and lifestyle behaviors. The membership of each social class is also relatively or comparatively different from the other six social class membership sets. Different, for example, in terms of their preferred attitudes, behaviors, and lifestyle choices.

Answers to "so what" questions are typically useful. The "so what" answer here is that consumers hailing from or currently residing in particular social classes are more likely to respond in similarly favorable or unfavorable fashions to the same promotions, pricing levels, or product values. Consumers from the same social classes are similarly more likely to desire the same sorts of products/brands as solutions in their lives.

In other words, consumers from the same social classes are more or less likely to "like" or "dislike" the same product or service options. Meaning, at net, the members of the same social class are likely to be attracted toward or repulsed by the same marketing mixes. By contrast, members of another social class likely will be turned on or off in a similar fashion by different marketing mixes. Marketers should target specific segments and refine (adjust) and position their marketing mix values accordingly.

Social class membership may represent a more important segmentation criteria than most marketing experts think—and for reasons most people would rarely admit. Indeed, social class-based acts of bias or bigotry based on an individual consumer's perceived or actual social class membership may exist as the last broadly practiced form of discrimination inside contemporary society. (The only other form of practiced discrimination or bias that may compete head-to-head in this bias sweepstakes with social class-based prejudgments—yes, prejudice—is the typically unspoken prejudices that exist against overweight consumers. Yes, as noted during Module 5, this specific bias still dominates even as nearly two-thirds of American consumers are either obese or overweight.)

Then there is perhaps the most heinous of all social class-based biases: The bigotry of low expectations that are imposed on certain social classes.

We're not suggesting such social class membership-based biases are acceptable. (Or for that matter that the bias against "weight" is right.) We're instead purposefully explaining that this sort of prejudice definitely exists, in large portions. What's happening is that social class "uppers" frequently look down upon and disparage their perceived social class "inferiors" for no good reason. But these biased attitudes and behavioral responses flow up, as well. Members of lower social classes routinely disparage and criticize folks residing inside higher social class strata, again usually for no good reason. Social class membership clearly exercises material influences on the attitudes and behaviors of consumers.

Determinants of Social Class Membership

Social class membership is never determined by one single factor. Consumers' social class membership, or their status, consequently cannot be measured by a single factor. Instead, social class membership is determined/measured by a combination of several variables. Social class measurement factors/criteria include consumers' occupations; annual incomes; primary sources of income; educational attainment (highest level); accumulated wealth; primary residence neighborhood (zip codes); schools, as in universities, from which they graduated; or so forth. Marketers consolidate these variables into a single measure when attempting to determine given consumers' social class membership through marketing research.

The consumer memberships of social classes are often characterized by distinct brand preferences. These brand preferences often relate to clothing choices, home furnishings decision, neighborhoods in which consumers choose to locate their primary residence, leisure/entertainment activity choices, and automobile preferences that differing social class memberships typically display. Explained more simply: Which social class memberships are more likely to own and actually fire guns, travel to Europe, attend church, drink mainstream as opposed to boutique brewery beer, or drive big trucks? Is it the same social class? You know the answer is "hardly." And therein lies evidence exemplifying the differing sorts of preferred consumer decisions that an individual's social class membership can often inspire.

Social Status

Social status functions as a positional good.[11] Social status delivers positional value to consumers. This means that their social status elevates certain consumers above certain other consumers—you

---

11. The definition, nature, and significance of the term "positional goods" is discussed during Module 9.

know what's being discussed here, you learned everything and more than you need to know about the topic as you passed through middle school. Social status is a value that many people covet—even if comparatively few readily admit it.

Social status works like this. To get or remain on top of any social heap, merely having fine things is not enough. Your things must be finer than anyone else's things, particularly those anyone(s) who occupy the same social sphere as you do.

Many, though certainly not all, human beings are obviously status-conscious and status-seeking and status-driven creatures. This is likely an evolved natural trait rather than a learned behavior.

When coupled with social media, our natural tendency to seek higher social status for ourselves probably created a situation where it was inevitable that celebrity-based status would become the weird mutant phenomenon it has become—once the "right" social networking technologies were introduced broadly to the market. Many people sit in the audience, but only a few stand on the stage. So of course many consumers naturally look up toward or look down upon celebrities, dependent upon the particular audience (market segment) in which those individuals reside, and thereafter passionately seek to buy or do things that will make them more like or less like the celebrities who have grabbed their attention.[12] All because status- and celebrity-conscious consumers want to be more like/less like . . .

Acts of consumption routinely play out like highly competitive but still understated games. Say, someone in your social sphere who buys a more expensive watch or car to climb up the social ladder. These singular acts often force other social climbers, possibly you, to buy more or better watches/cars to stay even or climb up toward their aspired social status. Fashion, in particular, is indicative of many things. Fashion is visual iconography that represents and captures both the past and present. At the same time, fashion is also a leading indicator of consumers' displayed economic and social status.

Consumers' pursuit of higher social status benefits marketers. The same pursuits empower, grow, and sustain the domestic economy.

Does their pursuit of higher social status benefit consumers' psyches or their emotional well-being? Often not. After all, people are not what they consume . . . despite what marketers of prestigious brands often seek to finesse consumers to believe. Social comparisons are routinely made, and routinely generate net negative outcomes. Comparisons are the thief of joy largely because happiness is reality minus expectations. Whenever consumers compare themselves socially to others (I've got more and better stuff), they find folks upon whom they can look down, and may revel in unmerited pride. Whenever consumers compare themselves socially to others (crap, those "others" have more

---

12. A tendency to engage in something akin to celebrity worship is probably baked into consumers' genetic cakes. Historically, celebrity followership likely involved people looking up to the leaders of their tribe of 150 or so people. However, back then built-in and incentive-based mechanisms likely existed for tribal leaders to not get too big-headed about their elevated status because of the potential negative consequences of not ruling well over a bunch of people you knew personally. But such natural-arising human constraints likely ran off the rails more than a little once modern social networking technology got involved. Now millions, rather than dozens, of "consumers" worship or criticize another few individuals. From there, it's watch-out time, because as the adage suggests: power corrupts. Or, perhaps we should not quickly or reflexively criticize consumers who follow celebrities. There's much that consumers can learn from celebrities that will help them improve their lives and make them better people. That's why this book religiously recommends following and trying to emulate truly intelligent and highly inspiring celebrities such as *Paris Hilton* or the *Kardashians*, or *Harry & Megan* and *William & Catherine*. Or not.

and better stuff than me), they feel envy, covetousness, and dissatisfaction. While dissatisfied feelings definitely motivate greater amounts of consumption, which helps marketers and the economy, feelings of envy, pride, and/or covetousness create all day long net-emotional or net-psychological negatives for many if not most consumers who engage in such social comparison games. Watch out: envy eats our bones.

Envy Plays "Special Roles" Inside Social Classes

Feelings of envy, in particular, are incredibly powerful negative motivators. One primary reason why is because for many consumers the only thing worse than not getting what they want is seeing other consumers that they know get what they want. This powerful emotion is the prime factor that props up the *German* word *schadenfreude*. This nasty word is now routinely used inside the English language too. *Schadenfreude* describes the pleasure individuals sometimes experience as they learn about or observe other people's misfortunes.

By the way, is anyone interested in experiencing a bit less envy inside their interior emotional lives? Thought so. Then stop making comparisons. The best way to ruin the receipt of a good thing or the feeling that finally, one has enough, is to compare what we have to other supposedly better things or feelings. Constant comparison games, every bit as much as entitlement or unrealistic games, are a trap. Run your own race; enjoy your own life; and remember, envy can consume consumers, nearly everyone.

Of course, on the macroeconomic downside, if every American consumer instantly began following these restorative courses of action the economy would slowly then immediately fall into a depression from which the nation might never recover.

There's not much need to worry about this happening, however. As economist *Thomas Sowell* recently tweeted, "when people are presented with the alternatives of hating themselves for their failures or hating others for their success, they seldom choose to hate themselves."

Membership Groups

Other social factors beyond social class may prove important to marketers as they segment, target, and seek to create uniquely desirable positions for brands residing inside their organizations' product portfolios by managing their marketing mixes.

Membership groups can be used as one such segmentation criteria. Fraternities/sororities, *Rotary Clubs*, CPAs, church congregations (specific religion type matters too), the *NAACP*, motorcycle clubs, the *NRA,* or *AARP*; these are all examples of membership groups. The fact that they voluntarily decide to belong to any one or more of these membership groups often impacts consumers' decision-making and subsequent behaviors. As does the fact that many consumers often aspire to one day belong to a particular membership group. You might, for example, want to belong to a motorcycle club. Well now, likely everybody would agree that a good first step to earning membership would entail deciding to and then actually buying a "cool" motorcycle. *Harley-Davidson* sounds about right.

Family

Consumers' families and family membership are used by marketers to create fruitful market segments. Families exercise a huge influence on consumer decisions and behaviors. Various consumption-related family roles must be performed by someone inside the family. For example, decision-maker roles, gatekeeper roles, actual user roles, purchasing agent roles, influencer roles, and financier roles exist. Any given family member may perform one or more of these roles across time and perform in certain roles when, say, washing machines/dryers are being purchased or in different roles when groceries, grooming products, or home repair services are being acquired.

Which family member generally leads the way when decisions about automobiles, vacations, home purchases, or restaurant choices are made? Is it the same family member all the time? Usually, not. Instead, one family member is likely deemed as expert decision-maker for automobile purchases; another for home furnishing purchases. Children usually perform inside either user or influencer roles, or both. For certain product categories, the role that children play as members of the buying unit should be carefully analyzed as marketers develop/execute strategic marketing plans.

The traditional nuclear family unit, one featuring two heterosexual married parents living together as marital partners with kids living together in the house, still exists. But only as a surprisingly small minority of family types. Many other types of family units also exist today, and B2C marketers often seek to create unique-and-uniquely-desirable marketing mixes for each sort of family unit that exists in the broader marketplace. As they should. The most desirable family segment for many marketers has long been labeled DINKs—as in, Double Income No Kids. DINKs often represent a sweet spot for marketers selling high-end vacations, jewelry, automobiles, and so forth.

Reference Groups and Opinion Leaders

As noted, the human propensity to reference certain select groups in order to secure cues and guidance about how to behave or what products to purchase/use apparently represents natural rather than learned behavior. For example, did you know that a gathering of flamingos is known as a flamboyance? Why is knowing this factoid relevant? The answer is simple. It is because groups exercise large influences over most consumers' habits. In particular, groups influence the products that people buy and how others identify them. Animals also routinely gather in groups for safety, especially when they eat. Flamingos obtain their flamboyant pink color from the food they eat (i.e., brine shrimp). Thus, flamingos are identified as a group based on the products they consume collectively. Just like humans often are . . . .

Reference groups exercise a tremendous influence on many consumers' decision-making processes. Reference groups (which groups do consumers voluntarily choose to reference for guidance or for cues before making certain purposes?) are consequently extremely important to marketers as those marketers engage in either segmentation or targeting processes. Consumers look toward reference groups to secure insights and implicit recommendations regarding what they should or should not consume and/or how they should or should not behave.

Reference Groups, Two Basic Types

Two basic kinds of reference groups exist. The first type is called aspirational reference groups. As the name implies, these are groups to which consumers aspire to belong. Consumers who reference them typically attempt to model the consumer behaviors of aspiration reference groups. Consumers engage in such modeling behaviors even if they do not or never will belong to the group. Simple example: few males reading this will ever play in the *NFL* or the *NBA*. That does not mean that ample portions of generally younger men aspire to be more like *Zeke* (Elliot) or *Zion* (Williamson) by wearing the same gear each baller wears or drinking the drink that either endorse.

The second type of reference group that proves extremely important to marketers are called opinion leaders.[13] Again, this is because opinion leaders often exercise extreme effects on consumers as these potential customers seek, and sometimes struggle, to find "advice and counsel or recommendations" about how to make the best possible consumption decisions. Opinion leaders are generally well-known individuals who are recognized as experts about particular product categories. That is, they are well-known or viewed as experts among the individual consumers or consumer segments being influenced. For various reasons opinion leaders enjoy the opportunity to sway consumers' thoughts and behaviors related to products/brands for which opinion leaders are known and viewed as experts upon.

Politicians, business leaders, community leaders, journalists, educators, celebrities, and sports stars can function as opinion leaders and often actively seek out the label or designation as opinion leader. But opinion leaders are more likely to be regular folks whom other consumers know personally, and whom they like, trust and, again, view as experts about particular product categories. Opinion leaders function as unpaid, uncontrollable, highly believable—and consequently highly-influential—ambassadors on behalf of any brands they praise or condemn.

Opinion leadership works. The process is powerful. The reason, primarily, is because human creatures default naturally toward imitation of each other.

These default responses arise in aspirational ways. I want to ball like *Zion* so I will dress like young Mr. *Williamson*.

Sometimes these default reactions actually arise inspirationally. For example, I am already in, part of, this group. The group might include males or females; *Dallas Cowboys'* or *New York Giants'* football team fans; or Goths versus Hippies versus Preppies groups. Since I already belong to the group, should I dress like them? The usual consumer response will be yes.

Their Absence of "Original Sin": Why Opinion Leaders Are So Influential

Opinion leaders are usually perceived as true experts for only one or a few product categories. Consumers who voluntarily choose to reference their opinions may directly solicit their experience, knowledge, and/or expertise because they perceive the individual opinion leaders are highly knowledgeable—experts—about, say, electronics, movies or music, fashion, or automobile product

---

13. Contemporary opinion leaders are often also called and/or aspire to be known as "social media influencers."

categories. In turn, marketers often directly target opinion leaders,[14] perhaps by offering special incentives that encourage known opinion leaders to check out the innovative choice, as new products are introduced. Marketers do this in the hope, the expectation, that these thought leaders will then endorse their brands to others.

Opinion leaders can exercise tremendous sway over other consumers who occupy the same general social sphere as them. Their powerful influence derives in no small measure from the fact that opinion leaders are free from an original sin from which few marketers could ever complete absolution. This original sin derives from the inarguable fact that most everything marketers say to prospective or actual customers is directly or indirectly said for the money. And most B2C or B2B customers explicitly or implicitly recognize that this condition exists. Marketers' motives, as they communicate product-related information, advice, or counsel are therefore always a little suspect. Or should be . . . a little suspect . . . if and when prospective customers possess much more than half a brain themselves. Rarely, if ever, should anyone blindly take advice from anyone who stands to benefit from the device, absent long—say seventy-two or so hours—deliberation.

No reason exists to criticize marketers because they are guilty of this specific original sin. Marketers cannot help having the ultimate intention of selling products for their own monetary gain. This fact, however, can prove problematic for marketers primarily because discerning customers always suspect marketers' motives. Again, as they should . . . Consequently, the foremost source of the awesome marketing power embedded in opinion leadership, which is a type of WOM, derives from message recipients' assumption and belief that this motivation is missing from WOM endorsers. Opinion leaders are absolved from the original marketing sin and as consequence are typically more persuasive and influential than marketers themselves.

CATEGORY 3: PERSONAL STIMULI

Various personal stimuli also affect the decisions that consumers make. These same personal stimuli consequently also influence consumer behavior. These stimuli include the general ages; family life cycle status; occupation and current economic circumstances; and lifestyle choices of consumers. Again, their lifestyle choices are generally reflected in the psychographics, dominant personality traits, and/or the self-concepts of consumers.

Psychographics, AIOs, Lifestyles

Psychographics, AIOs, and lifestyle measurements can be used separately, collectively, or in any combination for segmenting, targeting, and, ultimately, positioning purposes.

Psychographics, as a measure, is a combination of consumers' preferred AIOs and their dominant personality traits. AIOs essentially measure what consumers prefer to do or contemplate (think

---

14. Contemporary marketers can easily identify individuals who function as opinion leaders within specific product categories by monitoring their behaviors on social networking sites. Marketers, for example, might be seeking the woman who reads and talks about trucks, including her own, all the time. Or marketers might covet a relationship with the man who is constantly perusing restaurant or movie reviews. This is how marketing research operates in real time inside modern markets.

about) during their free time. AIOs consequently capture portions of consumers' beliefs, attitudes, and opinions. The acronym AIOs stands for (consumers') Activities, Interests and Opinions. Their preferred lifestyles profile individual consumers' patterns of acting and interacting with other people and various stimuli, including marketing stimuli, within the world.

Personality

S/he has a big personality. You've likely heard similar sentiments expressed. A "big personality" is usually a statement of how engaging or entertaining someone is. But a more formal definition of the word personality itself includes people's habitual ways of thinking, feeling, and relating to others. ("Habitual ways," in this context, means how people regularly or routinely behave.) Most people understand that individuals differ along certain personal characteristics and tendencies. Such differences may reveal themselves along people's tendencies to display more or less introversion or extroversion; fondness for details or attention to detail; tolerance for boredom; willingness to be helpful to others; determination or grit; and other personal qualities.

What people often fail to realize, however, is that the personality qualities that most of humanity value most highly are not randomly distributed. A far from complete list of such highly valued personality characteristics might include individual consumers' kindness, their tolerance for others, or their willingness to honor their commitments. These "valued" personality tendencies tend to exist as sets, collections, or constellations of personality "traits" that are recognizable and reasonably stable over time. Knowing this, marketers position themselves and their brands to take advantage of their knowledge in ways that may either help or hurt individual consumers, or for that matter help or hurt the larger environment.

The personality characteristics that most of humanity definitely does not value also often cluster together in similarly predictable ways, and these too are easily exploited by marketers. Such attributes might include individual and generational collections of consumers' impulsivity, their speed and propensity to grow angry easier, or their self-centeredness. These "less desirable" personality tendencies similarly tend to exist as sets, collections, or constellations of personality "traits" that are recognizable and reasonably stable over time. Knowing this, marketers position themselves and their brands to take advantage of their knowledge in ways that may either help or hurt consumers or the larger environment.

By the way, did you hear that *Copernicus* just texted to remind *Gen Y* that its consumer cohort, or market segment, is not "the center of the universe," any more than *Millennials, Gen X, Baby Boomers,* or any other generational cohort that ever lived (there have been hundreds) who also once thought they too were the center of the universe during their formative years. If you don't get the "center of the universe" reference *Google Copernicus*. Read about who he got in big trouble with, all because Copernicus was either brave enough or dumb enough to tell the truth.

Personality Defined

Personalities exist as sets of unique psychological characteristics associated with consumers that lead them to engage in relatively enduring and consistent responses to stimuli as those stimuli arise inside those consumers' environments. Those stimuli could include marketing-initiated and therefore marketer-controlled stimuli. This definition is complicated, yes. It is also powerful, correct, and useful.

From marketers' perspective, key personality traits include consumers' self-confidence; desire to exercise dominance; degree of sociability; willingness to broadcast, as on social media, to others; willingness to adapt; willingness to take risks; and venturesome nature. Yet marketers also have successfully profiled and segmented consumers based on their relative possession of five additional major personality traits. Those consumer personality traits are openness, conscientiousness, agreeableness, extroversion, and narcissism.

Marketing organizations often develop these consumer profiles today by analyzing consumers' *Facebook* posts where they express likes or dislikes, and by analytically coding and then classifying what consumers write online. *Tweets* are mapped to determine how often consumers are serene, alert, depressed, tense, or elated.

Aligning Brands with Consumer Personalities; Aligning Consumer Personalities with Brands

Consumers often select brands that they believe are consistent with, would favorably reflect upon; and/or would help them express their personality. Brands, it turns out, can also have personalities. Brands can be perceived by consumers as, say, rugged, competent, sophisticated, sincere, exciting, or sexually desirable in their personalities. If you are male and badass, what brand of beer will you likely drink? Hint, what beer brands have earned rugged personalities? If you are a young heterosexual male and a "player," what clothing brand will you likely give females as a gift? Hint, what female-targeted clothing brands have earned "sexy" personalities?

Jeep vehicles or *Wrangler* jeans are generally perceived to have a rugged personality.

Each *Big-Four* accounting firm has strategically cultivated competent brand personalities.

Consumers generally deem and identify *Rolex* as a brand that simultaneously evinces a sophisticated, stylish, and tasteful personality.

The *Hallmark* greeting card brand, meanwhile, is widely perceived as utterly sincere in nature—and personality.

These perceptions of sincerity likely represent one reason why consumers so willingly pay $6.95 to $8.95 or more for card products that likely cost a nickel or a dime to make and ship. Yet despite their pricey prices *Hallmark* greeting cards dominate inside their product category and market sector. This dominance is surely also based in part on the brand's positioning tagline, "When You Care Enough to Send the Very Best."[15] Here, as often occurs, the positioning tagline also operates as a branding slogan.

---

15. *Hallmark* does not take a back seat to any marketer when it comes to the precision and effectiveness of its market targeting, either. *Hallmark* produces different types of cards for every occasion: birthdays, anniversaries, deaths, graduations, promotions, marriages, and for all we know divorces, and so forth. But then *Hallmark* produces cards targeted with razor-like precision at consumer subsegments existing inside each of these card-based product categories. Among birthday cards, and they alone, for example, *Walmart* shelves feature *Hallmark* cards targeted, by category, toward birthday girls and boys and birthday women and men who are sons; daughters; mothers; fathers; grandfathers; papas; grandmothers; nanas; merely "thinking of you(s)"; merely "missing you(s)"; "you're like a daughter/son to me"; coworkers; church friends; nieces; nephews; aunts; uncles, and so forth. Then, adding additional targeting precision to already eloquently-targeted cards, differing *Hallmark* birthday cards are available that feature refined, serious, funny, solemn, profound, sexy, religious, elegiac, goofy, poetic; plaintive, nostalgic, and so forth messaging styles. And we're just describing cards available on two *Walmart* shelves here; not some fancy greeting card store that is full of card shelves and selections. How do we know these things? Simple, one author did a little marketing research by walking into a *Walmart* store and perused the two greeting cards aisles.

The positioning statement rocks on two fronts. First, buy branded greeting cards other than *Hallmark*, and givers self-evidently did not care enough about the getters to spend a little more to send the very best. Sad, or at least that's what Hallmark wants getters to think. Second, what consumer doesn't want "the very best," particularly when someone else is gifting it to them.

But, of course, at least one other reason exists to explain why consumers pay so dearly for the ideas expressed inside *Hallmark*-branded cards is those cards. Turns out that *Hallmark's* card's words and wording solve customer problems. Consumer problems related to "what to say" and/or "how to say it" at the advent of the product recipient's birthday, anniversary, illness, birth, loss of a loved one, and so forth.

Hallmark truly does appear to have a card available to say just the right thing for every occasion. And the particular type of value that *Hallmark* cards provide is clearly worth the extra costs in dollars that consumers must pony-up to acquire it. Were this not the case, consumers would not purchase the high-priced cards. *Hallmark* should be lauded, not criticized, for its high prices. Because those high prices underscore the degree to which the *Kansas City*-based marketer has its consumer behavior-management game on by elevating the perceived value of their cards so high that their high prices became less important considerations among customers.

Self-Concept

The self-concepts of consumers are best described as how those individuals feel about themselves. Yet self-concepts can also be defined as mental images consumers hold deeply inside their minds about their own personal strengths, weaknesses, "coolness quotients," abilities to influence or exercise power over others, or social status and end up having to enjoy or endure about themselves.

Consumers' self-concepts are essentially their self-identities. Consumers constantly make buying decisions that support or allow them to maintain their self-identities because consumers are pre-programmed psychologically to try to behave in ways and consume brands that reinforce or enhance their self-concepts. Consumers want to buy and consume brands that make them feel better—about themselves. These wants are often desperate and therefore highly motivating in nature. Motivating to the point where these mere wants are often experienced by affected consumers as acute needs.

Consumers' self-concepts can be expressed in various ways. For example, deciding to engage in terrorism or school shootings gives losers the chance to ascend from zeros to heroes inside their minds; thus, consciously if usually temporarily elevating their self-concept. Please note that deciding to engage in terrorist acts or school shootings, actually, also a terrorist act, are each behavioral choices.

Most Americans, in their private hearts, embrace internal images—continuously rolling mental motion pictures—not of who they actually are but of who and what they desire to be. No worries here; most B2C marketers will happily help consumers see all their dreams come true. The preceding statement is not a joke. Self-concepts are important. Consumers' opinions of themselves matter more than the opinions of strangers. Or at least they should. Take that, *Facebook*.

CATEGORY 4: PSYCHOLOGICAL STIMULI

Four psychological stimuli often play huge roles as they influence the choices that consumers make. By name, these four basic psychological stimuli are perceptions, learning, beliefs and attitudes, and motivations. Motivations are also called motives or drives. Motivations or motives or drives all express themselves or play out as needs inside most consumer decision-making contexts.

Perceptions

Perceptions capture processes by which people select, organize, and then interpret or attempt to make sense of stimuli. Stimuli can consist of old or new information. Consumers create perceptions in an effort to develop meaningful and useful pictures of the world around them. Their cultural and social class memberships affect consumers' perceptions. As do how consumers are feeling during the moments in which they're exposed to particular stimuli. Their feelings, as in, are those consumers being exposed to marketing or other stimuli feeling tired, angry, full, happy, sad, or randy right now?

The point is that consumers often don't interpret stimuli as they, the stimuli, are. Instead consumers interpret stimuli as they, the consumers, are—and often as they are right in that moment. Another way of saying the same thing is that consumers' points-of-view are materially affected by their points-of-viewing.

Three primary types of perceptions exist. First, there is selective attention. Consumers do not pay attention to most stimuli to which they are exposed. For example, some people will listen to everything that *Donald Trump* or *Mitch McConnell* say on *FOX* because they are conservative and *FOX* is a right-leaning media outlet. Those same people would generally ignore anything *Joe Biden* or *Kamala Harris* said on the same television medium, if indeed *Biden* or *Harris* agreed to answer questions asked by *FOX* anchorpersons. But right now, at least, it's unlikely that either liberal *Democrat* politician would visit *FOX* because the network's viewers are highly underrepresented inside these two *Democrat's* normal target segments, or audiences. Things really are all marketing all the time.

Selective distortion (of perceptions) also. The takeaway here is that consumers usually perceive and interpret new information in ways that support what they already believe. This is the primary reason why changing people's minds is so difficult. Which in turn underscores why segmentation and targeting is so important.

Finally, there is selective retention. Selective retention suggests, correctly, that consumers tend to retain information that they perceive supports attitudes and beliefs they already hold.

The bottom line right here is that human beings naturally exhibit strong tendencies to hear/see/believe what they want to hear/see/believe and to filter out or reject what they don't. Rolling combinations of human emotions and biases almost always influence how consumers respond to existing and new information but also how and whether they pay attention to and thereafter accept the information embedded inside the stimulus.

All people engage in each of the three perceptual activities at one time or another. Knowing this, successful marketers manipulate consumers' perceptual tendencies in ways that generate positioning and profit advantage. Consumer decision-makers who fully understand how often marketers are playing them are difficult to find.

Learning

Learning describes changes arising in human behaviors as a result of experiences. Or, for that matter, changes that arise in canine, rodent, or aviary behaviors as a result of their experiences, given that most of the content that follows in this brief section is based on what clinical psychologists or psychiatrists learned as they studied the learning responses of laboratory animals as they, the animals, were manipulated—there's a reason why clinical psychologists and psychiatrists are often branded as "rat runners."

But on a more human and humane level, the three-year-child who touches a hot stove top, but only once, offers a classic and easily understood illustration of how classical learning works.

Learning arises from a four-way interaction between (1) consumers' motives; (2) stimuli, including marketing cues, to which consumers are exposed and elect to pay attention to; (3) consumers' decisions and behavioral responses to the stimuli; and (4) rewards or punishments resulting from consumers' behavioral responses. Those emerging rewards or punishments then function either as positive or negative reinforcements to those behaviors.

Rewards function as positive reinforcements. After their receipt of positive reinforcements, consumers will likely engage in the rewarded behavior again. They repeat the behavior because it has been "learned." Punishments function as negative reinforcements. After their receipt of negative reinforcements, consumers will likely not engage in the punished behavior, again. Consumer decision-makers generally will not repeat the behavior because they learned to avoid the negative consequences visited upon them.

If the consequences of their learned decisions work well for them, consumers continue making similar choices. If the consequences turn out poorly, consumers learn something new and unappealing, and ultimately will likely purchase something new. One fundamental takeaway: consumer decisions always generate behaviors that in turn always generate consequences. These decision-making fundamentals or some close variation of it has already been expressed four time. This repetition should signal the importance that the authors place on the basic idea.

Beliefs and Attitudes

Beliefs are descriptive thoughts that consumers develop, have, and hold about something. The "something" might include people, ideas, places, or products. Whatever the something is, it has, by definition, functioned as a stimuli in that consumers formulated perceptions about it.

Stimuli may arrive in the form of products, messages, brands, shapes, colors, words, music, designs, styles, customers, or some combination of many of these potentially influential factors. Or, stimuli may arrive in the form of ideas, experiences, or people.

Attitudes, by contrast, capture consumers' relatively enduring, consistent, and more deeply-held evaluations, feelings, and tendencies toward stimuli, whatever their form.

Consumers' attitudes are more deeply held than their beliefs. Their depth makes attitudes more influential than beliefs on consumers' behaviors. In a general sense, attitudes are comprised of multiple beliefs that have been bundled together, linked with, and inter-connected with each other. Think about suspension cables under which long and heavy bridges can be hung. Now think about the spectacularly long, strong, and thick cables that support the *Golden Gate Bridge* that spans the relatively narrow waterway between the *Pacific Ocean* and *San Francisco Bay*—the bridge's cables are like attitudes. Finally, think about the thousands of narrow wires that are bundled to comprise the cables—the individual wires are like beliefs.

Key Takeaways

Consumers' behaviors follow consumers' decisions follow consumers' attitudes—a lot of the time, though not always. Explained more succinctly, consumers' attitudes drive their decisions drive their behaviors—again, most of the time, but not universally.

The idea that most marketers should attempt to change consumers' attitudes is generally "stupid." Most marketers would go quickly broke if their initial or ongoing success depends on changing people's attitudes. A superior strategic marketing approach would entail making sure the products that marketers initially create and subsequently promote, distribute, and price in order to deliver "value-propositions" align with consumers attitudes that already exist within targeted segments.

Products deliver benefits, value, and solutions. These benefits, values, and solutions coalesce inside the value propositions of products. That value proposition ideally aligns precisely with the types of consumer attitudes already present within targeted market segments. Presumably, differing target segments are characterized by differing sets of prevailing attitudes.

Value propositions, generated by combining all possible benefits/values/solutions created through marketing mixes, incentivize consumers. Incentives, in turn, motivate consumers.

Motives (Drives)

Motives or drives function as needs that are sufficiently pressing to direct individual consumers to seek satisfaction and solutions to whatever problems have triggered their motives or drives. Some needs are biological in nature. Humans "need" food and water, nourishment, sex, or sleep. Other needs are psychological in nature. Humans "need" to feel loved, as if they fit in, safe, and as if others view them as "cool."

The five types of basic human needs are depicted in the well-known pyramid shape known as Abraham Maslow's "Hierarchy of Needs." The five types of needs are described as physiological, safety, social, personal (self-esteem), and self-actualization, in that order, ranging up from the bottom to the top of "the pyramid."

An assumption that different needs will motivate the same consumer at different times drives this hierarchy. Consumers are motivated to satisfy their most pressing, the most basic physiological, needs first. This premise is reflected in the fact that Maslow's Hierarchy of Needs is pyramid-shaped, and in the fact that all pyramids feature disproportionally large bases. Consider that fifty-seven varieties of sadness exist. Turns out, the number 57 is not just a *Heinz 57 Sauce* thing. The thing is, however, that all but about 7 of the 57 number turn out to be problems that can be easily cured with a little flour and sugar—joking?

Humans get hungry. They also get horny, especially the younger male human specimens. To respond in these ways is imminently natural. Either human sensation—that of hungriness or horniness—represents both a physiological and a basic human drive. Neither need has to be created by marketers (although each desire is often stimulated by marketers). Moreover, all manner of needs follow as a consequence of the hungry or horny sensations—including about fifty shades of agitation, peevishness, or sadness when either of these needs are insufficiently satisfied.

The core takeaway here is that basic human needs matter. Were we kidding when we wrote "57"? Not really. Basic needs matter, and until they are satisfied few to no other outcomes or things really matter to humans; nothing else can actually make us feel happy or experience a sense of satisfaction until our baseline problems are solved. After all, the hunger need is really basic, basic as in it is located at the base of Maslow's pyramid.

Whatever their core nature is, once these lower-level needs are satisfied, consumers move up the pyramid toward the next "need-level" that has yet to be satisfied. Consumers continuously move up and down the hierarchy. No need is ever permanently satisfied: Fill your belly to near bursting today and you will be hungry again tomorrow. Feel good about yourself on Tuesday, meaning your self-esteem need is temporarily satisfied, but then something happens to bring you down emotionally by Wednesday. Knowing this, anyone can similarly figure out how comparatively easy it is for marketers to yank consumers up or down this hierarchy of needs as if the humans were puppets and the marketers their masters.

Products can be targeted and positioned based on the hierarchical need that they are intended to satisfy. Some products can be positioned to successfully satisfy more than one need. A fine house (home) for example, might satisfy safety, social, and self-esteem needs. Any consumer's opportunity to own and/or drive prestigious and therefore well-branded automobiles might achieve exactly the same ends.

These omnipresent human needs often play out in unexpected ways as their presence inspires unintended consequences. Take the basic human need to feel safe and secure, for example. One author entered a *JCPenney* store, the physical not the virtual site, for the first time in more than one year during January 2021. He discovered that *JCPenney* had spaced its counters and shelves seemingly much more than six safe feet apart in an obvious response to the then still-pressing COVID-19 threat. The safety need, or at least the implicit need to apparently respond proactivity to an unseen but definitively present threat (the COVID-19 virus itself) was clearly ruling the day inside this specific store location. Ruling the day even as, to your authors' frankly experienced retailing eye, the new merchandising design made *JCPenney's* store interiors appear even more empty and less exciting or inviting in the process. As always, and no implicit or explicit criticism in play here, the need to satisfy or to convey the perception of satisfying consumers omnipresent and always-pressing safety need had clearly won the day.

Motives matter. Sometimes the reasons why consumers decide to do something or purchase anything are as or more important than what they actually decide to do or to purchase.

Disproportionally Powerful Roles Played by Fear, Love, and Greed

Successful B2C marketers generally understand the degree to which most consumers are motivated much of the time by one or more of three specific motives: fear, greed, or love. Whenever marketers strategize about how best to develop effective advertising messages and then to inspire consumers to pay attention to them, which should be always, they would do well to design messages that either scare or piss-off consumers exposed to them. Nor should marketers ever forget or ignore the role that consumers' pursuit of pleasure and/or the desire to avoid pain plays is motivating their choices.

Modern media, for example, cannot thrive on agreement. "Us versus them" types of messaging generally must be, and is, used first to obtain and then to sustain consumers' attention. Conflict that is powerful and/or persuasive enough to piss-off or terrify the consumers of specific media needs to be ginned up. *FOX News* uses its particular genre of fear- and/or anger-inducing messaging, swinging right. *CNN*, meanwhile, uses another genre of fear-inducing and/or anger-inducing messages, but now swings hard left. When this happens *FOX* or *CNN* loyalists become more likely to listen to, see or read the channel or website; hang around on the medium; revisit the medium and spread the good or bad word around about the messages heard or seen on the media platform that is transmitting them. Each communication outcome represents a win for the media, regardless of whether an actual or e-based newspaper, any sort of social media, or any subset of news- or editorial/opinion-based television programming is being used.

The preceding five descriptions of what really motivates humans to pay attention and/or to care may appear simplistic. Perhaps the descriptions appeared harsh. Yet these accounts are accurate. Stop DVR-ing television programs or clicking away from *YouTube* advertisements for a day or two. Start actually watching the advertisements. You'll quickly observe how marketers rarely miss out on opportunities to subtly or brusquely stroke the erogenous zones [arousing feelings of fear, greed, love, pleasure, pain] of the audiences targeted by the advertising stories.

The idea that fear so forcefully motivates consumer behavior may surprise. Yet no one should be shocked. Consumer fears are rampant and subject to being ramped up easily by marketing promotions. Fear among consumers is only natural, it appears, as people grow afraid of what they are or are not, or remain afraid of what they have become, or may not become—as marketers strategically pull targeted fuel on their natural fears. If generating unfounded consumer fears were a football game, marketers would be winning 66–3.

Democrat political products (okay, candidates and office holders) routinely attempt to stir up fear among their targeted voters or likely voters. So do *Republican* products. Typically, *Democrats* seek to invoke one of three types of fear. One, fear about the environment. Two, fear about presumed social injustices such as racism or other forms of perceived or actual discrimination. Three, fear about the economy, which usually arrives in the form of marketing stories that emphasize income inequality. More recently, during 2016–20, *Democrat* political marketers inside government and the marketing party's allies in the media strategically tossed in moral fear, as in "look at how repugnant *Trump* [or insert another future or current *Republican* political product's name here] is."

Yet *President Franklin D. Roosevelt*, another *Democrat*, presumably was trying to calm a panicked America when, in the midst of the *Great Depression,* he insisted that, "The only thing we have to fear is fear itself." Notably, *FDR* (his branding identifier just like *JFK* was *Kennedy's*) made this assertion during the 1932 Presidential Campaign. The candidate clearly was engaged in nothing more or less than marketing.

The sum of all consumer fears ranges far and wide and deep. Humanity's collection of fears is nearly as diverse as humankind itself. Americans, in a recent survey,[16] tabbed government corruption as fear #1, followed in declining percentages by concerns about the health-care system, the environment, personal finance and war inside the Top Ten. Spine-tingling triggers such as public speaking and claustrophobic spaces ranked high, as well; while lower ranked, clowns were scarier than zombies who induced more fear than ghosts.

Okay, back to more traditional marketing—even though zombies have proven a dominant television and cinematic marketing theme for nearly ten years. A primary reason why consumers struggle with fears is because they, being wholly human, are simultaneously too primitive and too evolved for their own good. The aforementioned reptilian portions of our brains are cold-bloodedly efficient. Environmental stimuli that shout danger speed to the threat-perceiving amygdala (one of our three brains) within 74 milliseconds. This resounding promptness, across eons, has saved humankind from extinction. It's also promoted countless false alarms. Our ancestors' oldest fears are still with us, and that's part of the problem. Babies exhibit fight-or-flight responses to pictures of spiders and snakes due to instinct, not experience. Deeply-embedded aversion-responses to these and many other more manageable stimuli can pervert consumers' perceptions, their imagined-realities, and the processes by which these consumers make sense of stimuli to which they are exposed.

The more human portion of our brains, the larger brain parts that promote higher consciousness and reasoning, are supposed to help consumers sort out real- from imagined-fears. But, at times, even these smarter portions of our brains appear more committed to throwing out unfounded what-ifs about potentially imperiled loved ones or ourselves. Decades in the making, an entire body of risk-perception research specifies how badly consumers fall short of accurately determining which dangers are actually worth worrying about—and which can safely be ignored or dismissed. Consumers habitually overestimate the prospect of death by floods, murder, or lightning. Indeed, many multiples more people are killed by falling coconuts than by lightning in this world. Consumers, in the meantime, consistently underestimate much more genuine threats of death by asthma, stroke, diabetes, fast-food, stress, sugar. Or . . . because the subject is context relevant, consumers routinely estimate the risk of going broke before they die by failing to save and invest more now.

Do you suppose sophisticated marketers know these things? Do you think sophisticated marketers cultivate new and exploit such old and near fears? If you thought, yes, you're correct, both times. For example, marketers such as *Facebook, Google,* or *Instagram* absolutely have created a new fear. It's called FOMA; the Fear of Missing Out. But FOMA is not really a new fear. Humans have always feared missing out on good times, as it were. Today, however, this naturally-arising fear has reached

---

16. 2017 Survey of American Fears; *Chapman University*.

previously unthinkable heights because of consumers' incessant exposure to electronic steroids—or dopamine.

Creating Feelings Rather Than Thinking

Marketing messages targeted at consumers are more often designed to make them feel rather than think. Messages designed to stimulate outrage, fear, or low-grade but persistent anxiety in order that they, the stories that are generated, take up rent-free residence inside targeted consumers' minds. Such stories are often intended to eliminate rational and logical assessments of products' true value from customers' decision-making equations. These targeting and message approaches, as executed through their marketing mixes, make sense for marketers. Unfortunately, consumers often end up being manipulated without their knowledge.

How can this happen? The answers are relatively straightforward:

- Anger makes consumers optimistic and risk-seeking—more likely to buy. Yet anger also increases consumers' feelings of self-righteousness and clouds their judgments. This combination routinely plays out to the advantage of manipulative marketers.

- Fear makes consumers pessimistic and risk-averse—but marketers can finesse consumer fears in ways that cause them to pay attention and end up choosing products that they perceive will elevate their spirits or lower their sense of danger.

- Sadness and its cousin pessimism make people anxious to buy things to release them from their perceived plight. However, pessimism does have its place—the emotion fosters caution along with the pursuit of solutions.

- Disgust makes consumers less likely to buy anything at all.

Knowing these things, marketers routinely message and position—communicate about—their products in ways that are specifically designed to stimulate anger or fear among consumers. At times, marketers even attempt to ramp-up sadness among consumers they target.

The greatest obstacle to human pleasure is not pain but delusion. Any consumers' inordinate or unwarranted desires exist as a natural enemy of their happiness. But the fantasy that we somehow might attain something—remember the *Ferrari* sports car or six-week-long *Tuscany* sojourn—that exceeds what our financial or professional or family circumstances allow us to obtain is often effectively sold by marketers. And for now, we'll leave it up to readers to determine whether they think such marketer behaviors are ethical.

The desires of consumers to avoid pain or to secure pleasure are perfectly reasonable—who could argue against either consumer motive. But consumers are becoming or remain unhappy because of boundless natures of their imaginations. Human lives are finite and mortal; we are gripped by illusions about the infinite. Consumers' fantasies about infinite pleasure drives their susceptibility to be captured by marketers' presentations; for example, marketers' incessant promotions of idealistic versions of romantic love. It's foolish, however, to not accept that reasonable limits to pleasure or that limits to pain do not exist and immature or short-sighted to not realize that too much pleasure often leads to pain.

Continuing this painful—or is it pleasurable—discussion. Consumers (i.e., here readers) might benefit from understanding and accepting the fact that pain is always housed in their brain, although it's obviously felt elsewhere (sometimes our legs or back really do physically hurt). The fact that pain is always housed in the brain means that numerous ways exist for marketers to inspire pain's purported or actual arrival and to then introduce and position their brands as solutions that supposedly contravene against pain's negative influence.

Yet pain is nothing more than anybody's brain registering a departure from whatever state the body's brain has previously regarded as "normal." This description applies to both emotional and physical types of pain. If consumers were to train themselves to view pain as normal, their pain will cease to exist. But such an argument has no relevance here and won't happen among anywhere but the most fervent *Buddhists*, and then only on an intermittent basis.

What is relevant here is that often what is actually happening when "pain arrives" is that one's mind is mourning for the way things used to be. For example, marketers could and do stand-up advertisements that use songs to purposefully evoke nostalgia among targeted consumers for a favored decade of life that is not long past for them, and no matter how they long, cannot be recaptured. And of courses do exactly this.

Alternatively, what is actually happening when "pain arrives" is that one's mind is mourning for the way things inside one's life could be but currently are not. This is an even easier game for many B2C marketers to play—and win. All such marketers have to do to win is stand-up an advertisement that "shows" the wonderful outcomes and happy times that "will happen" and be yours once you make the right brand choice, versus the crap that will remain in your life if you fail to make the right choice.

This is the basic promotional game that many well-branded and well-positioned B2C marketers play like maestros. And the damnable fact for consumers or the redemptive fact for marketers is that few consumers realize how adroitly their presumed-pain-points are being played. Any readers' "take" whether this fact is bad (damnable) or good (redeemable) depends upon their point of viewing; their perception. If you view this state of affairs as good, you have adopted the B2C marketer point-of-view. If you view this phenomenon as bad, you have adopted the point of view that a now better informed and safer consumer would generally possess.

Now, you are ready to be either a successful B2C marketer, or a happier and healthier consumer. Each outcome, in fact, appears attractive. Can you enjoy both possibilities at the same time? Sure, you could. But while you are pondering those possibilities please reflect upon how often our perceptions—our points of view—about what is right or wrong or better or worse are determined by our points of viewing.

MODULE 7.4

How Consumers Make Decisions

A five-stage consumer decision-making model is presented below. The model explains how most consumers make B2C decisions most of the time. However, before this discussion begins, four disclaimers should be considered.

First, the following discussion below combines extensive and limited consumer decision-making processes into one presentation and one model. (Detailed definitions and discussions of extensive- and limited-consumer consumer decision-making processes also follow.) Second, consumers inside a given market or market segment need not necessarily pass through the same consumer decision-making stages at the same time. Third, no need exists to assume that all consumers necessarily pass through all five stages. Consumers can enter/exit any one stage at any time they choose. Fourth and finally, consumers often do not pass through the stages in the order presented below.

Despite these disclaimers, most consumers do pass through all five stages in the order presented below. This outcome is especially likely to result when consumers are engaging in high-involvement purchase decisions. High-involvement decisions arise when consumers are making decisions about products that are genuinely important to them. Those sorts of products are called "high-involvement" products. A more refined definition and more detailed discussion of the role that "consumer involvement" plays as it influences consumer decision-making processes also follow.

THE CONSUMER DECISION-MAKING PROCESS

When the buy or do-not-buy decisions that consumers are making are genuinely important to them (i.e., a high-involvement decision), decision-making becomes more a journey than an instantaneous reaction. Most of the important decisions that consumers make unfold in procedural stages. These stages are explained below.

Stage 1: Need Recognition . . .

Or, stated differently but the same, consumers' recognition that some problem exists in their lives always functions as the trigger that launches their decision-making processes. Problems or needs arise when consumers "recognize" that something is actually or merely perceived as wrong, missing, or lacking in their lives. Needs or problems arise when ideas, notions, or feelings such as "I need" or "I want" arise inside consumers' minds. Once the recognition of problems or needs has occurred, consumers begin moving forward rapidly or methodically toward solving the problem.

Yet occasionally, consumers don't move at all. When questions regarding whether and how to solve their problems arise, consumers simply elect to *Let It Be*, as *Lennon & McCartney* wrote. "Let it be," as in doing nothing and making no decision.

Consumers sometimes apply reason and logic as they enter these problem-solving processes. But a lot of the time neither logic nor reason enters the picture as consumers evaluate both their options and next steps.

Is it fair and reasonable to suggest that adult lives unfold as a series of problems? We believe the suggestion is fair and reasonable, even among, and at times especially among, even the seemingly best-off, got-the-most human beings. The best-selling book of all time expressed the exact sentiments in a famous statement that is paraphrased below: "in this world there will be troubles."

The suggestion becomes even more fair and reasonable if one acknowledges that not all problems are equal. In fact, an argument can be made that life is full of problems. No one should think that bad things might happen. Everyone should know that bad things will happen. Just wait a while. "If only because evil is not the exception, it is the rule," as *The Walking Dead* character *Gabriel* suggested during season 10—*Gabriel* is the minister in the show.

And when the bad thing—the problem—inevitably arises some marketer's brand should be there, well-positioned inside an evoked set your inside your brain as top-rung-on-the-ladder first choice to eliminate the bad or solve the problem. That's why the management of market mixes—as tools that generate desirable brand positions—should never take days off. Marketers' positioning processes, their efforts at creating or sustaining differentiation, should never sleep.

Need or problem recognition amongst consumers can be stimulated by internal or external sources. Stimulations that arrive from internal sources imply the problem-initiating stimuli arose inside consumer minds or bodies. This point is easily illustrated: Guy or gal got hungry. Stimulations that arrive from external sources imply that the problem-initiating stimuli emanated from controllable marketing stimuli or uncontrollable environmental stimuli. Another point that's equally simple to demonstrate: Guy or gal was driving along the interstate. Guy or gal saw a *KFC/Taco Bell* co-branded billboard advertisement. Consumer then got "hungry."

What happens inside your mind and then in what external behaviors do you engage when you recognize you're experiencing a pressing problem—or need? You try to solve the problem or need, right? Other consumers do this too—you're not a freak. This is why consumer decision-making processes always begin with the recognition of problems—or needs.

While marketers cannot create needs, they can trigger awareness of problems that are experienced as needs. Or make vague or faint needs appear more pressing—by "working" consumers' emotions;

manipulating their feelings, creating unfounded anxiety in service of making mild, at worst, issues appear more pressing or dire. This sort of thing happens all the time. Certain professional marketing sectors that succeed or fail primarily based on their ability to market their own ideas often promote division by advocating victimhood.

Genuine victimhood is a big-time problem. But even merely perceived victimhood creates intense emotional responses among those who rightly or wrongly perceived they are victimized or those who think, rightly or wrongly, that others have been victimized. This whole process, which is intentionally stimulated by marketing agents more often than many suspect, gives "these others" who "worry" about the "wrongs" that others have suffered the opportunity to feel better about themselves because they are so obviously virtuous.

The following statement summarizes an iron rule that explains why human nature is often squishy and easily manipulated: Emotional consumer responses generally push out rational consumer thoughts. When this happens the marketer who instigated an emotional as opposed to a rational consumer response usually wins.

Whether marketers employ such manipulative tactics is their choice. If these thinly-veiled promises are disrobed to reveal real underlying value, more the better, because the choice to engage with consumers in this manner with consumers is ethically defensible. And successful marketers do these things, along with persuading targeted consumers that their brand, and it alone among all other competing brands inside the product category, is best suited to solve those consumers' problems. This process plays out during consumer decision-making Stages 2 and 3.

Stage 2: Information Search . . .

Information search may or may not take place. If it does, consumers seek out information about available solutions and which solutions are preferable from many information sources. These information sources include personal references, such as friends, family, or co-workers; commercial or marketing-controlled sources; one's own experience; and various public or internet sources.

The importance of specific information sources varies greatly. Some sources may be completely ignored or utterly rejected as useful or invalid information sources. The value of such information sources is at best discounted. Still other sources of information may be highly esteemed and actively sought out by consumers. This variance in the value of information sources often depends on individual characteristics of consumers as well as the characteristics of the problem itself.

Stages 2 and 3 essentially occur simultaneously. But there is value in breaking them into two stages, as the following discussion demonstrates.

Stage 3: Alternative Evaluation . . .

The evaluation of brand alternatives stage similarly may or may not take place. Sometimes, careful consumer evaluation of competing brand alternatives and their product features, attributes, and benefits (FAB) occurs. At other times, little to no evaluation of competing brand alternatives occurs. In those situations consumers may engage in impulsive or intuition-based purposes. Or perhaps, consumers have already developed high levels of brand loyalty toward a particular brand. Indeed, their preexisting possession of greater brand loyalty is a primary reason why consumers would not engage in any (brand) alternative evaluation.

Every decision that consumers make is shaped by their essentially simultaneous evaluation of each alternative branded product's price versus each alternative branded product's costs versus each alternative branded product's associated incentives laid out before them. This idea called "associated incentives" is best understood as the unique and hopefully appealing bundle of values—or value proposition—that will be obtained and enjoyed if consumers choose one branded as opposed to another alternative branded product option.

Exchanges entail gets of value and gives of value. Every decision consumers make is shaped by their perceptions of the "relative costs" or "their give" associated with each of the respective brand alternatives, measured against their perceptions of the "benefits" or "their get" received through each alternative brand choice that those consumers could make.

Consumer evaluations of alternative products usually occur along several features, attributes, and benefits that are perceived to be associated with each of however many brands are being deliberated seriously, as alternative choices, by consumers. Some product attributes are clearly more, or less, important than other product attributes to certain consumers. The prices of the various alternatives that s/he may choose for the big formal "dress-up" event always weigh heavily on some consumers' minds; other consumers would barely concern themselves at all about price in the exact same decision-making context. The prestige of the apparel item's brand name may matter greatly to some decision-makers, or matter not at all to others. The quality of the fit of the apparel item and the degree to which it emphasizes or camouflages the right or wrong body parts matters greatly to some consumers; other decision-makers could care less whether the apparel item lets things all hang out or smooches everything together in just the right or wrong manner. You get the point; different strokes (product attributes) for different folks (segments), and different product attributes either matter greatly, matter a bit, or don't matter at all for different segments of consumer decision-makers.

Marketers often divide consumer markets into consumer segments based on the brand attribute or attributes that individual consumers deem most important as they are choosing which brand to purchase from inside a given product category, such as say, the chainsaw product category. Then those chainsaw marketers may, and certainly should, create uniquely-desirable marketing mixes for these targeted segments. Marketing mixes should be designed such that they feature exactly the attributes and values most strongly sought by the segments that each chainsaw marketer is targeting.

Attributes[17] deliver benefits. Benefits deliver solutions. Solutions deliver values. Values, their very presence, create opportunities for marketers to create perceptions of genuine or merely perceived differentiation. The presence of differentiation facilitates opportunities for marketers to position their brand's specific bundles of values more effectively.

---

17. Product attributes, or brand characteristics, distinguish one brand from other brands competing inside the same product category. Any product's size, shape, color, features, design, style, quality, functionality, durability, reputation, quality, or price; these and other possible product characteristics exist as potential product attributes, or brand characteristics, that marketers might strategically choose to emphasize as they "position" their brands. Product attributes affect the appeal, levels of acceptability, and/or levels of desirability of individual brands.

Stage 4: Purchase Decision . . .

Whether actual purchases of products occur or fail to occur, this stage typically begins with consumers' purchase intention. As noted, when consumers decide to not decide they still have a decision; just not a purchase decision.

As decision processes unfold, attitudinal factors may intervene and overturn the original choices that consumers have made. Such factors could consist of attitudes toward others who are important to consumers who would not, in the decision-makers' perceptions, approve of the purchase of this particular product/brand. Or, these attitudes could consist entirely of the decision-makers' own attitudes. Unexpected or predictable situational factors may also enter the picture and cause consumers to choose another brand alternative or decide not to buy anything right now. Such situational factors might include economic dips or gains, unexpected exposure to a previously unknown competitor's lower prices, or consumers simply changing their minds.

Stage 5: Post-Purchase Decision Behaviors . . .

Things are deceptively simple.

When consumers' expectations about the value that they will receive from a product they purchased are met, consumers are satisfied. That's better than a mud sandwich. But few sustainably successful marketers are satisfied with merely satisfying their customers.

When consumers' expectations about the value that they will receive from a product they have purchased are greatly exceeded, they're delighted. Truly, truly; that's more like it, profits are coming or have already arrived. All because marketers effectively segmented, targeted, positioned, and managed their marketing mixes. Good on them. Rinse and repeat, for a while, until it's time to again toss in some new or take out some old marketing mix ingredients, and then mix things up, again.

In competitive markets, marketers' profits reflect the value of the market's delight created by marketers' innovative and effective management of their marketing mixes, because their marketing mixes also create value. If consumers are not delighted with the values marketers are offering, customers either will create the value themselves, choose to do without, or more likely will seek to acquire delight-generating value from some other marketer. Profits create wealth not just for marketing-me(s) but for society's collective-me.

Marketers would generally do well for themselves by moving away from an exclusive focus on profit and loss as a success criteria and moving toward a greater focus on the role that "customer delight" can play in ensuring or negating true marketing success. *Apple* is not a mega success because of how effectively it manages P&L balance sheets. *Apple* is a mega success because its products and therefore its brand delights customers. Marketing success likewise usually has little to do with greed. Successful marketing instead is predicated on marketers' ability to weed out good ideas from bad ideas. Bad ideas generate disdain, neglect, rejection, and loss for marketers. Good ideas that lead to good products and to better marketing mix management. These two outcomes, in turn, generate greater delight across markets and higher profits for the same marketers. If you are a marketer, your job is not about you. Your job instead is about customers—and determining how best to delight them.

When anti-marketers or socialists see profits, they should not think, fat cat. Instead, they could ruminate about all the delight that had to have been created and delivered to make that individual marketer or organization successful. Consumer delight, in many though not all marketing contexts,[18] represents the ultimate social value. By the way, how did socialists light up their homes before some entrepreneurial marketer created candles? You're right, the answer is electricity.

Meanwhile, back to the main storyline. When consumers' expectations about the value they thought they bought are not met, they're dissatisfied. The emergence of complaint behavior is likely—people love to complain, doing so is instinctual, for reasons explained more fully below. Negative WOM is quite likely to arise here, often playing out as marketers' worst enemies because WOM is so believable to those consumers who solicit and/or receive it.

A consumer experience called cognitive dissonance is likely to arise at this point (that is, the point after consumer decisions have been made and products have been purchased), dependent on size and risks associated with consumer decision. Cognitive dissonance, defined, entails a mental state of having inconsistent thoughts, beliefs, or attitudes, especially relating to decisions made about important, risky, high-involvement products. Cognitive dissonance arises when customers voluntarily hold two opposing thoughts inside their minds at the same time. The phenomenon of dissonance is similar to a paradox. Cognitive dissonance is perhaps more commonly described as buyers' remorse.

One possibly surprising but logical takeaway is that marketers sometimes do better for themselves by lowering customers' expectations and then greatly exceeding them. This expectations-management tactic is so easy to execute that it is like dunking on eight-foot-rims.

Marketers should emphasize different marketing mix activities during each stage of the consumer decision-making process.

Marketers, for example, should primarily engage in promotional activities in order to stimulate need or problem recognition during Stage 1.

Marketers should mostly engage in information provision activities as consumers pass through the information search and alternative evaluation stages, or Stages 2 and 3. These communication efforts usually aspire to create perceptions of differentiation in order to establish unique-and-uniquely-desirable-positions for their brands among precisely-targeted segments.

Reinforcing-activities are the marketing mix order of the day as consumers pass through post-purchase cognitive processes, or Stage 5. Reinforcing activities would include metaphorical "hand-holding" or legitimate marketing attempts to encourage and calm doubts or concerns. Marketing mix initiatives, at this point, should fundamentally reinforce the "great choices" that, for example, new homeowners or automotive buyers have already made. Note how new home or automobile purchases each entail high-involvement consumer decision-making.

---

18. Marketers, for example, have benefitted and will continue to benefit from bringing delight, albeit of a temporary nature, to opiate addicts. This specific customer delight generates no overall net societal gain, or value, however.

INVOLVEMENT LEVELS AFFECT CONSUMER DECISION-MAKING

Humans care more and think more and sweat the details more when they engage with topics, product categories, or brands (products!) that are more important to them. Consumers are similarly more likely to engage more deeply with—be more highly involved in—decision-making processes associated with topics or brands that are important to them.

Consumers can care deeply about a given idea, issue, or product category (for example, abortion rights, an issue; whether abortion should or should not be legal, an idea; or abortion services themselves, a product). Consumers can care a little about an idea, issue, or product category (fast-food, whether fast-food consumption should be regulated, and hamburgers & fries). Or consumers could basically give a crap and not care at all about an idea, issue, or product category (professionals shooting balls at hoops, whether players are overpaid, the *National Basketball Association*).

Consumer involvement is akin to consumers having skin-in-the-game. Do you have skin-in-the-game? If the answer is yes, "I got a lot," then as a decision-maker you are highly involved in the decision-making process and in the consequences that any good or bad decision will generate. Got no skin-in-the-game? Your involvement then would prove low to nonexistent.

Consumers' involvement levels materially influence how they pass through the five decision-making stages. Consumers' higher or lower involvement levels impact the amount of effort they expend during their decision-making processes. An old marketing joke explains the difference between involvement and commitment. Envision, first, a breakfast featuring ham and eggs. Having given his all to this endeavor, the pig was deeply committed to the breakfast. Whereas the chicken, having merely laid an egg, she is only highly involved.

Involvement matters. After all, differences exist between not being asleep and being fully awake, as in being completely engaged. Whether consumer decision-makers are paying attention; are fully engaged; and believe what is happening and what they are evaluating is important and imposes huge differences on how deeply consumers process information and on what and how much information those consumers process in route to making whether- and what-to-purchase decisions. Their levels of involvement materially influence whether they decide to buy a specific brand from within a particular product category or decide to not buy another specific brand or for that matter any brand from the same product category. Ask any preacher, priest, professor, or professional salesperson whether these points are valid. Each marketing professional is consistently expected to communicate with potential or actual customers who are highly involved and/or not involved at all with what he or she is telling and selling.

Inside consumer decision-making processes, the level of involvement of consumers is consistently impacted by:

- ▶ The degree of importance they assign to a particular purchase related decision;
- ▶ The costs associated with purchasing a given brand from the product category being evaluated; and/or

- Whether high perceived risks are associated with using the product or making the wrong product choice.

For example, most prospective brides, when buying wedding dresses for first or starter marriages, are highly involved during the purchase decision-making process. Lots of risk, time, monetary costs, and stress/anxiety are present in such a decision. The fear of making a less-than-perfect choice that itself will be displayed in a highly public fashion is also associated with wedding dress purchases. Entire buying teams, including the bride; her mother; perhaps a wedding advisor; and other members of her family or entourage who influence decision-making processes. When wedding dresses are being purchased the best solution is usually not already known. But that the absolutely best solution be found is critical. Extensive consumer effort is usually expended, which makes sense because the consumer bride is experiencing an extended and extensive problem-solving decision-making scenario.

But what if our bride were buying a can of *Campbell's Pork & Beans* or a *Walmart* store brand gallon of 2% milk? She clearly would be far less involved in such decisions. In fact, the decision-making processes she has to engage in here are absolutely routine. The best, or good-enough, solutions are already known, and what is known works fine. Routine consumer decisions typically feature (a) little to no risk; (b) low relative costs, including the costs associated with making a bad choice; and (c) little to no information search. Our bride is engaged in routine problem-solving—the solution is already known.

Finally, our bride might be facing a consumer decision-making "problem" wherein she must choose a restaurant in which to have lunch with her three best girlfriends, say, to discuss wedding or reception plans. While deciding to choose one and not another restaurant (say, *Luigi*'s versus *Giuseppe*'s because she knows everyone in her four-member crew likes or loves *Italian* food), she likely engages in limited problem-solving. Here she chooses one from among several known restaurant alternatives. Each restaurant is relatively or quite familiar to her. Our best marketing recommendation is that she should reject the restaurant that the *Bridesmaids* movie bridesmaid chose for her "girlfriend wedding planning" luncheon.

ROLE-PLAYED BY WORD-OF-MOUTH

Word-of-mouth, as a marketing communication process that marketers can influence but not control, involves oral or written recommendations made by satisfied or unsatisfied customers to prospective or actual customers of branded products. Products, here, would be defined broadly as products, services, ideas, places, or people. Interpersonal word-of-mouth messages can be conveyed face-to-face, text-to-text, via the mail, during actual phone voice conversations, and so forth.

Human beings have been hard-wired across unknown millennia to more highly trust and esteem opinions, views, and recommendations originating from members of their own groups or tribes over messages emanating from other groups or tribes such as inherently self-serving marketers. Knowing this, no one should be surprised WOM is so persuasive. But everyone should understand why WOM is so important to marketers and consumers. Successful marketers do everything possible and reasonable to stimulate positive WOM and to dampen negative WOM. Negative WOM travels more rapidly through and penetrates more deeply into the collective mind of any market than positive WOM does. Managing customer satisfaction and effectively handling any purchase-related problems as they arise is crucial to brands' long-term success.

The primary reason: most humans love to "dish-the-dirt." The famous early twentieth-century satirist *Dorothy Parker* synopsized this human tendency by writing, tongue-firmly-planted-in-cheek, "If you don't have anything good to say about Mr. or Miss X, come right down here and sit by me." Behold the power and allure of gossip, and gossip works pretty much the same way as WOM does. Many people love to dish.

The evolution of linguistic ability amongst humans enabled them to gossip for hours on end. Reliable information about who could be trusted meant that small bands could develop into larger bands, as humans developed tighter and more sophisticated forms of cooperation and communication. At first blush this theory of gossip may appear silly. Assuredly, it is not. Even today substantial chunks of human communication—whether in the form of emails, texts or tweets, phone calls, or newspaper columns—is gossip. Do you believe accountants sit around at lunch talking about the latest accounting theory? Sometimes. But more often they talk about accountants who got caught cheating on their spouses.

That gossip arises so effortlessly among humans is neither accidental nor coincidental. Gossip actually functioned as a force-multiplier that accelerated the evolution and development of human language.

Gossip usually focuses on the negatives, wrongdoings, or shortfalls of others. Hence, huge concerns arise for marketers who somehow muck-up things and subsequently fail to address and correct the real or imagined wrongs. Combine these gossipy human tendencies with the fact that so many e-social networking exchanges feature snarky and barky communiques of a sort that would rarely be exchanged face-to-face—and you have a world in which marketers must do the best job possible of avoiding any outcomes that could lead to negative WOM. Oh wait. This is exactly the world in which almost all marketers already operate.

Gaining new customers usually costs marketers many multiples more time, effort, and money (the "3Ts" stated a bit differently) than retaining existing customers. Unhappy customers are much more likely to evangelize about product or purchase experiences, by about an 8–1 ratio. Except here, evangelists definitely will not be spreading good news.

These conditions underscore the need that exists for marketers to satisfy existing customers by providing them with value that exceeds the costs associated with owning or using a product. In addition, marketers similarly need to provide value that exceeds the value provided by their competitors. Finally, marketers must manage their marketing mixes in ways that generate levels of value exceeding the amount consumers perceived they would receive in order to become or remain successful; here again, notions of exceeding customer expectations and generating customer "delight" are raised.

Success pivots, time and again, based on whether marketers give customers enough differentiating value that those individuals buy their brand and not buy other marketers' brands or choose to not buy anything at all. The presence of superior differentiating value incentivizes customers to choose one marketer's brand rather than other marketers' brand alternatives.

Doing these things inspires greater customer loyalty and higher propensities among customers to engage in positive (favorable) word-of-mouth/WOM about the brand. In traditional-marketing or e-marketing settings, WOM entails people influencing each other in personal conversational settings, which could occur in person, over the phone, or occur electronically through various devices. Negative WOM, spreading at the speed of baud during an internet-mediated age, amplifies the downdraft to the point where even future good news can be degraded.

WOM functions as a positive or negative force-multiplier for marketers. This notion should readily come to mind as marketers contemplate and discuss how best to stimulate positive or avoid stimulating negative WOM. Force multipliers such as WOM elevate the power and persuasiveness of any positive story issued about or by marketers and their brands by many multiples. That's great for any marketers that are being praised.

In the meantime, WOM exercises the same multiplying effects whenever negative stories emerge from any source about brands and the organizations or individuals that market them. That's horrific for marketers being criticized.

This is why traditional WOM, or its electronic cousin, e-WOM, often represents the best-friend or worst-enemy of marketers.

THE TRADITIONAL ECONOMICS TAKE ON CONSUMER BEHAVIOR

Economists are increasingly accepting what most thoughtful people have long understood. Economists now understand and account for the fact that average people fall well short of rationality in their daily decision-making. For decades most economic models had pre-supposed that people as decision-makers are well-informed and rational.

Contemporary economists have also learned other genuinely important things about the behaviors of normal consumers. For example, research has shown that consumers experience their losses more acutely then their wins. This naturally-arising human response to losses or even the threat of loss leads to endowment effects, which also influence CB. The presence of these endowment effects further implies that consumers typically ascribe higher values to assets simply because they own the asset. Ever wonder why many consumers experience so much difficulty parting with old worn-out things? Wonder no more.

Or, did you ever think about this? Almost all parents think their children are special. Yet most of these parents are actually wrong. In fact, a combination of logic and observation decrees that most parents must be mistaken. Were things otherwise, there might not be so many ordinary adults planted right here on earth.

What's that four-letter word again, the word that identifies the effect that radically influences consumers' perceptions and their decisions? Oh yes, the four-letter word is B-I-A-S.

Economists have also learned that consumers usually compartmentalize and then agglomerate when pondering money; ultimately "clumping" together certain similar types of spending or income. The phenomenon drives humans' tendency to tackle cognitive problems in pieces rather than as wholes. But this tendency can promote negative outcomes. Taxi drivers who aim to earn a certain amount each day, for example, often stop work earlier on busy days and later on slow days. This is a stone-cold silly business strategy because taking the opposite approach would maximize their weekly or monthly earnings.

Economists also now understand that human brains feature two cognitive parts. First, a doer-part focused on short-term rewards, or incentives. Second, a planner-part focused on longer-term rewards.

Their willpower restrains doers-parts from saying the heck with the short-run. But exercising constraint is costly, and strategic marketers make the exercise of constraint even costlier by constantly throwing short-term incentives at consumers. Feeling like getting high on anything, anyone? Some marketers would have consumers believe that getting high is great for the short-run; while doing so regularly obviously would play out negatively for most consumers in their long runs.

These internal human struggles play out continuously. Successful marketers understand that individual consumers' preferences and choices rarely remain constant across time—whether Joe consumes one more beer than Joe should drink largely depends on his brain state in that moment. The perpetual and omnipresent nature of these mental processes implies that presenting internet users with choice architectures that favor planner-brains over doer-brains enables marketers to subtly influence choices and behaviors, and for the better. The simple but highly strategic decision to make employee-enrollment in retirement investments the default choice has generated huge benefits for those consumers.

Finally, economists now understand that consumers almost universally prefer fairness in their own and others' behaviors. Consumers hate price gougers and punish marketers who act unfairly. Consumers do this if that means lower payouts for themselves.

Bottom lines from the bottom-up.

- ▶ First, consumers find fairness attractive.
- ▶ Second, consumers experience difficulty exercising self-control.
- ▶ Third, consumers hate losing what they already have. Fact is, the prospect of loss can shut many consumers down from deciding to do anything from anything at all. Inertia, as a natural physical and consumer decision-making phenomenon, again rears its head.

Knowing these consumer and human tendencies, strategic marketers should respond accordingly as they segment, target, and develop positions by managing their marketing mixes.

EXHIBIT 7.1
Maslow's Hierarchy of Needs (Hierarchy of Motives)

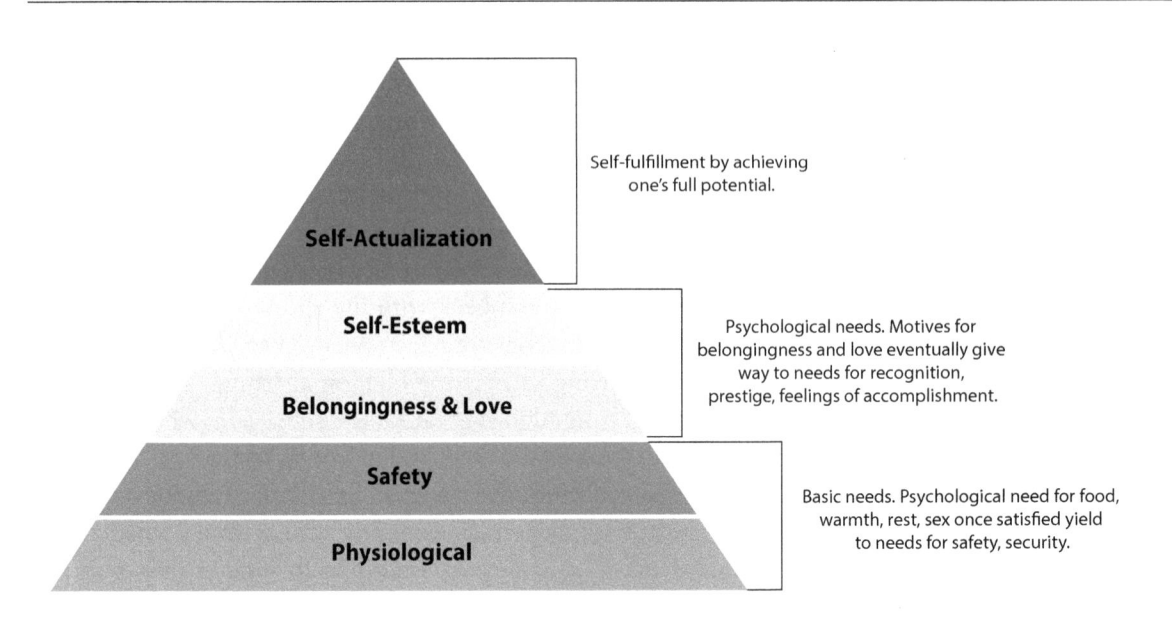

- **Self-Actualization** — Self-fulfillment by achieving one's full potential.
- **Self-Esteem**
- **Belongingness & Love** — Psychological needs. Motives for belongingness and love eventually give way to needs for recognition, prestige, feelings of accomplishment.
- **Safety**
- **Physiological** — Basic needs. Psychological need for food, warmth, rest, sex once satisfied yield to needs for safety, security.

EXHIBIT 7.2
A Model of Consumer Buyer Behavior

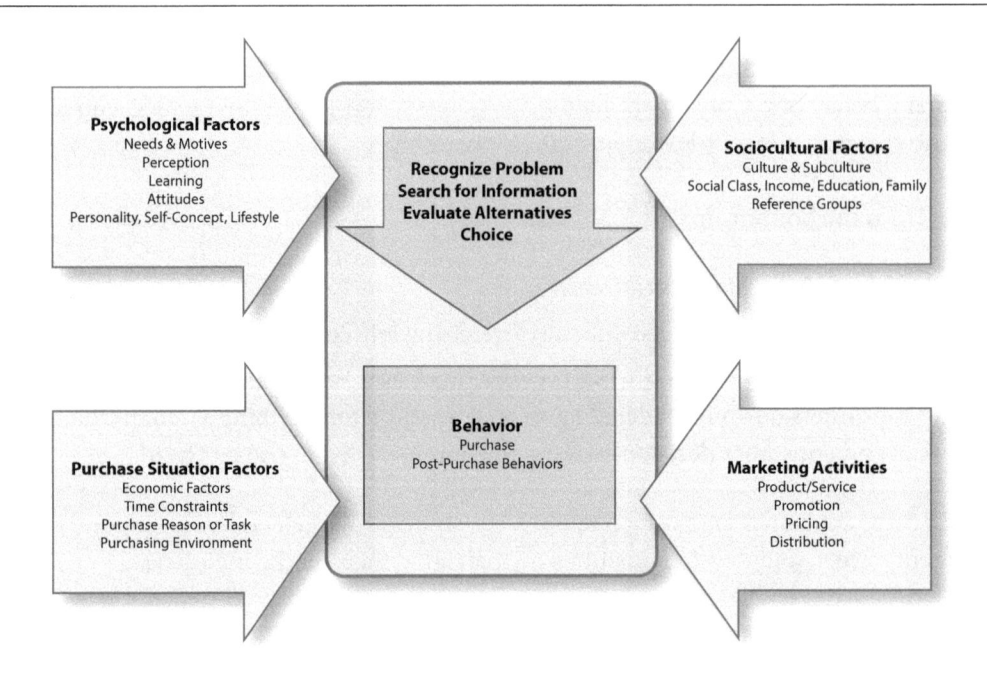

Psychological Factors
- Needs & Motives
- Perception
- Learning
- Attitudes
- Personality, Self-Concept, Lifestyle

Sociocultural Factors
- Culture & Subculture
- Social Class, Income, Education, Family
- Reference Groups

Purchase Situation Factors
- Economic Factors
- Time Constraints
- Purchase Reason or Task
- Purchasing Environment

Marketing Activities
- Product/Service
- Promotion
- Pricing
- Distribution

- Recognize Problem
- Search for Information
- Evaluate Alternatives
- Choice

Behavior
- Purchase
- Post-Purchase Behaviors

EXHIBIT 7.3
Range of Consumer Decisions

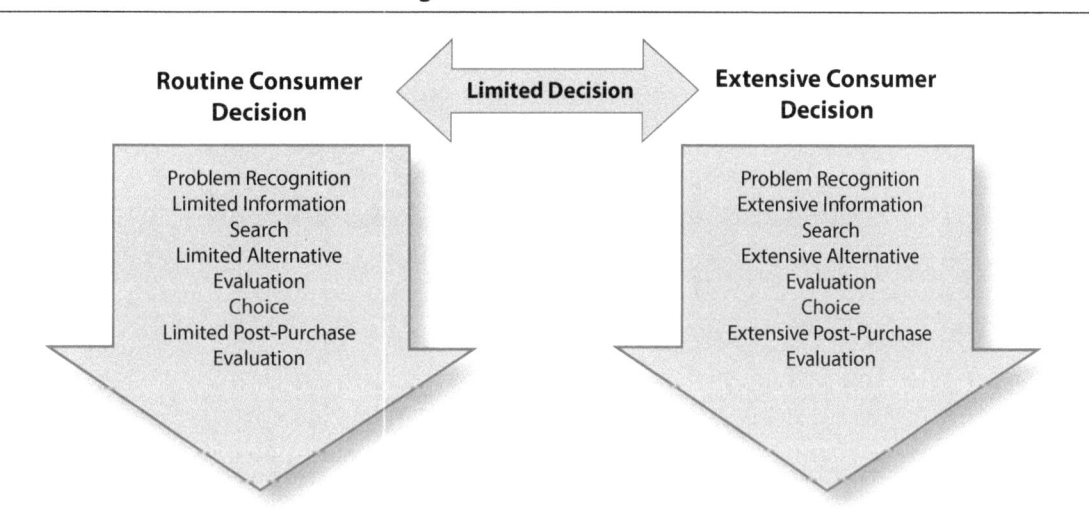

Routine Consumer Decision ←— Limited Decision —→ **Extensive Consumer Decision**

Routine Consumer Decision:
- Problem Recognition
- Limited Information Search
- Limited Alternative Evaluation
- Choice
- Limited Post-Purchase Evaluation

Extensive Consumer Decision:
- Problem Recognition
- Extensive Information Search
- Extensive Alternative Evaluation
- Choice
- Extensive Post-Purchase Evaluation

EXHIBIT 7.4
Factors Affecting Consumer Decision Complexity and Involvement

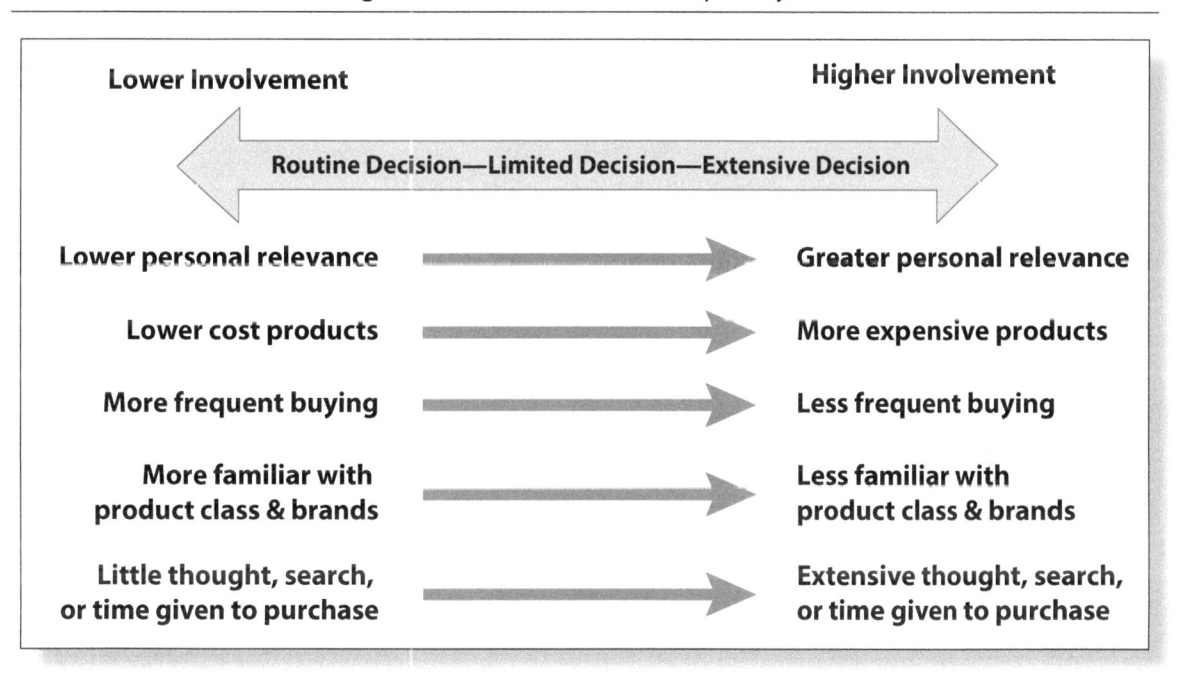

Lower Involvement ←————— Routine Decision—Limited Decision—Extensive Decision —————→ **Higher Involvement**

Lower Involvement	→	Higher Involvement
Lower personal relevance	→	Greater personal relevance
Lower cost products	→	More expensive products
More frequent buying	→	Less frequent buying
More familiar with product class & brands	→	Less familiar with product class & brands
Little thought, search, or time given to purchase	→	Extensive thought, search, or time given to purchase

EXHIBIT 7.5

Cultural values define norms for behaving, sanctions for misbehaving, and ultimately consumption behaviors.

```
Cultural Values & Norms  <--->  Marketing Activities
              \                 /
               \               /
                v             v
              Consumption Behaviors
```

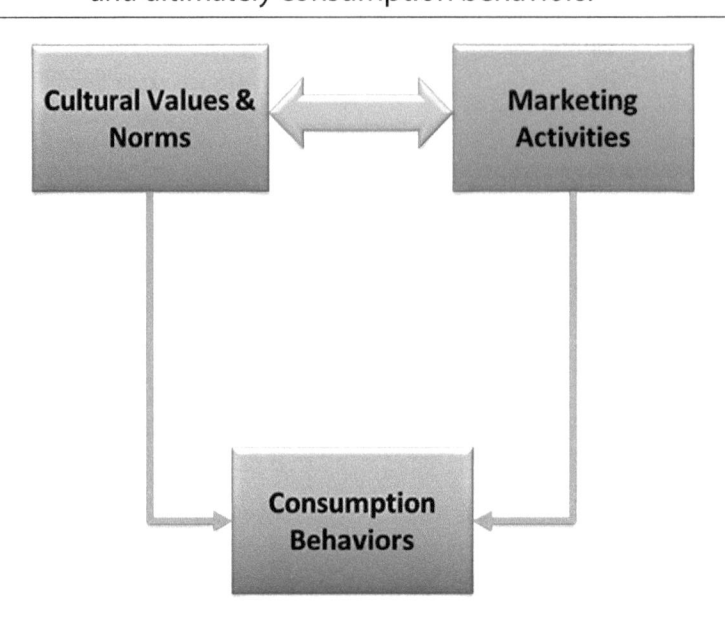

EXHIBIT 7.6

The Dimensions of Self-Concept

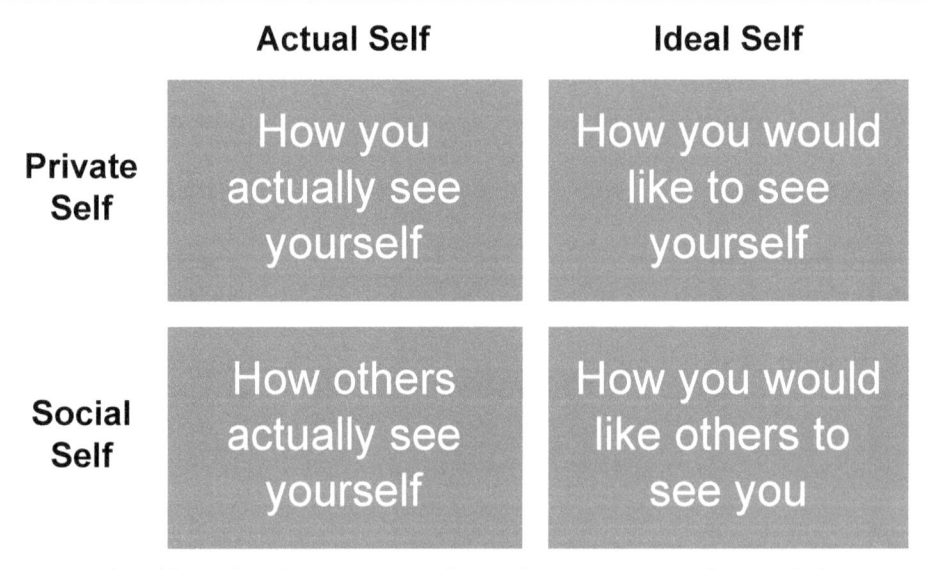

	Actual Self	Ideal Self
Private Self	How you actually see yourself	How you would like to see yourself
Social Self	How others actually see yourself	How you would like others to see you

Source: Adapted from Del Hawkins, Roger Best, and Kenneth Coney, Consumer Behavior, 9th ed. (New York, NY: McGraw-Hill, 2004): 422.

EXHIBIT 7.7
Marketers match elements of brand image to consumers' ideal self-concepts to build positive attitudes for brands.

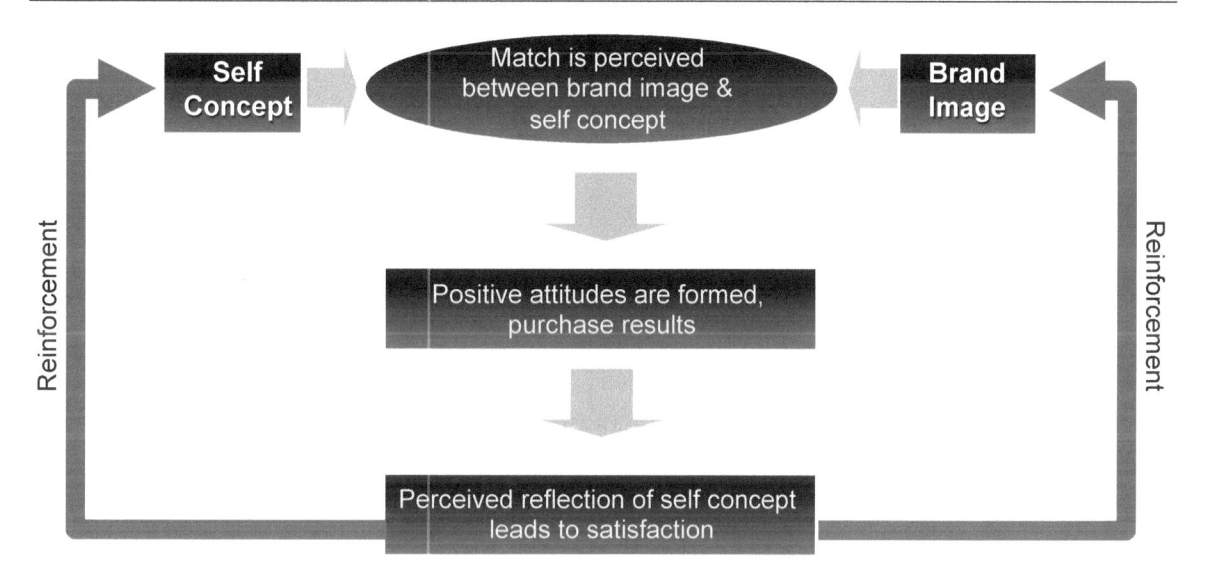

```
Self Concept → Match is perceived between brand image & self concept ← Brand Image
                            ↓
          Positive attitudes are formed, purchase results
                            ↓
       Perceived reflection of self concept leads to satisfaction
```

Reinforcement (left loop back to Self Concept)
Reinforcement (right loop back to Brand Image)

MODULE 8

Marketing Ethics and Social Responsibility

MODULE 8.0

Few creatures, including humans, are inexorably evil. But all creatures, including humans, get hungry, and begin feeling needy—to put things nicely. At that point all creatures begin putting themselves and their needs first, and that's where the fun—and ethical transgressions—typically begins. Even humanity's best friend, the canine, unquestionably runs faster and eats more aggressively when hungry.

Identifying the right (ethical) decisions versus the wrong (unethical) decisions to make is not that difficult inside most marketing or marketing managerial contexts. Choosing between the right wrongs to pursue, however, is much more challenging. The necessity to choose between the right wrongs may arise more frequently than many may assume. That's because sometimes less than completely ethical choices represent the only options that marketers have available to make. The reasons why are explained below.

ETHICS AND ETHICAL DECISION-MAKING IS . . .

. . . Reflected in what people elect to do or to not do when no one is looking. Ethics is likewise reflected in what people choose to do or not do in those decision-making situations where no one will ever find out what has been done—or where decision-makers assume, obviously often erroneously, that no one will ever find out.

Ethics and ethical considerations arise whenever and wherever questions or doubts arise about the right or wrong choice to make in a particular situation. Right, here, means moral. Wrong, means immoral or less moral. These descriptions of ethics and ethical considerations remain appropriate regardless of whether business or nonbusiness decisions are being deliberated.

Questions, concerns, and doubts about what is or is not the moral choice often feature philosophical and religious underpinnings. Notably, the five major global religions (*Buddhism, Christianity, Hinduism, Islamism,* and *Judaism*) are always philosophical in nature. But some philosophies are emphatically not religious.

Almost all organizational or religious and philosophical systems impose explicit or implicit sets of moral expectations on their membership. These sets of moral expectations often exist inside formal codes of ethical conduct. The *American Marketing Association* boasts a formal Code of Ethics, as do various other accounting and managerial associations.

Contemporary *European American* ethical guidelines are usually grounded either in ancient theories created by *Greek* philosophers such as *Thales, Aristotle, Plato,* or *Socrates* or in *Judeo-Christian* religious texts. This makes sense given that the most basic moral codes are timeless and unchanging. Paraphrasing *C. S. Lewis*, a well-known *English* scholar, lay theologian, and writer (*The Chronicles of Narnia; Mere Christianity*), one could no more create a new moral code than one can invent a new color—although many progressive marketing organizations are clearly wont to try.

Ruminate, for example, about these ancient guidelines. A decision to follow the standard embedded in each guideline would clearly foster more ethical marketers and higher satisfaction among customers. Each guideline is taken from the generally more redemptive *Christian New Testament*.

- "Let each of you look not just to your own interests, but also to the interests of others"—*Philippians* 2:4.
- "Simply let your 'Yes' be 'Yes,' and your 'No', 'No'; anything beyond this comes from the evil one"—*Matthew* 5:37
- "Don't seek your own advantage, but that of the other"—*1st Corinthians* 10:24.

Each ethical admonition is entirely consistent with the business philosophy called the marketing concept. A philosophy with which all readers are already familiar. The three admonitions are all also entirely consonant with the sort of strategic reasoning that would not just illuminate but also sustain any marketer's pathway to success.

Another ethical guideline, one that might similarly function as ethical North Star for marketers, emanated from the typically harsher and less redemptive Jewish Old Testament.[1] This book suggests, on forty-six separate occasions, that the "haves" of the world should leave grain behind in the corners of the field after the harvest for the widows and orphans. Widows and orphans is Bible-speak (or a *Christian* dog-whistle phrase) that means poor and dispossessed people—or the "have-nots." Marketers should be socially responsible as well, and indeed many are. A decision to act routinely in socially responsible fashions would generally elevate the value of marketing brands because the resulting strategic behaviors would burnish marketers' reputations, especially over the long-run.

Useful ethical guidelines that most individual or organizational marketers seem to follow flow organically from theological thought. However, if anybody is getting upset by these overtly religious ties to marketing ethics, s/he should ponder the following indisputable point:

- "People or firms that consciously act to further the interests of others, groups to which they belong or seek to serve, are ultimately serving their own self-interests."

This profound piece of ethical advice again ties directly to the marketing mix and to how this tool should be managed, but it was written by *Ayd Rand*. Ms. Rand is probably modern history's

---

1. The *Old Testament* is primarily driven by The Law, explanations and justifications of these guidelines, discussions of sinfulness and their consequences, and God's acts of punishment (check out *Judges*). The *New Testament* is primarily driven by love, grace, and God's forgiveness.

best-known atheist, and author of *Atlas Shrugged*. She also developed the philosophy of enlightened self-interests. The philosophy of enlightened self-interests is a broadly practical and typically beneficial ethical theory.

Feeling uncomfortable with religious or atheist points of view? Okay, not a problem. Let's turn toward some purely philosophical reasoning as we continue to develop an understanding of what ethics is and what being an ethical marketer actually entails. Question:

▶ "Is the world too small for anything but truth?"

The preceding question paraphrases a statement written by *William Sloan Coffin*. The question could never be conclusively answered inside anyone's lifetime—unless one holds resolutely to notions of absolute truth that prevail inside some religions, and it is inappropriate to enter that domain in this setting. However, issues raised by asking the question are still worth pondering in markets that have increasingly shrunk, due to technology, and in markets while social media and traditional media are each locked in on love embraces that spawn great passion for outing anybody or any idea or behavior that anyone perceives is wrong. And indeed, parameters of what constitutes right or wrong—the truth—are fluid across time. Perhaps there was a day when certain people or institutions could literally get away with murder? The fact is such days once existed and still do exist. But the size of this world is waning. The straight and narrow, difficult though it remains to traverse, represents the most logical path to follow among marketers seeking success.

Back to our original question:

▶ Is the world too small for anything but truth?

The truth is that we are not qualified to opine. Two revealed truths are certain, however. First, every lie that is told incurs a debt to the truth. And second, many well-respected marketers owe a great debt for their success to their willingness to walk resolutely in the truth, no matter the short-term costs.

Had it up to here with religious, atheist, or philosophical thought leaders? Well, how about some sports-related ethical advice? Quoting former *NFL* coach and current television analyst *Tony Dungy*:

▶ "Remember . . . what happens in the dark usually comes to light."

Should readers agree with *Dungy's* statement? Yes, usually they should. To be sure the statement implies that "the world [indeed] is too small for anything but truth."

Yet sometimes it's not the presence of darkness but rather an absence of light that causes ethical problems for all sorts of decision-makers. You may be familiar with the saying "sunlight is the best disinfectant." But as one ponders both the question and the possibility of whatever unethical actions you decide to pursue or whatever aspects of those actions eventually comes to light, understand that successful marketers should expect more than collective agreement about what ideas or behaviors represent "the truth." That's because societies and cultures often collectively agree upon what behaviors represent truth and/or morality in morally challenged ways. Those marketers who are seeking to position their branded selves as ethical practitioners and their behaviors as ethical examples should commit to routinely rising well above whatever highly malleable standards that societies or cultures establish as the truth.

ETHICAL REALITY CHECK 1

Research has shown that the three factors contributing most to professionals' success are their IQs, their birth family socioeconomic status, and their self-control.

Which factor is most controllable? I.Q. supposedly is driven about 50 percent by heredity (arising from the intersection of your genetic parents' intelligence and other inheritable traits) and 50 percent by environmental factors, particularly during the first few years of life. Yet professionals never get do-overs on their birth parents or on how the first few years of their lives played-out. And as far as birth family sociocultural status goes, again people cannot select their birth parents. At this point, then, we are left with one non-ironic choice, "self-control" represents the only controllable factor for aspiring or actual professionals.

Self-control, as would be reflected in basketball players' commitment to not end vigorous two-hour practice sessions until after they have made eight straight foul shots, right at the point when they're most tired and most likely to experience difficulty shooting straight, in order to simulate what crunch-time, winning-time, at the ends of games actually entails. Self-control, as could be illustrated by students completing their homework, editing presentations one more time, or not eating the extra cookie. Self-control, finally, as in not chiseling customers; even when cheaters will not be outed until months or years after they have left their current marketing gig. Maybe that's what the "cheating their customers" bank *Wells Fargo* or master of the financial pyramid scheme *Bernie Madoff* somehow thought would happen.

The right set of ethics, including one's work ethic, along with the imposition of personal self-control, deliver the sorts of professional values that never go out of style. The sort of ethical professional values that have no sense of what "an expiration date" actually means, in other words.

ETHICAL REALITY CHECK 2

Professionals are often second-guessed by somebody—who is either jealous or an unpaid critic—whether they succeed or fail. Consequently, people need to be comfortable doing what they know is the right thing. Doing the right thing, as in the moral thing, helps marketing professionals and their organizations win in the end. Doing the right thing because "right" is what you are supposed to do, not for recognition or reward. Never being proud about doing the right thing, just doing it—oops, we accidentally slipped in a reference to *Nike's* owning a word, or three words, thing. (In doing so, you may recall that *Nike* was honoring our fifth Marketing Law.)

The fact that there is never a right way to do the wrong thing is worth remembering. Similar to how strategic decision-makers don't want to find themselves in the right place at the wrong time and miss out on a golden opportunity, thoughtful marketers should never assume that the wrong thing can ever be done right.

ETHICAL REALITY CHECK 3

Professionals almost always know what to do inside their respective fields or disciplines. Their "knowing" is what makes them professionals. Professionals likewise almost always know the difference between right and wrong. Question—So why do professionals choose wrong so often?

Dr. Martin Luther King was previously referenced. Let's turn now to his namesake *Martin Luther*. *Luther* was a *Catholic* priest whose disdain for prevailing *Catholic* polities in his time (ca. 1517 AD) promoted protests that culminated in the formation of a new product that was called the <u>Protestant Church</u>.

Luther is also credited for fathering the *Lutheran* principle and *Latin* phrase *incurvatus in se*. The *English* transition of this *Latin* phrase implies that humans are all "curved inward" toward themselves. Which makes perfect sense, because we humans are. We are all naturally bent in, focusing selfishly on ourselves, and on our actual or perceived needs. These conditions make humans all highly prone to selfishness. Humans are literally born that way.

Consequently, when humans get hungry, in any sense of the word, their innate selfishness motivates them to lean in toward sinfulness. Selfishness arises when one individual is trying to gain more advantage at someone else's expense. The omnipresent influence of *incurvatus in se* implies that the good behavior of consciously striving to improve one's own morality is always comingled with the bad behavior of always selfishly preferring oneself.

The two most common elements in the universe are hydrogen and human selfishness. Joking? Well, yes, but not really.

The English word *conscious* originates from an early Greek word, *sunseidesis*, that meant to know with another. Today, most people would agree that a "conscious" is our inner voice that says we should know better. As we generally do. So why do people so routinely fail to do the right thing? The answer relates to people's inherent self-interests, and how inexorably our own naturally arising selfish natures and instincts motivate us to routinely engage in unethical behaviors as we seek to serve our own interests at the expense of the interests of others. *James Dobson* was right when he described the human conscious as a fallen organ.

Some experts suggest the word sin, which in the original "Hebrew" meant missing the mark, should actually be spelled sIn. Note emphasis on the "I"—the role that the self plays—in facilitating sin. If you are harboring any doubts about how easily sinful or unethical people can be produced, conduct this experiment. First, take two bucolic two-year-olds. Second, place them, seemingly alone, inside a safe room. Third, toss a single super-badass toy that only one child can play with at a time. Fourth, record how quickly one and possibly two young sinners will inevitably magically appear as each child instinctively pursues his or her best self-interests.

What best self-interests will likely be pursued? Typically, the ones that bring these young consumers the most pleasure! Another irrefutable fact that's worth remembering about the intrinsically humanness of sIn: No one in the history of the world has ever had to teach a child to be disobedient

Does this quick and possibly unexpected spin toward sIn upset anyone? We hope not. But if you're feeling upset, consider this. That people sin and do so routinely resides among the most widely observable and empirically provable facts in the world. The empirical evidence supporting this premise is likely exceeded only by the power and pervasiveness of the observable evidence confirming that gravity always exists and has its say.

ETHICAL REALITY CHECK 4

Question—Does everybody cheat?

The answer is yes, apparently almost everybody cheats . . . if and when two conditions are simultaneously present. Condition 1—the stakes involved are deemed sufficiently high, exceedingly appealing, by the cheating parties. Condition 2—the probability of getting caught, again in cheaters' estimates, must be sufficiently low. These insights come from a book called *Freakonomics*.

And if most readers don't believe this, they're possibly lying to themselves. You know, in that low grade, "really-doesn't-hurt-anyone-too-bad" way that many college students misrepresent the fact that they did not write their own papers or did access any number of new e-products that are designed to help students find answers to standardized online exams. *Quizlet*, anyone?

Many reasons exist why cheating is wrong. But do you know the worse thing about cheating, at least arguably? Cheating is unethical because leaders, organizations, or nations who don't cheat are getting exploited.

Entire school districts across multiple states have cheated by giving students answers to standardized questions, because administrator and teacher pay raises depended on students' standardized scores. Money motivates, doesn't it? Consumers, time and again, have been shown to steal the bagel without throwing the dollar in the money dish. Free food apparently motivates too. Students find new ways to cheat (technology is magical) at a rate that surpasses professors' technological ability to capture them. *Disney World* stopped allowing families with disabled members to go to the head of the line during 2013 because too many customers were hiring disabled people to join their group.

Traditional marketers cheat as well. But they are not the only ones who swindle, commit fraud, or double-deal. In the investment world, retail- or consumer-level investors are branded as *dumb money* due to their tendency to buy high and sell low—to jump out during moments of panic or to jump in during moments of exuberant mania. The key phrase here is moments, the antithesis of long-run. But truth be written, financiers—analysts aside—actually are traditional marketers. Not all marketers sell tangible items such as shoes, used cars, or *Brooklyn Bridges*. In fact, few do. In modern economies marketers more likely sell services, expertise, or money (or rather the promise of access to new or more money), as financial advisors do.

Yet marketing firms, and marketing activity generally, consistently receives more than their fair share of ethical-based criticism from various quarters. Much of this criticism is deserved; some is not.

Why is marketing so subject to ethical criticism? The answer relates to . . . icebergs. What portion of icebergs are visible about the water's surface? About 10 percent. What portion of firms is most visible; above the surface of the water, as it were? The answer, yes, is the marketing part. Critics are more likely to accuse what they can see than what is not visible when assigning cheating accusations.

This is not to suggest many marketers aren't routinely poised to prey on gullible and often not-so-gullible consumers. Some marketers, seemingly including entire industries, are well-positioning to do exactly that. For example, there are more payday lender locations than *McDonald's* and *Starbucks* locations combined operating in the *United States*. This is worth noting because payday lenders routinely charge punitive interest rates on scales that would make *Mafia* loan sharks blush. We are not exaggerating. At least *Mafia* loan sharks usually know the customers they are cheating.

ETHICAL REALITY CHECK 5

Question—Can adult marketers, or any other sort of adult professional, be taught to become more ethical?

The answer is probably not. People's moral compasses are established well before they enter college—unless they begin college around age seven or eight. But everyone can learn more about the positive long-term consequences for their career-long success prospects that emerge if and when they righteously earn a reputation for "doing-well-by-doing-good." That is, earning a brand-like reputation was "doing-well-for-oneself" by "doing-good-for-others."

Correspondingly, anyone can learn more about the negative long-term consequences associated with making unethical decisions that lead them or their firms to engage in unethical behaviors. Just as anyone can learn certain key ethical guidelines to follow as well as mind tricks to use when encountering moral dilemmas. And they should, because reputations matter . . . greatly. Funny thing about reputations and how to leverage them to earn personal or professional branding advantage. Similar to nuclear weapons, reputations exist as power cards that almost certainly prove more effective when held in hand rather than played.

Whenever professionals persistently tell others how powerful or patient or perceptive they are, they are preemptively and presumably unknowingly diminishing the prestige of their reputations. That is because these sorts of desirable personal traits, if present, would already be reflected in their personal branding reputations. *Margaret Thatcher*, former *British Prime Minister*, embraced the branding identity laid on her leadership style by, of all sources, the *Soviet Union* press. Mrs. Thatcher was professionally branded as *The Iron Lady* because of how resolutely she held to her ironclad conservative principles. *The Iron Lady* also wonderfully summarized the point made in this paragraph's opening: "Being powerful is like being a lady. If you have to tell people you are a lady, you aren't."[2]

Ethical conflicts often arise in exchanges between firms and their customers; in exchanges as firms interact with society, or in exchanges as firms engage in relationships with other firms. The preceding "exchange-dominant" statement should not surprise. Almost everything that matters in marketing and in business happens during exchange processes that themselves unfold inside supply chains.

Customers act unethically too. Pre-*Great Recession*, did home buyers who knowingly signed up for mortgage loans they knew they could not afford to pay off once higher interest rates kicked in act

---

2. "The Best of the United States and International Media," *The Week* (June 19, 2019): 19.

unethically? Absolutely, as did their colluding lenders. According to *Michael Lewis*, author of books such as *Moneyball, The Blind Side*, and *The Big Short,* deciding to blame banks "who lent the money for the real estate bust during the early 2000s is like blaming crack dealers for creating addicts." Takes two-to-tango, or something to that effect, right?

Know anyone who has ever purchased a beautiful gown on Friday afternoon, worn it Saturday evening at the wedding or gala, and returned the item for a full refund on Monday? Returned the item, we must add, as a then-used garment that could never again be retailed at an appropriate price in that same store. Victim? The retail store. Victimizer? The unethical consumer.

Or, finally, remember *George Floyd*? Sure you do, the 2020 crises that emerged in *Minneapolis, Portland, Seattle,* and so forth following his death are not buried deeply into history's recesses.

But did you know that consumers/looters involved in the peaceful protests that followed on *Chicago's Miracle Mile* have been caught fencing their stolen goods on *EBay*? In the manner that a lot of expensive *Christmas* toys like *Barbie Houses* that are donated by charities to poorer people end up getting sold for cash by the adults that received them. A lot of *Toys for Tots* were never gifted to needy children. Their flimflamming parents simply turned around and sold them. Big re-marketing opportunities abounded for unethical consumers. As has been written, everyone is a marketer.

ETHICAL REALITY CHECK 6

Many of the ethics-related questions that seemingly have been blithely asked throughout this discussion are surprisingly difficult to answer. Often that's because no one best answer exists to any of these questions. But hey, that's marketing. Far more than *Fifty Shades of Gray*, in either branded book or movie form, routinely prevail inside marketing practice—and it is an undeniable fact that sometimes people do bad things for good reasons. Stated differently but the same; sometimes people actually consciously and correctly think that they must do immoral things for moral reasons.

Beyond question, the presence of all these "gray" decision-making contexts greatly bother many readers. We accept that. Yet isn't it often "better to have questions that cannot be answered than answers that can't be questioned"? *Richard Freyman,* to whom this quote is attributed, certainly thought so.

But such descriptions don't apply to the following inquiry because the question addresses the natural relationship between ethical and legal behavior. Here's the question:

- ▶ Adherence to which standard (i.e., the law or the relevant ethical standard) leads to higher moral standards for marketers as they encounter situations where questionably moral decisions must be made?

Clearly, the answer is ethics. Ethical standards abide, they rise up, well above legal moral standards. The law in any land merely represents the lowest common denominator that could be agreed upon within the relevant culture and society about what sorts of behaviors are moral and socially responsible. That's often a rather low bar. In many instances marketers could plan all day long to ensure that they operate within the boundaries of what's legal but still engage in activities that fall outside the boundaries of what's ethical.

Same story, different frame: Nothing is illegal unless you get caught. But all the while a whole lot of behaviors remain unethical—or immoral. Unfortunately, when legal and ethical standards collide with each other, ethics usually gets the worst.

Consider, for example, selling cigarettes. One of the few if not the only legal US products that, when purchased and used as directed, eventually kills its consumers some 35 to 40 percent of the time.

Is the legal marketing of cigarettes too harsh or too scary? Well then, consider the legal marketing of all manner of overly salty, sweet, fat-laden, heavily branded "stuff" as actual eatable food. Hello, epidemic-like outbreaks of diabetes, heart disease, and colon cancer as more consumers grow heavier throughout *America*. Creating outcomes and consequences that eventually lead to the premature deaths of many heavy consumers of the products.

Then there is that other popular smoking option. No, we're not talking vaping. Recreational marijuana is an increasingly legal product (as of this writing eighteen states, plus the *District of Columbia*, and growing)[3] that, also when used as directed, decreases customer attention, focus, and memory. Cool, man. That's right, recreational marijuana inarguably produces these solutions in a marketplace of ideas that is currently more complicated and competitive than at any point in history. Uh huh, smoking cultivated leaves to knowingly escape everyday pressures and responsibilities sounds like a great product solution to us. (The immediately preceding phrase was intended as a joke. The following sentence is not.) Talk about consumer decision-making whose consequences will generally separate the world's winners from its losers. But recreational pot as a product is increasingly legal, and may be moral too. Well, at least inside those situations where morality is a choice individual consumers must make for themselves.

ETHICAL REALITY CHECK 7

This is a big-time reality check for marketers and also represents an ongoing source of ethical quandaries for many firms. That is, a source of ethical conflict if we can logically assume that *Wendy's, Pizza Hut,* or other dozens of competitors don't actually want to be partially at fault for America's obesity epidemic.

Giving customers what they actually want as opposed to what they should want represents an ongoing source of ethical conflict for contemporary Western marketers. Yet this exact strategy represents a near-certain path to sustainable marketing success.

What do most people want when it comes to food? More and better taste represent an easy and accurate answer. But more and better tasting food is typically accompanied by some combination of higher fat, sugar, and salt. Neither of these elements promote heathier humans when consumed in excessive quantities. Yes, but each of these ingredients are delivered in cannot-help-but-prove-delightful

---

3. Medicinal marijuana, which has been shown to help ailing consumers in various ways, is legal in thirty-three states plus DC—and also counting. Another sixteen of the seventeen remaining states that have not yet legalized marijuana have decriminalized its use.

combinations and portions at affordable prices by a vast and highly sophisticated industrial-fast-food-marketing-complex.

Or, consider alcohol. Alcohol consumption inside the *United States* annually kills far more people than smoking. A drug itself, legal alcoholic drinks and legal alcohol drinkers surely ruin more lives annually than illegal drugs and druggies.

Yet . . . drinking will undoubtedly endure as part of too many cultures to reference here because the choice offers so many rewards, incentives, and values. Talk about a can't-miss value proposition for marketers. Drinking alcohol promises and delivers confidence for insecure people; clarity for uncertain people; comfort for lonely or hurt people. Consuming alcohol helps users attain a soothing bliss. Alcohol succeeds because it gives consumers what they want, short-term, even if the longer-term consequences that arise are often not what drinkers need. Alcohol succeeds because customers rightly or wrongly perceive that drinking solves their problems. Drinking succeeds not because it makes users funnier, sexier, or smarter, but because the branded beer or wine makes drinkers think they're funnier, sexier, or smarter. And the alcohol culture will not just endure but prevail inside a domestic marketplace where only three of the major players in the domestic beer industry collectively spend more on advertising each year than the entire Gross Domestic Products (GDPs) of more than forty countries.

ETHICAL REALITY CHECK 8

Times arise inside personal, professional, organizational, and business lives when *not-to-do lists* prove more important than *to-do lists*. This is where ethical considerations often kick in.

Daniel Moynihan, a truly honorable *Senator* from *New York State*, is famous for many things. One thing is his statements that "People are entitled to their own opinions. They are not entitled to their own facts." Such ideas are rarely more apropos than when they're applied to scenarios where professionals are attempting to skate by or away from their ethical transgressions.

ETHICAL REALITY CHECK 9

There are situational and sustainable ethical values. Marketers and everyone else should pursue and apply sustainable ethical values.

Professionals guided by situational ethical values generally do whatever the situation allows them to get away with, without regard to the wider longer-term interests of their firm or themselves. They usually do this because, for various reasons, these decision-makers care less about the long-run than their own immediate term.

Professionals guided by sustainable ethical values do the opposite, making decisions as if they realize they or their descendants will always be here. They're consequently more likely to behave in ways that sustain and lift up. Sustaining and lifting up employees, customers or suppliers, the environment, their country, and/or future generations they might propagate.

One approach, as a defensible basis from which to make more ethical marketing decisions, clearly makes more sense. Presumably we're all able to identify which . . .

MODULE 8.1

Right or Wrong?

Many marketing professionals routinely confront ethical dilemmas and unresolved moral questions. Those that do not encounter such dilemmas or questions routinely still usually come eye-to-eye with them occasionally. Indeed, marketing decision-makers often have no choice but to select least worst alternatives from menus of decisions that feature no morally palatable dishes—or choices. For example, should marketing organizations:

- ▶ Knowingly create and market purposefully addictive products? The following list of addictive products is long but hardly exhaustive: smartphones; Facebook; tobacco; opiates as painkillers; sleeping pills; highly fattened, sugared, or salted elements posturing as food?
- ▶ Get involved in local or regional communities, and at what levels should marketing organizations allocate portions from their 3Ts in order to support socially responsible purposes?
- ▶ Always be utterly honest, truthful, and fair in all their marketing practices and "communications" with customers?
  - ◆ Hold on here, before you automatically respond, well yes, a man-bites-dog conversation is presented in Module 8.5. (Man-bites-dog-conversations typically involve discussions or thoughts that invert conventional wisdom or conventional thinking.) [4]
- ▶ Use animals in product testing? Seriously, how many rabbits need to die to make cosmetics customers more beautiful than they already are?
- ▶ Overbuild safety fail-safes into their product designs?
- ▶ Always accept full responsibility for innocent mishaps or mistakes that are only tangentially associated with the "confessing" firm or brand?
- ▶ Trade with repressive regimes or with regimes that generally act against the best interests of the United States as a whole and thus represent threats—as we have defined environmental threats—to the domestic economy? Any list of repressive regimes necessarily must include *North Korea* and *Saudi Arabia* as well as *China* and *Russia*.

---

4. As more experienced readers know, the conventional wisdom is often neither conventional nor wise.

DANGEROUS GROUND

A discussion of marketing activities in which ethical dilemmas and unethical accusations often arise follows.

Pricing

When pondering pricing inside ethical contexts, the possibilities of price-fixing, price-discrimination, price-skimming, and price-gouging or extortion should stray far from moral marketing minds.

Price-fixing occurs when two or more firms get together and agree mutually that each organization will set prices at some predetermined though not necessarily the same level. Price-fixing is illegal and unethical.

An unusual assembly of competitors who purchase the same product teamed up during 2020 to sue a purportedly independent group of marketing organizations who happened to sell the same product. Allegations of price-fixing drove the lawsuit. The competitors who purchased the same product, who partnered in the lawsuit, and who alleged "price-fixing" included *Golden Corral* and *Chick-fil-A* who compete in the restaurant marketer sector; *Kroger* and *Albertson*s who compete in the grocery marketer sector; *Target* and *Walmart* who compete in the big-box mixed merchandise discounter marketer sector; *Sysco* and *U.S. Foods Holding Company* who compete in the food distribution marketer sector; and *Campbell's Soup* and *Kraft Foods* who compete in the food manufacturing marketing sector. Presumed and putative competitors who were accused of price-fixing included *Glaxton Farms, Perdue Farms, Pilgrim's Pride, Sanderson Farms,* and *Tyson Farms*. The price-fixing lawsuit alleged that these marketing corporations reduced production levels in order to raise prices, colluded in their pricing strategies, and generally engaged in anti-competitive behavior.

What unifying and nearly universally loved product is being bought and sold? You've guessed it: chicken. Between them, these five domestic marketers produce and sell nearly 37 billion pounds of chicken annually. The lawsuit was not settled before this book went to press. But unlike millions of chickens per year, the question of price-fixing remains very much alive and kicking, even today.[5]

Price-discrimination arises when marketers sell the same product in the same quantities at different prices to different customers or groups of customers. Discrimination, indeed. Definitely seems illegal and unethical.

But is it? Well, yes and no; laws are written by lawyers, after all, and attorneys routinely write laws in purposefully fuzzy and/or subjective ways in order to create more marketing opportunities, for . . . lawyers. Do women get in free during *Lady's Night* in bars and dance clubs? What about movie tickets? The real kids, those twelve years old or younger, and older kids, those aged somewhere between sixty and sixty-two, pay less to enjoy the flick than do the masses of consumers featuring in-between ages. Autos? Do different customers pay different prices for the same *Honda Civic* sold on the same lot?

---

5. Dave Sebastion, "Target Adds Its Suit Against Poultry Farms," *The Wall Street Journal* (December 8, 2020): B1.

Price-skimming; also known as skimming-the-cream pricing. A strategy where marketers establish relatively outright high prices for new or existing products and then gradually lower prices, generally in a planned fashion, over time, and after those firms have created the perception or reality inside targeted customer minds that their brand is worth the higher cost.

Price-skimming is neither illegal nor unethical. Indeed, the ability to leverage the strategy is a logical result of great marketing planning, execution, or both. *Apple* and *Gillette* have used exactly this pricing strategy; in the case of *Gillette*, for more than 130 straight years—and counting. The *Gillette* Corporation was founded by an entrepreneur named King Gillette in 1890.

Price-gouging exists wherever sellers extort, exploit, take huge advantage of, buyers just because they can. Gouging is likely to arise during periods of extreme, unanticipated scarcity. Doesn't matter, the activity is still wrong; $90 cartons of water really were being sold in and around *Houston, Texas,* immediately after *Hurricane Harvey*. This is unethical, illegal, and many perps were rightfully locked up.

Price-gouging, which exists as a virulent subset of price discrimination, occurs more often and on larger scales than many suspect. After an *Amtrak* passenger train crashed outside *Philadelphia* en route to *Washington, DC,* from *New York City* during 2015, four domestic airlines (*American, Delta JetBlue, Southwestern,* and *United*) immediately and radically raised their flight prices to and from *Washington, DC,* and *New York City.* Some increase could be justified through the context of increased demand. But in one recorded case prices rose up to $2,300. Realistically, this price total appears a bit high for a direct city-to-city nonstop trip encompassing only 217 miles!

Or, price-gouging may be more vague and cagey than most realize. *Johnson & Johnson*, lauded earlier as an exemplar of doing the right things right when the *Tylenol* tampering tragedy arose, markets three basic types of *Tylenol*. There is an adult version, a children's version, and an infant version of the well-known and well-branded pain medication. The child and infant versions feature exactly the same ingredients. Yet the infant version costs approximately three times more. The infant version also contains a syringe in order to ensure that exact measurements of dose levels may be extracted and given to baby patients. The child version features a measurement cup, a less precise dosing device. Beyond question, getting dose levels exactly right—not merely close to right—is far more critical to the health and welfare of the patient when this or any other medication is administered to infants. But does the inclusion of a syringe in order to achieve greater precision justify a price that is three times higher? We'll leave the choice to you.

Two closing thoughts follow. First, competitive brands similarly charge about three times for the baby formula versions of their children's pain relief medications. Likely, they're playing a follow-the-leader pricing strategy inside the oligopolistic *Big Pharma* marketplace. Second, syringes themselves retail for between 10 and 30 cents each inside *Walmart* pharmacies.

Anti-Competitive Marketing Practices

Anti-competitive practices arise whenever marketers from inside two or more competing organizations knowingly engage in practices aimed at eliminating or lessening competition. These acts of collusion frequently take the form of secret agreements or unspoken cooperation, typically between firms, and are done for illegal, deceitful, or unethical purposes. Usual suspect lists might include local gas station owners. There's no way that so many stations share precisely the same underlying cost structures as their gasoline and diesel prices move up or down in concert. Or, brace yourself, breakfast cereal companies.

Three of America's favorites—here we are referencing the *Big Three Cereal* marketers named *Kellogg's*, *General Mills*, and *Post*—got together, time and again (during the 1940s, 1950s, 1970s, and 1980s), and agreed to not compete on the basis of price but rather to compete based on advertising (*Captain Crunch* versus *Tony the Tiger*) and new product development. Win, for those marketers and their shareholders. Loss, for customers who paid artificially elevated rates to acquire overprocessed grain-like fluff laden near equally with sugar and salt.

Situations also arise in which one firm prices below its actual costs of making and marketing a product in order to injure another firm and eventually to eliminate the targeted marketer as a competitor. This unethical practice is called dumping. Dumping is a form of predatory pricing in which typically foreign-made products are priced at extremely low levels in comparison to the prices of products that are normally present inside the product's country-of-origin. With good cause, *Chinese* or *South Korean* companies are consistently accused of dumping. The *Chinese* and *South Korean* governments each subsidize certain national industries such that domestic firms operating within the sectors can produce, distribute, and deliver products such as steel to American markets at prices that nonsubsidized domestic (US) steel producers cannot match. Because steel is a commodity, price alone often proves a powerfully differentiating buying criterion.

Potentially Unethical Promotional Practices

Green-washing is an unethical business practice that should be illegal insofar as the practice entails an outright lie. That green-washing exists at all underscores the reality that some managers or marketers are so cool about and good at prevaricating that they could lie their way to hell and back and never break a sweat. Green-washing arises when marketers report or infer that their branded products or organizations themselves are green—as in beneficial to the environment—when the fact is they are not.

The disturbing truth, however, is that the majority of brands that proclaim themselves green are misrepresenting the truth, at best. What happens then is that not only is the environment not being helped or sustained, customers are also actually being hurt. How so? Because green brands inevitably are more expensive to purchase than regular products from within the same product category.

Interestingly, customers who purchase green often do so motivated more by a desire to signal their virtues to others than to help the environment. This practice, of course, is called virtue signaling.[6] Noticing how mixed-up, bungled-up, and jumbled-up the consumer and marketing worlds can quickly become, particularly as those two worlds intersect.

---

6. Virtue-signaling entails conspicuous publicly-issued expressions or demonstrations of one's superior moral values. The wealthy might signal their charity; the religious might signal their piety; the environmentally-conscious might signal their green bona fides. One major irony is often associated with contemporary virtue-signaling: "Virtuous" citizens routinely signal their virtues by boldly proclaiming how much they hate something or someone.

Pink-washing is another unethical promotional practice. Pink-washing arises when brands brag that the proceeds garnered through sales of branded products will be used to support worthy causes—such as the *Susan B. Komen Race for the Cure* for breast cancer. Inside pink-washing scenarios branding marketers are technically telling the truth. But the percentages of proceeds actually going-to-support-the-cause are often shamefully miniscule. The *National Football League*, which promotes its support for breast cancer research by having players wear pink every October, promises that proceeds from League-endorsed goods go to *The Race for the Cure*. Again, these NFL representatives speak truth. But the percentage of total proceeds that actually go into Komen coffers should embarrass the billionaire owners.

The morally questionable game being played by the *National Football League* recently came to light in the broader media marketplace, who love a good scandal unless it involves their favorite political flavor. In response, and in a blatant attempt to avert further damage to its brand, the *NFL* blitzed the media with reports that it had stepped up its donation to the anti-cancer cause in a big way. One might rightfully write that the *NFL* woke-up, instantly.

Green-washing and pink-washing have been around for a long time. Woke-washing is a new promotional phenomenon that sometimes slides over into the realm of the morally-questionable. Woke-washing entails offering support for causes in highly visible ways in order to benefit an organization's or individual's brand by signaling virtuous attitudes or behaviors. These virtuous signals are in part pure marketing and pure cynicism, in many instances. Think ex-*NFL* player *Colin Kaepernick's Nike* ads or *Lacoste's* replacement of its crocodile logo with the phrase "endangered species." Some woke-washing is spinelessly transparent. Think, for example, about *Goldman Sachs* very public refusal to finance fossil fuel projects. All that needs be said here is a veritable paradigm of virtue this specific investment bank is not.[7]

We're not debating whether or not fossil fuel projects should be funded, although almost all of you have routinely ridden in a gas-powered car, train, or plane or resided inside a building heated either by burning coal to produce electricity or by burning natural gas during the last year and therefore probably are not willing or able to walk everywhere you go. Nor are many readers, not even citizens of Texas, willing to forgo heated homes during those cold February nights. We are instead debating whether *Goldman Sachs* initiated this promotional Passion Play—virtual-signaling as fast and vigorously as it could—in an effort to rehabilitate or defend its always imperiled brand reputation. Some woke-washing is strategic. *Twitter* and *Facebook* continuously attempt to fend off federal regulations by publicly issuing ever-changing policies on exactly what type of content represents misrepresentation than outright lying.

Nor are we calling out woke-washing as a universally unethical practice. But the topic is definitely relevant in this context for two reasons. First, woke-washing is currently experiencing its first fifteen minutes of fame. Second, the woke-washing promotional practice hues closely to the fine line that distinguishes outright lying and merely engaging in slightly less moral forms of misrepresentation

---

7. Virtue-signaling is far from just a corporately-inspired promotional power play. Regular citizens/consumers also routinely signal their intrinsic goodness to others. But they, like corporations, should be careful what they ask for and how they ask.

than outright lying. Yes, this second reason is vague. But the genuine reasons that motivate the strategic use of awakened promotional practices are rather vague themselves.

Turning away from the vague and toward the real let's consider beef—the real red meat. Beef exercises a greater impact on the climate than any other category of food. (Cashews do give cattle a run for their money—in terms of the relative amount of water required to grow one pound of either product. Of course, higher consumption of cashews has never been statistically associated with higher rates of colon cancer, as is the case with beef consumption, or with massive increases in CO2 emissions.)

Meanwhile, if the world's cattle formed their own nation, call it *Cows-R-Us*, the nation would boast the world's third highest rate of methane-generation.[8] *Cows-R-Us* would trail only *China* and the *United States,* in that order. There's more environmental degradation to report, however, 1,590 gallons of fresh water are required to raise one pound of beef.[9] Hmm, anyone else feeling like those *Chick-Fil-A* cows really do have it going on when they admonish us, as part of *Chick-Fil-A's* positioning strategy, to "Eat mor chikin"?

Bait and switch practices are unethical. But they're still used even by prominent retailers. *Best Buy*, for example, might promote a great price, for a limited time, on a new-hot technology toy.[10] And specify that this ridiculous "low" price is available this Saturday only. This is actually true. But what's left unsaid is that only three such items are in the store's inventory. Meanwhile, consumers by the hundreds show up on a busy Saturday, lured in and incentivized by the price-deal bait. But as customers arrive and ask for the product, they are told truthfully that the last one has already been sold. Can I show you—switch you to—an alternative brand (now that I have "baited you in")? That's how bait and switch promotional practices work. And use of the unethical promotion does work.

Pyramid schemes, frequently branded by critics as pyramid scams, are business models that recruit new members via promises of payments or the provision of services-in-kind in exchange for enrolling others into the scheme, rather than supplying investments or assistance in sales of products or services. As customer or client membership in the scheme proliferates, recruiting as well as successful marketing at individual levels becomes difficult if not impossible. The net result is that most members who are sucked into the scheme are unable to profit. As such, pyramid schemes will eventually prove unsustainable. These multilevel marketing organizations are almost always unethical and often illegal. Pyramid schemes have existed in the world for at least two millennia under different labels.

Inside pyramid schemes, organizations force the individuals who want to join to pay entry fees. In exchange, the pyramid promises new members a share of the money taken from every additional member they recruit. Founders or directors of the pyramid (those living at the top, or who got in early) also receive a share of these payments. For founders and directors, the scheme is potentially lucrative—whether or not they do any work, these marketing leaders have a strong incentive to

---

8. Greenies and non-greenies alike agree that too much methane is never a good thing for the environment.
9. B. Duckworth, "How Much Water is Required to Raise One Pound of Beef?" *Livestock* (January 4, 2018): 26.
10. This passage is not asserting that *Best Buy* has ever done this. The brand name *Best Buy* is being used to illustrate larger points about the "bait & switch" practice.

continue recruiting others to funnel their money to the top of the pyramid so they can continue to cash their checks! On average, pyramid schemes suck. *Bernie Madoff*, founder of the most famous pyramid investment scheme in recent history, rightfully and only recently died in prison. *Mary Kay Ash*, founder of *Mary Kay* cosmetics, died rich and famous and well-regarded. Many of her fast-followers[11] ended up driving real *Pink Cadillacs* because they made so much money. Many later entrants ended up losing thousands of dollars. *Amway, Nutrisystems,* and *Herbalife* have also been described, often with good cause, as pyramid schemes.

Advertising content is likewise often singled out for its ethical shortcomings. Attack advertisements in politics that essentially are unmoored from any truth, overly-sexualized advertisements, or immoral or harmful stories issued to promote some products or services at the expense of others' branding reputations are often rightfully called out for their ethical shortfalls.

As are, especially, advertising that targets children. Children are not little adults walking around in miniaturized bodies. They do not reason like adults; children generally believe what they see or are told; including what they see or hear inside advertising stories, and this condition can quickly devolve into genuine ethical problems. Notions that advertisers of junk food should be allowed inside schools is a jump ball, ethically speaking. The facts are that marketers pay big money for the privilege of "entering" schools' promotional firewalls and that many schools surely need the money. But what about those thirty-to-sixty-minute-long TV or internet-hosted programs aimed at children that essentially unfold thirty-to-sixty-minute-long marketing stories for the products that sponsor and produce the show?

Marketers are often also criticized for cutting corners on product safety in order to lower costs. More about this issue follows.

---

11. Fast-followers is a term used to describe organizations or individuals that recognize other organizations' or individuals' good ideas early on, and then move quickly (fast) to integrate those ideas into their organizations or lives. These "good ideas" generally relate to new product development.

MODULE 8.2

Critics—Who's Right, Who's Wrong?

Ethical criticisms against marketers and their practices generally arise from either consumer, sociocultural, or business/economic quarters. Sometimes such criticisms are well-founded. Other times, the criticisms are ridiculous. Marketing ethics consequently can be examined and understood from the perspective of:

- Marketing managers or executives and their decision-making;
- Marketing organizations and the impact that the decisions of one organization can have on other organizations; or
- The ways in which ethical or unethical marketing decisions affect consumers, the economy, society, or culture.

CONSUMER-RELATED ETHICAL CRITICISMS

Harming Consumers Through Excessively High Prices

Those who find fault with marketing practice often suggest consumers are harmed through excessively high prices. Are they? Yes, sometimes. But only, logically enough, when consumers are actually forced to buy the excessively highly priced products. When the price of milk is far higher than overall market averages in stores located inside poor inner-city neighborhoods, as routinely happens, consumers indeed are hurt.

But are inner city retailers/marketers who are charging higher prices for milk merely responding strategically by raising prices in situations where little competition exists? After all, far more stores that sell alcohol than milk are typically present inside such neighborhoods. Or are prices higher because marketers know poorer people often don't have easy transportation available to places where less expensive milk is available? The possibility also exists that marketers are strategically responding to the fact that it costs more, say, insurance wise or theft wise (more shoplifting occurs), to do business in poor neighborhoods.

On the other hand, consumers who possess the financial means to exercise the option are never actually forced to buy *Mercedes* or *Prada* brands, to purchase $1,000+ *Apple* smartphones, or to grow house-poor by living in larger, more expensive homes than they can afford.

Using Deceptive Marketing and Promotional Practices

Marketing critics often suggest marketers engage in deceptive practices. Do marketers deceive? Yes, some surely do. The 2006–08 mortgage industry, anyone? Or, according to the best available verified evidence, the bank that uses the brand *Wells Fargo* at pretty much anytime during this century.

Should marketers engage in deceptive practices? Emphatically not because "what happens in the dark usually . . ." And then recall the values intrinsic to the marketing concept. The values that are prominently featured inside the marketing mix firmly suggest marketers exist to help customers solve problems rather than to create new and different problems for their customers to solve. And when marketers build sufficient value and appealing solutions into the brands they're selling, the need to deceive disappears.

Underserving Certain Market Sectors

Relatedly, critics argue that marketers provide poorer or fewer services to disadvantaged consumers or regions. Is this true? The answer, often, is yes. Inside certain communities finding fresh fruit at any price is many times more difficult than finding stale beer. Is it economically justifiable? Same answer; usually yes. Is *Albertson's* or *Kroger's* job one to satisfy their investors or their customers? Actually, the answer is both. But to satisfy investors sometimes marketers may need to satisfy fewer customers. This was not an easy explanation to write. Nor are these easy questions for these organizations' leaders to ask to themselves. But the successful acquisition of sustainable marketing success, which is driven in near equal parts by branding reputation and revenues secured/costs expended, is not an easily-mastered task, either.

Using High-Pressure Selling Tactics

Critics of marketer's ethical standards, or lack of such, often argue that marketers engage in high-pressure selling tactics. This is true. Unethical marketers have always pushed people to purchase products or services that they don't really need and/or cannot afford.

But consumers themselves have been known to desperately desire products and services that they don't need, absent much if any intervention from marketers.

Who's at fault, then? As discussed below, consumers enjoy the right to not purchase anything they do not want.

In an ideal marketing world, marketers should never have to pressure anyone into buying anything they neither want nor need. And marketers would not need to exercise pressure, not if they create sufficient perceived or actual value for their brands by effectively managing their marketing mixes. Marketers should reflect on an additional factor; that being, they should never pressure people into buying stuff they don't currently need unless those individual or organizational marketers are willing to bear the risk of never again selling anything to those specific B2C or B2B customers. Relationship management, present and future, always matters.

Apple has never directly pressured anyone to lay out more than $1,000 for its latest generation of phones. To the contrary, *Apple* brand loyalists, whose ranks are legion, routinely stand in line to exercise their privilege to be the first to fork out a special-K for new *Apple* stuff. *Apple*, however, seemingly has mastered the task of indirectly pressuring people to overspend for now-non-extraordinary products. It's just a smartphone. Consumers' fears about not keeping up or no longer leading the social/status pack are emotional strings that *Apple* has adroitly plucked for decades as the marketer leverages positioning and ultimately profit advantages. But hats-off to *Apple*; the firm does marketing extraordinarily well. And apologies to any *Apple* loyalists who now may feel pissed-off. Your perceptions about *Apple's* value are no less valid than this book's, a condition that makes both parties right.

Cooling-off regulations and laws exist, and consumers can use them to gain escape from "bad deals" where they feel they have been pressured into buying products they really don't want or need. Regulations and laws that are available essentially, to help consumers extricate themselves from the consequences of purchases they now regret. Part of the body of legislated consumer rights, cooling-off periods exist where buyers may cancel the purchase, return the goods (even keys to autos/homes, along with the autos/homes themselves!), and receive full or near-full refunds. Cooling-off timelines vary from state to state, but typically range between forty-eight and seventy-two hours.

Marketing Shoddy (Unsafe) Products

Even today, despite ample countervailing evidence, the profession's detractors routinely suggest marketers often market shoddy (low quality) or unsafe products. Yes, but contemporary marketers sell their products in an incredibly transparent (internet) and competitive global marketplace. Markets where firms that fail to bring their A-games in customer relationship management each day often don't get to play in next week's game. There has never been a better time or place to be a consumer than right now, in America. Today, higher or high quality is pervasive and generally prevails over crap. Marketers are marketing and customers are making buying choices during an era in which those firms that don't sell high-quality products rarely stick around very long.

Need evidence? The average age of an automobile on American streets and roads has risen to 11.8 years. The rate of increase is slowing, people do want new rides and few quality curves will ascend forever. But average vehicle ages surpassed twelve years during 2020.

Yet this high-quality phase was hardly the rule inside the domestic automobile industry during the 1970s and 1980s. What's more, the entire domestic industry, which currently features only 2.5 fully domestic marketers rather than the four brands that the US hosted during the early 1970s, still pays high indirect prices today, decades later. Do you know why your first author (entering his latter sixties) has never purchased any *General Motors, Ford,* or *Chrysler* products? The answer is because his father bought an expensive, at the time and for him, *Chrysler* branded vehicle in 1971. The new car was quickly revealed to be a total POS, and the after-sales service of the *Chrysler* dealership proved even worse. Not our problem, was the dealer's prevailing attitude! That's a lot of lost domestically-made potential automobile sales from one consumer during the intervening fifty-plus years.

And what's more he grew up to be a professor who routinely spreads this poisonously negative WOM about the *Chrysler* brand, its products, and its services. Has the *Chrysler* brand improved its marketing and customer relations management game since then? *Chrysler* indeed has stepped up its game. But the *Chrysler* brand, like all brands, only received one chance to make a good first impression inside this particular situation, as is generally true of any other brand competing inside such a globally competitive marketplace. And all *Chrysler* brand-related parties at the time blew their one audition all those decades ago.

What point has been referenced time and again throughout this book? Okay, many points have been referenced over and over. But the one being referenced here, again, is that customer relationships REALLY matter.

Even so, bad stuff, often inadvertent or unknown at the point of its arrival, happens. Mull over what happened to *Mattel*, a few *Christmas* seasons back. Turns out, the esteemed toy marketing brand truly was selling both unsafe and shoddy products during that Christmas season, because *Mattel* had inadvertently/accidentally/unknowingly allowed lead paint to be inlaid upon many of its new toys.

How did this happen? *Mattel*, like many iconic brands, actually did not make the products it markets inside America. *Mattel* still doesn't make anything itself . . . the opportunity to lower costs of production and earn economies-of-scale by partnering with actual manufacturers inside Asian supply chains is too appealing. And understandably so. In this case, partnering with a *Chinese* toy manufacturer (i.e., *Mattel's* supply chain partner). A *Chinese* toy manufacturer that outsourced the painting of the toys it made to yet another supply chain partner—a firm that specialized in intricate industrial-scale painting. Right now, for those keeping score, we are two *Chinese* firms levels up the supply chain from *Mattel*, the famous American retailer and supply chain captain. Now as it happened that supply chain painter partner firm, as the need to achieve and sustain modern-day efficiencies generally dictates, did not produce its own paint. No, the responsibility for paint production slid further upstream to a *Chinese* paint manufacturer.[12] If you're keeping score we're now three supply chain levels[13] up inside the supply chain from *Mattel*, the originating marketer. The unethical *Chinese* paint manufacturer, competing based on its provision of lower prices inside a commoditized market sector, used lead rather than more expensive and safer elements to produce its paints but failed to inform any downstream customers (such as the *Chinese* toy manufacturer). Again, *Mattel* was not aware that any of this was happening until it was too late. The bad news for *Mattel* and its brand, when it did break, broke bad, fast and hard, as is usually the case. But the lead on *Mattel* toys did happen, and this highly unethical and actually illegal transgression ultimately was viewed, correctly, as *Mattel's* fault. *Mattel* paid a heavy reputational and actual cost price, and withdrew all its toys from real and virtual holiday shelves during that *Christmas* season.

---

12. Lead paint degrades cognitive processing among children who are exposed to excessive amounts of it. And children, particularly toddlers, often chew on toys, and so forth, which is where some major problems can begin. However, the use of lead in paint when making paint lowers costs of production. Hence, there is an economic, or cost-based, incentive to use lead paint.

13. Supply chain levels are defined and further discussed in the Supply Chain Management Module.

Finally, have you ever been to *South Louisiana*, to the self-designated and heavily promoted *Cajun Country*? No such thing as low-quality, low-taste, as in low-fat restaurants survive there, for long. South Louisiana restaurants cannot succeed long-term unless they bring the taste value. Yet most food consumed in those restaurants trended big-time toward the unhealthy. Is that unethical?

What's an Unsafe Product, Anyway?

The preceding discussion leads logically to the question of what is an unsafe product, anyway? Cigarettes? Well, surely they're hazardous, but cigarettes are legal, even though when used as directed for about thirty years, the products begin killing users at ridiculous rates. Beer, wine, liquors?

Well, yes, but . . . see previous discussions about alcohol, ice cream, hamburgers/pizza, the dispensation of HUGE portion sizes in restaurants; well, yes, but . . . isn't this just . . . what . . . consumers . . . want? Yes, it is; and that's exactly where a perpetual ethical dilemma for marketers resides.

Using Planned Obsolescence

Mindful of consumers' welfare, cultural critics of marketing practices often accuse marketers of pursuing a strategy called planned obsolescence. Here, the critics are correct in their accusation, but absolutely wrong to assume that any ethical transgressions arise when markets employ planned obsolescence. Planned obsolescence is a useful and highly effective strategic marketing practice wherein marketers design, produce, or market products that purposefully feature artificially limited useful lives so they become prematurely outdated in terms of function or fashion (fast-fashion, anyone?). Or, in a more prevalent scenario, where marketing organizations' new products, which usually command higher prices at their successful points of market entry, are strategically replaced by additional new products emanating from that same firm.

Apple, again, has mastered this tactic.[14] The mega-brand has successively and successfully introduced *iPhone* generation after generation, and always commands high prices—first topping $1,000 during 2017—at the point of the new products' entry to the marketplace by using this strategy. So has *Gillette* with its razors, in an uninterrupted winning streak extending back to 1890—yes, 130+ years ago. Video game marketers, *Beyoncé, Jay-Z,* or *Beyoncé/Jay-Z*, musically-genre-wise, yes, yes, all are guilty as charged of planning and executing planned obsolescence.

The *Hebrew* word *paleios* is the root word for the *English* word obsolete. *Paleios* meant "to be old when it comes to usefulness" during ancient times. *Paleios* also meant "useless or worn out." Hebrews, a chapter inside the *New Testament*, states that what is becoming obsolete and growing old is ready to vanish away. Many forward-thinking marketers who have successfully engaged in New Product Development (Module 10), as well as consumers who reflexively yearn for new stuff that concurrently appears fresh but feels familiar, think exactly the same way. When executing planned obsolescence strategies, marketers gently make their own existing brands appear less useful, worn-out, or less than

---

14. Yes, one really could write full marketing books by describing just *Apple* or beer brand marketing.

utterly stylish, but only in comparison to the "wonderful" new products that the planning marketer itself has strategically introduced. Planned obsolescence strategies are often used by those marketing fashion or electronic items.

Should marketers engage in planned obsolescence? Sure, why not—if and when they can execute the strategy successfully. The plan and its planned intent is to obsolete one's own product before competitors do it to your firm. In such market domains it's far more preferable to do onto yourself before others do onto you. Planned obsolescence is neither illegal nor unethical. Hardly, the tactic is broadly used by many of the world's best marketers.

Consumers don't have to buy the new versions of existing products as those new products are introduced. The now-older versions rarely leave the marketplace instantly; they remain widely available. The only reason why most consumers buy new versions of existing products is because the new products deliver new and highly appealing value that incentivize consumers to switch. Switching (changing what they are already buying), after all, is difficult for most people to do. A physics principle called inertia[15] inveighs against change, even for humans. Marketers really must get or keep their "A" game on to entice existing customers to willingly switch from an existing product to a new product.

SOCIETAL-RELATED ETHICAL CRITICISMS

Ever since corporations were granted the privilege of limited [financial] liability during the 1850s, debates have raged about how many and what type of obligations marketers have to society. Marketers certainly should do their fair share to grow overall societal welfare. And believe it or not, most marketers do. For example, growing the economy by creating jobs because marketers are creating demand for their products and services absolutely benefits society.

One point is clear, however. Marketing organizations are absolutely obligated to customers and to investors. A worthy motto that all professionally minded marketers should not just live but will also succeed by: Do more than your duty.

The first job of ethical marketers is to satisfy customers by solving their problems. The second job of ethical marketers is to reward investors in exchange for the risks they incurred by financially supporting the firm. Fail to honor one, the other, or both obligations, and soon enough marketing organizations will require the undertaker's services. No problem, funeral homes are marketing organizations too. And in an ironic twist, funeral homes exist and operate as marketing organizations that often actually do exploit vulnerable customers. Funeral home customers are especially vulnerable, because they are making expensive B2C purchasing decisions during highly emotional and stressful times in their lives. Please note that no intimation is in place suggesting that all funeral homes exploit their customers. But the ethical reputation of the industry as a whole is far from stellar, with good—or is it bad?—cause.

---

15. Inside physics contexts—yes, the actual scientific discipline—the phenomena called inertia explains why objects at rest tend to stay at rest. Inside marketing contexts, inertia relates to the pronounced tendency of customers to choose nothing or to remain locked-in on decisions or behaviors they have already made or are living out.

Marketing Practices Negatively Impacting Sociocultural Values

Perceptions broadly exist that marketing practice exercises a negative impact on society/culture as a whole. But, is the more valid criticism that society/culture at large has negatively impacted marketing practices? Glaciers, anyone? Even so, societal critics accuse marketing of creating false needs and too much materialism inside domestic society.

Human needs, however, are real rather than false. Needs arise instinctively, absent marketing intervention. Marketers, however, are clearly capable of transforming one-time customer wants into customer desires that feel as pressing and motivating as actual needs. A sweet spot for any product entails actually being or merely being perceived as a necessity people can neither provide for themselves nor live without. Especially when the branded item is not a necessity—as usually is the case.

Effective marketing activities—a combination of branding, product development, promotional and ultimately positioning efforts—often create false needs. Or, such activities sometimes may simply tap into and grow wants that already exist into needs. Again shades-of-gray prevail.

Marketing Practices Generating Too Few Social Goods

Marketing critics sometimes argue that marketers create too few social goods, such as highways, public universities, or less pollution, while creating too many private consumable goods. This is a silly critique. The creation of public or social goods is not the job of business—although this sort of creation still sometimes happens indirectly as a result of the value that marketing and marketers create. Social goods are supposed to be generated through the taxes paid by citizens to governments. One can either futilely hope or fruitfully pray that governmental marketers will steward this task more effectively. And in between the "where-we-are" and some critics would "like-us-to-be" marketing profits create wealth that benefits not only investors and employees but society as a whole, because those investors and employees each pay heavy taxes on their gains.

When marketers operate based on profits and losses, as all ultimately must, light is shed on whether or not marketers have created delight. Successful marketing is fundamentally based on who is better at weeding-out bad ideas from good. Bad ideas generate net losses; good ideas generate customer delight. Delight generates marketer and societal profits.

Hewing closely toward a profit and loss orientation, and remaining constantly oriented toward satisfying customer needs, cannot help but point marketers toward providing what society really wants. Because marketing success, foremost, requires satisfied customers. Customers, in turn, comprise society. It is not marketer's fault that what society wants often proves harmful, long-term, for individual members of society. Or is this the fault of marketers? As noted, shades-of-gray often prevail. It is the truth that telling the truth is hardly the same—morally or otherwise—as not telling a lie.

Marketing Practices Polluting Culture(s)

Critics sometimes suggest marketing practices generally degrade, if not outright pollute, domestic culture. Citing ample evidence, they might point toward advertising clutter. This makes sense. *Yankelovich Research* reports *American* consumers were exposed to around 500 advertisements a day during the 1970s. Today? As many as 5,000 daily.

Detractors further suggest marketers are responsible for excessive assaults on consumers' privacy. This makes sense, again. *Facebook's* entire business model is based on pirating private information from its consumers and selling the data to marketers. *Facebook* consumers have always known this, and willingly gave up the goods. Perhaps, not for that much longer; certainly, teens are no longer as inured to *Facebook* as teens were even three or four years ago. (No, this segment leans heavily toward being Instagrammers or TicTokers these days. And the day after that, ???) Meanwhile, few consumers really still really love *Facebook*. Instead *Facebook* customers generally only love what the communication medium can do for them. Fewer people are wanting to perform out their lives publicly now in ways similar to what they relished until recently. Perhaps due to cultural factors. And certainly due in part to *Facebook's* failure to initially admit and ultimately manage the proliferation of fake news through their e-ways.

Those who criticize the ethicality of advertising similarly sometimes emphasize the, say, loose morality displayed in and propagated through ad messages. Clearly, such critics are correct. It's difficult to mount a defense when evidence supporting their case abounds. Take, for example, a 2018 ad sponsored by *New Mexico Democrat* political candidate. The ad featured three, and only three, words, "Fck the *NRA*."[16,17] The political advertising message was a bit course, of course. But the fact is that sociocultural norms and expectations have evolved/devolved to the point where the word was freely disseminated throughout *New Mexico* markets and printed in another product, this book. For what it's worth, the *Federal Trade Commission* decreed in 2003 that the F-word could be used as an adjective but not as a noun inside most media. A factoid that helps most marketers only to the extent that they know the difference between nouns and verbs.

Marketing Practices Consolidating Much Power Inside Few Hands

Marketing faultfinders likewise lament that too much economic and political power end up in too few peoples', marketing organizations', or other institutions' hands; while repeatedly singling-out marketing practice as the chief culprit. Yes, this sort of consolidation of power has happened and

---

16. *NRA* is the branding acronym used as a primary branding identifier for the marketing organization called the *National Rifle Association*. And the *National Rifle Association* uses the branding identifier so effectively that most readers already knew what *NRA* meant.

17. Final word on the ethicality of the use of the word f__k. F__k is a powerful word in large part because it can be used in so many different ways. But when speakers or writers use f__k too many times the word loses its power and makes users look stupid, or at least vocabulary-challenged. Balance, in most things, generally proves useful. And for the marketing record, the *United States Federal Trade Commission* decreed a few years ago that the F-word could be used as an adjective but not as a noun inside various media, including regular television stations (channels). Marketers took notice and in the intervening decades produced legions of television programming products that are now liberally peppered with the word.

will continue to happen. But remember, many organizations, people, and brands legitimately earned branding power by being innovative and willing to take risks that paid off. And yes, a lucky few who won the genetic lottery actually were born on third base due to their non-earned wealth, natural athletic ability or good looks but somehow concluded they had hit a triple all by themselves. But that's marketing, and that's capitalism, and without marketing inside a capitalistic marketplace the domestic society, culture, and economy would each be markedly different. Different in ways that are sometimes worse, but usually different in ways that are better.

This is business life, yes, but also sort of like real life itself. Marketing, globalization, and capitalism are each harder on losers than on winners—just like life itself is obviously harder on so-called "losers." But so-called losers inside capitalistic economies and markets are not necessarily losers. They too are still typically far better off than they would be if marketing, globalization, and capitalism did not prevail inside the *United States*. These so-called losers instead are often folks who failed to keep up, plan, change appropriately with the times, master new technologies, or properly brand themselves and the values they create. In the world marketing has created, there are real winners or losers, that's fact. But mostly because people are better or worse choosers.

Here's another benefit associated with capitalism. Capitalism is so powerful and effective that capitalistic marketers can easily accommodate a little socialism. Informed *American* citizens routinely call this touch of socialism the "safety net," and they are usually delighted that it exists. Capitalistic-funded safety nets are socialistic, and that's okay. If citizen consumers slip up for whatever reason, often for reasons not of their own making (factories do shut down unexpectedly as people lose jobs; people actually do become deathly ill and unable to work), the net catches them before they totally crash.

Problems arise when people perceive the social net as a replacement for the creative engine that only capitalist sparks can fire up. Capitalism plus a safety net; wonderful. Socialism as the safety net; well, then you have *Venezuela*.

Socialism, of course, is being marketed widely as an appealing idea (product) inside contemporary *America*. Many find the idea of socialism attractive. Likely, this is because the word "free"—as in zero-priced college tuition and health care, or universal income—proves so determinant inside many hearer or reader minds. Nothing is free, however. Everything, and every choice, arrives with an associated price. Someone always has to pay.

These thoughts represent our learned and experienced-based opinions. Readers are free to formulate their own. But for us, socialism is better understood as trickle-up-poverty—and how ethical is that in the long-run? The long-run, as in as you know, the place where everyone hopes to one day live.

Capitalism, best understood as the greatest secular idea that humanity has ever created. Marketers, and this book has since established that every successful organization is first a successful marketer, make money by creating value that solves problems for others; make money by producing goods and services that people want and can afford; and make money by creating paychecks for employees, returns for investors, and benefits for communities. Capitalism, from both an ethical and social responsibility standpoint, creates greater amounts of shared value, not for the few but for everyone. In the long-run, how ethical is that?

Marketing Practices Killing or Debilitating Customers

Cultural critics also exist who have observed the presence of more diabetes, colon and lung cancer, heart disease, and obesity than otherwise should exist; and who ascribed blame to marketers. Primarily blaming food marketers, and particularly fast-food marketers. Maybe they're right. Or, are fast-food marketers simply acting rationally by developing and promoting products and satisfactions that consumers crave based on their natural (instinctive) responses? Consumers, after all, are only human. Sincere question: When a powerful marketing complex offers more salt; fat; sugar[18] buzz, highs, or the thrills associated with more caffeine or shock entertainment, what's not to love? And what's wrong with selling the Unholy Trinity of Fat, Salt, and Sugar in *America,* the Land of the Free, where consumers enjoy a medley of Constitutional and legislated rights to buy-eat/not buy-not/eat exactly what they please?

Regardless, attributions—acts of finger-pointing—of blame by cultural critics has long since emerged as the number one spectator sport inside America. Hence, much of the madness arises inside social media. Inside these media anybody can say anything, and usually does. After all, the emergent brand name "*The Mob*" is increasingly used to describe unhappy sheeple who flock to and spend too much time on social media. Social media are a mirror, yes, but they are also megaphones that are designed to amplify the worst—and do a great job of that.

Two ready-made and relevant marketing research-worthy questions emerge organically:

▶ First, do unhappy sheeple naturally migrate toward social media?

▶ Or second, does social media migration and the grazing that happens there naturally manufacturer unhappy sheeple?

Likeliest answer: We have stumbled across a paradoxical situation where the answer to both questions is yes. Talk about cognitive dissonance—and a real-time ethical dilemma begging for a viable marketing solution.

Ronald's Responses

What is *McDonald's* doing in response to cultural criticisms directed at the role it plays in creating and expanding this growing epidemic of domestic obesity? The answer is a lot.

McDonald's, for example, took cheeseburgers and chocolate milk off its *Happy Meal Kid's Menu* in response to sociocultural criticisms about the possible intersections that exist between growing segments of overweight kids and the general unhealthy nature of its food. Did you know, for example, that there are more than seventy ingredients in a *McRib* sandwich (reintroduced in 2018 and again in

---

18. Sweetness—sugar was not "discovered" by *Western* culture until around 1425 or 1493 AD [disputes exist over the exact time; notably, *India* and other regions had wide access to sugar by 500 AD]. Envision the first time a *Medieval European* consumer tasted sugar. Wow! Talk about wants instantly transforming into needs. Understand that *European* consumers had experienced sweet through honey and berries. Further understand, however, that *European* consumers could not have possibly fully understood the true meaning of "sweet" until they encountered sugar. Did you know that the consumption of sugar triggers the same sort of physical bodily responses as does the consumption of *OxyContin*?

2020)? At least one of those ingredients is rumored to be pork. Yuck. All that processing. It cannot be good for either hogs or people.

McDonald's senior management has long since opted to delete several traditional items from its existing menu in an effort to reduce the amount of calories, saturated fat, and sugar that kids consume inside its restaurants.[19] Parental purchasing agents still can ask by name for cheeseburgers and chocolate milk and acquire each for their growing children. But *McDonald's* strategists rightfully concluded that not listing such products would decrease how often they are ordered. *McDonald's* reports that since soda was moved from *Happy Meals* in 2014, orders for soft drinks with *Happy Meals* have fallen 14 percent. Hamburgers and *Chicken McNuggets* still remain the main entrees on the *Happy Meal* product mix. *Happy Meals*, a branded product offering that is more than forty-seven years old, has been targeted by health advocates and health-conscious parents for years. *McDonald's* has introduced many product and menu tweaks across the years, including decreasing the amount of fries and adding fruit. These menu changes continue. An old apple juice was recently displaced by a new one featuring less sugar.

Love or hate the brand, *McDonald's* is trying to "Do Well For Itself By Doing Good For Others." *McDonald's* has long since offered more socially responsible product choices to parental segments seeking to protect or recover their kids' health. One surefire and simple solution, parents could stop driving their kids to *McDonald's* stores (i.e., follow *Occam's razor*). Readers presumably recall that *Occam's razor* suggests that the best solution to complicated are usually the simplest ones. And questions about how best to act in more ethical and socially responsible usually represent complicated problems for most marketers.

McDonald's fast-food competitors are not all similarly buying into the socially responsible platform. Nor does any ethical obligation exist for them to do so. *Hardee's*, for example, continues to honor the "all-the-fun-fat-&-flavor—and you'll get it all fast" principle that has traditionally driven the success of fast-food marketers. One of *Hardee's* recent positioning taglines argued that fast-foodies should "Eat like you mean it!" Hardee's is honoring the principle that marketing success is based, in part, on standing-out rather than fitting-in.

Other Marketers' Deeds and Misdeeds

Truth be written, times occasionally arise when marketers and marketing practices clearly hurt individual consumers. But overall marketing practice emphatically helps society at large, in many ways and for many reasons. And as far as the prospect that consumers might also pursue dietary solutions that would almost always improve their health, allow us to repeat the terse counsel offered by dietary expert *Michael Pollan* several years back: "Eat food. Not too much. Mostly plants." *Pollan's* simple approach almost certainly features more value than advice generally embedded inside legions

---

19. Please note two issues primarily because each issue appears later. First, when *McDonald's* added or cut items from menus displayed inside *McDonald's* restaurants or drive-through lanes, the fast-food giant was changing its marketing mix. Second, when *McDonald's* has added or eliminated items from menus displayed inside *McDonald's* restaurants or drive-through lanes, they were also engaging in new product development.

of advertising and promotional stories issued by the fast-food sector—whose messages, at net, are akin to eating pseudo food fast. All the time.

Our physical, spiritual, and intellectual bodies operate like sewers. What we get out of these three bodily parts, long-run, aligns closely with what we elect to put or to not put into them. This statement, yes, is meant to apply to pseudo food. But obviously the statement applies similarly to unethical ideas or practice.

How might marketers counter these social-cultural criticisms?

The behaviors of an entire global business sector—*Big Pharma*—sheds useful light. Perhaps in recognition of the wicked marketing games that some pharmaceutical industry members have played, but certainly in recognition of the need that existed to burnish the sectors' dinged branding image, five of the top-ten corporate donors to charitable causes[20] are *Big Pharma* marketers. By name, the top three Pharma donors, in descending order from largest to smallest, are *Pfizer, Merck,* and *Eli Lilly*.

What wicked games? Well, for starters was and is the wicked marketing game in which an addictive opiate-based brand called *OxyContin* has ended up wrecking several hundred thousand lives. *OxyContin* was surely marketed expertly and over-exuberantly by *Purdue Pharma*. Then there was the wicked pricing game played by ex-pharmaceutical CEO and current convict *Martin Shkreli*. *Retrophin*, the firm that *Mr. Shkreli* founded and led, purchased the rights to sell a life-saving medicine called *Daraprim* and immediately hiked the price from $13.50 to $750.00 (not a misprint) per pill. Not coincidentally, patent-protected *Daraprim* has a short shelf life. Yet consumers who permanently needed the solution when they needed it to survive had no lower priced alternatives available. They had no choice but to keep buying and rebuying. The *Retrophin* marketing strategy was both a sham and a shame.

More inside baseball. While the organization should be lauded for donating, *Pfizer* donated less than .004 percent of its actual revenues. Most of the donations related to in-kind giveaways of free or heavily price-reduced distribution of their actual products to targeted, often underdeveloped markets. But when *Pfizer, Merck,* or other corporate sector brethren give away *AIDs* drugs for free in *Africa*, as each does, pharmaceutical marketers aren't truly giving drugs away for free. *American* consumers and health insurance marketers pay for more than they should to cover the costs of any presumed giveaways that occur. The purpose of this paragraph is not to criticize purportedly charitable donations given in the name of corporate social responsibility. Instead the purpose is to shed sunlight—supposedly the best disinfectant—on the other side of the donor coin.

Little to None of This Is New

There's one last thing to understand about how these societal criticisms of marketing ethical practices are playing out.

---

20. Charities, also marketers. Charities are classified, correctly, as not-for-profit organizations. Charities certainly compete vigorously against one other to secure donors and larger amounts of charitable funding from them.

A book called *Ecclesiastes* taught long ago there is nothing new under the sun. True that. Meanwhile, from a literal physics perspective we know that matter cannot be created or destroyed. We understand, further, that everything is constructed from matter. But you soon will also learn (Module 10) that existing elements of matter—including ideas—can be re-bundled, re-packaged, re-stored, and eventually even re-positioned in order to create new products not from nothing new but instead from old, as in existing, stuff. The new ideas that buttress consumer or marketing institutional demands for divestiture, for de-marketing or for eliminating morally suspect assets; for boycotts of products ranging from *Goya Beans* to blood diamonds; or for promoting ethical sources for dolphin-safe tuna or fair-trade coffee have deep, historically-planted, roots. And these deep historical roots and the ideas that sprouted during those long-gone times emerged from marketers' strategic responses to society's ethical criticisms. Each and every one of them!

Among the earliest expressions of an *American* branding identifier[21] was the non-importation agreement generated by a marketing association of Boston merchants that was supported by local Boston consumer households' boycotts of overpriced and overtaxed goods imported from *Great Britain*. To both promote and enforce the new agreement, local Boston retailers and their customers held a party. Historians called this soiree the *Boston Tea Party*.

Ethical capitalism emerged a long time ago. One early example is when marketers first began targeting conscientious consumers who flocked to acquire free-labor products and to signal the virtues of one brand of sugar that was promoted through one big positioning idea. The positioning idea simply said: "East India Sugar Not Made by Slaves." That was the entire marketing message.

This happened during the mid-eighteenth century (the 1750s). At the time sugar was a luxury good, and existed both as a specialty and positional good,[22] available only in the most minuscule quantities or rarest occasions to all but the most privileged and wealthy.[23]

BUSINESS/ECONOMIC RELATED CRITICISMS

Critics routinely argue that three strategies exist through marketing practices that harm other companies and reduce competition.

Competitive Acquisition

The first strategy entails acquiring competitors. By definition, the acquisition of smaller competitor organizations by a single larger competitor organization reduces competition. Also by definition,

---

21. Speaking of branding identifiers, these original issue "Americans" then immediately adopted a flag. So what, and so where is the brand? Here's the answer, in the form of two more questions. What's a flag if not a symbol? And what's a symbol if not a brand identifier?
22. Specialty goods and positional goods are discussed below.
23. Bronwell Everil, *Marketing to Abolitionists: Not Made by Slaves* (Cambridge: Harvard University Press, 2020).

smaller or weaker competitors, especially those associated with start-up firms, frequently want to get acquired. Surely the founders of *Instagram* and *Snapchat* were respectively delighted to receive more than $1,000,000,000 and $3,000,000,000 for the privilege of being swallowed whole by *Facebook* all those years ago.

Creating Barriers to Entry

The second strategic approach entails creating barriers-to-entry.[24] These barriers-to-entry (BTEs) function to dampen the success prospects of new organizations seeking to enter the market. BTEs exist when entry-to-market is made more difficult or denied to new firms because existing absolute capital costs, branding-power, or economies-of-scale (EOS)[25] impediments to successful entry prove too substantial for those "new guys" to overcome. Over time, conditions where fewer competitors exist usually produce higher prices and fewer customer alternatives (available choices). No, this does not sound very appealing to us, either. For decades, the domestic automobile enjoyed huge economy of scale- and brand-based advantages. But those resource advantages did not last forever. Just ask *Toyota, Mercedes, Hyundai, Honda, Volvo,* or any number of other foreign competitors who began entering the domestic automobile market *en masse* during the 1980s and soon thereafter began grabbing more than their fair share of market.

Creating Extreme Marketing Power

The third strategy entails the creation of extreme marketing power; which is generally reflected in the existence of greater branding power and stronger brand equity.[26] Firms that create branding power for products inside their portfolio often enjoy the opportunity either to engage in predatory-pricing[27] or again, to block competitive entry by keeping their prices low while building both their market shares and economies-of-scales. But even marketers who are powerful enough to pursue predatory

---

24. The term barriers-to-entry is an economic concept. The term is used to describe the existence of high start-up costs or other obstacles that prevent new competitors from easily entering existing markets. Patents or special tax benefits can function as barriers-to-entry. From more purely marketing perspectives barriers-to-entry also might include strong brand identities, brand loyalty, established and efficient supply chain relationships, high customer-switching costs, or the presence of economies-of-scale.

25. As a reminder, economies-of-scale refer to the reduced making and marketing costs per unit that automatically arise from increased total output of products and their marketing processes. Simply stated, larger scaled factories can make and market batteries at lower-per-unit prices than smaller scaled factories can produce and market them.

26. Brand equity (power) is derived from the goodwill and name recognition that a branded product, service, or organization has earned. Marketers enjoying brand equity generally can raise prices without losing much if any marketing share. The nature of and role played by brand equity and by brand power are discussed in detail inside Module 11.

27. Predatory pricing, also known as undercutting or dumping, entails pricing products or services at extremely low prices in order to drive weaker competitors who cannot match the lower prices long-term out of the market or create cost-based BTEs that block new competitive entry.

pricing usually cannot prey forever. Truly predatory pricing inevitably invites new competitive entries; governmental intervention at federal regulatory levels; or both results.[28]

Does predatory pricing always invite new competitive entries or governmental intervention? The answer is no, suggests *Los Angeles Times* reporter David Lazarus. During 2020 Mr. Lazarus wrote about how *Big Pharma* marketer *Eli Lilly's* insulin product cost $21 in 1996. Today, the cost/price of an *Eli Lilly* brand called *Humalog* approaches $300. During the same year *Eli Lilly* purchased another pharmaceutical firm, which also sold insulin, for $8 billion. David Lazarus happens to be diabetic. These are, for him, matters of life and death. Another twenty-six-year-old diabetes patient died during the same year because he could not afford the monthly bill for his daily doses.

Between 2012 and 2017, the cost of insulin for the average domestic consumer nearly doubled, from $2,900 to $5,700 annually. *Big Pharma's* response? Essentially, pointing accusatory fingers at insurers and pharmacy benefits managers. *Big Pharma* claims that the issuance of rebates and coupons—sales promotions—cover much of the costs. *Big Pharma* then typically goes on to argue that the real problems follow from high deductibles and other cost-savings insurance services.[29]

Each implicit and explicit criticism is legitimate. Yet a countervailing argument that if marketers had not effectively targeted, positioned, and managed their marketing mixes; created correspondingly high levels of genuine/perceived value; and created huge swaths of satisfied customers based on their value creation, none of these three sources of competitive advantage would have emerged is also legitimate. Moreover, don't B2C or B2B customers usually only pay amounts that are roughly equivalent to what they perceive given products' or services' value is actually worth? The answer is yes. Yet, prices and pricing strategies are more than occasionally designed to be manipulative, complicated, confusing, and more than a bit unfair.

---

28. *Alcoa* was split into three separate firms by the *Federal Trade Commission* during the 1940s. The three brand names—*Alcoa Aluminum*, *Kaiser Aluminum*, and *Reynold's Aluminum*—remain rather well-known today. The primary reason for the split was that *Alcoa* owned near-exclusive rights to a mineral called bauxite inside the *United States* at the time. Aluminum cannot be produced without bauxite. *AT&T* was split into dozens of firms during 1984. This governmental regulatory decision made *Ma Bell* mother to many tele-children corporations. These corporations were originally branded as the *Baby Bells*.

29. David Lazarus, *Los Angeles Times*; Axios.com.

Module 8.3

Consumerism

Marketers have rights. So do consumers. These conditions are natural and should be honored.

The goal of consumerism is to improve the rights and power of buyers in comparison to the rights and power of sellers. Consumerism, as a movement, has been around for more than 100 years inside the *United States*. But the movement regained its footing and materially moved forward during the mid-1960s with the publication of a book by erstwhile presidential candidate *Ralph Nader*. The book was titled *Unsafe at Any Speed*. The book primarily discussed a *GM* automotive brand—the *Corvair*—that actually was unsafe at any speed. *Unsafe at Any Speed* accurately accused *GM* and other domestic automobile marketers (*Ford, Chrysler*, and *American Motors*, at the time) of refusing to introduce certain known life-saving devices because they cost too much to implement. Design-wise, the *Corvair* brand was appealing. The look of the car was absolutely ahead of its time. These aesthetics largely explained the brand's temporary popularity.

The consumerism movement eventually specified certain core buyers' and marketers' rights. These rights remain largely intact, with but a few additions, today. Buyers' have since enjoyed the rights to:

- Not buy something that they don't want to buy.
- Expect the product to be safe. Except for what, cigarettes, alcohol, ice cream, or smartphones? Not an easy question to answer, is it?
- Expect the product to perform as claimed.

Marketers themselves currently enjoy the rights to:

- Sell anything, so long as what is being sold does not injure anyone or anything.
- Charge any fair price for the product, so long as no discrimination exists against any group of buyers.

- Promote products and spend any amount they desire on promotion, so long as the associated stories are genuinely accurate or understood to be so outrageous a claim that no sane person would believe them, which is puffery.[30]
- Use any product message they choose, so long as the product message is not misleading or dishonest or offensive to any particular oppressed group.
- Use incentives, typically arriving in the form of direct or indirect financial rewards. Incentives motivate most customers. Economists agree, correctly, that most big or small decisions made by humans are directly or indirectly motivated by incentives.

The importance of the word introduced after the fifth bullet point, "incentives," would prove difficult to exaggerate. Almost every decision that almost everyone makes is motivated by an incentive. Yet marketers themselves often do more than merely tangle incentives like bait in front of actual or potential customers (prospects) in attempts to lure them onto websites or into physical stores in order to eventually sell them something that presumably has value. Instead, marketers themselves are often also heavily motivated by the promise of incentives.

Climate advocates, for example, come in two basic product types. They are generally either scientists or activists. But the product type does not really matter because both scientists and activists are heavily incentivized by the opportunity to "discover" additional and/or to exaggerate "existing" climate-related problems in order to secure greater amounts of funding to support themselves, their work projects, and possibly their life missions. These behaviors are entirely predictable. The opportunity to secure more funds (revenues) to support one's own self-interests is highly incentivizing. Doing so by creating or revealing and then emphasizing a certain sort of climate-related problems toward targeted funding sources. In the process literally creating dilemmas that demand solutions of the sort only the marketing agent as alarmist is uniquely qualified to provide. Hmmm, this process just described sounds like marketing to us.

Which is, actually, not really the point. The point to be understood and taken away is all this alarmist or purely motivated (your choice) signaling about problems that in the end will help "me" and my cause is motivated at its core by the presence of personal incentives.

ETHICAL VERSUS LESS ETHICAL PRODUCTS

Some marketers enjoy the opportunity to create and sell products that are inherently more ethical than other products. Few unethical ways would exist to produce or market asparagus, one might assume. No matter, however, because every marketer has the opportunity to manage their marketing mixes more ethically. Marketers, for example, have the option of marketing products that deliver immediate or long-term satisfaction to customers. But marketers ethical or unethical options continue.

---

30. In advertising contexts, puffery entails purposefully exaggerating the benefits, attributes, qualities, and so forth associated with branded products. But doing so in ways that consumers understand is an exaggeration. Puffery is discussed in greater detail during Module 14.

For example, marketers might market products that harm (fail to benefit) or help (benefit) customers either in the short-term or over the long-term. Other marketers enjoy the opportunity to market products that offer short-term/immediate or long-term benefits to customers. Those same products may never provide any material short-term or long-term satisfaction to customers.

Imagine, please, two dimensions. The vertical dimension captures a spectrum of satisfaction. This satisfaction-spectrum ranges from the immediate-term to longer-term satisfaction. The horizontal dimension captures a spectrum of benefits. This benefit-spectrum ranges from the immediate-term to longer-term benefits.

Next, create an intersection between the two dimensions, and by default a two-by-two matrix featuring four cells or categories has been created. Almost all tangible products or intangible services can be classified into one and only one of those cells.

Some cells are more ethical than others. One cell is completely unethical.

Deficit Products

Times arise when certain products don't solve anyone's problems, failing to create any sort of discernable value for those who consume them. Instead the only people those such products or services help are the people or organizations who market them. Such products are deficit.

Deficit products are understandably difficult to market. Small wonder why; how would you like to promote products that fail to deliver either immediate satisfaction or long-term benefit? Yikes. Diet pills, for example, apparently have never helped dieting consumers lose weight (i.e., the benefit). Otherwise, one can only assume far fewer overweight people would populate America, because basically most plump people would prefer to lose weight. Diet pills do, however, materially increase the amount of time users spend in the bathroom. They deliver zero long-term benefit and zero immediate satisfaction, as such. Such morally- and practically-challenged products rarely succeed. And honestly, does anyone really think throwing pills at physical problems always represents the best solution?

Pleasing Products

Pleasing products, by contrast, deliver immediate satisfaction and consequently are easier to market. *Krispy-Kreme* or *Marlboro Lights*, anyone? Pleasing products may actually injure people who consume them because they often generate radically non-beneficial longer-run consequences. Pleasing products are less-than-morally-ideal, to say the least. But again, they are easy to market. After all, pleasing products provide panaceas to individuals seeking short-term pleasure.

The pursuit-of-pleasure or desire-to-avoid/mitigate-pain exists as prime behavioral motivators for most earthly citizens. Pain can arrive in myriad forms—and you'd best believe many marketers are masters of ginning-up pain. Mental, physical, emotional, spiritual, relational, in varying degrees or combinations, to identify a few.

Were this not so, would so many customers become addicted to the pleasurable sensations that the aforementioned *OxyContin*, heroin, porn, or other alcohol-based pain relievers initially provide to the point where consumers literally use these solutions to death?

Salutary Products

The word salutary suggests that unpleasant or unwelcome experiences sometimes actually generate beneficial longer-term effects. Salutary products are characterized by low immediate appeal (failing to deliver much short-term satisfaction) while featuring high potential for benefitting customers longer-run.

Exercise programs or broccoli drive home this point. These highly-ethical products are certainly saleable. But they are more challenging than pleasing products to market because consumers often live-in-the-moment rather than plan-for-their-future. Such consumers aren't worrying enough about their future-selves because they're too busy satisfying their today-selves.

Desirable Products

Desirable products provide both immediate satisfaction and long-run benefits to customers. Awesome; and not just because desirable products are rather easily marketed. High-quality, classically-designed wool sport jackets for men or high-quality, classically-designed little-black-dresses for women fit in this highly-ethical category. You know, products that look and feel great when we initially slip them on but that can be used for years because good taste is always fashionable and rarely goes out of style. Such product types represent yet another sweet spot for marketers seeking to do well for themselves by doing well for others.

A relevant question follows; one that is applicable to many organizations. Can marketers therein be sufficiently creative to conceptualize, produce, and promote such products?

MODULE 8.4

Making Good, Better, and Best Ethical Marketing Decisions

Marketers always have the opportunity to do-well for themselves by doing-good for others. This guideline is important, applies universally, never won't work, and should be pursued whenever possible. Marketers might do-well by doing-good by:

- Supporting the right causes with their time, talent, and treasures.
- Doing exactly what they say they will do, every time; keeping every promise made.
- Being environmentally-neutral, worst case; or environmentally-beneficial, ideally.
- Following each guideline associated with the marketing concept.[31]
- Being scrupulously ethical in all activities, marketing or otherwise, that the marketing organization pursues.

Doing-good, from any marketer's perspective, could also entail:

- Honestly and completely informing customers to the extent that those customers need to be informed to make good decisions. This exact point is more fully addressed below.[32]
- Never marketing ethically-questionable products, or using ethically-questionable promotional or pricing practices.
- Marketing, whenever possible, products that improve customers' quality of life.
- Never marketing products that directly/indirectly injure customers' welfare/well-being.

---

31. As a reminder, the marketing concept prescribes that the satisfaction of customer needs should come first (for marketers) and further suggests that the pursuit of mutual gain between customers and marketers holds paramount importance.

32. Interested readers could Google Brooke Hamilton and David Strutton's 1990s-era research on truth-telling.

A strategy that was recently executed by *AMC Theatres* exemplifies the idea of doing well, both for the *AMC* brand and bottom line, by doing-good, for others. A deluge of children have been diagnosed as autistic, for largely unknown reasons, in America during recent years. *AMC* recognized this environmental trend and responded to this demographic shift by addressing a specific problem that autistic children's parents often control.

The problem: Autistic children, like most youngsters, enjoy watching kid-appropriate movies inside theaters. But autistic children often get over-excited by cinematic stimuli in ways that annoy families who did not know what was happening or who did not want their viewing experiences disturbed.

The solution: In a doing-good-for-others strategic plot twist *AMC* recently began showing movies to autistic children and their families and friends in dozens of its theaters. And only to those kids and their support units. This tactic was and remains laser-like market targeting. Naturally, *AMC* only promoted special showings of child-appropriate movies. How cool is that? Cool thing, indeed, because *AMC* made (these were pre-COVID-19 days) greater profits per screen at this time of weekend mornings or summer days than would otherwise be earned, while doing-good for others. And yes, clear reputational benefits arise.

Another marketing lesson follows: Marketers do not always generate revenues and especially profits the way that most laypersons would believe they create sales or profits. Movie theaters make some profits from each film they show. But these margins are skinny, because these revenues are disproportionately shared with upstream marketers in the cinematic supply chain who actually produce movie products. Actually, this is not a problem for movie theaters. The cinematic products that movie theaters literally project merely function as "bait" or an "incentive" to lure fannies into seats. And those butts don't necessarily remain in those seats, or delay sitting down, because they are hungry, thirsty, or both, and willing to pay exorbitant fees to eat and drink. Can you handle a dirty little marketing secret? Sure you can, by this point. Movie theaters don't exist to show movies. Theatres exist to sell exorbitantly-priced soda, popcorn, hot dogs, candy, and so forth, because that's where the real profits reside.

Years ago the slightly higher-end (price-wise) fresh fast-food firm called *Panera Bread* decided to begin singing off the same sheet of doing-good-for-others marketing music. St. Louis-area *Panera Bread* stores, during the bottom of the Great Recession made and kept a promise to consumers who had lost their jobs, or were afraid they might lose their jobs, *but who still wanted to eat out occasionally*, to pay what they could afford at *Panera*. Or to pay nothing at all. Have a meal on *Panera Bread*, if you currently cannot afford to eat out; that was *Panera*'s positioning ploy. *Panera* also asked guests who could afford the meal to pay a little more.

The results were great. *Panera* profits tilted up, a little; *Panera* store traffic, grew a lot; *Panera's* reputation and level of goodwill in the *St. Louis* region, went through the roof. The goodwill, the brand's rightfully-enhanced reputational advantage hopefully continues to this day. You read about this, after all.

The mega bank named *Wells Fargo* recently exemplified the wrong sort of managerial reasoning—or non-reasoning. The bank developed and executed a "ravage and ruin" its customer-base strategy in exchange for short-term profits. The savagely unethical strategy entailed covertly selling and charging customers for unneeded banking accounts. One can only assume that the bank's senior management must have really felt they needed to score their year-end bonuses—another example of incentives? (The answer is yes.)

Revelations slowly and then quickly came to light that the bank had opened more than 2,000,000 credit-card accounts without unsuspecting client's knowledge. The strategy worked, generating billions in unwarranted fees and unearned millions for the executives who fostered and supported the unethical and presumably illegal act. Not nice; in fact, the act entailed doing well for one's own firm while doing extremely bad things to others.

The rest of the story: In a 2018 response to the consequences produced by these clear ethical transgressions, *Wells Fargo Bank* begin promoting a new positioning story. The message simply said, *Established in 1875, Re-Established in 2018*. Good luck with the re-positioning strategy, *Wells Fargo*, especially since a wrath of entirely new ethical missteps were uncovered during 2018 and 2019! Legions of former customers have long since rode off into the sunset, and surely aren't looking back.[33]

SERVING ONE'S OWN INTERESTS BY SERVING OTHERS' INTERESTS

Doing-well-for-oneself by doing-good-for-others makes strategic sense, most of the time. But continuously pursuing this ethical standard, and it alone, does not represent a sustainable marketing strategy. Marketers, even the not-for-profit variety, still should be driven by bottom-line considerations. Marketers, the same as people, who fail to feed themselves, first, will eventually become unable to feed anyone else.

One remaining issue should be deliberated before leaving this topic: Seemingly unselfish deeds—not just marketing activities—are also often actually driven by highly self-interested and selfish motives. Why? First, because doing unselfish things makes us feel better ourselves. Second, because engaging in unselfish or seemingly unselfish behaviors allows people or organizations to signal their virtues to others. Virtue-signaling, when executed well but not to excess, can enhance doers' reputations in marketing and non-marketing settings.

During 2018 *Starbucks* announced it would eliminate straws from all 26,000+ stores by 2020. The coffee chain currently used more than 1,000,000,000 straws annually. The company also promised to remove dome lids from all beverages except *Frappuccino*. Starbucks could simply be virtue-signaling its *Green* bona fides. Or, perhaps, the firm really is committed to saving the world one overpriced cup of coffee at a time.

Virtue-signaling may now be emerging as America's newest national pastime. Virtue-signaling occurs when folks or firms strategically strike poses and publicly display the right behaviors toward targeted audiences, publicly support the right causes, or purchase and publicly display the right products. The right causes might entail supporting "green" or the rights of illegal immigrants. The right products might entail purchasing Priuses or solar panels. Virtue-signaling is tailor-made for the world that Facebook and Instagram have created.

If green is good then plastic is bad. Then virtue-signaling about how bad plastic is should work out well for most marketers, right? Well, maybe.

---

33. What just happened is a negative word-of-mouth (WOM or e-WOM endorsement).

During 2020 a *Vancouve*r grocery store called the *East West Market* opted to signal their virtues and to shame their customers into bringing their own reusable bags by only offering them plastic bags festooned with the following external labels: "*The Colon Care Coop,*" "*Dr. Toew's Wart Ointment Wholesale,*" and "*Into the Weird Adult Video Emporium.*" But many *East West Market* customers thought these bags were funny and began started asking for the bags by name. We'll give the grocery chain an "A" for effort and for caring for the environment but an "F" for execution and not doing enough research to anticipate their customers' likely responses.

Perhaps the grocery chain could have driven more customers toward greener choices had they offered bags that detailed exactly what customers had bought and placed inside. Labeling recyclable bags with positioning slogans such as "*Cheap Beer to make the Pain Go Away until the Divorce is Finalized: She's Taking Me for Everything*"; "*Assorted Lunch Meats for my Stupid Brats: They're Making My Life Hell So I am Feeding them Scrappy Crap*"; or "*A Birthday Card for Someone at Work I Can't Stand: His Success Was Built on Others' Dashed Hopes*" might have worked better.

East West Market management apparently did not consider that many people, customers all, thrive and strive for attention, and how *East West Market* had actually decided to give away attention to consumers for free. Who wants a bag that just says *CVS*? And more seriously, if stores really want to eliminate plastic bags why do cashiers still put only one or two items in each bag?

Yet choosing to demonstrate virtue based on self-marketing and self-branding calculations, and them alone, demonstrates little more than the virtue of vice. Which is not virtuous, at all. The point, readers' take away, is that marketing professionals and organizations should strive to do the right thing not because the action helps them out but because doing the right thing is always the right thing to do. In the end, the goal is to be better and in the doing do what benefits customers. The goal is not to feel better, for one's own benefit. Even though those who consistently do right inevitably will ultimately feel better about themselves.

DEONTOLOGY: A GOOD ETHICAL THEORY

Ethical behavior (i.e., acting morally) features a strong upside. In the long-run, ethical behavior pays off for corporations and individuals. Reputations for being ethical and fair players are reflected in higher corporate stock-market valuations, which most experts agree are the fairest arbiter of value because investors vote with their money inside stock markets.

These points remain valid although individual people and organizations surely exist who occasionally get away with shady marketing practices. Over the long run, however, most don't. *Enron's, Countrywide's,* and *Bernie Madoff's* pyramid-scheme-based financial empires come to mind as unethical houses of cards that quickly collapsed once sunlight entered their data files.

The major downside associated with using ethical rules is that no set of ethical standards or principles exists, or ever has existed, that could successfully address and resolve every possible ethical quandary that businesspeople, medical practitioners, legal professionals, politicians, and so forth might encounter. An at-this-point-in-history self-evidently true statement that brings us to an ancient ethical theory called deontology. In quasi-contemporary times, the deontological ethical philosophy is most closely associated with *Immanuel Kant*, a German philosopher who died in 1904. Deontology theory suggests ethical rules should be established and that those moral guidelines should then be followed. Having such ethical guidelines in place is necessary and useful inside any contemporary organization. But their presence is rarely sufficient, in and of itself, to ensure ethical behaviors follow.

Rule sets such as the *Ten Commandants* or the *Hammurabi Code*[34]—216 *Babylonian* laws created around 1763 BC—have existed essentially since formal leaders and any groups following them have existed. And these same rule sets have not been strictly followed, nor much paid attention to, for about the same length of time. For example, how many of the *Ten Commandants* did you break last month? Did you kill anyone? Its doubtful, but still possible dependent upon the marketing organization for which you work. Did you covet anything that anyone has? Well, uh . . . inside America it's a pity that envy is not a cash crop. In socially networked markets where "everyone" sees only the best of what people strategically curate and choose to display modern Americans would doubly become the richest consumer realm in the world. Doubly, because American consumers are richest in terms of their goods, services, and expenditures.

But back to the commandments themselves. Ever take God's name in vain? Hope not, but possible. But did you ever do or think anything, were the deed or thought brought to your parent's attention, that would fail to bring honor to them? Oh, heck. Now we've probably figured everyone, including us, were our parents all still alive.

Within the Ten, please note that only four of the Commandants point up toward God, advising humans about how they should enter and manage relationships with Him or Her or It. By contrast, six of the *Ten Commandments* extend horizontally left and right—dealing with how human-to-human relationships should be managed right here on earth. The clear intent was to govern how people enter and manage relationships with other human beings. Apparently God, as presumed historical author of the Ten Commandments, understood the importance of humans successfully managing relationships with other humans in ways that add to rather than subtract from the value of harmonious, collaborative, and cooperative relationships. Well, given that he has been positioned and branded as omniscient by all religiously-oriented marketing organizations, of course God knew.

How many commandments did the Jews eventually write to supposedly govern their behaviors? The answer is 613. Thirty-nine laws alone, for example, are associated with keeping the Sabbath holy. Did the Jews uniformly follow these Laws, then? Readers know the answer. And yet knowing and honoring each additional ethical law still would not counter all the ways to cheat, lie, distort, or otherwise act unethically in today's world. If you think the *Ten Commandments* being posted in a school or ethical standards being posted in a workplace will fundamentally change the behavior of children or employees, you most similarly envision that a world exists, somewhere, where "Employees Must Wash Their Hands before Returning to Work" signs in *McDonald's* or *Burger King's* bathrooms keeps urine traces out of their french fries.

Having rules in place to determine and govern what decisions and behaviors should be deemed ethical or unethical simply does not work. A major if not the primary reason why devolves directly from one natural human condition. What condition is that? The condition is a naturally arising character trait that apparently resides deeply inside most human beings. This character trait dictates

---

34. The *Hammurabi Code* is another deontological ethical rule set. The origins, the issuance of the *Hammurabi Code* predates the *Mosaic* issuance of the *Ten Commandments* by 800–900 years.

that we humans are prone to (1) create rules and then to (2) almost immediately begin to bend/rationalize/break those rules in ways that redound to our own advantage and, if we are not entirely self-interested, to the advantage of our families and close friends or partners. Did anybody else just think about what appears to happen naturally to previously well-meaning politicians, staffers, or lobbyists shortly after they arrive in *Washington, DC*, or in any other capital city inside all fifty states?

So what? Beyond question it is better to have ethical and moral rules in place as guidelines than not have anything at all. Ethical rules represent a good start. But their mere presence will not finish the job.

The *U.S. Constitution*, for example, represents both another ethical document and a concession to humanity's fallibility. Human beings tend to abuse power after they have acquired it, often by declaring fervently on their routes to the top that they would never behave like their previously powerful predecessors. Being wise beyond all reasonable expectation, the *Founding Fathers* of the *United States* dispersed federal power by establishing a constitutional set of rules or guidelines that created a three-part federal rule: an Executive Branch, a Congressional Branch, and a Judiciary Branch. To preserve liberty and to promote ethical management of the public's interests requires not just intentions but also institutions.

Reiterating, it is still better to have ethical rules in place than have no guidelines at all.

UTILITARIANISM: A BETTER ETHICAL PHILOSOPHY

An understanding of the underpinnings of utilitarianism and the willingness to make decisions and take actions based on the theory will push marketing decision-makers further up toward an ethical ideal. Utilitarianism is also known as consequentialism. *Jeremy Bentham* (1747–1842) is the father of the utilitarian theory of ethics. Bentham wrote that "The right thing to do is that which maximizes utility." Stated differently but the same, inside marketing contexts the right thing to do is the choice that generates the highest overall happiness. Consequently, arguments could follow that even murder is not wrong but instead could prove useful and ethical if the kill increases overall happiness. So long, that is, as any decision and consequences that follow generate the greatest good for the greatest number.

This means that the ethical choice is always the one that does the most good; delivers the most value, for the most people—even if some people are injured, perhaps badly and forever, as a consequence. Yet, this theory is as harsh and as unfair to the few who are left behind or perhaps even injured as it sounds. Marketers should always weigh the consequences of their decisions. In fact, everyone should make decisions now as if they could envision themselves looking back from some future point at the good (moral or ethical) or bad (immoral or unethical) consequences that the decisions they made today engendered.

What follows is a metaphorical rocket blast from the past. *Mr. Spock*, from original *Star Trek* television crew, is speaking to *Captain Kirk* during the second movie in the eventual movie franchise. The highly-ethical Vulcan said: "Jim, remember, the needs of the many always outweigh the needs of the few." *Spock* was utilitarian in his ethical philosophy. He was quite intelligent and always logical. Spock must have been right.

Weighing out the good and bad consequences of decisions creates more ethical value than does following deontological rule sets. Yet deontological rule sets still have their time and place.

Perhaps surprisingly, enlisting utilitarianism as a means to making more ethical decisions is easier than one might think. All that decision-makers have to do is choose the lesser of two evils.

ENLIGHTENED SELF-INTERESTS: THE BEST ETHICAL PHILOSOPHY TO APPLY INSIDE MARKETING DECISION-MAKING CONTEXTS

The core ethical philosophy of many marketing and other professional types appears to constitute a reasonable akin to "do whatever you want but don't get caught." Other deeper thinkers about the subject matter philosophical takes are a bit more complex. *Ayd Rand* was one such deeper thinker (and a doer as well). Her aforementioned ethical philosophy known as Enlightened Self Interests (ESI) suggests that marketing decision-makers who consciously act to further the interests of others, including the interests of the group to which they belong or customers that they seek to serve, are ultimately serving their self-interest. ESI theory is correct to suggest this. ESI strengthens the doing-well by doing-good ethical argument. Deciding to act in ways that promote enlightened self-interests represents the preferred courses of action in most marketing settings. When making decisions inside such situations, marketers should analyze the:

▶ Role and importance of their reputation. How difficult are ethical reputations to create? How easily can ethical reputations be destroyed? The answers should inform marketing decision-makers before they make their choices.

▶ Fact that when marketers plan well and work hard driven by the goal of creating genuine and differentiating value they can more easily tell the truth and sell exactly what they promise. Working hard is so important for so many reasons. After all, the only place where success comes before work is in the dictionary.

People or organizations can become or remain more enlightened marketers by becoming or being:

▶ Extremely customer-focused; strategically organizing marketing activities from customers' points of view.

▶ Tightly focused on value-marketing; strategically investing resources in activities that create more true value for customers.

▶ Perpetually socially-focused; strategically evaluating customers' wants, their long-term needs, and society's long-term interests first—along with the strategic imperative that their organization also must profit—before doing anything.

Honestly, and how could one not be honest while writing about ethics, the ESI philosophy provides the soundest ethical decision-making tool. First, because the theory promotes the idea of doing-well for oneself by doing-good for others. And second, because use of the theory is entirely consistent with the core principle that drives the marketing mix (i.e., focusing intently on solving customers' problems).

NOT A PHILOSOPHICAL, BUT STILL A USEFUL, ETHICAL GUIDELINE

The Newspaper [today, Facebook] and Your Mother Ethical Test falls short of any expert's about grounded ethical philosophy. Yet there are three reasons why the "Your Mother Ethical Test" comes highly recommended as an ethical guideline. First, the *Facebook* and your mother test is practical and easy to use. Second, the test is virtually assured to make decision-makers more ethical if they employ it. That is, unless their mom is an unethical mess herself.

Assume you're working late, struggling after-hours to identify the most ethical choice in a situation where the most ethical alternative is less than clear. Assume, further, that you are sincerely motivated to remain or become your ethical best. Then apply the following criteria, understanding that decisions always generate consequences. You also realize that consequences produce generally good or ethical outcomes while others generate generally bad or unethical outcomes.

Okay, you're ready to go. If you're comfortable knowing your mother will read all about the consequences generated by your choice on *Facebook* tomorrow morning, you've made what was, in this situation, the most ethical decision. If you're not comfortable knowing your mother will read all about the consequences generated by your choice on *Facebook*, you have not made, given the circumstances, the context, the most ethical decision.

Because few people would want their mom to learn tomorrow morning that she raised an unethical... Right?

SHOULD MARKETERS TELL THE TRUTH? YES, USUALLY

The idealized notion that people or firms might occasionally sacrifice their own interests by always telling the truth appears admirable—in the abstract. But marketers live and work in a concrete world. In the real marketing world such magnanimity often causes more harm to or creates less good for innocent, fully disclosing, entirely truth-telling marketers than does realistically accepting the fact that times will arise when not all customers need to know everything.

One universal marketing recommendation—tell the truth. Then marketers don't have to worry about or remember all the lies they told, either injuring their reputations or looking stupid when the truth comes out. But inside marketing settings, truth-telling means giving customers full and fully accurate disclosure of information to the extent that the information provided is necessary for the consumer to make a well-informed, well-grounded, and safe purchase decision.

As far as actually lying goes, no, that's never acceptable. Anytime any individual marketer or marketing organization has to lie to make his, her, or its point, the marketing entity has no point to make—presumably because he, she, or it has no value to promise or to deliver to prospects or customers. No reasonable option exists at that point other than to revert back to strategically mixing and managing the marketing mix in ways that generate genuine value.

One implication is that pharmaceutical product marketers face higher truth-telling standards or expectations than smartphone marketers. This is because when consuming pharmaceutical products, what consumers don't know can hurt or possibly kill them. Or leave them stuck sitting around all day in bathrooms.

But most everyone reading this already knew these things, whether they recognized it or not. All readers that is, who have seen a thirty-second ad for a prescription drug on television, and actually paid attention. If this is you then you know that such advertising stories invariably use their opening five to six seconds to explain the health problem (sometimes not such a genuine problem, but that's another manipulative-marketer story that we discussed earlier). Then the same ad spends another five to six seconds discussing how the branded pharmaceutical product being promoted or advertised will solve the problem. Okay, ten to twelve seconds into the thirty-second message. The ad then spends another ten to thirteen seconds discussing the possibly offensive to downright horrible side effects. Four-hour-long erections, as the promotional proponents of the brand *Viagra* subtly imply may arise as an unpleasant side effect of taking the drug, may or may not be unpleasant [highly context-dependent]. But dying because you took any medication is almost always a horrible side effect. The ad then exhausts whatever remains of the remaining thirty-second message offering uplifting, possibly redemptive music along with user testimonials about the problem and how the medication resolved the dilemma for them.

Seems like even *Big Pharma* is able to discern when it needs to tell the whole truth. Another possible side exists to this story, however. A *New York Times* article reported a study suggesting that a drug described as being able to generate such serious side effects actually may make users more confident in its power to cure. Talk about unintended consequences.[35]

Yet similar criticisms and truth-telling expectations need not be applied to marketers selling smartphones. Not knowing what they don't know about smartphones will not hurt or kill customers—unless we're talking about customers having their attention spans, their ability to pay attention, get killed by falling into an uncovered manhole or onto a highly trafficked street, or feeling horns grow out of the backs of their teenage necks as their bodies respond naturally to the pressure placed on their necks by growing bone matter as teens repetitively bend their heads down to read or send texts. Are we suggesting that times may arise inside marketing contexts when a little bit of truth can go a long way; that times may arise when marketers face no moral obligation to tell the whole truth in its entirety? Such as, for example, those organizations that make and market bubble gum do not have to spell out in excruciating detail that chewing too much highly sugared gum is generally not good for the chewer's teeth. Yes, that is exactly what we are suggesting.

By the way, what is one of the surest ways to discern whether someone is lying to you? The answer is straightforward. Your conversational partner, or whomever, is often lying whenever s/he answers a question you did not ask while ignoring the query you did make. Watch for it.

---

35. What are "unintended consequences"? Consider this: One, though not the only marketing-related, reason why so many Americans are overweight today is that so many fewer consumers smoke today. Is being overweight worse for consumers' health than smoking? No, definitely not. But the gap between premature morbidity attributed to the dead person being overweight as opposed to the dead person dying from smoking-related causes is not as large as most would assume.

MODULE 8.5

Bottom Lines

Marketers who aspire to remain or become more ethical should learn the rules offered below. These moral guidelines relate to ethics, social responsibility, and sustainability. Sustainability, which can be described simply as conservation practices whose unwavering goals entail using none (fossil fuels), using less (fossil fuels), or repurposing what's already been used (plastic bottles, 99 percent or so of plastic is sourced from chemicals made from fossil fuels, by the way) encompasses an increasingly important point of and opportunity to achieve sustainable differentiation and positioning advantages. Following even a few of these rules would usually facilitate greater marketing success. Following all these rules would typically ensure greater marketing success of the sort that proves sustainable. As former President *Theodore Roosevelt* said, "Knowing what is right doesn't mean much unless we do what is right."

Ethical Rule 1

Accept that the best way for organizations or individuals to be socially responsible, to support sustainability and social responsibility, and to act more ethically is to succeed as marketers.

Various desirable societal values, such as enhanced employment opportunities, a more robust economy, and greater numbers of more highly satisfied customers are almost always generated when marketers succeed by offering values to their customers that are different from and perceived as superior to the values offered by their competitors. There is little to nothing that is unethical about any of these marketing-induced outcomes.

Ethical Rule 2

Marketing organizations and individuals should never act unethically by taking advantage of any customer or supply chain partner, even when they can get away short-term with the abuse, unless those marketers plan on never doing business with those customers or partners, again.

Ethical Rule 3

Marketing organizations and professionals should never view others simply as a means to marketers' own selfish ends.

Nicolai Machiavelli, original purveyor of the ends-justify-the-means worldview, was a successful marketing consultant; okay, full-truth, he was part-political counselor and part-public relations advisor, but full-time genius at each. And in his *Renaissance* era-defining book that was titled, *The Prince*, Machiavelli never wrote that "all" ends justify "any" means. The marketing master instead wrote, and we paraphrase, that only ethical ends justify the means. When applied inside this context, ethical ends stand in as a synonym for ethical goals and means functions as a synonym for marketing activities.

Ethical Rule 4

Too few marketers are like *Abraham Lincoln*, about whom the following was written: "[Lincoln] never remembered any slight and never forgot any kindness" conferred to him by another human being.

Maybe, indeed probably, this statement is nothing but an apocryphal anecdote about a great leader. Even so, the premise represents a goal all should strive to honor; although most, if not all, humans still would fall short in their efforts.

Ethical Rule 5

Marketing organizations and professionals should always take the long view when deliberating whether decisions are or are not ethical.

The value of taking the long view is well-synopsized in this Russian Proverb:

- "Is there ever a good reason to piss into a well today that you might need to drink from tomorrow?"

Ethical Rule 6

Once marketers have the long view in sight and focus on it, they should find it easier to mindfully learn to be nice to the people they are passing on their way up.

Why? Because marketers often see those same people on their way back down.

Ethical Rule 7

Marketing professionals should understand that ethical decision-making is not about being clever in a moral crisis but about forming the sort of character that does not realize it has experienced an ethical dilemma until the crisis is resolved.

Ethical Rule 8

Marketing organizations should recognize the degree to which they, as humans, are programmed to forget or never even recognize their own ethical transgressions and to remember their grievances.

Might knowing this fact now affect how marketers manage their future professional relationships? It should.

Ethical Rule 9

Marketing professionals should take the high road.

If nothing else good happens, any traveler traveling this path will encounter less traffic and consequently enjoy better chances of standing out.

Ethical Rule 10

Marketing professionals should appreciate the extent to which getting away with not telling the truth requires an incredible memory.

Even so, people are rarely entirely truthful. Most people are lying much of the time. This is the world, marketing is part of this world, and people have created the sociocultural and marketing worlds that reside therein. Many marketers, unfortunately, are also lying in ways big and small much of the time. Lab tests conducted during 2016 revealed that samples of store-brand aloe vera skin gel sold by *Walmart, Target,* and *CVS* actually contained no aloe vera, notwithstanding the fact each retailer's store brand listed the skin soothing plant as its number one or number two most prominent ingredient. The *Food and Drug Administration* does not approve cosmetics before they are sold. Nor is there any legal penalty for peddling fake aloe. Of course not; it's not as if *Target* was selling knock-off *Gucci* or *Prada* totes.

Why do human beings, including managers, lie so much—in marketing, and other venues? Because, at critical points, everybody makes choices based on incentives and their own perceptions of what option best serves their best self-interests. Humans are first and foremost concerned with self-preservation. People do what they want to do and routinely make choices that they perceive will most benefit themselves.

These are natural human laws. Best to understand them, as well, and to live open-eyed in the real world rather than an idealistic world that almost everyone presumably would love to enjoy but surely will never attain.

That's the story, and we're sticking with it.

EXHIBIT 8.1
The Scope of Corporate Social Responsibility

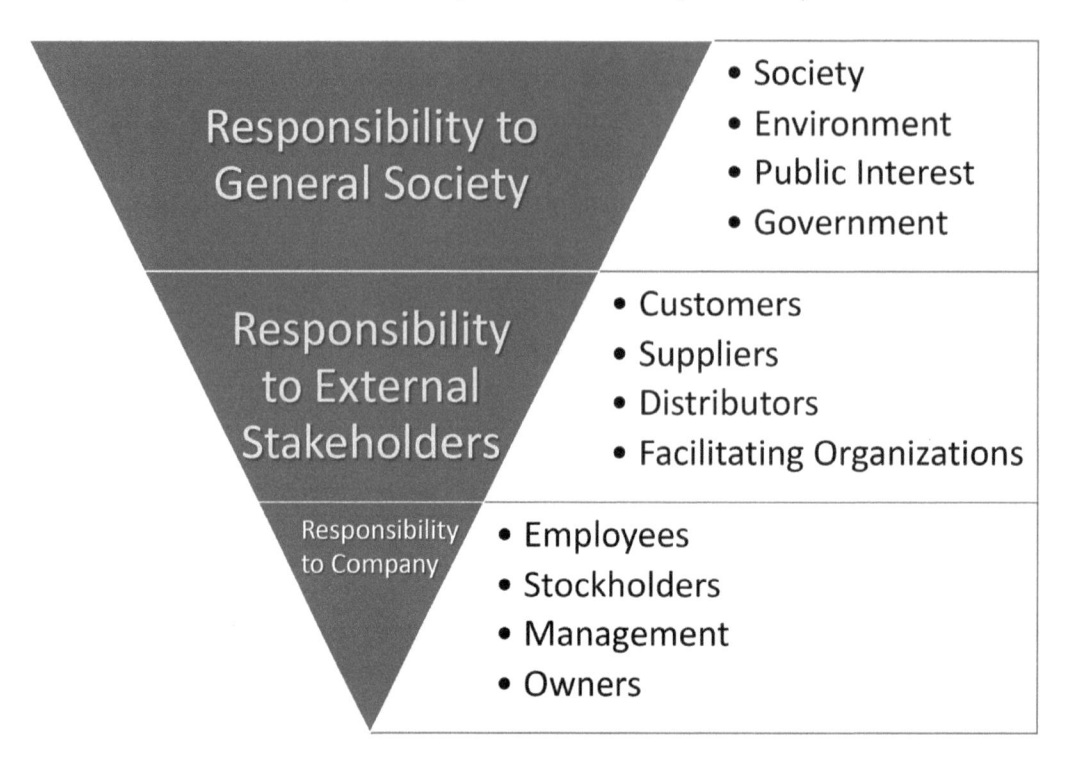

Responsibility to General Society
- Society
- Environment
- Public Interest
- Government

Responsibility to External Stakeholders
- Customers
- Suppliers
- Distributors
- Facilitating Organizations

Responsibility to Company
- Employees
- Stockholders
- Management
- Owners

EXHIBIT 8.2
Ethics/Legal Continuum

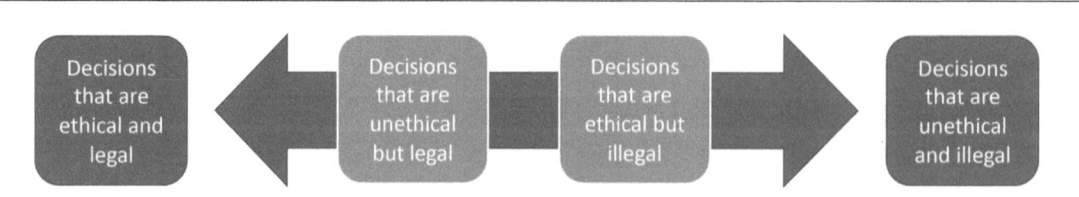

Decisions that are ethical and legal ← Decisions that are unethical but legal | Decisions that are ethical but illegal → Decisions that are unethical and illegal

EXHIBIT 8.3
Benefit Matrix for Ethical Products

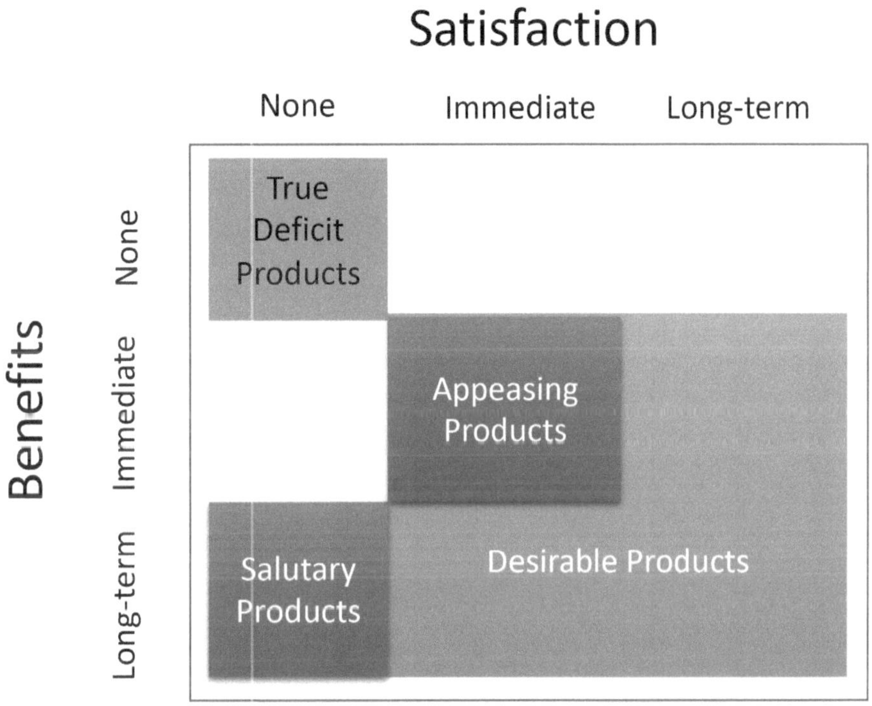

	Satisfaction: None	Satisfaction: Immediate	Satisfaction: Long-term
Benefits: None	True Deficit Products		
Benefits: Immediate		Appeasing Products	
Benefits: Long-term	Salutary Products	Desirable Products	Desirable Products

SECTION III

Managing Key Marketing Activities

MODULE 9

Managing Products, Services, and the Product Life Cycle

MODULE 9.0

Products

Cosmetics marketers are not just marketing cosmetics. Cosmetics marketers also market renewed hope or sustained hope; the prospect of greater beauty; the possibly of more confidence;[1] younger looks for mature users; more mature looks for younger consumers; and so forth. These values are among the supposed solutions that cosmetic products promise to users as those customers seek to solve perceived or actual problems that they are "confronting."

The global cosmetics, apparel, and general beauty industrial sectors each reside in the frontline of a colossal consumer-dissatisfaction-creation industrial complex. And each sector stands exactly there, as a vanguard, for good reason. The good reason is because if their female or male users instantly became and remained more satisfied with how they look without the "makeup solutions" that cosmetics bring to them, the beauty industries would immediately enter a world of hurt. Thus, an irony arises: while successful marketers absolutely operate inside in the satisfaction-creation business—how else could customer problems get solved—many successful marketers concurrently operate inside the dissatisfaction-creation business.

For now, the dissatisfaction-creating cosmetics marketing sector is clearly winning battles for dissatisfied space inside targeted consumers' minds. Many middle-aged or older women likely agree with Thressa Strutton's statement that she believes "Women should look as young as they can afford to look." One reason why cosmetics or apparel marketers routinely triumph inside the dissatisfaction-creation wars they are waging inside consumer minds is that most men have not historically been judged by or held back/advanced in any manner because of their perceived attractiveness. Yes, the world constantly changes and exceptions surely exist in certain professional sectors. Yet many women of certain ages and even women younger than those ages understand quite well about the degree to

---

1. Interesting fact about confidence. When people have confidence they often feel that they will never lose it. Meanwhile, if and when confidence is lost people may feel their winners' mojo will never return. For example, inside highly competitive golf or basketball competitions where fame, fortune, scholarships, and glory or ignominy are all at stake, it may take hundreds of made shots to gain confidence. Yet only two or three missed shots in the right—as in wrong—situations can utterly destroy the confidence of golfers or basketballers. But hopefully not yours, to the extent that all good marketers realize that each failure takes them one step closer to ultimate success. And you thought we were only talking about cosmetics.

which the same sociocultural "rule" does not apply for them, regardless of whether anyone actually publicly speaks its ugly name.

And therein lie additional differences that discriminate—separate—how women, as opposed to men, make marketing choices related to cosmetics or the prospect of plastic surgery. Women remain far more likely than men to use cosmetics or have-work-done. Yet men are materially closing the gap. For now, however, gender-based segmentation within these product categories still makes sense.

Gender-grounded sources that spur customer dissatisfaction also rise up from less than purely marketing sources. Namely, from cultural shifts that readily change in ways that remain relatively unmoored from focused marketing initiatives. One such cultural shift entails the Two-Betty's Paradox. The Two-Betty's Paradox encompasses a dilemma that contemporary women sometimes confront. A paradox that frequently twists modern women into spools of dissatisfaction. Betty 1: *Betty Crocker*, and the promise of a happily productive life as mother and wife. Betty 2: *Betty Friedan*, and the promise of fully-liberated and fully-independent and fully-successful professional womanhood. Achieving both Betty-outcomes simultaneously is possible, but often difficult to pull off successfully.

But now that we have thought further about the issue, we rescind our previous statement. Each Betty is a marketer-created phenomenon. Even though one product is merely a marketing idea (Crocker), and the other product (Friedan, who died in 2006) was a real-life human being.

This notion of dissatisfaction can be easily and productively pushed down another fascinating avenue. Ambitious marketing professionals—and every professional is a marketer—are never fully satisfied. Their low-grade yet perpetual dissatisfaction subsequently drives ambitious professionals to greater success while keeping them from ever being fully happy, at least with their current professional status, for longer than scant moments, weeks, or months at a time. Then, after their brief encounter with satisfaction, it is push themselves forward-again-time, again.

WHAT'S ACTUALLY BEING SOLD, REVISITED?

Let's continue by returning to a point made earlier about products. Remember, value-based retailers are not selling ½-inch drill bits. Instead, value-based marketers sell holes featuring varying dimensions. Why? Because those B2B or B2C customers who are attempting to purchase just the right drill bit for them have a problem for which the best solution is a ½-inch, ¼-inch, or ¾-inch hole.

PRODUCT DEFINITION, REVISITED

Products were previously defined as anything that can be offered to individuals, segments, or entire markets for their attention, acquisition, use, or consumption that might also satisfy those same individuals', segments', or entire markets' wants and needs while solving their problems—and profiting marketers in the process. We stand by that definition here. Products can exist in the forms of tangible products, intangible services, actual people, new or old ideas, or actual physical places.

Tangible products, such as jeans, shirts, or coffee tables are products.

Intangible services, for example, might include solutions provided by CPAs as they prepare consumers' taxes; hair cutting or coloring solutions that hairdressers provide as they prepare consumers' hair; and/or solutions provided by any medical, entertainment, hospitality, consulting, and so forth service provider.

The idea that people exist and are marketed as products is illustrated by celebrities, politicians, or your own professional self. Each of these people as products entities also exist and are marketed as brands.

Ideas such as pro-choice versus pro-life or arguments that corporations should display greater social responsibility and concern about a greener world as opposed to merely and voraciously pursuing higher profits exist as product. Each idea, each product form, is regularly promoted and routinely sold or purchased as if it were a product that generates value and solutions for some person, group, or cause.

Places, regions, cities, or states; these too are also marketed as products. Marketed as products for the best possible reason. Because they actually are products. *Vermont*, for example, simultaneously exists as a state, a place, and a marketed product. While the locale is beautiful, *Vermont* has experienced great difficulty convincing talented younger native-born Vermonters to stay home—not much cutting-edge professional opportunity resides in the *Green Mountain State*. In response, *Vermont*, logically promoting itself as a product, recently began offering $10,000 annual grants to anyone willing to live and pay taxes in the state while working remotely for marketing organizations located in other states.

Tangible Versus Intangible: Comparisons-Contrasts

Tangible products feature intangible service dimensions. The warranty associated with a tangible automobile brand is an intangible service dimension.

Marketers are increasingly differentiating tangible products based on products' ability and marketers' promise to deliver memorable experiences. Marketers that differentiate tangible brands based on memorable experiences recognize that consumers purchase brands based on their perceptions of what the offering will deliver to them in terms of experience-based benefits, values, and solutions, not just based on the products or services themselves. The key value, the key utility associated with differentiating tangible products through the use of experiences is that experiences rarely get stale, as in "same-ole, same-ole," as rapidly as tangible products do. So not only does the initiating marketer win, it continues to win for a longer time inside the differentiating wars waged by all marketers and marketing organizations.

The evergreen nature of experiences derives primarily from the fact that experiences prove harder for consumers to get used to. Each experience unfolds as a unique event. No one ever experiences the purportedly same experience exactly like the preceding, supposedly same, experience. Like wise folks say: People never see the same river twice, because rivers constantly change as do the folks perceiving them. Similar descriptions apply to experiences, to greater or lesser degrees. From one day to the next the same experience changes, if almost imperceptibly at times. (The next one is still "different," as are, of course, individuals who perceive the experiences.

Intangible products, or services, typically feature tangible dimensions. The physical surroundings in which services are delivered or the service provider (a tangible person) who creates and delivers the service are part of the value created by service providers. Take legal services, for example. Enter law offices looking like they escaped from the television show *Better Call Saul's* set, and those physical surroundings would preemptively inform visitors about the quality of legal service they would likely receive. Enter law offices appointed like the one portrayed in once highly popular television shows (television shows are products) such as *Ally McBeal* or *Boston Legal*, and altogether different conceptions, perceptions, and ideas about what this high-end, presumably high-quality legal service will cost clients would immediately arise.

Or consider nail salons. Nail salons are service-oriented marketing organizations that operate inside physical surroundings. These physical surroundings themselves project or cast-out cues to customers or prospects. Nail salons provide manicures, pedicures, and acrylic treatment services—or solutions. Yet upscale salons, as demonstrated and exemplified in terms of their furniture and furnishings such as art on the walls, rugs on the floor, or for that matter floor surfaces themselves (all tangible physical surroundings, or the seventh P), often throw in an inexpensive, lower quality glass of wine (another tangible product) for free, and then charge $70.00 or more, before an anticipated 20 percent tip, for their nail services. The tangible aspects of nail services integrate seamlessly with their intangible dimensions.

Positioning, Revisited

In their positioning efforts marketers should strive to make-old-things-appear-new. You knew this. This "precursor to marketing success" was among the first ideas taught inside *The Inside Skinny*.

One logical way to achieve this end is to associate meaningful intangible experiences with even highly-tangible products. The delight emanating from most fun or cool experiences generally outlasts the allure of shiny new [tangible] objects. Consumers often get bored with shiny-new-objects in hours, days, or months—at most.

Marketers can also differentiate tangible products such as automobiles through the quality and extensiveness of the supporting services they attach to them. Those supporting service-related attributes presumably provide additional new benefits and value adds to the original tangible product. Quickly revisiting *Hyundai*. Marketing problems arose for *Hyundai* during the first ten or so years after the brand entered the American marketplace. Too few domestic consumers trusted or wanted to buy *South Korean* autos. However, this marketing problem was eventually resolved by the *Hyundai* brand by strategically associating a desirable intangible service with a tangible product (i.e., the physical automobile). That service was a ten-year, bumper to bumper, 100,000 mile warranty.

PRODUCTS FEATURE THREE LEVELS

All tangible or intangible products potentially feature core benefits, the actual product, and an augmented product—or three levels.

Core benefits are the truest, most basic problem-solving attributes associated with branded products. Core benefits are what customers actually buy at the most fundamental level. A narrowly-defined but still core benefit associated with smartphones is that they let people speak (literally voice-to-voice in that moment) with whomever. A more broadly-defined core benefit of smartphones is that they also allow people to communicate with others through non-voice-to-voice means.

The actual product entails a given branded smartphone's features, design, quality level, brand, and packaging[2] as well as, perhaps, its shape or color.

The augmented product includes other over-and-above services (i.e., warranties, free delivery, etc.); features, attributes, and benefits (i.e., FAB); and ultimately, any new, unusual, and at times unknown solutions that are also attached to/associated with, for example, a branded small phone. Augmented means supplemented, enhanced, or expanded, which is exactly what happens here. Most smartphone users, for example, probably don't even know, must less understand, all the augmented features, attributes, and solutions available on or made available through their phones. The same description would apply to most owners of new, all the bells and whistles, SUVs.

Each level of any product should produce additional customer value. Each level of any product also represents another platform from which marketers can promote, differentiate, and position a specific branded version of the product. Marketers should exploit each product level to varying degrees as they promote, price, and seek to position products or services to different B2C or B2B segments based on their core benefits, actual product, or augmented levels. This is because the same benefits, values, and solutions won't appeal to customer segments in the same ways or to the same degrees of favorability.

TWO BROAD CATEGORIES OF PRODUCTS EXIST

The first product category is industrial/business/governmental goods, which entails B2B marketing. B2B goods can further be classified as production goods or support goods. Production goods enter into the production processes of final products. Production products often arrive in the form of raw materials or component parts. Support goods assist, directly or indirectly, in those production processes.

The demand for industrial/business goods is derived. Derived demand implies that the market demand for industrial, business, or governmental goods is directly or indirectly derived from—or based on—the demand for consumer goods. When consumers, *en masse*, feel more optimistic about

---

2. Some comments about packaging appear appropriate, given that packaging is only occasionally discussed below. Their critics have often said, as they described various politicians, that "nobody says nothing better than them." Follow-up clichés such as "all talk, no action" practically write themselves. Yet having little to nothing of value to say or contribute wrapped up inside attractive packages still works effectively for many politicians as effectively-branded and therefore successful products. Does the well-packaged political product look good or sound great on television, *YouTube* clips, or tweets that a marketing aide writes and "sends" in their name? Often that proves sufficient to get a politician's brand selected among the meticulously identified to within an-inch-of-their-lives segments that their marketing teams target oh so carefully. However, this type of all-attractive-exterior-messaging (wrapped inside glorious packaging) but deliver no genuine, differentiating and/or determinant interior value ploys rarely plays out well during the long-run for more tangible and traditional products.

their futures, industrial/business demand booms. That's exactly what happened during most of 2021 as fear and concern about COVID-19 subsided.

When consumers feel gloomy about their future prospects, derived demand dips. That's exactly what happened during the last seven months of 2020 as mainstream marketing media perpetually ramped up consumer fears and concerns about COVID-19 and its consequence. *Big Media* such as *The New York Times, CNN*, and the *Washington Post*, and so forth waged highly competitive marketing warfare with each other in a struggle over who could scare the most people the fastest and attract and retain the attention of the viewers, readers, or listeners as a consequence. Two major marketing sectors (products) emphatically did not suffer any net negative fall-out as consequence of COVID-19. One, the *Federal Government*; who possessed the power to create their own revenues (it's called deficit spending); two, *Big Media*, who enjoyed their highest ratings (usage rates) in history.

The second product category is consumer goods, which entails B2C marketing. Consumer products are purchased and used by end-use consumers in order to solve or satisfy their own problems/wants/needs. Or, consumer goods are purchased and used to solve or satisfy some other individual consumers' needs/wants/problems. For example, fathers buying groceries for their children.

The decision to classify products into one or the other broad B2B or B2C category depends on whether the product's end users are consumers or organizations. When consumers buy power drills or fluorescent lights to use in their home, a consumer or B2C good has been sold. Yet if an organization purchases the same power drill or fluorescent light and uses either to build a dormitory, an industrial or business goods exchange transaction has just been consummated.

The success of B2B marketing efforts, generally, is driven by the satisfaction of customer needs. The success of B2C marketing efforts, generally, is driven by the satisfaction of customer wants. This difference is meaningful. This difference also materially influences how marketing organizations create, promote, and seek to differentiate and position the values of their branded products.

CLASSIFYING CONSUMER-ORIENTED PRODUCTS

Consumer products can be further classified as convenience, shopping, or specialty goods. Or, consumer products might be classified either as unsought or positioning goods. Sometimes the same product might be classified concurrently as both a specialty good and a positioning good.

Whether a product is deemed convenience, shopping, or specialty in nature is based on:

- ▶ The amount of consumer effort expended to acquire the product.
- ▶ How frequently consumers purchase the product.
- ▶ The level [or extensiveness] of marketing distribution (i.e., how widely available is the product in the marketplace).
- ▶ The degree of comparison that consumers make between alternative brands available inside the same product category.

This classification scheme—these four metrics—only apply when a marketer is seeking to categorize convenience, shopping, or specialty goods. The metrics do not apply to unsought goods or positional goods.

Convenience Goods

When consumers seek to purchase convenience goods they do not expend much effort. Convenience goods are usually purchased frequently. The product is widely available but consumers typically do not engage in much brand comparison. A classic example of a convenience good would include a gallon of milk, regular or 2% fat milk, originating from a cow, as opposed to soy or goat milk.

Shopping Goods

When consumers are deliberating whether to purchase shopping goods they expend considerable effort in an attempt to make the best possible choice. Substantial brand versus brand comparison inside the relevant product category (trucks versus trucks; phones versus phones) is likely. Shopping goods themselves are typically purchased infrequently. But shopping goods themselves are widely available. Their level of distribution throughout the marketplace is considered extensive.

Most clothing brands fit into the shopping goods. A man might compare *Levi's* versus *Lee* versus *Wrangler* jeans. Women might more likely compare *True Religion* versus *Calvin* versus *Pepe Jeans London* jeans, although she surely might compare *Levi's*, *Lee's*, or *Wranglers*. A given auto shopping brand, such as *Toyota* versus *Honda* versus *Hyundai* more similarly can be applied by consumers whose lifestyles or attitudinal preferences led them to prefer more efficient brands.

Specialty Goods

When consumers decide to purchase specialty goods they generally don't expend much effort or engage in much if any brand comparison. Customers have already decided which brand inside the product category is most special to them; no need exists to further shop around. Nor are specialty goods widely available. Neither in terms of distribution or their affordability. But then again, were specialty goods widely available and broadly affordable, they're no longer special.

Consider consumer fashion goods such as *Prada, Gucci,* or *Hermes*, or luxury auto brands like *Ferrari, McLaren,* or *Lamborghini*. Clearly, most auto or clothing brands are shopping goods. However, a relative handful of prestigious auto or clothing brands are better classified as specialty in nature.

Unsought Goods

Unsought products fit into a category all their own; a category unlike either of the first three. Unsought goods are products/brands that no one typically seeks out. The implication is that some marketer truly has to sell them. Life insurance, gym memberships, burial plots . . . these sorts of products illustrate the unsought point.

Positional Goods

Certain product and service goods have recently come to be labeled as positional goods. Positional goods can generally also be classified as specialty goods. But not all specialty goods are positional goods.

Positional goods are tangible products or intangible services experiences that consumers perceive as valuable largely because other consumers occupying their same broad social sphere (social class membership and social status) cannot have or enjoy them. Many people define their value and self-worth by comparing themselves to others. Sometimes these comparing parties are up, winning—because it seems to them they have more, and they presumably feel happier. Sometimes these comparing parties are down, losing—and presumably feel worse because consumers perceive they have less than those individuals to whom they are comparing themselves.

Yes, a nasty and unflattering human calculus is being described. But a calculus that is very much part of human nature—and that proves surprisingly beneficial to the entire domestic economy. The economy grows because more people end up buying more stuff, including lots of goods and services that they actually cannot afford, simply to stay even with or stay ahead of others in their social spheres.

Luxurious paintings hung on walls; magnificent sculptures displayed in gardens; fine, as in very expensive, wines served in the best, in the coolest, places; high-end sports cars that are more widely shown or admired than driven; extraordinarily expensive stays in luxury accommodations or locales; exorbitantly-priced bags installed on shoulders or outfits draped on male or female bodies; these products or services belong to positional goods categories.

Positional goods, say in the form of art, are particularly popular amongst the truly wealthy 1 percent because it is considered gauche for them to hang gold bars on their home's walls. The purchase and typically public or public/private displays of positioning allows some consumers to compete and prevail against other consumers in social-status wars. After all, only the privileged few even get peeks. Apparently consumers operate under an assumption that the folks who die owning the most, and/or the most expensive gear win a higher high rise apartment inside heaven.

The preceding statement may have come off as harsh. But social competitiveness exists. Indeed, verifiable reality suggests that the existence of these fierce social comparisons exist is probably biologically and evolutionarily pre-determined. For example, which male peacock gets chosen as her mating partner by female peacocks? Is it the male bird with the merely good-enough tail? Or is it the male with the best tail? You know the answer.

Even so, people generally want to be like everyone else, only better. One other thing, however, that most people would benefit from knowing: Excessive comparisons of "what we have" to what we perceive others have steals human happiness, as noted. Someone always has more, meaning the perpetual social comparer loses. Consumers playing the comparison game can never win in the end. Because someone will always have more and better stuff.

Positional Goods: Breakout, Breakdown

Once consumers achieve a certain level of material abundance, some but not all consumers' consumption behaviors shift away from the acquisition or use of ordinary goods and services and toward more experiential forms of consumption. The lines between so-called "ordinary goods" and "experiential goods" are not distinct. For example, consumers who order $1,000 bottles of wine in luxurious restaurants are not necessarily paying for aged grape juice. Often, what they instead are paying way extra for is the act of ritual consumption and a passage into the state not of having but of "having had" a taste of 1986 *Bienvenues-Bâtard-Montrachet*. Well-to-do aficionados characterized by a taste for wildly expensive wines but who could not distinguish a *Bordeaux* from a *Brunello* under threat of imprisonment belong to a well-established consumer category. And notably, such enthusiasts are certainly not phonies or snobbish inside their respective minds.

Luxury and/or positional goods such as the "*1986*" combine acts of both physical and psychic consumption. Extremely expensive watches are not about "telling time better" any more than the uber-rich denizens who visit the California-based *French Laundry* restaurant do so to satisfy their naturally-arising physiological hunger needs. Indeed, the most rarefied levels of consumption often dissolve into almost purely experiential acts of consumption that do not feel like conventional luxury at all. A photo with the President, a personal audience with the *Dalai Lama*, or a dinner photo op with the young, sexy Governor might qualify.

The great marker of positional goods-driven social status is the line that separates prestigiously branded products that are merely expensive from prestigiously branded products that money alone cannot buy. Owning a *Ferrari* represents one sort and source of status symbol. Having one's offspring enrolled at *Princeton University* is another sort of positional good and status. This sort of rarefied consumption is thankfully not reserved exclusively for the super-rich. It is one of the benefits that subsidizes volunteer work in churches and civic organizations, in which discerning status-conscious and presumably upwardly mobile consumers may engage-in in order to enhance the prospect of forming relationships with socially prominent members of their local marketplace.

Higher prices reduce the demand for most products. However, positional products, services, or experiences invert this economic law. When positional goods are bought, buyers actually have purchased, as in acquired, evidence that they have forked out a bundle—and were capable of doing so. Consequently, when their prices rise purchasers of positional goods are rarely disturbed. In fact, such status-seeking consumers may be pleased. That is because higher prices make their positional goods purchases, and consequently them, more exclusive still.

Yet positional goods don't have to be off-the-hook expensive. Certain brands of bottled water, expensive inside their product category but still not fortune-busting, could be viewed as positional. Brands such as *Aqua Deco* or *Veen* come to mind as examples that likely reside inside many consumers' evoked sets.

Luxury brands often fit into the positional goods category. Luxury brands, similar to positional goods, typically confer social status to their owners/users. Luxury brands and positional goods are often synonymous—that is, one and the same. Luxury goods are often wildly popular but never widely accessible. As noted, most consumers cannot afford them. People purchasing *Prada* pay for exclusivity. *Prada* purchasers pay more not to fit-in-with but to stand-apart from and above the crowd, status-wise. Devils who counterfeit *Prada* (play on the movie and book called *The Devil Wore Prada*) erode this exclusivity. Devils who counterfeit *Prada* actually impose extra costs in the form of higher prices on people who can afford to purchase genuine *Prada* brands.

Some consumers are motivated to purchase *Prada* as acts of self-expression. Others purchase *Prada* as acts of social emulation, or imitation, reflecting feelings such as "I want to be more like . . . . Researchers suggest *Chinese* consumers are more likely to purchase *Prada* for the second reason. Likely, most *American* consumers are similar to the average *Chinese* consumer in their motivation for buying this exclusive—and positional—brand.

OTHER PRODUCT TYPES EXIST

As noted, the following entities are also marketed and positioned as products. A non-exhaustive list of these things includes:

- Organizations *(Facebook* versus *CNN* versus *Fox* versus *MSNB* versus *Newsweek* versus the *Wall Street Journal* . . . as sources of news).
- Places (*New Orleans* versus *Las Vegas* versus *Macaw* versus *Monaco* as physical places in which to win or lose money while gambling).
- Ideas (Former President *Trump's The Wall* [not *Pink Floyd*] versus President *Biden's* Borderless America; *Right to Life* versus *Right to Choose*?)
- People (Celebrities, professional brands, politicians).

Speaking of people functioning and being marketed as products, perhaps politicians should be outfitted like *NASCAR* drivers or *PGA* golfers, professionals who sport numerous brands on their uniforms, so that the targeted market segments can more easily discern who is sponsoring them. What do you think? The *NRA* brand for *Republicans*; the *Planned Parenthood* brand for *Democrats?* This is no joke but rather illustrates the omnipresent nature of marketing, which emphatically is no joking matter. Because marketing, like technology, changes everything either for better or worse.

LEVERAGING QUALITY TO DIFFERENTIATE PRODUCTS

Quality—defined—is freedom from defects. Or, if one prefers, freedom from flaws.

The presence of quality is directly proportional to the presence of efficiency. Stated differently, when quality grows, so does efficiency. When quality fades, so does efficiency.

The presence of higher quality and well-branded products generally, though not always, brings higher quantity . . . of sales for those brands.

From the 1960s until well into the 1990s the *Maytag* repairman was successfully positioned time and again in a string of print and television advertisements as . . . "the loneliest man in the world." A series of droopy-faced male actors played a character who was lonely and sad because no one ever called because his repair services were never needed due to the reliability and durability of the *Maytag* washing machine-dryer sets. The same advertising message was delivered as the "Big Idea" that drove decades of different advertising campaigns. This core advertising message was a huge, memorable hit. The message eventually evolved into a cultural touchstone that nearly everyone knew—and understood. This core advertising message, which humorously and memorably signaled *Maytag's* durability and reliability, demonstrated high quality of the brand, and simultaneously justified the premium price tags affixed to *Maytag* and explained the primary reasons why consumers should purchase the brand. *Maytag*, you see, was differentiating and continues to differentiate and position its highly respected brand based on quality and reliability. Quality and reliability exist and operate as two sides of the same marketing coin.

Quality once was, and to some degree remains, a major positioning tool inside the *United States*. This makes sense; consumers want things that last. Many consumers are aware of the adage that "the-cheap-pay-twice." The cheap pay once when they buy products. Second, the cheap pay again when pre-maturely replacing the cheap products they originally purchased.

Then there is the presumptive fact that, as a minor character from the television show *Yellowstone* put it during Season 3, "Cheap sh-t ain't cool, and cool sh-t ain't cheap." Cheap stuff isn't cool, and cool stuff isn't cheap, and higher quality rarely comes cheaply, either.

Even so, inside most contemporary American market sectors quality functions more like an ante inside a highly competitive poker game. The presence and/or the perception of quality is the cost (price) that must be paid to get into the poker game and sit at the table, compete, and possibly win differentiation (positioning wars) inside given market sectors. Even so, quality, and it alone, rarely wins the day, today. Still, absent quality, brands did not even get to play in the game. Domestic consumers are no longer living during an 1970s/1980s era in which domestic automotive marketers—that would be, at the time, *General Motors, Ford Motor Co., Chrysler,* and during part of that period, *American Motors*, mostly sold less than high-quality vehicles—and that's stating things nicely. Not coincidentally, this was also an era during which foreign competitors were not nearly the pressing environmental threat they have long since become—and before domestic automobile marketers were forced to step up their game.

Yet even today, the phrase "high-quality vehicles" does not mean the same thing to everyone. Some automotive products, for example, are built to be fast (and highly maneuverable/aesthetically appealing), but not built to last. Many automotive aficionados ascribe this exact description to several higher end German automotive brands, including *BMW, Porsche,* and *Mercedes*.

LEVERAGING FEATURES TO DIFFERENTIATE PRODUCTS

Product features and attributes can function as competitive tools from which one brand as opposed to another brand can be differentiated. Product features and attributes are strategically-attractive, primarily because features and attributes can be added, eliminated, augmented, promoted, or ignored by marketers; dependent on the segment being targeted and the positioning and promotional tactics being employed.

Features can be added, cut, or augmented to improve products' performance and their ability to differentiate.

When features are added, eliminated, or augmented with respect to any product, a new product has been created.

Whenever product features are added, cut, or augmented new marketing mixes are also created.

And whenever feature-driven additions, deletions, or expansions have occurred, the changes should be emphasized in marketers' promotional efforts as they seek to position or reposition their brands and brand values. After all, it is not the job of customers to determine whether any changes have been made to the features or attributes of products that might increase their value or appeal. Instead the job of marketers is to inform, persuade, and/or remind customers that such changes have been introduced and as a result, the now "new" product is simultaneously more valuable and appealing. Unfortunately, this does not always happen.

Features and attributes ignored? Yes, this routinely happens but many features and attributes are ignored at the marketer's own risk. Again, it is not customers' jobs to figure out which obscure or unannounced features should-be-highly-valued inside any branded product. Instead, marketers' job is to reveal and emphasize, to promote, the features that should be important to customers as they choose which brand to buy from a given product category.

All product features and attributes should have a purpose. Features and attributes should deliver benefits. Hopefully those benefits prove meaningful, important, and valuable or "determinant" to consumers as they make decisions. Remember FAB, or Features >>> Attributes >>> Benefits >>> Solutions >>> Successful Differentiation >>> Desirable Market Positions.

LEVERAGING STYLE TO DIFFERENTIATE PRODUCTS

Style describes the appearance of products, down to their websites, packaging, or the colors they use that accompany, complement, or emphasize the brands of products. In fact, everything that directly or indirectly communicates anything about brand relates to those brands' style.

Style should not be confused with fashion. No need exists for people or products to be fashionable in order to be deemed stylish. Edgy Bohemian, Goth, or Hip-Hop gear are often purposefully unfashionable when viewed by the dominant culture, but the dominant brands inside these product genres can surely rock their style effectively inside the specific market segments being targeted.

Over the long run the value of substance generally trumps the value of style because real distinctions exist between style and substance. Style is generally shallow in nature; design is generally deeper. However, great depth of meaning sometimes can be derived from stylistic surfaces of products—their obvious aesthetics. German philosopher *Frederic Nietzsche* actually argued "existence can only be justified on aesthetic grounds."[3] And there's no point denying that superficial things often punch above their weight—matter more than experts might suspect—in marketing matters.

---

3. H. De Lubac, *The Drama of Atheist Humanism* (San Francisco: Ignatius Press, 2008).

LEVERAGING DESIGN TO DIFFERENTIATE

Design is far more likely than style to contribute to the substantive value of any product. As it should, because design goes to the heart and the functionality of a product. Design is generally far more substantive in nature than is style.

A primary reason why *Apple* is such an incredibly powerful brand is because *Apple* has passionately specialized in developing minimalist technological designs that simply work better inside that most important of places, *Apple* customers' minds. This is largely why the mega-firm boasts the Apple brand name . . . as one of the most powerful brands in marketing history. *Steve Jobs*, the man, the innovator, and the brand, cared passionately about design. Too much caring may be creepy, yes, but perhaps not when one cares about the right things. Jobs cared about the right marketing things as those "design-related-things" exponentially elevated the branding image of his products, company, and professional self.

Jobs died far too young from pancreatic cancer. This is widely known. Less well-known, however, is the fact that Jobs lived years longer than the original diagnosis suggested he would. Less well known, as well, is that the man rudely flung the first five oxygen masks back into the operating room nurse's face before he agreed to be sedated for his first pancreatic cancer surgical procedure—a procedure that easily could have killed him inside the operating room itself. Why worry about dying from a surgical procedure, though, when you can worry about the design of the oxygen mask. Jobs hated, and clearly was repulsed by, the designs of these initial five oxygen devices, and adamantly refused to have them placed on his face. The man deeply cared about design and the role that *Apple* product's designs first played in bolstering and eventually sustaining the brand's success.

Jobs famously dropped out of college. But after he was no longer enrolled he still hung around *Reed College* for a year or so longer, sitting in on whatever courses he wanted. His favorite course was calligraphy—learning about elegant letter and inscriptions, and how to develop them, if you will. Do you think this college course played into his passion for design, or that his passion for design led him to designate calligraphy as his favorite course? Spectacularly great *Apple* designs, likely due to their pure simplicity (more about the relationship between simplicity and great design follows immediately), also made/make many of the brand's products more addictive. Smartphones were designed from their origins to be addictive. Pull (scroll) down, refresh, there will always be something new to tease your attention.

What legal substance could be more addictive than that? As noted elsewhere, humans love the new, the fresh, and the familiar, so long as it is not too new. The specific customer-machine design interface originated by *Apple* operates exactly how *Las Vegas* slot machines operate, designed not just to keep users/customers coming back but to keep them from ever leaving.

Making Customers Happy

Great design does more than just solve—and occasionally create—customer problems. Great design also usually makes customers happy. Usually makes them happy if for no other reason than because merely good design does not make customers unhappy. Not making people unhappy is hardly a small differentiating advantage in a world as fraught with dissatisfaction and unhappiness as this one is.

Great design features a perfect marriage of performance or function and purpose or form in ways that suggest product meaning to customers or prospects, facilitate product functionality, and enable better product performance. The development and provision of extremely well-designed products consequently represents another strategic path through which sustainable differentiation and competitive advantage can be achieved, because great designs are difficult for competitors to emulate, much less improve upon. These differentiation-based advantages are further amplified when "your firm's brand" is the first in the market to feature such "exquisite design."

Products usually should be designed to appear or be as simple as possible. Simple-to-use, easy-on-the-eyes. Like great art, great designs should create more energy inside than they remove from any setting. Rarely if ever is it useful, necessary, or appropriate to speak, write, or design using three syllables in an increasingly one-syllable-world—this is a practical and contemporary nod to the power of simplicity.

Great design strengthens any product's brand. Great design contributes to the perceived or actual usefulness of a product. Great design makes products more appealing. Great design helps marketers position their products as different and better. Great design drives innovation. Innovation, best defined as new things that are also useful things because the "new things" solve new or old problems in new ways. Great designs can be nearly universal in their appeal. In fact, the goal of universal design is to create environments and products that can be used in the widest possible range of situations absent much or any need for user (customer) adaptation or adjustment.

Design also might relate, for example, to how buildings are structured or to how furnishings inside rooms inside buildings are arranged. Rooms inside those buildings are also designed. Yet the layout and types of furniture inside those rooms also can be designed. In each structural setting design can be leveraged to create either the perception and reality of additional space or the perception or reality of greater coziness. All readers who elect to mix in a little effort, creativity, and muscle power with a few dollars can achieve similar design outcomes—in the process creating more "space," "coziness," "buzz," "cool," or feng shui—inside most rooms inside any house or apartment in which they reside.[4] Not based on counsel from us, however. For such advice one should turn toward interior design marketers.

Great design often functions as an indispensable precursor to great style. The novelist *Ann Padgett* wrote that art stands on the shoulders of craft. To successfully develop art, one must master the craft. Think of design as the craft.

Meanwhile, to create winning styles, marketers would usually first need to master design. Because great style similarly stands on the shoulders of effective design.

---

4. In fact, in his latest self-help book, cultural values guru *Jordan Peterson* suggested, "Try to make one room in your room as beautiful as possible." Barton Swain, "The Man They Couldn't Cancel," *The Wall Street Journal* (May 1, 2021): A-13.

The Power of Simplicity

The task of creating great designs represents a huge challenge for most marketers. Largely because so many different consumer personalities, ideas, and options much be considered as either B2C or B2B marketers. Each create carefully-designed products that are strategically targeted at specific customer segments. These design-related tasks are another part of the marketing mix management process that successful marketing organizations must master.

Meanwhile, most successful marketers generally understand they should design products in ways that simplify those offerings to their fundamental essence. Inherent design value apparently can be readily developed by hewing closely to the core design concepts known as "simple" and "simplicity" as one actually designs products. (Obviously, the preceding statement does not apply universally; but the preceding point is relevant far more often than it is not.) *Steve Jobs*, him again, claimed that "Simplicity is the ultimate sophistication." Dare we add, and yes we will, simple or simplicity might be better spelt as speed. And who among us does not want many things speedier? Well, then, it follows that most normal consumers want things to be simpler, as well.

Envision *Egypt's Pyramids* or America's *Golden Gate* or *Brooklyn Bridges,* the *Washington Monument,* or the *Empire State Building.* There, you just visualized five of history's most iconic designs. Now consider this: An average six-year-old child could accurately copy and sketch out all six designs in five minutes or less. That's because each design is so simple. Just as the child could easily copy the alluringly simple curves and silhouette of *Volkswagen's* classic *Beetle* design.

The Power of Three (and Other Odd Numbers)

When designing anything or for that matter orally presenting any topic, many successful marketers understand the power associated with using threes in design, and if not threes, at least using odd numbers. God, nature, and consumer-kind apparently each love the power of three. There is, for example:

- Religiosity—Father, Son, Holy Ghost (3).
- Human Beings—Mind, body, spirit (3).
- Time—Past, present, future (3).
- Physical Shapes—Height, depth, width (3).
- Matter—Gaseous, solid, liquid (3).

Note the not-so-subtle use of five examples to illustrate the power of odd numbers.

Or, more mundanely, consumer, the power of three as it plays out among marketing and marketed places:

- *Dallas, Fort Worth, and Denton*—a brand marketed internationally as *The Metroplex.*
- *Raleigh, Durham, and Chapel Hill*—a brand marketed internationally as *The Research Triangle.*
- *Greensboro, Winston-Salem, and High Point*—a brand marketed nationally as *The Triad.*

There's more to the power of three than that, however. Three factors motivate humanity to compete with great vigor and occasional viciousness. People, particularly males, compete most heartedly based on their possession and the presence of personal pride; unit or team pride; and hate for the other. Tailor-made for military, football, or basketball competitions, each of which clearly inspire fiercely-competitive passions. Or for business-versus-business competitions, which often also burn fiercely across decades, usually to the benefit of customers because increasingly superior solutions continuously emerge. As noted, the *Tesla* versus *Westinghouse, Gates* versus *Jobs, or Pepsi* versus *Coke* wars materially benefitted customers and in the case of the first two examples, the entire world.

Playwrights or scriptwriters—these folks are often great storytellers—surely understand the power of three inside marketed products. Director *Mike Nichols*, best known for the movies *The Graduate* and *Carnal Knowledge*, wrote that every theatrical play focused on either seductions, negotiations, or conflict, or some combination of these three elements.

And finally, the Bible actually treats seven—another odd number—as the symbol of completeness and as the "perfect number." The same source designates six, an even number, as the symbol of incompleteness. Product designers and presenters alike should honor the value of sevens or fives when they cannot reasonably use "threes."

LEVERAGING EXPERIENCES TO DIFFERENTIATE PRODUCTS

De Beers, the globally dominant *South African* diamond marketer, now attempts to position and differentiate diamond purchases as uniquely desirable experiences. The diamond brand far and away dominates global markets inside the diamond product category, and now routinely conveys messages to customers and prospects about where its diamonds are from; how those diamonds themselves were formed; how they were mined; and all the good or value creation these diamonds have generated on their journey from the dirt to some beloved person's finger, ears, wrist, or wherever.

Whether that presumed good arrived in the form of contributions to local economies in the neighboring nation of *Botswana*; whether the presumed good entails educating young girls in regions where female children are normally not educated, *De Beers* promotes experiences that the brand strategically associates with its diamonds.

A reality check and an important point to understand is that *De Beers* purportedly controls the sources to about 90 percent of the world's known supply of raw diamonds. (Knowing marketers can also describe this amazing fact as a "resource advantage," a "core competency," and a "source of sustainable competitive advantage" [an SCA]). And *De Beers* hoards diamond, exploiting its particular resource-based core competency, to invent/create perceived scarcity. After all, scarcity often equals preciousness in the minds of malleable consumers.

Love the strategy, hate the strategy; this is hard-ball marketing reduced to its core. *De Beers* ruthlessly but strategically leverages the strongest core competency it owns. This strategy also illustrates, in real time, the law of supply and demand as how it operates in the global marketplace.

One more positioning message related to the marketing of diamonds. "Nothing lasts forever," despite what *De Beers* would have us believe. Certainty not love (lots of times) nor will the seemingly eternally-increasing value of diamonds last forever. Three global market forces are—all largely uncontrollable external environmental factors—at work that eventually should degrade *De Beers'* now-enviable market position. First, technology has advanced to the point where man-made diamonds are now indistinguishable from the real thing. Second, the rising power and prevalence of socially-aware consumers. Blood diamonds are bad, really bad, in their estimation. Third, tighter governmental oversight that has nominally reshaped financial sectors in the wake of the COVID-19 crisis and the *Great Recession*. Diamond intermediaries who perform indispensable functions inside diamond supply chains now often struggle to secure the necessary financing power.

As a partial positioning solution, the diamond sector unveiled a new branding slogan: "Real is rare." This positioning strategy presumably was employed to satisfy another millennially-aged and younger consumer craving (i.e., authenticity). Or, for *The Real Thing*. Oops, sorry, *Coke* already coopted that obviously inauthentic but magnificently effective market position.

Notably, turning toward a gender-driven, or demographic, sociocultural environmental trend, greater numbers of single and married women are buying more diamonds, including diamond rings, for themselves.

How prevalent and how powerful is marketing? The answers to this double-barreled question are everywhere and incredible. Ponder this: Apart from their utility as cutting devices, after all diamonds are earth's hardest element, what actual value do diamonds deliver to the world? The answer is none to very little, apart from the value that marketers across millennia have consciously cultivated for the comparatively scarce mineral. Diamonds are worth relatively little apart from imagined meanings and realities marketers have created for them. Now, hopefully, you are more fully sensing marketing's powerfully pervasive nature.

NEVER GO OR STAY THERE

The most dangerous market position for any brand to occupy is stuck-in-the-middle—absent obvious or perceived cost-, innovativeness-, or quality-advantages. The brand power, pricing power, and sales of *JCPenney's, Macy's,* or *Dillard's* department stores have suffered for years because this non-positioned position is primarily the place where their brands have resided.

MODULE 9.1

Services

Facebook, Google, and *Amazon* each offer wildly popular services. The service values provided by these technology behemoths collectively generate solutions that permit consumers to communicate, navigate, search for information, buy stuff, and socialize in previously inconceivable ways and means. Services marketing is important . . . hugely so. Indeed, at this point the *United States* features a primarily service-driven economy.

This condition does not hurt the US economy. Instead a services-dominated domestic economy stands as a reality that most professional Americans must navigate successfully if they are to enjoy successful careers.

China, by contrast, is widely viewed as the world's factory. *China* primarily manufactures tangible products that thereafter are largely distributed across the world through global supply chains distribution. (Yes, *Chinese* consumers also purchase many of the myriad products produced inside *Chinese* factories.) The *United States* is increasingly viewed as the world's greatest provider of professional services. This situation generally represents a desirable condition. The profit margins associated with making and marketing professional services typically materially exceed margins recouped from making and marketing tangible products.

SERVICES: DEFINITION AND DESCRIPTION

The development and delivery of marketing services involves applying specialized competencies and performing deeds and processes for purposes of benefiting others that also profit the service provider. These specialized service competencies include service-related knowledge and service-related skills. The phrase "benefiting others" (as referenced in this paragraph's first sentence) generally means customers' problems are solved (i.e., their needs are satisfied). Marketing services include the development and provision of medical, accounting, consulting, lawn maintenance, hair care, hospitality, travel, restaurants, investment, banking, lending, flight, and so forth values and solutions.

The successful development and marketing of professional services is fundamentally important to the overall health of the *American* economy. How important? The *United States* manufacturing sector only accounts for about 13 percent of America's gross domestic product. Any guesses regarding the type of product that accounts for the lion's share of the rest of the domestic economic output? Good guess. The answer is intangible services.

Customers never actually own services. At best, they are renting the values and solutions delivered by services.

However, four additional special characteristics associated with intangible services distinguish them from tangible products. These should be deliberated by marketers as they develop, deliver, and market services—and manage the 7Ps[5] that are embedded inside the marketing mixes for services. The four service characteristics, which make all the difference in how services must be marketed, are:

- Intangibility—Services cannot be touched, seen, smelt, or stored up. When communicating about services, marketers often seek to make their brands appear more real.
- Inseparability—Little to no separation usually exists between the point-of-service-production and the point-of-service-consumption. Services cannot be inventoried in anticipation of periods of peak demand.
- Perishability—Marketing organizations cannot store up, or inventory, services to satisfy customer demand during high demand periods. Perishability is related to the inseparability characteristic.
- Variability—The quality of services, as they are provided, vary to greater degrees than does the quality of tangible products. Everyone, including service providers, has bad days. More problems with customer dissatisfaction are likely to arise when marketing services, as opposed to marketing products. This creates situations where internal marketing becomes more important.

The management of internal marketing issues become extremely important to marketers that are seeking to differentiate and position their services effectively. Internal marketing refers to marketing efforts targeted toward marketing organization's own service providers. Professional service providers must be highly trained and motivated. First, in order to do their jobs well. Second, in order to satisfy customers—and to keep them satisfied.

Internal marketing specifically involves training and creating highly-engaged service teams. The continuous focus and goal of such teams should be to develop, sustain, or at times restore customer satisfaction. Specifically, to restore customer satisfaction in situations where some sort of service failure has occurred. That service failures will occur is predictable due to the inevitably variable nature of service quality delivery.

---

5. The 7Ps are the now standard, for readers, Product, Price, Place, & Promotion—along with the Physical Surroundings in which services are developed and delivered; the Processes through which services are developed and delivered; and the People who develop or deliver services.

The need that nearly all service marketing organizations face to engage successfully in internal marketing in order to generate highly motivated and competently- or better-performing professional service providers is more important than many uninformed people likely would expect. Some public K-12 schools operate as service monopolies. This monopoly label primarily applies to educational service providers located inside cities or neighborhoods where the local politicians fail to support charter schools because they are in bed, donation-dependency-wise, with their public education union benefactors. Such public schools do not have to "compete" for students (customers), because their parents usually have no choice but to "purchase" (use) the school's deficient educational services no matter how poor the quality of those school's educational services are or become. One result is that public school teachers, who supposedly operate as professional service providers, are on average, less motivated than charter school teachers to perform effectively.

This circumstance exists apart from the fact that many public school employees are unionized. (Unions themselves operate as, yes, another marketing organization. Educational unions' customers typically include their teacher and administrator memberships and local/national politicians—and that's about it.) Teachers' unionized status simultaneously serves to protect the incompetent or worst among their ranks and tends to demotivate others who otherwise might dedicate themselves to become star performers themselves. Why? Because all union members typically receive the same negotiated raise, a raise primarily based on time-served-in-rank rather than by differences in any actual educational value produced by any individual teacher's service delivery. Union-protected teachers can be and typically are retained and paid regardless of whether their customers' needs are satisfied, whether students are educated and learn what they are supposed to learn. Naturally, many teachers' intrinsic motivations decline as internal marketing efforts either fail or are not initiated in the first place.

The highly-targeted services that are marketed by unions insulate their memberships—be they teachers, governmental, or automotive workers—against the costs/prices they otherwise would pay for being wrong or doing stupid or unethical things. When service employees are insulated from their wrongs or mistakes you get a lot of wrongs and mistakes. And over time union leaderships quickly adopt the mindset that the protection and welfare of the union takes precedence over the protection and welfare of unionized schools', unionized governmental institutions', or unionized automotive marketers' customers.

Most professional service marketers save perhaps public schools or governmental institutions, can only survive to the extent that they can attract and retain clientele. Compulsory attendance inside public schools eliminates that customer service challenge and its associated problems for many public schools, again especially among specific educational marketing institutions that enjoy actual or near monopoly power. Meanwhile, also due to this monopoly power, public schools often do not even have to compete against themselves. That is, against other educational organizations, schools, who are delivering similar union protection in the educational service product category.

None of these service quality-debilitating descriptions apply to most charter or parochial (generally religious, such as *Catholic),* schools. All students, or more so their parents, matriculating charter or parochial school are enrolled there based on voluntary and discretionary decisions related to financial expenditures and analyses of costs and benefits (values). Indeed, the parents of children who attend most charter or parochial schools actually pay double for their children's educational experience. If those parents own property, local school taxes are still due on top of tuition fees. The moment charter schools even hint that their educational services provision is not far superior to their public competitors those customers are out of there.

Marketing, incentives, and value-driven (think, money-driven) decisions dominate everywhere.

When attempting to differentiate/position services, careful management of interactive marketing relationships is also hugely important. These interactive-inside-interactive service marketing processes relate to the marketing exchange encounters that occur between service providers and customers. Physicians, teachers, attorneys, CPAs, bank tellers, hairdressers, airline pilots, professors, and so forth are all professional service providers. Each service provider routinely interacts with clients, customers, or students. The quality of these buyer-seller relationships directly impacts customers' perceptions of the quality of the service that service-providers create for and deliver to them. Again, especially when service failures arise.

Adults are always responsible for managing exactly 50 percent of the extant relationships in their lives. This percentage-obligation to the relationship expands radically to the service provider side when human customers enter relationships for purposes of providing or receiving professional services. Service customers don't owe anything, including provision of their satisfaction, loyalty, or hard-earned dollars, to marketing service providers—as we revisit a theme discussed earlier in other contexts. This customer satisfaction, and their loyalty and payments, essentially must be earned every day by service providers. Professional service providers, as well as their service organizations themselves, consequently should do whatever is possible and necessary to bring their A-games every day.

INVERTING CONVENTIONAL WISDOM

Not all service encounters unfold swimmingly. Even unintentional service mistakes or misfires often upset, piss-off, customers. Conventional wisdom would suggest that failures to provide expected levels of service quality are always bad—even in situations where the service providers themselves learn from their mistakes. Indeed, such conventional thinking is often correct. But in a man-bites-dog inversion of conventional marketing wisdom, service failures can actually be managed in ways that ultimately create greater customer loyalty.

Good service failure recovery can turn formerly disappointed or even angry customers into more loyal customers. This can happen when failed service encounters are converted into successful service encounters. Service recovery from an initial service failure may earn greater customer loyalty and future purchases than if things had gone well in the first place. But here, an interesting paradox arises, because successful recoveries from service failure often create stronger relationships with customers who previously had every right to be upset. After all, the service provider had originally failed them!

Service failure recovery processes function much as damage control units do on warships after they have been struck by enemy fire and would have sunk absent quick and strategic intervention. Naval or service marketer organization damage control teams, as they execute their recovery and restoration tactics, quickly reestablish a sense of normalcy and order so that deeper and more intricate processes can be enacted in order to fully restore working relationships between people or parts. Except what's being restored inside the physical surrounding and processes where marketing services are created and delivered are the damages that otherwise might be visited on the offending—the failed—service's brand.

Starbucks surely understands these exact principles and as a result teaches a LATTE service failure recovery process to its employees. The LATTE service-failure-recovery process suggests that when service encounters go badly, employees should Listen to the complaint; Acknowledge the complaint; Thank the complainer, then give him/her a new cup or dish; and finally Explain what went wrong—and why.

Chick-fil-A; they got this point too. Consumers routinely rhapsodize over the service quality experience they encounter at *Chick-fil-A*. There are several reasons why *Chick-fil-A* customer service is so good. First, the franchise or corporation requires that franchisees or individual store owners work in their own store. Second, franchisees are allowed to only own one store. Third, the *Chick-fil-A* franchising system supposedly only accepts 100 of 10,000, or 1 percent of applications. That's an exclusive club. Fourth, the franchise loves pull-yourself-up-by-your-own-bootstraps stories. So, franchise fees are only $10,000, a number that was recently raised from $5K. Plus, everybody gets Sunday off. Plus+, stores close at reasonable hours. These policies and practices are all part of an internal marketing plan.

These service tricks, which actually are not tricky at all, are not difficult to learn or execute. But they surely motivate service providers, including the owners, to do their best. But no *McDonald's* franchisee runs their multimillion dollar investment in a similar fashion. Hence, *McDonald's* service levels are often very much hit-and-miss.

As noted, *Chick-fil-A's* corporate mission dictates that ownership must work in the store because doing so is a key to good customer service. Plus, *Chick-fil-A* doesn't let anyone hide in their restaurant office—as most multi-location fast-food owners tend to do. There's more, of course. At *Chick-fil-A* orders are read back to customers at the speaker, and again when they arrive at the window. Common sense, right? When was the last time that happened to you at a *McDonald's*? *McDonald's* customers are foolish to pull away from the window until they've verified the bag's contents.

By contrast, how often does *McDonald's* ask customers to pull ahead to the parking spot so they bring your order out to them? Not at *Chick-fil-A*. Some *McDonald's* have designated parking spots for drive-thru customers waiting for their order—how insane is that? If there are three cars in a line at *McDonald's*, drive on. But customers can visit *Chick-fil-A* as the fifteenth car in line because *Chick-fil-A* posts staff outside with *iPads* taking your order, offering customers a snack while they wait, and they will be in and out within five minutes. Customers can wait five minutes at a *McDonald's* even when they are the only people in line.

BUILDING PROFITABLE SERVICES—AND PRODUCTS

Marketers usually should avoid price competition. That is, unless an organization's entire business model is structured to support the successful delivery of lower-than-average sector prices. *Southwest Airlines, Walmart, Aldi's,* or *The Dollar Store* come to mind as examples of marketers that feature such low-cost business models—and who relatedly have succeed across the decades because they position/differentiate based upon their "Cost-Leadership" "Core Competency."

Lowering prices to match or beat competitor's low prices typically ends up helping only consumers—many of whom naturally crave lower prices—while hurting both marketing competitors. In the end, neither price-cutter's market shares will likely change much. But during the price-cutting process, each competitor's profit margins will definitely decline.

The best practical way for most firms to avoid price competition is for them to make price a less important consideration in customers' minds when they're deciding which intangible or tangible brand to buy. To avoid damaging price competition, service marketers should create strategies that enable them to:

- Offer innovative (i.e., difference-making) service or product features.
- Deliver consistently higher levels of product/service quality and reliability than competitors.
- Develop/deliver superior environments in which services or products are delivered.
- Design and deliver superior service or product delivery processes.
- Develop differentiated images for either products or services through branding, symbols, and remarkable and memorable promotional efforts.
- Develop more capable and reliable customer contact service professionals.

MODULE 9.2

Product Life Cycles

The US horse population fell almost 90 percent between 1915 and 1960. All because something better, as both a means of facilitating everyday travel and powering farm work, came along. That something better was a superior solution that arrived in the form of a different product. Welcome to the combustion engine, and the cars, trucks, tractors, and other farm implements such engines empowered.

Only about one century into this particular transformational process, domestic automakers like *Ford Motor Co.* can no longer escape the obvious. Demand for traditional four-door sedans among American consumers is drying up and dying out. As part of a massive cost-cutting initiative, *Ford* recently announced its plans to walk away from the traditional passenger car sedan business after decades of declining sales. Domestic consumers are abandoning sedans and choosing trucks and SUVs, showing preferences for vehicles that are higher off the ground and roomy enough to accommodate families. Consumers' tastes and preferences change constantly. As do the consequences of those changes on marketers. "Ford's sedan-killing move is a bet on the future of driving, and the vehicles drivers will be using," says *Market-Watch.com*. Nothing lasts forever, say your authors. Except for maybe . . .

Been to the movies recently, for example? If the answer is yes—stop right there, because you differ from most other Americans who emphatically have not been to the movies lately. Movie theatre attendance hit a twenty-five-year low during 2018, well before concerns about COVID-19 really kicked theatre-based movie attendance (demand) in the head. This, despite a booming macroeconomy. Revenues also sank as prices rose. Hmmm, something better, again in the form of a superior solution, must have arrived on the scene. Hello *Netflix, Hulu*, and seventy-two-inch flat screens.

When *The Beatles* broke up approximately five decades ago, all four ex-Beatles released solo albums during the same calendar year (1970). The best-selling album among the ex-*Beatles* was recorded by the so-called *Quiet Beatle* (a label that functioned as George's branding identity). *George Harrison* titled his album *All Things Must Pass*. So it was with *The Beatles*, as a product and musical act. The *Fab Four's* time had come and passed.

What about *The Beatles* music itself? Pretty much every band or musical performer in history has had its unique sell-by date. Yet contrary to what should have been expected, their song catalogue has enjoyed a surprisingly looo…ng Product Life Cycle. In fact, *Beatles* music was either the highest or second highest (expert sources actually disagree) selling musical brand—amongst all musical genres; including rock, pop, rap, hip-hop, country, blues, classical, and so forth—during the decade ending in 2009. Some experts argue *Beatles*' sales volumes barely bested *Eminem*'s decade-long sales volume during the 2009 *Christmas* season, which arrived right after *Apple* secured the licensing rights to release *The Beatles*' music on *iTunes* for the first time.

Why has the no-longer-new but actually-rather-old *Beatles* music successfully hung around near the top of sales charts for so long? Success can be explained to some degree by the fact that great music never goes out of style. But to larger degrees, because technology, first in the product form of vinyl albums, then cassette tapes, then CDs, and finally e-music kept giving new life to old tunes, or products. Who knows which new technical form music will take next?

GROWING AND SUSTAINING SUCCESS

Marketers must continuously develop successful new products to initially succeed or to sustain success long-run. Post-introduction, the same marketers must also effectively manage those new products throughout their product life cycles. Strategic managers seeking to manage their product's life cycles more effectively (all of them?) must continuously monitor three factors.

Factor One: Changing Consumer Tastes

Marketers should remain ever mindful that customers' wants, needs, and consequently their tastes evolve constantly across time. For example, consumer tastes in what constitutes luxury, and what products are more or less desirable change constantly. Chicken, of all things, was considered fancy food in Britain before about 1950. Oysters, by contrast, were deemed plebian—low-resent and less desirable. Lobsters were fed to pigs during colonial New England.

Or consider that until recently the open concept interior design for "family" homes had demonstrated remarkable staying power. You know, those design plans that typically combined entryway, kitchen, living, and dining room into one mega, so-called "great room" and dominated new home (or new product) designs since the late 1970s. Why were open concept homes so appealing for so long? Because the format solved multiple family problems or, stated differently, delivered so many family values (solutions). For example:

- ▶ Open designs facilitate benign state-like surveillance over young children with kitchen islands functioning as parental command centers. (Check, for parents marketing the right values to their children.)
- ▶ Loft-like atmospheres delivered hints of Bohemian—no, not Rhapsodies—lifestyles for youngish or young-thinking customers. (Check-plus for cool consumers promoting their

coolness to targeted others; these days no one lets anyone into their homes unless they belong to a valued target segment.)

- Open floor plans provided stages for real estate agents to rhapsodize about—this space is so airy; those tall windows. (Obvious check plus for this marketing cohort.)
- Real estate developers loved the open concept design style because construction costs plummeted; fewer walls. (Another plus-plus for these venturesome new product developers.)
- Open floor plan designs naturally facilitated familial familiarity; okay, togetherness. (Who doesn't "supposedly" value togetherness as this praise-fest screeches to a stop?)

Suddenly, however, new homes featuring more but much smaller room floor plans are the cat's meow. Or, newly constructed walls and barriers are being integrated in existing property products. So, what happened?

The answer, probably, is that nothing really happened. It's more a combined matter of nothing lasting forever, and as noted, consumer tastes changing. During large portions of 2020 or 2021 we could have constructed a case involving COVID-19 and its negating effects on the notion of the value of togetherness. But do you really want to ascribe everything happening that's either good, bad, or different on one environmental trend? We don't, either. What really happened is that consumer tastes changed.

Factor Two: Changing Technological Trends

As already noted, why spend $10–13 a ticket and $8+ for popcorn to sit in a dark room with loud, unpredictable strangers when you can watch the same flick two months later on that seventy-two-inch screen while sitting on your couch?

Factor Three: Changing Competitive Trends

Competitors and their marketing mix management and targeting strategies will constantly change.

Consequently, new products or new positions for old products must be developed in a routine basis. The sort of new products that can lead or ride the crest of new hot trends while providing superior solutions to evolving customer problems is what should be developed. Any firm's existing products, no matter how successful, eventually will be replaced by newer products in the end. Not even *Coca-Cola*, the original classic soft drink and *The Real Thing*, will not last forever. Eventually, however, may be a long time coming.

New products often fail. However, they generally do not fail at the rates reported in most textbooks. Still, the risks associated with innovation—and thus new product development—are high. But the rewards associated with successfully innovating are higher still. As for the punishments that will be meted out among those marketers that fail to innovate; well, they're also extremely high.

INTRODUCING THE PRODUCT LIFE CYCLE

Every product category experiences—passes through—a life cycle. The Product Life Cycle concept, or PLC, concept is similar to the biological life cycle. The biological life cycle informs us that all living entities on earth—trees, fish, humans—are born; hopefully grow rapidly; eventually level off in their growth while entering, often through a combination of strategy and good fortune, an extended maturity stage; and then, inevitably, experience decline and death.

Product category concepts are similarly born; pass through several stages of new product development; are launched ("launched" means introduced directly into markets) (Stage 1); hopefully grow in terms of both the revenues and the market share that they generate after they are launched (Stage 2); eventually reach maturity or plateau stages in terms of their growth in either sales revenues or market share (Stage 3); and inevitably one day begin to decline—finally, to die, which is akin to exiting the market (Stage 4). Product life cycles begin again and again as newer branded products enter markets. If, but only if, those new products do a better job of serving and satisfying evolving customer needs and problems they will grow, albeit not forever. These new products typically reside—consequently compete and seek differentiation—inside the same product category.

Marketers should always attempt to obsolete their existing, or old, products by introducing their own new products before competitors obsolete them. This strategic marketing process and practice is called planned obsolescence. Planned obsolescence is a desirable marketing practice, is executed routinely and successfully by many powerful marketers and marketing brands, and is also part of the creative destruction processes that routinely play out inside First-World marketplaces.

The fact that entire product categories are always subject to these conditions and inevitably will pass through life cycles is normal, expected, and something that should be addressed by strategic marketers. The reality and the presence of product life cycles demands that successful firms continuously acquire or develop new products to replace aging predecessors inside their product portfolios. Otherwise, those successful firms will not remain successful for long.

Even the best, most beastly brands, marketed within formerly dominant product categories, can slowly and then quickly fade away. The *Washington Post* recently reported "and then there was only one [*Blockbuster* video rental marketer] left." During *Blockbusters'* 2004 peak, the franchiser boasted more than 9,000 American retailing storefronts. Things change. *RedBox, Netflix*, and other forms of digital video providers soon ate into the classic retailer's profits, and stores began to shutter. The last store standing, by the way, is in *Bend, Oregon*. Who knows for how long?

The PLC concept only applies to entire product categories (i.e., fizzy soft drinks), as opposed to individual brands within the entire fizzy soda drink product category (i.e., *Coke, Pepsi,* or *RC Cola*). Other examples of product categories could include automobiles powered by combustion engines or by batteries (that's two distinct product categories); phones tethered to land-lines or to the cloud (again, we see examples of two discrete product categories); or books printed on paper or on screens (two separate categories of books). Automobiles, phones, or books each constitute separate product categories. And yet, inside each product category we will find additional subsets of product categories. The takeaway: Product categories can exist inside product categories.

PLC STAGES: BREAKDOWN DEAD AHEAD

The Introduction Stage

During the Introduction Stage, a primary goal is to develop awareness among the targeted audience. Distribution in the market may be limited. Consequently, collaborative and cooperative supply chain relationships also should be developed and refined—see Module 12. Because few to no competitors exist, prices can be comparatively high to quite high. Marketers may employ skim-the-cream pricing strategies. Promotional, or communications, efforts should generally orient toward educational and/or informative messaging. As written, the overarching communication goal is to stimulate awareness. This is because no one has ever bought anything until they first were aware the anything existed. Note how each stage of the marketing mix for products was just discussed.

The Growth Stage

During the Growth Stage, marketers face more competitors because the product(s) they introduced were successful. Success always begets imitation, in football, basketball, or any other form of marketing competition.

Meanwhile, B2C or B2B customers enjoy more options from which to choose—which benefits them. During the Growth Stage a primary goal is to gain market share or to protect existing market share, especially if the marketer was first-to-market in its new product development efforts. A second goal entails promoting greater differentiation and establishing stronger positions. Specifically, positioning the branded product choice as different-from and better-than competing alternatives in that most important of marketing places—inside targeted segments' collective minds. Distribution is not as important an issue during the Growth Stage—although supply chains' relationships cannot be ignored. Marketers should attempt to sustain higher pricing levels during this stage. Yet competitive pressures often make this task difficult to achieve.

The Maturity Stage

The highest levels of competition prevail throughout the marketplace during the Maturity Stage. The product category itself is now well known and firmly established. Inside the product category sales may remain high for individual brands as weaker brands drop out or decrease their promotional efforts. In fact, sales may remain as high as ever for individual marketers if they do everything reasonable to convert maturity into a long-standing plateau.

Yet individual brands and entire product categories are no longer the shiny-new-object and therefore alluring product or service it once was. In response to this condition, marketers should attempt to make their brands feel fresh, again. Other primary goals include sustaining brand loyalty; defending higher prices; protecting market share; engaging in reminder promotional efforts that are initiated to retell stories to targeted customer segments that explain why the brand they once loved is still best; and increasing efficiencies (lowering costs) and improving service levels inside already established supply chain relationships.

Even if the product category is cast in the best possible light, newspapers are still well onto the going down escalator portion of their Maturity Stage. Similar to how video killed the radio star (yes, the name of the song that introduced the *MTV Age*, as performed by one-hit-wonder *The Buggles* during 1979), technology has killed traditional newspapers. Technology has also killed the sort of customer attention spans that are required to read "the paper" deeply enough to extract value from the activity. In 2018, combined circulation for print and digital newspapers was 28.6 million on weekdays and 30.8 million on weekends. This represented a year over year drop of 8 and 9 percent respectively. *Starbucks*, leading indicator of all things or ideas that are good and awakened, stopped selling newspapers at all 8,000+ of its US locations during 2019.

The Decline Stage

During the Decline Stage, marketing strategists must determine whether their firm's sunk costs[6] and/or their customers' switching costs[7] are sufficiently high to merit keeping on inside declining product categories. Competitive strategies and behaviors should be carefully monitored. As other firms drop out of the market, competitive pressures clearly decline. Marketing organizations that strategically decide to remain "left behind" in the fading product category still may market successfully for decades.

Recall how the US horse population rapidly declined throughout much of the twentieth century? This decline was surely accompanied by declines in the sales of buggies or buggy whips. Even so, for various reasons, certain customer groups beyond *Amish* or *Mennonite* (religious-based) market segments are still buying buggies and buggy whips in *Pennsylvania, Ohio,* and *Indiana* among another twenty-eight states. (However, approximately 63 percent of *Amish* and *Mennonites* live inside the first three states.) Which means, at net, at least a few marketers are still successfully making and marketing buggies and buggy whips.

The *Yellow Pages*, classified ads, movie rental stores, landline phones, VCRs, ash trees, ham radios, answering machines, cameras that use film, milkmen, handwritten letters, honey bees, analog TV, and family farms each reside inside product categories that have already entered their Decline Stage. As have paper maps, in a GPS world, *Greyhound*-like long-distance bus travel, or golf, which takes too long in today's speed-up world. Televisions, the product with a screen and speakers, and fast-food are likely in their mature and possibly the decline phase of their Product Life Cycle stage inside the *United States*. However, this does not mean that televisions or *Whoppers* will exit Planet Earth anytime soon. Sadly, new production of the beloved *Volkswagen Beetle*, also branded as *The Bug*, stopped cold during 2018.

---

6. Sunk costs, inside business decision-making, are costs that have already been incurred and cannot be recovered. Their literal opposite number is prospective costs. Prospective costs are future costs that may be incurred or retracted if certain decisions are made.

7. Switching costs, which exist inside and influence B2B customer- or B2C consumer decision-making alike, are encountered when customers or consumers switch to another brand inside the same product category or switch into new product categories. Most switching costs are monetary. Switching costs, however, also relate to outlays associated with time-spend, inconveniences-incurred, learning-required, or psychological-challenges encountered.

Then there is *NASCAR*, a product and brand that is experiencing decline. The recent decline of *NASCAR* as product and brand validates the marketing theory of "mess too much with something that's already working and you might eventually screw up a good thing." *NASCAR* changed in an ultimately futile attempt to become mainstream instead of catering more directly to their base or core market segment.

The changes failed to attract new people to the sport but alienated many old fans. *NASCAR* should have focused on its core market, locking in the brand's appeal while strengthening loyalty among its core audience, and then branched out from there in its efforts to expand the stock car racing market. Oh well, folks who ignore certain core marketing principles often get bit in the butt by those same principles. *NASCAR'S* now lamented changes, by the way, boil down to two words. Those words related to the introduction of "restrictor plates" inside engines. The restrictor plates simultaneously lowered the maximum speed of race cars and the appeal of the *NASCAR's* brand because they changed, lowered, the value and appeal (read "damn the danger; full speed ahead") that formerly was associated with the brand.

One piece of good news about the Decline Stage inside the life cycle of any product category is that the stage can last a long time. Any good axman or woman can cut down small *Douglas Firs*, insert their stumps in water, and sustain their greenness for weeks. Consumers label these obviously brandable products as Christmas trees. In brief, and this is the truth, Christmas trees continue to breathe even though they are dead. Some brands or product categories experiencing their declines states can similarly breathe for long times if their owners water and generally give their marketing mixes sufficient care. Even though their prospects for ongoing life across the long-term are dead and gone.

A second piece of good news about the Decline Stage is even after a product category has entered it that product category's life cycle can be resurrected—and yes, the products inside the category can experience renewed life. The life cycles of product categories can occasionally come back around again, essentially returning to the beginning of and repeating the traditional product life cycle process.

Vinyl (music) records, for example, cycled from their original introduction as 45s in 1949 (containing three or so minutes worth of music, tops, plus a B-side song) to their evolution into so-called LPs (Long Players), or 33s (containing up to forty-three minutes of music), the sales of which faded away to near zero as additional new products such as, in order, eight-track tapes (an innovation arriving in 1964), cassettes (a second innovation also arriving in 1964), and compact disks or CDs (an innovation arriving in 1979) were introduced to the music marketplace. But about ten to twelve years ago, after wallowing in the category's Decline Stage for around three decades, vinyl records, in the form of the old 33s, have returned to market as a smash hit despite their clearly premium prices.

Why have vinyl records' normal product life cycles fundamentally recycled themselves as the product category began again as it were new again? Likely, the reintroduction of vinyl as a preferred music median has rolled out due to a combination of nostalgia and a younger, cooler, and hipper generation (at least inside the segment's own collective mind) began exhibiting a strong preference for the superior sound, including hisses, and were willing to pay premium prices to obtain, play, and "show off" those values to their equally hip or cool friends. Vinyl records, at first slowly but then suddenly, became and remain as popular as at any time since the mid-1980s.

THE TRUE VALUE OF THE PLC, BUT WITH A CAVEAT

The true value of the PLC concept is that if strategists understand the stage of its life cycle the products/brands they manage are in, they will understand better how to manage the marketing mixes of those products/brands.

But one problem arises... and it is the same problem that arose during the BCG Product Portfolio Planning Matrix discussion that was conducted during Module 2. The problem, then and now, is that determining exactly what stage of its life cycle a given product/brand is in during "real time," as is right now, often proves extremely difficult. The only way to know for certain the stage of their life cycles that brands are currently experiencing requires planners to look backward at historical data to determine what has happened. This tact, looking backward, may appear acceptable and reasonable, at first. After all, the past offers myriad lessons to those willing to investigate and learn from what historically went right or wrong. But by the time marketing managers discover these historical insights about their brands it may already be too late for them to respond strategically in ways that enhance their brands' current or future prospects for marketing success.

One can easily drive from *Wilmington, North Carolina,* to the *California* border. Locate *US Interstate 40* as you leave the city and head west. There genuinely are no turns to make. But who wants to traverse those 2,800+ miles driving forward while only looking backward at where you had been through your rear-view mirror? Not many people, we suspect.

Some Things Are Difficult to Know

Consider the following illustration. Artificial intelligence, as an incredible product category that features multiple product category subsets, is probably still experiencing its Introduction Stage. But who knows for certain?

The AI product category always features a computing system and is vaguely modeled on the biological neural processing network otherwise known as the human brain. Like our brains, AI systems learn and progressively improve their performance by gathering and analyzing amounts of environmental data; acquainting themselves firsthand with the information by engaging in thousands or millions of trial-and-error experiments in order to determine what solutions or approaches work or do not work well; and then adjusting AI systems' behavior in response to feedback about what went right or wrong. Products classified with the broader AI product category reprogram themselves by reacting to patterns present in incoming data, rather than relying and remaining locked-in on previously learned rules. Just the way our human brains should operate, in other words.

With capabilities like these, once AI does hit its Growth Stage spurt, which should occur anytime now (but no one knows for sure), sales and profits should blow up. By the time the category reaches maturity, AI, the category, will probably remain in place inside that stage for a long time. Probably until AI begins creating its own AI, hello, *Terminator V*. But again, no one knows when this stage will arrive, either.

Here's one more peek into a version of the future for which many domestic managers and workers should prepare for.

In the future whatever can be done more effectively and less expensively by machines will be done by machines. Primarily because machines don't complain, join unions, go on strike while demanding higher pay, or call in sick on Mondays or Fridays because they're hungover or traveling to visit distant girlfriends/boyfriends.

Yes, it's true. Machines literally are high maintenance; machines actually do break down. But that's where highly trained or well-paid professionals arrive on the scene to maintain or fix those machines. During this *Rise of the Machines*-era human jobs will be preserved and likely expand in volume because human beings are also required to conceptualize, design, build, ship, install, and yes, market, the machines.

Robots at *Amazon*, as of 2019, were capable of assembling 600 to 700 delivery or distribution boxes per hour. That's right, making six to seven boxes per second. These *AI* machines cost about $1,000,000 each and replace twelve employees per machine times three shifts per day. Run the numbers, add in the human constraints noted just above, and one clearly sees who—the machines—is destined to win in the end.

Small wonder that Amazon has grown into the world's largest "company store."

EXHIBIT 9.1
The Levels of a "Product"

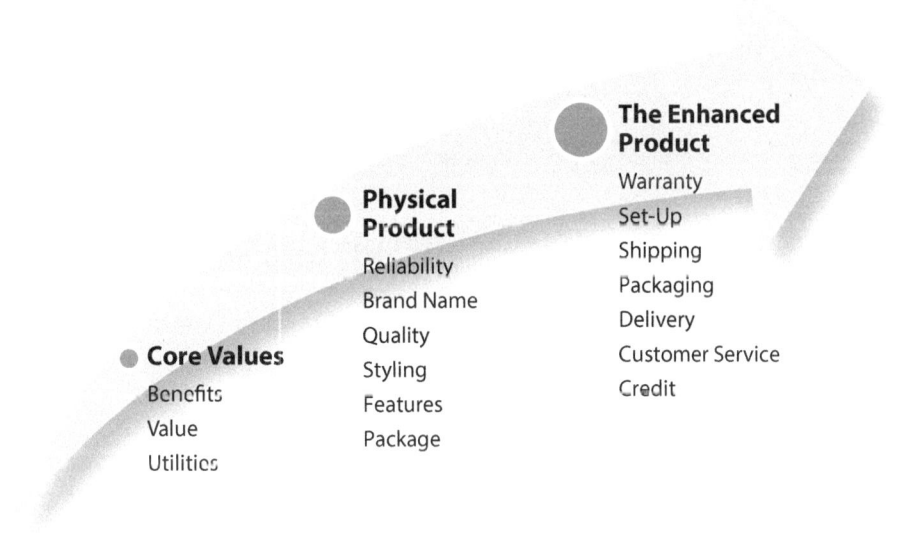

Core Values
Benefits
Value
Utilities

Physical Product
Reliability
Brand Name
Quality
Styling
Features
Package

The Enhanced Product
Warranty
Set-Up
Shipping
Packaging
Delivery
Customer Service
Credit

EXHIBIT 9.2
The Goods–Services Continuum

	Automobiles		Entertainment
	Major Appliances		Airline Travel
Grocery Products	Restaurants	Personal Service	Health Clubs
Personal Care Products	Tailored Clothing	Automotive Repair	Insurance

← Goods—Service Continuum →

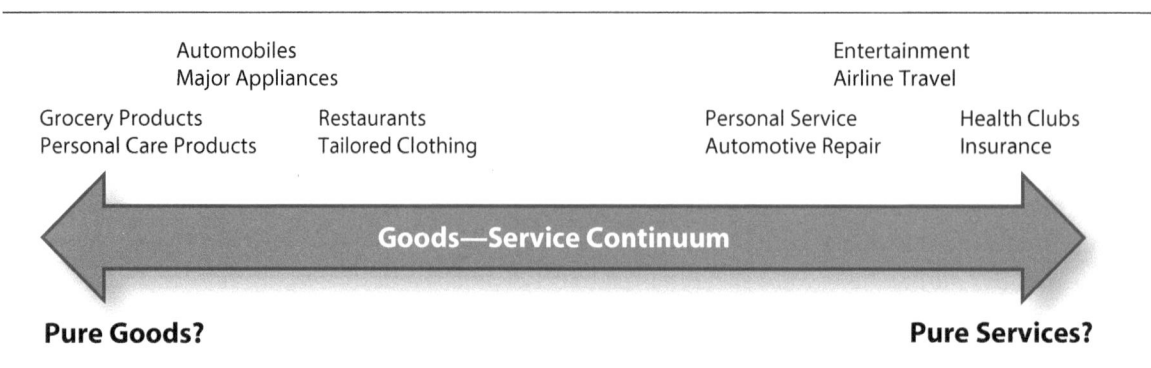

Pure Goods? **Pure Services?**

EXHIBIT 9.3
Marketers Match Elements of Brand Personality to Consumers' Ideal Self-Concepts to Build Positive Attitudes for Brands

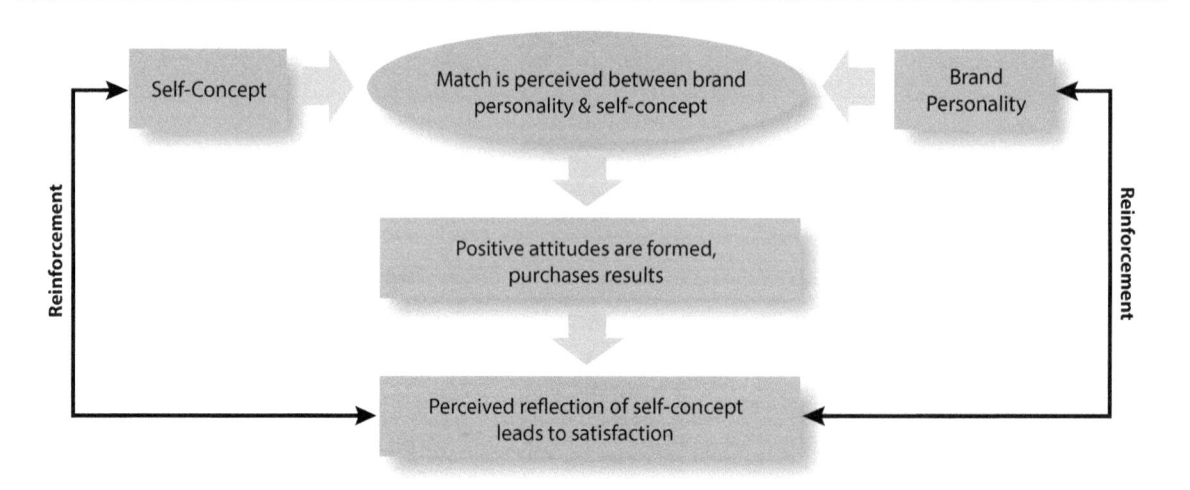

Self-Concept → Match is perceived between brand personality & self-concept ← Brand Personality

↓

Positive attitudes are formed, purchases results

↓

Perceived reflection of self-concept leads to satisfaction

Reinforcement (loops back to Self-Concept and Brand Personality)

TABLE 9.1
The Scope of the Product Management Decision

Product Item	Description
Benefits	The benefits the product provides to customers that fulfill their needs and expectations.
Attributes	The specific attributes or characteristics the product must possess to provide customers with the desired benefits.
Branding	Family brand vs. individual brand. Specific brand name to use. Brand mark or logo to be employed.
Legal Protection	Trade marking. Copyrights. Licenses.
Packaging	Desired functions of the package. Package design and costs. Package labeling. Legal obligations with labels. Package disposition and recycling.
Quality Level	Desired level of quality the product should possess.
Product Safety	Design and build in safety features. Test to ensure safe to use.
Warranties and Guarantees	Warranty coverage for the life of the product.
Life Cycle Management	How the product should be managed over its life cycle in terms of features, services, quality levels, branding, pricing, etc.

EXHIBIT 9.4
The classification of consumer goods is based on how much effort consumers are willing to expend to acquire them.

Amount of effort expended in the purchase process

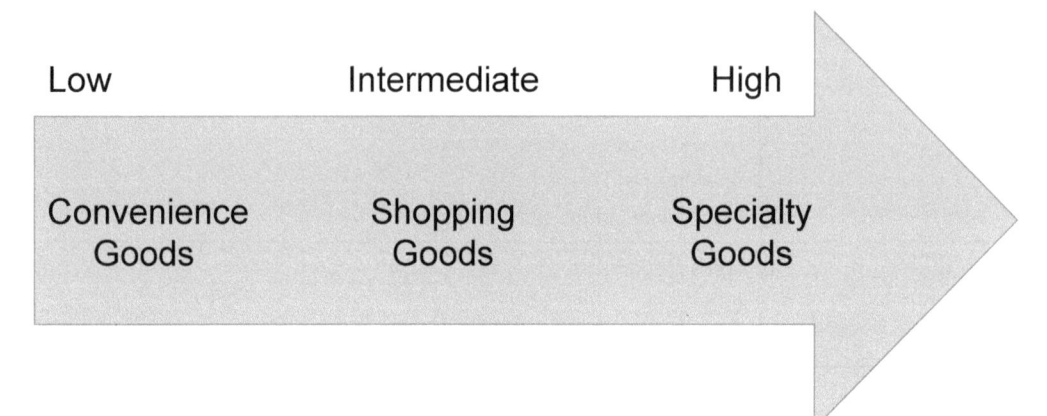

Low	Intermediate	High
Convenience Goods	Shopping Goods	Specialty Goods

EXHIBIT 9.5
Stages of the Product Life Cycle

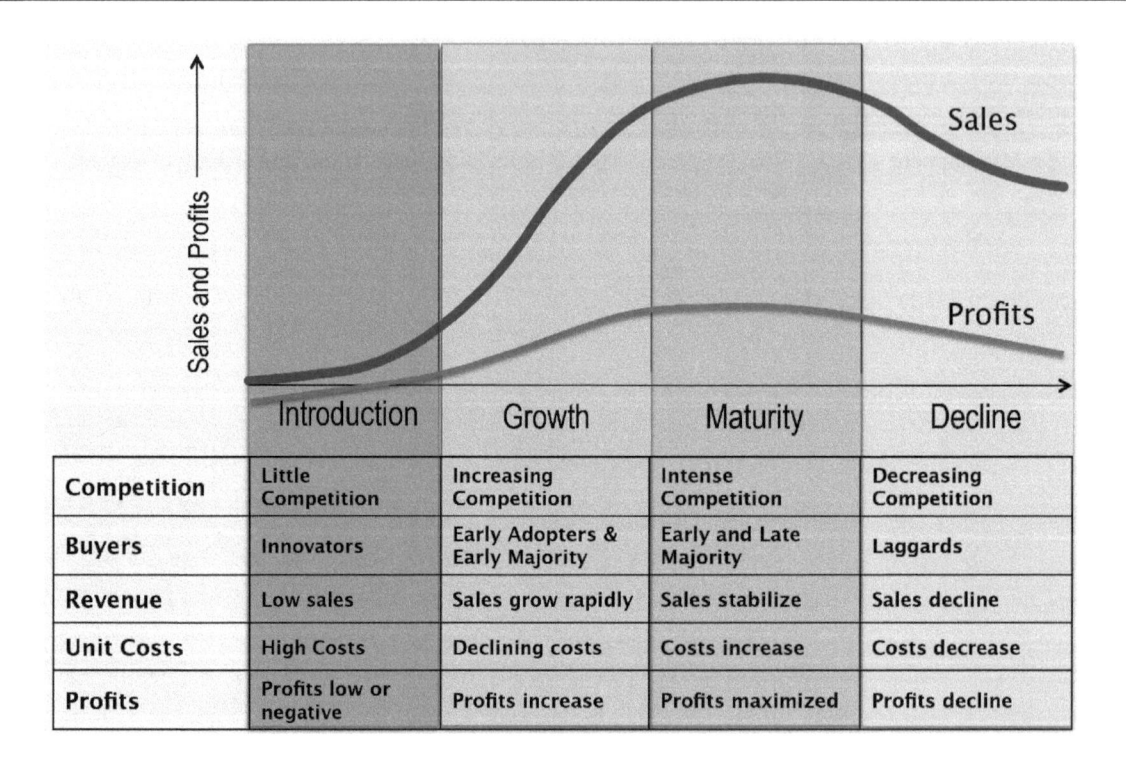

	Introduction	Growth	Maturity	Decline
Competition	Little Competition	Increasing Competition	Intense Competition	Decreasing Competition
Buyers	Innovators	Early Adopters & Early Majority	Early and Late Majority	Laggards
Revenue	Low sales	Sales grow rapidly	Sales stabilize	Sales decline
Unit Costs	High Costs	Declining costs	Costs increase	Costs decrease
Profits	Profits low or negative	Profits increase	Profits maximized	Profits decline

MODULE 10

Managing New Product Development

MODULE 10.0

Ideas

Marketers can expend all the strategic effort and finite resources that they want in efforts to reposition old brands as somehow new, again. But marketers can never truly make existing products completely new again. (This is always true, despite earlier admonitions that successful marketers should always make "the old appear new.") Products get to be truly new only once every bit to the same degree as people never receive second chances to re-generate their lost innocence.

This natural condition exists as both a problem and a challenge. The condition, however, also exists as an opportunity because marketers as well as consumers can derive tremendous value from successfully introducing and actually acquiring or using new products.

Ideas rule the world. Good to great ideas create success and wealth. Mediocre to poor ideas facilitate failure and hardship. Marketing professionals are not what they eat. They are what they think.

True or false? New product development, hereafter NPD, is often similar to bearing children for the first time. After delightful intervals where creation occurred, months of waiting—check. Agonizingly complicated deliveries as well as extensive preparations for delivery—check. Knowing that after babies . . . products . . . are born your life, for better or worse, will never be the same again—check. So the answer is, "true."

For hundreds of years humans have burned waste to generate energy. For hundreds of years the resulting carbon emissions billowed into Earth's atmosphere. Processes through which garbage could be transformed into clean sources of energy, however, remained a "Back to the Future" sort of fiction.

But as this book was going to press a handful of companies were seeking to convert household trash into low emission (cleaner) fuel for "Planes, Trains and Automobiles." What had happened slowly then suddenly was that new product developers had taken an existing idea (burning trash), combined old practices and behaviors with a new idea, and created an entirely new solution (cleaner sources of recycled energy). An entirely new product delivering an entirely new solution that allowed the corporations who began selling it to honor the need and imperative that so many marketers face to position themselves simultaneously as purveyors of sustainability and practitioners of green had finally emerged, not out of nowhere but very definitely out of somewhere.

The entirely new and cleaner idea is known as waste gasification and involves cutting and drying non-recyclable trash from homes and offices, and beyond that the details of the new idea and process don't matter. What does matter, however, is that you understand the ideas from which successful new products emerge generally result from combining old and new ideas, from combining old and old (existing) ideas, or from combining new and new ideas. Creative success emerges from and through the development of combinations—or intersections.

BUILDING INNOVATIVE CONTEXTS

The world is full of challenging problems. Low-hanging fruit, it's been picked. Most of the important marketing challenges remaining today exceed the capabilities of individuals, working alone, to solve. To solve the biggest problems, the combined expertise of people from diverse backgrounds who can bridge gaps between different disciplines and professional skills is required. The spark for the big ideas that create solutions to big problems like those proliferating today rarely arise in solitude.[1]

Few lone geniuses stride the earth today. Not because people aren't smarter than they used to be; on average, they are. Better nutrition and more education actually worked—that is, until recently when their continuous engagement with smart devices began lowering children's IQ's of inside all developed countries [fact, not an opinion; validate the assertion by googling it]. It's just that today too much knowledge exists for one person to know enough of it to make a huge difference. *Bill Gates* had *Paul Allen*, who now owns the *Seattle Seahawks NFL* football team. *Steve Jobs* had *Steve Wozniak*. *Mark Zuckerberg* had *The Twins*—made more famous in *The Social Network*. *Mark Cuban* had *Todd Wagner*. *Batman*, yes, *Robin* has his back.

Two takeaways are revealed. First, most people today can either work successfully together with others or fail alone. Second, great value can be derived from the mutual creation, critical evaluation, and eventual exploitation of intersections and intersectional ideas. This is the second time we've mentioned the word intersection; time to take a peek at why.

How powerful are intersections? Consider the little-known fact that dragons existed as mythological creatures inside virtually all ancient cultures. This is probably because dragon like imagery itself creates a near-perfect intersection of three basic human fears. The first fear being that of serpents and other reptilian creatures. The second being the fear of rapacious flying birds. The third being fear of animals that feature large and powerful claws.

INVENTION, INNOVATION; RECOMBINATION

The acts of invention and innovation are actually acts of recombination. This is because ideas have sex. What would eventually happen were two [or more] potentially fertile ideas get together and repeatedly engage in [sexual] exchange? That's right, baby ideas are born. The combined ideas produce a third

---
1. We've probably encountered another reason why governments are often so bad at solving problems. Yes, it's true, people inside government often have diverse backgrounds. But once in government these people usually fail to work together in ways that maximize the best of their combined expertise and experiences.

[new] idea. And then it is off to the races, so to speak, in terms of the inventions and innovations that may be reproduced.

Professionals need to remain open-minded, particularly in terms of seeking and accepting constructive criticism, when developing or vetting ideas. Constructive criticism leads to more and better new ideas. Why? Because constructive criticism encourages others, including anyone reading or writing this sentence, to fully engage with their work and the ideas and work of others. That is, unless we fold-up like a cheap lawn chair at the first whiff of criticism. Hint, inside business settings, don't be this person.

Criticism can be unfair and untrue. Criticism can be unfair but true. Criticism can be fair and true. Little to no experiences of criticism will be deemed constructive by its recipients unless the criticism, as well as the critic, is to be both fair and true.

The Importance of Form, Formulation, and Function

Invention refers to a dimension of uniqueness—newness related to the Form, Formulation, or Function of something. The something in question here is a new product. Form factors address what the new product is. Formulation factors address how the new product is made. Function factors address what the new product does; what problems does it solve? Inventions are often patentable; innovations usually are not.

Innovation, the word, refers to an overall process whereby inventions are transformed into commercialized and marketable products that can be sold profitably. Innovations must deliver practical or perceptual value that benefits someone; someone must be willing to give up something of value in order to obtain or use the innovation. For new products to be described as innovations they also must be useful. There are more inventions than innovations.

Human history is a by-product of innovation. New or once-new products, including now everyday tools such as wheels, plows, or analog and digital computing devices, inevitably generate new social, cultural, and economic orders. Winners and losers result—those who create usually win; those who fail to create or who refuse to accept changes that creativity brings usually fall behind. Whole civilizations rise—and fall.

The development of voice-based technologies such as recording devices, telephones, or the radio has imposed epic impacts on the course of political history. And naturally so, given that well-rehearsed but seemingly ad-libbed speeches along with prepared rhetoric has always resided at or near the core of all forms of persuasive marketing efforts. Nothing new to see here. Across the ages new and useful media have always sprung up as newly innovative products that convey these presumably persuasive words.

Radio broadcasts of *Adolf Hitler's* rallies brought the *German* nation under the sway of an *Austrian*-born *National Socialist*—since branded as *Nazi*—dictator.[2] Both radios and radio broadcasts were radically new and widely marketed during the 1930s—and remain so to this day. *Franklin Roosevelt's*

---

2. Some historians suggest that the nation of *Austria* has successfully pulled off one of the greatest re-positioning and re-branding campaigns in world history. That is because the nation has largely succeeded in convincing the world that *Adolf Hitler* was *German* and *Wolfgang Mozart* was *Austrian*. The fact is, however, the exact opposite; national genealogy abides. Ah, the power of marketing.

fireside radio chats nudged American sentiment toward acceptance of the war that eventually toppled the dictator. (Of course, the *Japanese* sneak attack on *Pearl Harbor* facilitated this outcome, as well.) This all happened some seventy-nine to eighty-eight years before *Alexa*, and her various artificially but highly intelligent e-cousin brands, began manipulating contemporary consumer hearts, minds, and emotions.

THREE TYPES OF INNOVATIONS EXIST

Three basic types of innovations exist: continuous, dynamically continuous, and discontinuous innovations. Most innovations are continuous. Honestly, not much is new about continuous innovations. Something minor is typically added to or removed from existing products to formulate continuous innovations. The musical history-changing *Sgt. Pepper* album, created and released by *The Beatles* during 1967, was still only a continuous innovation. Broadly viewed by critics as a great work of art, *Sergeant Pepper* was among the first concept albums or albums to integrate non-musical sounds into musical recordings. But in the end the album was just four talented and creative guys laying down tracks on vinyl. By the way, art, as in "a work of art," can be defined and described as any object that creates more energy than it consumes.

Discontinuous innovations, by contrast, are new and useful products that change everything. Discontinuous innovations are few and far between. The internet, the first telephone, the first wheel, the printing press, sanitation systems, combustion engines, the airplane, dynamite; these were all discontinuous innovations at the point they were introduced to the world. But discontinuous innovations need not be utterly epic all the time. The transportation (traveling) service providers called *Uber* and *Lyft*, as one-time innovations, have proven disruptive in terms of their effects on traditional taxi, limousine, and bus services, as well as how radically they changed users' ride-hailing behaviors.

The difference between the two types of innovations depends on how-radically-new-and-different the new products are, as well as how much customer learning is required before they can adapt to and use the innovations in their intended manner.

As noted, dynamically-continuous innovations exist. But this specific topic is not discussed further here, or elsewhere in this book. That is because discerning the difference between continuous and dynamically continuous innovations is a difficult task indeed, and in the end the differences themselves don't truly much matter.

"IN THE BEGINNING" THERE ARE IDEAS

Successful new product development[3] begins with the creation of good to great new ideas, as stated above. Hopefully, the great version of new ideas. Because with great ideas, the sort that lead to great new products, one thing leads to another.

---

3. NPD is the process through which new products or services are developed. NPD processes may be executed to improve established products in order to re-position them to compete more effectively in open market competitions. NPD processes also may be executed to develop completely new product or products that are new-to-the-firm in order to counter new environmental threats or pursue new market segment opportunities.

When the printing press[4] was invented, throngs of consumers began reading suddenly far more widely-accessible books. Even more suddenly, many new book consumers realized they had a problem (i.e., farsightedness). Their awareness of this problem facilitated other marketers' creation of a solution. We now call this innovation eyeglasses. But as craftsmen worked more precisely with glass and lenses, both the telescope and microscope quickly followed. These two new products facilitated huge advances in other disciplines. For example, astronomy, note *Galileo*, with his pivotal science- and religious-altering idea that the Sun did not revolve around the Earth. Or, microbiology, as pioneered by a physician named *Fracastoro* who identified germs and infections. Relatedly, increasingly efficient European glassworkers improved technologies that made superior mirrors possible. More effective, more broadly available mirrors allowed more people to see themselves clearly for the first time. Whoops, another problem. As *European* consumers examined themselves more carefully, did they become more introspective or more self-critical? Perhaps both. If so, the initial consequence may have fostered philosophical debate and progress. The second may have decreased self-esteem? If so, greater numbers of more effective camouflaging products—we now call them cosmetics—probably emerged.[5]

Or not. Still, this chain of ideas, events, consequences, and new products as arriving solutions *to new problems* is not only possible but plausible. All one has to do is believe, *One Thing Leads to Another*, as *The Fixx* sang a few decades ago.

How to Identify Not Just "Good-Enough" but "The-Best Creative Ideas"

Innovative people often know that the underlying ideas from which successful new products can be developed have promise when the value of the ideas and the resulting new products themselves appear obvious in retrospect. The simple idea that sailing west from *Portugal* (situated at *Europe's* western shore) to reach the trading riches of *China*, for example, appears obvious in retrospect (retrospect means "when looking back"). Yet *Christopher Columbus's* idea had so much promise that it changed world history. The real underlying issue is why did various other *European* powers—all of which had the means, motive, and opportunity to improve trade relations with Asia—take so long to act upon the idea.

Or take sitting. Sitting is supposedly the new smoking because of the degree to which too much sitting proves injurious to people's health. Perhaps, but don't tell that to old smokers who themselves sit around all day.

Too much sitting, often while staring into little glass-covered machines, has been recognized as a problematic villain as US citizens have steadily grown heavier and began dying earlier. So why did it take so long for marketers to develop desks that people work out at while sitting down or standing up.

---

4. The printing press was history's second most important innovation; yes, the wheel remains number one. Yet if one thinks deeply about this point, the wheel probably arrived comparatively easily. Someone surely had watched roundish rocks or logs rolling downhill, making the wheel relatively easy to envision. Ah, but those axels that make wheels work, that was likely the genuine innovative breakthrough.

5. Raymond J. Seeger, *Galileo Galilei, His Life and Works* (Oxford: Pergamum Press, 1966).

In retrospect, such a product sure seems like an obvious solution for otherwise sedentary white-collar workers, after all.

At least five additional creative criteria exist through which the best new NPD ideas can be identified. A discussion of each criteria follows.

First, is the idea simple enough, and if not, can the idea be made simpler? Complexity represents the easy way out for lazy marketers. Complexity could entail giving too much product/contractual information; providing too many options and choices; or building too many features into new products. By contrast the virtue of simple ideas, yielding simple solutions, is that each generally offers an easier path to success.

However, there's usually nothing simple about achieving simplicity. Except inside rare and revealing contexts. When current *GM* CEO *Mary Barra* directed the corporate Human Resources Department, she chopped down a ten-page single-spaced report that advised employees about how to dress to two words: "Dress appropriately." There is power and clarity inside simplicity. Anyone surprised that Ms. Barra became the first female to ascend to the CEO rank for *GM*?

Most of the time achieving simplicity demands adherence to three principles. Namely, the ability to empathize—by accurately perceiving customers' needs and expectations; the ability to distil—by reducing to their essence the substance or value of new products; and finally, the ability to clarify—by making new products easier for customers to understand or use. The keys to achieving empathy entails receipt of the right sort of feedback, listening to that feedback, and then responding accordingly to address and resolve consumers' reasonable desires and problems.

The value of *Occam's Razor* should always be respected. The Razor—as explained earlier in *The Inside Skinny*—prescribes that the best solutions to complicated problems, or here, the best idea that might facilitate highly creative solution, is usually the simplest one that works and accounts for all the data.

The next four criteria are more easily explained, perhaps in homage to Occam. Second, is the new idea unexpected? Third, can the new idea be made to appear more or is it already concrete as opposed to abstract in nature? Fourth, does the new idea appear credible? Fifth, will any new product resulting from the new idea resonate emotionally or logically inside targeted B2C or B2B segments? The word resonate means "speaks directly to someone."

The order in which potential innovators ask these questions is immaterial. However, if two or more questions are answered negatively material amounts of work likely remains—because the best possible new idea remains unidentified.

Product quality is directly proportional to product efficiency and ultimately to quantity of units sold, as discussed during Module 9. Here, however, readers should note that the quality of creative NPD ideas is directly proportional to the quantity of purportedly creative NPD ideas and ultimately to successful creativity. It turns out that usually many ideas—often, dozens—must be evaluated and eliminated to arrive at one or two high quality ideas.

This circumstance runs counter to what is normally required to earn success in marketing. Meaning, first, marketing success is typically a matter of addition—as readers have read. And meaning second, NPD success typically begins with a matter of subtraction. Specifically, the sort of subtraction that entails removing the fewer great ideas that are actually suitable for additional NPD consideration[6] from the higher quantities of less-than-best-ideas that are not suitable for the same purpose.

THE UNSPOKEN BENEFITS OF "NEW" THINGS THAT ARE FRESH AND FAMILIAR

Successful NPD benefits society because winning innovations increase productivity and economic growth. The primary cause of economic growth, in fact, is marketer-produced, competition-prompted, customer-satisfying innovations. Think about the once innovative product called the internet and how its introduction radically increased economic growth throughout the 1990s. Economic growth creates more and more highly paying jobs.

Innovations increase efficiency. Innovations stimulate demand. The hopefully uniquely new and useful value that must be present inside innovations operates as force-multiplier that can deliver sustainable marketing success. Few firms can remain successful for long absent the ongoing introduction of new products. This has always been true. Customers love the new when it relates to new stuff. Just not-too-new, because humans simultaneously crave and fear the new.

Okay, but so what? As previously discussed (again!), the sweet spot for marketers are NEW songs, movies, or books that simultaneously feel fresh and familiar to consumers. Actually, the best bet for all manner of marketers entails creating new products that simultaneously feel fresh and familiar. Marketing generally and new product development specifically are activities in which both innovation (fresh!) and imitation (familiar!) abound. And activities in which innovation and imitation simultaneously function as keys to new or sustainable success.

NPD is big business. Beyond that, however, the biggest reason to understand NPD is that new products offer the best solution to most firms' most-pressing challenge. Their most-pressing challenge, among most firms, relates to the difficulties associated with achieving sustainable differentiation and earning the ongoing brand loyalty, brand equity, and ultimately pricing power that results from "owning" SCAs. Competitors can do the most damage to any marketer when that marketer has failed to create product differentiation. At that point, competition regresses to price wars where every competitor loses profits as consumers chalk up a win. Product differentiation is best earned through successful NPD.

Greater creativity, and the successful NPD that the existence and execution of creative ideas can inspire and deliver, allows marketers to earn lasting differentiation and competitive advantage. And what about readers as current or future professionals? All readers are also marketers. And all readers are more likely to be successful if they are or become more creative. This principle applies now. But the principle that creativity is absolutely critical to professional success will apply to greater degrees in the future as international and technologically generated threats tamp down the success prospects for many domestic professionals.

---

6. An uncompromising culling of the fewer greater NPD ideas from the many good but not good enough NPD ideas is similar to processes that great writers or presenters usually master. That is, the process of editing-out the parts of the story that readers or hearers either don't want or don't need to read or see.

The willingness and ability to think and act creatively is one personal asset that anyone can develop and possess that increases in value over time. Take youth, beauty, physical strength, flexibility, energy; with the passage of time each asset fades in power. Meanwhile, the power of anyone's creativity, once established, never fades. No modern economy needs more past their sell-by-date professionals—or for that matter recent college graduates—to replicate the performance of tasks computers can already do more efficiently and less expensively than people. Instead, greater numbers of more creative professional thinkers are needed. More than that, more creative professional problem solvers are demanded. The sorts of marketers equipped intellectually not just to solve problems but to also imagine new solutions to problems that do not even exist yet.

CREATIVELY INNOVATIVE PROCESSES FEATURE NO END POINT

How many readers have pondered the nearly miraculous creative NPD progress entailed in the movement from whalebone-bound corsets to spandex-enabled *Spanx*? These two markedly different yet highly innovative-in-their-time products were developed to address exactly the same human problem. The problem in question flows from females' desire, likely reflected in male desires, to shape and re-form the natural curves of their bodies. No, not all women desire this outcome, but many indisputably do. Consequently, what we're discussing is a problem that has not fundamentally changed across millennia. Yet a problem whose solutions have clearly radically changed during the last 150 or so years.

Innovations always evolve. The solutions used to solve the darkness problem by producing light have evolved across millennia. Let's see; from wood fires, requiring hours of chopping to fuel brief, flickering blazes, to sesame oil lamps to tallow candles to whale oil lights to electric lights to incandescent lights to *LED* bulbs. What's next? Who knows? The story is not complete; the evolution of lighting innovations will continue. Such issues are never in doubt; the only question is who will lead lucky marketing organizations to the new promised land first. And yes, riches and possibly fame will await those innovators.

Another outcome is certain, however. The full effects of innovations are often unpredictable because the effects of creativity and innovation can prove erratic. Innovation effects may play out over decades or centuries.

Innovations often change the balance of economic or market power on global scales. Barbed wire, for example, allowed American pioneers (the word "pioneers" also a marketing synonym for first-movers, typically into new marketers as first-mover firms introduce new products and marketing mix strategies) who staked out claims to land ownership in the *Old West* to gain the upper hand over *Indian* tribes and cattle herders who claimed rights of use. Barbed wire also allowed fewer World War I soldiers, while fighting defensively, to kill far more attackers from far larger ranges.

Innovations always produce intended and unintended consequences. Never assume that innovations offer nothing but solutions. After all, when new products are solving problems for someone or segment they are often creating problems for other individuals or segments. Robotics, anyone? Yes, technology eliminates old jobs, and increased automation is scary. But innovations involving AI or robotics also creates higher marketing demand for people who can imagine new ways in which technology can be leveraged to help consumers and communities solve their problems. But long-run, watch out; because robots are better at acting like humans than humans are at acting like robots.

All the while, however, innovative successes are mostly written in sand. The phrase "written in sand" implies that innovativeness must be pursued constantly as marketers commit themselves to continuously moving forward. Innovative-ness must continuously push forward toward the leading edges of new value.

Successful new product developers and innovators must perform as orchestrators. Teams of product developers, rather than *Lone Ranger* I'll do it myself genius-types, are generally necessary in order to generate winning innovative ideas today.

Marketing innovativeness and marketing innovations each must be pushed. Innovativeness and innovations each represent and require change. The introductions of innovations usually impose change. Most folks, however, don't want to change. Customers—those internal and external to the firm—rarely jump up, shouting . . . I want that [change].

Marketing innovations often prove disconcerting. Yet such disruptions are basically unavoidable. That is primarily because when everyone is comfortable, growth and change become less feasible. However, inside those situations where no one is comfortable growth also becomes more difficult to achieve.

By this point you're presumably realizing why innovative processes, which necessarily require change, often play out as unnatural, discomfort-producing events. Organizational roadblocks and *Debbie Downers* must be overcome. Oh, sorry, we don't do that sort of thing around here. . . For reasons discussed below, associative barriers that exist within ourselves and others must be overcome.

The successful management of innovation imposes conflicting sets of demands upon marketers. First, new products must be developed and delivered that feature attributes that satisfy current or prospective customer needs in ways and to degrees that are superior to existing product alternatives. This single task alone represents a huge challenge. Second, new products usually must feature unique design characteristics. Another daunting test. Third, the marketer usually must be able to reach and penetrate either existing or newly-targeted market segments quickly. Here, new product developers or their surrogates must manage existing or new supply chain relationships successfully.

These three demands are interlocking. These demands usually must be managed and satisfied in an essentially simultaneous fashion. Fail at one task and the entire NPD process collapses. It is flat-off tough to do NPD well. One might assume that this is the primary reason why marketing organizations and individuals who manage NPD processes effectively end up doing so well financially.

Successful new products actually must be or merely be perceived as superior to products they are replacing in order to succeed. Again, most people, including customers, do not want to change. Thus, NPD success comes down to differentiation. Differentiation in ways and along dimensions—dimensions that feature benefits and solutions—that are important and meaningful to customers. When the new product's dimensions differ from dimensions present in existing products and those differences are important to targeting customers, the dimensions are determinant.

REVISITING TWO KEY POINTS

The following points were introduced during previous modules. Each is sufficiently important to revisit now.

- First, many consumers, much of the time, take things for granted after an often short period of time; products, people, places.

When people buy new cars or acquire other new "things," even including most new friends or lovers, they surely cherish "the new" for a few weeks or months. But typically within a year, or less, people get totally used to the formerly new thing. Blah . . . and slowly then suddenly people find fault with something they formerly loved and often but not always begin looking elsewhere . . . for . . . something . . . else . . . new to make them happy, again. Well, then, marketers continuously need to give consumers products that are new and useful, again, as a predicate to the sustainable success of those marketers. Then those innovating marketers should rinse and repeat the NPD process, and thereafter continue to rinse and repeat their new product development processes.

Even so, most successful new things must remain useful to remain successful. But not always, and most exceptions to this rule usually speak directly to the persuasive power of marketing communications, or promotions, and to the development of branding power. Diamond engagement rings were once a new but never a useful new product; implying, correctly, that diamond engagement rings once were an invention but never an innovation. By the way, whether readers accept the premise that diamond rings bring no utility to anyone's table other than contrived and therefore merely perceived values and associations (images of everlasting love, and all that) that diamond marketers have carefully constructed inside primarily (targeted) female minds that they target does not matter.

What matters instead is understanding the difference between merely new products, as in inventions, and new and useful products, as in legitimately valuable, or genuinely useful, innovations.

- Second, most marketers, all the time, should understand that the best opportunity they have to achieve mega-success is to create a solution to a problem the world did not realize it had yet. Moreover, "problems" actually can exist without the world having known about them only because these pseudo problems are often not real.

For example, food lovers—even true connoisseurs of fine cuisine—cannot truly know, understand, or conceive the taste that they, even as food lovers, most desire if the taste they desire does yet not exist. Stated differently, but the same, human minds cannot know what human tongues desire until after the satisfactions [solutions] for the desire are available for the affected human tongues to sample and savor. The two preceding and embarrassingly esoteric statements (i.e., this is no way to tell an effective story) fundamentally implies that humans usually don't know whether they'll like or loath a new food taste until after they've tasted it. Or for that matter, like or loathe most radically new "any things" until after consumers have experienced them. Beyond the simple power of sampling, that is.

Culinary marketers seeking to engage in new product development consequently face two tasks. Task one, to create new food tastes by creating new products—a process that involves engagement in ideation and in physical activities wherein existing food ingredients are creatively re-combined. Task two to convince targeted portions of say, differing foodie market segments, that consumers who populate these segments have problems if they do not have the new solutions. That's marketing! And this sort of "that's marketing" is happening all around America right now to the point where domestic consumers' tastes about their taste are dramatically changing inside certain B2C segments.

Not long ago, for example, if the trendy side of the "power you" had invited a "power couple" over to your home for a meal of charred anything, your guests would have assumed you were apologizing preemptively for your decision to burn something—and then to serve it. But today (2022), "charred" food options are hot. The modifier "charred" significant signifies that the food item is robust, deeply flavored, and prepared through "modern methods," whether the meal was prepared on hot skillets or grills or inside ovens.

Tastes change from one generational cohort—think an age-based segment—to another. These descriptions of tastes applies to the keywords—this dish is "charred!"—now being used to promote and differentiate foods as well as the marketers of those foods themselves. These shifts in marketers' promotional vocabulary and consumer food preferences mirror wider environmental trends unfolding across domestic cultures or subcultures. The fact that charred vegetables and fermented everything are now in vogue is spurred by growing concerns for healthiness and domestic arrival of more globalized attitudes toward food preparation and food itself inside certain demographic segments. Many consumer segments have long since spurned old beliefs that French cuisine was the only language spoken inside upscale kitchens. The *Indian* word "tadka" and the *Mexican* word "sofrito" have assumed honored places alongside the *French* word "mirepoix"—with each formerly-foreign but now domestically-coopted *English* word simply describing how finely chopped, spicily-flavored vegetables are prepared inside consumer kitchens.

Similarly new, new product taste trends are playing out inside grocery sectors as well. During the 1990s, grocery stores began affixing premium prices to "imported" food items. The marketing word "imported" inferred foreign and fantastic as well as different and glamorous. Most importantly, the word imported underscored that the associated food items were worthy of their higher prices.

But today locally sourced foods, as opposed to more distantly imported foods, rule. The word "local" currently signals sustainable, seeds-to-table, fresh, and yes, healthy. These four product values now function routinely as key points of differentiation that are highly prized and deemed worthy of their higher prices by many sub-culturally tuned-in and turned-out consumer segments. During previous generations cooks or chefs would have uniformly recoiled in disgust at the idea of serving smashed carrot salad as a failed carrot puree. But contemporary tastes dictate that such rough-hewn dishes are healthy and natural especially if they are sourced from local foods and therefore should be well-received by those lucky enough to consume them.

MODULE 10.1

Foundational Insights

WHAT ARE NEW PRODUCTS?

New products or new services can be classified in various ways. The classifications range from truly new-to-the-world to substantial improvements to simple additions to or deletions from existing products.

Most new products fit into this latter classification. This process generally entails taking something bad out of existing products or putting something good into existing products. The taking away something bad could be as simple as *Pepsi* removing sugar from an existing drink. The putting in something good could be as simple as *Pepsi* adding vitamins to the same drink.

Or, as we continue hanging out in the junk food grocery aisle, *Reese's Corporation*, of *Reese's Peanut Butter Cup* fame, released a new 2021 product that was designed to appeal to a peanut butter lovers-only segment. The new product eliminated chocolate for the original *Reese's Peanut Butter Cup*. Jury remains out, for us. Peanut butter without chocolate sounds like *Jordan (Michael)* without *Pippin (Scottie)*. Or, *Astaire (Fred)* without *Rogers (Ginger)*.

The key to remember, however, is that these product changes are executed to create, reposition, and deliver new, different, and enhanced value to targeted consumer segments. Here, for example, is a small ball innovation that can make a material difference for customers. *Bays English Muffins* recently integrated resealable packaging into its six-pack of English muffins. Now consumers who pull out two muffins to toast and eat at breakfast no longer have to worry about the remaining four muffins getting stale over the next couple of mornings. Little things can mean a lot, right?

Such addition/deletion processes, however, often prove more complicated in nature. The *Miss America* contest deleted the swimsuit competition from its product during 2018. This NPD action was surely logical, from a public relations perspective, in an entertainment marketplace that was then being dominated by *#metoo*-like movements. The deletion also made sense insofar as men generally weren't watching anymore; consequently men did not miss what they were no longer watching anyway. Years ago men more routinely watched because the show provided one of the few venues in which they could secretly ogle scantily clad women without pissing-off the women around them. Today the male demographic has free or "reasonably" priced internet porn to ogle. Internet porn, yes, was once an innovation too. What has really happened is that societal/cultural, demographic, lifestyle, and technological trends co-mingled in ways that portended and necessitated that NPD-related changes be introduced to the old-school brand that is *Miss America*. Societal/cultural trends include the #metoo movement. Lifestyle trends include changing male preferences. Technological trends include readily available, literally "24/7/365 everywhere" porn.

The beauty pageant, a marketing competition, has become more a women's thing. Thus, the event's marketers logically spend more time focusing on aspects of the show that cater toward a female demographic—here, the targeted segment. For the product and brand to survive for a few more years *Miss America* marketers had to dramatically change its marketing mix and target marketing tactics.

Truly new-to-the-world products also exist. At one time in history time there were no personal computers, and then desktops were around. The first cell phone, or the first smartphone (2007), were introduced to worlds that previously had neither seen nor experienced any values of the sort that either new product conveniently offered at the time.

There are also new-to-the-firm products. Marketing organizations will generally acquire new products by purchasing existing firms, whole, or by acquiring the rights to market an existing product themselves. Either product acquisition strategy would generally be executed either to eliminate competitors or to secure access to new market segments.

Finally, strategic efforts aimed at re-positioning or re-targeting existing products for new or existing customers also constitute NPD. As do cost reductions (i.e., developing newer, less expensive products that are intended to replace older existing, more expensive products).

Professionals should take NPD personally. They should personally embrace the prospect of earning a reputation for creativity or re-position their professional brands as the go-to, first-choice creative alternative if the label already fits and is appropriate and opportune for them to pursue. Earning and benefiting from a brand image that identifies you as a creative thinker and doer will never go out of style in any marketing context. When accounting, financial, managerial, IT, or marketing professionals upgrade themselves or what they're doing and consequently add value to their brand, they're re-branding and creating a new and improved product. When professionals stop doing something negative that was detracting from their value, they are engaging in the same positive repositioning or rebranding processes. By the way, whenever professionals stop doing stupid stuff, letting the world know about these positive changes through subtle means is probably best.

Professionals should always view themselves as brand-able products.

WHAT ARE THE TWO MOST BASIC NPD STRATEGIES?

Most marketers must develop steady streams of successful new products and services or else they cannot succeed long-term. This not-new statement remains true and relevant even though some, perhaps many, of these new products fail. Firms must move forward continuously for the same reasons that sharks must continuously swim forward—unless they (organizations or sharks) are ready to die.

Marketing organizations generally develop new products through two methods. The first method entails acquisition. Acquisition might entail buying entire companies whole, acquiring rights to patents, or acquiring licenses to produce someone else's products. *Facebook*, which by all measures is a creative company, has bought *WhatsApp, Instagram,* and *Messenger*. This is called a buy NPD strategy.

The second method entails actually engaging in NPD activities themselves. NPD activities entail developing original products, making product improvements, introducing product modifications, or launching new brands/renewing positioning strategies through marketers' internal management of their marketing mixes. At other times, marketers save money and presumably lower their risk and effort by copying competitor's products and creating close facsimiles. Not for nothing did the phrase "imitation is the sincerest form of flattery" long ago enter the Western cultural vocabulary. This is called a make NPD strategy.

When marketing organizations develop new products they often gain entry to new target market segment opportunities.

HOW DO NPD PROCESSES USUALLY UNFOLD IN REAL MARKETING LIFE?

During NPD processes marketers strive to create *new* products or services that promise and deliver *new* practical or perceptual value to targeted customers. Hopefully, the value delivered through those new products/services also differs from and is better than other values currently being marketed by any competitor firms.

When focused NPD processes begin, marketers may not always know exactly what those new products or services will end up being. This is because NPD is based on ideas. This is where creativity comes into play.

At the start, marketers may not exactly understand how much the new product/service will cost to make and market. However, marketers engaged in NPD should have a sense and create a rough budget. Marketers should always have a plan.

At the start of the NPD process, marketers may not know exactly how the new product, once developed, will be distributed, promoted, or priced. But still, marketers should possess or quickly create reasonably accurate insights about whether and how their current marketing mix or prospective marketing given resource constraints and expected returns.

At the start of the NPD process, what happens is somebody or some team creates a new idea that proves convertible into new product or service offering values that appeal to somebody—hopefully to a large and identifiable targeted segment.

This is roughly how NPD processes unfold, or should unfold, in real marketing life.

WHAT'S NECESSARY TO EXECUTE NPD SUCCESSFULLY?

Three factors clearly contribute materially to successful NPD efforts. The first factor is strategic planning. The second factor is effective managerial execution. The final factor is individual/organizational creativity.

WILL SUCCESSFUL NPD ALONE ENSURE SUCCESS?

The universal answer to this question is no, because even for marketers as powerful as *Nike*, the basics still must fit—and work properly. Thirty-three seconds into what many experts deem the greatest rivalry in sports (*University of North Carolina* versus *Duke University*; NCAA Men's College Basketball), boom—things blew up instantly. The 2018–19 freshman phenom *Zion Williamson*, all 6'7" 285 pounds of him, got injured when he drove to the rack, pivoted right, and his *Nike* shoes literally split in two. *Zion* missed the next nine *Duke* basketball games and *Nike's* public relations nightmare began.

Social media exploded—again in an instant. Even NBA star *Paul George*, namesake of the sneaker brand Williamson was wearing, tweeted . . . "What happened?" *Nike's* stock tumbled the next day. This all happened while *Nike* was promoting some cutting-edge technology, such as self-lacing shoestrings.

This sort of thing has happened before. Well-meaning and properly innovatively-minded executives and managers take their eyes off the ball—here, *Nike's* core business mission of marketing performance-enhancing [not physically-incapacitating] and well-fitting shoes, which is, after the giant's core business model—to chase a shiny new invention. Let's face it, machine-tied shoes are unlikely to prove determinant when any individual consumer or organization is deciding which brand of shoes to purchase. Relatively silly, only presumably innovative improvements often don't end well if the basics get ignored in the process because corners have been cut. Even the most creative firms should never get so busy chasing tomorrow's products that they forget key success fundamentals such as quality, reliability, and promised and delivered performance that earned them the past success that they have enjoyed right up until today.

Other more subtle yet naturally arising reasons exist why successful NPD alone is not enough to ensure success. Such reasons typically wrap around our own natures as humans. For example, it's human nature to resist change. This resistance to change often leads to huge problems as marketers attempt to gain market acceptance for new product ideas and solutions.

An *English* innovator named William Petty observed in 1679: "When a new invention is first propounded, in the beginning every man objects . . . not one (innovator) out of one hundred outlives this torture."[7] Mr. Petty was right. Keep in mind that all these products once were, but also still remain, innovations. Innovations such as vaccinations, anesthetics, steam engines, railroad transportation and travel, and electricity all encountered serious market and consumer resistance when they were first introduced. Yet each formerly disruptively-innovative product category is still around. And especially in the case of vaccinations or analgesics which are still innovating as rapidly as possible. Witness the new *Johnson & Johnson, Moderna,* or *Pfizer* COVID-19 vaccinations that were developed during 2020 and introduced to great acclaim to the US consumer market during 2021.

Or take bicycles, introduced as an innovation to the world in 1817 as a branded new product called the *Swiftwalker.* Bicycles did not become popular until the 1880s. In part, this was because numerous cultural and medical critics feared that bicycles would create a generation of hunchbacks given that riders leaned forward constantly. Bicycles were also subjected to accusations that sitting on bike seats would make women infertile. Female riders were further chastised for risking the emergence of "bicycle faces." The unfounded concern was that clenching one's jaw and focusing one's eyes while balancing on two wheels would force women to get stuck in unflattering facial grimaces.

We're not ridiculing these historical consumer cohorts or cultural critics. Similar sorts of anxieties have generated contemporary pushbacks against innovations such as the internet, video games, genetically modified organisms, and stem-cell research. But in the end, each contemporary innovation obviously delivered desired values, provided solutions that were clearly superior to the solutions that prior products competing inside the same category had delivered, and were accompanied by relentless marketing efforts. It was no surprise that each innovation was quickly and broadly accepted within their targeted market segments.

This is not to suggest that some fears about certain innovations are not well founded. Innovations generate consequences. Those consequences will break good or break, with interpretations of whether the changes were good or bad generally dependent upon one's point of viewing. Traditional cultural values are routinely disturbed by innovations; again, for better or worse dependent upon one's point of view. Innovations, particularly of the primarily technological sort, will destroy some old jobs and professionals even as they are creating some new ones. Friction results, and individuals who are either unwilling or unable to change see their future professional prospects bruised if not outright destroyed.

---

7. Johan Norberg, "Why We Can't Stop Longing for the Good Old Days," *Wall Street Journal* (December 26, 2020): C. 6.

Module 10.2

Creativity

Why is creativity so important inside NPD contexts? One answer is revealed in the three ready-for-their-on-a-poster-inscription, verses that follow:

"Every morning in Africa, a gazelle wakes up.
He knows he must run faster than the fastest lion, or be eaten.

Every morning in Africa, a lion also wakes up.
She knows she must outrun the slowest gazelle, or starve to death.

In Africa, it doesn't matter whether you are lion or gazelle.
When the sun comes up, you had best be ready to run."

Are you more lion or more gazelle? What's your preference? The answers to either question actually do not matter. Because if professionals plan to compete and earn/retain decent or better jobs inside today's globalized marketplace,[8] they had best wake up every single day ready to run—hard, fast, and long.

Today's domestic marketing lions or gazelles realistically cannot hope to out-compete, out-work, or out-cheap their foreign professional competitors. For starters, domestic professionals simply cannot afford to execute their services at the same low salaries foreign professionals will accept. Domestic professionals will not routinely outsmart foreign competitors either. After all, many of their foreign competitors attended the same universities as domestic professionals did. And all of them use the same technology tools that contemporary domestic professionals use. The only long-term hope for US professionals is to out-create their foreign competitors. By the way, no reference has been made

---

8. In today's globalized marketplaces most domestic professionals compete at least indirectly with foreign professionals, robotic devices, or other AI forms that can perform the same job just as well but less expensively than them. Yes, even physicians, attorneys, professors, or accountants.

here regarding the threat that AI imposes upon entire professional sectors. But that threat is already real and destined to radically expand, as was discussed above.

Another rationale exists underscoring why today up-and-coming professionals should grow into the most creative version of themselves. C-Level executives were recently asked to identify the "Top Ten Traits" they seek from new hires. In decreasing order of importance they responded:

> Critical problem-solving skills, critical thinking skills, creativity, people management skills, coordinating with others; emotional intelligence; judgment/decision-making skills, a service-orientation, negotiating skills, and cognitive flexibility.

Seven of these "Top-Ten" most desirable hiring traits relate directly or indirectly to creativity.

DEFINED AND DESCRIBED

Creativity entails seeing or experiencing the same stimuli as everyone but being willing and able to think about and develop something new that others don't think about or develop. The new something often involves creative ideas that harbor great potential value. Creative ideas portend great value because they may lead to new and useful solutions (i.e., innovations) that solve customer problems.

Creativity entails the ability to produce intangible or tangible things that are novel or original and useful or adaptive. Creativity, however, never requires that something be created from nothing. As if it were possible to create something from nothing. This is an argument that *Christian* apologists often make when arguing for their case that an Intelligent Designer—apologists designate him God—created the universe and the earth within it.

The exact opposite of creating something from nothing prevails among creative marketers. Creative marketers almost always create new products by combining or recombining elements that already exist. What's more, creative marketers consciously or unconsciously refashion things. These refashioning processes usually necessitate the thoughtful execution of one or more of three NPD activities—bending, breaking, or blending.

Bending, Breaking, Blending

Bending involves taking something and altering a property, aspect, or dimension of the original element or object; as in redesigning. Take the human heart, for example. No need exists to over-romanticize or over-complicate the human heart because hearts are nothing more or less than bags full of muscles that pump. The artificial human heart was a great new product, if one ever existed. Initial researchers copied the human heart as closely as possible, beats and all. But continuous beating led to excessive wear and tear and consequently shorter shelf-lives for artificial hearts. Continuous beating was also completely unnecessary because all hearts must do is pump; *Dr. Dre*, we're sorry but when the subject turns to hearts beats don't matter. Today's new artificial hearts are continuous flow in nature—no more heartbeats required. Less wear and tear results. Products and solutions last longer. Better value emerges.

Breaking entails taking whole things apart and reassembling something new and useful from the pieces. Breaking is analogous to reengineering an existing entity, including products. Modern presidential campaigns, operating as marketing endeavors promoting uniquely new products (remember, people are products and politicians, purportedly, are people), have existed since 1960. No such campaign, however, featured the mold-breaking approach used by *Donald Trump* during the 2016 US presidential election cycle. Candidate *Donald Trump* took an existing product (traditional presidential campaigning), and broke the whole traditional thing apart. First, by largely bypassing traditional media by using tweets and texts. Second, by degrading his opponent's branding power by derisively nicknaming them ("*Lying Ted*" or "*Crooked Hillary*"). Third, by communicating with potential voters using everyday, often near-street language rather than prewritten and presumably soaring rhetoric that had been focus group-tested to within inches of its persuasive life.

Blending involves mixing solutions from previously related or unrelated sources together in new ways. *Constellation*, a *Canadian* brewer, is chasing a new type of buzz. The beer marketer is seeking first-mover marketing advantage by developing drinkable cannabis products containing alcohol. The NPD blending process is analogous to creating new intersections. An intersection was established at the point where the ideas to create products that combined pot-highs with beer-buzzes first got together and engaged in sex with one another.

Other products currently being developed by US marketers in the growing numbers of states where pot is legal include buzz-inducing sodas, coffees, and fruit elixirs. Wine and spirits marketers are not sitting still, either, as marijuana continues to be legalized in more states. This environmental trend represents a threat to some and an opportunity to other marketers. But hopefully, for their sakes, no brewers or distilleries are ignoring the trend.

CREATIVE PROFESSIONALS ARE . . .

Creative professionals are usually better at solving complicated problems. They excel at problem-solving often because the most creative professionals are typically oriented more toward thinking in terms of "we/us" than "me/mine."

Creative professionals problem-solve effectively because they consciously couple "so what" questions with "why not" questions. Consciously coupling as in creating intersections.

Creative professionals usually occupy go-to roles inside organizations toward who others go to for solutions when big, hairy, or audacious problems arise. Likely, in no small measure because creative professionals are oriented to think beyond simply asking "What should we do" questions toward asking "What could we do" questions. Hmmm, seems like creatives are not only oriented toward answering questions, they typically willingly ask questions too.

Creative professionals are much, much better than average at recognizing obscure relationships between previously unconnected stimuli, events, or ideas that less creative people ignore or altogether miss.

Creative professionals are better at establishing associations and connections between existing and new ideas. This discussion smacks of intersections again, doesn't it?

Creative people often see old things in original ways.

Creative professionals often see or experience stimuli, events, or ideas that others don't even sense—perhaps those others are too busy peering into phones.

Creative winners, and that's what they usually are, typically do things that non-creatives either fear doing, or are too lazy to do, or both.

Creative professionals typically work much harder than average professionals in their specific fields. Probably because they almost always love their work and are paid substantially more than most other marketers who share their field for doing it.

Creative professionals are often accurately described as polymaths. The brand-like polymath designation implies that creative professionals typically possess and are driven by broad interests across many fields. Polymaths are people whose base of knowledge touches many subjects and was usually self-taught.

One would be foolish to sell short the creative value and power of polymaths, or the value associated with becoming a polymath oneself. Serial polymaths helped create the disciplines now known as:

- Sociology;
- Semiotics, the study of signs, or branding-power;
- Cybernetics (the science of communications and automatic control systems inside both machine and human minds);
- Biometrics (ways to measure people's physical characteristics to verify their identities) and the like.

Why it just so happens that a polymathic marine biology student who became a physiologist ended up creating the discipline known as psychoanalysis. His first name was Sigmund. His last name was discussed during the research module.

Creative people are also often described as autodidactic. High-creatives typically teach themselves rather than waiting to be fed by others—that's what autodidacts do. *Bill Gates, Steve Jobs,* or *Mark Zuckerberg* come to mind as uber-successful college dropouts. The minds of autodidacts function like grappling hooks that reach out and tightly grab any subjects that attract their attention. The objects that capture their attention are usually many and varied. The extreme value of the intersection concept, again, becomes apparent.

Autodidacts usually have much, much quicker than average minds. You knew that, even though before you read the preceding paragraph you may not have known what an autodidact is.

Maybe you're autodidactic yourself. Hope so. Autodidacts, on average, are rather effective jugglers—usually of ideas.

The apparel/fashion market sector is one of the few marketing mediums that can fully accommodate high-end autodidactic thinkers. A primary reason is because single garment or bag items can easily accommodate a dozen ideas at once.

Creative people often share similar personality traits. They are, generally, more venturesome and exploratory. Creatives knowingly and willing take more and bigger risks. Creatives usually travel a lot and read widely. Notably, each personality trait can be cultivated.

Creative professionals typically understand and accept that the best creative work occurs at the frontiers of what is known. Which is cool, and important, because when professionals work at the creative edge of what is known, they frequently get cut—and bleed. Bleeding is like failure in at least one important way, each hurts. And all non-masochistic people prefer to avoid pain. The pain that accompanies failure hurts creative people; they're human, after all. But failure's pain either hurts or restrains creatives less, in comparison to non-creatives. Creatives soldier on when experiencing failure. Creative people persist, despite rejection or occasional failure, because they believe in themselves and in the value of what they do. And perhaps creatives persist because they understand, by dint of their wisdom, experience, or inborn grittiness that sometimes you must take risks, overcome failure, or work harder before you get the biscuit.

Love it or not, most *Americans* live in a winners take, well, if not all, most of the dollars and acclaim that are available for some bright and assertive person to grab. And true creatives are more likely to be big winners. The reason why is simple. Creative professionals are far more capable than less creative professionals to solve important problems.

GROWING CREATIVITY—SHOULD DO[S]

Few if any marketers cannot convert from paint-by-numbers status to *Vincent van Gogh* levels of creativity overnight, but most can evolve upward toward greater creativity by rigorously honoring a few simple principles. For example, the willingness to act based upon the following five simple, easily acquired behaviors and skill sets would inherently make professionals more creative inside their interior thought-lives. People who become more creative in their thinking are more likely to generate higher quantities of more creative ideas. Which is everything insofar as successful NPD always begins with ideas.

No contemporary idea that appears antiquated today exists that was not once modern—absolutely cutting- or bleeding-edge. No contemporary idea is so modern today that it will not one day be viewed as antiquated—so last year. Ideas can and do arrive from anywhere. Ideas must be appreciated when found and cultivated and appreciated when they are not readily available—when the fruit is not hanging low enough to be easily plucked.

Capturing for Oneself

So how can professionals consciously cultivate—grow—their own creativity? To begin with, professionals should capture for themselves. Capturing involves preserving new ideas as they occur and preserving ideas without judging them. Many ways exist to capture new ideas.

Dr. Otto Loewi won the *Nobel Prize in Medicine* for creating solutions that he developed based on an idea about cellular biology that he almost failed to capture. He had the idea in his sleep, woke up, and scribbled the new concept or idea on a pad. But the next morning he couldn't read his notes or remember the idea. When the idea appeared again in his dreams the following night, he used a better capturing technique. The professor wrote the idea down more clearly, put on his pants, and went straight to his lab! Of course today Dr. Loewi would have captured the idea on his smartphone.

This notion that creatives are likely to do their best and most creative thinking out of the office is borne out in recent experience, as well. Only 10 percent of professionals say they do their best thinking—creatively foraging through ideas—at work. During 2019 the *Wall Street Journal* reported that 49 percent of professionals said they do their best thinking at home. No one who knows creativity could be surprised by this information.

Challenging Oneself

Professionals seeking to become more creative in their thoughts and actions should strategically challenge themselves. They could, for example, ask their boss to assign the toughest problems by name to them. In challenging situations, multiple thoughts and behaviors must compete with one another inside our minds. That's a good thing—for creativity. These forced interconnections—intersections—create new behaviors and promote new ideas.

According to the recently-deceased *Dallas Willard*, a mind-life that fully and simultaneously integrates the secular and spiritual is a life likely bursting with creativity, especially since he further argued that God is the original source of all creativity. This is no small thing, in business or in life; or inside scientific, technological, or humanitarian thought. Inevitably, the best thinkers and doers inside any discipline have combined, inside their own minds, mastery over scientific thinking in combination with deep knowledge of or strong appreciation for humanitarian thought.

Broadening Oneself

Literally coming back to earth professionals who aspire to greater creativity should also strategically broaden their interior thought-lives. Broadening involves exposing oneself to more intersections and intersectional thinking. Reading extensively—processing real text, rather than texts—helps. As their knowledge bases broaden and automatically diversify, professionals can more readily establish interesting and useful interconnections inside their professional lives. All professionals have wonderful opportunities to boost their creativity as laid out before themselves to boost their fun and creativity. All that's required is a willingness to learn interesting new things.

Surrounding Oneself

Professionals could also further elevate their creativity by surrounding themselves. Surrounding implies that professionals should consciously immerse themselves among and around people and ideas that continuously force them to change or upgrade the quality of their thoughts and reasoning. Many professionals enjoy the opportunity to manage their physical and social environments. The more interesting and diverse the ideas and the people around them are, the more interesting those professionals' subsequent ideas should become.

Does anyone get better at playing chess, tennis, or wrestling by competing against people who play chess, tennis, or wrestle worse than you? The answer is no, and with that professionals should see the creative value inherent in this simple proposition.

Embracing Boredom

Professionals seeking to become more creative should embrace boredom. Boredom is good.

Boredom that is boring the way that hot, empty afternoons in late July used to get during the *Baby Boomer* generation's summer break from school; that's the good stuff. Not boring like the eighth season of a reality TV show is boring where, yes, lots of inauthentic crap is happening but none of the infotainment is real which means none of it actually means anything or thought-provoking. (Thought-provoking; that is the key phrase here.) In brief, not only is there nothing new to say or think about this sort of boredom, no new ideas are likely to emerge, either.

However, a great way to embrace and to create the right type of boredom in these current times is to stay off technology for pre-ordained periods of time, possibly extending for a day or two. People's minds run free and wild when they get bored. Minds running free and wild often stumble into unexpected intersections. Intersections facilitate creativity.

Humans biologically require boredom to let their minds roam toward newer and more exciting arenas. Technology makes us forget or never learn much of what we ought to know about life . . . and never allows us to get bored because with each new click tech pours more dopamine into our brains. Or, for that matter bored with things that should never bore us, such as sex. Yes, internet porn was just discretely referenced again, but again in a completely appropriate fashion given that internet porn was once a new product and did more than any other marketed product to spur the astoundingly rapid proliferation of the internet that began in earnest just less than thirty years ago. Internet porn, as a carefully segmented, highly targeted, and frankly successfully positioned product, also that did more than anything that did not arrive with a screen attached to grow internet-marketing into the vast, industrial-sized beast it has long since become.

INTERSECTIONS REMAIN CONTINUOUSLY IMPORTANT INSIDE CREATIVE PROCESS

Intersections—their creation, presence, and exploitation—are incredibly valuable. The fact that intersections should be created as a means of enabling creativity is also entirely logical. Combining existing concepts to make new concepts is essentially the purpose of algebra, and nothing is more logical than math.

Liberals need conservatives, for example. Liberals' political ideas—their new and old products, and presumed solutions—are deficient because they are insufficiently diverse.

Conservatives need liberals. Conservatives' political ideas—their new and old products, and presumed solutions—are deficient because are insufficiently diverse.

Yet were the naturally-divergent ideas offered by libs and cons actually forced to contend for supremacy inside the middle ground that the creation of intersectional settings would offer, were the free and open exchange of ideas not just be permitted but encouraged inside political marketing practice, better ideas and new and superior political solutions would result. Of course, inside heavily socially-networked media and political settings where the intersectional mating of opposing—and diverse—ideas is generally not only not permitted but implicitly or actively discouraged, the exact opposite happens. So honestly, today's political failures are driven largely though not entirely by marketing media, including not just the cable news networks but also social networking media.

The evidence—what has this lack of intersectionality created—is clear and incontrovertible. When and where one and only one ideological perspective is permitted, the creativity of emergent ideas and solutions diminishes. To illustrate the point, consider how the livability and survivability quotients that prevail inside cities such as *Detroit, Chicago*, or *San Francisco* have materially deteriorated during the five decades where one party rule has prevailed. Only one ideological point of view was played out because few to no intersections were allowed to exist inside these cities. Meanwhile, the consequences endured by most of the citizenry in these places have proven dire.

And new, useful, and quality political solutions soon disappeared from anyone's consideration set, simply because creative solutions are never born in the first place. Who suffers? Not competing sets of marketing pols. They get paid anyway, while in and especially after leaving office. The marketplaces that are full of voters whose needs/problems politicians are typically not solving, they're the ones getting screwed.

MORE ESOTERIC PATHS ALONG WHICH CREATIVITY MAY BE GROWN

Brainpower, important as it is, will only take anyone so far. Simple luck, as in the sort that some people appear to involuntarily accrue, well, that juice eventually also dries up for almost everyone. Even when one tosses in hard work and adds it to brainpower and luck, no guarantee of success follows. No, creativity is the missing ingredient for most smart and hardworking professionals who have yet to earn success. Creativity is the secret sauce inside the secret recipe that when combined with brains and hard work will transform any marketing professional into the entire package. So, what are some other paths along which marketers can grow their own creativity?

We count five such paths. Each follows.

First . . . Create Intersections

To become and remain more creative, marketing professionals should establish more intersections in their interior thought-lives. Okay, inside their minds. All new creations emerge from this exact locale. Intersections were in play when marketers crossed waffles with doughnuts; *Jewish* bagels hooked up with *Italian* pizza; and *German* frankfurters were combined with *Mexican* chili. The new products now known as wonuts, pizza bagels, and frankfurters emerged as a result. Leave it up to the fast-food sector to discover exciting new ways to force more consumers to purchase two airplane seats—for themselves. Perhaps *American* or *Delta Airlines* should send the domestic fast-food industry a thank-you note.

Intersections are produced whenever anyone introduces two or more sets of disciplinary thinking inside their own mind. In effect, intersectional-minded marketers create cross-disciplinary deliberations inside their heads. The process can be straightforward. When solving complex problems, marketers could consciously decide to ruminate about how a marketer combined with an accountant combined with a *Navy Seal*—all wrapped inside one professional mind—might try to solve the problem. That's an intersection, and that's intersectional thinking.

In history's greatest point of creative intersection, great scholars worked for more than a millennium in the ancient library that *Alexander the Great* established in *Alexandria, Egypt*. Before the product[9] was destroyed by *Islamic* invaders in 642 AD, *Euclid* developed geometry there; *Archimedes* discovered pi and laid the foundation for calculus; and *Eratosthenes* posited that the earth was round and calculated its circumference to about 1 percent accuracy. Astronomers postulated a heliocentric universe; *Galen* revolutionized medicine; and geometers deduced that a year's length was 365.5 days and proposed adding a leap year every fourth—while each set of disciplinary thought-leaders were housed inside this intersectional residence. Geographers working inside the library speculated that voyagers could reach *India* from *Spain* by sailing west; in-library engineers developed hydraulics and pneumatics; and anatomists discovered that the human brain and nervous systems represented one unit and developed cardio and digestive track system principles that remain unchanged to this day. Nutritionists even conducted food experiments—the original marketing researchers?

An impressive list of creativity and innovative progress, for certain. But that's not the primary point. No, the major point instead is that no overarching doctrine or philosophy drove this NPD. Instead, a global intersectional cosmopolitanism, a determination to assemble accumulated knowledge absent regard for culture, nation, or origins, arose and coupled (i.e., had unprotected sex). New and useful ideas could not help but emerge.

Yet intersections don't always work. The purportedly accidental union of peanut butter and chocolate, as was once prominently promulgated by *Reese's* as the firm advertised its Peanut Butter Cups, actually degraded the amazing independent appeal of each life-affirming food group in the eyes of some.

Intersections exist as the key to creative success at personal, professional, or organizational levels. How do people create more, stronger intersections inside their own minds?

Second . . . Lower One's Own Associative Barriers

To create more and stronger intersections inside their thought lives, marketing professionals could lower their and others' associative barriers. But mostly their own. That's because associative barriers inhibit marketers from making connections between heretofore dissimilar things.

---

9. *Alexandria's* library surely generated great value in solving myriad problems and therefore merits this designation as a "product."

Among the first things law school students are taught is that one of the worst arguments they could ever make is that "we have always done things this way." That sort of thinking is also death to creative thinking. So, what are associative barriers? Associative barriers are those typically intractable mind-notions that we should not change because "we have always done things this way."

Associative barriers function like chains holding down professionals, restraining them from thinking more creatively when facing the sorts of complicated business and customer problems that need to be solved today. The presence of associative barriers increases professionals' sense of certainty, even in situations where individual professionals' known solutions are wrong and their current perspectives are not up to the task. To enhance creativity, marketers should loosen their grip on [their] certainties—their associative barriers—to expand their range of possibilities. We're guessing many otherwise best-selling books have been prevented by earnest, well-informed and associative-barrier burdened teachers or editors.

Associative barriers are not all bad. The presence of associative barriers is in fact, what makes professionals professional inside their respective fields—accounting, systems management, logistics, finance, marketing, medicine, the law. So in this regard associative barriers are useful. Indeed, their existence is necessary for professionals to perform professionally because associative barriers readily provide known solutions to known problems. But these known, frankly simpler, problems—the low-hanging fruit noted earlier inside this Module—have mostly already been solved. This final condition represents the real problem, and most pressing creative challenge.

Shortly after his three-year official ministry began a Jewish rabbi named *Jesus*[10] discovered that he had to push back against nearly all other *Jewish* religious leaders of his day. And all he was doing, at net, was to market a few creative ideas about religion and to "slow-play"—imploring his disciples to not tell anyone about this—his performance of a few miracles. Talk about new and useful solutions. The real reason Jesus needed to push back against The Man was simple. Seems the creative ideas he taught were antithetical to what the *Jewish Pharisees* and *Sadducees* already "knew" was true. Those *Jewish* leaders were bound up in associative barriers about the best (right) ways to explain various unknowable phenomena and the Law they applied to solve particular problems.

The presence of their associative barriers neither distinguished nor differentiated those *Jewish* leaders. All humans have associative barriers. In fact, the more professionals learn about any given discipline (i.e., marketing, logistics, accounting, physics, chemistry, psychology, sniper-ship, baseball), and the more experience professionals accumulate inside those disciplines, the more likely they are to get wrapped up in and weighed down by their associative barriers. Cliché-alert, such professionals find it difficult to think outside the box. Which is death to creativity, creative processes, and inspired solutions. The most pressing challenge to creating intersections and becoming more creative themselves that most professionals will ever confront are the associative barriers that exist inside their own minds.

Highly creative thinking is necessary to solve today's most pressing problems. When only highly creative reasoning and solutions will solve problems, successful marketing professionals must eliminate their own associative barriers. The question thus becomes, how?

---

10. A history book called *Antiquities of the Jews*, written by Roman historian *Flavius Josephus* in 93/94 AD, makes two direct and one indirect reference to a "Jesus of Nazareth." The word rabbi means teacher.

Third . . . Integrate Multiple Perspectives to Lower Associative Barriers and Build Intersections

Marketing professionals should consciously integrate multiple perspectives into their lives. This integrative process might involve thinking like a marketer, like a logistician, like a financial analyst, like a historian, like a philosopher, all at the same time, when seeking to develop ideas creative enough to solve pressing problem. Of course, individual professionals can integrate this sort of diverse thinking inside their own heads, in and of and by themselves. People who know a little about a lot are much more creative than those who know a lot about a little. Deep divers tend to remain stuck in holes they have dug for themselves. We called those holes associative barriers. Of course, as just reported, associative barriers are not all bad. But the presence of high and strong associative barriers spells nothing but trouble for professionals seeking to become more creative. Meanwhile, people who know little about anything aren't likely to respond creatively to pressing problems, or to turn professional for that matter.

The serially entrepreneurial marketer *Elon Musk*, *Tesla's* daddy, and his thought-crew, employed multiple perspectives when asked to solve the problem that arose when twelve young Thai football players and their coach were stranded in the cave during 2018. The solution, which involved a submersible escape capsule constructed of rocket parts, likely would have worked had the scuba diver solution failed.

To create multiple perspectives inside their minds, professionals might consciously choose to watch FOX and *MSNBC* news or to read the *Wall Street Journal* and the *New York Times*. Every day. The experience might hurt, but not kill, certain close-minded professionals. Their thought-spectrum and solutions-bandwidth would radically expand. These newspaper media giants address the same basic issues every day, except on Sunday in the case of *The Journal*. These highly-divergent—in terms of their editorial views—news and informational sources invariably propose radically different solutions to the day's most pressing problems. When two radically-different takes exist on the best way to solve problems, where do you believe the best possible solution exists? Yes, us too. Someone in the middle.

Or, multiple-perspective seekers might opt to simply read, while shelving technology. Professionals might visit as many different domestic places and countries as possible—even if only online! Everyone could choose to share workday or school day lunches as often as possible with people who do not look like them. People who don't look like us generally have different experiences and insights from us. Readers may be amazed at how their perspectives and *creative prowess evolve.* As *British* political economist *John Stuart Mill* wrote, "He who only knows his side of the case knows little of that." Viewing complicated issues through a single lens is unhelpful.

Not really into reading, especially long articles or books with real paragraphs? If this description describes you that's too bad, but non-deep-reading readers surely have lots of company today. Even so, individuals who are seeking broader perspectives in order to enhance their creativity could begin visiting new places and consequently experience new experiences (perspectives!), drawing the strength and motivation to do this from knowing that one day of seeing and experiencing things firsthand is worth more than a month of teaching.

Multiple perspectives is code-speak for diversity. Diversity, in turn, is the answer to the question: Besides intersections, what's the best source of new creative ideas? Human beings gradually accumulate new ideas which lead to new solutions. This has happened forever. New products—each of which function as technologies—from stone axes to smartphones almost always emerge from the interaction of many individual problems solvers rather than lone geniuses. Cultural evolutions emerge slowly or quickly but inevitably as a consequence.

A central challenge of cultural evolution is how to manage imitation and innovation. Imitation allows creators to take advantage of all the ideas that their creative ancestors discovered before them. Innovation naturally also remains crucial. If everybody precisely copied everybody else, no creative progress would occur. So what's the best approach for solving real-world problems for creating the new solutions that we call products? Intersections and diversity, these are the keys. Rather than the random contributions of occasional lone superstar creators (who actually do exist and have existed), the combination (intersection!) of different kinds of knowledge, perspectives, temperatures, and humble tweaks and bold leaps is what produces creative new solutions.

Fourth... "Don't Fear the Reaper"—Okay, Failure

Professionals, marketing and otherwise, could consciously avoid certain creativity-defeating psychological traps that influence how they respond to risks and the prospects of failure that accompany failure. The most damaging psychological trap that most people ever confront is their often-irrational, often-bordering on debilitating, fear of failure.

Prospect Theory is a *Nobel Prize*-winning economics theory. *Prospect Theory* uses complicated analytics to explain a simple, nearly-universal principle that exercises a disproportionate amount of influence on human decision-making. The principle is that most people hate/fear losing far more than they love/crave winning.

The consequence of this principle is that too many people refuse to even try in risky situations because they fear the painful prospect of failure. A situation similar to what a minor character in *HBO*'s norm-breaking 2000's-era show *The Wire* arises. She said, "You cannot lose if you do not play." To which we'd respond, you're right. But you cannot win, or in this context become more creative, either, unless you play.

Marketing professionals who feel this way, that is, who feel and respond like most humans feel and respond, then often confront two undesirable options. Inside the first option, most people endure *Henry David Thoreau*-like lives of quiet desperation. You know what Henry David mean: Concerned mostly with paying bills on time, keeping their kids happy and healthy, preserving their property, and keeping families safe. Not worried about vacationing in *Europe* or owning a condo on *Lake Tahoe*. Yep, even the successful pursuit of these ordinary outcomes is a beat-down in today's hypercompetitive markets.

Or inside option two, people live out mediocre lives—perhaps occasionally whining about how the rich and powerful get all the breaks, while foreswearing their chance of becoming rich and powerful themselves because they refused to try. If professionals consciously refuse to take risks or to act creatively during a ridiculously dynamic marketing era,[11] they likely will live out average professional

---

11. This ridiculously dynamic era has already arrived but is poised to become even more of what it already is—faster still.

lives. And average professional lives may or may not suck. Depends on what individual professionals want. No value judgments to follow here.

Fact is, once creative professionals commit to avoiding this psychological trap, they won't so much think outside the box as destroy the box. The very box that once constrained them from thinking more creatively.

Fifth . . . Learn from Failures

Professionals could consciously commit to learning from failure's lessons and subsequently become comfortable with managing the prospect of failure and the need to leverage the opportunity to learn from failure. English majors might know *Samuel Beckett*, also known as the bard of noble drudgery. He famously wrote: "Fail again. Fail better." His two phrases, in a nutshell, epitomize the attitude that persistently creative people have adopted, and that those aspiring to become more creative should adopt. Most everything that everyone does will always fall short of its full potential as it first leaves the gate. That doesn't mean that creative people ever will or should stop trying.

Kemmons Wilson was a serial entrepreneur, meaning, essentially, that he regularly failed as he attempted to convert his new and creative ideas into new products and business formats. But he also had a lot of creative ideas—and was relentless. Mr. Wilson lived and worked in a pre-internet age (the 1950s and 1960s) and created the idea that eventually led to a franchised motel chain called the *Holiday Inn*. The concept behind the *Holiday Inn* was a paradigm-shifting innovation at the time.

The breakout success of *Holiday Inn* was facilitated by the concurrent development of the *U.S. Interstate Highway System*. The new interstate highway systems functioned as an uncontrollable environment trend that Mr. Wilson's idea clearly exploited. And thank goodness the idea was exploited. So, once this then-new interstate system was in place automobile drivers suddenly enjoyed opportunities to travel 600–700 or more miles a day, and end up in to them unknown regions. Naturally, these drivers experienced big problems, at least inside their own minds, if they did not have available a known, safe, reasonably-priced place in which to sleep. Mr. Wilson franchised the simple but undeniably appealing value proposition embedded in the creative idea that the same known, safe, reasonably-priced motels,[12] places that even featured the same sized black-and-white televisions, would appeal to long-distance automobile travelers. His then unique *Holiday Inn* solution to the newly emergent "OMG, where are we going to sleep tonight?" problem eventually spread along new *U.S. Interstate Highway* intersections across the entire *Lower 48*. And indeed, spread rather quickly.

Wilson once was lecturing to *MBA* students at the *Harvard Business School*. His lecture's primary topic was failure. During his lecture a student stood up and asked, "Mr. Wilson, considering how successful you are how do you profess to teach us anything about failure?" To which Mr. Wilson replied . . . "Young man, I have probably failed more times than you have even tried," as he explained how fortunate he was to have finally succeeded, despite so much initial failure.

---

12. "Hotels" have existed "forever" as hospitality-based buildings where travelers could pay for lodging and usually for food. Motels, as created by Mr. Wilson, were new and useful innovations; particularly at the moment they were introduced during the late 1950s. But now, these hospitality-based buildings were places where motor (automotive motor) travelers could pay for lodging and find known, safe, reasonably-priced sleep-based solutions virtually anywhere they traveled. Sleep is a basic need, after all. Just ask *Dr. Maslow*.

Marketing professionals should learn from their failures. They should also learn how to address failure or to address the prospect of failure from the proper perspective.

Viewing Failure from the Proper Perspective

What does it mean to view failure from the proper perspective?

Acknowledging, first, that lessons can often be learned and applied from failure.

Learning, second, the extent to which bold failures often preview more successful futures.

Understanding, third, that big-time winning is more about overcoming losing than most uninformed people suppose. When ambitiously creative people win, they remain happy for perhaps an hour. Okay, maybe a weekend. And then they begin contemplating the next opportunity to win. When people lose, they are cogitating on the loss and how things must be done differently to avoid losing next time. The choice is yours. You adopt the mind of creative winner or that of a stuck-in-defeat loser.

A fourth lesson on how to view failure from the proper perspective emerges from four now-ancient rock & rollers. The brand of the band was *The Kinks*. For a period during the mid-1960s *Kinks*' songs rivaled the popularity of *The Beatles* and *The Rolling Stones* music. The band continued to make relevant music well into the 1990s. One such song is called *Celluloid Heroes*. Its lyrics opine: "But those who are successful be always on your guard, [because] success walks hand-in-hand with failure down Hollywood Boulevard." We beg to differ, only slightly. Failure likely walks slightly ahead of success down any creative path, even each outcome continues to hold hands.

Another valuable lesson and take (perspective) on failure entails viewing the prospect or reality of fear-inducing challenges as opportunities where much might be gained (won) rather than as threats where much might be lost. Let's face it. Failure, or merely the prospect of failure, stinks. Then again, so does fertilizer or the prospect of having to spread it, largely because one especially stinky element is prominently featured in many fertilizers. But the thoughtful management of failure, like fertilizer, often proves necessary before one's ideas can grow into fully blooming successes. Even the most creative ideas rarely arrive on Planet Earth as full grown trees. New ideas are more akin to acorns or other seeds that feature loads of potential for growth into who knows what if and when they are properly nourished, and should be treated as such.

Speaking of professionals, namely professional baseball players, the sport is probably the only field of endeavor, as well as of dreams, in which professional participants can succeed only three of ten times and still be viewed as successful performers. Come to think of it, new product developers who experienced three NPD hits out of every ten NPD ideas would be deemed great performers, as well.

We Have No Secrets

In the end, there are few to no secrets to successful NPD. Successful product development is a matter of preparation, hard work, a willingness to learn from failure, and the capacity to get or remain more creative. Mistakes, at times, represent little looks forward toward what is actually possible.

Safety, as in making no hard choices or taking no risks, is no one's enemy. Heck, safety ranks number two on *Abraham Maslow's* Hierarchy of Needs hit list.

But when safety, as would be reflected in an insufficient willingness to take risks, is prioritized over all other values, three things will happen to marketing professionals. First, safe marketing professionals will rarely if ever fail. Second, said marketing professionals will exhibit little to no creativity. Third, the probability that those safe professionals will even sniff major success approaches zero.

Defaulting to safety is rarely an acceptable option for marketers who are seeking to stand-out from rather than fit-in with the professional crowd based on their creative prowess. Hold fast to the truth that few people have ever distinguished themselves until after they have learned to accept the risk of being laughed at. It's true. People cannot lose when they do not play. The downside, however, is that non-players cannot win, either.

Tolerable Risks

The preceding commentary brings to mind the following question: How does one evaluate the risk associated with not doing something, of not taking the chances that necessarily must be taken before one can become and/or remain creative? There are actually many ways to answer this question but one thing known for certain is that conducting such a risk assessment is difficult. But the risks associated with not taking any risks in service to the pursuit of creativity and to the furtherance of one's career are extremely high, especially for the many who will pursue marketing careers. Moreover, essentially everyone who reads this already is or will benefit from understanding marketing, if only to become more persuasive or influential themselves, as noted.

Yet one more reason exists for marketing managers to take reasonable risks by planning to get or remain more creative. We'll leave it up to you to determine whether we're joking: God, after all, rewards those who plan, strive, and fight to make themselves better, when and if necessary, over those who merely sit at desks and play computer games or watch *YouTube* clips while munching on chips and getting high.

S/He Got (Creative) Skills: What About You?

The pursuit of capability and inspiration to pursue greater creativity within oneself is not a race. Even equivalently-dedicated and talented would ascend the same creative curve at different rates. But the rate at which new perspectives on how to become more creative are learned and integrated into one working or personal life is important. The primary reason is that both knowledge and the propensity and willingness to act more creatively build upon themselves.

Consider any acquired skill. The skill could entail playing piano, playing poker, playing basketball. The skill could even entail the ability to exercise impulse control or the willingness to take measured risks. The earlier one begins to learn the new skill the better one's chances of "getting better all the time become," as *John Lennon* and *Paul McCartney* wrote. For those born during the last fifty-plus years since the *Beatles* broke-up, "getting better all the time" inside this context means becoming more creative.

One additional idea is worth remembering, however. It's never too late in one's professional or personal life to begin learning how to be a more creative thinker and doer.

EINSTEIN KNEW

Albert Einstein, who understood creativity and everything else, wrote that: "You cannot solve problems by using the same sort of thinking that created them" [in the first place]. This statement alone provides a sufficient argument about why aspiring marketing professionals should do whatever they can to become more creative in their thoughts and deeds. Same-old-same-old no longer cuts it; certainly not among marketing professionals yearning for success. A strong grounding in how and the willingness to act more creatively feature no expiration date. The value that will materialize from becoming and remaining more creative continuously expands across professional lifetimes.

CREATIVE DESTRUCTION

Within a twelve- or so month period that spanned portions of 2015 and 2016, *Playboy* and *Penthouse* magazines both halted production of the printed versions of their formerly popular products. Then, during 2019 a more worthy magazine—*Mad*—also ended its fifty-plus-year run. Creativity yields the opportunity for new and useful solutions to arrive; creativity also destroys opportunities for the no longer new or quite so useful to survive. Creative destruction[13] is a real thing.

But creative destruction is hardly all bad all the time. The same creatively destructive process obsoleted the *iron lung* because better, safer, and more comfortable breathing solutions came along to solve the problems of people suffering from breathing disorders.

The entwined and indeed intersecting power of globalization and digitalization has accelerated the velocity with previously-mentioned 1940s–1950s era *Australian* economist *Joseph Schumpeter's* old school notion of creative destruction is wreaking havoc throughout contemporary professional sectors. The successful professionals that are creating and leading this *brave new world* often emerge from obscure places such as *Estonia* (*Skype*) and *Galicia* (*Inditex*). And then suddenly, the products and solutions they have developed reach across the globe. Internet-based technologies permit these new business ventures to grow huge essentially overnight.

The velocity and scale of these success stories have understandably proven disconcerting and disruptive to old and even contemporary orders. The marketing organizations that champion and drive these creatively destructive successes (not an oxymoron!) generally employ minimal human capital (workers) and physical resources, partly because digital services are highly automated and party due to outsourcing. *Blockbuster* operated more than 9,000 domestic retailing stores and employed

---

13. The creative destruction process captures what happens as long-standing and by definition formerly successful products or processes are obsoleted, dismantled, and/or displaced by new, superior, and more useful, and consequently innovative products and processes. Creative destruction creates consequences. In turn those consequences benefit creative individuals or organizations who willingly embrace change. Yet those same consequences injure or outright destroy other individuals or organizations that fail to either create or to adapt.

83,000 workers as recently as 2007. *Netflix*, the primary blockbuster-buster, employs only about 2,500 workers and rents the computing power for its streaming videos from *Amazon*. The *University of Michigan* report that the 1,200 or so firms that have held initial public offerings (IPOs) in the *United States* since the year 2000 employ, on average, only 700 employees worldwide.

This new and highly creatively destructive marketing paradigm is pitiless. Today's winning marketers must constantly reinvent, reconfigure, and reposition themselves to delay the fates that befell formerly could-not-miss and could-not-possibly-fail parentage firms such as *AOL, Nokia,* or the aforementioned *Blockbuster.*

NPD drives and is driven by creative destruction processes. *Professor Schumpeter* used the label creative destruction to describe those processes by which new and innovative firms or technologies displace stodgy ones and subsequently drive long-term economic growth. Creative destruction processes are difficult on the displaced; professionals who get caught holding the short end of the innovative stick. But creative destruction benefits everyone else. Which represents two additional reasons for readers to learn how to become more creative themselves.

Unfortunately, the normal and expected effects of the economic process known as creative destruction apparently do not apply to most governmental programs. Seems like most "putatively new and useful" governmental programs that have been born are destined to live on forever.

MODULE 10.3

Managing NPD Processes

Not-To-Do lists sometimes prove as or more important as To-Do lists. Especially given the extensive discussion about failure that just transpired. While the preceding discussion about creativity and how best to develop original ideas correctly suggested that professionals should learn from failure, most professionals would still surely prefer to not fail at all. Similar to the useful lessons that flow from experience, one major problem with using failure as a teacher is that the losses and their associated pain come first, while the revelatory and presumably useful lessons that can result from failure only arrive later.

So, given that failure is generally not desirable, what lessons should marketers learn about how best to avoid NPD failure? One set of lessons to learn is that the risk of NPD failure rises substantially if the:

- Demand present within the target segment is overestimated.
  - This condition represents a strategic planning and marketing research problem.
- NP design is weak or flawed; this condition represents a design problem.
- Marketing mix is poorly planned or poorly executed.
  - This condition represents a pricing, positioning, communications, or supply chain management problem—or some combination of these problems.
- Concepts in question, that is, the ideas initially driving NPD processes are pushed through anyway despite non-supportive marketing research results.
  - This condition represents an NPD procedural problem.
- New products fail to deliver sufficient new value and sufficient differentiation does not exist.
  - This condition epitomizes flawed NPD processes.
- Costs of making, promoting, or distributing NPs prove higher than expected.
  - This condition represents a resource-allocation and planning problem.

- Competitors strike back more vigorously than anticipated. Here, the marketer that engages first in NPD processes and eventually engages in target marketing should have understood that when marketers choose segments to target they're also choosing firms against which they'll compete.
  - The condition represents a targeting problem.
- Dogs don't want to eat the (new) dog food, for whatever reason. Sure, marketer and NPD teams may have been creative and actually produced a superior new dog food. But what happens if nobody wants or needs the new products that are created? That answer is easy. Failure is what happens.
  - This condition typically represents a marketing research problem. More specifically, either the wrong sorts of tests were used or the right sorts of tests were used, while the negative results of those tests were ignored by NPD champions who pushed their new products to market anyway.

This meme about "dogs not eating the new dog food" is neither conjecture nor hypothetical. One can easily envision dog food marketers such as *Purina* or *Fancy Feast* actually creating a new dog chow brand that improves the health of dogs and consequently expands their life spans. This solution clearly solves major problems; certainly in the eyes of dogs' purchasing agents, those dogs' human pets. But these human purchasing agents rarely eat the dog food themselves. What if the taste of the new product genuinely proved repulsive to canine palates? While the new product might initially leap off grocery shelves (after all, human purchasing agents will love the promised solution), after one or two failed trial runs where Alice or Sophia refused to eat the food, it remained on the purchasing agents' pantry shelves. And then the new product is never bought again.

ADDITIONAL NPD SUCCESS LESSONS

NPD Success Lesson 1

Marketers should only deliver uniquely superior new products to market. After all, if new products are not better than existing products that they presumably are supposed to replace in the marketplace . . . why bother? Uniquely superior products, at a minimum, would be truly higher in quality. Or they might legitimately deliver superior features, attributes, benefits, solutions, and ultimately value. Perhaps the new product is actually less expensive or easier to use—again, we encounter an underlying value that simplicity confers. The relative advantage, value-wise, of the new product over existing products that the new product will supposedly supersede is indispensable to NPD success.

The amount of value that the new product provides to actual or prospective customers, relative to the older existing products, that's what matters. Products always exist to provide value and satisfy customers' wants or needs and/or solve their problems. In any decision-making situation where customers possess free-will and the means to purchase any of various competing brands from within the same product categories, customers inevitably choose the brand they perceive will deliver them the most value. And remember, value—perceived-value inside customers' minds—can arrive packaged in many forms.

If readers are sensing they have heard this same tune and these same lyrics played and sang before, they are right. And that's on purpose. This book knowingly states some critically important points over and over because repetition is the mother of skill. Repetition, or repeated exposure to the same stimuli, also motherly nurtures knowledge and the ability of readers to recall and remember. Readers who eventually become professional marketers would relatedly do well to remember this admonition as they are communicating with their customers and prospects. (Readers will encounter a communication principle called the Three-Hit Rule during Module 14.)

NPD Success Lesson 2

Once upon a time, but a time from the not so distant past, consumers of all ages were highly satisfied with the delivery options they had available to play their music. *CDs*, cassette tapes, radios, even boom boxes that muscled-up dudes toted around on their shoulders, these product alternatives were up to the job of delivering music to listeners' ears. The world was down with this. No pressing problems existed, music-delivery-wise.

Then MP-3 technology entered the world, as a new product; along with the *iPod*, as the new product category's preeminent brand. *iPods*, from their start, allowed users to store up to 10,000 songs (many more now, of course); snatch, catalogue, and classify the songs by artist or genre; play whatever song they wanted when they wanted; and take their music anywhere. The new solutions offered by this new product were so superior to prior musical solutions that consumers almost instantly felt they had a problem if they did not have the solutions now available through various MP3 technology enhanced brands. Marketing nirvana, brought to life. A new branded product that could be marketed in ways that enable the new to satisfy heretofore unrealized needs or wants or problems that customers previously did not even realize they had yet!!!

NPD Success Lesson 3

Marketers should only deliver new products based on well-defined product concepts or ideas and strategies; new products for which discernible, well-defined, and substantial target markets exist; and/or new products that deliver benefits, values, and solutions that are important to targeted segments' membership.

NPD Success Lesson 4

The only marketers that logically should pursue NPD are those characterized by relentless commitments to succeed despite an awareness that failure happens, occasionally, along with relentless commitments to engage continuously in innovation. Before professionals commit themselves fully to any important endeavor, they should ask themselves whether there is anything that they could do to talk themselves out of the commitment. If the answer is no, you are ready to go.

NPD Success Lesson 5

Marketers usually should only introduce new products that are as simple as possible for purchasers to use. Relatedly, marketers should only introduce new products whose benefits can be easily discerned by users. Some new products are so complex by nature that even in their simplest forms few could accurately describe them as simple to use. That's life in the big city; this is marketing reality.

The word simplicity, used in this context, proxies the relative ease with which new products can be used or their benefits easily understood or communicated either to primary users or purchasers.

For example, any new book is a new product. Unless they are written for target audiences so erudite or esoteric that their members cannot extract their own noses from their own behinds, new books should be written to be read, not deciphered. So should most other forms of writing. Making new books simpler to read and understand entails avoiding technical terms or analytics whenever possible, and when such jargon is sometimes unavoidable, providing definitions—as happens here.

Descending to earth, again, mull over tennis racquets—and tennis, a sport that American men once played well on a global stage. Until the early 1980s tennis racquets were roughly 70 percent the size they are today. Using the once so-called oversized but now-normally sized tennis racquet imbues players with greater power and control than the racquets that preceded it. Greater power allowed players to generate higher ball speed. Greater racquet control facilitated more accurate shot placement. The new thing beat the tar out of the old thing. What's more, the new thing was used exactly like the old thing, it just produced far superior player outcomes. The benefits were clear; the oversized racquet was easy to use. What was not to love? Nothing, and among serious players, the new replaced the old within three months or less. Game, set, match.

NPD Success Lesson 6

Marketers usually should only introduce new products that are compatible with the existing ways users do things or with the users' attitudes, beliefs, likes or dislikes, or preferences. The original *iPod* and the first oversized *Head* tennis racquet were entirely compatible with how potential users—tennis players—already did things.

NPD Success Lesson 7

Marketers, finally, should only introduce new products that are easily divisible. Divisibility, here, relates to the ease with which a new product or concept may be tried out on a limited basis How easy was it for prospective users to try out their playing partner's original iPod or oversized tennis racquet? That's right; quite easy.

Small wonder these products were so successful almost instantly.

FUNDAMENTALS ALWAYS REMAIN FUNDAMENTAL

Marketers committed to NPD processes should understand that new products have never succeeded until after targeted markets knew they existed. Nor can new products succeed unless the targeted market segments understand the problem the new entity is supposed to solve for them. And if the problem being solved by the new product is deemed important by targeted customers, well, all the better.

New product developers should never function as inventors that develop solutions running around seeking-out problems to solve, without finding them. This has happened before and will happen again.[14] Remember: Creative solutions must be new and useful in order to be designated as innovative.

Marketers who introduce their new products successfully generally understand they also need to:

- Manage absolute costs to customers effectively, as would generally be reflected in their pricing strategies.

- Make switching costs appear less onerous to customers. Switching costs are costs—measured in time, money, stress, frustration, cognitive dissonance, and so forth—associated with switching from the old product that was once used but that now is being replaced by the new product.

- Manage customer perceptions of the degree of risk/uncertainty that is involved in their decision to adopt (purchase) and/or actually use the new product. (New products are often purchased by one customer and used by another customer.) Essentially, marketers must provide assurances to customers or to prospective customers that the new product will work as promised. New product marketers must, at net, communicate effectively to targeted customer segments.

- Manage and mitigate the level of social approval required to adopt the new product. This principle would not always apply. The importance of the principle would generally pivot based on the degree to which the new product is consumed in a socially conspicuous fashion. But for some new products the question "Will my friends still like me if I use this?" is both real and a matter of grave consideration. Such factors, superfluous though they may appear to some, materially influence the rate at which certain types of socially- or conspicuously-consumed new products or ideas diffuse throughout social systems. The social system of interest here would generally exist as market segments. But remember, a market segment might consist of entire cultures, subcultures, or generations such as *Millennials, Gen X,* or *Gen Y.*

---

14. This is exactly what happened with GPS tracking devices. For years after their introduction to the marketplace GPS tracking devices were accurately derided as solutions seeking problems. Essentially, GPS devices were ridiculed right up to the point when *Walmart* strategically decided to require all its supply chain sourcing partners to use GPS devices to track the positions of incoming products as they flowed downstream from their originating sources toward the retailer. Then, all of a sudden all of *Walmart's* big-box and not-so-big-box retail competitors decided they wanted their incoming products tracked too. Next thing the business world knew, formerly homeless GPS tracking devices were suddenly welcome everywhere. Sourced from Nelson Liechtenstein, *The Retail Revolution: How Walmart Created a Brave New World of Business* (New York: Metropolitan Books, 2009).

NPD STAGES: DESCRIBED . . .

To create successful new products, marketing organizations generally must understand their competitors, consumers, relevant marketplace conditions (trends, trends, trends), and then develop new products that deliver superior value to prospective, brand new, or existing customers. A systematic new product development process also should be established. Specifically, a systematic process that permits new product concepts (ideas) to be discovered or developed and strategically commercialized into successfully marketable products; that's what's needed. The process features five stages:

- Stage 1: New Product Strategy—Developing a new product strategy first entails identifying and prioritizing the best new marketing opportunities. The following questions also should be asked and answered: Does our firm seek market leadership in a particular product category? What are the goals? And what customer problems—new problems, old problems, or as yet unidentified or felt [by customers'] problems—will our new product solve?

- Stage 2: Concept or Idea Generation—Here, derive various concepts, all developed based on an initial assumption that each will help the firm reach its marketing goals, as denoted during stage 1, are created. Yes, this is where creativity comes into play.

- Stage 3: Concept or Idea Screening and Evaluation—Here, logical and process-driven efforts are pursued to ascertain how good each new idea is, whether each or any might lead to successful new products either now or in the future. Most new ideas will be eliminated for further consideration at this point.

- Stage 4: Development—The development stage includes the big pair of quasi-simultaneous activities called technical and marketing development. Technical development includes developing a prototype. Cost estimates become living budgets; manufacturing processes become factories (if tangible products are involved); marketing plans become marketing promotional and positioning efforts.

- Stage 5: Market Launch—This commercialization stage involves developing, implementing, and commercializing strategic go-to-market plans for the new product that has been developed. Strategic go-to-market plans should flow from the same sorts of processes introduced during Modules 2 and 3.

IS NPD MORE ART OR SCIENCE?

The following answer may surprise readers who deeply considered the earlier portion of this module. That's because while successful NPD practices and processes emphatically require substantial artistic-like thinking those same processes and practices, in order to be successfully executed, require even more scientific-like thoughts and practice.

Art is largely based on intuition, emotions, hunches, or gut feelings. These qualities and personae exercise more dominance when NPD decision-makers lack experience or the proper knowledge on which to base decisions. And creativity—being, thinking, acting creatively; accepting manageable risks; operating willingly outside comfort zones—is critical to successful NPD.

What is art? Or better still, what sort of entities merit descriptions as art? As noted, art is anything that creates more energy than it consumes inside whatever setting it resides.

Art, or the arts, are important to all types of marketers, if for no other reason than life actually does imitate art. Police did not start calling "Sting Operations" sting operations until after a 1973 movie starring *Paul Newman* and *Robert Redford* called *The Sting* was released. The *CIA* did not begin calling embedded spies "moles" until novelist *John le Carre* used the word in his novel "*Tinker Tailor, Soldier Spy.*"

By contrast science is based on the results produced by empirical tests. Empirical, here, means NPD decision-makers collect samples of information to factually answer questions in order to determine which idea or stage in the NPD process (see immediately above) should or should not be pursued next. The results of empirical tests support or invalidate certain hypothesized relationships. Science is also based on already established concepts, principles, or laws, and existing theoretical relationships between the concepts and principles.

Science ideally should operate like an unfeeling machine bent solely on the production of facts about the observable world. Science should be relentlessly skeptical.

In plainer English the preceding two statements mean that hypotheses—research questions—must be tested and confirmed as correct time and again before conclusions derived from the answers to the questions can be "scientifically confirmed."

The "Iron Rule of Explanation" keeps science running and makes any science a science. The Iron Rule of Explanation functions as a resolute set of standards—or tests—by which all scientists are expected to abide. These standards—these tests—determine what counts as scientific evidence and what doesn't.

The purpose for which all empirical tests are conducted is to sift the wheat of facts from the chaff of falsehoods. Empirical tests control and should ultimately determine which NPD ideas come out on top. When left to its own devices, any scientific discipline will advance and eventually save its constituent scientists from themselves. These statements apply equally to social sciences (such as marketing or psychology) or to physical sciences (such as chemistry or biology).

NPD developers should never shy away from the value of a good test. And, thus, the need for good tests. Three specific tests are integral to the success of most NPD endeavors:

- ▶ The Concept Test—NPD and indeed all innovative processes begin with ideas, or concepts. The concept test is conducted to determine whether intended new product users are likely to either want or need the proposed product. Scientists—be they marketing, medical, or metallurgical in their professional orientation—are taught from the outset of their academic training that they should approach every new idea with skepticism. (Skepticism is actually the basis for the philosophy of science, and for all theoretical advancement.) While they must welcome new ideas, new product developers should similarly remain skeptical of them, which means they must test those new ideas. At their cores concept tests reveal useful insights such as whether the dogs are likely to eat the dog food. What was it that happened when Beauty refused to eat the new healthier fare? No-go, failure, is what happened. Literally doesn't matter what the owner wants if the dog won't eat the new dog food. Had a concept test been conducted, this product taste-related problem presumably would have been revealed and hopefully resolved before the new product was launched.

▶ The Product Use Test—Product use tests are developed and executed to determine whether prototypical products, as they are developed, will actually satisfy that customer want or need and in the process solve the problem it was intended to solve.

▶ The Market Test—The market test determines whether the firm already possesses or could create an effective strategic marketing plan, an effective marketing plan, and the resources necessary to successfully commercialize the new product. Commercialize means actually bringing—introducing—the new product to market.

Art itself, artistic endeavors, and creative thinking are all good, necessary, useful, and appropriate at various stages during NPD processes. But primarily only during the initial two stages of new product development. Beyond question, however, empirical testing and adherence to certain insights derived from those tests should play guiding roles during later NPD stages.

MODULE 10.4

Truly Creative Creativity: Is It Always a Good Thing?

Readers should self-determine whether they want to accept or reject the ideas that follow. After all, readers are simultaneously the prospective and actual customers for the following thoughts. Prospective customers, in turn, get to vote with their feet by walking away from any creative new ideas and the products (presumed solutions) that those ideas may create—if they so choose. Therefore, readers have that option, as well.

Many if not most technology companies purposefully design their new products to be habit-forming. A generation of *Silicon Valley* executives trained at the *Stanford Behavior Design Lab* in the *Orwellian* art of manipulating the perceptions and behaviors of the masses. The lab has isolated the elements necessary to keep users of an app, a game, or a social network coming back for more. The benefits of incentivizing enticements such as variable rewards—envision the anticipatory rush you experience as you wait for your Twitter feed to refresh, hoping to discover new likes and replies. Introducing such rewards to an app or a game quashes the regions of the brain associated with judgment and reason while juicing the parts associated with wants and desires. Indeed, that brief lag between refresh and reveal is not *Twitter* crunching data—it's an intentional delay written into the code that is designed to create the responses just summarized above. What do you think?

Obvious dangers are inherent in such manipulation. Is having an *iPhone* like having "a slot machine in your pocket"? Yes, absolutely. Many *iPhone* features mimic those built-into the most addictive games present on any casino floor. *iPhones* are hardly unique in their ability to hook consumers. On *YouTube,* for example, the auto-play function deprives viewers of a natural moment at which to disengage. But it's not just that the site keeps queuing up new clips to watch. *YouTube's* algorithms are designed to hold your interest by serving up content you can't resist, and the algorithms have gotten very good. Way back in 2017, users were already watching a collective one billion-plus hours of *YouTube* videos a day.

More than 70 percent of *YouTube* content is targeted specifically toward individual users through the use of algorithmic recommendations. Hang onto that preceding thought: More than two-thirds of the *YouTube* videos you watch are specifically targeted at you by some marketer. How do you feel about that? Do you feel finessed or relieved that "someone" cared so much about securing and maintaining your attention?

This creative integration of addictive traits into their new products drives the business models of many of most powerful brands in the world. Brands and companies naturally, with which many readers engage every day. The power of creative addiction has fundamentally shifted the balance of power between consumers and producers. This was not always the most likely outcome of the digital revolution. In many facets of our lives, technology has improved transparency and given potential buyers access to a wealth of information they previously lacked. During the long-tailed analog age, prospective car buyers had little more than the *Kelley Blue Book*—and their own time, willingness to kick tires, and tolerance for listening to self-interested salespeople—to steer them to the best deal. But now you know that *Instagram* algorithms know whether we are seventeen or seventy and whether we prefer the music of *Cardi B* or the *Bee Gees*, and markets to us accordingly. By now, of course, you should also realize that the more reliant consumers become on a given app or platform, the more opportunities its creators have to observe individual consumer behavior—and the better marketers understand consumers' behavior, the better prepared those marketers are to manipulate customer behaviors to their own ends, whether their business model is serving ads or directly selling products to users of the site or device.

This cycle is virtuous for marketers. But is it vicious for consumers? As noted, the choice is yours to make. But we barely recognize that we're participating in the spin cycle because the barriers to participation are so low. Many of the most addictive platforms lure us in with the promise of a free service. But *Snapchat, TikTok,* and *Twitch* can be considered free only if users decide that their time or the personal information they are surrendering has no value.

THE DIGITAL LIFE: ALREADY CREATED BUT STILL CREATING

The digital life has by now been around for quite a while. But arguably digital as a product category still remains in its infancy inside the Introduction Stage of its Product Life Cycle. And certainly, the powers of the corporations that govern your digital life are still growing.

Digital marketers are continuously researching issues such as consumers search for; what subtly incentivizing nudges are consumers most likely to respond to; and what times of day will consumers most likely to engage in certain online behaviors. Soon, cameras and sensors will likely be tracking what frightens, amuses, and arouses consumers, allowing researchers and marketers who benefit from their collected data insights to know more about those consumers than many of them perhaps even know about themselves—not written as a joke. *The Wall Street Journal* also recently reported how popular *iPhone* apps that track customer users' heart rates and menstrual cycles were forwarding such information to *Facebook. Facebook* did not deny this description. Instead *Zuckerberg's* marketing and public relations teams merely asserted that the information was not being used to *Facebook's* advantage.

Any suggestion that consumers should be shielded from such creative marketing tactics might appear as paternalistic or overly regulatory, because the government is the only entity powerful enough to offer such "protection." Moreover, if you buy into the classical economist case that consumers are rational actors then the only logical choice is to let consumers decide for themselves whether they are willing to give up no small measure of privacy for the joy of getting friends' photos or the convenience of tracking their own heart rates. But an addiction economy relies on an asymmetrical (one-sided) exchange of information (one side in the buyer–seller relationship gives up far more value than it gets inside the exchange), and the technologist side of these exchange relationships are clearly creating greater asymmetry on a continuous basis.

HERE WE ARE

Here's the inside skinny about digital creativity.

Digital users are expected to blithely surrender their private information to gain access to highly creative and therefore desirable services. The marketing data—or is it debt—collectors, meanwhile, fiercely guard their own privacy. *Big Tech* typically steadfastly refuses to reveal what information they have, to whom they are selling these marketing research insights, and how these insights are being used to manipulate consumer behavior.

One thing is certain. Digital new product developers, big and small marketers alike, are creatively manipulating consumers' behavior. *Harvard Business School's Shoshana Zuboff* notes that the ultimate goal of "surveillance capitalism" is to turn people into marionettes. Marionette is *French* for a "puppet" [on a string], doing the bidding of the puppeteer. *Pokémon Go* was a putatively harmless game that proved a raging hit back in 2015–16. Players use smartphones to stalk their neighborhoods for the eponymous cartoon creatures. The app creatively leans into a system of rewards and punishments that would herd players to *McDonald's*, *Starbucks*, and other stores that pay its developers for foot traffic. Was this a digital innovation or an addictive innovation, or both? The answer shouts out its name. Marketers were able to induce consumers to show up at their doorstep, whether they sell their wares from a website or a traditional brick-and-mortar location. And if those consumers were not ready for a *Big Mac* or a latte? Well, they can manipulate that too. *Facebook* has boasted of its ability to subliminally alter our moods. Boasted not to naïve users, but to corporation shareholders. What do you think, now?

Yes, of course, *Facebook* claims that it does use these manipulations to promote targeted ads; others, however, will surely take advantage of our vulnerabilities. Consider "drunk shopping," a bad habit Americans have acquired in the age of the Buy It Now button. Marketing researchers suggest this trend is already a multibillion-dollar phenomenon. It's not difficult to imagine any number of technology platforms determining when we're likely to be high—or discerning it from speech slurs or text typos—and using that information to time their pitch.

Creative marketers are leveraging consumers' reliance on them—and those creative marketers' knowledge of those consumers as individuals—to get them to shell out more for their products. By following consumers' purchasing patterns (what they will pay for an airline upgrade; how sensitive consumers are to price increases, called *price elasticity*, see Module 13), these digital marketers can and do extend offers based on what each individual is willing to pay rather than what the market will bear.

The price of headphones displayed in *Google* search results varied depending on users' web history, with prices going up—by a factor of four—when past searches suggested affluence.

Another study, by *Benjamin Reed Shiller*, found that while marketers having access to basic demographic information about a specific buyer can gain 0.3 percent more profit than the market price would produce, marketers with access to the same consumer's browsing history can increase their profit by 14.6 percent. We bet we can predict what you are thinking now. The first word among your two-word response is probably holy . . .

Here's one certainty, however. A core benefit of capitalism is under assault. Buyers have traditionally benefited from what economists call a consumer surplus. The consumer surplus is defined as the difference between what consumers would pay for a product and what marketers actually charge, price-wise, for that product. Because many marketers now often enjoy huge intelligence—think information-based—advantages, those sellers can retain far more of that surplus for themselves. Whether or not the average American understands the concept of consumer surplus, individualized pricing violates a sense of fairness. Unless we're purchasing automobiles or auction items consumers have long assumed—such as *John Wanamaker* (again, see Module 13 for additional information)—that the price you pay is the price that I pay. Well, assume this no longer.

This is not an argument against creativity because creativity—new ideas, folks—is the foremost driver of progress and economic growth; echoing a point emphasized earlier inside this module. Technology has helped create a world of convenience and abundance, and it will continue to do so. Properly channeled, creative technology can improve the functioning of a market economy. But for society to harness technology's potential, we must understand how it is reshaping our lives.

During most of the last one hundred years people were naïve enough to entirely trust *General Motors* or *General Electric*. This was true even though not a single potential or actual customer had to worry whether *GM* or *GE* were warping their natural desires or stealing their time or human agency. The phrase human agency, as used here, is a marketing, economics, and psychological term that describes the capacity that human beings normally enjoy to make choices and to impose their choices on the world. Some citizens clearly possess more agency than others. But presumably all citizens of the *United States* should enjoy the agency to freely decide, absent undetected external manipulation, what they choose to buy or not buy, assuming that the product or service is affordable.

Is anyone surprised to read that the biggest, best-known companies in the contemporary US economy—*Facebook, Amazon,* and *Google*—are now being viewed with growing suspicion and mixed emotions? Such sentiments emerge in part from the growing realization that these and other tech giants have hooked us on their services in order to profit from us. But users of all ages are increasingly acknowledging the scale of their own finite that they have blown—weighing out, if you will, how much they have lost versus how much they have gained. Increasing numbers of consumers/users are becoming dismayed about how they've been spending their days, while feeling powerless to abandon their new bad habits.[15] Millions of consumers/users who deleted, but eventually reinstalled, their *Facebook* apps can attest to the nature of the challenge.

American consumers have long treated habit-forming products differently from non-habit-forming ones. Alcohol and cigarettes, their consumption is restricted based on age and location (you cannot smoke inside schools or offices). Gambling, until recently the activity was illegal in most places, and closely regulated. Big BAAD Tech has largely been left alone to insinuate addictive, potentially harmful products into the daily lives of millions of Americans, including children, by giving them away for free and even posing as if these creative solutions were social goods. The most addictive new devices and apps one day should be put behind the counter, as it were—packaged with harsh warning about the dangers inherent in their use, and sold only to customers of age. Human behavior being what it is, that course of action would likely only make the products more desirable. Who knows? But all would benefit from understanding that not so recently cigarettes were sold in front of the check-out counter, and condoms behind it. Things change.

---

15. The most effective ways to change now-traditional bad habits such as sitting too much while staring and poking at screens usually entail more than good intentions or even written reminders about alternative behaviors in which we should engage more or less. "Too much sitting" has long been characterized as the "new smoking" insofar as each consumer activity imposes negative health effects. One universally effective method of changing traditional bad habits entails creating small obstacles that force us to take action. Professionals could alter their home or corporate work offices in ways that force them to remove their fannies from their seats more often. Folks who *Zoom* frequently as part of their professional obligations, for example, could engage from separate areas that have been specifically designed to conduct video based exchanges absent any chairs. Those working from home might keep files in other rooms for the same general purpose. Or, professionals could habitually use those bathrooms located furthest away from the office or on different floors in order to force stair-walking. As far as changing new technology-induced bad habits, well, that's an entirely different challenge.

MODULE 10.5

The Diffusion of Innovations

Diffusion, defined scientifically, entails the movement of atoms, molecules, or particles—for simplicity's sake, objects—from areas of greater concentration to areas of lower concentration. Were someone to open a large bottle of malodorous cologne at the front of your classroom, the aerated molecules would diffuse from the point of highest concentration (i.e., the top of the opened container), to the point of lowest concentration (i.e., the back of the room). This is how diffusion works in the physical world.

Diffusion, defined in marketing and NPD contexts, entails the *rate of new product adoption*—the rate at which the new product sells—throughout a particular market, population, or social system (for simplicity, just market). The adoption rate for any innovation is measured from the point at which the product is introduced to a given market to the point at which, theoretically, the last customer in the market has adopted the new product for use. This process unfolds over time.

ADOPTER CATEGORIES

Naturally, not everyone in a given targeted market adopts an innovation at the same time, and some people may never adopt the new product. Customers and prospective customers have traditionally been classified into one of five adopter categories based on the rate at which the new product is adopted (Exhibit 10.2). There are five adopter categories: Innovators, early adopters, early majority, late majority, and laggards:[16]

Innovators (about 2.5%)

Innovators adopt innovations first and comprise about 2.5 percent of those consumers who will eventually adopt the innovation. Customers in this category, on average, enjoy higher social status, are better informed and more knowledgeable about the innovation in question. Most importantly,

---
16. Everett Rogers, *Diffusion of Innovations,* 5th Ed, (New York: Simon and Schuster, 2002).

innovators possess the financial means to acquire new products and are more willing to take purchase or usage-related risks. Innovators typically possess the resources that permit them to recover from any losses that may arise due to the innovation's failure.

Early Adopters (about 13.5%)

Early adopters comprise the next 13.5 percent of adopters. The characteristics of early adopters mirror those of innovators. On average they enjoy high social status, are better educated, and possess greater financial resources in comparison to latter adopter categories. Early adopters are, however, more judicious in their product choices than Innovators. This category of adopters is crucial for the diffusion process because it contains opinion leaders who readily pass on "word-of-mouth" about new products to other potential adopters. This characteristic makes early adopters extremely important to marketers. Their propensity to evangelize favorably or unfavorably about their experiences with the innovation make them either a marketer's best friend or worst enemy.

Early Majority (about 34%)

The early majority adopter category contains roughly 34 percent a product's potential adopters. Consumers in the early majority category adopt the innovation much later than members of the initial two adopter categories. This segment enjoys above average social status. Members of the early majority likely know one or more other early adopters who may have influenced their adoption decision. However, adopters in the early majority category are much less likely to function as opinion leaders. Still, the early majority may influence some future adopters. The early majority, along with the next category, the late majority, comprise the mass market for the new product.

Late Majority (about 34%)

We have passed the hump and are now sliding down the diffusion curve. The late majority, the next 34 percent of adopters, is generally skeptical about most innovations. They are usually less well off financially and lack social status. The late majority will exercise little, if any, opinion leadership. But, given the comparative size of this cohort, firms still attend carefully to the late majority as a significant proportion of the mass market for the new product.

Laggards (about 16%)

Laggards "lag," meaning they adopt an innovation last. They usually assign higher values to tradition, are concurrently more satisfied and comfortable with how things are currently being done, and thus sense little reason exists to change. Compared to other adopter categories, laggards trend older, lack financial resources and social status, and are adverse to assuming the risks associated with new innovations. Members of this category typically do not adopt an innovation until it is on the verge of obsolescence.

Membership in any of the above adopter categories depends on the type of innovation under consideration. An innovator or early adopter for one type of innovation may be a laggard for another. For example, a technologically proficient computer user may be an innovator with respect to new computer hardware and software, but a later adopter for, say, digital music devices.

FACTORS THAT INFLUENCE THE DIFFUSION RATE FOR INNOVATIONS

New innovations will spread more rapidly through social systems based on the degree to which they possess the following characteristics:[17]

Relative Advantage Over Existing Products

Relative advantage is the degree to which an innovation is perceived to be better than what it replaces. Innovations that score high on relative advantage tend to diffuse more rapidly. Consider, for example, the game of tennis. A form of tennis (*jeu de paume*) was introduced as a new product in France during the 1200s.[18] Early forms of tennis were played bare-handed, much like today's handball. Tennis was widely played in France and England in the 1500s. England's King Henry VIII built England's first tennis court in 1530. However, tennis as we know it today was designed and codified in England in the 1870s. The modern tennis racquet was introduced in 1583. The head (the striking area) of the original racquet maintained approximately the same size until 1976, even though the composition of racquets and their strings had evolved across the centuries.[19]

In 1976 *Prince Manufacturing* introduced the then-oversized Price Classic tennis racquet that boasted a 110 square inch head. This racquet, along with other oversized branded racquets that quickly followed, featured a substantially larger sweet spot. The Prince Classic also provided players who were performing at all levels of proficiency, the immediate ability to hit balls faster and more accurately, as compared to prior generations of racquets. The scale of the Classic's relative advantage over existing racquets was epic. The Prince Classic became history's best-selling racquet, a record held to this day.[20]

---

17. Ibid.
    John T. Gourville, "Note on Innovation Diffusion: Rogers' Five Forces," Harvard Business School. https://alertlogic-hb4e.hbsp.harvard.edu/api/courses/372244/items/505075-PDF-ENG/sclinks/0b67796224d121eb84cf205259ab113c (accessed July 1, 2018).

18. Olympic.Org, "A Brief History of Tennis," (May 3, 2017). https://www.olympic.org/news/a-brief-history-of-tennis (accessed July 1, 2018).

19. Tennistheme.com, "History of Tennis—Origins of Tennis Game." (2009–2010). http://www.tennistheme.com/tennishistory.html (accessed July 1, 2018).

20. Bernie Carlson, "Howard Head And The Prince Tennis Racket: A Journey From The Personal To The Democratic," *Forbes* (December 1, 2017). https://www.forbes.com/sites/berniecarlson/2017/12/01/howard-head-and-the-prince-tennis-racket-a-journey-from-the-personal-to-the-democratic/#323fb4974a8e (accessed July 1, 2018).
    Active.com, "Prince Celebrates 40 Years of Tennis Innovation." https://www.active.com/tennis/articles/prince-celebrates-40-years-of-tennis-innovation?page=1 (accessed July 1, 2018).

Comparatively Low Complexity

Complexity, in this context, captures the relative ease or difficulty associated with:

- Using the innovation.
- Understanding the benefits and value delivered by the innovation.
- Communicating the value and benefits of the innovation to others.

The Prince Classic was easy to use. The innovation was used (i.e., swung exactly as earlier racquets had been wielded). The only difference was a marked improvement in the Classic owner's ability to play tennis. Classic users, as well as competitors playing against Classic owners for the first time, clearly saw and experienced—one positively, the other player negatively—the new product's value. As far as communicating the value and benefits of the product to others, the Prince practically spoke for itself.

Some innovations are adopted and diffused slowly because they are too complex for many consumers to initially understand and use, even though the innovations may possess extremely high relative value. The introduction of the micro-computer offers a case in point. The relative complexity of the computer's operating system and the functioning of associated applications software were daunting hurdles to many potential users who otherwise recognized the computer's merits. Adoption and diffusion thus were quite slow.

Compatibility

Compatible with what, obviously? Compatibility, building on our tennis racquet example, with the existing ways in which tennis players were already using existing generations of tennis racquets. As well as compatibility as with tennis players' existing attitudes, beliefs, likes or dislikes, and preferences. The 1970s-era tennis players did not have to change any aspect of how they used tennis racquets or played the game; they simply played tennis better. The new racquet was highly "compatible."

More broadly, compatibility includes both compatibility with existing product usage patterns (as in the Prince Classic example) and compatibility with existing societal norms or ways of behaving. Consider, for example, the introduction of microwave ovens or automatic dishwashers. Both products suffered slower than anticipated diffusion rates due to their incompatibility with the wife's perceived role in the kitchen. The wife who used either product was perceived as lazy and less caring for the welfare of her family. Thank the stars that such perceptions are no longer a reality![21]

Divisibility or Trialability

Divisibility, in this context, captures the ease with which new products can be tried out on a limited basis—the degree to which new products can be sampled on a low-risk basis. For convenience goods, marketers enhance a new product's divisibility by providing incentives such as coupons, free samples,

---

21. Rosanna Garcia, Fleura Bardhi, and Colette Friedrich, "Overcoming Consumer Resistance to Innovation," *MIT Sloan Management Review*, 48 (4) (Summer 2007): 82–88.

rebates, lower prices, and trial sizes. For shopping goods and services, trialability is enhanced with such things as test drives (cars, usually), free trials (services), and generous return policies or cancellation policies.

Observability

New products that can readily be observed, such that their benefits become easily recognized, will diffuse more rapidly. For example, an insect poison that kills on contact will be more readily adopted than one that inhibits the insect's reproductive capacity. Products whose qualities are relatively hidden don't score well on observability. Consider, for example, furniture. A recliner sofa may look great in the showroom. But its construction, functionality, and reliability probably cannot be judged until the consumer actually experiences the sofa. Many of the attributes that contribute to the sofa's qualities are hidden and cannot be readily inspected prior to purchase.

EXHIBIT 10.1
Classifying New Products

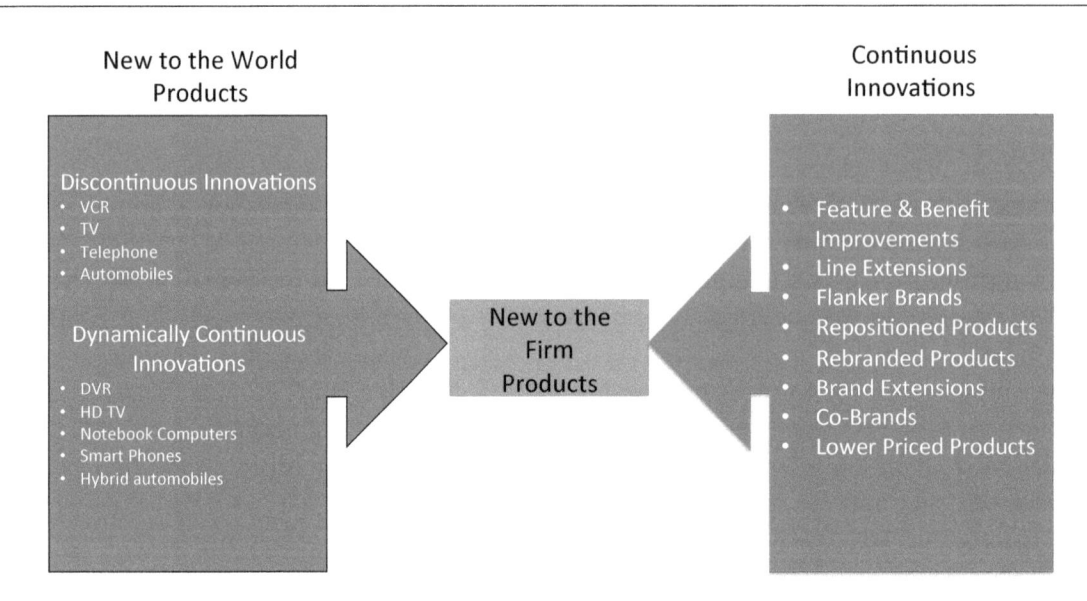

New to the World Products

Discontinuous Innovations
- VCR
- TV
- Telephone
- Automobiles

Dynamically Continuous Innovations
- DVR
- HD TV
- Notebook Computers
- Smart Phones
- Hybrid automobiles

→ **New to the Firm Products** ←

Continuous Innovations
- Feature & Benefit Improvements
- Line Extensions
- Flanker Brands
- Repositioned Products
- Rebranded Products
- Brand Extensions
- Co-Brands
- Lower Priced Products

EXHIBIT 10.2
The adopters of a new product are distributed along a normal distribution.

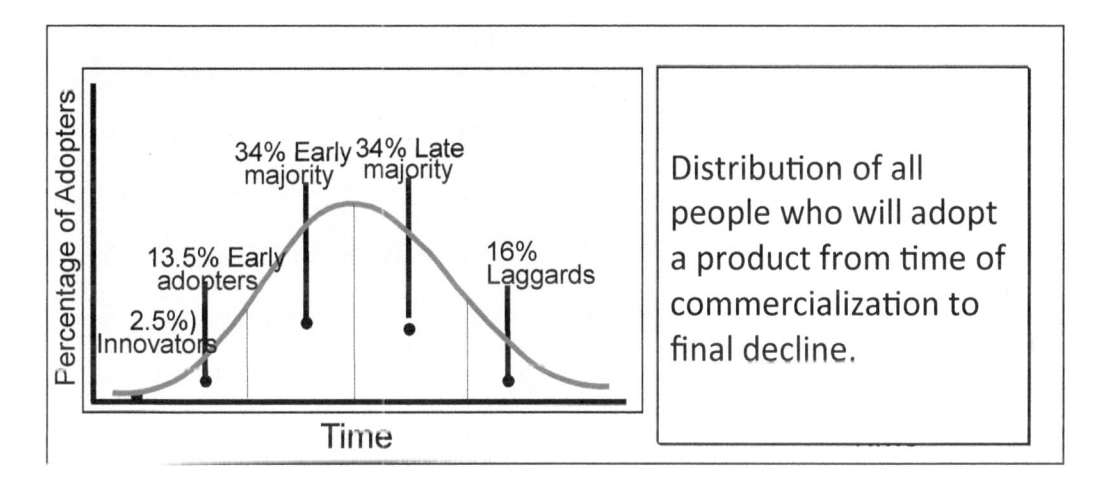

- 2.5% Innovators
- 13.5% Early adopters
- 34% Early majority
- 34% Late majority
- 16% Laggards

Distribution of all people who will adopt a product from time of commercialization to final decline.

MODULE 11

Managing Brands and Branding

MODULE 11.0

A Major Key to Marketing Success

Two outcomes contribute most to the marketing success of all B2C and most B2B organizations. Only two outcomes. That's it. No reason exists to make the end goal of marketing management more complicated than necessary.

- ▶ The first outcome entails building appealingly differentiated brands.
- ▶ The second outcome entails successfully delivering the right messages about these appealingly differentiated brand's values to targeted market segments.

However, the primary problem associated with brand-building and targeted brand-value delivery is getting complex marketing organizations to execute based on such simple ideas. A secondary problem is getting marketing organizations to understand the degree to which brand management is crucial to their success. Every marketing plan that organizations make and every marketing step that organizations take should be executed only after due diligence has been given to consideration of how the marketing plan or the marketing activity will strengthen the power, prestige, and/or position of a new brand or sustain the power, prestige, and/or position of a currently successful brand.

If right now you are thinking and feeling something along the lines of this means "everything is about the brand" then you are thinking and feeling the right things.

Two truths characterize modern capitalist markets. An awareness of and the ability to successfully manage these two truths also contributes materially to the marketing success of all B2C organizations and to most B2B organizations.

- ▶ The first truth: The most precious resource that any marketing organization can possess in today's noisy, crowded traditional or digital marketplaces is the attention of customers.
- ▶ The second truth: Most consumers don't just seek utility (usefulness, or pure problem-solving ability) from products and values that they buy; many consumers often also seek meaning from the products and values that they choose to purchase.

The intersection between these two truths is precisely where the power of brands and brand management as success-facilitators enter the scene—and the market. The best brands, after all, essentially command attention. The best brands also confer meaning to the products with which they, the brands, are associated. Typically, the best brands simultaneously command attention and confer meaning.

These two outcomes are remarkably important. Consumers often wield and leverage specific brands and their unique power to signal meanings about themselves to others who see them driving, drinking, wearing, visiting, and so forth, the brands or the places those brands identify. Sometimes consumers use brands to signal their virtues—driving a *Prius*, for example, simultaneously signals how green and socially-responsible they are. At other times, consumers exploit brands to signal their wealth, sophistication, sexiness, sincerity, intelligence, and so forth. Individual consumers, in brief, often use brands to command that attention be turned toward them as individuals. Not all of the time, of course. But enough of the time that these two factors—attention-getting and meaning-transference—prove sufficiently crucial to marketing success (failure) that most B2C marketers should consider each issue all of the time as they strive to effectively develop or manage their brands.

DEFINED AND DESCRIBED

Brands are names (words), signs (symbols), designs, colors, songs, or combinations of these dimensions that identify and distinguish the marketer of a product/service.

Brands, regardless of their dominant form, exist and function as symbols. Branding symbols matter. Symbols can say in an instant what words cannot. Symbols capture consumers' beliefs and aspirations; symbols can capture and create consumers' prejudices and fears. Symbols themselves possess no inherent value—or meaning. Symbols can be as simple as *Golden Arches* signifying *McDonald's* or inverted peace signs welded into or onto trunks or hoods to symbolize *Mercedes* and the brand's promise of higher product quality; greater prestige, as conferred to brand owners; and higher prices, as must be paid to acquire the power of the symbol.

The meaning-value of symbols derives from how people use them. The meaning and value of symbols evolves over time in concert with symbol-bearers'[1] behaviors or actions. Consider, for example, the contemporary symbolic meaning associated with the *Confederate Battle Flag*. Or that the *Nazi swastika* brand originated thousands of years ago in *India*. When the swastika was first developed, it meant, among other positive things, "Good Will." *Hitler* and his *National Socialist* crew surely degraded that value.

No one should sell short the value of the potential branding power that can emanate from successfully leveraging the brand-ability of the right sign or symbol. The *American Flag* is both branding sign and symbol. *McDonald's Golden Arches* are also both a branding sign and a symbol. That the meaning of one symbol is profound while the meaning of the other symbol borders on the profane matters not a whit inside this discussion.

---

1. Symbol-bearer equals brand-bearer.

And moving from the patriotic (*Old Glory*) to the routine (*Mickey D's*) to the sacred, how many *Old and New Testament narratives* begin or end with the issuance of signs? A Fast-Five could include *The Cross* (signifying victory over death, inside *Christian* minds); *The Lamb* (signifying both sacrifice and a covenant promise); *The Rainbow* (signifying covenant relief from future floods); The *Burning Bush* (signifying the unknowable and mysterious countenance of God, again inside *Judeo-Christian* minds); and *Water, Wind, Fire,* and *Oil* (signifying the Holy Spirit) inside *Christianity*.

Worth noting, the idea of *Christianity* exists as a well-branded[2] global philosophy and religion that positions itself as a problem-solving and value-adding product. As does the global philosophy and religion of *Islam*. Both religions—*Christianity* and *Islam*—routinely engage in evangelical-like and have evangelized for a long time, albeit through radically different marketing methods. Inside these two particular marketing contexts the word evangelizing means that each religious institution promotes its ideas and in doing so seeks to strengthen relationships with existing customers or to create new relationships with prospective customers. These customers, of course, as labeled by turns either as believers or the faithful. If that's not marketing, then what is?

Signs and symbols are not necessarily reality. Given that each is symbolic how could they be? But signs and symbols often point consumers toward a greater reality. However, in the context of this branding discussion, this greater reality is undoubtedly often merely a perceived reality. And yet perceived realities alone frequently prove enough to create real and lasting differentiation for various marketing goods, services, places, people, and ideas.

Well-managed brands gift the marketers that build them with formidable barriers against successful competitive imitation. The presence of these barriers makes it difficult for competitors to copy or dissipate the stronger brand's competitive advantage. Well-managed brands, transformed into powerful brands, exist as powerful barriers to competitive entry.

Ironically, however, the idea that consumers engage deeply with brands applies to only the smallest subset of high-involvement product categories and brands. The preceding statement is true beyond question despite the ample attention given to high consumer involvement discussion during the Consumer Behavior module. The truth, on average, is that consumers spend only about thirteen seconds deciding to buy one brand as opposed to another branded option from the same product category. Most decision-makers spend less than ten seconds. This condition does not denigrate the power of or the necessity for branding and branding power. In fact, this fact of marketing life elevates the power of both brands and branding power because the need is underscored for marketers to successfully "sell-the-brand's-story" before customers find themselves inside a situation where they must decide "which-brand-to-buy." In this regard, successful brand management presells products.

Marketers should not ignore the potential value of using music, songs, as brand identifiers and differentiators. A *Bob Seger & the Silver Bullet Band* song called *Like a Rock* was a medium-sized *FM* radio hit when it was first released during 1986. Then during 1991 *General Motors (GM)*, presumably after paying a healthy fee for the song's licensing rights, coopted the song and closely aligned the *Like a Rock* song as both the theme and key value proposition for its *Chevy* brand of trucks.

---

2. Critics may disagree with this characterization. Disagree, as expected, insofar as conflict naturally arises inside all supply chains.

The song and *Chevy Truck* advertising campaign ran continuously until 2004. Advertisements featuring *Like a Rock* were particularly likely to run during televised football and basketball games. This made great sense from both segmentation and targeting perspectives given that these sports events drew and still draw primarily male viewers and consequently lots of truck-buying prospect. (No suggestion is afoot that women do not purchase trucks. They do. But not in the percentages that males buy trucks.) Why embed the song so prominently inside truck ads run during televised sporting events? Because televised sports programming products primarily drew male eyes and ears to the then-big screens. (Ever notice how as technology got bigger other non-television screens got smaller?) And, with gender-based segmentation and targeting marketing considerations very much in play, which gender primarily—through obviously not exclusively—purchases large rugged trucks?

And the song/brand-management/advertising marketing campaigns still occasionally runs today. Truly a great job, *GM* marketing team. And tens of millions of consumers of a certain age can neither hear *Like a Rock* on classic rock venues without thinking of the truck brand, nor can those consumers encounter the truck brand on the road without thinking of the song. The "tens of millions" include nearly everyone old enough to have watched sports on television from the early 1990s and through the mid-2000s. Worth nothing, those fourteen or so years were emphatically a pre-DVR and fast-forwarding through ads era. Otherwise known to marketers as advertising heaven. Win-win, on huge scales, for the brands of both *Chevy* and *Bob Seger*.

BRANDS: ORIGINS AND PURPOSE

An original purpose of brands was to provide assurance to customers about the reliability or dependability or quality of a product or service. This job remains important today. Another original purpose of brands was to distinguish the maker/marketer of one product from other makers/marketers of the same product. This job remains crucial too.

The use of brands as differentiating devices began long ago. No one knows exactly when or where. But situations where *Medieval Age European* shoe or candlestick makers living in towns or cities where other families also made shoes or candlesticks prominently displayed special signs, symbols, codes of arms, or insignias inside their home factory-retail store (all housed in the same structure) windows can easily be envisioned. Signs, symbols, family codes of arms, and various insignia might have been displayed to identify and differentiate the products that their family unit produced from products made by other marketing units. Nothing has fundamentally changed about the purpose of branding between back then and right now.

The term brand was originally used in a prominent fashion in the *Old American West*[3] for purposes of designating and distinguishing one owner of horses or cattle from other owners. Imagine any branding scene you've ever seen in cowboy movies or television programs and you've got it. Now, think how branding irons were used to designate or identify and distinguish or differentiate the owners of said livestock. The purpose for which branding efforts were initiated then—identifying cattle or horses as belonging to one ranch and not another—remains the primary reason why branding is used

---

3. The *Old American West* itself is a well-branded and heavily-marketed idea—even if the *Old West* is not always an accurately-branded idea.

today. The other reason for using branding irons—attempting to distinguish the quality or features or uniqueness of one's product or work—still applies to contemporary branding.

WHAT'S IN A NAME?—PART I

The Bible suggests that to name something is to exercise and retain dominance over that something. Yet more value than dominance or control is associated with the opportunity to coin or re-coin a name in a brand-dominant world. How many mountains in *Colorado*, for example, are higher than *Pike's Peak*? The answer is thirty-one. And how many of those thirty-one other *Colorado* mountains can you name? In all likelihood, none. Ah, an informative peek into the explicit power of a strong brand name. Or conversely, an informative peek at how less-than-stellar brand names can drag name-bearers down.

Dunkin' Donuts, for example, recently removed donuts from its brand name as the marketer strategically focused on becoming more a beverage-led brand. Makes sense in a trending sociocultural environment where fat—inside food or on the outside of people—is increasingly castigated as a villain—except, of course, among body-positivity marketing-movements.

The brand name *Subway*, for example, has interesting origins. The first store in the eventual sub sandwich franchise chain was called *Pete's Super Submarines*. The owners changed the brand after a second store opened in 1966. The reason was that customers kept mishearing the name as *Pizza Marines*.

Megabrand *Starbucks*, a brand name powerful enough to convince untold millions of American consumers that paying five bucks or much more for a non-refillable cup of coffee made sense, opened in Seattle during 1971 as a single coffee shop that was named *Starbucks Coffee, Tea and Spices*. This first store was named after a character—yes, named *Starbucks*—from *Moby Dick*, the classic *Herman Melville* novel. Entrepreneur *Howard Schultz* bought the coffee shop in 1987 and quickly deleted the brand's references to tea and spices. Smooth move, Howard. You were right to focus strategically on only capturing one rabbit, coffee, as opposed to diverting resources, including customers' attention, to tea, spices—and coffee.

The technology firm *Yahoo!* began life in 1994 as *Jerry and David's Guide to the World Wide Web*. The original company was named after founders Jerry Yang and David Filo. One year in Jerry and Dave changed the brand name to something a bit catchier—and more memorable.

But when the subject is names, as in brand names, things are not always yummy, caffeinated, or ice cream-like. *Planned Parenthood* is a well-branded marketing organization that has positioned itself successfully as a women's health care provider. Yet the *Planned Parenthood* organization is often completely divorced from actual parenthood, other than preventing it. However, the brand name "preventing parenthood" would not have the same appeal or social acceptability, would it? Especially if and when prospective customers realize that *Planned Parenthood* was co-founded by *Margaret Sanger*, a famous advocate of eugenics.

The complete history is that Ms. *Sanger* founded the *American Birth Control League* in 1916. Then, in 1942, the *ABCL* organization merged with another similarly-focused (i.e., draconian) birth control marketer and successfully repositioned its brand as *Planned Parenthood*.[4, 5]

BRANDS TELL STORIES

Successful brands are more than logos, taglines, or campaigns. Successful brands are also experiences wrapped up tidily inside stories. Marketers are rarely wasting time when they tell their brands' stories. Instead they're investing in a better future for both their own profitable interests and their customer's welfare and happiness. Yes, good brands make their loyal customers happy, if for no other reason than good to great brands really disappoint their loyalists.

Great branding is not about one ad, one piece of content, one moment in time. Great branding is definitely about more than data and technology—even though marketing research insights are important. Great branding, which can only result from great marketing mix management (often including new product development), is about an endless, relentless, lasting commitment to building and telling branding stories, and waking up every morning inspired by the opportunity to help write the next new, even more compelling brand story.

Storytelling provided the means through which, for example, humans learned to hunt cooperatively. Stories were—and remain—how humans achieve an understanding of themselves, their history, and their place (yes, their "position") in the world. Each of the world's so-called *Five Great Religions*[6] is grounded upon a series of narratives told by and about prophets, tyrants, and redeemers. The idea that a right side to history exists and coalesces around a belief that, in the long run, the great narrative of humanity will end on terms that humans is embedded within most of these religions.

The stories behind all great brands makes similar promises to their loyal customers; that things (i.e., the experience or the solution) will end on terms that consumers like—but only if customers insert themselves in the story by buying the product. Remember, please, that products can include branded services, people, places, and most germane inside this context, ideas.

A brand is a narrative—part of a story—that confers meaning to distinct systems of benefits that branded products promise to deliver.

The best brand stories are unique—can any other competing brand stories claim the same story-ground? The best brand stories are authentic—can hearers or seers comfortably believe the narrative? The best brand stories are relevant—will hearers or seers care about, will they "feel," the tale? The best brand stories are motivating—will the narrative move people to action? The best brand stories are sustainable. Sustainability, in this context, implies that the story has legs, it will last, and more often than not various layered narratives can be laid upon the original tale.

---

4. Eugenics is the name given to the science of improving humanity through controlled breeding practices to increase the incidence of desirable heritable characteristics. No, we're not feeling eugenics as a "cool science," either.

5. Charles A. Donovan and Robert G. Marshall, "Margaret Sanger Was a Eugenicist to the End," *The Wall Street Journal* (2021): A-19.

6. Listed alphabetically, the world's five great—and indeed the world's most powerfully-branded—religions are: *Buddhism, Christianity, Hinduism, Islam,* and *Judaism*.

Well-Branded Stories Are Not Always True

Did you know that astronauts can see the *Great Wall of China* from outer space? You probably did; almost everything knows this amazing truth. And isn't this story, that narrative, incredible? One author heard this cool little factoid from friends some time ago and began telling everyone he knew about this cool trivia nugget; spreading the good word (of mouth), and all that in ways that made both *NASA* and ancient *China*, the branded entities that respectively made space travel possible and who built the *Great Wall* each appear more powerful as a consequence. Spreading the kind of story that would make people want to become astronauts or to visit *China* or do both.

What really blew the author away was how almost everyone he told had already heard this and agreed with him that this indeed is a cool fact. A human-made wall you can see from outer space; that's simply awesome. Or would be "simply awesome" were it true. You see, the story is not true—not even a little. The marketing organization known as *NASA* as well as multiple individual astronauts have debunked this myth. Yet much of the general public believes it to be a fact, as *NASA* points out. But why? The narrative; this story—and its power. That is why. There are few things more potentially powerful or more potentially destructive in today's world than a good or bad (or true or false) narrative.

Any successful brand's narrative is simply an assumption or set of assumptions widely accepted by its targeted market segment. As we know, facts cannot be changed. That is why they are facts. But the fact remains that facts can be reshaped or reinterpreted to make almost whatever key point any scrupulous or unscrupulous marketer wants.

BRAND STORYTELLING: FIVE RULES (OR STRONG SUGGESTIONS)

Brand Storytelling Rule One

As already noted elsewhere in this book, the first rule of successful brand storytelling is to make me care. Or, inside marketing contexts make targeted segment audiences for the story care about the story. Care enough to look or listen, to pay attention, to remember, to repeat and to share, through WOM or some other evangelizing channel—core elements of the story.

Brand Storytelling Rule Two

The second rule of storytelling is to leave-out or eliminate[7] the parts of the story that no one cares about or consequently wants to hear, see, or experience. Marketers, as they message or story-tell in

---

7. How does one eliminate the parts of the story that no one wants to hear, see, or experience? Success surely requires hard work and focused refinement. But storytellers could take heart and guidance from words uttered by the *Renaissance*-era art *Michelangelo*, whose most renowned work is the seventeen-foot tall statue of *David*, which was carved from pure marble. When asked how he created such a magnificent work of art, *Michelangelo* famously replied, "Every block of stone has a statue inside it and it is the task of the sculptor to release it" as well as, "I saw the angel in the marble and carved until I set it free." While few of anyone's stories will ever qualify as masterpieces, it remains the responsibility of every storyteller who aspires to create stories that inform, entertain, engage, inspire, or persuade others to remove the unnecessary rubble inside any written or oral stories they deem worthy of telling, before they tell them.

service to building or sustaining their brand and its equity should always honor this iron rule. Bet you've noticed how the more that even powerful people say the less that people actually listen to them. Or how, alternatively, the less that powerful people say, the more others will generally listen to them.

Relatedly, and in this context often sadly, have you ever noticed how many people who feel as if no one is really listening to them (and unfortunately, such people exist for myriad good and bad reasons) often confound their "no-one-listens-to-me" problem when they do receive the opportunity to speak? How? Yes, such folks often exacerbate their "no-one-listens-to-me" problem by then electing to speak too much.

Brand Storytelling Rule Three

A third rule of storytelling is to take measures to ensure that to the extent possible the most important parts of the story are also the most interesting parts of the story. Wow, think about how challenging this specific brand management and messaging assignment might prove. But then think about the rewards that would be available for you—and your brand—to claim when you successfully completed the mission.

These initial three storytelling rules are so nice that we have knowingly repeated them twice. The triad has also been repeated because almost all successful marketers must be storytellers—no point in exaggerating the point by claiming all marketers. But think about professionals who have enjoyed meteoric rises. Almost all were successful storytellers or were riding the crests of engaging stories told by others. Either way these storytellers were functioning as free-market preachers.

However, by now, readers are ready for two more storytelling rules.

Brand Storytelling Rule Four

The following chunk of basic storytelling advice will never not apply:

▶ Read the room.

If a given narrative or some dimension of the branding story is not working, as in not resonating with or outright being rejected by the audience, change that part of the narrative, unless storytellers have good reason to remain absolutely dogmatic in their views. Or, to the extent that storytellers can still skew close to the truth, change the brand story itself. In either scenario, stop . . . digging your hole.

This counsel is akin to the sort of thinking that works exactly like this. If you don't like what others are saying about you, then either change the story you are telling or give those presumably targeted others a reason to change the story they are telling each other about you.

Brand Storytelling Rule Five

Finally, one additional brand-related storytelling nugget to consider. This one emanates from a famous social scientist's most famous book. The famous social scientist is *Daniel Kahneman. Professor Kahneman* was referenced during the *New Product Development* module as one of the two fathers of *Prospect Theory*. The famous book features the brand name *Thinking, Fast and Slow*. In his book *Kahneman* suggests that human brains are only able to effectively process parcels of information for about 2.5 minutes at a time. The takeaway: once anyone has passed the 2.5-minute limit in their story-telling they have already entered an inefficient time zone. The time has arrived for the teller to alter their story's subject or theme, ask a question to "the audience," or perhaps either tell a joke or—hold your breath—just stop.

Not for nothing did the now-clichéd but always relevant phrase "brevity is the soul of wit" long ago enter the cultural vocabulary almost immediately after *Shakespeare's Hamlet* uttered it. Notably, both *Hamlet*, the play's character, and *Shakespeare*, the playwright, who are each roughly 500 years old, remain extremely well-branded and widely discussed, even today, inside many other places behind this book. Coincidence? We think not, believing instead that the *Hamlet* and *Shakespeare* brands remain firmly ensconced inside so many learned consumers' evoked sets is because each "person" told such wonderfully compelling stories. No wonder that the equity of their brands resonates so powerfully even today.

The phrase "brevity is the soul of wit" features multiple meanings. Let's examine the two meanings that are most relevant to this part of our branding story about storytelling.

In one sense, the phrase "brevity is" means that any good piece of writing, speechmaking, or storytelling should be brief, as in concise. Otherwise, the power of any wisdom, intelligence, or knowledge embedded in the story ends up diluted.

In another sense, "brevity" means that witty—wit is generally manifested inside the intersection between funny and wise—stories should be short. Otherwise, their power and punch will be diminished.

REAL BRANDING STORIES, SYMBOLIC BRANDING STORIES, OR SYMBIOTIC BRANDING STORIES?

Ideally, the branding stories told by marketers are real—fact-based. But successful branding stories also can be merely perceived as real, or true. Which is okay . . . Fiction, after all, is often the lie people must tell themselves and sell to others before those other customers or prospects can either explain or understand the truth—this is fact-based, as well.

Consider *Coors Light* and its ongoing branding story. Most know the narrative, because the story has been around for a while. The gist of the story is that *Coors* is brewed by people who care as they use beautiful *Rocky Mountains* stream water. Okay, sure. But the facts remain that not all *Coors* beer was brewed using water taken from *Rocky Mountain* streams. Particularly *Coors* beer brewed in *Eden, North Carolina*. Turns out Eden has wonderful water that flows down from the *Meadows of the Dan* on top of *Lovers Leap*, a nearby *Virginia* mountain. But the *Dan* and *Smith Rivers* that flow together, intersecting, inside *Eden* are also approximately 1,600 miles from the nearest *Rocky Mountain* stream.

By and large, such distracting facts don't much matter to beer-drinkers and surely is not going to hurt them. This particular sort of not-telling-the-whole-truth doesn't really matter because the telling it is non-material, does not hurt anyone, and entails a puffery-like transgression that falls into a "no-harm, no-foul" territory. That is, if this book is permitted one more basketball metaphor.

Brands, after all, are never what marketers say they are. Instead, brands are always what prospects/customers say they are. And brands are destined to remain so, until and unless marketers successfully define and position their brands by implanting compelling stories about the brand in the collective minds of targeted customer segments.

All marketers should persistently position their brand as the one and only option that is distinctively different and better than all other brands from the same product category competing in the same market space. At times when they are telling and selling marketers should act like they are the boss. This is one of those times. And bye the bye, if brand managers don't believe their brands represent the best options available at a given price inside the product category and market in which they are managing, then they are not doing their jobs. Those brand managers have either failed to plan well or failed to manage their marketing mixes properly (particularly the promotional element), or failed at both tasks.

THE STORIES—AND SUPPOSED SYMBOLIC MEANINGS—BEHIND SEVERAL POWERFUL BRANDS

How do these branding messaging management as compelling storytelling processes actually work? The following examples explain part of the story behind the story of what drove the success of various well-known brands.

- Look at the *FedEx* branding sign carefully to find the hidden message. An arrow resides between the letters "E" and "X." The arrow represents *FedEx's* forward-thinking ways and outward look toward the future.
- The brand name *Coca-Cola* came into existence with the help of its original ingredients—extracts of coca (yes, cocaine) and kola (caffeine, extracted from the kola nut).
- The arrow in the *Amazon* brand symbol that looks like a smiley face underscores Amazon's mission-driven goal to keep customers happy. The arrow stretches from A to Z, underscoring the vast variety of products available through Amazon. Well-designed branding symbols, like *Amazon's*, often exist, in their final forms, as works of art.
- *Mobil's* red and blue brand letters features primary colors, on purpose. The red represents strength. The blue represents the faithfulness and security provided by *Mobil*.
- The bitten-into *Apple* logo represents—subtly embodies—a bite from the forbidden tree of knowledge. The bite also epitomizes and represents a computer byte.
- From the 1960s, rumours abounded that *McDonald's* customers supposedly unconsciously recognized the *Golden Arches* as symbolizing of two nourishing breasts. *McDonald's* wanted to change its logo even back then but never did and now never would. An alternative explanation for using the Golden Arches as branding devices exists, however. Franchise founder *Ray Kroc*

purportedly wanted *The Brand-able Arches* to rise high enough in the air that people driving on distant streets or highways could still see them. Two brothers, Ray and Dick McDonald, actually created the production-line-like burger and fries preparation processes that led to the first incredibly successful *McDonald's* restaurant in *San Bernardino, California*.

▶ The three ellipses depicted in the *Toyota* logo symbolize three hearts. The heart of the customer, the heart of the product, and the heart of progress, with boundless opportunities for improvement in the future.

▶ The white lines passing through the *IBM* brand insignia give the appearance of the equal sign in the lower right-hand corner, symbolizing equality.

▶ The globe in the *AT&T* logo is three-dimensional, representing the growing depth and range of products that *AT&T* was committed to providing its customers.

▶ The *Adidas* symbol represents a mountain, underscoring the obstacles people must overcome along their pathway toward success.

▶ *Google's* branding logo features four primary colors in a row before they are broken by a secondary color. *Google* was signifying its playfulness without making its logo too big or overwhelming. The branding logo also subtly signalled that the brand did not play by the rules.

▶ Giving that the parent company's roots are in aviation, it makes sense that *BMW's* branding symbol was designed in a way that justified and reflected those heavenly roots. The blue and white *BMW* branding symbol is meant to epitomize a propeller in motion, with the sky peeking through.

▶ From its origin, *NBC's* peacock logo was extremely colorful, which was supposed to drive viewers toward color televisions. Not coincidentally, the National Broadcasting Company Corporation had a stake in a color television manufacturing firm at the time.

▶ The star embedded in the *Mercedes-Benz* symbol represents the firm's dominance in style and quality over land, air, and sea.

Subtle brand messages, yes. But powerful stories nonetheless. Especially when repeated repeatedly across decades.

OTHER USEFUL STORIES ABOUT USEFUL BRANDING STORIES

Brand stories should be told clearly—and in other news, water is still wet. Yet the point must be made. The same simple and basic branding story themes should be consistently turned over and twisted together. And assuredly, the best branding stories are constructed and told in compelling fashions. What's the point of telling even the best stories if targeted customer recipients cannot understand, do not remember, or are not impacted by them?

The best branding stories are authentic or genuine. American politicians, for example, continuously seek to tell the sorts of stories that will brand them as authentic. Most fail. The problem with many politicians as they seek to establish or burnish the power of their brand is that they are so bad at intimating actual human beings.

The best branding stories also are benefit driven.

The best branding stories are likewise appropriate for, as in appealing to, the segment being targeted.

The best branding stories exist as promises. All marketers are promise-makers, as you know. You likewise know that successful marketers—at least across the longer-run—are also promise-keepers. Branding promises represent commitments made by marketers that their products will deliver specific features, benefits, services, experiences, cache, prestige or status, solutions, and/or values . . . every time.

If promises about a value that will be delivered are not kept, for whatever reason, marketers must make things right. Otherwise, brand equity declines, brand reputations slip, and favorable marketing positions and brand loyalty disappear. Powerful brands, however, function as insurance policies. Policies that give marketers the time and opportunity to cover their losses if promises are occasionally unintentionally broken.

The best branding stories exist and unfold as living entities with whom customers can have relationships. Such relationships can take years to build. Such relationships, however, might be destroyed in hours or days—or seconds if a customer experiences say, a horrific service encounter?

The best branding stories take up rent-free residence inside customers' minds. Imagine what this statement means, along with its associated implications. Then think, positioning.

The best consumer brands carefully craft their own personae, portray those personalities in public, and perpetually polish them in pursuit of the brand's posterity.

Each of these desirable branding outcomes are best accomplished through sustained and strategic storytelling.

HOW SUCCESSFUL BRANDS HELP MARKETERS

Successful brands help marketers and buyers alike. Successful brands permit marketers to raise prices. *Ralph Lauren* polo shirts cost consumers far more than polo shirts. *Coke* without the logo is just a cheap, terrible-for-your-health, sugary soda. Successful brands earn differentiation; hold broad appeal among distinct groups of consumers; and foster customer loyalty. Loyal consumers, in turn, drive brand profitability, because brand loyalty permits marketers to raise prices and sustain higher prices longer.

Successful brands give meaning to distinct systems of benefits—as noted. Brands are living stories that are produced by and produce differentiation. The real story underlying *Harley-Davidson's* long-term branding success is that owning and riding the brand often provides forty- to fifty-ish-year-old, generally slightly overweight white-collar male professionals an opportunity—inside their minds—to drive into small towns and scare their citizens. The preceding statement is sort of factual, fact, though it may play like fiction. And the fact remains that this specific point of differentiation, when promoted across time, permitted *Harley-Davidson* to raise the prices of their bikes to striking heights.

Successful brands help marketers differentiate/position, develop, and introduce new products. The basic strategy entails introducing new products as extensions—using the same branding icons or names—of known, established, and well-liked brand names—and attaching the already established and respected/loved brand name to new products. The brand name *GE* comes to mind as an example. Every new and existing product that this iconic firm markets has the *GE* brand attached or affiliated with it.

The fact that the brand name is already well-known helps marketers that have developed new products secure shelf space, market attention, and investment or start-up funding more easily.

HOW SUCCESSFUL BRANDS HELP CONSUMERS (AND OTHER CUSTOMERS)

Successful brands help B2C or B2B simplify their consumption lives. Consumers and other types of customers typically choose brands that they already know and in which they already trust. Time, hassle, stress, and/or emotional energy are conserved or avoided as a result.

Consumers love trustworthy brands. How much do consumers love them? So much that they often allow many certain popular brands, particularly from among technology-based product categories, to babysit their children.

Consumers—being human—are meaning-seeking creatures. The brands that consumers buy, wear, drive, drink, and/or are seen with are frequently used by consumers as symbols and signals that express their identities. Typically, consumers are not really motivated by brands or marketing firms themselves. Consumers instead are motivated by other people associated with particular brands. At times, however, it's more important for marketers to convey messages to targeted consumers that they're the factor that is making this brand appear cool. Not only does this consumer-affirming approach help marketers execute their brand management tactics successfully, it features the added benefit of actually being true!

Brands also help buyers seeking to express themselves or build or project their personalities based on brands they boast, bear, wear, drink, drive, and so forth. The best and generally most prestigious consumer brands often deliver meaning, in other words. For categories such as automobiles or clothing, brands do more than signal quality and performance. Brands also help consumers present and promote their actual and wannabe or "wish-I-was" self-identities more effectively. The decisions to shoulder *Fendi* bags or to drive *Harley* bikes tell special stories about consumers—especially when she is wrangling each branded product at the same time.

MODULE 11.1

Branding Basics

BRAND LOYALTY

Brand loyalty is a crucial asset—a core competency and a source of competitive advantage—for marketers who manage their brands effectively enough to earn it. The term brand loyalty is used to describe strongly held customer preferences for particular brands. The presence of brand loyalty provides marketers with an opportunity to raise prices without losing excessive market share.

Brand loyalty, however, is declining throughout the *American* marketplace. Primarily, because domestic consumers are better informed about available brand alternative and have more brand product choices available than at any time in history. Domestic consumers are better informed because internet sites and online WOM reviews exist. Globalization, during the same era, has increased domestic competition by making more brand choices available.

Brand loyalty has also declined because consumers, especially *Millennials* and *i-Gen*, are extremely cynical. More so than any prior generation from any point in US history. Which makes sense in many ways for many reasons. After all, who or what should younger consumers believe or trust? Religious leadership, governmental deep state bureaucrats or politicians, entertainers, media spokespeople or thought leaders; corporations and their branding promises; each marketing entity has routinely (though not always) have let them down.

Some brands are used to identify distinctive products, such as *The Economist*, a high-priced but highly informative magazine, and to inspire customer loyalty toward the brand. Other brands confer distinctions upon otherwise homogeneous products; plain old soda versus *Coke*, for example, while also functioning in ways that enhance loyalty for the brand.

The fact that brand loyalty toward service marketers such as banks or insurance companies is usually shaped less by advertising than by customers' experiences with the service providers themselves is worth noting. This condition underscores the important role played by service-provider>><<service-receiver relationships as services are marketed. However, the use of advertising represents the usual

pathway that is followed when marketing organizations are seeking to build brand loyalty for more tangible products.

BRAND EQUITY

When the asset is present, brand equity generally permits firms to charge higher prices for their well-branded products. The presence of brand equity likewise permits marketers to attain and sustain higher market shares despite their higher prices. When brand equity exists more efficient communication programs can be more easily developed. Better communication programs generally facilitate effectively-differentiated brands. These communication programs usually feature a combination of advertising and other promotional efforts.

Brand equity reflects the extent to which customers willingly pay more for particular branded products as opposed to other branded products from the same product category. Brand equity functions as a proxy for the level of pricing power that has been built into and is associated with well-branded products. Brand equity permits marketers to command greater customer loyalty and earn stronger distribution power in markets themselves and often block competitive attempts to enter the same market space. Brand equity, likewise, facilitates earlier customer trial of new products branded with the same brand name. Marketers that enjoy equity thus can more easily extend existing product lines into new markets. Finally, those firms that enjoy brand equity usually enjoy greater amounts of positive WOM endorsements.

The price of one-day passes to *Disney's Magic Kingdom* first surpassed $100 (beginning at $105, actually) way back in 2015. But the three-digit price tag didn't dampen visitor demand. Actually, the opposite happened. The *Magic Kingdom* experienced an *increase* in attendance during all five years preceding 2015 despite the fact that admission prices also continued to substantially rise during each succeeding year. This trend—steadily increasing prices without experiencing decreases in demand—likely exemplified a combination of brand loyalty, brand equity, and pricing power. Pricing power exists whenever marketers can raise prices or sustain already-higher pricing levels without losing substantial market share.

The *Banana Republic* apparel brand enjoyed substantial pricing power back in its heyday. During this four- or five-year period the once-hip apparel retailer simply did not discount its prices. No need existed to cut prices in order to move over-priced t-shirts and khakis out store doors. No longer. Branding success is never guaranteed. Branding success first must be earned and then re-earned every day.

Brand equity likewise may be described as the physical and mental availability brands carve out for themselves inside targeted customers' minds. Physical and mental availability is best understood as customers' propensity to think about specific brands when confronting problems for which known product categories provide solutions. Deliberating about the specific values associated with and promised by specific brands, insofar as brand "X" is situated—positioned—high up on the top rung of those ladders that exist inside customers' evoked sets.

Brand equity, at net, also captures customers' perceptions and feelings about branded products—and the value, performance-power, and/or meaning that those consumers ascribe to those brands. These consumer feelings are generally positive, although the possibility of negative feelings does exist.

Brand equity is an inestimably valuable asset that marketing organizations earn for their products, usually over time and by dint of hard, focused, and ultimately strategically successful marketing mix management. Brand equity is rarely if ever gifted. Brand equity almost never happens by accident or through coincidence, at least not the sustainable sort of equity. Brand equity inevitably emerges as a consequence of strategic decision-makers having executed one or more elements of their marketing mix extremely well over an extended period of time. *Nike,* as well as *Apple,* have simply done product development (the product element) and advertising (the promotion element) better than most or all of their competitors for decades. By contrast, *Walmart* has executed the place, or supply chain management, element of its marketing mix at world-class levels for more than fifty straight years. Unsurprisingly, all three brands have experienced their fair share of criticism across time. Haters are going to hate, after all. But despite the presence and persistence of these brand naysayers and detractors, the power of the equity of their brands continues to sustain and even bolster the marketplace prominence and positioning of *Nike, Apple,* and *Walmart.*

CO-BRANDING

Co-branding occurs when two established brands of different companies are in relation the same product. Usually, one firm grants another organization the right or license to use its brand name in exchange for some sort of financial remuneration. Co-branding generally permits one marketing organization to expand its existing branding power into new product categories or marketplaces that otherwise might be unavailable to the co-branding marketer. This is the primary benefit.

Amazon primed its branding power to push customers to shop more at *Whole Foods. Amazon,* a mega-brand, acquired *Whole Foods,* a well-known-but-struggling brand, during 2017. *Amazon* immediately integrated the two brands. Aside from ensuring that the brands retain their separate and distinct identities, which is what co-branding partners generally do, the two brands' strategic union was executed in ways that benefitted each corporate entity. *Amazon* now delivers *Whole Foods* groceries; *Whole Foods* now sells *Amazon* brands such as the *Echo* or *Kindle;* and *Amazon Prime* customers—paying $119 annually to join the club—receive substantial discounts on numerous products at all *Whole Foods* store locations.

Before the brand merger, *Whole Foods* had been trying but failing to reduce prices to compete with lower-priced grocery brand alternatives since 2015. For years prior to 2015, *Amazon,* through *AmazonFresh,* had been trying but failing to get its grocery division flying as high as other offshoots from the Mothership have flown.

So far, its win, win, win, and win—full-speed ahead. Win for co-brand one, *Amazon;* win for co-brand two, *Whole Foods;* win, for *Amazon* customers; and finally, win for *Whole Foods* customers. This is the sort of mutually shared differentiating and positioning power that well-executed co-branding strategies can produce.

Co-branding is not just a foodie thing. *Apple* and *Goldman Sachs* partnered during 2019 to jointly issue a credit card that offers new features on *iPhones*. The *Apple Paycard* uses *Mastercard's* payment infrastructure to provide extra features on *Apple's Wallet* app. The features permit users to establish spending goals, track their rewards, and manage their account balances, concurrently solving three common consumer problems.

This was *Goldman's* first credit card. The investment bank has created customer-support call centers and built a $200 million internet payment system. For *Apple,* the cards embodied a broader incursion into their customers' financial lives. *Apple* hopes the card elevates use of *Apple Pay,* which has barely caught on among users and retailing merchants. These retailing merchants are supply chain partners with *Apple;* see Module 12. Yes, the new card risks alienating other banking partners. But we're talking *Apple*, so why should that killer brand worry about what banks think—and yes, the preceding is a bit tongue-in-cheek.

MODULE 11.2

Building Powerful Brands

POSITIONING BRANDS

Brands should be positioned inside the collective mind of targeted segments comprised of actual or prospective customers. More powerful brands have established their space inside customers' thoughts, perceptions, beliefs, and feelings—creating elbow room inside the minds of markets! By now this logic should be second nature to readers.

Brands can be positioned based on:

- Attributes promoted as being uniquely associated with the branded product/service in question.
- Successful promotional efforts to associate the brand name with one uniquely desirable customer benefit/solution that the brand actually or purportedly delivers.
- Customer beliefs, values, and emotions that are associated with the brand.
- Personalities that are created and thereafter managed for respective brands.

The personalities of brands might be perceived by targeted segments as rugged (*Jeep*), exciting (*National Basketball Association*), sincere (*Hallmark*; "when you care enough to send the very best"), competent (*Edward Jones*), sophisticated (*Rolex*), or sexy (*Victoria's Secret*).

Brand personalities are generally reflected in the type of person the brand represents. A brand's personality provides depth, feelings, affinity, and liking to relationship between brands and customers.

Marketers attempt to align the personalities of their brands with the consumer personality traits (again, rugged, exciting, sincere, competent, etc.) that dominate inside specific target market segments. Consumers often seek to purchase brands whose personalities reinforce what they, consumers, already are; or what those consumers aspire to become. Either way, consumer's preferred self-identities are in play as these decision-makers seek to reinforce existing and to create new and more desirable personality traits within—yes—themselves.

BUILDING SUCCESSFUL BRAND NAMES

Effective brand names often suggest or directly reference primary benefits and values that are presumably delivered and are certainly promised, as it promoted, by the branded product itself.

Big Ass Fans, for example, should really blow. *Nair*, as in, one can only assume, no-hair. *Drano*, as in, well, most everyone knows the problem that *Drano* solves, right—the problem relates to drains. *Keeps*, for a hair loss prevention product. *Rainmaker*, as a more than decent brand name for a yard irrigation control device.

But is *Planned Parenthood* an effective brand name? Truthfully, the brand name may represent half a good choice insofar as the affiliated organization is definitely about planning but rarely about achieving parenthood, as noted elsewhere.

Less evocatively, one might consider the brand name *CounterCraft . . . A Counter Revolution*. This particular brand name works effectively as a signifier of what and how this brand delivers the values and solutions that it delivers. The brand itself—*CounterCraft*—speaks to the fact of what benefits and solutions this product delivers. Countertops, which have been crafted, for certain. But the branding tagline *A Counter Revolution* also speaks directly to edgy, innovative, cool, perhaps even dangerously different spirit through those promised solutions are *Crafted* (created) and provided.

Typical Characteristics of Effective Brand Names

Sometimes the best brand names are distinctive. Brand names that effectively set apart successful brands from other brands occupying the same market space. *Udder Cream*, for example.

Times arise when effective brand names are extendable to new products that the parent firm might develop. *GE* is the ultimate extendable brand. Effective product this marketing behemoth makes has one brand and symbol affixed to it: *GE*.

Good to great brand names are often memorable and/or easy to recall. *Monkeybutt Cream* comes to mind and once that particular brand lands inside anyone's mind, it tends to stick around.

At other times the best brand names are easy to pronounce and recognize. Or not.

Volkswagen, the well-branded *German* auto maker, successfully positioned its global brand inside the United States based on the *German* word *farfegnugen*[8] for more than a decade. American consumers, to whom this branding story was targeted, found *farfegnugen* neither easy to pronounce or to recognize. But *Volkswagen* persistently stuck with the branding identifier. And once domestic consumers basically understood and could generally pronounce *farfegnugen*, the name certainly stuck in their minds.

---

8. In German, *farfegnugen* means "driving pleasure."

Closer to home but further back in time, the 1970s–1980s era US southern rock band named *Lynyrd Skynyrd* (pronounced Len-nerd Skin-nerd) illustrated the potential virtue associating with purposefully creating brand names that prove difficult to properly pronounce, but likewise difficult to forget once the word—or intended market target—does get the word, along with its pronunciation and implied meaning. *Lynyrd Skynyrd* also exemplified the case for being successful by being different, by sounding at the time like no other band but themselves. Their music soon exemplified what came to be known as *Southern Redneck Rock*. This positioning designation distinguished the *Skynyrd* brand from *The Allman Brothers Band's* brand.

At the time the *Allman Brothers* were accurately promoted and positioned as *Southern Hippy Rock*. *Skynyrd* came across to its stage and radio and album audiences—these were pre-MP3 player days—as rough, tough, from the country roads, dudes. Because the band's membership actually were. The band made their predominately poor to lower-middle class white Southern male fans (who often willingly embraced the brand and positioning label: redneck) proud that they were also working class. Talk about marketing segmentation, targeting, and positioning—or the basics of any successful marketing strategy.

Yet even successful brand names don't always mean what targeted others think the names mean, or even exhibit any connection with reality. *Greenland*, for example, is almost entirely covered with ice and snow, not much green grass growing there. *Iceland*, however, actually is overflowing border to border with flowing grass hills throughout much of any year. Approximately 11 percent of *Iceland* is covered by glaciers; about 80 percent of *Greenland*, meanwhile, lies under glaciers. Now, as a prospective tourist destination, which product has more curb appeal for you?

Twenty-plus years after its market introduction as a discontinuous innovation and new product, the brand name *Viagra* remains extremely well-known—and highly successful. However, the brand name *Viagra* is not a real word. Even so, the name subtly suggests the benefits, values, and solutions delivered by the product with which the brand is associated. The brand name *Viagra* emerges from the strategic intersection between the words Virality, as in potency and strength, and Niagara, as in Falls.

Viagra was clearly a distinctive brand name, and quickly grew into one of history's most successful brands. Of course, the fact that *Viagra* solved a major problem—erectile dysfunction—for huge swaths of the middle-aged and older male population also helped stimulate its success. As did the fact that the brand was first-to-market.

Viagra, the brand, proved so powerful that its development and marketing introduced an old but previously-generally-not-mentioned, problem into the broader consciousness and lexicon of the global marketplace. Viagra came to own the word *ED*, if you will, in the male market's collective mind, reminding us of the marketing Law of Focus that was first introduced during Module 2. *ED* encompassed a kinder, gentler description of the soul-sapping, psychological-abusing problem that erectile function actually visits upon many men who suffer the affliction.

Trader Joe's, the *California*-based grocery retailer, generally targets overeducated but relatively underpaid consumers as its core customer segment. If you are a second seat-violinist who holds two master's degrees and performs in mid-sized city symphonies, *Trader Joe's* may have you in its targeting sights. While the grocery retailer's prices are not especially inexpensive, *Trader Joe's* itself is notably frugal. The grocery chain, for example, habitually locates new store sites in the lowest rent districts inside generally high rent neighborhoods and zip code regions. That's smart, strategic marketing; manage those costs!

Trader Joe's has long been identified as a brand name that understands to which descriptive words cost little to nothing, and consequently piles on evocative adjectives as prefixes to its food brands. Once such branded products are literally extricated from *Trader Joe's* shelves, one can see their evocative adjectives include words such as "fresh," "fancy," "flavorful," and naturally "organic" or "environmentally-sound." Those descriptive prefixes are nothing more or less than simple brand identifier words. But these particular words simultaneously thrill, appeal to, or chill-out targeted customers (*Trader Joe's* brand image is undeniably hip), while materially differentiating otherwise not-all-that-special generally discounted grocery options. These branding identifiers coalesce and conspire to create a discounted-upscale brand image and equity for the *Trader Joe's* brand inside the minds of many of its loyal consumers.

GOOD BRAND NAME CATEGORIES—BUILDING BRANDS FROM BIRTH

Human babies born today might reasonably expect to live out ninety-plus years on Earth. Do you think that naming such a newborn might prove difficult, especially given that today no new parent would dream of branding their newborn as a Mary or Jane, or a John or Michael? (Or for that matter, Alexa.) Now imagine the difficulties associated with assigning the just-right (brand) name to your newborn marketing organization, which may survive for centuries, all while attempting to tag the just-right branding label.

This naming issue and potential marketing problem is real. The well-known chemical marketer that bears the *DuPont* brand was founded and named in 1802. The well-known consumer goods marketer branded as *Colgate* was named in 1806.

Onomasticians are experts who study the origins and meanings of names. Thus, by default, this oddly named set of professionals studies the origins and meanings of brand names. Naming scholars have identified seven basic categories from which most corporate brand names appear to emerge. Those seven basic brand name categories are labeled, yes branded, as:

▶ The "Plain Vanilla" Brand Category—Vanilla brand names plainly, practically, and functionally describe the products and solutions that the marketing organization provides. *United Parcel Service,* now, *UPS; General Motors; International Business Machines,* now, *IBM; or Quaker Oats Co.* fit precisely inside this category. So does *Radio Corporation of America,* now known as *RCA,* which proved a ridiculously successful brand during *The Roaring Twenties,* as the decade that preceded our current decade by exactly one hundred years was branded.

▶ The "Places" Brand Category—Place-based brands adopt the focal locale in which these named organizations were launched. *Texas Instruments; Southwest Airlines;* the *Kansas City Southern Railroad; The Southeastern Conference;* or *Kentucky Fried Chicken,* now *KFC,* each easily come to mind. The phrase "easily come to minds," of courses, implies that each brand, with the likely exception of the railroad, is well-positioned inside the evoked sets of many readers' minds.

- The "Founders" Brand Category—Founder-sourced brand names are, no surprise to follow, named for the person who birthed the brand. *Mary Kay Cosmetics; Ford Motor Co.; Eli Lilly and Co.; Wendy's;* the *Boeing Co.;* or *Macy's* or *Wanamaker's* in the departmental store domain to illustrate the point. Are you surprised that *Apple* is not named *Jobs*, *Microsoft* is not called *Gates*, or that *Facebook* does not roll off the tongue as *Zuckerberg's DreamDates*? Don't be. Because each founder just referenced chose wisely when selecting an alternative brand name that more effectively captured and projected the key branding values, the positioning vibe and value, or atmospherics that were delivered by their once-infant-like corporations as each grew up.

- The "Mashup" Brand Category—Mashed-up brands are what etymologists (experts on sources of words) call neologisms. Neologistic, okay, mashed-up, brand names emerge from the distillation into one word of two major benefits delivered by the brand. While this discussion may appear esoteric at this moment, let's clarify things by pronouncing several well-known brand names that simultaneously and more simply illustrate the points just made. These category features current or rising superstar brand names such as *Netflix, Facebook, Snapchat, GoPro, Pinterest, WhatsApp, GameStop,* or *Trupanion*, an up-and-coming marketer that sells pet insurance. Talk about the pairing of creative intersectional ideas—remember the "intersection" concept that was originally introduced inside Module 10.

- The "Inspirational" Brand Category—The brand name *Telsa* was inspired by *Nikola Tesla*, the now for more famous than when he actually lived inventor of too many electronic innovations to name here. As does *Planet Fitness*, a planet full of fit people; now that's inspirational, aspirational, and therefore forward-looking, and a good brand name. Even so, perhaps the *Nike* brand best fits here, inspired as the brand was by the *Greek* word for "victory," "outstanding achievement," and basketball dominance. Okay, just kidding; we actually meant football dominance.

- The "Whimsical" Brand Category—The apparel marketer *Lululemon* boasts one of the best whimsical brand names. This alliterative label implies nothing much more than cute, as far as we can cipher. Hmm, let's see, implying nothing but cute for a product targeted primarily at youngish females. Yes, that's probably sufficient. The name *Under Armour* is whimsical too, and presumably purposefully misspells armor—which is whimsical, isn't it? The power brand name *Google* is surely whimsical, given that the word "google" represents a purposefully misspelled take on an obscure mathematical term—the googol—that textually symbolizes the number 10 to the 100th power, or 1 followed by one hundred zeros.

- The "Metaphorical" Brand Category—Metaphorical brand names are rare but effective probably because they prove highly descriptive. A prime example is the *Chicken of the Sea* packaged food provider. The long since well-established brand was first used as a positioning statement (slogan) by the *Van Camp Seafood Co.* in 1914. But as a seafood differentiation device "*Chicken of the Sea*" is so catchy a lure for consumers that the *Van Camp* marketing team quickly changed its entire name. The *French* phrase for seafood, or at least seafood listed on menus inside restaurants, is *Fruits de Mer*—or "Fruit of the Sea." Perhaps that's what a marketing maker had in mind when, way back in 1856, a company that almost everybody knows and has probably worn more than once or twice began selling its underwear products. Yes, the name of that company, and the branding label literally affixed to each item of clothing the company markets, was and remains *Fruit of the Loom*. Playing the marketing long game, perhaps? Yes, of course, and nearly every other marketing organization and its brand managers should play the long game, as well.

POWERFUL BRANDS, OR NOT?

Powerful brands, by definition, have earned strong brand loyalty and brand equity. The process of developing brand equity can take years to complete. *Coca-Cola*, inside the *Japanese* marketplace, and *Mercedes*, inside the *United States*, are brands whose power was strategically developed across several decades.

Sometimes, however, the process through which branding power is developed seemingly blows up overnight. *Google* and *Facebook* underscore this point. As does GEICO. GEICO is a marketing organization that has operated profitably inside America since 1927 as the Government Employees Insurance Company. Then, in 1999, the *GEIGO Gecko* made his debut, and cliché alert, the rest is branding and advertising history.

And sadly, from a marketing perspective, the loyalty and equity of former powerful and favorably differentiating brand names can degrade rapidly or across time. *Lance Armstrong, Enron, New Coke, British Petroleum, Bill Cosby, Facebook, Ford sedans, Toyota,* and *Tiger Woods* come to mind. Of course now that Tiger is on the prowl again by winning the 2019 *Masters Tournament*, he eventually may rehabilitate much of the luster once associated with his fallen brand, assuming that Tiger is able to rehabilitate his body after his limb-shattering 2021 car crash.

Is the Power of These Brands Coming or Going?

The jury remains out on some other popular brands. Is their star waning or rising?

The *NFL* brand once was highly successfully positioned based on scarcity and violence. Don't sell violence short; many people, they're usually called men, absolutely love watching it. For many there is no other reason to slow down around automotive wrecks than to score a more accurate body count. And for decades its emphasis on scarcity and violence was enough to firmly impact the *NFL* brand residing among the world's most powerful. The brand is currently losing power because football is more widely available and less violent; while the foibles of its players, owners, and leadership have become more public.

Some relevant background. The *NFL*, since the 1960s, has staked a non-significant chunk of its brand personae and brand position on patriotism. Not for nothing do *U.S. Air Force* or *U.S. Navy* fighter pilots fly their jets over stadiums right before the *Super Bowl* kick-off. Player-led protests against the *American flag*, embodied by decisions to take a knee as the *National Anthem* is played, have been perceived by many fans as blatantly unpatriotic. Voting with their ears, eyeballs, and most importantly, their non-engagement, average viewership for the typical regular season Sunday game declined to 14,000,000 during 2020 from 16,000,000 fans the preceding season. Co-incidence, or causality, you decide. What is certain, however, is the *NFL's* brand loyalty, brand power, and brand equity have been damaged. Will a further deterioration of the league's *pricing power* soon follow?

Some perspective is merited, however. The power of the *NFL* brand has waned but remains strong. *Game of Thrones'* final episode was shown on May 19, 2019. The event garnered a huge initial audience. The total audience count, however, was merely equivalent to the seventy-third highest viewership for NFL games played during the 2018–19 regular- or post-season.

The *Major League Baseball (MLB)* brand was once successfully positioned based on tradition, statistics, and the chase of historical records. The brand has long been losing power . . . despite some wonderful recent World Series . . . because the game takes too d—m long in a speed of baud age. Consumers really do live in fast times, in busy worlds, don't they? There's never enough time to do all the nothings—texting, *Facebook*-ing, what-evers?—that modern consumers want to do.

Despite the slippage in branding power reported above, professional baseball and football remain hugely popular and highly marketed products throughout the United States. Yet the marketers who manage how each brand is delivered to targeted domestic markets are wisely continuously changing their products.

Features that once dominated inside football were eliminated in order to reduce the risk of permanent injury to players and preserve the game's brand image. (This was new product development.) Changes in how *MLB* is played were recently instituted for purposes of speeding up the game and making the sport more television-friendly. (Again, this was new product development.) Each brand's senior leadership was seeking to preserve and/or upgrade its long-term value by holding onto the best of the old while integrating changes into the traditional game that essentially were forced upon them as uncontrollable opportunities and threats, but primarily threats, rose up inside their external environments.

For the time being, one still dominant domestic sports brand continues to hum along nicely. The *NCAA* Men's Basketball brand is still successfully positioned on the related ideas of *Cinderella* and *the Glass Slipper* and the fact that she might have a shot at attending an annual fancy ball called the *Final Four*. The *NCAA's* Division I basketball brand is gaining power still because even old male sports fans apparently still believe in fairy tales.

That's likely because capable marketers adroitly convinced these old guys that the slipper might yet fit their team.

ONE TRUE SOURCE OF POWERFUL BRANDS

Do most powerful consumer-oriented brands emerge primarily from what marketers say about the products associated with the brands? Or do most powerful consumer-oriented brands emerge primarily from what other consumers who use or endorse the brands say about the products associated with the brands?

Framed differently, the same two questions could read as one: Do most consumers buy the brands that they want or purchase the brands that they perceive others would want them to want? The correct answer, both times, is embedded inside the second part of all three questions.

What others think or what we think others think about individual brands matters more in the long run than what marketers say about their own brands.

This makes sense. After all, what are consumers going to believe about particular brands? The things that obviously but also understandably self-interested branding marketers say? Or, will consumers generally believe what others who are important to them and who exercise some degree of subtle or direct influence over them are actually saying and, more importantly, doing?

The power as well as the need that marketers routinely confront to efficiently manage word-of-mouth or e-word-of-mouth processes, reference group relationships, and existing relationships between marketers and customers themselves again is underscored.

MODULE 11.3

What's in a Name?—Part 2

What's in a name? The answer is simple. Typically, more power and success lies ahead in the future of those people and organizations who coin the right term, word, label, brand, or name.

Names have power. And brand names have the power to separate consumers from their hard-earned money. Which is an outcome that is invariably good for marketers and more than occasionally not great for consumers. None of this should surprise. After all a famous book long ago wrote that a good name is to be valued more than great riches. Although, as has been made clear throughout this book, good names often lead to great wealth.

The costs for pharmaceutical firms to name and brand new drugs frequently exceed $3,000,000. This sounds like a lot of money until one learns that the domestic pharmaceutical market alone is a $450,000,000,000 business. So, there's a lot at stake whenever firms strategize to do branding well, after new products have been developed.

That's why *Big Pharma* firms don't assign the branding-the-new-thing project to white-coated pharmacist teams who sit around big tables, cleverly shoot the bull, order pizza, drink beer, and brainstorm branding ideas onto whiteboards. Instead, these assignments are usually allocated to branding agencies—the branding equivalent to advertising agencies—whose entire mission entails naming and branding new drugs. From the start, the assignment is more complicated than most assume. Not least because new prescription drugs must feature three different names. First, the chemical name, such as ibuprofen. Second, the generic name, such as *NSAID*—or nonsteroidal anti-inflammatory drug. Third, the actual brand name itself, such as *Advil* or *Tylenol*.

These brand-naming companies, such as *Zinzin*, the *Brand Institute*, or *Catchwood*, work through months-long to year-long processes to create and subsequently pick just the right names for new pharmaceutical solutions. The following sort of process is generally followed.

First, agencies must fully understand and flesh out the new product's purpose. Second, agencies compile dozens to hundreds of plausible brand names, which are then subjected to rigorous tests in accordance with various culling criteria in order to shrink the account to seven to ten finalists. Names must be cross-referenced through databases to ensure the name has not been taken. Foreign language databases must be electronically perused to make sure that names don't translate into something appalling or scandalous in another language or culture. These checkpoints actually bear fruit. In *Mandarin Chinese*, "Coca-Cola" roughly translates into "bite the wax tadpole." Marketing masters that they are, *Coke* executives wisely changed the brand to *Kekoukele,* which means "crazy fun" or something close to it in *Chinese.*

The *U.S. Food and Drug Administration* (FDA) and the *European Medicine's Agency* play hardball, and with good cause. Their mistakes, omissions, or errors can and do kill customers. To decrease the likelihood of prescription error, names cannot contain any medical modifiers, prefixes, suffixes, or numbers that could confound with dosage levels. The *Institute of Medicine* reports that about 1.5 million Americans are annually killed, injured, or sickened because of prescription or dosage mistakes. Docs surely should write more legibly, the increasing use of keyboarding certainly should help, but the takeaway lesson is that brand names matter in ways having nothing to do with brand's myriad marketing purposes. Naming firms seek to prevent such mistakes by asking numerous test subjects to write out the brand name to confirm that it cannot be confused for other brands due to sloppy handwriting.

In 1987 *Interbrand* earned the right to name a new product that *Eli Lilly and Company* was about to introduce. The new product was an antidepressant that featured the chemical name *fluroxetine hydrochloride.* After months of work similar to that ascribed above, *Interbrand* branded the new product as *Prozac,* claiming "the name sounded positive, professional, and full of zap." The truth was that the brand name meant absolutely nothing (not unusual) but provided an ample platform on which consumers could hang any attributions they wanted. Which is exactly what has happened insofar as during the intervening thirty-something years it has been prescribed to more than 55 million adults, children, dogs, cats, parrots, elephants, and polar bears—this is the truth.

The *Viagra* naming story was touched upon earlier during this Module, but the full version follows. In 1992 Arlene Teck, creative director at branding agency *Ixxeo Healthcare,* conducted a focus group with urologists to discuss erectile dysfunction. The malady is a normal and frequently occurring health condition that happens as men age, experience various health issues, or drink/drug too much. Erectile dysfunction has long since been powerfully branded as *ED.*

Ms. Teck asked a physician what a man felt like after his erectile dysfunction had been cured. The doc said visualize a "strong stream." Okay, Ms. Teck reasoned, what stream could flow stronger than the *Niagara River* at the falls, over which the entire outflow of the massive *Lake Erie* flows. Mindful of this, Ms. Teck created an intersection between the words "vigorous," "virile," or "vigor" and "*Niagara*." And suddenly, the once new brand name *Viagra* magically appeared. *Pfizer* shareholders have never halted their cheering. *Pfizer* is the *Big Pharma* firm that owns the rights to the *Viagra* brand name and the combined drug ingredients themselves.

Viagra was first to market and thereafter has remained first in the mind of the market, as well. Perhaps that's why the brand name *Viagra* popped up first in this Module, arriving as it did before any other branded products that are also classified and positioned within the new product category that the introduction of *Viagra,* as new product, actually inspired. Shortly after *Pfizer* introduced the big

"V," other *Big Pharma* competitors proved to be fast followers by quickly introducing their own ED solutions. *Eli Lilly* was first to enter the new marketplace. *Eli Lilly* had no choice but to bring its "A" creative game as it began the brand naming process. *Eli Lilly* and its naming agency reasoned that if *Viagra* captured the "action" market position resulting from use of its drug then it could capture the "feeling" market position resulting from use of its new product. *Eli Lilly* and agency began with the word *ciel*, meaning sky in *French*, and added the *French* word for bliss to arrive at the brand name *Cialis*.

Not to be outdone, the *German* pharmaceutical firm *Bayer*[9] and the *British* firm *GlaxoSmithKline* also quickly partnered to introduce a third major new solution to the impotence market. Yes, *Levitra*. *Levitra's* naming agency intended the name to make potential users think of words such as lever, levitate, and leverage. The creative team was aware of but judiciously overlooked the fact that LEV stands for Low-Emission-Vehicle in the automobile sector.

Can effectively named and well-positioned brands such as *Viagra* take up residence inside consumer minds? Yes, absolutely. And because brands that do take up mind-residence would generally be viewed positively by the consumers who own the minds, marketers should do anything possible to ensure that their brands' residence ends up being both permanent and rent-free.

---

9. *Bayer* legally created and briefly successfully commercialized the product now called heroin in 1898 (the century is correct). Guess what brand name *Bayer* ascribed to its new product. The answer is that the product was branded as *Heroin*. Buzz kill?

MODULE 11.4

The Inside Skinny behind a Remarkable Brand

The *United States Marine Corp* has an illustrious history, a birthday (November 10, 1775), a brand, and a prestigious and notably short list of slogans (words) that have been used to build and buttress its brand. *Marine Corps* birthday celebrations feature a traditional cake-cutting ceremony that would put your usual event marketing to shame. For this, a commanding officer cuts the cake with a *Mameluke* sword, the first piece going to the oldest Marine present, which is then passed along to the youngest. During the annual birthday celebration, Order No. 47 is read. Order No. 47 says in part, "it is fitting that we who are Marines should commemorate the birthday of our corps by calling to mind the glories of its long and illustrious history." Marines are understandably proud of their history.

History and tradition coalesce inside the *Marine Corp*s brand. Many branded expressions that have entered the American cultural vocabulary are related to the *Marines Corps*. For example, the brand *Leathernecks* hearkens back to 1776 when the Second Continental Congress designed new Marine uniforms and along with green coats, buff breeches, and black gaiters, mandated a leather collar to protect the neck against cutlasses. Oh, and to help maintain proper military bearing. Marine "packaging" has changed over the past 239 years—they have the best dress uniforms of any of the services—but the name stuck! The brand name *Devil Dogs* comes from the *Battle of Belleau Wood* during 1918. Their *German* foe called the *Marines* fighting through a steep forest terrain that was thought to be impenetrable, who captured ground thought to be an absolute German stronghold, "Teufel Hunden"—The Hounds from Hell. Modern Marines sometimes call themselves *Jarheads*. This brand name has its source in the "high and tight" haircut that many Marines prefer. The style purportedly makes Marine heads look like jars.

The most famous and differentiating Marine Corp branding identifier, however, is *Semper Fidelis* (*Latin* for "Ever faithful"). Marines are renowned for being fiercely loyal to country and to each other. Semper Fi was adopted in 1883 and at the time replaced three traditional but unofficial branding slogans. The first unofficial branding slogan was *Fortitudine* (*Latin* for "with courage"). The second was "*Per Mare, Per Terram*" ("By sea and by land"). The third was "To the shores of Tripoli," amended in 1848 to "From the halls of Montezuma to the shores of Tripoli." Those words were incorporated into the "Marines' Hymn," which yes is part of the USMC brand. Marines stand when the song is played or sung, a real tribute to the Mad Men of the '50's who counseled you could identify a hit brand, theme song, or campaign by "running it up the flagpole, to see if anyone saluted it." Marines continue to do so. Oh, and when they talk about a song being "top of the charts with a bullet," in this case *The Marines* mean a real bullet! When the subject is fighting, the Marines come strong. When the subject is marketing, the Marines play a strong game too. And when you think about things, that's not many brand slogan changes for a product that's 246 years old (Take a look. See how many times *Coca-Cola* has changed their branding tag line. And that *Coca-Cola* is only 135 years old!).

But the six words that USMC and the Marine brand itself are best known for today are, *The Few. The Proud. The Marines*. Primary credit for this brand slogan credit goes to ad man *J. Walter Thompson* for that. The famous slogan that Mr. Thompson's advertising agency developed helped transform The Corps into the elite brand it stands for today. *The Few, The Proud, The Marines* is the most-cited, most-recognized, and most-respected brand slogan of any U.S military service. The slogan even appears on *Madison Avenue's Advertising Walk of Fame*. But, like most things Marine, the brand slogan is also deeply rooted in history. On March 20, 1779, Captain William Jones of the Continental Marines placed a recruiting advertisement in *The Providence Gazette* (digital banner ads being unavailable at the time), which read in part "The Continental ship *Providence*, now lying at *Boston*, is bound on a short cruise, immediately; a few good men are wanted to make up her complement."

If you're seeking a celebrity endorsement regarding that practice, here's one. *George Washington* later commented: "It is infinitely better to have a few good men than many indifferent ones." Even during an age when Mr. Washington and many of his Southern contemporaries are subjected to new-age criticism, having George endorse your brand through word-of-mouth carries more than a little water—and a whole lot of weight. *The Few, The Proud, The Marines*. A branding identifier that just wins, like the Marines themselves.

EXHIBIT 11.1
What Is a Brand? Brands Exist at Four Distinct Levels

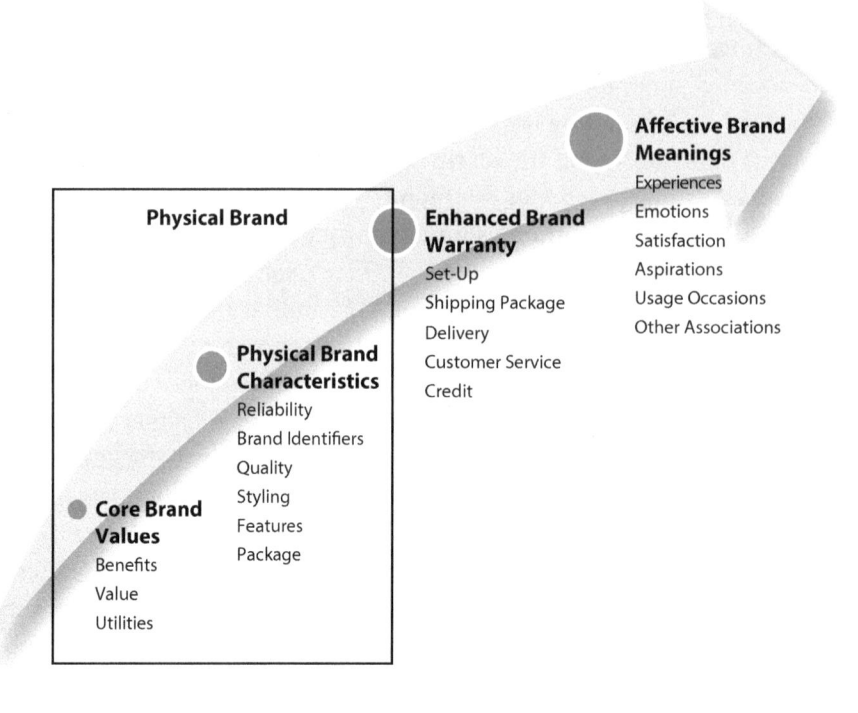

Physical Brand

Core Brand Values
- Benefits
- Value
- Utilities

Physical Brand Characteristics
- Reliability
- Brand Identifiers
- Quality
- Styling
- Features
- Package

Enhanced Brand Warranty
- Set-Up
- Shipping Package
- Delivery
- Customer Service
- Credit

Affective Brand Meanings
- Experiences
- Emotions
- Satisfaction
- Aspirations
- Usage Occasions
- Other Associations

EXHIBIT 11.2
Marketers Match Elements of Brand Personality to Consumers' Ideal Self-Concepts to Build Positive Attitudes for Brands

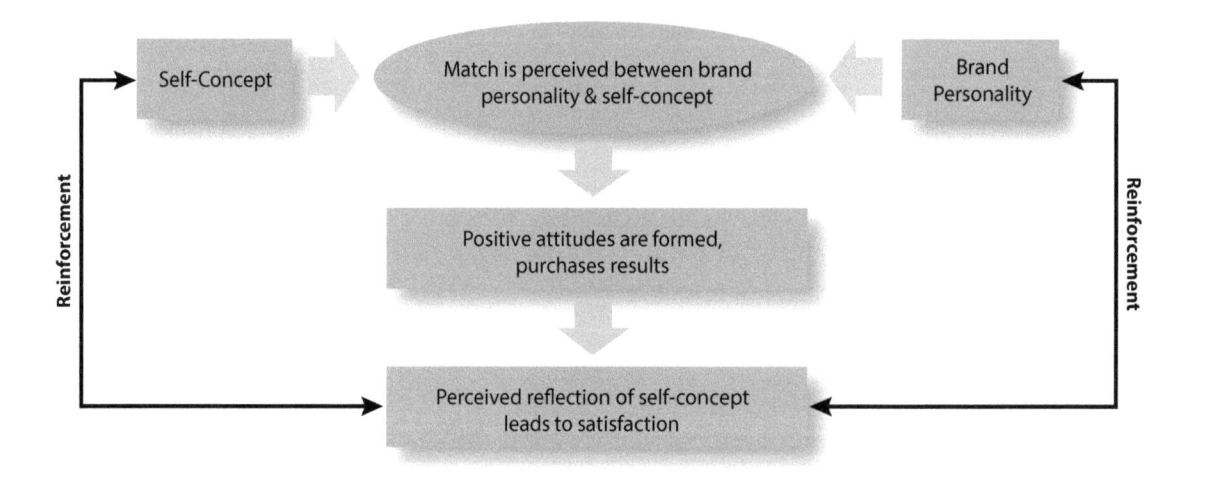

Self-Concept → Match is perceived between brand personality & self-concept ← Brand Personality

↓

Positive attitudes are formed, purchases results

↓

Perceived reflection of self-concept leads to satisfaction

Reinforcement (both sides)

MODULE 12

Managing Supply Chains and Logistics

Module 12.0

Establishing Context

Layer Cake is a criminally under-recognized *Guy Ritchie*-directed gangster movie. The 2004 flick starred *Daniel Craig* just before he broke big as the then-new *James Bond*, a branding icon if one has ever existed. Two key characters suggested, once near the beginning, and then again exactly as the movie ended, that:

▶ "The key to succeeding as a businessman (and marketer of guess-what?) is to be a great marketer and middleman. You must be a great go-between."

Or, using contemporary supply chain parlance, the key to being a great marketer and businessperson is being a great intermediary.

Nice, but . . . isn't this about the ninety-ninth time this book has tabbed a principle or an idea as being "a key to success"? Well, the truth is we have made similar points before, but this time we really mean it. Or do we? After all, hasn't this book also taught readers on a couple of occasions how best to "fake sincerity" inside certain contexts?

Truth be written the answers to the preceding questions don't much matter, because supply chain management actually does represent the last best chance for most marketing organizations to earn competitive advantages of the sort that will actually prove sustainable.

Are humans typically better off living and working together—or alone? Unsure what to think? Then imagine a blazing fire inside a contained campfire. Now imagine that you separate all the logs, one from the other, ensuring that the still burning logs no longer connect with one another. How well and for how long will those now-isolated logs burn? The answer is not well, and not for long.

This particular fireside chat[1] applies to humans and their inexorable need for interconnectivity. Yet the story similarly relates to organizations and the need they experience to partner and work

---
1. The "fireside chat" is the branding identity that *President Franklin Delano Roosevelt* assigned to his radio communiques as he spoke informatively and persuasively to the US population during most of the 1930s—or *The Great Depression* era. Radio was a new era-changing innovation of the time, and *FDR* (the President's brand identity) spoke into a microphone while sitting next to *The White House* fireplace while citizens often sat next to their fireplaces listening to their radios. The advent of the fireside chat and its delivery through radio was driven by political marketing goals. The communication mode and the message's mode of delivery also embodies an era-defining and era-changing marketing communication innovation. The "fireside chat" as marketed product truly was "new and useful."

cooperatively/collaboratively with each other. But the metaphor doesn't stop there. People also need to play well or work well with others before most of them can reasonably aspire to create successful professional lives for themselves. (Yes, some professionals still succeed and have succeeded despite being jerks. But inevitably such individuals succeeded because of the power and creativity of their ideas.)

The preceding descriptions apply to organizations too. In order to succeed organizations likewise have no choice but work and play well with others. The importance of interpersonal relationships as well as more corporate sorts of connections has long been acknowledged. During 1623 the poet *John Donne* wrote in *Devotions:* "No man is an island. Every man is a piece of the continent, a part of the main."

Human beings, each of whom are consumers, necessarily and naturally depend upon each another. The world is challenging. Most folks cannot manage worldly affairs much less repair their own broken stairs or ceiling fans efficiently and effectively by themselves. Mr. Donne was inveighing against the threats and dangers of too much isolation. Yet to degrees that might make current Senator and former Presidential Candidate *Mitt Romney* blush, the personal relational principles that Donne espoused about individuals also apply to corporations and the relationships that those "impersonal" organizations establish with each other in the persons of their human constituents. Now-*Senator Romney* was ruthlessly pilloried by the media during the 2012 presidential marketing campaign for uttering a sentiment about corporations being people.[2] The press also laid a general beatdown on Romney based on his response to a question about the role women would play in his administration. Mitt's tone-deaf answer was . . . no worries . . . "I have binders full of women." Yes, a pretty dumb response by such an otherwise intelligent man. Sometimes you have to wonder what politicians are thinking or even know when they don't have a marketing guy or gal putting the right words in their mouths. The right words, also known as those having been pre-tested and pre-selected by focus group or other research initiatives (Module 6).

MARKETING CHANNELS

This discussion of contemporary marketing supply chains ironically should begin by referencing an old-school concept called marketing channels. That's because the contemporary school concept known as the supply chain emerged directly from the idea of marketing channels. Marketing channels are organized collections of independent organizations that interdependently partner in order to execute the processes that must be fulfilled before products or services can be made available for

---

2. Here's the real "inside skinny" on this issue. Critics insist that corporate personhood, the idea that corporations enjoy certain legal and constitutional rights, is a fiction because corporations are not living, breathing human beings. The progressive take is that corporate personhood was foisted upon the *United States* by radical conservatives who were motivated by one purpose: helping Big Marketing. However, the fact that corporations are equivalent to people exists as a matter of long-standing legal precedent. Corporations have enjoyed personhood status since the beginning of the *Republic*. Corporate personhood is deeply rooted in the legal and constitutional traditions of the *United States*. Another useful thing to known and understand about corporations: Corporations will never pay higher taxes. They collect higher taxes in the form of higher prices imposed upon their customers, along with a ready-made excuse, lower wages paid to existing or fewer employees, or lower dividends paid to investors.

use or consumption by B2B customers or B2C consumers. These products or services might include *ESPN* sports entertainment content, political opinion magazines, or the *Ticonderoga No. 1* brand of pencils. The truth is that anything and everything of value that has been bought and sold or acquired and used by consumers or organizations has been touched by and passed through marketing channels or their contemporary successors, supply chains. Supply chains are ecumenical (unifying) because of the solutions they provide. Supply chains are universal (everywhere) because of their fundamental importance (we human consumers literally could not live with them) and consequently their universal reach.

The organizations that comprised traditional marketing channels generally included manufacturers, wholesalers, agents, shippers/transportation firms, warehouses, retailers, and ultimately customers themselves. The marketing channels used to distribute and market popular pharmaceutical brands such as *Lisinopril* or *Elixir* would classically include manufacturers (i.e., *Pfizer*) and wholesalers (i.e., *McKesson*) and other intermediaries (i.e., middlemen such as warehouses or shipping/transportation firms) and retailers (i.e., *CVS Pharmacy*)—and typically middle-aged or older customers.

What thoughts do you think come to mind first for most people were they asked to consider the word "channels"?[3] If you're feeling television channels or river/harbor navigation channels then you're thinking along the proper lines. How many different marketing channels does *ESPN* use to deliver its product content to viewers, listeners, and readers? *ESPN*'s content, regardless of its delivery mechanism, exists as a marketed product that has value and presumably solves customer problems related to what to do or watch next. Consider some of the ways in which *ESPN* monetizes its live and taped sports content across multiple channels platforms: Four or more *ESPN* television channels (*ESPN1, ESPN2, ESPNU, ESPNClassic*, each with slightly or notably different foci); *ESPN, the Magazine*, now delivered only in an "e" form; *ESPN.com*; *ESPN Radio*; and myriad *WatchESPN* mobile applications. Each channel permits the *Entertainment and Sports Programming Network*—that's what the branding acronym *ESPN* denotes—to deliver different products or services to different target audiences.[4]

The Atlantic is a progressive monthly magazine that thoughtful conservative thinkers should read if they are striving to introduce multiple perspectives into their creative lives. *The Atlantic* is an insightful, provocative, and useful magazine. But in this post-internet, 24/7/365 news cycle era (i.e., today), the magazine's once-a-month publication schedule often proved a barrier that diminished the timeliness and relevance of its reportage and opinion pieces. No longer. *The Atlantic* overcame the limitations of traditional print and once-a-month publication dates by making all its original content;

---

3. You were just asked a question related to top-of-the-mind-awareness and the evoked set, by the way.

4. *ESPN* ratings have been decreasing for years, shedding viewers like sheepdogs shed hair in *Texas* summer heat. Most experts agree this is because *ESPN* has lost its "core focus," chasing political and social responsibility rabbits having nothing to do with the sports-entertainment values that most previously loyal viewers had tuned-in to watch (i.e., actual live sports and videoed sports highlights programming). In response, *ESPN's* senior management engaged in a focused new product development initiative. The new product development initiative, at its core, entailed precluding show hosts and other talking heads from talking incessantly about politics, and particularly from expressing progressive opinions that unnecessarily but absolutely alienated roughly 50 percent of *ESPN's* actual and potential market audience. Perhaps those senior managers got a memo suggesting that if ESPN's sports addicts wanted to hear all political talk all day long they could change the channel to the *MSNBC* or *FOX* networks. The whole scenario convincingly underscores one key point. Rarely if ever is it a good idea to insult the political or cultural views of half or so of your customer base—that is, your targeted market segment.

new products, all, available through six different supply chain platforms. These supply chain—distribution—platforms are: A large, vigorous website; *Atlantic Studio* that provides video content; a live-events division; podcasts; a new membership program called *The Masthead*; and naturally, the traditional monthly 150-plus-year-old magazine that consumers can receive in the mail or purchase directly for themselves inside bookstores or on newsstands. Regardless of how they acquire the magazine, consumers can hold real paper in their hands.

SUPPLY CHAINS

Most Americans work in a knowledge economy and spend their professional days creating and passing information and services back and forth from one to other locales or persons. But *Madonna*, yes, the original 1980s' era *Material Girl Madonna*, was right to write: "*We are All Living in a Material World.*" So how does all that tangibly physical stuff get to our bathrooms, garages, closets, or television screens?

The answer is through supply chains. In many ways the descriptive terms "supply chains" and "marketing channels" are synonymous with one another. Except for one important difference. Marketing channels fail to account for the role played by firms that exist and operate upstream in the channel by functioning as sources to manufacturers or assemblers. Supply chains, by contrast, account for these "source" firms and the roles they play.

The pharmaceutical marketing channel discussed above began with a manufacturer firm. *Pfizer* is the name of the corporation that markets *Viagra*. The active ingredient in *Viagra* is sildenafil citrate. From where is this raw material sourced? We really don't know, and the answer really does not matter, other than we are certain that all individual crystalline elements compounded into sildenafil citrate originate somewhere in somebody's dirt. What is also known for certain is that *Pfizer* obtains these and numerous other raw materials from various other "partnering firms"; then compounds (assembles) the right chemical elements in the right proportions; next markets, merchandises, distributes, brands, and even colors the final product (*Vitamin V* blue, a color that is part of the brand's design); and finally helps make primarily older male customers feel younger again after having driven them half-insane by slamming "problem-recognition" into their collective minds through incessant advertising and other promotional initiatives. And voila, another marketer; here in fact, another set of collaborating marketers has succeeded, again; by working together inside a supply chain, all by solving their customers' differing problems.

What about automobiles? Their traditional marketing channels would kick off with manufacturers such as *General Motors*. But does *GM* actually make or merely assemble the automotive products that it markets? You know the answer. Next question. Does *GM* make the tires, windshields, batteries, navigational devices, pistons, bumpers, or the vast majority of the 30,000 or so parts, down to the smallest screws, that collectively make up their vehicles—yes, assembly is required. You got this, again. No, various other source firms make them. The book's use of the descriptor "source" in front of the word "firms" makes sense. After all, the key ingredients blended together to create *Viagra*, *Levitra*, or *Cialis*, the three dominant *ED solution* brands, or the thousands of parts that are required to assemble *Chevy*, *Ford*, or *Dodge* trucks must originate somewhere from some source.

What about the humble pencil? The wooden pencil—sharpener not included—is a simple writing technology. Yet the intricate set of genuinely global supply chain processes that must play out efficiently and effectively for traditional *Ticonderoga* or *Dixon Yellow No. 1* or *2* school pencils to be birthed and delivered to wherever consumers or businesses purchase them are stunningly complex in their intractably networked complexity and globalized nature. Even simple basic yellow pencils themselves are too complicated for any one organization or person in the world to make within reasonable timelines and at economically-feasible costs. That's because byzantine-like and highly sophisticated networks of producers and assemblers, processes and processors, nations and supply chains each must collaborate cooperatively and efficiently with one another in order for pencils, this modest technological solution, to be built.

For example, some networked set of organizations had to make the saws to cut the wood that ultimately is transformed into pencils. Another network set existed and executed in order to mine the ore that was congealed into steel. Another set of networked marketing organizations existed ship the steel to where it was repurposed into saws. We should quickly realize how many additional boats or ships, trains and trucks,[5] as well as various warehouses are inextricable pieces of the multiple supply chains that must be successfully managed to successfully manufacture simple pencils. Yet some other supply chain of marketing organizations had to make and market and man those boats or ships, and trucks or trains, and warehouses.

Perhaps dozens of globally networked systems of marketing organizations must process, make, ship, store, and/or assemble the various raw elements and finished goods that must arrive at the right time in the right place and in the right quantities and forms in order merely to make the lacquer that coats pencils' exteriors. Lacquer, of course, is only one of many constituent parts inside the deceptively un-simple pencil. What about the lead, which is actually graphite; the tinting; the ferrule; or the rubber plug, which is not rubber but rather factice? By the way, what is factice, where does its supply chain begin, and how is it made, shipped, stored, and sold? These additional individual pencil "ingredients," along with nearly a dozen others not mentioned above, similarly must be processed, made, shipped, stored, and/or promoted/sold/marketed by various additional globally-networked-systems comprised of collaborating marketing organizations that had to cooperatively be present at the right time in the right place in the right quantities and forms in order to make and market any single one of the finished goods or raw materials that collectively constitute a pencil.

Are you beginning to more deeply understand how complicated and indispensable supply chains and their management are? And how complicated and important supply chain management remains even when unpretentious and decidedly low-tech products are marketed?

DIRT-TO-DIRT

Supply chains almost always extend all the way back to the dirt. Or conversely, supply chains almost always begin in the dirt. Think about the various *Apple* or *Samsung* products that many consumers

---

5. What should readers think of whenever they hear another train whistling down an already busy railroad track or see another truck slogging down another crowded interstate highway? Seers or hearers should recognize another sign that a free market-based economy and marketplace are doing their jobs well.

own, love, and regularly use. Didn't all the component parts of these products, including their covers, actually begin their lives in the dirt? What is silicon if not dirt? Almost all kinds of sand, clay, or minerals contain silica in one form or another. Estimates are that more than half the Earth's crust is silica-based.

Of course every tangible product comes from the dirt, from the screws that hold cars together; to the tree or minerals that make up pencils; to the cotton likely covering your back or backside at this moment.

And supply chains eventually flow forward all the way back to the dirt again. Because some future day will arrive when the tangible things that we buy now grow old inside our minds, yes even the pair of *Levi's* jeans or *Bassett*-built piece of furniture that we currently completely love, and we decide to rid ourselves of them. Garbage-time or recycling-time? Who knows? One known thing, however, is the fact that possessions we currently love grow old and pass away as we become less passionate about them. This naturally-arising circumstance represents another reason why successful new product development (NPD) is necessary for all marketers to sustain their success. These two processes similarly illustrate the nature and value of the product life cycle (PLC) concept.

Dirt-to-dirt, dust-to-dust; these are two extremely well-branded *Old Testament phrases*. Each phrase, however, remains highly relevant inside contemporary supply chains.

SUPPLY CHAINS: IN THEIR BEGINNING, AND AT THEIR END

Supply chains always begin with source firms . . . continue to flow downstream through focal manufacturers, assemblers, or marketers (i.e., *Apple*) . . . extending through wholesalers and other distributors such as warehouses or shippers . . . and apparently end with retailers (*Apple Stores, Best Buy,* kiosks inside malls) or e-tailers . . . and ultimately, customers. But supply chains need not necessarily end with customers, as just noted, because older products are often recycled or repurposed.

All organizations and people who operate as organizations between original source firms and retailing firms function directly or indirectly as intermediaries. The word intermediary means in-between. Or, in the common business vocabulary, middlemen.

Supply Chain Intermediaries Unite the Marketing World— and Other Entities As Well

Intermediaries are everything and exist everywhere—similar to marketing itself. The presence and participation of intermediaries adds a miraculous range of values to the world. The presence and effects of "supply chain-like" intermediaries are evident even inside some likely unexpected places.

Core *Protestant Christian Church* doctrine, for example, positions *Jesus* as the intermediary between here on earth and *Christianity's* conception of heaven. *Protestants* routinely and actively seek out *Jesus* as their direct intermediary when facing dire problems that often seemingly have no earthly solution.

By contrast, *Catholicism* doctrinally envisions and uses *Mary* (the mother of *Jesus*), along with Jesus and other saints, in the same manner—as intermediaries. *Catholics* enjoy the opportunity to engage with many more intermediaries when seeking to establish problem-solving connections between earth and their conception of heaven. The supply chain extending between earth and heaven in the *Catholic* conception consequently features many more levels and/or possible designs than the *Protestant* supply chain, because the *Catholic* supply chain features many more intermediaries, including, for example, *the Pope*.

The Pope, meanwhile, is further branded and positioned as *"The Pontiff"* inside the *Catholic Church's* organizational structure, as an estimated 1.2 billion Catholics know.

Pons, in *Latin*, means bridge. Bridges, all of them, offer connections and passageways. So do all supply chains, so long as they feature intermediaries. We reiterate: Marketing is everything and marketing is everywhere, as are supply chain-like relationships—and intermediaries.

Promiscuous or Strategic?

Apple, like numerous for-profit and not-for-profit firms, freely engages in dozens of supply chain relationships. As does *Dillard's*, the retailer. Or, as do various other various less well-known corporations that mine and market zinc, copper, or coal.

Strategic marketing organizations would rarely limit their supply chain partnering options to only one choice. Retailers generally engage in relationships with multiple supply chain partners, primarily in the form of manufacturers and marketers. Plano-headquartered *JCPenney* buys men's pants from multiple apparel marketers. These manufacturing source firms include *Haggar Manufacturing, Levi Strauss, Liz Claiborne, Dickies,* and *Ralph Lauren* . . . . Retailers such as *JCPenney* essentially function as *Haggar's, Levi's,* or *Liz's* sales force and promotional agent as they sell through their supply chains to end use customers, or consumers. Which is only right because these supply chain partners function as *JCPenney* source firms.

But the same manufacturers engage in multiple supply chain (and marketing) relationships with different retailers, who simultaneously function as both their customers and sales force (i.e., marketers). Dallas-headquartered *Haggar,* for example, sells men's pants to multiple retailers . . . including *Walmart, JCPenney, Dillard's, Kohl's,* and so forth. These retailers essentially market these pants downstream through their supply chain to end-use consumers, a group that would include most though not all males reading this passage now.

The fact that none of these American apparel manufacturing brands actually assemble any apparel items they sell to and through, say, *JCPenney* inside the *US* is worth noting. This is a difference with a distinction. Many supply chains that originate or end inside America are actually global in nature. Essentially, this condition means at times that raw materials grown inside (for example, cotton) the *United States* leave the country, typically being shipped to *Asian* destinations, and rather quickly return to the Mothership, *America,* as finished shirts, pants, or other apparel items.

Have you ever considered how many different marketing organizations supply tangible products in the form of finished products to *Walmart* in order to flesh out the giant retailer's inventory inside its lawn & gardening or automotive parts product merchandise categories? Or how many different sets of supply chain relationships that *Netflix, Microsoft, Toyota,* or any hotel, hospital, or university must manage? The numbers should not only impress. The numbers should also underscore the global depth, breadth, scope, reach, and fundamental importance of supply chains.

Marketing Success Always Flows from Supply Chain Exchange Relationships

All these exchange activities, all these supply chain relationships, are necessary. Things cannot differ.

Indeed, one overarching goal and unifying purpose that prevails inside almost every supply chain entails the creation and efficient maintenance of flows that operate as friction-free as possible. This goal applies regardless of the nature of the supply chain activity itself. This unifying purpose—achieving frictionless flows—remains relevant regardless of the specific nature of the supply chain activity itself and whether physical, possession, payment, promotion, or informational flows are entailed.

Modern marketing organizations cannot exist, operate, or compete effectively as islands unto themselves. Contemporary organizations cannot succeed absent contact and engagement with other organizations situated on-the-mainland with them. Not inside modern marketplaces and economies that should logically and accurately and strategically view the opportunity to develop extreme specialization, to focus on their specific specialties, and to therefore develop the opportunity to earn impressive cost efficiencies as "must-haves" rather "it-would-be-nice-to-have-this-opportunity."

Suggesting that various highly-networked sets of social, technological, business, economic, academic, governmental, and military organizations exist as nothing more or less than one huge set of intricate and inextricable supply chain relationships is not hyperbole.

Exchange relationships exist as the simple and not-so-simple element that connects everything. Nothing is more important in marketing than exchange and exchange processes. Few things are more important in life, either.

Cotton Balls and T-Shirts Exemplify What Supply Chains Do

First, consider that tens of thousands of bales of cotton are grown annually in *West Texas* cotton fields. Next, contemplate the three-packs of *Hanes* T-shirts sold in any *Walmart* store. In addition, note that six miles of thread, or what apparel manufacturers call yarn, are woven into each T-shirt. Finally, consider how another seemingly simple product is actually extremely complex, particularly as more is revealed about the intricate supply chain processes required to make and market apparently simple T-shirts as apparel solutions. Yes, first pencils; now T-shirts. Thank goodness we haven't been discussing cell phones or televisions.

How does cotton exit *West Texas* cotton field dirt as raw material and return boasting finished-product status to *Fort Worth, Texas,* where T-shirts supply particular value to end-use consumers; after having traveled back and forth not only across the *Pacific Ocean* but also across some 1,300 American miles from *West Texas* to *Long Beach, California,* for a relatively short stay in *China*? Do you think numerous *American, Chinese,* and *Swedish* global shipping sea carriers or domestic rail or trucking firms had intermediating roles to play as these T-shirts experienced their journey; just like various company-owned or independent warehouses, manufacturers, and assemblers also had their own indispensable say? You'd better bet your T-shirt they did. Just as you should classify *Michael Jordan, Kevin Bacon,* or *Charlie Sheen,* who are or who were at one time celebrity spokespersons and brand endorsers for the *Hanes* brand, as integral parts of *Hanes'* T-shirt supply chains. Why? Because each gentleman has also traditionally played a prominent promotional role in *Hanes'* brand positioning processes.

Supply chains always consist of upstream and downstream business partners for any marketing organization that is participating in a supply chain. As almost all firms do, because almost all organizations must! Upstream means moving up or backward toward the originating sources of any product. As in, for example, the original source for raw cotton is cotton fields or ultimately, dirt. Downstream means "flowing" down toward final selling retailers and/or customers. These intermediary[6] business partner organizations generally include suppliers; intermediaries (including but not limited to agents, warehouses, and shippers such as trains, trucks, planes, pipelines, or marketing researchers and bankers); and customers to each intermediaries, along with various sorts of traditional and internet-based retailers.

All supply chain partner firms either sell to or buy from each other. Each organization functions either as B2B marketers or B2B customers. Then, customer organizations literally reverse course, turn around, and transfer into marketers that are selling the now value-added product to the next partner downstream in the supply chain they all share.

---

6. Intermediary organizations are for-profit or not-for-profit organizations, including individuals such as agents or manufacturers' representatives, that play fundamental roles in facilitating, promoting, or encouraging B2B relationships between marketing organizations or B2C relationships between marketing organizations and end-use consumers.

MODULE 12.1

Values Generated

Throughout history wise warriors have fought battles and indeed entire wars based on strategy (Modules 2 and 3). Yet warriors, wise or otherwise, usually have won or lost battles, but especially entire wars, based on how effectively they or an important adjutant team managed logistics and supply chain processes for their fellow fighters.

Supply chain management is similarly a fundamentally important marketing topic.

SUPPLY CHAIN MANAGEMENT IS . . .

Supply chain management . . .

> ▶ . . . Involves planning, implementing, and controlling the flow and storage of products and services from their points of origin to their points of consumption, with the end goal of satisfying customer needs always fixed in place.

If asked, supply chain managers might accurately describe how their professional efforts enable B2B customers and B2C consumers to obtain the right product or service at the right time in the right place at a price customers, by definition, must consider right. Otherwise, customers won't purchase. And if they are gabby, the same professionals might discuss how crucial their role is to satisfying B2B and B2C customers alike, and that supply management is crucial from cradle to grave—or from dirt to dirt.

SUPPLY CHAIN VALUE ONE

Supply chains permit the individual marketing organizations that partner inside them to focus on doing what they do best. Creating opportunities for those firms to become the best in the world in their area of expertise, for example. The strategic need to specialize; the need for firms to focus on doing and improving what they do best; along with strategic imperative that marketing organizations confront to pursue, sustain, and strengthen their specialized marketing capabilities and skills was introduced earlier.

Nike currently does not make anything it sells, and rarely has. Not even back in 1964 when founder *Phil Knight* sold his first few pair of Tiger brand shoes, the precursor brand to *Nike,* out of the trunk of his *Plymouth* to *Bill Bowerman* who was the then-renowned track coach at the *University of Oregon*. The *Tigers* had been made in *Japan*. Instead, *Nike* brands executes NPD processes, and manages the 112 independent supply chain partner organizations that currently coordinate with *Nike* in the manufacturing and assembling of those shoes and other sports gear. (Yes, this 112 figure likely has changed by now.)

Apple is another fabulously famous brand that has never made anything that it has sold. And presumably never will.

Hmmm. These facts surely help explain why supply chains exist and how they contribute materially to marketing success—or failure.

The need to achieve specialization and to then focus on creating and/or sustaining one or two core competencies invariably prevails inside supply chains. This need for specialization generally plays out in the form of one marketing organization's ability to perform a given supply chain function more effectively than its partnering firms could perform the function for themselves.

The need for and the desirability of achieving greater specialization inside individual organizations is the primary reason supply chains exist. This need also represents the primary reason why firms enter supply chain relationships in the first place. Supply chains specialize in specialization.

Supply chain member organizations, which include all firms because—for the last time—"no firm is an island," should be allowed to concentrate on doing what they do best. Source organizations should provide necessary parts and raw materials to manufacturers and assemblers. Manufacturers and assemblers should make or assemble. Transportation firms should transport. Warehouses should store and manage inventory. Retailers, finally, should merchandise, promote, and retail.

Inside supply chains, those marketing organizations that are best able to perform given functions most efficiently and effectively should perform the functions. This idea is as strategic as it is logical. The idea's underlying principles extend back to economist *Adam Smith* and his 1776 publication of *The Wealth of Nations*.

This opportunity to focus, their opportunity to specialize in specialization, permits marketing organizations to leverage and further refine their core strengths and competencies. Core competencies, in turn, provide foundations on which differentiating marketing values can be established, promoted, and delivered. Core competencies, finally, provide bases on which firms can establish sustainable competitive advantages by managing their marketing mixes to create desirable positions. Yes, the "core competency" concept actually has been referenced in seven previous Modules. This ongoing refrain should signal how important the pursuit, development, and exploitation of core competencies are to the success of individual or corporate marketers.

The Illustrative Tale (Story) of Topsy Tail

What's a *Topsy Tail* and why should readers care?

Readers should care because *Topsy Tail* was a 1990s-era brand that quickly made many millions by marketing a little piece of plastic that allowed young girls or for matter women to easily pull their hair back or up, and create a hairdo. As a reminder, back during the 1990s the opportunity to make $1,000,000 actually meant something.

Okay, nice story. But what's the real point?

The supply chain takeaway is that *Topsy Tail*, the entire corporation, consisted of three people. *Topsy Tail* outsourced the performance of all supply functions to independent supply chain partners. From there, the innovative *Topsy Tail*—itself based only on one great idea—focused on doing what it did best.

The one great idea, by the way, involved offering a quick and easy inexpensive solution to harried mothers whose young daughters always wanted mom to "give them a hair-do" or "give them a ponytail." The idea led to an only-cents-to-make but ultimately highly profitable plastic loop that moms or dads could pull their daughters' hair through. Voila; happier kid; happier parent; happier household. This little piece of *American* marketing and supply chain management history began in 1991.

SUPPLY CHAIN VALUES TWO, THREE, FOUR, FIVE

The Generation of Economies of Scale (Value Two)

Producers (manufacturers or assemblers) usually seek to make narrow assortments of products in large quantities. Their ability to focus and specialize on making fewer products in huge quantities allows supply chain partners to increase efficiency[7] and lower costs by exploiting the core-competency-based advantages and values delivered by economics of scale. Economies of scale refer to the reduced costs *per unit* that will arise from increased *total* outputs of products. For example, larger factories will produce drill bits at a lower per unit cost, and larger medical systems, at least in theory, should reduce costs per medical procedure. Various *Asian* firms, but primarily *Chinese*-headquartered *Foxcomm*, play their role in annually producing millions of *iPods*, *iPhones*, and *iPads* that bear the *Apple* brand

---

7. The ability to increase efficiencies generates certain sustainable strategic advantages all its own and on its own. When organizations or consumers engage in production or consumption practices that use more resources than are needed, the world experiences waste, and *Green* advocates should shudder in response to that prospect. The willingness and capability to continuously create and sustain greater efficiency ultimately may prove to be the *Greenest* tool in anyone's environmental capitalistic toolkit. Which is important insofar as everybody wants their children and grandchildren to live in environments that are better than the environments that currently exist. Capitalists love, desire, and wish to facilitate *Green* too. In all likelihood, capitalists support *Green* for two reasons. First, because they love or will support future or current children and grandchildren. Second, because they love or will love whatever marketing actions that will enhance their branding reputations and consequently fill up their coffers. Strategies should "always dance close to revenue lines," right?

The Generation of Product Assortments (Value Three)

But even customers who are fiercely loyal to the *Apple* brand usually still want to buy broad assortments of products in narrow quantities (i.e., one iPod, one iPhone, or one iPad). Or, for example, seek to acquire one automobile; thirty blood pressure pills; or one, two, or three tubes of toothpaste at a time.

The presence of supply chains creates this specific value for consumers by transforming mass assortments produced by manufacturers into the onesie-units that buyers want to acquire. This value, one that is created by and though supply chains, results from this sorting, or breaking-bulk, function.

The Bridging and Closure of Gaps (Value Four)

Supply chain members and the relationships they share with one other likewise add value by bridging the time gaps; place gaps; and possession gaps that separate organizations that generate products and services from the organizations or individual consumers who seek to purchase and/or use them.

When time gaps are bridged, the right products are made available to customers at the right time.

When place gaps are spanned, the right products become available to customers in the right place.

When possession gaps are bridged, the right products can be accessed by customers in the product's most appropriate or useful form.

These fundamental customer rights are fulfilled through supply chains. Customers, naturally, decide what products, times, and places, as well as pricing levels are right for them.

A true story follows:

Once upon a time there was a lobster named *Larry* who met an unfortunate and ill-timed fate. Of course, other people, including the *Washington lobbyist* who consumed Larry's lobster tail, perceived his ending differently. The fact these two disparate points of view could co-exist was due to the value-adding (think: price-elevating) power generated inside *North America's* lobster supply chain.

Long-story-shortened: The takeaway from Larry's supply chain tale is that he was caught and lifted out of the water by a *Nova Scotia* lobsterman. A seafood agent bought Larry live off the dock. The intermediary paid $2.75 per pound for the privilege. Six to eight days later Larry got sold again, but this time by a high-end *Washington, DC*, restaurant at exactly $37.99 a pound. This increase in Larry's street value (the supply chain for cocaine produced in *Nicaragua* actually could have been used to illustrate the same point) resulted because value was added to his tail at each of the four succeeding levels in the lobster supply chain that Larry passed though from the time he was plucked from the North Atlantic to the time when he was plated at a high-end DC restaurant where most patrons pay for their meals using someone else's money. Notably, Larry's supply chain and its special processes kept him alive until about eight to nine minutes before he was served, whole-tail, likely to some fat cat brandishing corporate plastic. During his journey southeast toward the *Washington, DC, swamps*, Larry received a colonic, which improves taste and thereby adds value; had his claws clamped, so he could not kill and eat his relatives and friends, thereby maintaining value; and allowed to swim inside cold Northern Atlantic water, maintaining his fresh taste, yum, value-added, again.

No one should assume lobster actually tastes like chicken, by the way. But let's segue to chicken, anyway, for purposes of illustrating how poultry supply chains add great value to the humble chicken. Chicken has long been the world's most widely traded and consumed meat. The total mass and weight of farmed chicken inside *America* alone surpasses the mass and weigh of every other farmed and wild bird in the rest of the world, as noted elsewhere in this book!

Supply chain-wise, chickens as a product are the opposite of automobiles as a product. Chickens are produced whole, inside supply chains. Unlike autos, which are assembled from parts, which themselves are sourced piece by piece from upstream supply chain partners.

But the value of chickens is maximized as the product is broken up or disassembled. Beaks, feet, meat, legs, thighs, breasts, feathers; each chicken part generates different sorts and amounts of additional value. Automobiles, just the opposite. Value is added to autos by piece as they are assembled.

Managing and Satisfying Product Demand by Providing Product Supply (Value Five)

Marketing success derives in near equal measures from ability of organizations or individuals to first create and to thereafter manage and satisfy customer demand. This fact is supply chain management itself has moved from being consumer-aware to consumer-driven. Most supply chain management decisions should be demand-based. Making accurate demand projections—largely derived from successful marketing research—is really important. Supply chain executives are increasingly listening to the voice of consumers.

Successfully managing demand, ultimately, entails successfully fulfilling demand. This is the ultimate value created and provided by supply chains. The four rights (see above) that *American* customers enjoy and take for granted to the point that few ever consider the functionally-miraculous activities that had to be executed before they can enjoy what they now enjoy only because of values that were first created and subsequently fulfilled inside domestic or global supply chains.

Modern supply chains deliver remarkably-underappreciated solutions. Contemporary supply chain processes are astounding in their complexity, efficiency, and effectiveness. Most American consumers fail to fully appreciate, must less understand, how all that stuff they consume on a daily basis gets into their pantries, bathrooms, or closets. The wonderful things that supply chains do, as well as the values that supply chains create for them are consequently often taken for granted by those benefitting most. Such a lack of appreciation is not without historical precedent.

Values One through Five Follow from Hopefully Seamless Flows

A book called *Exodus* describes how manna miraculously appeared to nourish the Israelites as they wandered, desert-bound, for forty years after leaving captivity in Egypt. No one knows how manna arrived in the right form at the right time and place each night from heaven—it was quickly simply accepted as God's gift. And unsurprisingly, its arrival was soon taken for granted. Just like the toilet paper in our bathrooms. Ever wonder how those valuable products arrive, seemingly seamlessly?

(Seamlessly is how supply chains ideally should flow.) The answers are not actually miraculous, but each is fascinating, complicated, and important in its own right. The answer, yes, is through supply chains.

One additional play-an-imaginary-game-thought: Imagine how crappy the day would be if and when toilet paper stopped showing up, first inside stores, and thereafter, inside bathrooms.[8] Of course this possibility—a day without toilet paper—became very real very fast and presumably actually visited a handful of American households during 2020 as the consumer marketplace began hoarding toilet paper during the early stages of the COVID-19 environmental threat. Remembering this eventuality not as possibility but as recent reality should make readers cognizant of the fact that they should never take supply chains—even the less sublime versions—for granted.

---

8. Excerpted from David Strutton, "Logistics: Getting the Toilet Paper (and Everything Else) to the Right Place at a Right Time," *Fort Worth Star-Telegram* (May 27, 2006): 1–12.

MODULE 12.2

Logistical and Supply Chain Functions and Flows

The successful execution of logistical or supply chain processes is driven by the presence and reciprocal flows[9] of information. This information presumably is gathered through the proper metrics (measurements) and freely distributed within individual firms for logistical management purposes or among partnering firms for supply chain management purposes.

Supply chains that possess and exploit superior information usually win marketing competitions against other supply chains that possess and can exploit roughly equivalent amounts of resources or core competencies, but that fall short on the supply chain information front. To a degree that would likely surprise most readers, modern marketing competition are often more about entire supply chains (*Nissan's* versus *Ford Motor's* supply chains) competing against each other than it is about individual firms (*Nissan* versus *Ford Motor*) competing against each other. The firm who partners inside the best supply chains almost inevitably wins, long-term, in other words. Other things being equal, the best supply chains are those that have the best information available as they formulate their marketing strategies and execute their marketing mix decisions.

Superior information is determinant; a prime difference-maker. Superior information is more accurate, reliable, and valid in nature than other available information. Note that the descriptive terms used to characterize superior information—accurate, reliable, valid—were originally discussed during Module 6 (the Research Module).

The same broad descriptions apply to logistical and supply chain managers themselves. Managers who possess and exploit superior information usually win marketing competitions against managers who can lay claim to roughly equivalent amounts of resources or core competencies but who possess deficit information.

Logistical processes involve getting the right product to the right place at the right time. Again, as do supply chain processes. Individual marketing firms certainly still compete against each other. But most of the time the efficiency and effectiveness of the relationships cobbled together by logistical processes

---

9. In this context reciprocal flow refers to information that passes back and forth, in each direction, between partnering supply chain organizations.

playing out inside their supply chains determine which firm—again, *Nissan* or *Ford*—prevails during these competitions.

HISTORICAL ILLUSTRATION (AGAIN)

Logistical and supply chain matters matter greatly. More than one-half ton of material, products that were almost always made in America, was required to keep a *World War II*-era American soldier fit for one month's service inside *Italy* from between 1943 and 1945. America's supply chain and logistical efficiencies were perhaps the major reason why the *United States, Great Britain,* and the *Soviet Union* eventually won the war by defeating *Germany, Japan,* and *Italy.*

Keep in mind that America was waging war on multiple fronts (*Europe* and *The Pacific*), each located between four to ten thousand miles from the homeland, and still kicked logistical ass. To what degree did America kick logistical ass? Consider this evidence: US soldiers' rationed daily allotment for toilet paper was 22.5 sheets. During the same 1943–45 period their *British* allies, again fighting in *Italy*, were only allotted three sheets per soldier.[10]

THE THREE CORE LOGISTICAL FUNCTIONS

Three primary logistical functions must be performed inside any supply chain. In no particular order these functions are storage, order processing, and shipping.

Storage involves inventory management and warehousing.

Order processing is important mostly in terms of ensuring nothing goes wrong; meaning, fundamentally, that raw material, component parts, or finished product ordering processes unfold as expected and promised. Notably, the first-generation *Affordable Healthcare Act* (better known, brand-wise, as *Obamacare*) website experienced extreme enrollment and payment—order processing—problems). These technical flaws badly damaged the new product's brand power, image, and equity during the Introduction Stage of its life cycle.

Shipping, which entails the provision of transportation services for the planned movement of raw materials, component parts, or finished goods, is a highly specialized supply chain function. Many supply chain organizations perform the shipping function and it alone. Examples include the trains, planes, trucks; ships, boats or barges, and pipelines noted earlier.

Today's globalized shipping companies have achieved mind-boggling economies of scale. Mega ships now routinely carry 20,000 twenty-to-forty-five-feet-long shipping containers while crisscrossing oceans; automated cranes, trains, and trucks are currently loading and unloading ships at record rates. Maritime supply chains bring American consumers bottled water sourced in *France*, shoes manufactured in *Cambodia*, and phones assembled in *China*—all at prices that the average *American* consumer perceives as affordable. Because, if the water or shoes or phones were not deemed affordable, they would not be purchased.

---

10. Rick Atkinson, *The Day of Battle: The War in Sicily and Italy* (New York: Henry Holt and Company, 2007).

These shipping companies face the same relentless downward pressures on costs and prices as every other supply chain firm faces. Many developing countries bankroll new ports and vessels and subsidize shipping to tip trading scales in their favor. Shipping rates in certain global trade corridors have actually fallen below costs. *China* has been especially aggressive in providing national subsidies; creating a global marketplace in which it sometimes costs more to ship products and material from city point to city point inside the US (say, from *Boston, Massachusetts,* to *Cleveland, Ohio*) than to transport products from *Guangzhou,* in southeastern *China,* to *Boston,* in the *Northeastern United States.* Keep in mind that products crossing from *China* to *Boston*, situated on the *Atlantic Ocean Seaboard,* either have to travel across the US continent, sail through the *Panama Canal,* and then up the Atlantic Seaboard, or travel below the southern tip of *South America* and then sail 11,000 or so miles north to *Boston.* The mind boggles at the economics of scale involved. (Yes, many modern container ships are too large to use the *Panama Canal*.)

Logistical managerial processes primarily occur inside organizations, such as, for example, the *U.S. Army.* These same logistical processes, however, also knit otherwise independent organizations together as they partner inside supply chains. Even so, logistical processes unfold as inputs to firms; as through-puts inside firms, and as out-puts, when exiting firms. Logistics is primarily about me—my firm's inbound, outbound, and through-bound flows of raw material, components, products, information, and money.

Supply chain management processes, by contrast, unfold between firms. Supply chain management is more about all of us—everyone—inside the entire network or system of companies inside the supply chain who presumably partner and work together for every supply chain firm's mutual benefit. Supply chains are like rivers; they will run (flow) whether or not they are managed. But, unlike wild rivers, which sometimes should be left alone, it is always best to manage the flows that stream up or down through supply chains as demand is created and demand is satisfied.

Traditional rivers only flow in one direction; downstream. Not so with supply chains, however. Inside modern supply chains, the rights, obligations, and responsibilities of partnering firms flow reciprocally, back and forth upstream and downstream. Like *Louisiana Bayous,* supply chains can and do flow in either direction. Information, in particular, flows up and down supply chains in both directions. In exchange for downstream partners' customer patronage and money, upstream partners are responsible for providing quality and value-enhancing services.

Here comes some old news. But news so worthy that it merits another hearing.[11] When operating inside supply chains, participating (and partnering) organizations should concentrate—as in focus—on doing what they do best. In brief, the partnering firm that specializes in performing a key supply function—key supply chain functions are described in the next section—should be permitted and indeed encouraged to perform the function. When this happens, firms that specialize in, say, shipping, inventory management, or order processing, clearly benefit. But so does every other partnering firm inside the supply chain.

---

11. Bayous typically flow in one direction. But when extreme amounts of rain falls downstream, bayous often quickly back up on themselves and begin flowing in the direction that formerly was upstream.

KEY SUPPLY CHAIN FUNCTIONS

Additional supply chain functions exist apart from the three classic logistical functions discussed above.

- Providing production capabilities.
- Sorting—or creating right-sized assortments for customers. The sorting function is also called breaking-bulk. Consumers typically want to buy one or two tubes of toothpaste at a time, not, for instance, a "dozen"—or a gross—at a time. Toothpaste manufacturers, by contrast, want to produce tens of thousands of tubes a day. The sorting function allows customers to buy the quantities they seek to acquire. The sorting function allows marketers to make the quantities they seek to manufacture. Both parties in these buyer-seller relationships win. Sorting was discussed above.
- Delivering and executing various forms of promotion, including selling, advertising, sales promotions, and direct marketing.
- Negotiating final prices and product placement on retailer shelves. Not to be confused with market positions as places inside customers' mind, product placements makes literal reference to retailers and their store shelves. Product placement is often executed by supply chain professionals called agents and jobbers. (Product [brand] placement also occurs inside movies, videos, or television shows when brands are prominently displayed [placed] in key character's homes or hands, etc.—but that's a different promotional story.) Matching sellers-with-buyers or matching supply-with-demand.
- Information-gathering; fundamentally, this activity entails executing the marketing research function.
- Risk-taking, which usually is financial in nature; because inexorable risks are associated with the known and unknown costs of executing marketing, inventorying, or shipping functions versus the expected returns.
- Financing sales and purchases. Supply chain relationships and supply chains themselves normally come into play here; even in unexpected places such as marketing IPOs.[12] Few to no IPOs can succeed without first successfully managing supply chain relationships with sale-side analysts at investment banks and buy-side analysts at asset-management firms. Investment banks function as sales agents for firms engaging in an IPO. Buy-side analysts generally function as IPS firms' primary customer base, or target segment.

---

12. IPOs, or Initial Public Offerings, basically entail the selling (marketing) and the buying of stock shares that are issued, for the first time, by marketing organizations. Often these marketing organizations are recent start-ups.

Supply Chain Partners Sell to, and Buy from Each Other

The extent to which supply chains themselves operate as networked systems of marketing organizations selling to and buying from one another is underscored by the depth and breadth of these functions has been revealed.

The curtain likewise has been pulled back on the extent to which this world is a marketing world, and we're all living, working, and playing inside it.

Finally, the extensive nature of these supply chain functions has underscored the degree to which the marketing activities that have been described or that readers soon will encounter actually largely occur inside supply chains.

CUTTING OUT MIDDLEMEN (INTERMEDIARIES)?

Perhaps you've heard the saying or something to it: If we could just eliminate middlemen, or intermediaries, imagine how much money we could save. The theory of the case unfolds like this:

- *Iowa* wheat farmers receive about $8.00 a bushel for the product they grow in the dirt of their fields. US bushels measure dry weight volume and equal 31 liters, or 8 dry gallons. About forty-two loaves of bread, the sort available at *Kroger's*, are produced from each wheat bushel. On average, bread loaves retail for $3.00 each in domestic grocery stores. And remember, during certain family life cycle stages, bread represents not a nice-to-have but a must. After all, what are families with school-age children going to do? Send their kids to school with gobs of peanut butter and jelly slathered inside their backpacks?

What's wrong with this story? Hard-working farmers—it's hot in today's air-conditioned tractors—getting about $8 for a product that generates about $126 in "bread" value that is sold at retailer grocery supply chain levels? Does this appear unfair; shouldn't farmers either get more money or consumers pay less money?

The answers to these three questions are *nothing, does not matter,* and *no*. Farmers get about what they deserve. Consumers pay about what they should. How much more would consumers have to pay in time, inconvenience, learning, sweat equity, tools and skills acquisitions, renting or buying land, and lost opportunities to spend time performing other activities—including sleeping—that would generate more real or perceived value were they to have to grow and prepare bread themselves? Further, how much less money would farmers receive were there no bakers, intermediaries, and retailers to process, distribute, and market their raw materials into something offering far greater value as a finished good? The difference between the $8 and $126 is accounted for by the fact that each level in the wheat-to-bread (or again, dirt-to-dirt, what happens after you eat) supply chain adds substantial value as wheat is converted from raw material to a finished and literally consumable good.

What's more, supply chain middlemen can never be eliminated. That's because the solutions and values created by each function these intermediaries perform cannot be eliminated. Well, actually, intermediaries themselves could be eliminated. But then performing the functions necessary to transform wheat into bread would cost many multiples more than is currently the case because either farmers or consumers would have to perform the supply function themselves. Or you, as a consumer, feeling like an expert baker or fertilizer maker today? Didn't think so.

The only relevant question, then, is who, as in which marketing intermediary, will perform which function? The question of whether a given supply chain function can be performed is irrelevant. Some firm must perform each function. No single supply chain function exists that cannot be performed (i.e., that somehow could be eliminated). However, any member of any supply chain could choose to perform more functions by itself.

An Opposing Point of View (Which Is Also Correct)

Even so, certain situations might arise where the elimination of an entire supply chain level, and consequently eliminating certain intermediaries themselves, make sense. Perhaps the time is approaching when it will make sense to dust automotive dealerships, to ditch the traditional car dealership model. The process by which consumers acquire other big-ticket items such as appliances (refrigerators) or furniture (couches or dining room tables) is relatively straightforward. Decide what brand and/or design of product you want, check. Learn what your preferred option costs, check. Pay the price you deem fair, check, as well as enjoying the opportunity and the exact price that the retailer posted.

Car buying, among regular consumers. It's nuts. Or is it a screw job? Many readers know the drill. Even in an internet age, most consumers drudge from dealer to dealer in the rain, heat, and/or traffic. Each dealer features supposedly distinct but truthfully only slightly different inventories, or product portfolios. Each dealer displays its own fake sticker or window prices. Most dealers actually force consumers to enter anachronistic, stressful, and aggravating haggling process—although a few do shoot straight, these days at least. Add to these hassles the fact that consumers are expected to pay added costs to the dealership. Somehow the idea of you paying extra costs to acquire that $2,000 refrigerator never happens at *Sears* or *Best Buy*, who each also function as the final retailing link in their respective supply chains. The sad fact is that for most automotive dealers to reap profits they must force customers to pay extra, unnecessary markups.

If car manufacturers sold directly to customers, like *Tesla* does, automotive supply chains would be shortened and car prices would drop as much as 8 percent, overnight. For products costing them $20,000 to $60,000, or more, 8 percent in consumer savings is real. Many states, however, bow to politically powerful dealership networks and have banned direct sales. Donors pay, politicians play, what can you say? The only supply chain entity or partner who absolutely positively all-the-time loses here are consumers who purchase autos from traditional dealers. This is one supply chain that could and perhaps should be shortened, by eliminating an intermediary, as long as other intermediaries operating between auto assemblers and end-use customers step up and perform the same retailing function that dealerships now provide, but at lower costs.

Yes, we just contradicted an earlier point. But so what? Marketers should be open-minded; should realize that one-size-fits-all-answers rarely if ever exist to any major question; and should feel comfortable changing either their opinions or attitudes when the facts of the case in question change.

FLOWING DOWNSTREAM THROUGH SUPPLY CHAINS

The processes and functions that enable raw materials, component parts, and eventually finished goods to flow from their originating upstream sources downstream toward final customers should unfold seamlessly. Raw materials, component parts, and finished products ideally should flow absent a hitch, creating efficiencies and new values at every supply chain level.

You recall *Larry the Lobster* exiting his cold-water trap fully alive and landing steaming hot, fully cooked, and obviously deceased on a *Washington* lobbyist's plate some six to eight days later. Or how an inexpensive raw material called wheat was cut directly from the dirt and processed into the much pricier finished product known as bread arrives on *Kroger's* shelves thirty-something days later. These outcomes were each made possible through the efficient management of various supply chain flows.

Revisiting Those Ideally Seamless Flows

The marketing institutions that collectively constitute supply chains are connected one to another by various, hopefully seamless flows.

These marketing institutions may be operated completely independently from each other. These marketing organizations might also operate inside vertically-integrated and consequently operate inside precisely defined relationships with each other—because one supply chain partner functions like a hoss, and calls the shots.

As explained, organizations that collaborate, cooperate, and partner with one another inside supply chains are selling to and buying from each other, and they are also connected by flows.

These connective flows may be one-way in nature, say they're going downstream.

Or the connective flows may be reciprocal—or simultaneously going upstream and downstream—in nature.

The most basic supply chain flows include:

- Physical flows of raw materials, component parts, and finished products, from firm-to-firm-to-firm-to-customer. How does *Viagra* get constituted (compounded), again?
- Ownership or possession flows, from source to firm to firm to customer. Ownership need not necessarily change hands at each level inside supply chains.
- Promotional or communication flows.
- Payment flows.
- Information flows.

Information flows are the most important of these flows. That is because without information supply chains cannot flow seamlessly. Nor can strategic plans entered into mutually be successfully pursued without ongoing information exchange. The true gift of the information age is not the opportunity to secure large amounts of information. Yet the true gift of "information flows" (and indeed "the information age" itself) is the opportunity that the free and easy change of information provides the opportunity for partnering organizations to engage in greater collaboration with one another inside supply chains. One charm of collaboration, meanwhile, is that blame gets shared if the collective effort fails—which may or may not be offered as a joke.

In reality, of course, the opportunity to engage in more collaboration inside supply chains is neither a small nor a joking matter. *The Wall Street Journal* reported during 2021 that today's managers must excel at fostering collaboration as they manage inter- and intra-organization (supply chain) relationships because up to 70 percent of a manager's workload will be replaced by automation and artificial intelligence by 2024.[13] The general idea is that current and future managers will need to win others over to their way of thinking, or perhaps to just past halfway there—as opposed to blithely issuing directives and dictates. Contemporary managers, as well as their future associates, must learn to lead through, and in some cases, actually drive rapid change.

THE ONE AND ONLY . . . PLACE

Supply chains are the exact location where most marketing decisions and marketing activities actually occur. These marketing decisions relate to marketing activities such as pricing, promotion, some new product development; and the entire set of typical marketing mix activities. Any marketing organization's supply chain decision directly affects every other marketing mix decision made by the firm—or at least it should. Those marketing mix decisions might address how marketers price their products, what products; marketers choose to make or manufacture, display or discuss; and how those marketing organizations promote those products.

This is why marketing organizations should never make fundamental supply chain decisions in isolation from other marketing mix considerations.

A Place Where Long-Term Commitments Should Dominate

Supply chain management decisions usually involve long-term commitments with other marketing organizations. Management consequently should carefully define, evaluate all available information, and only then establish their supply chain relationships. Management should always establish supply relationships with an eye cast toward understanding today's as well as tomorrow's environments. This is largely because supply chain relationships are more similar to marital than dating relationships. Marriages are supposedly long-term; designed and entered into benefit both parties, right? So are supply chain relationships, obviously.

Are supply chain relationships really similar to marital relationships? Yes. Similar to marriages, supply chain relationships can be entered rather easily. And once that happens either relationship—supply chain or marital—generally proves extremely painful to exit. The takeaway is that organizations or people should choose their supply chain or marital partners . . . carefully.

---

13. Kathryn Dill, "All Together Now," *The Wall Street Journal* (January 15, 2021): R7.

Yet this is not where the similarities between supply chain and marital relationships end. Successful marriages, among humans, are not entirely about finding the right partner. Successful human marriages are also about being the right partner. No one should assume that successful supply chain partnerships much differ.

Can the preceding be taken to imply that supply chain relationships are similar to friendships? Yes, maybe. One known certainty is that having the right friends in one's life will multiply your pleasures (yes, values!) and divide your pain (yes, problems!).

Having the wrong friends around, well . . . Another thought: People wiser than us have suggested that if you show them your friends then they can show you your future. Beyond question, similar future values can derive from having the right supply chain partners in place.

A Place That Is Not Just Important, But Indispensable

The importance of supply chains should never be sold short. Shipping, logistics, distribution, inventory management, delivery, promotions, pricing, finance; supply chains exist near the root of everything. The four small *British Islands* that comprise the *United Kingdom* built and sustained a global empire that lasted for centuries. The *United Kingdom* primarily achieved this amazing feat based on its possession of the logistical ability and mobility to attack wherever it pleased.[14] The global nature of the internet provides all marketers with similarly global reaches. The internet is nothing but a supply chain that facilitates rapid and globalized flows of information.

Supply chains are rarely glamorous. But contemporary supply chain relationships are pivotal in terms of the power they exercise. Inside supply chains and the relationships that bind together partnering firms, partners/collaborators/competitors would each do well to remember the following description of power: Power is not just you or what your side has but also what your partner/collaborator/competitor thinks you have. (One "dirty little secret" about personal or professional relationships: the person who wants or needs the relationship least always enjoys the most power.)

A Place That Offers Most Marketers Their Last Best Opportunity to Achieve Genuine SCAs

Well-managed supply chain relationships offer many marketing organizations their last and best chance to secure sustainable competitive advantages (SCAs).

Walmart is *Walmart,* the hugely successful firm that it became and has remained, because of how effectively it has managed supply chain relationships to lower its costs of doing business during a fifty-plus-year period. Only rarely have *Walmart's* competitors been able to compete successfully against its sustainable competitive advantages, primarily in terms of the lower customer costs and broader

---

14. How small are the *British Isles*? Most readers realize that *Texas* is a large state. *Texas,* however, is still only one state. Yet *Texas* alone is almost three times larger than the combined size of *England, Scotland, Wales,* and *Ireland*. Talk about a nation that punches way above its weight. Yes, the nation is the *United Kingdom*.

product assortments (for customers to acquire) that *Walmart* is able to generate through adroit supply chain management practices.

The entire business model of *Walmart* is strategically structured to allow the retailer to compete and win based on its development of cost leadership. Remember cost leadership; one of three ways for any firm to differentiate its value and brands. The other two ways to differentiate, that's right, entail achieving greater customer intimacy or achieving technological leadership.

About 95 percent of Americans shop at *Walmart* once or more a year. *Walmart* boasts three square feet of shopping space for every American adult and has sunk $83 billion into a fixed asset base that is the fourth largest owned by any domestic firm. Expects have compared *Walmart*, as well as *Amazon*, to boa constrictors that are swallowing capitalism. In the case of *Walmart* this status is the direct result of how efficiently *Walmart* manages supply chain relationships. (In *Amazon*'s case, sustainable advantages derive from the giant's skillful exploitation of technological advantages.)

A Place Where the Bottom Line Is Massaged

There's one more major reason why supply chain relationships are so important.

Cost advantages or disadvantages that are gained or lost inside supply chains go straight to corporate bottom lines in the form of either profits or losses. That means organizations selling $100,000 worth of goods annually and earning 10 percent profits or returns on this top-line revenue would have to generate $10,000 in additional sales in order to equal the amount of extra bottom-line profit that $1,000 worth of cost savings generated inside the firm's supply chain relationships. Seeing and feeling the power of supply chain management?

MODULE 12.3

Managing Supply Chain Relationships

If other supply chain members are identified that can add more value than existing members, old supply chain members often should be replaced so new partners can be added. Cold-blooded, or calculated, yes, either label applies. But this strategic supply chain decision is also appropriate and defensive because supply chains feature business rather than marital relationships.

The previous conflation of marriage with supply chains was merely an analogy, used for instructive purposes. Yes, supply chain relationships are like marriages. But they are not marriages. The success or failure of supply chain relationships often ultimately pivots based on five factors. Spelled out, the five factors are M.O.N.E.Y.

Of course, what else but money would coalesce into the five most important factors inside supply chains? In business and marketing planning or execution players can follow the action, which can prove distracting—so much is always happening. Players can follow their instincts, which are often wrong. Or players can follow the money, which almost always leads them toward the information about the true source of the problem or genuine nature of that opportunity that you need to know. Is an existing supply chain relationship making me and my firm money; or saving me and my firm money? If the answer to either side of this double-barreled question is no, time to reconsider the relationship.

MONEY MATTERS

Money matters mightily inside supply chains and everywhere else. Because, at some point inside everyone's life either you singularly or you inside some legally-sanctioned marital partnership or cohabitating relationship will be the sole or commingled breadwinner. Responsible for paying for the mortgage, auto loans, a child or children, educational savings, gasoline and food, and so forth.

Inside that brave and challenging world more professional decisions than you might now readily envision really will come down, to a degree that now may shock many younger and more idealistic readers, to which planning alternative will generate the most money for me and mine while generating the least damage to you and/or psyches and emotional welfare. Summing up "why" money matters, because at some point unless you were born to a trust fund you currently are or soon will then . . . "be the breadwinner." Humanity may not live by bread alone, in accordance with wisdom imparted by an extremely popular book, but try living without the bread that money buys.

Don't think money doesn't matter almost without regard to context or even to life and death threats? Was it just us or did it seem that the people who supported continued COVID-19 lockdowns during 2021 were mostly the people who keep getting paid during lockdowns? Hint: It wasn't just us.

Even so, money isn't everything. This book is not attempting to make that argument. As humorist and satirist *Dorothy Parker* said: "If you want to know what God thinks about money, look at whom he gives it too." Was she joking? Readers should make that decision themselves.

Nothing about this logic or argument is new. The thirteenth-century *Welsh* culture featured a prominent saying, "Diwedd y gan yw y geiniog." Roughly translated, the saying—or adage— suggests, correctly, "The end of every song is money." The following statement should arrive as no surprise, then:

▶ One additional overarching goal that generally prevails inside supply chains is that of securing and retaining partners who can perform supply channels functions quicker, better, or less expensively than alternative partners.

Marketers generally should only partner inside supply chains with organizations that permit them to save money, secure greater efficiencies, or both. "Faster, better, cheaper" has long since emerged as a governing supply chain mantra. So much so that one or more of the following words or phrases— faster, better, "less expensive"—is usually directly present inside supply chain firm's mission statements and/or brand positioning statements.

GOOD, BETTER, BEST

When evaluating or measuring efficiency inside managed supply chain relationships, another governing mantra is "good, better, best." This principle is worth remembering for many reasons. Foremost, however, because successful supply chain managers understand that good isn't good-enough if they still can do better. Those same supply chain managers should understand further that better is still not good enough if opportunities to achieve best possible supply chain efficiencies still exist.

Deciding to end existing supply chain relationships if new prospective partners that can generate superior value are discovered is neither illegal nor immoral. Instead, a decision to terminate often represents a smart business strategy.

Yet because supply chains still consist of inter-organizational personal relationships, interpersonal relationship management remains important. Extremely so, in fact. Supply chains are more than information management systems communing and communicating with other information management systems. Supply chains are business ventures, of course, but can also be highly personal in nature.

And here, again like marriages, supply chain relationships that successfully bind together marketing organizations as collaborative and cooperative partners inside supply chains they share, despite occasional conflict, are generally based on the presence of:

- Shared trust, or the belief that promises made will be promises kept, and/or when things go wrong they will be made right again by the erring party, to the extent possible.
- Collective acceptance among the engaged and partnering parties that shared benefits and mutual gains must result from the relationship.
- Mutually-shared, long-term commitments for the future amongst supply chain partners.
- The social norms known as solidarity and reciprocity.

Solidarity is embodied in the sense that even when times are challenging, we are in this thing together and will work things out, together.

To understand the role that reciprocity should play inside supply chain relationships, reflect upon the consequences that typically emerge from offering open handshakes as opposed to closed fists to an adversary. Open handshakes are generally reciprocated with open hands, in return. Closed fists are generally reciprocated with opponents' closed fists, in return. Stated differently but the same, supply chain professionals who give-good generally get-good, in return. Supply chain professionals who give-nasty usually get-nasty, in return.

On an individual level business and marketing success or failure inside B2B settings, probably around half the time, comes down to one factor. Do I like or not like this person? Whether you or anyone else likes your professional B2B counterpart typically comes down to one additional factor. Do I trust him/her? Because absent trust, the prospect of "liking" becomes nigh on impossible. Or put differently, consider this analogy. Relationships without trust are like trucks without gas. You can stay in them for as long as you want; but the trucks are not going anywhere.

MODULE 12.4

Managing Conflict inside Supply Chain Relationships

If they do not operate in a class by themselves, supply chain relationships operate inside a class that features an extremely short roll.

Supply chain relationships are unusual because they frequently, freely, and concurrently offer feelings of, "I'm winning," to both buying and selling participants. Both sides winning at the same time, mind you. Which, of course, is not possible. Yet if the decision to consummate an exchange relationship did not feel right to each selling and buying entity inside every supply chain partnership, neither party would participate. The indisputable truth, however, is that one supply chain partner is always either winning or losing, at least a little.

Supply chain participants consequently might benefit from trying to avoid winning or losing too big. Yes, avoid winning too big. Following this simple rule will not eliminate conflict. Buttheads—a-holes—certainly do exist.[15] But following the rule should mitigate some otherwise negative consequences that accompany the resulting strife, struggle, and conflict.

Essentially, avoiding winning too big means never taking the last dollar off negotiating tables—even in situations where the size or power of marketing organizations would allow them to grab far more than their fair share. Marketing organizations might grow materially or acquire exceptional power based either on brand equity, leading to extreme pricing power of the sort that *Nike* enjoys, or earned economies of scale of the sort that *Exon Mobile* possesses. Or both core competencies, as is true of *Apple*.

Why? Because individuals or partnering firms from whom the "big dog" takes the last dollar may well spend the rest of his/her/its natural life wanting and waiting to get back at, in their perceptions, the "bad dog." And one day that opportunity may arise.

---

15. A useful piece of marketing as well as life counsel about buttheads or more dauntingly, a-holes, and how to recognize and deal with them. The advice is paraphrased from the well-known novelist *Elmore Leonard*, AKA "father" of the book *Justified* and character *Raylan Givens*. Said Raylen: "If you ran into an a-hole in the morning, you ran into an a-hole. If you run into a-holes all day long, you're the a-hole." Walk away either from the a-hole or from your former self, according to where the description applies. Relatedly, as *Maya Angelou* wrote using more genteel language: "When someone shows you who he is, believe him."

Mighty oaks always begin life as little acorns. More ominously, little puppies often grow into big dogs. Canines combine long memories and self-righteous motivations with fierce desires to go for the throat of the perceived or actual exploiter.

ONE BUYER, ONE SELLER; TWO PARTNERS

Every supply chain exchange relationship features one buyer and one seller. And the fact is that usually, either the buying or selling partner is wrong while the other partner is right. Wrong, because the value gotten from the seller during the exchange was less than the value the buyer gave up to obtain the object of exchange. Or right because the value given up by the seller during the exchange was less than the value the buyer gave up to obtain the object of exchange.

Supply chain decisions are further complicated by the fact that inside them human people rather than corporate firms actually enjoy or endure relationships with each other.[16] Inside these human relationships, especially those where negotiated allocations of money are constantly exchanged, conflict eventually arises. This is largely because whenever the you-and-yours side or team take away more value from any exchange than me-and-mine side or team necessarily takes away less value. "Everybody wants some," in *Van Halen's* immortal words. But "you can't always get what you want," as *Mick Jagger* and *Keith Richards* wrote. It's only natural, then, that conflict arises.

Another conflict-facilitating factor that also plays out inside supply chains likewise follows from human nature. Humans typically judge other humans by their actions, which typically makes other people appear impure and self-interested. Meanwhile, humans typically judge themselves based on their own interior motives, which make perfect sense and appear utterly rational to them. This instinctively-arising human response—and the misattributions that follow—creates intentional distancing and higher prospects for disagreement. Like most mutual activities involving humans interacting with each other inside relational settings, supply chain management can devolve into conflicting goals, squabbling, missed deadlines, flawed processes, and efforts deemed by the other as insufficient.

Winston Churchill shared a valuable insight about how conflict inevitably arises even inside indispensably valuable and mutually beneficial relationships. The esteemed *British* leader wrote "There is only one thing worse than fighting with Allies [think supply chain partners], and that is fighting without them." In *Churchill's* case his allies—or supply chain partners—were *Americans* and *Russians*. And the Brits, Yanks, and *Russians* formed an unusual but ultimately successful capitalism-communism alliance in a genuinely fight-to-the-death struggle with *Hitler's National Socialist Party*, yes, the real NAZIs, in *Germany*.

So it is with partnerships inside supply chain relationships. The managerial leadership inside many successful firms sometimes likely assume that that they cannot live with their supply partners. Yet hopefully, those firms and their leadership—if they plan to continue to succeed—must come to

---

16. Funny thing, one firm's information management system rarely gets angry at partnering firms' information management systems. Okay, this never happens. But the professionals who own and/or administer those computing systems for the respective firms can surely get into conflict with each other.

understand the extent to which they cannot live successfully without partners who continuously and successfully perform their assigned supply duties or responsibilities.

What did this book previously assert was the key value provided by supply chains? Yes, that's right, their:

> Participation inside efficient and reasonably conflict-free supply chains should allow each partnering organization to concentrate on performing and getting better at performing what it does best.

The preceding summarized both the opportunity and the need to engage in supply-based partnerships in order to achieve greater specialization.

RESOLVING CONFLICT

Even so, some measure of conflict is inevitable inside supply chain relationships. Unavoidable because inside life or supply chain relationships there is a "me-and-my-family-side" to any conflicted-issue; a "you-and-your-family's-side" to the issue; and a "when one side gets more; the other side gets less" issue, as in problem, that must always be managed. For many business professionals, the "me-and-my-family" category of issues also includes the organizational team to which they belong.

The debate over whether the desire to create war—the ultimate form of conflict—is inherent in human nature or the result of culture and social institution likely will never be resolved. What is undeniable however is that supply chain management and the onset of conflicts are interwoven to the degree that one cannot understand how to manage one entity (supply chain) without understanding how to manage—and mitigate—the other entity (conflict).

Inside supply chains, participating partners should not seek out conflict. Supply chain partners should never act like the *Proverbial Irishman* who was walking down the street and who sees, to his delight, two men viciously fighting each other. He is so happy, in fact, that he stops the struggle to ask whether this is a private fight, or can anyone join in the fun? But when the stakes in play inside the conflict are sufficiently valuable clashes should not be avoided, either.

Supply chain conflict usually arises from concerns and questions about "which partner gets what, and how much of it," as finite and fungible resources are being allocated between or secured by "partners." Stated more clearly, people and therefore supply chain partners are highly likely to fight over who gets the most money. As noted, one key to preventing or making it easier to resolve these struggles entails establishing and sustaining norms where mutual respect, trust, and reciprocity govern relationships among supply chain partners. Norms, as might arise inside supply chains or anywhere else, designate and distinguish right or appropriate behaviors from wrong or inappropriate behaviors. One norm that broadly applies in life and inside supply chains is that in the long-run people or partners usually will get what they deserve.

The norm called reciprocity is nearly always in play and enjoys its day largely because things usually average out, regressing toward the mean, over the long-run. The nineteenth-century *German* leader *Otto von Bismarck* conjured up a maxim that effectively summarizes this premise. *Bismarck*, well-branded by his advocates and detractors alike as the *Iron Chancellor*, wrote that "a generation that has taken a thrashing is following by a generation that deals out the thrashings."[17] He was speaking about *France* after its ignominious defeat during the 1870–71 *Franco-Prussian War*. And *Bismarck* was right, because next time *Germany* and *France* fought each other, during *World War I* (1914–18), the *French* fought with remarkable tenacity.

In blunter *English*, however, reciprocity means this:

▶ Act like an ass, you'll usually get treated like an ass.
▶ Act honestly and fairly, you'll usually get treated honestly and fairly.

But, of course, this averaging out of affairs does not always happen.

Another key to preventing conflict inside supply chains follows from the build-out of a shared sense, or understanding, that if the respective marketing organizations work together driven by the unifying goal of developing and sustaining a long-term relationship, each will be better off, during the long-term. Better together, as noted earlier fires whose logs hang together burn longer and more fiercely. Then when supply chain conflicts arise, and they will, quarrels can be resolved more easily.[18]

There's more, however. Marketers generally, and supply chain partners specifically, should play the long-game. Playing "long-games" entails many elements. But perhaps foremost among these elements is to not take everything, value-wise, off the table even when you can, as has already suggested in another context. That way marketers get to shear the sheep and benefit from selling the wool every year rather than slaughtering the animal—okay, customer—once and only getting paid that one time. Or, continuing the barnyard motif, as every pork farmer knows: pigs get fed while hogs get slaughtered. Hogs, of course, are known for overly greedy consumptions habits. Think about it.

TEN SUPPLY CHAIN CONFLICT MANAGEMENT AND RESOLUTION (CMR) RULES

The ten supply chain conflict resolution rules are ecumenical in their nature and application. The word ecumenical, as used here, means that knowing and deciding to use the rules should also prove useful in contexts having nothing to do with supply chains.

▶ *CMR 1: Pick Battles Carefully.* Don't take on everything that bothers you; otherwise constant turmoil will arise. Distinguish between annoying behaviors or habits and actual problems that impede the effectiveness of the partnership. Understand that the primary danger associated with declaring war is that you then have to fight it. Yikes. The preceding three sentences reflect kinder and gentler ways of suggesting that "negotiators" should know when they should give a hoot and understand when no need exists to bother with the hassles that always accompany skirmishes.

---

17. A. J. P. Taylor, *Bismarck: The Man and Statesman,* Mass Market Paperback (London: Harper-Collins, 1967): 199.
18. David Strutton, Lou E. Pelton, and James R. Lumpkin, "The Influence of Psychological Climate on Conflict Resolution Strategies inside Franchising Relationships," *Journal of the Academy of Marketing Science* 21, no. 2 (1993): 201–17.

Winston Churchill actually experienced combat firsthand while leading men who were fighting inside *World War I's* bloody trenches. He knew firsthand about the nature of the topic he was discussing when he said: "Meeting an artillery attack (emphatically and definitively high rates of conflict are reflected therein) is like catching a cricket ball. Shock is dissipated by drawing back the hands. A little give, a little suppleness, and the violence of the impact is vastly reduced." According to Churchill, then, only rarely would the need exist for any supply chain partner to fight absent any possibility of compromise, any prospect of giving and taking—fighting to the last breath, as it were—in the midst of most conflicts that might arise inside supply chain relationships. There is almost always room for some horse-trading back and forth or for what *Chinese* negotiators would understand as a little "yin and yang" inside negotiations aimed at resolving supply chain conflict.

- CMR 2: *Don't Feel Guilty.* Healthy supply chain relationships are not conflict-free relationships. Instead they are relationships that have learned better how to deal with conflict. Disagreement is not hate; nor is it discrimination. What disagreement is instead, is natural—especially inside meaningful supply chain relationships. Nor is there any point in pointing out the other side's flaws given that your side is probably burdened with a few flaws itself.

- CMR 3: *Become Aware of, Understand, Accept, and Make Reasonable Accommodations for the Other's Cultural Norms.* Be aware that geographic, ethnic, and corporate cultural differences exist. Understand and account for the fact that the cultural norms and values governing negotiations for the right to lease land to drill for oil in *Montana* differ radically from the norms and values that govern the same sort of negotiations in *Yemen*. Accept that these differences exist. Then make reasonable accommodations when accommodations are reasonable. Or that, the *German* cultural view, when confronting any serious crisis or conflict: The situation is serious, but not hopeless. The *Austrian* cultural view when confronting the same scenarios: The situation is hopeless, but not serious. The *French* view: What crisis?

What's the point of making such points? The point is that what constitutes polite in New York City is not necessarily polite in Dallas, Texas. The fact that two words, "f—k" and "you" basically function as prerequisites to negotiating success inside many *New York City* business settings does not mean that the first of those words is even acceptable inside similar *Texas* circles. Or that what represents truth in *Charlotte, North Carolina*, will not represent truth in *Beijing, China*. And that is the truth. Such divergences must be dealt with and accommodated.

Learn and benefit from embracing and thereafter acting based on the axiom that, "Blessed are the flexible, for they are far less likely to be broken." This axiom will prove especially true over the long-run.

- CMR 4: *Don't Overthink.* Little to nothing will be gained from overanalyzing *what* could go wrong during conversations about how to resolve a conflict. Instead look more broadly at the need and opportunity to address a key issue and resolve a pressing problem. No one can plan an entire conversation. So do your best and go with the flow.

▶ *CMR 5: Work to Improve Your Vision.* When attempting to solve supply chain conflicts correcting one vision defect almost always pays off. The defect derives from an inability to see both sides of every issue.

A known percentage of humans—a quantity that does not matter here—are born color-blind. People born with this defect are unable to distinguish reds and greens. For managers failing to see both sides when conflicts arise, the missing color is gray. Yet the ability to see gray is important. Few issues in which conflicts arise are as black and white as color-blind opponents often perceive them to be.

The problem, and actual source of the conflict, is often our absolutes. No one side has the total story. It is only when we see merit in another's opinion that we will be able to solve our problems.

▶ *CMR 6: Don't Rush through the Awkwardness.* Easy conflict resolution is not necessarily good conflict resolution. Spend time outlining the situation rather than assigning blame. That way, the supply chain participants who are experiencing conflict will enjoy better and less nonjudgmental insights into the nature of the problem causing the conflict. People who understand the core causes of any problem are well down the road to resolving it.

The absence of conflict is not necessarily a positive. This condition may prove a powerful signal of mutual or individual apathy toward the relationship—not a good sign. But there is always zero value in having everyone sandbagged intransigently inside their own positions, resentfully resisting any challenge to their views. The trick is creating relational environments in which people enjoy productive arguments and view them as part of their jobs. Each party to any exchange should agree to consciously separate conflicts related to tasks or what actions to take next from conflict about personalities. It's one thing to have different personal views and to use the heat of the moment inside disagreements to forge better solutions and another to allow that same heat to melt down relationships.

This last point transitions us logically toward the seventh CMR.

▶ *CMR 7: Don't Reflexively Conflate Arguing with Fighting.* Thinking of arguments as fights undermines the use of logic. Viewing every argument as a fight also degrades the ability of supply chain partners to learn from any information that is exchanged during arguments. Deeming every argument a fight often makes otherwise capable and reasonable negotiators less willing to engage in so-called argumentative conversations while disagreeing agreeably.

▶ *CMR 8: Understand and Accept That Once the Fight's Over, It's Really Over.* Once conflicts are resolved, get over them. Holding grudges only ensures that new problems will arise more quickly. People or individuals who seek or hang onto a desire for revenge, especially after conflict supposedly has been resolved, eventually dig two graves. In the form of one six-foot-deep hole for the partnership, and another similarly sized hole for themselves. Remaining angry or bitter after having encountered some now-resolved real or imagined wrong from one's partner is like drinking poison that degrades your own logic or spirit and hoping the prior "offender" is the one who suffers.

> *CMR 9: Accept the Possibility That Your Side May Be Criticized—So What?* People can be immobilized by the slightest criticism and begin to defend themselves as if they were in a battle. In truth, however, criticism is nothing more than an observation by another person about us, our actions, or how we think about an issue that fails to align with the vision we have about ourselves.

When we react to the receipt of criticism with knee jerk, defensive responses we're signaling that the criticism hurt. When we feel attacked we typically feel a need to defend ourselves or to offer countercriticisms. Our minds fill up with angry or hurtful thoughts directed at ourselves or at the person issuing the reproach. An enormous amount of mental energy is consumed; relationships are injured if not imperiled. But what might happen if you consciously and strategically decided to agree with the criticism?

We're not suggesting that anyone turn into a doormat (walk on me) or that anyone should abandon all measure of self-respect by accepting all negative shots headed their way. We're instead suggesting strategically agreeing with some measure of the criticism that has created a supply chain chasm; thereby defusing the situation at least a little; defusing the situation, allowing partners to express their points of view; and accepting that the receipt of this criticism gifts you with an opportunity to learn something new about yourself or more importantly your marketing position. Give this bend but not break negotiating approach a try now and then, and you may discover that agreeing with occasional criticism generates more value than costs.

> *CMR 10: Remember Enforcements.* Before so-called final agreements are reached, each party to the conflict should take measures to ensure that enforcement mechanisms are in place to reward partners who "play by the new rules" that both parties have just established and to punish the partner that still elects to "not play well with others" by failing to honor the agreement. This rule is incentivizing, to say the least. Following the rule would not just incentivize superior conflict resolution but also ensure that resolutions made are resolutions kept.

Incentives can be negative or positive. That's a given. Another given is that the use of incentives work; nothing motivates good or bad choices and behaviors than the arrival and distribution of the right or wrong incentives.

Tamping down expectations—and demands—usually generates better outcomes throughout the entire conflict resolution process. Folks who demand everything, all the time, often end up with nothing. The reason why is because because their "opponents" naturally push back and then dig their own trenches from which they prepare to fight it out! Talented negotiators learn how to finesse situations by offering minor concessions without actually conceding. Talented negotiators likewise learn how to make aggressive demands without appearing aggressive. The why and how to achieve these outcomes goes beyond the scope of this book. But the topic is worth reading about elsewhere.

Another mitigating factor that is essentially certain to exist inside supply chain or other sorts of relationships is that the party who more fervently seeks resolution inevitably occupies the weaker position, and resides there from the jump. Supply chain partners should care, but not too much, about the stakes in play inside the conflict. The partner who wants the relationship least—the party genuinely prepared to walk away—usually enjoys the most power. Everyone should always carefully choose the hills on which they are willing to die. Such hills, hopefully, are few and far between. If not, people are going to die a lot.

Supply chain partners bumping up against one another on a particular issue should likewise understand and accept the fact that no one ever learns anything from anyone else who totally agreed with them.

They should likewise understand and accept that conflict; like sht, happens. Conflict, as noted, arrives naturally.

Understanding that the first person to ask for forgiveness in the middle of conflict is likely the bravest is another useful insight, especially inside situations where your side has knowingly or unintentionally done something wrong. Yet there is more. The first person in such settings to offer forgiveness is also usually the happiest. But the first person to forget about the whole affair, regardless of what triggered the enmity, is definitely the smartest. Few things are more beneficial than peaceful sleep-filled nights, regardless of one's age, health, or profession.

Conflict is an experience that few sane people enjoy—or willingly seek out. The presence of conflict and one's engagement with an "opponent" inside the grip of conflict will mercilessly reveal the character of most participants.

AN IDEALIZED TWIST

Finally, let's take an idealistic turn by imagining supply chains in which everyone lived out *Don Miguel Ruiz's* Four Agreements as covenant promises in their professional lives. The four covenant promises entail:[19]

- "Being impeccable with your word.
- Not taking everything personally.
- Not making assumptions; particularly about the other party's motivations.
- Always do your best."

Talk about a righteous recipe for preventing conflict.

By the way, when writing "imagining supply chains" we could have written "imagining the entire business world." That's because not enough space exists between the supply chain world and the entire business world to slip a credit card in-between. The whole business world is nothing less or more than an intricately interconnected series of supply chain relationships.

---

19. Covenant promises were serious matters, not to be broken, in the original *Jewish Law*. To break covenant promises consigned promise-breakers to being sliced in half. Similar to how sacrificial animals were sliced in half to honor God. Then the faithful person who conducted the sacrifice walked through the two halves, acknowledging what would happen to him if the promise were broken.

MODULE 12.5

Designing Matters

Supply chain design-related questions generally relate to how many firms should marketing organizations partner with inside each supply chain in which they participate. When marketing organizations partner with numerous other firms in order to market their products to final customers, organizations are said to have longer supply chains. Long supply chains feature many levels. When marketing organizations partner with fewer firms in order to market their products to customers, organizations have shorter supply chains. Short supply chains feature fewer levels.

Supply chain design-related questions also relate to what types of firms does any firm choose to partner with inside each of its supply chains? Will a manufacturer, for example, strategically elect to partner with an advertising agency, with a series of warehouses, with two or three different transportation firms, or with one or multiple retailers with their own internal sales forces? Or will that same manufacturer elect to perform all these typical supply functions itself, and to not outsource any of these activities?

The advantages or disadvantages of one supply chain design versus another supply chain design generally pivot based on managerial decision-makers' preferred answer to one cost versus control question. Specifically, supply chain managers must ask:

- ▶ Will my organization be better off if it lowers costs by outsourcing marketing functions that are then performed by other organizations operating as partners with my firm inside the supply chain we share? If the answer is yes, then your firm makes a buy decision. The deciding organization then buys the performance of marketing functions from other firms. Here, buy means the performance of the supply chain function is outsourced or acquired by hire by the buying supply chain partner.
- ▶ Or, will my organization be better off if it maintains greater control over how various marketing functions are performed? If the answer is yes, then your firm should choose a make decision. Here, deciding firms perform—or make—the supply chain function or functions themselves. Execution of the function is kept in-house.

When marketing organizations choose to perform supply chain functions themselves, they pay more, because developing the ability to and then executing the function costs more. But the upside is that marketing organizations would then maintain control over how said functions are performed. What we do for ourselves, we control, right?

When marketing organizations partner with firms inside supply chains that they share for purposes of having those partners perform a function or functions, firms usually spend less for the performance of a function or functions. But the downside, if one wishes to label it as such, is that the firm gives control over how exactly those functions are performed. Things are that simple.

Even so, additional questions emerge: Which outcome is more important to the firm? Does the firm care more about the lowered costs that result from having supply chain functions performed by other partners? Or does the firm care more about retaining greater, actually total, control over how supply chain functions are performed? Which, as noted, is what happens when marketing organizations decide to perform functions themselves.

Supply chain members exist and succeed inside any supply chain because they add value. Supply chain success, similar to individual marketer's success, is based on determining which combination of partnering organizations adds/creates/delivers the most value. And then moving forward strategically based on those insights.

This idea is similar to the premise that consumers, as decision-makers, usually make choices that they perceive—in their imagined realities—will generate the most value for them.

SUPPLY CHAIN DESIGNS

Two basic supply chain designs exist.

Vertical Marketing Systems

First, there are vertical marketing systems (VMS). VMS are highly vertically integrated supply chains where one 800-pound-gorilla[20] organization controls or owns other firms in the supply chain system. Vertical integration entails to the degree to which firms own/control upstream toward sourcing-from-the-dirt suppliers or control/own downstream shippers, other intermediaries such as warehouses, or retailers toward end-use B2B customers or B2C consumers.

Old-school *Hollywood*, which used to function as the epicenter of domestic film production, once operated as a series of nearly completely vertically integrated supply chains. Old-school *Hollywood* studios completely owned and fully controlled the means of creating, producing, and distributing movies to end-use consumers. The means of creating movies included writers, directors, producers (financiers), and so forth. The means of producing movies included physical studios themselves, set designers, camera and lighting operators, cameras, sets, costumes and make-up artist, actors, and so

---

20. Where does the 800-pound gorilla sleep? The answer is wherever he wants. What does he eat? The answer, again, is whatever he wants.

forth. The means of distributing, or delivering, included complete ownership of all movie theatres themselves within which *Hollywood* studios logically also kept profits from sales of popcorn, soda, and candy to themselves. The *Hollywood* of this era rocked. *Hollywood* rocked largely because a handful of oligopolistic studios—marketing organizations one and all—managed their respective supply chains with ruthless efficiency.

The most remarkable year in movie history was 1939. That's the year when *Gone with the Wind*, *The Wizard of Oz, Stagecoach, Dark Victory,* and *Wuthering Heights* were all released. But *Hollywood* also got a little full of itself, at least in the eyes of the *U.S. Senate*, during 1939. The misstep involved the release of *Mr. Smith Goes to Washington. Mr. Smith* broadly castigated the inept, inane, unethical, greedy, and inefficient political practices of the day. Yes, we're feeling it too—the more things change the more they remain the same.

By 1940, *Washington, DC,* began successfully dismantling the *Hollywood* studio movie machines, or their vertical supply chains. The Senate's first move entailed outlawing a lot of "titillating fun" from films, thereby making the resulting products less entertaining. Too bad, so sad. The second regulatory act entailed actively decoupling actual movie theater operations from studios' direct vertical supply chain ownership. This was probably a great move. Remarkably, however, many of those same studios still operate today. Branded names such as *Paramount, Warner Brothers, Universal, MGM, Columbia,* or *Disney,* do any these brands still ring familiar today? Apparently, the ability to adapt, be creative, and operate based on contingency planning never goes out of fashion. Or more pointedly, never fails, long-term.

Marketing organizations generally create vertically integrated marketing systems (or supply chains) in marketing contexts where they can earn and leverage economies of scale. *Kimberly-Clark* is more than just a manufacturer of toilet paper. The giant marketer also owns forests/trees that are harvested and processed to make toilet paper. *Kimberly-Clark's* supply chain is partially vertically integrated.

Inside the global oil sector, *Royal Dutch Shell's, British Petroleum's (BP's),* and *Exxon Mobile's* supply chains are even more vertically integrated. Each oil marketer owns the rights to drill on land or the land underneath oceans, seas, or gulfs; owns or controls drilling and refining capacitators; owns or controls various shipping modes such as ships, trucks, or pipelines; and markets their gas and diesel products at the retail level inside gasoline stations and convenience stores that they own or control.

Italy's *Luxottica* is one of the world's most powerful brands but remains nearly unknown inside America. *Luxottica* is the world's largest maker of glasses frames. The firm is close to achieving complete vertical integration. The firm controls nearly every level in its supply chain, from the mining sources and suppliers of metal alloys used to produce eyeglass hinges to the retail stores where eyeglasses are sold. After a series of audacious takeovers, *Luxottica* acquired brands such as *Ray-Ban, Oakley,* and *Persol. Luxottica* signed exclusive agreements with fashion houses such as *Armani, Ralph Lauren, Chanel,* and *Prada.* And *Luxottica* recently acquired *Vogue. Luxottica* has built factories in *China;* acquired vision insurance schemes inside the *United States;* and now outright owns and primarily controls myriad retail stores located on four continents. Only one major level—optical lenses themselves—

was missing in the supply chain link. No longer, *Luxottica* and *Essilor* recently agreed to merge. You guessed it. *Essilor* is one of the largest manufacturers of optical lenses.[21] That's vertical integration.

Conventional Marketing Systems

Then there are conventional marketing systems which operate as the second basic supply chain design. Conventional marketing systems exist when independent organizations voluntarily agree to partner with one another. A unifying expectation that exists inside these relationships and indeed that binds the firms together is that each organization then can specialize or concentrate with great focus on executing its own one or two core competencies. A related underlying premise is that the partnering organizations then can collaborate and cooperate in order to produce greater efficiency and more value than either firm could generate alone. Greater efficiencies facilitate lowered costs; higher values facilitate superior solutions—each partnering firm ultimately wins along with end-use customers. Such is the beauty of and the case for participating as partners inside supply chains.

Everything sold at the retail level by *JCPenney* or *Walmart* is produced by another supply chain partner. Everything sold at the retail level by either giant merchandiser is also at least partially shipped and inventoried by another chain or set of firms. *JCPenney* and *Walmart* participate in many dozens of conventional supply chains.

As does *McKesson*, the world's largest pharmaceutical wholesaler. *McKesson* neither makes nor markets pharmaceutical products to end-use consumers. The supply chain partner instead functions as a classic intermediary by partnering with various organizations operating upstream from *McKesson* toward the sources of pharmaceutical products (*Pfizer, Johnson & Johnson,* and *Merck*). Yet *McKesson* also partners with various organizations operating downstream toward end-use consumers (*CVS, Walgreens,* even *Walmart*). Upstream, toward the dirt, which is surely where most chemical products and processes originate. And downstream, toward consumers, the customers who actually purchase and consume pharmaceutical products and their presumed solutions.

Similar conventional supply chain membership descriptions apply to battery manufacturers such as *Albemarle Corp* or *Elcoa Advanced Materials,* given that few to no intermediaries [middlemen] exist that wholesale only batteries or retailers that exclusively sell batteries.

THE BEST SUPPLY CHAIN DESIGN

What is the best supply chain design?

The answer to this question logically begins and ends with answers to two other questions related to customer needs. Specifically, questions about what customer needs or problems exist and what is the best way to solve those needs.

---

21. *The Week* Staff, "The Secretive Firms Behind Your Glasses," *The Week* (July 20, 2018): 36–37.

Indeed, answers to these two hugely important questions should provide core baselines from which most strategic marketing decision-making can begin. The satisfaction of customer needs should function as a determinant factor in any supply chain decision. Which should not shock anyone . . . how best to, as well as whether this decision will, satisfy customer needs should be considered during any strategic marketing decision.

The best supply chain design is always the one that does the best job of satisfying customer needs at an optimal cost. Delivering higher levels of supply chain service simply costs more—no way around that.

Yet satisfaction of customer needs must be balanced against marketing organizations' strategic supply chain goals/objectives and their cost and resource constraints. On average, for example, the needs of *Walmart* customers differ radically from the needs of *Neiman-Marcus* customers. The nature of and costs associated with managing these two retailers' respective supply chains will likewise radically differ, and differ based on this fact. Decisions about which type of supply chain design would prove most efficient and effective for *Walmart* or for *Nordstrom's* would also differ substantially.

Three additional supply chain design-related decisions must be made. The decisions entail choosing the:

- Types of intermediaries that the marketing organization will use (i.e., manufacturers, wholesalers, agents, or retailers, etc.);
- Number of supply chain intermediaries the marketer will use; and
- Amount and types of supply chain functions or responsibilities that will be assigned to each supply chain partner with whom the originating marketing organization partners.

MODULE 12.6

What's Happening at the End of a Well-Managed Supply Chain

Managing successful supermarkets inside American markets is more challenging than ever. Profits remain razor-thin, as always. Home delivery and online shopping options have changed how consumers buy food. Dollar stores and drugstores now sell groceries. Threatening environmental and competitive trends are exercising so much pressure that regional chains such as *Southeastern Grocers*, owner of *Winn-Dixie* and *Bi-Lo*, have recently filed for bankruptcy. *Save-A-Lot*, second-largest discount grocer inside the United States after *Aldi*, is deep in debt and can't afford to continue lowering prices without sacrificing profit.

Large companies increasingly dominate a progressively more oligopolistic[22] grocery sector, which had always traditionally operated as divergent networks of smaller, local grocers. Even *Walmart*—the biggest beast of all—is feeling the heat. Primarily from *Amazon*, which purchased *Whole Foods* during 2017 for nearly $14 billion.

But when Greg Foran, *Walmart's* CEO, used words such as "fierce," "good," and "clever" to describe an emerging competitor, he's not referencing *Amazon,* or national chains such as *Kroger's* or *Albertsons*; dollar stores like *Dollar General* or *Big Lots*; or online players such as *FreshDirect* and *Instacart*. Foran was referencing *Aldi,* the no-frills *German* discount grocery chain that's marketing aggressively inside America and along the way is reshaping grocery supply chain practice.

Aldi's. The rebel retailer expects customers to endure several minor inconveniences not typical at other US-based grocery stores. Shoppers need a quarter to rent a shopping cart. Plastic and paper bags are available only for a fee. And at checkout, cashiers hurry shoppers away, expecting them to bag their own groceries in a separate location away from the cash register. New customers are often shaken and stirred by their maiden shopping experiences at *Aldi*. But *Aldi* is still growing cult consumer-like followings, city by city. When the brand enters a new town, hundreds of people often turn out for the grand opening. The allure is all in the rock-bottom prices, which are so inexpensive

---

22. The influences of oligopolies are discussed more fully during Module 13.

that *Aldi* often beats *Walmart* at its own low-price game. Recently, *Aldi* has expanded its produce and organic offerings to attract more customers.

Consumers willingly do the extra work because prices matter. Not to everyone, clearly, but large segments within the American grocery marketplace. Fans even manage blogs about the grocer (see *Aldi Nerd*). An *Aldi* Facebook page exists featuring more than 50,000 members.

When marketing researchers visited a *New Jersey Aldi*, antibiotic-free chicken was $4.29 a pound. *Trader Joe's* "All Natural Chicken" and *Whole Foods'* "365 Organic Fresh Chicken," each competitors located right down the road, were $4.99 and $6.99 a pound, respectively. *Aldi* has planted more than 1,800 stores in thirty-five states but primarily geographically targets Midwestern, Mid-Atlantic, *Florida,* and *California* locales. *Aldi* is poised to become America's third largest supermarket chain behind *Walmart* and *Kroger* and plans to have 2,500 US stores by the end of 2022.

Aldi has forced numerous other domestic grocery supply chains to make big changes in order to retain their customers. *Aldi* has jumped right into *Walmart*'s grill—literally. The German Giant kicked sand in the American bully's face during 2018 by opening a *Bentonville, Arkansas*, store—about one mile from *Walmart's* corporate headquarters. But competitors fight back. Can *Aldi* hang on to its low-cost advantage? Can *Aldi* continue to differentiate successfully on what it calls, the "*Aldi* way"? A strategy based primarily on creating and sustaining supply chain advantage.

THE ALDI WAY: BEATING WALMART AT ITS OWN LOW-COST SUPPLY CHAIN GAME

There are few secrets about how *Aldi* keeps its prices so low. *Aldi*, for example, strips down the shopping experience in an unapologetically and brutally efficient way. The retailer drives out every cent of supply chain cost without compromising quality, which represents a difficult needle to thread. Industry estimates are that *Aldi*'s supply chain operating costs are around half of mainstream retailers. The company also knowingly accepts lower profit margins than competitors. *Aldi*, one may argue, is winning by out-Walmarting *Walmart*.

From consumers' point of view, the distinctive shopping experience begins with shopping carts, which are locked up. Rather than employ teams of often unreliable runners to retrieve carts from the parking lot all day, *Aldi* expects customers to return carts to the store after each shopping trip. *Aldi's* reverse-incentivizes by charging customers a quarter deposit that they get back when they return their carts. Reverse-incentivizes means giving back their own money to customers.

The idea may have appeared edgy, but it was not new. Several *American* grocers pursued the tactic during the 1980s and 1990s, but abandoned the practice after it annoyed customers who had come to expect more services at their grocery stores. New era, new environments; same strategy, different [and more favorable] response. *Aldi*, which opened its first store in *Iowa* in 1976, has hung with the distribution model, actually insisting that the deposit system mindset is key to its low-price strategy. Die-hard *Aldi* fans celebrate it, shouting hosannas when *Aldi* occasionally offers "quarter keeper" keychains. Some fans even knit their own versions. A search on *Etsy* for "*Aldi* quarter keeper" turns up more than 500 hits.

The lowering costs hits kept coming. When customers enter stores, they'll notice how *Aldi* store interiors look almost nothing like traditional US supermarkets. Featuring only five or six super-wide aisles, *Aldi* stocks around 1,400 products—in contrast to some 40,000 at traditional supermarkets and more than 100,000 inside *Walmart Supercenters*. *Aldi* displays items in their original corrugated paper shipping containers, rather than stacking them individually. Time, and money, that otherwise would be allocated to stocking shelves is saved. Time-starved shoppers have learned to love the simple layout and displays. Shoppers never experience vicious self-induced pressures to make the best choice from among twenty-seven different salsa options; too much analysis truly leading to paralysis and no purchase decision.

Is your nature to be brand loyal? Many people are. If you lean toward brand loyalty, good for you, but *Aldi* may not be your cup of tea, because most of your favorite brands are not stocked by the grocery chain. More than 90 percent of the brands Aldi sells are private label (retail store-owned) brands like *Simply Nature* organic products, *Millville* cereals, *Burman's* ketchup and *Specially Selected* bread. If you're familiar with *Trader Joe's*, and this sounds like TJ to you, you're right. The two grocers share a common ancestor.

Famous branding trademarks and colors be damned, apparently. The packaging and branding on *Aldi* products sometimes appeared so similar to brand-name alternatives that customers may do a double-take. *Aldi's Honey Nut Crispy Oats*, for example, are distributed through boxes that feature the same shades of orange, yellow, and brown as *General Mills' Honey Nut Cheerios*. Branding fonts, typefaces, are also highly similar. Aldi markets *Tandil* laundry detergent in an orange plastic jug with blue and yellow graphics reminiscent of *Tide*. *Millville Toaster Tarts*, a house brand, look patently similar to *Pop-Tarts*—but a 12-pack of the *Millville* version is $1.85 while a 12-pack of *Pop-Tarts* costs $2.75. And, surprise, *Aldi's* corn flakes taste exactly like the one with the chicken on the package (*Kellogg's*), at a fractional price. *Aldi's* entered American shores not to play nice, but to win.

Aldi's reliance on private-label brands is also helping win millennial hearts, minds, and wallets. This generational cohort is increasingly brand-agnostic and instead is drawn to lower prices and convenience, according to *Bain* data. *Nielsen* data recently reported that private-label brands products have experienced a recent renaissance and are now growing faster at supermarkets than the top twenty national brands. Private labels essentially boil down to in-store, or *Aldi*, brands.

Although the supply chain innovations are not obvious to most shoppers at first glance, *Aldi* leverages key design details in order to maximize efficiency at checkout too. On many products barcodes are either supersized or printed on multiple sides to speed up scanning processes. After groceries are rung up, the packaged or fresh goods don't stand around (getting in the way) because cashiers drop them directly into shopping carts below. *Aldi* doesn't waste time bagging groceries. Customers must drive away their shopping carts to bag their groceries in a separate section at the front. Since stores don't offer free bags, customers often scour the store for empty cardboard boxes to use instead. Oh, the humanity.

But the lines fly. Once customers experience this sort of efficiency, going back to other supermarkets annoys some. *Aldi* uses other tactics to keep real estate and labor costs down. Store size is one factor. *Walmart* supercenters average around 178,000 square feet. *Costco* warehouse stores average about 145,000 square feet. *Aldi's* small box stores, however, claim only a fraction of that space, averaging 12,000 square feet.

Makes sense that *Aldi* is winning. Appreciable portions of the domestic consumer marketplace genuinely value efficiency, simplicity, and frugality. It was not government issued public policy but a widespread and organic consumer movement that created and drove a "use it up, wear it out, make it do, or do without" mantra inside a widely-patriotic and highly united *United States* during *World War II*. This genetic code has passed along from many succeeding American generations—apparently right up to now.

There's more. Unlike other grocers, where clear divisions of labor exist—runners retrieve carts, cashiers check out customers, clerks stock shelves—*Aldi* employees are cross-trained. They can perform every function that must be executed inside grocery stores. Employee duties are also streamlined. *Aldi* displays products in their original cardboard shipping boxes, rather than stacking them individually. Employees save time that otherwise would be allocated to stocking shelves. Most stores don't list their phone numbers publicly. *Aldi* doesn't want workers spending time answering calls.

The result is that single *Aldi* stores might only have three to five employees in the store at any given time, and have only fifteen to twenty on their entire payroll. The company pays workers above industry-average wages (ensuring better workers), but still cuts labor costs by employing fewer people. These cost savings add up—supply chain-based savings always do—and in *Aldi*'s case are passed forward to customers in the form of discounted prices. *Aldi* claims its prices are up to 50 percent less expensive than traditional supermarkets. An independent analyst, *Wolfe Research*, reports *Aldi* prices are around 15 percent less than *Walmart* prices in the greater *Houston* and *Chicago* markets.

Despite the stripped-down store experience, *Aldi* earns higher customer satisfaction scores and benefits far more from positive word-of-mouth marketing than Walmart and other supermarkets. *Aldi* has an extremely high Net Promoter Score—a key measure of how likely customers are to recommend the brand to their friends and family—in the grocery sector, again according to *Bain & Company*. Net Promoter Scores fundamentally measure the amount of favorable WOM or opinion-leadership that particular brands have earned.

INEXPENSIVE FOOD CHOICES SITTING ON SHELVES; EXPENSIVE AUTO BRANDS PARKING ON LOTS

The *Great Recession* and the *American* economy's slow but steady recovery from its effects helped *Aldi*, a discount grocer, gain and lock in popularity among budget-conscious shoppers in the United States. *Aldi*'s latest expansion builds on that momentum. Even consumers who escaped the *Great Recession* relatively unscathed pay much closer attention to pennies on their grocery purchases than ever before. Indeed, one might argue that smart people love saving money on commodities and staples, products where real differences are difficult to detect, if they exist at all. One might further argue that smart people often become wealthier people because they spend smartly. As far as those individuals who did get badly dinged by the *Great Recession*, they're still worried that it could and will happen again. And, of course, eventually they will be right. Recessions, great and merely mediocre, cannot be avoided forever.

Aldi has played into and indeed exploited these environmental trends and human tendencies. A substantial chunk of *Aldi's* success derives from the brand's ability to appeal not just to low or middle-income shoppers, but to wealthier ones as well. *Aldi's* core shopper tends to make more money and have a slightly higher education level than the overall grocery shopper, according to *Bain Capital*. In recent years, *Aldi* has ramped up its efforts to appeal to (target) high-income shoppers by offering more fresh and organic produce as well as imported items like genuine *Irish* cheese, *French* brioche, and *Italian* pasta. The stores now offer private-label versions of kombucha, cold-pressed juices, an array of gluten-free products and peanut butter powder.

Aldi's appeal is not entirely based on all-lower-grocery-bills, all-the-time value, though lower costs remain the brand's primary differentiator. But *Aldi* also strategically promotes these discounts, across consumer income strata, and does so by making customers feel as if they're outsmarting higher-priced supermarket and big brands alternatives when they see their receipts. By positioning itself as the "smart shopping alternative," Aldi consistently spreads the story that traditional grocers and brands simply rip off consumers.

Is *Aldi* right? [The answer mostly depends upon customers' perceptions of what represents value.] *Aldi* hammers home such messages on in-store signage. Positioning statements such as "The same is always better when it costs less" or "New deals every week. Find them here. Brag like crazy" or "Switch and save" [dust your current grocery store] are hard for competitors to parry and difficult for customers to forget.

Two sets of evidence are in. The first is that America is paying attention, and you know how important consumer attention is to B2C marketing organizations. The second set of evidence suggests that strategies driven by extreme supply chain-based efficiencies and savings passed along directly to consumers in the form of lower prices are difficult for anyone, even *Walmart*, to beat.

MODULE 12.7

Creativity, New Product Development, and Entrepreneurship inside Supply Chains

Malcom McLean was recently described as one of the "least known people who changed the world"—even though most Americans have seen a tractor-trailer truck with his last name on it. Mr. McLean is the primary driver behind the idea that inexorably led to the now-ubiquitous use of the container for shipping cargo and went from driving long-haul trucks to developing the "on-the-ship," "off-the-ship," "on-the-train," and eventually "on-the-truck" container. The astoundingly efficient supply chains of today, which depend heavily on the use of containerized cargo, would be practically impossible without *Malcom McLean's* idea. Mr. McLean struggled long and hard to get his new idea and new product accepted, in no small part because implementation of the innovation immediately obsoleted the how once very powerful, literally muscular set of opponents. Those opponents were and still are called stevedores.[23] And not only were these stevedores union-based, inside most American ports they were *mafia*-supported at the time of their initial opposition. But creativity and the correspondingly higher profits that resulted proved a creatively destructive force that eventually outed and ousted the *mafia*.

The idea for transporting truck trailers on ships was put into practice before *World War II*. A regular connection of a daily luxury passenger train from *London* to *Paris*, and back again, began in 1926. Four containers were used to transport passengers' baggage. These containers were loaded in *London* or *Paris* and carried to ports, *Dover* or *Calais*, on flat cars in *Great Britain* and in *France*.

Malcom McLean decided to introduce the broader use of containers inside normal B2B and B2C supply chains during the early 1950s. By 1952, he was developing plans to carry his company's trucks on ships along the US Atlantic coast, from *North Carolina* to *New York*. It soon became apparent that "trailerships," as this invention was called, would be inefficient because of the large waste in potential cargo space onboard the vessel, known as broken stowage. The original concept was modified into

---

23. Stevedore is not a word that one sees every day. But stevedores, also called longshoremen, still exist everywhere, albeit in far smaller numbers than in past decades. Stevedore is the name for people who unload cargo—typically either by hand or by hook—after boats and ships have docked.

loading just the containers, not the chassis, onto ships, hence the new designation container or "box" ship—and in the process a mere invention was transformed into a new and useful innovation.

At the time, federal regulations did not permit trucking companies to own their own shipping (as in ocean-going ships) lines. McLean secured a bank loan for $22 million and in January 1956 bought two World War II-era oil tanker ships. He then developed plans to have the ships converted to carry containers on and under their decks. McLean oversaw the construction of wooden shelter decks, known as *Mechano* decking. This practice was commonly used in World War II to ship oversized cargo, such as aircraft or large caliber artillery that were disassembled before shipping and then reassembled after landing in *England, France,* or *Holland.*

The tasks of refitting the ships, constructing containers that would be carried on and stored below the vessels' decks, and designing trailer chassis that allowed containers to be easily removed or latched back on took a few years. But by 1956 one of the converted tankers was loaded and sailed from the *Port Newark Marine Terminal* in *New Jersey* to *Houston, Texas.* The ship carried fifty-eight 35-foot trailer vans, now known as containers, along with a regular load of crude oil.

McLean flew to *Houston* to be dock-side when the ship safely landed. In 1956, most cargoes were loaded and unloaded by hand by stevedores. Hand-loading or uploading ships cost $5.86 a ton at that time. Using containers, it cost only 16 cents a ton to load a ship, thirty-six-fold savings.

Containerization also greatly reduced the time to load and unload ships. Ships are made to sell, and never make money while sitting at docks inside harbors. McLean based his innovative business on the pursuit of such efficiencies. In 1957, the first full-bore container ship, called the *Gateway City*, began regular service between *New York, Florida,* and *Texas. San Juan, Puerto Rico*, was soon added to the route, and the rest is container ship, and container train, and container truck, and containers themselves history. The history is so vividly on display all around us today that no need exists to summarize it further.

But remember this all started with the creation of one single highly innovative supply chain idea that now appears so obviously appropriate in retrospect and with one creative thinker, *Malcom McLean,* who variously pushed and pulled the containerization shipping idea to the point where it now dominates the supply chain world.[24]

---

24. Marc Levinson, *The Box: How the Shipping Container Made the World Smaller and the World Economy Bigger* (Princeton: Princeton University Press, 2006).

EXHIBIT 12.1
A Traditional Channel of Distribution

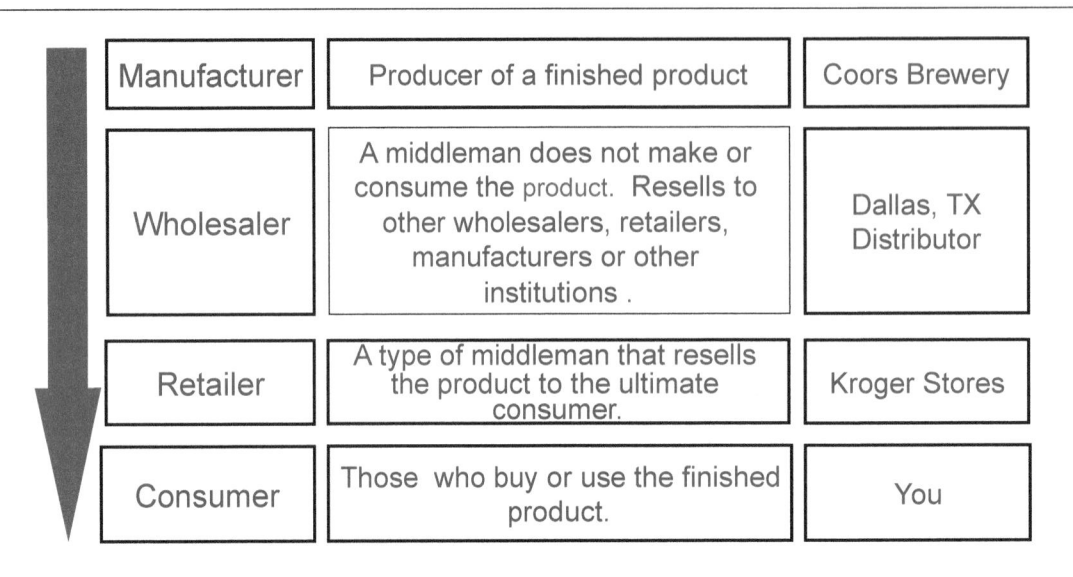

Manufacturer	Producer of a finished product	Coors Brewery
Wholesaler	A middleman does not make or consume the product. Resells to other wholesalers, retailers, manufacturers or other institutions.	Dallas, TX Distributor
Retailer	A type of middleman that resells the product to the ultimate consumer.	Kroger Stores
Consumer	Those who buy or use the finished product.	You

EXHIBIT 12.2
Relationship between Supply Chain and Logistics

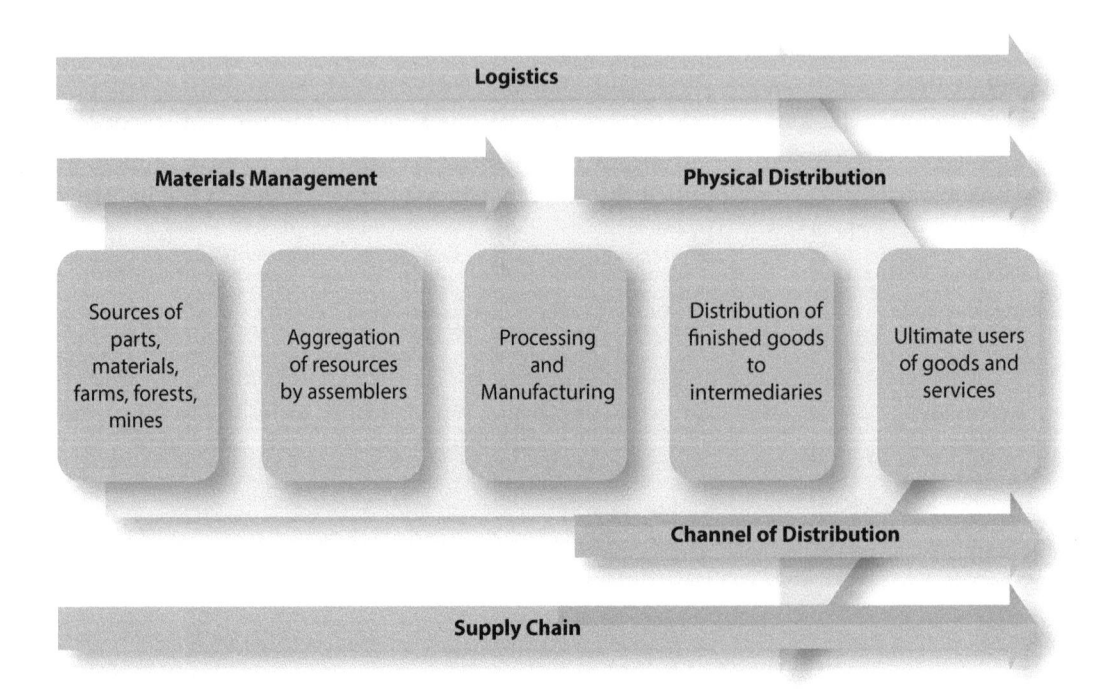

Logistics

Materials Management | **Physical Distribution**

- Sources of parts, materials, farms, forests, mines
- Aggregation of resources by assemblers
- Processing and Manufacturing
- Distribution of finished goods to intermediaries
- Ultimate users of goods and services

Channel of Distribution

Supply Chain

EXHIBIT 12.3
Number of Transactions Required for Producers to Reach Consumers in the Absence of Intermediaries

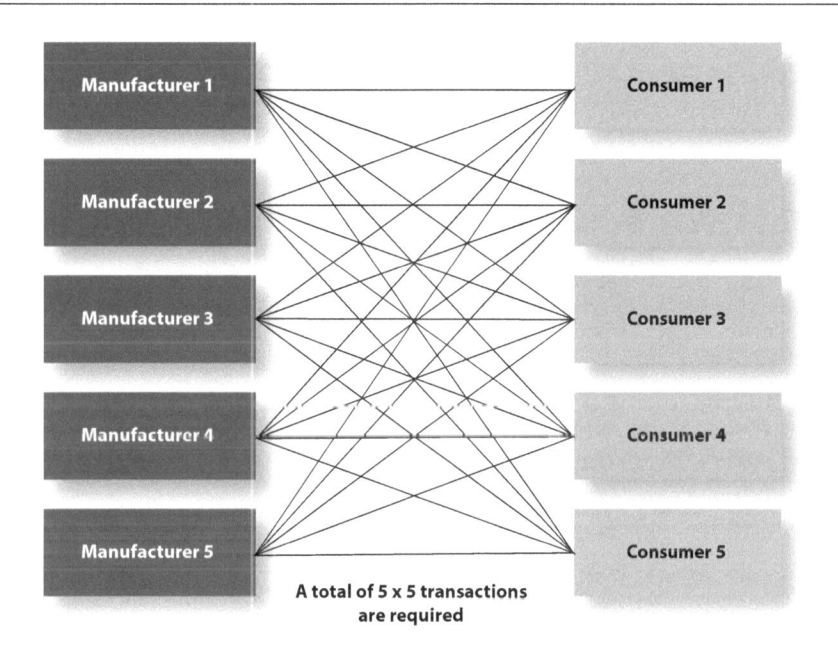

A total of 5 x 5 transactions are required

MODULE 13

Managing Pricing

MODULE 13.0

Pricing Points Worth Pondering

Stated simply, price capture what customers are willing to pay to acquire products. Stated alternatively, price is the amount of money marketers charge for their products or services. Stated more broadly still, price represents the sum of ALL values customers must give up in order to get the benefits or values associated with having or using products or services. Pricing and price-related decisions thus reside at the heart of marketing exchange.

Pricing at highest possible levels, when possible, makes sense for most marketers. For starters, because higher prices generate higher profit margins. Additionally, because the task of raising low prices and sustaining demand is far more challenging to execute successfully than is the task of lowering higher prices and either raising or sustaining demand.

These two references to demand may spur thoughts about the relationship between supply and demand. Supply refers to the amount of products available inside any market. Demand refers to how many customers want those products, typically at differing price levels.

The normal and expected relationship between supply and demand is that when products are perceived as too expensive by potential or actual customers, demand decreases. Conversely, when prospective or actual customers perceive that branded products are reasonably priced, demand for the brands is expected to rise.

THE EFFECTS OF SUPPLY AND DEMAND

How does supply and demand work?

The following example illustrates what happens when the supply of any product and its value goes up. If the domestic educational marketplace produces too many *Chilean* dance major graduates then the domestic marketplace gets flooded with supply, and the price paid by *American* consumers for the values that *Chilean* folk dancers produce through the development and delivery of their services will fall as a result. Alternatively explained, a higher supply of professional services tamps down the prices paid to acquire those exact professional services. This relationship between supply and demand is a major reason why the medical and legal professions impose high entrance requirements on those that are allowed to in either marketing sector.

Now, consider another illustration of what happens when the price of any particular product and its value goes up. Economist *Thomas Sowell's* well-known maxim related to the minimum wage argues that regardless of where governmental forces set the price the real minimum wage—the price of hiring workers—is always zero. Which represents the best possible explanation regarding why workers often have more to fear from well-meaning politicians than from capitalism. The minimum wage is a price. Employers will only hire as many workers as they can afford to pay. Increase the price of workers too much, and the amount of workers hired—the demand for workers—will decrease. Every single time; absent the artificial intervention of non-capitalistic forces. Meanwhile, professional or non-professional workers will only be hired—and paid—at pricing levels consistent with the value they are able to create. Just like any other type of non-human product that one might consider.

Rare exceptions to the normal principles that govern the relationship between prices and supply and demand do exist. Some of these exceptions are discussed below. Other exceptions were previously discussed during Module 9 when the positional goods concept was introduced.

TYPICAL PRICING OBJECTIVES

One or another of three key pricing objectives generally dominate thinking and practice inside strategic marketing organizations.

In no order of importance, marketers might establish price levels aimed at earning targeted profit margin returns (objective one).

Or, marketers might establish price levels in an effort to earn or retain targeted market share percentages (objective two).

Finally, marketers might establish or re-establish prices motivated by the goal of ensuring survival during challenging times (objective three).

A fourth pricing objective also exists and occasionally informs and steers pricing decisions. This objective plays out inside situations where marketers elect to and/or actually deliver socially-responsible-virtues. An industry norm that prevails among domestic pharmaceutical firms, for example, is to strategically price AIDS medicines at highly-discounted levels when targeting patients who reside in underdeveloped or so-called *Third-World Nations*. For example, this self-interested pricing tactic is often enacted in order to promote and to position individual pharmaceutical marketers, and in this case an entire industry, as ethical and socially-responsible marketing players.

Why is this pricing tactic described as self-interested? Because the strategy signals virtue. However, about 1,300 new pharmaceutical products were introduced last year in the developed First World. All but two or three of these new products were targeted at and sold exclusively at uniformly high prices to well-off consumers living in, by global standards, rich countries. "Rich" American consumers, or typically their health insurance service providers, pay heavily to acquire these solutions. Fact is, these consumers or their insurance providers pay out far more than enough to cover the lowered or zero prices occasionally offered in developing nations. The pharmaceutical sector has mastered the art of virtue-signaling through price management.

Yet certain marketing organizations exist, such as *Panera Bread,* that have successfully managed their pricing strategies in ways that deliver genuine social responsibility, as discussed during Module 8. Other marketing organizations, not so much or perhaps not at all.

Consider *Zuckerberg San Francisco General,* for example. Yes, the hospital was named after *Mark Zuckerberg* after the *Facebook Foundation* gifted it $75 million. San Francisco's largest public hospital takes no private insurance, and according to *Vox.com,* sends out bills exceeding $24,000 for a broken arm and $113,000 for a broken ankle. This is an egregious example of a national problem called surprise pricing. *Zuckerberg General* is an extreme case because it does not negotiate emergency room bills with major health insurance providers, unlike most other large health-care provider institutions. The problem is exacerbated for patients brought to the emergency room by ambulance, who are often still recovering from or actively experiencing trauma, and who have no opportunity to conduct research or choose another in-network facility. Insurers, protecting their self-interests, only pay the portion of the price they deem reasonable and stick patients with the remainder. In the case of one consumer patient's broken arm, the proportion of the bill that he was was stuck with was $20,243.71.[1]

SIGNALING VIRTUES THROUGH PRICING MANAGEMENT

Patagonia, a popular brand, has long employed a virtue-signaling-based pricing and positioning strategy. Panic recently erupted on *Wall Street* when *Patagonia* announced "It would sell its custom-made vests only to mission-driven companies," said *The Wall Street Journal.*[2] This announcement represented a sartorial blow to many men and women employed in business and financial sectors. Because for them, *Patagonia* vests embroidered with names like *JPMorgan Chase, Nomura,* or *BMO Capital* had become a *de rigueur* version of the contemporary three-piece suit or tasteful heels and pearls, signaling, one would suppose, their woke-ness. Nattily attired and nicely suited-up *Gordon Gekko* look-alikes, the focal character inside the paradigm-shifting movie *Wall Street*, no longer play on The Street.

The fleece-vest button-down *Patagonia* look first took hold in *Silicon Valley*, similar to many other trends. The fashion style soon emigrated to trading-room floors, which actually can get surprisingly cold. But when a financial communications firm recently placed an order for co-branded vests, it was denied. *Patagonia*, a marketing brand that long has positioned itself as a paragon of social awareness, said those hedge funds or banks hoping to make a purchase have to convince it that "they are helping to turn America green—and not just by making money," again according to the *Wall Street Journal*.

The *National Basketball Association (NBA)* brand has few peers when it comes to organizations that strenuously attempt to virtue-signal their collective woke-ness. Not merely content to being recognized as the world's best dunkers, three-point-shooters, or Euro-steppers who earn an average $9.5 million annually (that's the average price paid for their rarified service skills), NBA players became so awoke during the 2019–20 season that they canceled themselves by skipping out on several

---

1. Sarah Kliff. Vox.com.
2. "Vintage Patagonia Fleeces: Fluff That's Worth a Fortune," *Wall Street Journal* (2020): B:18.

scheduled playoff games—and shutting down the league. Yes, the preceding statement is supposed to be ironic, and definitely represents a riff on a progressively-engendered cancel-culture, but carries with it the virtue of actually being true. Or authentic, as any branding expert would tell you.

Virtual-signaling is, shall we say, generally okay. After all, who's really getting hurt? Usually, no one. But virtue-signalers would generally benefit and give others a break by learning or remembering, always, that the point of any promotional marketing tactic is to help the brand not to feel better about oneself.

Beyond this logical marketing advice, individual consumers should carefully consider what they are really asking for, making sure that they are genuinely ready to bear the consequences when "asking for something" through virtue-signaling, because they just may get it. So what does the preceding statement actually mean? Read on to find out. Not long ago, when students matriculating at *England's* highly prestigious *Oxford University* signaled their virtues by asking the university to divest its investments in fossil fuel-based energy firms (coal, natural gas, oil companies) the lead administrator replied (paraphrasing): Not a problem, so long as you agree there will no heat or hot water in your dorms, classrooms, or anywhere else on campus. Students quickly withdrew their request. Good intentions and virtuous signals aren't credible without the marketers or the customers who are issuing the signals appreciating and accounting for the costs. In fact, good intentions, absent a plan, are often accompanied by high reputational and financial costs.

REAL PRICE DEALS: PRICING FACTS SUCCESSFUL MARKETERS UNDERSTAND

Not only do most successful marketers know the real price deal. Successful marketers often also exploit what they know when developing and leveraging their pricing strategies to either create new value for or capture new value from their B2C or B2B customers. Which is exactly what marketers should do.

Marketers exist not only to satisfy customers and solve their problems at whatever prices customers deem appropriate,[3] they are also obligated to develop the highest possible ethical returns in terms of either higher salaries or dividends/higher stock prices to their employees and investors. These are plain marketing facts. What follows are fifteen price-related marketing facts that successful marketers typically understand and consider when establishing their pricing strategies and tactics.

Pricing Fact 1: Successful marketers realize few people wake up wanting to pay higher prices.

But at the same time, successful marketers understand that most customers seek value, striving to attain what customers perceive as valuable to them inside their own minds. By voting with their feet, walking away when they perceive deals are not "worth it" to them, customers determine what they are willing to pay.

Pricing Fact 2: Successful marketers relatedly understand that it is their responsibility to create, frame, and deliver their brand's value proposition and market position in ways that make the brand's value appear worth the price.

---

3. In capitalist economies and societies consumers usually vote with their wallets. If the price is not right, consumers move along and buy another brand or purchase nothing at all.

This is done by executing uniquely designed marketing mixes for each brand being marketed by the firm. (You got this!) Marketers likewise understand that when they execute NPD and/or branding processes effectively, prices become less important to customers. This earned condition represents a huge win for marketers because at that point they can more easily raise or maintain higher prices.

Pricing Fact 3: Successful marketers realize that no small number of highly loyal, addicted (written literally), or status-conscious consumers willingly pay higher prices, or are consciously unconcerned about high prices because for them money—or the price they pay—is no object.

Successful marketers understand that they should accommodate these folks too. No worries, they do. Such marketers understand that no need exists to assume all customers are constantly seeking bargains. Instead, large segments of consumers seek to maximize their value, as they define it. Remember the role that targeting and positioning play, and the existence of positional goods. *Apple* markets. Extremely well. And prices accordingly.

The following events are historical but still relevant. *Apple* introduced three new phones during September 2017. When doing so, *Apple* made the bold bet that a sizable customer segment would willingly part with more than $1,000 to acquire the premium iPhone X while other customer segments would also pay to upgrade regular models. *Apple,* as has almost always been the case, did NPD, branding, and their new designs extremely well. Knowing this now, it made sense then that *Apple* management knew their brand could command the formerly exorbitant prices that it did.

The pricing of these then-new phones placed them at levels closer to the prices of major in-home appliances such as stoves, washer/dryer sets, or refrigerators. The pricing strategy imposed a severe test on the enduring branding cache of *Apple* products, which were already the priciest in their field, but *Apple's* branding power ultimately prevailed.

Pricing Fact 4: Successful marketers understand that charging ridiculously high prices often works when the goal is to attract crowds of customers.

For two hundred or so years, along the *Florida Gulf Coast*, stone crabs, when they registered at all inside the minds of commercial fishermen, did so as junk catch. Stone crabs were deemed pests who snagged nets and were laboriously cut loose before being tossed, dead or wounded, back into the Gulf. Then a *Steve Jobs* of the oceanic set had a clever idea. Don't toss stone crabs, start selling them—and pricing them not at the bottom of the seafood marketing food chain but near the top. Successful fulfillment of this pricing goal required that stone crabs be repositioned as a delicacy appreciated by sophisticated consumers. This objective proved no problem, and indeed the rest of the story is now restaurant history. A nasty nuisance was quickly transformed into a luxurious delicacy. What started with fishermen bitching ended with *Disney*-like lines at various *Joe's Crab Shack* locations.

A singular economic and pricing principle is revealed, many consumers highly value what they cannot afford. The pricing premise is simple, actually. Consumers are human. Many if not most humans, in turn, appear inescapably wired to want what they cannot have, either because the choice is not available or because the choice is too expensive.

Pricing Fact 5: Successful marketers understand they should never use the word "cheap" to describe their prices or their brands.

Describing their pricing, positioning, and branding practices as economical, low-cost, discounted, competitive, value-priced, or lower-priced; that's okay. Describing them as cheap, not cool.

The underlying rationale rolls like this. Would you ever want to be described as cheap yourself? Rarely if ever, right? Get the point?

Besides this point, use of the word "cheap" connotes low or lower quality, not a good place for any brand to be positioned. Customers, meanwhile, usually perceive higher-priced products as higher-quality products, even when this is not the case. Such perceptions are particularly likely to arise in decision-making situations where customers cannot judge quality. Customers often lack the information, time, skill sets, or motivation necessary to judge brand product accurately. When consumers lack other supporting information, for them price becomes a huge signal of quality.

However, none of this discussion is meant to argue that the idea of "cheap"—even bragging about cheap, for example—cannot and should not ever be used as a point of differentiation. Try telling that to the owners of the obviously successful *Dirt Cheap* store the next time you enter *Meriden, Mississippi*, heading eastbound on Interstate 20. But conventional wisdom, which here has the advantage of actually being right, suggests that "cheap consumers" always pay twice. First, when they acquire cheap goods or services. Second, when they pay again to replace the cheap choices.

One thing your authors are not, however, are *Ivory Tower* (i.e., academic) snobs. Having each been relatively to extremely poor once ourselves, we recognize that many consumer segments realistically cannot afford anything other than deeply discounted, inexpensive, goods and services. Fortunately, marketers usually make lower priced alternatives available to more price-conscious segments for their consumption.

Pricing Fact 6: Successful marketers understand that $999.99 sells better than $1000.00.

In this psychological pricing ploy, the decimal makes the price number seem smaller. The use of psychological pricing is why about two-thirds of domestic product prices still end with 9. The assumption, again, is that consumers round down nines, making brands appear less expensive in their minds. Nature, along with consumers, apparently loves odd numbers, as in 1, 3, 5, 7, and especially 9, when the subject turns to pricing.

Yet buyers typically don't notice price hikes or drops that are less than 10 percent. Generally, B2C customers don't care about price hikes until the increase exceeds 10 percent of the original price. For example, the 35 cents that fast-food restaurants charge for a piece of cheese (cost—approximately 10 percent of a $3.75 burger's price) is generally not only not a show stopper but likely not even noticed.

Pricing Fact 7: Successful marketers understand how few consumers know the right price for anything.

Marketers further understand that rather than understanding the price totals they actually should be paying, most consumers mainly respond to price increases or decreases, or to comparative prices between one product/brand versus another product/brand; unless one brand has carved-out higher brand equity than its fellow brands that compete inside the same product category. Strategic marketers price accordingly.

Successful marketers also often re-frame prices to make the prices of brands from non-competing product categories appear similar. Customers perceive higher prices as more appealing or at least more tolerable when comparing them to other brands or choices whose prices appear trivial—at least in comparing customers' minds. Promoting the idea that a branded product costs less than your daily cup of *Starbucks* coffee across one year makes the daunting price of $999.99 or higher for a *Maytag* clothes dryer appear more palatable.[4]

Strategic marketers also know that B2C customers typically buy more when installment pricing options are available. Payment plans that are broken into multiple payments—three payments of $52.99 rather than a $149.99 single payment. That this strategy works is partly a function of consumers' logical desire to control their cash flow but primarily because most consumers cannot do the math in their heads. Presumably, however, consumers could do it on their phones if they took the time, but most don't.

And what, exactly, is the right price for perhaps the most important product that anyone ever consumes? Or, health-care services, as a product? Who among us could argue that health-care services are not the most important product whenever customers need specific medical solutions to save their loved ones or their own lives? Here we refer specifically to the domestic medical industrial complex (MIC), which has saved or extended the lives of millions of citizens at unbelievable cost totals—even though everybody's going to die sometime.

Inside the current *American* health-care marketing system, profit is a primary motivation that drives prices and pricing strategies. To assume otherwise is naïve, foolish, stupid—insert your own evocative adjective here. The domestic health-care marketing system has successfully negated every effort to contain its costs. Health-care consumers are perpetually victimized by predatory prices, in no small measure because most consumers have no idea what the right prices should be for health-care services.

Every marketing sector that operates inside the domestic health-care sector is guilty, none seemingly more so than another. The *Big Pharma* marketing sector plays small ball new product development games by introducing tiny changes to existing medicines in order to protect lucrative patent protections.[5] The nonprofit hospital marketing sector often though not universally on delivering the charitable care they are required to provide in exchange for their tax exempt status but often showers executives with lavish corporate style pay and perks. The health-care insurance marketing sector pushes prices up rather than containing them. Device makers, laboratories, and testing and diagnostic specialists, marketers all, pile on charges and perform unnecessary procedures such that the system is staggering under the weight of the resulting inefficiency.

Certain self-serving non-price-cutting pricing rules abide universally. Additional-for-pay treatments are somehow routinely viewed as more desirable by prescribing physicians than more logical, zero-new-cost-to-patients approaches of telling patients to get up off couches, walk around, stop eating crap, lose weight, and stop obsessing about "they-are-not-really-PROBLEMS" first-world

---

4. This re-framing pricing tactic surely puts *Starbuck's Coffee* prices in perspective.

5. How does "patent protection" work? A patent is a protective right that the US federal government grants to innovators. The protective right is designed to exclude others from making, using, selling, or importing, say, a pharmaceutical innovation throughout the US without the approval of the innovator or innovating marketing organization. The innovating individual or marketing organization may license or sell the rights defined by the claims of the federal patent to another corporation or individual, however.

problems. Physicians, acting based on marketing mindsets, regularly default to more expensive treatment options. No such thing as a fixed price or real price lists appear to exist pretty much throughout the domestic health care sector.

The ethics underlying all this conscious decision-making? Hmmm . . . the mind quivers as it considers. The health care sector profitability and customer costs that result from all this conscious decision-making. Hmmm . . . *American* consumers' minds should explode, in outrage.

Pricing Fact 8: Successful marketers understand the incremental value that they can secure for themselves by offering customers bundling options.

Bundling options increase add-on purchases. When confronting individual add-on options, consumers are less likely to buy when buying requires separate decisions. Consumers, by contrast, are more likely to buy when all options are bundled into a single package. The value of simplification is underscored, again. *Apple's* bundle-rich website illustrates the point.

Pricing Fact 9: Smart marketers, a synonym for successful marketers, exploit pricing anchors.

In pricing schemes that are virtually guaranteed to trick all but the best-informed consumers, marketers often toss out pricing anchors. *New York City* hosts a restaurant named *Norma's*. *Norma's* really, truly sells $1,000 caviar & lobster omelets. Had he been consumed at *Norma's*, our former friend Larry the Lobster really would have stepped up his value-add game big-time.

Few *Norma's* customers actually purchase the prominently-positioned (in a dominant place on *Norma's* menu) $1,000 caviar & lobster omelet. But the fact that this specific product is priced at $1,000 makes other less prominently positioned menu items, which remain rather expensive themselves (albeit not crazily so), appear less pricey by comparison. The anchoring pricing tactics work effectively because human minds assign disproportionate weight to the first information they receive when making decisions. When humans see exorbitant prices first, the still high but lower prices that follow then seem like a much, much better deal.

The availability of higher-priced alternatives, against which lower-priced options can be compared, unquestionably increases sales. Customers will more likely buy a brand after being exposed to more expensive alternatives. *Tesla Model 3*, originally introduced a few years back at a "low" $35,000 price tag, was the most pre-ordered car brand of all time in part because prospective buyers favorably compared it to *Tesla*'s existing and much higher-priced models that easily exceed $75,000-plus.

Pricing Fact 10: Successful marketers understand that other ways exist to trick consumers.

Tricking consumers is actually rather easy, especially when targeting low-involvement consumer decision-makers. Low involvement consumer decision-makers often pay much more for their products when they simply could have paid more attention to the B2C decisions they were making.

The pricing strategy being played here entails hoodwinking customers into believing they are getting more for less or more likely the same amount for the same price.[6] Trigger-alert; a beloved brand is about to be blasted. Some years back *Skippy's* indented its peanut butter jar such that the same-priced and seemingly same-sized container delivered 9 percent less peanut butter. Most consumers

---

6. These approaches were previously described as positioning strategies.

did not recognize this, happily continuing to buy the same quantity of *Skippy's* at seemingly the same price. But the price was not the same, because consumers were paying the same price for less peanut butter.

Full disclosure, *Skippy's* and its fast-follower competitors who employed the same pricing tricks, genuinely did face drastically rising raw material costs at this time as peanut prices rose, rose, rose.[7] Peanut prices themselves had shot through the roof as global demand exploded. For the peanut butter marketing sector, this trend represented an uncontrollable external environmental threat.

Naturally other variations on this pricing trick exist. Large airliners have been shrinking seat sizes for years, because by doing so they can earn up to $400,000 extra annual revenue per plane. More fannies on planes equals more dollars generated per flight. Makes sense, but only if the marketers in question do not care about satisfied customers—particularly during an era of radically-expanding passenger bottoms. The further inside pricing skinny is this, when every airliner competing across an entire oligopolistic market segment is doing the same thing, no single airline brand loses. As for the customers, well, if they're really unhappy they can always pay more to upgrade to a wider seat; usually wider on the order of two to three additional inches. Talk about being stuck with few to no good choices.

Pricing Fact 11: Strategic marketers, another synonym for successful marketers, understand that too many pricing decisions that marketers make are arbitrary in nature. Prices grounded in gut-based rather than research-based decisions.

The non-strategic pricing process often works like this. Managers get a hunch, and next thing you know they bet a bunch by pursuing non-strategic, going-from-the-gut, pricing strategies. Net, net, most marketers do pricing poorly. Then again, most marketers are not sufficiently strategic or successful.

Gut-based decisions, inside any strategic setting, have their time and place. Though the occasion is rare, pinning-back-one's-ears and going-for-it sometimes represents the preferred option, particularly given the potential value-add that is likely to result from the "surprise" that typically accompanies gut-based decisions. But the most basic problem associated with deciding to go with one's gut is that every piece of marketing research-generated evidence magically ends up being recast to support the feelings that previously drove the gut. Yes, a little hyperbole is in play here, but not as much as one might assume.

There's more, however, because times arise when business sector specialists themselves, operating during an era in which more marketing analytics-based information is available than at any time in history, still don't know the actual right price for something.

Optical lenses, discussed earlier, apparently abide as the pixie dust of the optical marketing sector. Barely anyone understands what optimal lenses are made of, how they are made or, even at high end

---

7. Diametrically-opposed quantity-versus-price tactics routinely play out inside women's fashion marketing sectors. Call this the paying-the-same-for-more pricing tactic. Due to the intersection between one uncontrollable-[to marketers]-environmental-factor and an innate human desire to be thinner that is shared among many (though not all) women, the old size 12 is the new 8, the old size 6 the new 4, and so forth. The uncontrollable environmental factor is that contemporary domestic women, on average, are heavier. The innately rising desire is that folks want to sustain the illusion that they are still able to wear the same clothing size. This is marketing, however. And what overarching goal that unifies marketers is to keep customers satisfied best through whatever reasonable means possible.

prices, exactly how optimal lens actually work. Profit margins within the optical lenses sector remain closely guarded secrets. But insiders who have given up the information goods on the inside pricing skinny explain that while optometrists might price eyeglass frames for two to two-and-one-half times their wholesale costs, lenses are the real money-makers. Markups around 750–800 percent are known to exist—inside closely guarded circles. The largest margins are on progressive lenses and protective coatings—features that cost *Essilor* a few pennies to make—but are sold for $25–$30 a pop. Nobody knows how much lenses cost or how much they should cost consumers to purchase.

Pricing Fact 12: Successful marketers understand that most consumers over-value certainty and assurance.

The point of introducing this human proclivity here is that most consumers unwittingly pay more than necessary to achieve presumed product value-adds known as certainty and assurance. This is why many consumers buy warranties that cost far more, in actual monetary terms, than the expected value of the loss, should it occur. When offered the choice between receiving a guaranteed $3,000 and an 80 percent chance of receiving $4,000, consumers typically choose the lower amount even when the alternatives expected value (i.e., $3,200) is higher.

This premise also explains why consumers willingly overpay for flat-rate plans—for example unlimited calling and data plans—when limited plans would likely prove less expensive.

Each premise is grounded in *Prospect Theory*, which was first introduced during Module 10.

Pricing Fact 13: Successful marketers understand that using similar prices for brands inside the same product category dampens demand.

More customers buy at least one of two "competing" products when the two alternatives feature slightly different prices. Meaning, two only slightly different branded T-shirts priced at $9.50 and $9.60, respectively, will sell better than if each is priced at $9.55.

Relatedly, strategic marketers understand that too much choice prevents purchases. Customers are more likely to purchase something, anything, when presented with fewer choices. Three to five choices, but usually three, appears to be the right number that marketers should provide to customers or prospects.

Fewer options permit people to more precisely select what makes them happiest. By contrast too many choices often leads to excessive analysis which facilitates future paralysis. Paralysis of mind, and thus either extreme difficulty or an outright unwillingness to make a choice, often results. We experience this same phenomena when scrolling through television programs or the thousands of entertainment options arrayed online.

Pricing Fact 14: Successful marketers know that customers willingly pay more in fancier places.

The fact speaks directly to the importance of the physical surroundings ingredient inside the 7Ps that comprise the marketing mix for services. Customers willingly but weirdly choose to pay many times more for the same product when the product is purchased in posh places. This is why upscale hotels can charge $8.00 for a $1.50 glass of milk.

Customers also buy more, even at higher prices, when they believe the brand is scarce. Customers pull out plastic more readily when told something won't be available in the future. For instance, the now-decades-gone *Pontiac* automobile brand comes to mind. A car essentially no one wanted until *GM* retired the brand in 2010. At which time every *Pontiac* vehicle still left on lots sold out inside two weeks. For what's it worth, did the *Pontiac* brand die because it had reached the end of its PLC, or because it was a Dog inside the BCG Product Portfolio Planning Matrix? Indeed, until its imminent departure was announced, the *Pontiac* brand owned a small share of a low-growth market, thereby designating the brand as a Dog.

Supply and demand still works as an economics and marketing principle. Of course, if the law did not work, the standing relationship between supply and demand would not remain a principle.

Pricing Fact 15: Successful marketers understand how human minds actually roll, okay, "work."

They know, for instance, that rational people respond to incentives. Pricing can be used as a tool that incentivizes customers. Pricing is regularly used for this purpose. But not always in ways that most people would normally suppose.

Successful marketers further understand that everyone is rational inside their own minds (males jumping off cliffs into uncertain depths of water to impress females must have impressed the jumpers as logical at the time), but that not everyone is rational in the same way. When any something becomes easier to do, less expensive to do, or more beneficial to do, consumers will do or buy more of it, right? Again, if people are rational they will.

But when weighing their choices, people bear in mind the overall constraints pressing on them—not just the costs and benefits of a particular choice—if they are rational. And consumers or other B2B customers consider the future consequences of their present/current choices, if they are rational. Yet who is rational, all the time?

Consider investing. Yes, your money in the stock market. When creating or managing investment portfolios, selling on bad news (when the prices of stocks you own are failing) or buying on good news (when the prices of stocks you are purchasing are higher) is usually completely irrational. These courses of action are precisely what stock market investors should seek to avoid if they want to pay lower prices and generate higher yields as they purchase stocks or mutual funds. Yet this is exactly what legions of individual investors do do when positive or negative environment news arrives. They are as predictably irrational as lemmings following each other as the entire flock falls to its death off cliffs. The only sure beneficiaries are stockbrokers; or stock marketers.

The truth is that when making price-based decisions about what to buy, most consumers are at least a little irrational some of the time. Marketers know this. In fact, marketers know that most consumer are *Predictably Irrational*—copping the name of a famous book by economist *Dan Ariely*.

EFFECTS OF BIASES AND OTHER CONFOUNDING FACTORS

Their inherently-biased natures lead most consumers to decide and to behave in predictably irrational ways. No need to worry, however. Human biases are natural, everyone has them, and are lying to whomever they are speaking—including themselves—if consumers claim otherwise.

The best way for consumers—all of us—to mollify their personal concerns about their own biases is knowing that biases exist inside everyone. For example, did you know that suicides greatly outnumber murders inside America, or that drownings outnumber fire-related deaths? Or know that throughout history—including today—many times more women have died in childbirth than men have died in battle? Or that the vast majority of people always think crime is getting worse, even when this is demonstrably untrue today?

The answer is that most readers knew none of these things. The reason why partially derives from their biases—and the biases of the media that consumers consume. Media interests are served by emphasizing the bad or disagreeable, thus stirring up anxiety and anger along with stress and fear among their customers, but attracting and retaining numbers of ears and eyeballs in the process. More troubling still, an issue that is truly worth worrying about, is that consumers are biased inwardly to the point where marketers usually can detect and "manage" these human errors or biases more easily than those same consumers can perceive their biases within themselves. Then marketers can and frequently do exploit customers' biases more vigorously than those individuals are able to defend themselves against their own internal biases.

The numbers and varieties of biases that degrade the quality of consumer decision-making related to what consumers willingly choose to purchase and how much they willingly pay are impressive. People are, for example, frequently irrationally estranged from concerns about their future selves and consequently make ridiculously stupid present-day spending and investment decisions. Saving money, budgeting, and not spending all that one makes today is analogous to choosing between spending money today or giving more money to a stranger years from now. The stranger, of course, is actually no stranger but the older you and/or your heirs.

There is, for example, the endowment effect. The endowment effect causes consumers to ascribe irrationally high values to things they already own.

There are also fundamental attribution errors. When assessing someone else's behavior, fundamental attribution error causes consumers to assign too much weight to that target individual's personal attributes and too little weight to external factors that are influencing their behaviors. Yes, it's true. Many of these external factors could easily be estimated through statistics. That is, if most consumers believed in or understood the value of statistics. Unfortunately, this is not the case.

Or, for example, a young, large, heavily muscled man may look like a great football player. But while "he looks like Tarzan he may play like Jane." The quoted material features no intentional or unintentional allusion to transgendered issues. The quote instead embodies a phrase from a circa 1970s critique of a football player uttered by his own coach. During this historical era football coaches rarely concerned themselves with players' feelings but did routinely fall prey to fundamental attribution errors. Particularly in contrast to today's more analytically-driven and yes, by necessity, more touchy-feely football coaches.

The anchoring effect, in turn, is reflected in consumers' tendency to rely too heavily on the first piece of information that marketers offer and to which consumers are exposed, as noted earlier. Naturally arising anchoring effects are exacerbated when the initial information is presented in numeric forms, particularly when consumers are making decisions, estimates, or predictions. This is why marketing negotiators usually begin with numbers that are deliberately too low or too high in the hopes that the ridiculous number will anchor subsequent negotiations.

Projection biases exist. Projection bias is reflected inside faulty assumptions that everybody else's thinking is the same as our own. Relatedly, bias blind spots exist. Bias blind spots are reflected inside feelings and perceptions that one's own self is less biased than the average person.

The gambler's fallacy, another irrational bias, makes people absolutely certain that if a coin has landed tails four straight times, it is now more likely to land heads on the fifth toss. Yes, you're right; the odds on the fifth, sixth, and so forth toss still remain 50–50.

Optimism bias leads consumers or other decision-makers to consistently underestimate the costs and duration of basically every product they ever choose or project they ever pursue. Seems like governmental planners are plagued by optimism bias too. Or perhaps they are biased as truth-telling and full-disclosure.

Availability bias leads consumers to believe that, say, traveling by car is safer than traveling by plane. Images of plane crashes are more vivid and dramatic in our memory and our imagined realities than are car wrecks. Such images reside on higher rungs upon the metaphorical "ladders" that exist inside the evoked sets of humans, and are consequently more easily and widely available inside our consciousness.

A type of prejudice called hindsight bias also exists. Hindsight bias describes the very human tendency to think, after the fact of its actual occurrence, that an event was predictable when it wasn't. This bias operates with particular force for unusually successful outcomes. Wealthy people overwhelmingly attribute their own financial success to hard work rather than to factors like fortunately being in the right place at the right time. Apparently, it's only human to more easily recall events and environmental trends that work to our disadvantage and are easier to recall than those events and trends that affect us positively.

The presence of hindsight bias can generate troubling effects. A growing body of evidence suggests that seeing ourselves as self-made—rather than as talented, hardworking, and lucky—leads consumers to be less generous or public-spirited. The presence of hindsight bias may even make purely lucky consumers (i.e., those born into loving and abundant family circumstances) less likely to support the conditions such as high-quality public infrastructure and educational opportunities that made their own successes more possible.

Then there is the mother of all biases, and a dominant source of irrational consumer decision-making. Confirmation bias arises when people consciously or unconsciously gather and accept data that supports their preexisting beliefs and consciously or unconsciously ignore or reject data that contests their current beliefs. In plainer language this means the presence or arrival of confirmation bias "encourages" consumers and other decision-makers to seek out evidence that supports what they already believe; to view all facts and ideas that they encounter as further confirmation, and to discount or ignore bits of factual information that support alternative views.

Confirmation bias has shown-up big-time inside political debates over the past ten years or so, wherein the only thing that members of the liberal or conservative camps appear to agree upon is that the opposing side's view could not possibly ever be right. The logical fallacy that promotes and sustains confirmation bias is that when they are testing a hypothesis they are inclined to believe people tend to seek out examples confirming it.

The right approach for consumers or other decision-makers to take would entail seeking out examples that disprove the hypothesis. This approach automatically defeats confirmation bias. However, as is often the case, this solution invariably proves far easier to describe than to execute or implement.[8]

Finally, there is liberal bias, or the belief that everything on the left is right and everything on the right is wrong. Or is such irrationality better described as conservative bias, which would mislead conservative thinkers/perceivers into believing exactly the opposite? The preceding two sentences may read as if we were joking. The joke is that this is no joke.

Also of note, and one might argue, something that is also notably funny derives from the fact that the human bias toward laziness or inertia may trump all these biases, excepting perhaps for the pro or con biases that most readers still experience when they read the word "*Trump*." The laziness or inertia referenced above reflects the tendency of consumers already seated on their preset prejudices to remain seated there. Many if not most consumers' bias toward inertia contributes mightily to brand loyalty, a desirable marketing outcome, and to consumers' natural proclivity to resist change, which often plays out as an undesirable human trait.

Robert Conquest wrote: "Everyone is a conservative about the things they know best." Conservatives, at their cores, want to preserve—conserve—things of the past which is also commiserate with things they already know and are doing. Which is one of the best explanations why consumer inertia exists and is so powerful. We are comfortable with what we know and uncomfortable about things—including new products—that we do not know.

A laundry list of potentially bias-induced decision-making problems was just introduced.

One solution to the negative consequences that routinely arise whenever marketing decision-makers or customers fall prey to implicit or explicit biases follows. The *Wall Street Journal* recently reported a study in which two researchers discovered that weather can influence consumers' ratings of their general life satisfaction and that "negative emotion," in turn, impacts their decision-making. The study also demonstrated that this effect was eliminated once people were reminded how gloomy weather can bring them down. In brief, the negative bias on mood imposed by the weather stopped influencing people's moods once they understood that the bias existed.

The takeaway for readers:

▶ Once people are aware that confirmation bias, fundamental attribution error, anchoring effects, projection effects, optimism or pessimism biases exist each bias should exercise fewer negative effects on their decision-making acumen. Which is a good if not a great outcome, insofar as our biases make us like *Van Gogh* than most of us would like to admit. That is to say, when biases dominate our thinking, we're only able to hear one side of any story (Vincent was the famous artist who purposefully cut off his ear.)

---

8. D. Kahneman, *Thinking, Fast and Slow* (New York: McMillian Press, 2011).

Dan Ariely's book *Predictably Irrational* features a passage about a medical procedure called internal mammary artery ligation. The medical service treats chest pains. The twist is that when a cardiologist decided to test the efficacy of this procedure by performing a placebo procedure the results revealed the placebo was equally effective, thereby undermining the effectiveness of the original surgery. This example illustrates the power of placebo in medical science.

That's nice, and the placebo effect of medicines has long been well-known. But this is a marketing discussion. So . . . while the effect of placebos has been knowingly and unknowingly practiced for millennia, the most interesting observation that author *Ariely* made was that prices of prescribed medicines can operate like placebos as well. The placebo pricing effect suggests that in the absence of other information or knowledge, patients usually believe higher-priced medicine will prove more efficacious than lower-priced medicine.

Similar principles and precepts apply to clothing, food, automobiles, wines, and so forth; essentially across most consumer product categories readers might care to identify. Marketers know this. Many marketers also exploit what they know about placebo pricing effects. As they should, at least insofar as use of the pricing strategy should benefit those marketers' investors, if not their customers.

EFFECTS OF CONSUMER MOODS ON JUDGMENTS AND DECISIONS

Most readers have likely noticed or suspected that their judgments and actual choices are affected by how they are feeling in the "decision-making" moment. Higher percentages still among readers certainly realize the judgments and decisions made by others are affected by their moods. Readers who once were young and experienced a parental unit who itself was happy, sad, or angry at given times or inside particular contexts have had empirical experience with these affects and can confirm that they exist. Happy Dad, happy home. Happy Mom, happy home. Sad or mad mama or papa, unhappy home.

Social scientists have developed surprisingly clear conclusions about how human moods influence human judgments and decision-making. (Surprisingly, because scientists rarely "clearly agree" on anything.) In brief, agreement was widespread that their mood materially influences what consumers think, what stimuli they are most likely to notice in their environments, what sorts of information consumers retrieve from their memories, and how consumers interpret these signals.

Social scientists also uniformly agree that mood exercises another, more startling, effect. The status of their mood actually and actively—actively, as in that instant!—changes how consumers think. But the effects of mood do not necessarily unfurl in the ways that many of us would assume.

Their encounters with good moods, for example, portends mixed blessings for consumers. And again surprisingly, being in bad moods often has silver linings. The benefits or costs of experiencing differing moods, apparently, is highly specific to the context in which judgments or decisions are being made.

Take B2B negotiations, the sorts that routinely unfold inside supply chains, for example. In such settings, good moods generally help. Decision-makers who enter negotiations in good moods are more likely to cooperate with their counterparts and to reciprocate good with good. The net is that happy negotiators generate better results than unhappy negotiators. Things get interesting, however, once one learns that individual negotiators who enter negotiations in good moods and then get sincerely or strategically angry (the notion of "faked sincerity" is reintroduced here) usually get better results. This is a piece of knowledge to glom onto and use when facing a stubborn supply chain partner, customer, or marketer—or quite possibly some combination of all three entities, because those individuals are often one and the same person.

Or take situations where consumers are deciding whether or not to buy what marketers are saying and/or selling. There, good moods make consumer decision-makers more likely to accept their first impressions as true and accurate, without challenging their initial thoughts much if at all. The takeaway is that consumers will more likely let their biases influence their thinking when they are in a good mood.

What about gullibility? Individual consumers, due to their human natures, are more or less prone to "bullshit-receptivity."[9] Yet among nearly all consumers the inducement of good moods makes them more receptive to bullshit and more gullible in general. Meaning, consumers become less able to detect deception and discern misleading information. The opposite circumstances apply when consumers are in bad moods. Oh, so that's why certain businesses are seeking to incentivize us by throwing inexpensive, or for that matter expensive, candy or wine our way.

Their moods even influence consumers' ethical judgments. Consumers experiencing good moods are more likely to employ the equivalent of utilitarian decision criteria (think the philosopher *Jeremy Bentham* or *Star Trek* television-movie character *Mr. Spock*). Hangry, tired, or plain-ole-pissed-off consumers will more likely make rule-based, or deontological judgment calls (think Babylon's *Hammurabi, Judaism's Moses,* or *Germany's Kant*).[10]

As always, the so-what factor should be considered. How should readers respond, either as marketers or consumers, to these insights? Two takeaways appear logical:

First, marketers should seek to manipulate decision-makers' moods in either positive or negative directions dependent on the marketing context that is in play—as long as those marketers remain with ethical boundaries. Or dependent on what, value-wise, marketers are saying and selling.

Second, customers/decision-makers should evaluate their current mood status before entering important decision-making contexts, especially when differing price levels are involved. Or, before making big purchasing or negotiating decisions. Let's take this advice one step deeper, however. Before this counsel would generate genuine value for decision-makers, choosers must understand the full range of consequences associated with their positive or negative moods. Otherwise, choosers might easily end up as losers.

In the end answers to questions about which side inside buyer-seller relationships will control the prime on average eight inches of real estate that lies between the ears on an average-sized adult hang in the balance. Whichever among the marketer and customer wins by taking away more value than the other side from the buyer-seller exchange, should no longer be determined by the effects of unacknowledged biases or unappreciated moods.

---

9. Bullshit has evolved into a more technical marketing term over the past few years. Essentially, since *Professor Harry Frankfurt,* a *Princeton University* philosopher, wrote a book called *On Bullshit*. The insightful book masterfully differentiated—or did it adroitly position—BS as being distinct from and in some ways better than in other ways worse than many other forms of human misrepresentation. Wow, more context-specific conclusions.

10. Daniel Kahneman, Olivier Sibony, and Cass R. Sunstein, "Good Moods Often Lead to Bad Decisions," *The Wall Street Journal* (May 15/16, 2021): C3.

MODULE 13.1

Strategic Issues to Consider

Before developing their pricing strategies and actually assigning prices to products or services, marketers should consider several related and unrelated issues. A breakout and a discussion of these issues follows.

ISSUE ONE: THE MARKETING MIX (WHAT'S HAPPENING THERE?)

Before establishing prices, marketers should evaluate what they are doing, or plan to do, with respect to the rest of their marketing mix. Pricing decisions/levels should align strategically with what the firm is doing with all other elements in its marketing mix. This is smart strategy. Not making pricing levels (i.e., higher or lower) consistent with what is happening with respect to any other firm's marketing mix ingredients is illogical.

Marketing organizations ideally should emphasize product-based features, attributes, benefits, and ultimately solutions; distribution-based alternatives (related to retailer choice or type [traditional or internet-based]); some combination of design, style, and/or quality-based differences; and/or promotion-based differences as they attempt to create real or perceived brand differences related to the value of their products inside the minds of targeted customer segments. (Brand differences typically generate greater brand loyalty and brand equity.) This paragraph began with a run-on sentence. The sort of sentence that most authors should avoid. Sorry. But the opening sentence also provides valuable insight into what the prerequisites for marketing success look like for most organizations.

When effective differentiation and positioning outcomes are achieved, firms usually enjoy an expanded opportunity to charge higher prices—while also sustaining market share. Properly executing the other three P's—Product, Promotion, or Place—presumably makes Price (more correctly, higher prices) a less important issue inside customers' minds. This represents a huge win for most firms.

ISSUE TWO: STRATEGIC GOALS

Before establishing their prices, marketing decision-makers should evaluate their organization's strategic goals. Pricing decisions generally should be based on whether firms are seeking to prevent new competitors from successfully entering their market segment; to generate higher profit margins; or to retain or grow their market share.

Ceteris paribus, certain outcomes generally emerge when marketing organizations raise or lower their prices, or when marketers launch new products that feature higher or lower prices from those new products' initial points of market entry. Specifically:

- Higher prices generally attract new competitive entry against firms.
- Higher prices typically improve margins and profits. But lower prices may produce more total revenue due to the nature of price-demand and price-quantity sold relationships.
- Lower prices usually preclude or discourage market entry by competitors.
- Lower prices allow firms to retain higher share of market. But firms' profit margins likely shrink.

During troubling times, the pressure to lower prices can be extreme. Troubling times might feature conditions which feature new competitive entry, changing customer tastes, falling market share, or the arrival of unexpected economic, technological or cultural environmental threats.

But lowering prices on existing brands works well as an ongoing strategy if firms are continuously engaging in successful NPD and thereby charging higher prices on newer, presumably more highly-valued "innovations." Essentially, a strategy that entails lowering prices works only if marketing organizations first obsolete the value of their existing products before their competitors obsolete those products. (Or, in situations where a firm's business model and strategic plans supports the ongoing delivery of lower prices.) New products, as you recall and as just noted, are usually accompanied by increased prices and consequently by increased profit margins. When firms are not ready or planning to replace their old-with-the-new, marketers must call on their ever-ready ally (i.e., increasing differentiation).

This process, of course, is called planned obsolescence. At this point *The Inside Skinny* has now offered exactly ten prior references to planned obsolescence. The larger point being that readers should by now be familiar with the concept and its associated implications.

ISSUE THREE: MARKET CONDITIONS

A third issue that marketers should also consider and evaluate relates to the impact that market conditions exercise on their pricing decisions. Market conditions, the term, proxy the type of market in which firms compete. Four basic market condition types exist.

Purely Competitive Marketing Conditions (Pure Competition)

In markets that feature pure competition no single firm possesses the absolute size, economies-of-scale, or branding power to exercise much effect on pricing. Examples of purely competitive markets include conditions where small family farms or ranches exist. Small family farmers, operating inside purely competitive markets, operate as price-takers rather than price-makers. Such farmers are described as "price-takers" because they exercise little to no control over the prices that others pay for the tobacco, corn, wheat, soybean, pork, or chickens that they raise and market. Purely competitive markets still occasionally pop up inside domestic marketplaces (and economies), but are still quite rare.

Monopolistic Competition Market Conditions

When monopolistically competitive conditions prevail inside any sector many sellers and buyers are present and competing against one another in the market. Said sellers, or marketers, price at higher, lower, and in-between levels. The ability of any single marketer organization to raise prices usually depends on how much actual or perceived differentiation that marketer's brand has achieved.

The grocery store sector that satisfies demand inside the *Dallas-Fort Worth-Metroplex* marketplace is monopolistically competitive. Grocery store brands exist that price at premium, or high, levels. If concerned at all, these premium brands are only interested in the prices of other grocery brands pricing at similarly premium levels. Rather than competing on the basis of price, these brands compete and seek to differentiate their value propositions based on the perceived quality, quantity, and variety of food choices, freshness, healthiness, and so forth associated with their product portfolios. *Whole Foods, Natural Grocers,* and *Central Market* occupy this market space.

The *DFW Metroplex* simultaneously features numerous discount and mid-priced grocers. *Walmart, H.E.B.,* or *Shop & Save* fit the former bill. *Kroger's, Brookshire's,* or *Albertsons'* grocery stores fall into the latter category. Mid-priced, or middle-of-road pricing "positions" are generally not great places for brands to reside. Retailer brands, similar to all other types of brands, should stand-up and stand-out for some particular, and hopefully determinant, value. The middle-of-the-road, in terms of its pricing strategies or any other marketing mix element, is rarely a desirable place for any brand to stand inside any competitive market. The opportunity to earn or sustain determinant types of differentiation consequently diminishes to near zero.

Regardless, grocery store brands that price at or below grocery market averages only need concern themselves about the prices offered by firms competing at the same level that they occupy.

Oligopoly Market Conditions

Oligopolistic markets feature only a few large competitors. At the same time, customers purchasing goods or services inside oligopolistic markets are often quite price-sensitive. When combined, these two conditions create situations where marketing organizations competing inside oligopolies bunch up at approximately the same pricing levels. As and after this bunching-up process happens, competitors play follow-the-leader pricing games. The same marketing organizations do not necessarily function as price leader year-in, year-out. Different firms may assume the leadership role. The global automotive, domestic airline, or domestic chemical supplies industries each exemplify oligopolistic market sectors.

American Airlines has long performed in a price leader role inside the domestic airlines sector. Back in 2008, *American* became the first legacy brand to charge for suitcases. The initial price hike was a what appears low by today's standards one-way $15.00 total. *Continental, Delta, American, United*, every major domestic legacy airline at the time, quickly followed this pricing path. The lone dissenter was *Southwest Airlines*. *Southwest* reasoned, correctly, that its brand would stand out favorably by strategically not fitting into this particular pricing scheme. The *Love Field*-based airliner has essentially hung its positioning, branding, and lower pricing banner on this singularly appealing and determinant hook ever since.

Southwest has failed to earn a profit during only one year since 2001. Everyone remembers what happened during 9/11/01. So, their pricing plan has rocked. That is not to say, however, that the other domestic airlines' *Bags-Don't-Fly-Free* pricing ploy crashed and burned. To the contrary, domestic legacy airliners reaped dozens of billions of dollars in extra profits from up-charges and fees such as these that were attached to regular ticket prices during the last decade or so.

The American health-care sector is becoming more monopolized at all levels. The prices of the various health-related services and products being sold within the health-care supply chain are naturally rapidly rising as well.

One marketing organization controls 84 percent of the syringe market. Between them, three firms own 68 percent of market share for IV solutions. Shockingly, two companies own 92 percent of the market share for dialysis clinics.[11]

Are these conditions likely to inspire price competition? We're not feeling it either. But health-care consumers and/or their insurers are feeling the pricing pain.

Did you know that on average domestic physicians earn about three times more than their European counterparts? This is but one of several marketing-based factors that explain why. Market-based competition, or the lack of such, will have its say.

Did you ever wonder why so many physicians practicing inside America were born and often even trained outside the *United States?* Well wonder no more. Markets, and marketing; or the potential for monetary gain is a powerful incentive; that what's in play here. Each force always has its say and uniformly exercises great sway. As has been previously argued, this is a marketing and marketers' world—and we're all living, competing, and consuming inside its constraints.

Monopoly Market Conditions

Monopolists, by definition, are the only or the overwhelmingly dominant competitor marketing inside monopoly market. Monopolists enjoy extreme pricing power and can generally maintain this power

---

11. *The Week: The Best of United States and International Media* (June 21, 2019): 16.

so long as they do not price at exploitative levels. Price exploitatively, and government regulators will often step-in and either impose price ceilings or break up the monopoly.

Such governmental breakups do happen. *AT&T* was famously broken up into seven *Baby Bells*; a list of brands and companies that now include *SBC Communication, Verizon Communication,* and *Century Link*, among others. *Alcoa*, the aluminum marketer, grew so large and monopoly-like that the government forcefully spun-off two additional aluminum marketers. By name, *Reynolds* and *Kaiser*.

Which monopolies will the government break up next? *Google* and *Amazon* readily come to mind as likely suspects. Frankly, government should at least occasionally consider breaking up monopolies that get too powerful for the good of society. The presence of monopolies reduces competition. Higher levels of competition are almost always a good thing, for customers, if not for marketing competitors themselves. Higher competition usually produces lower prices, generates additional brand choices that themselves are at varying price levels, and promotes the development of more innovative and therefore superior product solutions for customers to evaluate and possibly select. Moreover, the quality of both products and services almost always also increase in lockstep as levels of competition rise.

Yet one other factor is in play. Economist *Milton Friedman*—we have referenced him previously—wrote long ago that few companies ever become monopolies unless the government has given them one or two major sustainable competitive. His argument appears to ring true, even today. *Google, Tesla, Apple,* and *Facebook*, for example, have benefitted from huge governmental subsidies—mostly in the form of massive tax breaks—for years.[12] But *Big Tech* would do well to learn and to remember that whatever incentives and advantages governmental entities giveth they can taketh away.

Utilities own, enjoy, and benefit from lasting monopolies inside various product categories and markets. Natural gas (product category 1) and electricity service (product category 2) providers; at one time even cable television service (product category 3) providers, routinely competed as monopolies, though this was not universally the case within more competitive states such as *Texas*.

Hugely desirable and highly disruptive innovations can create temporary monopolies. Increasingly, *Google, Facebook,* and *Amazon*, in their own unique technology-based ways, essentially compete today as monopolies. What's different, however, is that tech titans don't just compete in markets. Increasingly, the firms themselves are the markets. This should not surprise. After all, *GFA* provide the infrastructure or digital platforms on which most of the digital economy operates.

Many of the services offered by *Google, Facebook,* or *Amazon* appear free. Increasingly, however, users know better. That's right, customers pay for the services by giving away their data and their privacy in exchange for them.

Their own personal data, then, is the currency that users spend, or give up, to acquire the value of the connective tech services. Tech giants receive valuable information on users—about their consumption behaviors, about who their friends are, and about those friends' purchasing behaviors, as well as other user behaviors. This sort of marketing information, which is easily converted into actionable strategic marketing insights, represents a true boon for firms seeking to create and manage positive E-WOM or target promotional messages.

---

12. Ethan Baron, "Google, Tesla, Apple, Facebook Rake in Massive Subsidies: Report," *The Mercury News* (July 3, 2018).

Then *Google, Facebook,* and *Amazon* sell the data to other markets. Marketing research is playing out on grand scales.

Market conditions also signal how well economies themselves are doing at various times at international, national, regional, or local levels. Is a recession in the offing, or has one arrived? When will the downturn end? Is the economy currently blowing up, going down, or likely to remain stagnant for a while? But if so, how long will either condition prevail? Such known and unknown but basically uncontrollable environmental trends exercise fundamental effects on pricing strategies, though not always in ways that non-experts would expect.

The prices of higher education, for example, appear recession-proof. Higher education prices defy the normal effects of economic downturns, which is to say education prices have rarely if ever declined during hard economic times. For starters, and perhaps primarily, because more formerly working people lose their jobs and realize their future employee prospects are almost always elevated through the acquisition of a degree and more refined skills. Meanwhile, higher education prices increase during good economic times because more families can afford to send their children to college or because the government is willing to extend low-interest and perhaps eventually students themselves no longer have to pay off loans. The type of loan, once one thinks about the matter, is likely to be everyone's favorite type. Despite the *Democrat* [marketing] *Party*, the jury remains out on whether this political promise will ever be fulfilled. Keep in mind, however, that whatever happens someone, namely the American taxpayer, will still have to pay the full loan price. (The assertion that "there are no free lunches" has long ascended into the status of cultural cliché. Its status as cliché does not make the statement any less true. In other words, someone always has to pay for lunch!)

By contrast, the prices of horses typically dip precipitously during downturns because middle and upper-middle class incomes and their stock portfolios become less stable, at best. Horses still must be fed and tended to while the prices for boarding fees, hay, and alfalfa pellets or veterinarian services typically do not fall. Horses become comparatively more expensive and the supplies of horses for sale rise in lockstep. Equine prices cannot help but fall.

MODULE 13.2

Other Factors to Consider When Establishing Prices

Apart from the strategic issues summarized inside the preceding section, marketing and product managers should evaluate the possible effects of other market factors when developing pricing strategies. A discussion of six such factors follows.

MARKET FACTOR 1: PRICE ELASTICITY

Price elasticity measures the degree to which changes in price stimulate changes in demand for the brand or product being priced. If demand for brands hardly changes, either up or down, when their prices change, again either up or down, then demand for those brands is deemed inelastic. Gasoline prices have historically featured inelastic demand—up to a point.

Between 2008 through 2010 average per gallon gas prices in *North Texas* slowly then quickly rose from less than $2.00 to more than $3.00. Demand remained constant, or inelastic. Then gasoline prices suddenly shot up like a rocket to just past $4.00. Demand dropped like a rock, as consumers carpooled, stayed home, or integrated two or three errands into one trip.[13] The point being made, and that should be understood, is that prices for products often remains inelastic, until some magical price barrier is breeched.

Meanwhile, if demand for products changes greatly (up or down) in response to their prices rising or falling, then demand for the product is considered elastic. Candy bars have historically demonstrated an elastic demand.

If demand is inelastic, marketers should seriously deliberate whether to raise their prices just a little, because demand for their products probably won't decline. The implication is that revenues and profits rise accordingly.

---

13. Funny thing about gas prices. Gas prices at the pump rise rapidly, seeming overnight—they shoot up like helium balloons. Then those same gas prices often fall across weeks—like that feather floating down during the opening scenes of the move *Forrest Gump*. Ever wonder why?

Indeed, strategic marketers should increase prices to barely below the point where the price difference would be noticed. This inflection point is commonly described as the Just Noticeable Difference—or JND. As noted earlier, most B2C customers don't notice price increases until their costs rise at least 10 percent.

Yet if demand is elastic, firms should consider lowering prices. In fact, marketing organizations generally should attempt to lower their prices to a point just low enough that typical customers notice the difference. Again, this usually entails a minimum decrease of 10 percent, or the point at which most consumers begin to notice differences. But marketers should rarely drop their prices much, if any, lower than that. There is rarely a reason to unnecessarily give away valuable products and profits. Total sales and profits should rise accordingly.

Strategic marketers should research the price sensitivity of their customers, a topic initially discussed during Module 6. Specifically, marketers should empirically analyze the trade-offs that targeted segments would generally make between paying higher or lower prices and receiving enhanced or lowered product values.

MARKET FACTOR 2: THE ROLE PLAYED BY REFERENCE PRICES

Customers carry around reference prices inside their heads. Customers reference these prices when contemplating whether to purchase one or another brand from known product categories. These "known" product categories typically would include frequently purchased items such as apparel, milk, or chicken breasts. Or products such as blue jeans or athletic shoes. Quite likely you carry around references prices for each apparel item inside your own mind.

Of course inside many purchasing contexts consumers don't possess sufficient skill or information to know, with confidence, whether they are paying appropriate prices. Marketers, however, often provide reference pricing cues to help consumers more easily make those choices.

If customers deem prices too high or too low, their radars are activated. Prices that are perceived as too low may signal buy now. Or alternatively, prices that are deemed too low may signal, oh crap, what's wrong? By contrast, prices perceived as too high may signal that it's time to switch to lower-priced brands; better purchase now before prices rise further; or better purchase now because the brand is hot.

Reference prices are created inside customer minds as they pay attention to current prices and/or remember past prices. Reference prices also emerge and become more important criterion as customers evaluate particular purchase situations and their personal economic status; are customers feeling relatively wealthier or poorer right now? Even genuinely wealthy people can feel comparatively poor on given days (the stock market dipped radically yesterday) or during particular time frames (OMG got to pay for Sally's wedding).

The existence of reference prices provides another reason why marketers, as they establish prices, should consider the impact of overall environmental trends, as first introduced during Module 5 and discussed throughout the book. Economic, demographic, technological, and competitive trends are perpetually changing. Economic trends, in particular, affect general pricing levels because this particular trend encourages strategic marketers to raise or lower prices based on how their targeted customers are feeling (i.e., scared/secure, happier/sadder, richer/poorer) essentially in the moment.

MARKET FACTOR 3: THE QUESTION OF CHANGING PRICES

When firms experience falling market share, they typically should lower prices. That is, when *ceteris paribus* prevails.

When marketers experience declining competition, they generally should increase prices. Again, assuming *ceteris paribus* exists.

Conditions of market scarcity exist wherever not enough products (supply) are available to satisfy demand. When firms market under conditions where market scarcity prevails, they should raise prices. But not excessively so. Raising prices too high or too quickly might entail predatory or exploitative pricing—and usually will be noticed by customers in ways that undermine the long-term interests of firms.

Situations arise in which emerging conditions of scarcity have nothing to do with anything the marketing firm has done. For example, motel and hotel space gets extremely tight with extreme speed during hurricane conditions. Prices then can be raised, but not radically so. Rarely if ever is it a good idea for anyone to get overly greedy. But this rule of thumb especially applies to marketers. As every pork farmer knows, pigs get fed, because there's still room from them to grow. Hogs, because they are already fat and craving more, well, they get slaughtered.

At other times firms may happily find themselves competing inside markets where the demand for individual brands exceeds the supply of that brand. These conditions often arise for the best of reasons; that being, marketers—*Apple* today or *J. K. Rowling* back in the day with her ongoing portfolio of *Harry Potter*-branded books—managed the other three (products) or six (services) non-pricing elements of their marketing mixes so effectively. Then those marketers should and typically do raise prices to better reflect and align with the values and problem-solving capabilities that customers perceive are present in the brand. Remember, powerful marketing organizations that have created strong equity for their brands will encounter little to no need to discount their prices unless lower prices are a key part of their brands' value propositions. As is the case, for example, with the *Walmart, Southwest Airlines,* or *Dollar Tree Stores* brands.

MARKET FACTOR 4: EFFECTS OF THE LAW OF SUPPLY AND DEMAND

The law of price and demand—as explained earlier inside this Module—illustrates and explains how the introduction of higher or lower prices will impact level of customer demand[14] for the brand being priced. Under normal market conditions, demand and price are inversely related. The relationship also features a downward sloping demand curve. What the prior two sentences mean, in plain *English,* is that when prices rise for a given brand, demand for that brand will drop—if other things are held

---

14. Demand is both an economic and marketing term. Demand refers to customers' desire and willingness to purchase certain amounts of brand goods or services at particular price levels.

equal, alternatively stated as when conditions of *ceteris paribus* exist. Or when the price of a brand goes down, demand for that brand will rise.

But in certain situations demand curves may slope upward. In particular, the demand curves for prestigious, well-differentiated luxury brands may slope up. An upward sloping demand curve means that when the price for a brand goes up, demand for that same brand goes up too. Or vice versa. Well-differentiated luxury brands also typically function and exist as positional goods, a term introduced inside Module 9.

When these anomalous supply and demand conditions prevail, consumers presumably assume that as prices of products rise their quality and other ancillary benefits also expand. Ancillary benefits, from individual consumers' perspective, might include considerations such as, "I can afford this 'XX brand' purse, and most if not all of the others I hang out with can't. Consequently, my (comparative social) increases and I feel better about myself." Yucky, yes, but all too true. This sort of internal logic arises naturally among many consumers—consumers who are, after all, only human.

This is exactly how the price-demand relationship for positional goods often rolls. This is also precisely why demand for many positional goods is currently off the chain. After all, consumers feel better about themselves during good economic times and also feel like they are worth the higher prices that must be doled out to acquire luxury brands (positional goods). With positional goods such as high-end *Chanel* or *Coach* bags, the fewer richer people who can afford them as prices further rise actually may be happy to pay higher prices—and even buy more bags. Higher prices, in such settings, function as an exclusivity tax. Higher prices keep less wealthy people from owning and displaying such bags. Customers consequently sometimes readily pay more to achieve exclusivity and greater social status.

Bear with us as we transition from what some would describe as "the ridiculous" (above) to an example that many more still would designate as "more ridiculous." According to the *Charleston Gazette* newspaper, more than 788,000,000 opiate pills were sold in *West Virginia* during 2016. The entire state of *West Virginia* boasted less than 1.7 million citizens at the time. Run the numbers.

Critics of the fifty-plus-year-long *American War on Drugs*[15] often suggest the problem is demand-driven. The argument rolls like this: If fewer domestic citizens wanted (demanded) illegal drugs, fewer illegal drugs would be produced in or illicitly imported to the *United States*. However, the facts suggest the opiate crises is still running rampant inside *West Virginia* and contiguous states such as *Ohio, Pennsylvania,* and *Kentucky* likely was provoked not by an excessive demand but an extraordinarily high supply of legal but ultimately addictively harmful painkillers when they are not used appropriately.

Apparently flooding the market with inexpensive treats—*Perdue Pharma* was the biggest but not only *Big Pharma* culprit—drove prices down to a point where artificial demand, primarily of a

---

15. Older readers may remember *First Lady Nancy Reagan's* famous 1982 "Just Say No" de-marketing illegal drugs campaign. The "Just Say No" slogan itself was created by advertisers Robert Cox and David Cantor. The de-marketing positioning statement was followed in 1987 by advertising depictions of chicken eggs frying inside a pan accompanying a "voice of god-like" spokesperson intoning: "This is your brain on drugs." Druggies of the time must have been paying attention. Why? Because shortly after the public service announcement began airing, hard case druggies would no longer say "Let's get high." Instead, their tune changed to "Let's fry an egg."

sampling nature, was created. One outcome is reasonably certain to arise when consumers sample addictive products two or three times. That's right, folks get addicted. Eventually addicted to the point where addicts pay any reasonable or unreasonable price to sustain their habit. The rest is a desultory marketing story whose ending remains un-authored because no one would want to take "credit."

The preceding is not intended to suggest that painkillers are not useful when they are used appropriately. But too often, this particular subset of painkillers has been inappropriately used.

Marketers and marketing practices have purposefully created tens of millions of additional consumers who are addicted to legal products that still might reasonably be characterized as dangerous drugs. To inspire them to eat more, the *Big Food* Industrial Complex lures consumers with low prices, dazzling packaging, fulfilled promises of greater convenience, and faked variety. One illustration among many: different colored *M&Ms* taste the same, but the availability of different colors tricks human brains into consuming more than if they were all just brown. Perhaps more astutely, *Big Food* has also acquired many big brands of processed diet foods such as *Weight Watchers* and *Lean Cuisine*. We'll allocate major props to *Big Food* marketing for being strategic enough to make money by helping consumers put on the extra pounds and to then profit again from selling typically fruitless solutions to consumers who are seeking to lose the pounds. Yes, it's like paying one marketer to start a fire and then paying the same marketer to extinguish the same blaze.

A 2021 book called *Hooked*[16] suggests the processed food marketing sector (*Big Food*) can reasonably be compared to tobacco companies such as *Philip Morris* or *RJ Reynolds* who lied about the harmful nature of obviously addictive cigarettes for decades. In the case of *Philip Morris & Co.*, marketers of tobacco and processed food long *were* the same company. Until recently, *Philip Morris* owned *Kraft* and *General Foods*.

Which reintroduces us to a dilemma and a question asked earlier (Module 8): who should be blamed here? No one is forced to eat at *Sonic* or to drink *Pepsi*. Few Americans don't already realize that eating salads with small amounts of low-fat dressing for lunch is healthier than bacon-wrapped[17] cheeseburgers and fries. But *Hooked,* the book, argues that consumers' "free will" is but an illusion, at least for many processed foods. *Hooked* is almost certainly right.

For most consumers, sugar is as addictive as cocaine. But from an evolutionary biological perspective, cocaine is actually as addictive as sugar. What? Yes, the preceding statement is true beyond dispute because the sweeter addiction exploits ancient genetic mechanisms inherited from distant ancestors that helped them acquire necessary calories. Meanwhile, most fast-foods are laden with sugar, as well as salt and fat. To stay healthy inside their endpoint on modern processed food supply chains, consumers must overcome their instincts and make choices over which they exercise little natural control by attempting to avoid sugar.

For legal reasons, *Big Food* may be safe in court right now. But the marketing sector's strategies should raise ethical questions. One such question: Should the prices that we must pay to marketers be judged solely on our costs and their profits or on how marketers' *Big Food* activities affect the world? Regardless of the legal and freewill that presumably will one day ensue, is it acceptable to

---

16. Nir Eyal, *Hooked: How to Build Habit Forming Products* (London: Portfolio: Penguin Books, 2021).

17. Bacon, of course, is the butter of fast-food. Bacon makes every other food it touches taste better—as does butter. So does that make butter the bacon of the dairy product category?

market breakfast cereals like *Cotton Candy Captain Crunch* to children? (The product is almost half sugar.) Such habit-forming foods have created bloated corporate bank accounts at the expense of over-fattening hundreds of millions of Americans, contributing to millions of premature deaths and debilitating illnesses as rates of heart disease, diabetes, and certain forms of cancer skyrocket. Billions of dollars in otherwise unavoidable health care costs are also expended. Even when consumers don't consume these junk foods themselves, they still pay a material price for the consequences produced by the "foods" that *Big Food* produces.

Consumers and their public policy watchdogs should also pay more attention to the relationship between quantity and quality of food. In recent decades, modern informed attitudes toward food have increasingly focused on nutrition labels that tell us how many grams of saturated fat, fiber, and other things are contained inside the foods we eat. These labels can make many highly processed foods appear harmless compared to higher calorie natural foods like avocados, salmon, and nuts. Yet, how many people eat too much healthy, unprocessed food? Nutritionist perspectives on food combined with the challenges of weight loss also generate confusion over the relative merits of alternative diets, sometimes promoting new types of messy eating when we Google the glycemic index of muffins or bananas, and most consumers end up wondering whether chocolate, eggs, or peanuts are good or bad for them.

No one requires a nutritional science degree to recognize that almost every traditional, unprocessed diet from every culture on the planet that isn't loaded with junk food is generally healthy. Plus, this natural stuff tastes great. The only remaining unresolved issue at this point is whether consumers can afford to eat healthy. Sadly, many cannot.

But back to the normal state of supply and demand affairs—and of how supply/demand/price relationships normally work. Despite the largely successful efforts of coffee retailers such as *Starbucks* to convince consumers otherwise about its brand, coffee itself remains a global commodity. And logically so, not that much genuine difference exists between individual coffee beans. The wholesale global price of coffee cratered from $2.20 a pound in 2015 to a low of 86 cents a pound during 2020. The cause of the price drop was highly predicable: In response to radically rising coffee demand, coffee supplies grew more rapidly still, primarily due to an influx of *Brazilian* and *Asian* growers entering the coffee bean production market. These plummeting prices proved a major factor that drove previously unheard of numbers of migrants northward toward the United States from *Guatemala*, where most coffee plantations have operated at a loss since 2017.

Two pricing principles are underscored.

One is the resolute law of supply and demand.

The second is the less predictable law of intended and unintended consequences. The fact that the consequences resulting from one environmental trend (declining coffee prices) promoted other environmental trends (radical increases in illegal immigrants crossing the southern US border) was entirely foreseeable yet completely unintentional. This immigration trend, as is true of most environmental trends, facilitated both opportunities and threats to marketers. Marketing beneficiaries would include coyotes (i.e., erstwhile supply chain "partners" [guides] to migrants fleeing their domestic poverty) or domestic firms that can build tall, strong walls fast at relatively low costs—if and when federal or state governments ever decide to build them again. Clearly injured marketing parties must already have overburdened domestic educational, health care, and social welfare systems.

We encourage readers to grasp the not-coincidental fact that each cause, consequence, trend, opportunity, or threat referenced above is marketing-related.

MARKET FACTOR 5: CUSTOMERS' INTERPRETATIONS OF PRICES CHANGES

Customers may view price cuts as a negative. Sometimes inside customer minds cuts suggest something is wrong with the brand or firm. Or, decreases, inside customer minds, might rightly or wrongly signal to them that prices will decline further in the future; best to hold off buying for now. These sorts of consumer responses happen routinely. Recent major examples arose during the 2008–10 stock market crash and the 2008–11 housing market bust.

Customers, conversely, sometimes view price increases as a positive. Apart from the value of the exclusivity tax (see just above), rising prices may infer that the value of the product is trending higher inside the market's collective mind, it's blowing up, and may become unattainable in the future. So, we had better buy now! This situation arises routinely inside real estate markets, especially at the level of individual neighborhoods. The sort of consumer mindset also routinely occurs inside stock markets (financial markets) and in no small measure the reason why irrationally exuberant—to adopt *Allen Greenspan's* famous phase—purchases of already overpriced stock shares often occur inside bull markets.

MARKET FACTOR 6: COMMODITIZATION . . . TO BE AVOIDED . . . WHEN POSSIBLE

Commodities are products produced and/or marketed by many different companies that collectively are experiencing difficulty achieving differentiation. Typical commodity examples include timber, oil, electricity, wheat, or pork bellies. Sausage and bacon come from pork bellies. Commodities essentially are uniform in quality across the firms that produce and market them. When commodities are sold it is difficult to detect any difference between the products being sold by various firms.[18]

Marketing organizations should avoid pricing at levels that prove low enough to convert products into commodities. Commodity pricing levels can destroy profit margins. More than ever, then, domestic marketers should do whatever is possible and legal to differentiate their offerings in home markets where larger and larger numbers of global competitors sell the same products at comparable or lower prices. This circumstance drags us, forcefully, back to the need to create value through differentiating, positioning, and establishing brand equity—which in turn promotes pricing power.

These imperatives reinforce and underscore the idea that firms can differentiate either by achieving greater customer-intimacy, technological-leadership or, in some cases, lower prices or customer costs. Yes, again reference is made to the three organizational core competencies, and the three paths that are available through which sustainable competitive advantage and differentiation may be achieved.

---

18. Then again, there is *"Morton's Salt."* The *Morton's Salt* example, as readers should recall, suggested that when marketers are sufficiently creative they can differentiate anything—even the most plentiful mineral on earth. Table salt, by all rights, should be a commodity. Telling apart one grain of salt from other grains is actually impossible. But due to marketing's magic, *Morton's* brand of salt grains emphatically is not commoditized.

MODULE 13.3

Core Pricing Strategies

During the 2016 *Democrat National Convention*, a gathering of impassioned marketers, then-*First Lady Michele Obama* famously declared, "When they go low [morally] we'll go high [morally]." Ms. Obama's admonition made sense, branding-wise, even though going-high emphatically did not reflect what actually happened on either marketing side during the *Hillary Clinton–Donald Trump Presidential Campaign*. Quite the opposite, in fact; both those marketing campaigns played out as way-down and real-dirty during the entire election cycle.

But pricing-wise, all marketers face two basic strategic pricing choices. Choice one is going high. Choice two is going low.

One choice that few marketers should ever make is staying middle-of-road when in terms of their pricing strategies. Middle-of-the-road is ordinary, unexciting, bland—and for those living in *West Texas* or *Arizona*, often laden with flattened (and dead) armadillos. Not a position—or a place—that many brands would want to occupy inside many customers' minds.

MARKET-SKIMMING, OR SKIMMING-THE-CREAM, PRICES

Market-skimming pricing is best understood as premium prices, going-high. Market-skimming is also called skimming-the-cream pricing. What happens when cows are milked and the milk is permitted to remain in pails? That's right, the cream rises to the top; it goes high. The cream is the fattest, tastiest, and richest, calorie-rise, part of the milk. Cream is also worth the most (i.e., commands highest prices).

Marketers that innovate and create desirable new products often can establish high prices as they introduce products and then skim off higher revenues and profits layer by layer from targeted customers across time. Such firms inevitably strategically decrease their prices for these older models over time; not coincidentally at the same time Apple is introducing its latest and greatest new products.

As noted, as *Apple* does today, and has done during approximately the last thirty years. Or how *Gillette Razors* has done since 1890.

Marketers that create extreme differentiation and/or branding power for their products are able to engage in market skimming practices. The outcomes, known as differentiation and branding power, are highly correlated with each other. Market-skimming pricing makes sense when the brand's quality, image, power, equity, features, benefits and values, design/style, or at net pricing power allow marketers to price at premium levels. Skimming makes sense when the higher costs associated with producing and marketing the smaller quantities of product that usually will be sold are not so high that they cancel out profit margin advantages gained from higher prices. When using skimming-the-cream prices, firms typically sell fewer units but earn higher margins on each unit sold.

Branding power need not actually be established on genuine or true statements/arguments. *Georgia*, the American state, not the former *Soviet Union* nation that separates *Europe* from *Asia*, has officially and successfully been branded as *The Peach State* since 1995. And *Georgia* was unofficially branded as *The Peach State* for more than one hundred years prior to 1995. Which is ironic and untrue; first, because *Georgia* produces far more blueberries per capita than peaches. And second, because one *South Carolina* country, *Chesterfield*, produces almost as many peaches alone as the entire state of *Georgia*.

MARKET PENETRATION PRICES

Market-penetration prices are best understood as drastically lowered prices offered for purposes of penetrating markets quickly and deeply, or for grabbing and then sustaining high shares of the B2C or B2B customer segments they target. The segments targeted by marketers employing penetration pricing strategies are inevitably price-conscious and price-sensitive. Market-penetration pricing strategies entail going-low.

Southwest Airlines, Walmart, Big Lots, Men's Warehouse, Jack-in-the-Box; the pricing proclivity of each well-branded marketer is to go-low.

Ideally, the higher sales volumes (demand) resulting from lowered prices contribute to economies of scale that ultimately decrease the costs associated with making and marketing branded goods or services. The primary marketing costs that are decreased by the presence of EOS are those associated with promoting, manufacturing or assembling, and distributing products. The primary distribution—or supply chain management—costs are warehousing, shipping, and order processing. Marketers then enjoy the opportunity to leverage economies of scale and decrease prices further should they wish or need to do so as part of their strategic plans. Or alternatively, to maintain current pricing levels while reaping higher margins.

For market penetration prices to work effectively, markets (i.e., the entire set of potential or actual purchasers of a product) should be price sensitive. Price sensitive means that decreasing prices markedly increase customers' desire for the product, while increasing prices produce the opposite effect.

The ability and/or willingness to charge lower prices tends to prevent competition from entering marketers' targeted market spaces. From those firms' perspectives, this result is desirable. When penetration pricing strategies are used, competitors are less able and willing to swoop into markets by undercutting higher prices.

One downside, however, is that once marketing organizations decide to offer lower prices, raising prices becomes difficult.

The preceding description remains true and valid, unless and until the product being sold is a solution that customers cannot live without, or a solution that customers perceive they cannot live without. Such products could include health care, gasoline, and higher education. In these three market sectors, the evidence is in and is clear: Inside these domains marketing providers can and do raise prices with impunity. The costs of higher education, for example, have more than doubled the overall inflation rate for nearly thirty straight years, and counting.

Some pricing principles will never not apply. One such pricing and positioning principle follows:

- ▶ The same is always better when it's lower priced—unless, of course, the same product is a luxury brand (positional good).

ADJUSTING PRICES

Price adjustments normally arrive in the form of price reductions. Price adjustments should be done strategically and enacted to account for differing customer needs or wants and changing marketing conditions. Price adjustments can be used to reward customers or supply chain partners when they engage in certain behaviors. Price adjustments can also be used to incentivize (motivate) customers or supply chain partners to engage in certain desired responses.

Desired customer responses that marketers might seek by adjusting their products' prices could include:

- ▶ Incentivizing customers to pay early, helping marketers address potential or actual cash flow problems.
- ▶ Motivating customers to buy in high volume, helping marketers ramp-up production, lower distribution or promotional costs, or earn economies of scale.
- ▶ Persuading customers to buy or buy more out of season, transferring inventory management costs downstream from selling firms to buying firms. Yet ironically as well as strategically, buyers should always buy out of season, when and where they can and when doing so is manageable, cost-wise. Why? Because those customers who buy out of season inevitably receive lower prices and usually receive better service.

- Or, inside B2C supply chains, getting customers—who in such cases would also exist as supply chain partners—to allocate more desirable shelf[19] space inside physical stores in exchange for receiving legal financial kickbacks or for agreeing to purchase other products bundled with the initial, usually more desirable, products that are being sold.
    - This entire arrangement is called slotting allowances or spiffs; is classified as a form of sales promotion (which is part of the promotional element [ingredient] inside "marketing mixes"), and is discussed more fully in Module 14. The slotting allowances topic is extremely important.

Price adjustments can take the form of discounts or allowances. Allowances themselves can be divided into promotional allowances and trade-in allowances.

Promotional allowances are payments, price reductions, or other discounts that manufacturers or dealers or distributors use to reward and help retailers with their advertising or selling efforts. Manufacturers, dealers, distributors, or retailers are all supply chain members.

Trade-in allowances are price reductions given to buyers in exchange for turning in old items as new items are purchased. Automobile trade-ins probably just entered your mind.

---

19. The most preferable shelf space inside retailers such as grocery stores is typically located at either end of aisles and at the eye level of average consumers.

MODULE 13.4

Tying Things Off

From marketers' perspectives, good pricing decisions should begin with an understanding of how customers' perceptions of a product's value impact their perceptions of what price levels are acceptable or unacceptable. Described more deeply, good pricing decisions begin with marketers' understanding what is, inside customers' minds, an acceptable amount of value to give up in order to get another sort of product-related value in return. The exchange process was just described, again.

All customers explicitly or implicitly evaluate the price associated with acquiring or using a branded product versus the benefits associated with owning and using that branded product. To customers, price is their costs. To customers, benefits are the values—solutions to given problems—they receive in exchange for giving up something else of value—generally, money but also customers' time, effort, and/or relinquishing the opportunity to own and/or use other brands that they could have selected.

Remember, marketing success or failure inside supply chains along with basically all marketing activities that play out inside supply chains are based on the willingness of both parties to engage freely in exchange. You know exchange; the process that entails a getting something of value and a giving up something of value.

HISTORY

Historically, price has proven a major factor that influenced buyer choices. But more recently, non-price factors have gained in importance as consumers choose what they choose or choose to choose nothing at all. This is because marketers, from the early 1960s-onward, got increasingly more proficient at finessing customers and their perceptions of value. Finessing, as in manipulating.

Most marketing organizations would be wise to not compete exclusively based on the planned provision of lower prices. Instead, those marketers should compete on the basis of the value they create by strategically managing other elements in their marketing mix.

However, pricing levels almost always materially impact the market shares and profit margins of marketers. Prices and pricing levels have always mattered greatly to marketers and customers alike. But marketers, usually, should do everything possible to make prices matter less to customers.

The immediately preceding strategic recommendation does not and should not apply to brands such as *Walmart* or *Southwest Airlines*. Each marketer's entire business model is designed to permit the firm to offer everyday-low-prices.

Marketplaces function metaphorically like battlefields where buyers and sellers engage with one another for purposes of determining who, either buyers or sellers, will secure the greatest value from the exchange process that each side is seeking to consummate. This exchange process almost always involves a giving and getting of money and a product, service, or a bundled product/service. The point at which the two contending parties agree upon a price represents a truce. Sometimes these truces are hard-earned, the product of great effort on each side of the buyer-seller coupling. Usually, these truces are more easily achieved.

Prices figuratively represent a buyer-seller agreement about the mutual value of two objects about to be explained.

The now-traditional practice of setting fixed prices inside stores or on web platforms for goods or services meant a cessation of the perpetual pricing conflict known as haggling—a truce, if you will. Yet having generally fixed prices for most products only took hold in the 1860s with a storeowner named *John Wanamaker*, in *Philadelphia*. As in most truces, each party surrenders something in the bargain.

Buyers were forced to accept or reject the one price imposed by the price tag. Mr. Wanamaker's price tag was an innovation—a solution based on an idea that created a new and useful solution. Buyers no longer had to haggle, meaning no one ever got completely screwed, anymore. This alone was a huge new and useful upgrade.

What retailers ceded, gave up, was arguably greater, as the extra money some people would have paid now could no longer be captured as extra profit. Retailers lost the opportunity to take naïve and/or less well-informed customers to the metaphorical cleaners. They abrogated the opportunity to exploit consumers' varying willingness to pay different amounts.

Yet retailers accrued several practical benefits. Hundreds of clerks no longer needed to be trained in haggling—negotiation. Fixed prices offered a measure of predictability to the accounting function, accelerating selling processes, and made possible the proliferation of printed retail advertising highlighting given prices for given brands and goods.

Mr. Wanamaker opened his *Grand Depot* store under the positioning statement, *One Price to All, No Favoritism*. The *Grand Depot* eventually morphed into *Wanamaker's,* which has operated as a prestigious department store chain throughout northeastern American states since the 1860s.

SHOWING THEM THE MONEY

Price is the only marketing mix element that produces revenue for marketers. Everything else in their marketing mixes represents a cost to firms.

Price is highly flexible. To suggest that price can be raised or lowered with a push of a button actually no longer fully describes the change process; prices now can actually be altered wirelessly. Price is far and away the easiest marketing mix element to change. Such changes can lead to problems, and frequently do.

Pricing is a big headache for many marketing executives. Consider *JCPenney*. Not too many years ago *JCPenney* badly bungled the implementation of a pricing system similar to the EDLP, everyday-low-prices strategy used by *Walmart*. The pricing plan failed miserably because neither Penney's supply chain infrastructure nor its core customer base were able or willing to support the strategy. Indeed, the core *JCPenney* customer base, which at the time consisted primarily of female shoppers purchasing good for their families, expected to see %-off! signage displayed every day as they entered. Once this no longer happened, those shoppers increasingly no longer entered *JCPenney* stores.

JCPenney is not alone. Many companies do not handle pricing well. Many marketers are loath to establish high prices, at the start, by creating more highly valued brands through marketing mix management. This often proves problematic. As noted, it's far easier to lower prices that are too high than to raise prices that are too low. Such marketers also often leave money—profits—on the table. Many other firms are seemingly too eager to lower their prices at the first sign of threat; thus, prematurely tossing away up-profits.

When possible, companies should avoid reducing prices too far or too fast to secure quick sales. Why? Because price cuts are the easiest thing for competitors to match. Once that happens, each business loses; market shares stay roughly the same, but profits for each firm normally drop.

Pricing, the process, should be treated strategically. Pricing should be viewed and treated as a marketing tool that both creates and captures customer value. Or, at least, pricing should function this way. Higher prices, when properly managed as a marketing mix element, can and do create perceptions of higher value in the minds of targeted customer segments.

MODULE 13.5

Specific Pricing Tactics

VALUE-BASED PRICING

Value-based pricing tactics use customers' perceptions of value, not marketers' costs, to establish prices. When using value-based pricing, marketers establish desired price levels before other marketing mix program ingredients—product, promotion, distribution, and placement—are considered, developed, and managed.

Firms that use value-based pricing tactics establish prices based on perceived customer value. Ideally, products that are priced on a value-basis deliver exactly the right combination of quality, good service, and performance, and do so at prices presumably deemed as fair by targeted market segments.

Before any marketer considers using a value-based pricing strategy, the "pricing" entity should have built its pricing power. Pricing power enables a firm to escape punishing price competition. Pricing power justifies higher prices in customers' minds. Pricing power allows firms to earn and enjoy higher profit margins, without losing excessive market share to lower-priced competitor brands. Firms may strategically attach value-adding services to differentiate service or product offerings and support higher prices, which in turn create higher margins. They may promote the heck out of them. Marketers may strategically ensure the right people are associated with their brand. And so forth.

Banana Republic once enjoyed tremendous brand equity for a few years that began about twenty years ago and ended some ten years later. The apparel retailer's possession of brand equity meant *Banana* also enjoyed the concomitant pricing power that generally accompanies the development of brand equity. The *Banana* brand was once extremely well-positioned as an eminent upscale casual apparel retailer. The retailer no longer enjoys these positioning and pricing advantages but still continues to market its apparel products successfully. These facts are referenced in order that three useful points might be introduced.

The first point is that for marketers—or anyone else—failure is rarely fatal. While some marketers may lose their jobs, most failures are akin to skinned knees. Skinned knees hurt temporally but ultimately prove superficial.

But, as noted earlier, marketing success is never final, either. That's the second useful point.

Here's a third. Marketers and marketing organizations must bring their best every day, never not leaving every value they bring to the table on the field. Bringing their best, every day, was a habit that was ingrained into victorious *Roman* generals. *Roman* generals, during the midst of city-wide *Triumph Festivals* that were carried out to celebrate and laud their conquests, routinely had slaves walk beside them whispering repeatedly: "This is fleeting." The message that "this is fleeting" is a lesson that *Banana Republic* probably learned the hard way, because the once mega-brand has long since lost its marketing mojo. But give credit where it is due: *Banana* is still in there swinging.

At times the best pricing strategy entails pricing above the competition and convincing customers the higher prices are worth it. Numerous companies/brands do this. This pricing approach relates to the growth strategy where new products are developed that offer solutions to problems that targeted markets did not yet realize they had, and then convincing those same targeted markets that they have those exact problems. Pricing above the market, in turn, requires well-managed promotional and positioning and NPD efforts. At net, well-managed branding efforts. As the marketers of *Carpe Diem* or *7 for All Mankind* jeans, and many other powerful brands have done.

COST-BASED PRICING

Cost-based pricing tactics are cost-driven. *IKEA*,[20] the *Swedish* firm that designs and markets ready-to-assemble furniture and household accessories, uses this pricing approach. As the corporation explains, cost-based pricing entails a situation where *IKEA product managers* determine an amount, for example, $299.99, that they want to charge for a new bookshelf that *IKEA* plans to develop.

From there, *IKEA*'s designers, manufacturers, and distributors—that's right, all part of *IKEA*'s supply chain—are expected to work together backward through their NPD, production, shipping and inventory management, and promotional efforts to ensure that *IKEA* can produce, distribute, promote, and sell and merchandise the new but disassembled bookshelf product at a $399.99 price and still earn acceptable profits. Cost-based pricing strategies begin with preset prices in mind.

COST-PLUS PRICING

Cost-plus pricing tactics involve adding standard markups to whatever amounts, cost-wise, are required to make, distribute, and sell, promote, or merchandise products. A markup is the amount added to the price of goods to cover the costs of overhead and secure profit. The pricing process is simple, which partially explains the pricing method's popularity.

Cost-plus pricing, however, ignores marketing demand and competitors' prices. Does not sound very strategic, does it? Even so, markup-based pricing remains popular. Primarily, because marketers are usually more certain about their own costs than market demand. And secondarily, because counting costs is easier than creating differentiating values.

---
20. The famous brand name, *IKEA*, is actually an acronym. *IKEA*, the word, was created by combining the founder's name (Ingvar Kamprad), the name of the farm where he grew up (Elmtaryd), and the name of his hometown (Agunnaryd).

This pricing tactic begins once costs are known. Costs always establish the floor for prices marketers can charge. Marketing organizations technically must charge prices that cover the costs associated with producing, distributing, and promoting products. Firms should also charge a price that delivers a fair rate of return for investors. No other legal or strategically logical alternative exists. There are exceptions, however. When *Amazon's Kindle* was introduced, the product was famously sold at a $199 price. Which is hardly remarkable in and of itself except for the fact that this price was below the $225 in costs that were associated with making and marketing each individual *Kindle* product. This pricing level, however, proved legally and strategically defensible because customers who purchased *Kindles* were also required to acquire books from *Amazon* to read on their *Kindles*, and to purchase them at emphatically not below cost prices.

If firms inside given sectors generally price on a cost-plus basis, industry prices typically bunch up. Consequently, price-based competition diminishes. This "bunching-up of prices" materially benefits firms and their profit margins. What about customers? Do they benefit? Hardly.

EVERYDAY LOW PRICING

Long ago (1962) inside the kingdom of *Rogers, Arkansas*, a town located near *Bentonville, Sam Walton* and his baby *Walmart* store pioneered a new pricing concept. Today the tactic is called EDLP, or Every-Day-Low-Prices. This tactic involves charging constant, everyday low prices with few temporary price discounts. This approach has worked well for *Walmart*. *Walmart* can pull off this pricing tactic because of cost efficiencies the retailer introduced and has maintained inside its supply chain. These efficiencies allow Walmart to post lower prices across broad assortments of products and still make sufficient profit margins, especially given the humongous amounts of different sorts of products and product categories sold by *Walmart*.[21] The entire Walmart business model supports EDLP.

As noted, *JCPenney* tried to use the same basic Every Day Low Price tactic to ill effect over ten years ago. The strategy failed miserably because EDLP confounded *Penney's* discounter department store image, proved incompatible with the *Penney's* business model, and conflicted with how the national retailer managed its supply chain relationships at the time.

JCPenney's discounter image had formerly signaled that when customers visited physical stores or the *JCPenney* website they could expect to see special price deals shouting out great deals everywhere. But once these signs and apparent discounts disappeared so did many *JCPenney* customers. This disappearing act transpired even though average prices throughout the entire store actually had declined by amounts greater than had been listed on all the previous sales signs!

That's humans, and their natures. Most consumers don't process at high-involvement levels, most of the time, as previously discussed. If consumers had really paid attention, they would have realized they were actually getting better pricing deals.

Usually, marketers take advantage of the fact that many consumers' ability or willingness to focus is so poor that they cannot even pay attention. This time, however, the marketer got mugged.

---

21. How large an assortment of products is available at *Walmart*? The answer is an assortment so vast that many consumers assume that if *Walmart* doesn't stock the product in its inventory the product does not exist. Note, as well, that the vast assortment of products inside *Walmart* stores or on its website is entirely due to the economies of scale that *Walmart* has created for itself by adroitly managing the myriad supply chains that supply the products that Walmart, as a retailer, merchandises and sells.

PRESTIGE PRICING

The pricing tactic known as prestige pricing is used when marketers establish higher prices based on the premise that quality-conscious, social status-conscious, or positional-conscious buyers will be attracted to the brand, due to its high price, the value that "higher" signals, and the potential buyers' ability to afford it, and thus become more likely to purchase the brand. Cars, perfumes, jewelry, and certain brands of clothing are known for successfully using this tactic. Think positional goods and/or luxury brands.

Joy Perfume, not long ago, proudly positioned itself as *The Most Expensive Perfume [Brand] in the World*. Ironically, *Joy* either was lying to customers or misinformed about global perfume prices. *Joy* was not the highest priced perfume in the world at the time. But *Joy* knew what it was doing and saying. Here's the inside skinny, if the generally female recipient of a gifted *Joy* bottle thought that her beloved loved her enough to spend that much; well, dare we write that his or her core mission was probably well on the way to completion. Score. *Joy* understood this, as well.

TARGETED PRICING

Marketers can price using targeted pricing approaches. Here, prices are established based on marketers' strategic estimate of the amount, no less, no more, that customers would be willing to pay for a product of this nature.

One might view this pricing tactic as a *Goldilocks* pricing approach. But rather than the porridge that *Goldilocks* stole from the Bear family in the fairy tale being not-too-hot or not-too-cold, *Goldilocks's* prices need to be just-right.

Just-right-prices are neither too high nor too low. When prices are too high, potential sales and customers are lost. Too low, and potential profits are lost even as market share is gained or held. Sometimes being positioned-in-the-middle, if the middle is the right place to be, makes strategic sense. Just this once. Because usually, being positioned-in-the-middle is a terrible place for marketers and their brands to occupy.

DYNAMIC PRICING

Oscar Wilde, yes him again, famously wrote that, "A cynic is someone who knows the price of everything and the value of nothing." If *Wilde's* maxim remains true, being a cynic is getting harder these days.[22] Marketers have always offered different prices to different groups of customers, without necessarily engaging in price discrimination—although discriminatory acts were sometimes unsheathed.

---

22. Few contemporary business books teach aphorisms or maxims. Yet marketing power and opportunities to educate and motivate readers readily derives from summarizing timeless truths in pithy maxims and aphorisms. Still, cultural maxims and aphorisms are often deemed superficial and meaningless. That's wrong. Because any intelligent person understands that "a penny saved is a penny earned" is more than a superficial comment. Combine a story about "saving pennies" with a story about "the power of compound interest" and any professional can easily retire a multimillionaire. All resulting from the creation of a strategic intersection of formerly independent story ideas. Does this intersection remind you of anything?

Harmless examples of dynamic pricing abound. Happy hours for consumers seeking an early jump on their drinking. Matinee specials for afternoon moviegoers who prematurely blew off school or work back when most people still either went to work, school, or the movie theatre. Steep discounts to incentivize students or elderly. But yes, some marketers also insert the same products into different packaging and charge different prices to different income level segments—and that actually is price discrimination.

Discrimination matters, usually—and naturally. When a parent favors one child over another for whatever reason—discrimination—not only do the children hate each other, one hates the parent. But adroit marketers can and do exploit discriminatory practices in ways that seemingly bother few.

Dynamic pricing takes the range of just barely ethical discriminatory pricing processes to new levels. Marketers use dynamic prices to change prices by the minute. Prices are tailored based on what is understood about the income, location, and spending history of individual buyers. Or even weather conditions, such as is the case of *Uber* pickups. The practice began during the early 1980s when *American Airlines* began to change their ticket prices daily to fight competition from discounter airlines such as *People's Express*. These dynamic pricing practices spread to other airlines, and to hotels, car-rental firms, and domestic passenger trains.

Now, given the degree to which e-commerce has proliferated, dynamic pricing has become the rage. The prices of goods sold online can be changed instantly and effortlessly, usually in alignment with the brand quantities and demographic/psychographic characteristics of consumers who are considering or actually making purchases. Competitors are monitored constantly and their prices are subsequently matched or bettered. *Amazon*, on average, updates prices every eight minutes. These actions are initiated based on data that is continuously collected. The practice is spreading to physical retailers as they install electronic price displays and borrow models from the e-tailers.

Dynamic pricing models benefit marketers in various ways. Besides smoothing out demand, dynamic pricing provides opportunities for marketers to cull higher profits from wealthier customers. The ability to smooth out demand lowers inventory management and other supply chain management expenses that otherwise would be required to maintain extra stock quantities to fulfill demand during peak demand periods

Dynamic pricing is accompanied by two risks. The first is psychological resistance to the practice among consumers—if and when consumers know the practice is playing out. And indeed, marketers' reputations can suffer if they offend customers' sense of fairness—see below. *Uber* experienced recently an extreme customer backlash when the riding service raised prices eight times during a mega *Northeastern United States* snowstorm.

The second risk associated with dynamic pricing is that use of the tactic potentially might lead to a race to the bottom. Firms that market primarily or exclusively online have been caught up inside wars waged to hang onto or secure the top slot on price comparison sites. In such settings a simple penny's worth of price difference can prove determinant to customers as they make price-based purchase choices. Physical retailers might easily fall into the same trap.

MODULE 13.6

Genuine Price Deals—A Consumer Take

This book has usually adopted and will continue to take the perspective, the side, of marketers and will continue to do so. This orientation toward marketers' side of the exchange processes was logical. The core purpose of this book is to equip readers with the sort of knowledge that is necessary to make them successful marketing thinkers and doers; to create potentially successful marketing managers. However, the discussion that follows inside this section contravenes this tendency. The purpose of this section is to make readers better consumers.

MISTAKES THAT CONSUMERS SHOULD AVOID

All people, whether or not they embrace the label, are marketers.

A less contentious but equally relevant fact is that all readers are also consumers. To help all of us as consumers the brief discussion that follows describes six pricing mistakes that consumers should learn more about and subsequently avoid.

Consumer Mistake 1: Don't Trust Yourself, All the Time

Never trust yourself, all the time, especially when it comes to past pricing decisions. Because mindlessly trusting prior choices that led to contemporary habits can end up creating big future problems.

Avoid doing something all the time, like getting a $5 or more latte. From time to time, question your long-term spending habits. People who don't learn from the purchasing mistakes of their past are doomed to repeat them. Seriously, are iced teas you're not going to fully drink in restaurants really worth $3 or $4 or more dollars, especially after extra taxes and tips have been added in, to you? Yes, the answer may be yes, and of course that's okay; we all perceive "value" differently. Yet other sorts of value may still be found by merely asking such questions to oneself. However, such questions should be asked mindful of the fact that people who consciously choose to pursue long-term financial goals are rarely viewed favorably by those operating in the short-run or in the moment. There are always prices to be paid.

One thing to remember or to learn about habits is that good routines are remarkably powerful processes that invariably generate positive outcomes. Consciously deciding to usually eat right, to regularly exercise, to wake up at the same time every morning, to dollar-cost average when investing, to spend less than one makes each month and to save the rest unless unavoidable circumstance makes this impossible, and rarely if ever overspending on commodities such as coffee that are available at lower prices elsewhere—these are all routines worth considering.[23] If and when they harden into habits, these six price-related behaviors will go a long way toward ensuring healthier and wealthier lives for most consumers who consciously choose to engage in them.

As *W. S. Auden* wrote: "Routine, in an intelligent person, is a sign of ambition." Who would not relatedly agree that ambition functions as a lever that buttresses the prospects of success?

Consumer Mistake 2: Don't Overvalue What You Own, or Overly Fear What You Might Lose

All consumers should learn about the natural human tendency to overvalue what they already own and consequently become overly fearful about what they might lose. Most people love to have stuff, and once they acquire new stuff are wired to somehow believe—fantasize, actually—that their stuff in some objective sense is the best stuff. But usually this is not the case—and no one is criticizing your stuff, here.

For example, never trust or assume home improvements will increase your home's value. Every consumer's taste is unique. Others may and indeed probably will see things differently. Knowing this, accept that home improvements may only increase the value of your home to yourself . . . which should prove enough.

But no, this discussion is not actually about home improvements. It's about sunk costs and how to treat them. Sunk costs cannot be recovered. That's why they're described as sunk. Once money is spent, it's gone. The past is past. When making decisions, only consider where you now are and plan to be in the future.

Consumer Mistake 3: Don't Believe the Hype

Never be naïve or disengaged enough that you fall victim to the magic dust spread by marketing words, images, and iconography. Follow the wise advice offered by *Public Enemy*, the great twentieth-century philosophers: *Don't Believe the Hype*.

If the description of a product's value or the process of consuming something is long-winded and overblown, you're almost certainly paying extra for that description or process. Who gives a crap, for example, about irrelevant claims describing all the effort that was expended in producing a product or about narratives recounting all the experiences the diamond in the ring went through—before it reached your or your loved one's hand.

Paying $200 for an artisanal hammer because it was handmade is rarely an intelligent purchase. The experiences your particular diamond encountered are irrelevant and often outright misrepresentations of the facts. Outright misrepresentations, here, means lies.

---

23. Of course, if consumers don't view coffee as a commodity then this last point flies out the window. And *Starbucks*, wonderfully effective marketing communicator that it is, has surely convinced tens of millions of loyal consumers that coffee is a specialty rather than commodity product.

Many new car buyers, perhaps surprisingly,[24] apparently are overburdened by fears of "what if" (they miss out on this feature and benefit) and end up spending scads of money for features that they rarely use. For example, how many times have owners actually needed the third row of seats in an SUV to seat seven people—unless, of course, they cart around volleyball teams.

Consumer Mistake 4: Don't Convert Expectations into Realities

Consumers should avoid converting their expectations into their realities. Expectations, once firmly embedded, give reasons that lead people to believe something will be good or bad. But expectations often falsely shape consumer perceptions and experiences without actually altering the genuine underlying value of the thing or experience.

Consumer Mistake 5: Don't Overemphasize Money

Learn to not overemphasize money. Prices are only one of several attributes that signal the value of things. Signaling value inside your or others' minds.

Prices, however, function as product attributes that most consumers can easily understand. Yet prices, customers' financial costs, are not the only product attribute that counts. Wise customers should move from indirectly comparing money to products to the point where products are directly compared to other products. When evaluating vacation alternatives, for instance, one might ruminate over the amount one vacation alternative costs in terms of numbers of movies or wine bottles you otherwise could afford to consume if you chose to not vacation at all or elected for another vacation destination.

Price is only a number in the end. And while price understandably plays powerful roles in most consumers' decision-making processes, price alone does not mean everything. Nor should it, not if marketers execute their value-creation efforts effectively.

Consumer Mistake 6: Do Slim Down Grocery Spending

The typical household spends most of its money on three purchase types: housing, transportation, food. According to *HuffingtonPost.com*, food is most susceptible to budget-draining conveniences, and thus to price-related mistakes. Paying for food in cash is inconvenient but does tamp down spending. When swiping plastic, a certain "detachment" from what is actually happening, budgetary-wise, arises. That's because consumers don't feel their resources dwindle in the same fashion. Consider building out a weekly food budget; withdrawing that amount in cash each week; and honoring your promise to yourself. Stop buying too much; Americans typically end up tossing 20 percent or more of their grocery purchases. Limit if not eliminate prepared meals; they cost on average $12.75 each. Consumers typically can prepare something as heathy or heathier for fractions of prepared meal costs.

---

24. The word "surprisingly" is used because for almost all consumers an automotive purchase represents a major, high-involvement decision. Automotive purchasing decisions force buyers into decision-making contexts where it's critical to not just make a good choice but the best choice. That's because long-term commitments, loads of money, conspicuous acts of consumption, and lots of risk are involved with nearly every decision that car buyers make.

MODULE 13.7

Conducting Cost-Volume-Profit Analysis

Cost-volume-profit analysis (CVP Analysis) consists of a series of tools and techniques designed to assess the profit impact of charging different prices for products. This section examines one such tool—break-even analysis. Break-even analysis is one of the most frequently used analytic tools by businesses. It can be applied to a wide range of business problems and decisions, in addition to price-related evaluations.

WHAT IS BREAK-EVEN ANALYSIS?

Break-even analysis entails an attempt to identify the level of sales, measured either in units or dollars, at which *break-even* occurs. Specifically, break-even analysis determines the levels of unit sales or dollar sales where total revenues equal total costs, or, alternatively stated, where profits equal zero.

Break-even analysis provides an indirect way to examine the impact of price on profitability. A more direct approach is to build a pro forma income statement (profit and loss statement) that attempts to project an accurate numerical estimate for expected profits. Pro forma projections, however, rely on obtaining solid estimates of the number of units that would be purchased at different target prices. A reliable assessment of the demand curve thus is necessary to produce realistic pro forma income statements. Yet this task is often unreasonable; demand estimation is prone to errors due to the potential influence of uncontrollable environmental and competitive forces. In addition, the process can be very time-consuming and expensive, particularly if experimentation is employed.

This is where the use of break-even analysis enters the picture. Break-even analysis does not require that precise estimates of demand at the price under evaluation be available. This makes break-even analysis an ideal technique for "backing into" profitability estimates when precise estimates of demand are not available or cannot be reasonably developed. But when they know the *break-even point*, managers can more readily estimate the likelihood that actual sales will surpass (or not surpass) the computed break-even point. Estimating break-even points is easier than precisely pinpointing actual unit or dollar sales anticipated at specific prices.

Assume, for example, the computed break-even point for a product is 100 units. Decision makers then can estimate the likelihood, or probability, that at least 100 units will be sold. If decision makers believe actual sales will likely exceed the break-even level of sales, the analysis indicates the price being considered is viable. By contrast, if management believes sales likely will not reach the calculated break-even point, alternative prices (and, probably, cost structures) should be evaluated.

Allow us to re-emphasize. Break-even analysis is extremely useful. The tool specifically benefits firms that are uncertain about how much demand will result from charging a specific price. By employing break-even analysis, marketers can acquire general insights about how many units must be sold in order to cover all relevant costs involved in making and marketing the associated product. With knowledge of this break-even point, managers can project the likelihood that sales will exceed (or not exceed) break-even.

Break-even analysis, therefore, is best described as a technique that allows firms to logically examine the potential profit impact of charging a particular price. The technique is also extensively used to evaluate the profit impact of changing various marketing mix and/or production programs. Marketers can use break even models to identify the level of unit sales needed to offset such things as increased advertising or sales promotion expenditures or adding personnel to the sales force.

THE BREAK-EVEN POINT: ITS RELATIONSHIP TO REVENUES AND COSTS

Exhibit 13.4 graphically illustrates how a break-even analysis is conducted. The "X" axis represents the number of units produced or sold. The "Y" axis represents both costs and total revenues. The cost dimensions on this graph should look familiar. When conducting break-even analyses, the relevant costs are fixed and variable costs. You should be familiar with each by now. Both total fixed costs (TFC) and total variable costs (TVC) at increasing levels of output are summed to generate the total cost (TC) curve. All that must be added is the total revenue curve (TR). The TR curve begins at the origin, where the X- and Y-axes intersect, and steadily increases to the right as sales increase.

The break-even point is the level of sales where TR=TC (total revenue equals total costs). Any sales in excess of those required to achieve break-even generate profits. This is illustrated in Figure 13.10 by the fact that to the right of the break-even point TR>TC (total revenue exceeds total costs). In contrast, to the left of the break-even point, TR<TC—total revenues are less than total costs. This latter situation results in a loss. There are no profits.

CONDUCTING BREAK-EVEN ANALYSIS

Building a break-even analysis is not difficult. For those familiar with Excel, the process may already be evident. One starts by building a spreadsheet that contains the relevant revenue and cost data. Then, from these data, the relevant curves are plotted on the break-even graph.

Assume we want to conduct a break-even analysis in which the price under consideration is $100 per unit and average variable costs (AVC) have already been estimated at AVC = $50. Similarly, total fixed costs (TFC) are $200,000. The resulting spreadsheet would contain six columns. The first column contains the values for the "X" axis. This is the relevant range of sales in units. The range of sales (Q) varies from 0 to 10,000 units. The second column, total revenue (TR), is obtained by multiplying price per unit (P) by each value of Q in the first column. The first entry in the total revenue column will, of course, be "0." After all, no units have been produced and sold. Remaining entries in the total revenue column range from $100,000 to $1,000,000.

The third column contains fixed cost information. Assuming that total fixed costs involved with producing and selling the product are $200,000, all entries in the TFC column will be the same—$200,000. This reflects the fact that fixed costs in total do not change with level of output. It does not matter whether output is zero units or 10,000 units. Fixed costs remain $200,000.

The fourth column tabulates total variable costs. Entries are obtained by multiplying values of Q by AVC = $50. Therefore, total variable costs will be zero when output (Q) is zero. TVC increases to $500,000 at 10,000 units.

Entries in the total costs (TC) column are, obviously, obtained by adding total fixed costs (TFC) and total variable costs (TVC). You should pick a few entries in the table and verify for yourself that the values in the total cost column correctly reflect the sum of total fixed and total variable costs at their respective levels of sales.

The break-even point can actually be identified directly from the data. Note that, at 4,000 units of output, the values in the total revenue (TR) column and the total cost (TC) column are exactly the same—$400,000. Four thousand units, therefore, is the break-even point in units produced and sold. At this level of sales, total revenue equals total costs, and profits are equal to zero. We have conveniently added a sixth column containing profit (TR-TC) to the spreadsheet, confirming that profits do indeed equal zero at the 4,000 unit point. Sales in excess of 4,000 units will yield a profit, while sales below 4,000 units result in a loss.

MATHEMATICS OF BREAK-EVEN ANALYSIS

The graphic approach to break-even analysis provides a solid conceptual understanding of the break-even point and its relationship to both revenues and costs. However, the break-even point can be found much more easily via direct computation. The formula for break-even in units sold (Q) is:

$$(13) \quad BE(Q) = \frac{TFC}{Price - AVC}$$

The break-even point in units (BE (Q)) is found by dividing total fixed costs (TFC) by the difference between price per unit and average variable cost per unit (P − AVC). The latter difference (P − AVC) is called the **unit contribution** (UC) or simply **contribution**. This is the per unit amount that is available to cover total fixed costs.

An example illustrates the computational procedure and helps clarify the meaning of the unit contribution. Using the data from our prior break-even analysis, the break-even point in units is found by:

$$(14) \quad BE(Q) = \frac{TFC}{P-AVC} = \frac{\$200,000}{\$100 - \$50} = 4,000 \text{ units}$$

Total fixed costs are, again, $200,000. These costs are divided by the difference between price, which is $100 per unit, and average variable costs per unit ($50). This difference is $50 per unit. Fifty dollars is the contribution per unit that is now available to help cover the $200,000 in fixed costs. Each unit sold contributes $50 to cover fixed costs. This means that the firm must sell $200,000/$50 = 4,000 units to fully recover the $200,000 in fixed costs. This 4,000 units is the break-even point.

Sometimes it is useful to compute the break-even point in dollars rather than units. Of course, a simple way obtain the dollar break-even point is by first computing break-even in units, as we have already done. The result then is multiplied by the selling price. In our previous example, the dollar break-even is obtained by multiplying 4,000 units by the $100 price tag. The result is $400,000. Not surprisingly, both the 4,000 units and $400,000 break-even values correspond to the break-even points on the X- and Y- axes, respectively.

Break-even in dollars can also be computed directly by dividing total fixed costs (TFC) by the percent contribution margin (or, more simply, the contribution margin). The percentage contribution margin is obtained by dividing unit contribution (P- AVC) by price (P). Percent contribution margin is, therefore, a ratio between the dollar unit contribution and the original selling price. The computation is:

$$(15) \quad BE(\$) = \frac{TFC}{\frac{P-AVC}{P}} = \frac{\$200,000}{\frac{\$100 - \$50}{\$100}} = \$400,000$$

Basic break-even analysis, as presented above, is immensely useful. Even if we stopped here with our presentation of break-even, you will carry away an application that will be one of the most important tools you will use in your business career. However, break-even analysis has many additional applications, or "extensions." For example, the break-even model, with a simple modification, can be employed to solve for the level of unit (or dollar) sales required to achieve some desired level of target profit. The modifications needed in the break-even formula are:

$$(16) \quad \text{Target } Q = \frac{TFC + \text{Target Profit}}{P-AVC}$$

Note that the additional desired profit is treated as an additional fixed cost in the revised formula. The numerator in the formula is now TFC + Target Profit. In addition, since the formula is solving for the level of sales required to achieve a target level of profit, it no longer makes sense to call the result "break-even" or use the variable name BE(Q). We have substituted the variable *Target Q* for *BE (Q)*.

Conceptually, treating the target profit as an added fixed cost makes sense. Achieving the desired profit requires selling more units beyond those required to break-even. The exact number of extra units that must be sold is a function of the unit contribution (i.e., P-AVC), just as in the standard break-even model.

Our last example can be extended to illustrate how this works. TFC remains at $200,000, but now let's add the stipulation that we want to earn $5,000 in incremental profit beyond break-even. Unit price is still $100 and AVC is $50. This means that the unit contribution is still $50. The formula becomes:

$$(17) \quad \text{Target Q} = \frac{\$200{,}000 + \$5{,}000}{\$100 - \$50} = 4{,}100$$

Note that the $5,000 target profit is added to the $200,000 fixed costs. The sum ($205,000) is divided by our $50 unit contribution. The result is 4,100 units. Recall from our earlier example that 4,000 units were required to break-even. Thus, an additional 100 units must be sold to achieve the $5,000 in profits. Of course, the number of additional units could have been computed directly by dividing the $5,000 by the $50 unit contribution - $5,000 / $50 = 100.

EXHIBIT 13.1
Demand curves can show a direct relationship between price and demand. Such curves are characterized as "inverse demand curves."

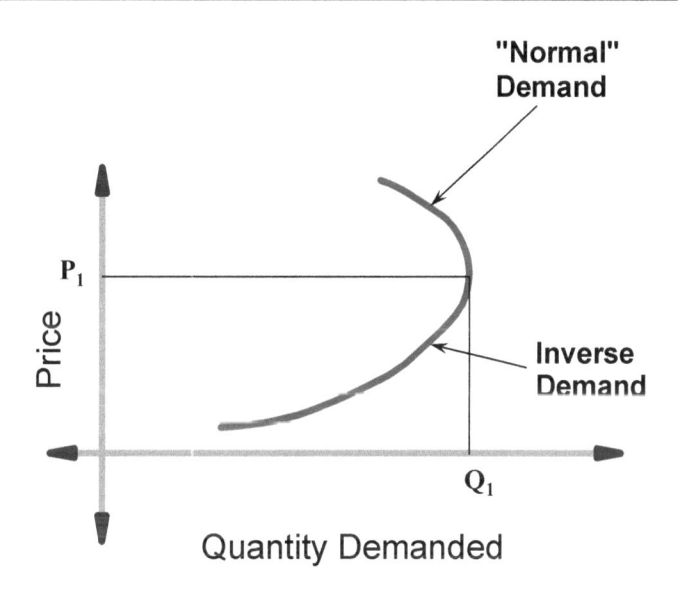

EXHIBIT 13.2
Demand can be price-elastic or price-inelastic.

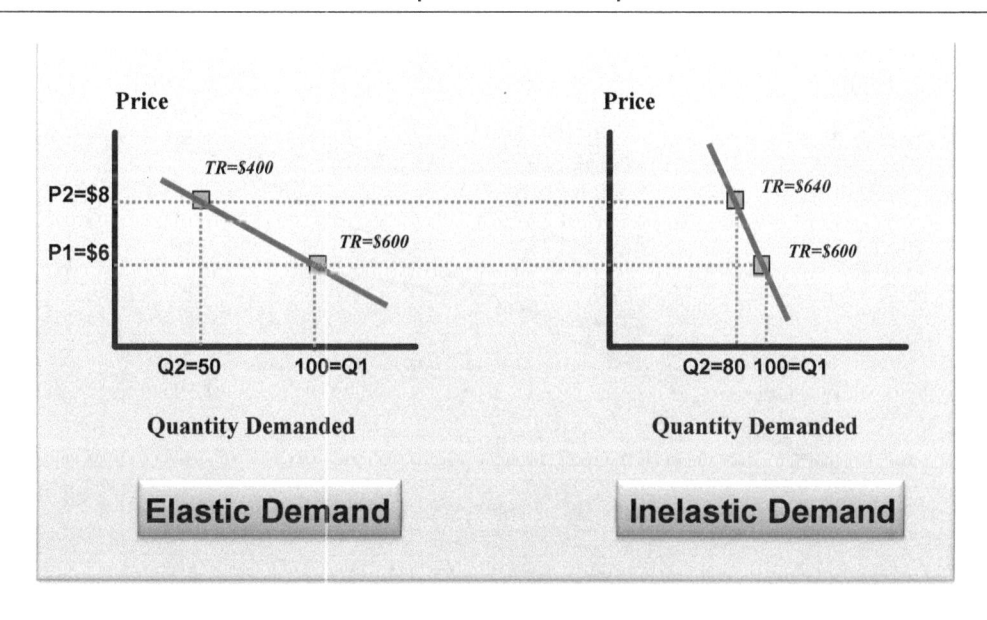

568 Section III Managing Key Marketing Activities

EXHIBIT 13.3
TI's use of penetration pricing for tapping the calculator market depended on the ability to predict cost reductions accruing from scale economies and experience effects.

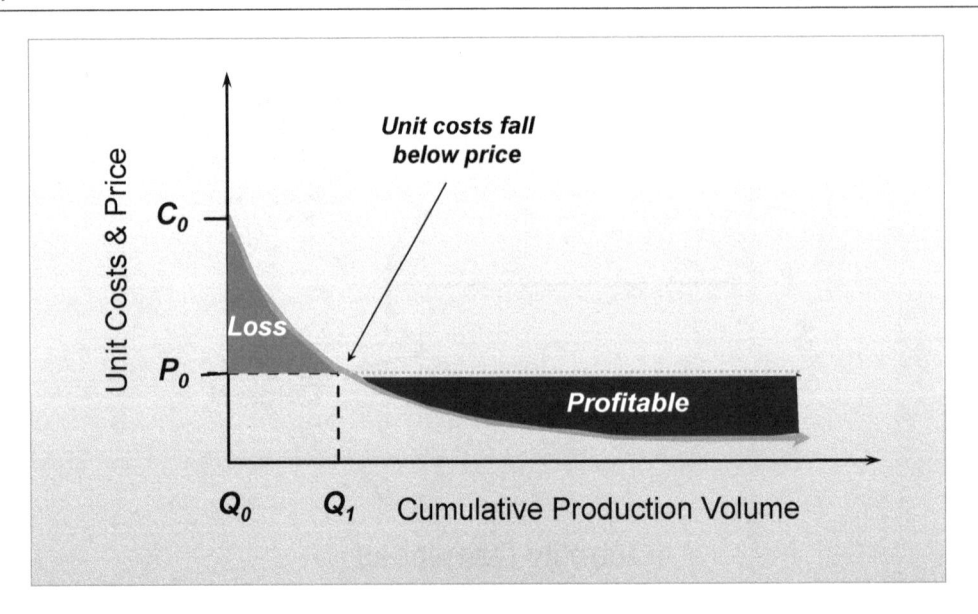

EXHIBIT 13.4
Relationship between costs, revenues, and the break-even point.

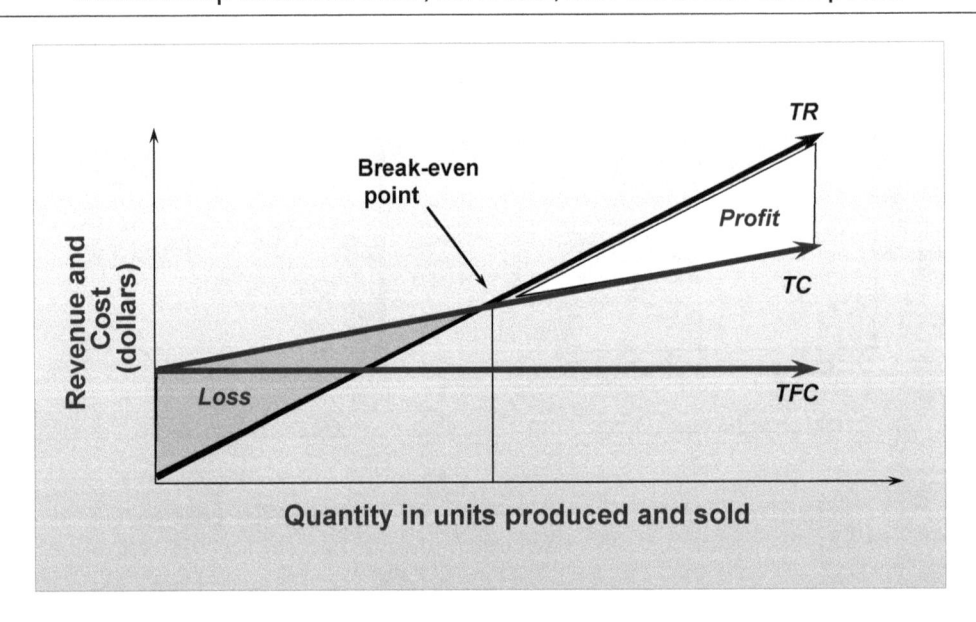

EXHIBIT 13.5
Weighted average prices and costs are used to compute a weighted average unit contribution.

Product	Ratio	Price	Weighted Price	AVC	Weighted AVC	Unit Contribution	Weighted Average Contribution
	(1)	(2)	(1)x(2)	(3)	(1)x(3)	(2) - (3)	[(2)-(3)]x(1)
1	30%	$1.30	$0.39	$0.50	$0.15	$0.80	$0.24
2	40%	$1.50	$0.60	$0.65	$0.26	$0.85	$0.34
3	30%	$1.70	$0.51	$0.80	$0.24	$0.90	$0.27
Sum	100%		$1.50	-	$0.65	=	$0.85

MODULE 14

Managing Marketing Communication

Module 14.0

Requirements for Successful Communication

"How then will they call on him in whom they have not believed?" Beliefs, yes, they are perceptually- and attitudinally-driven.

"How are they to believe in him of whom they have never heard?" Metaphorically-speaking, the "he" in question was human man, a new idea, and an innovative product and brand. And the requisite beliefs referenced in this paragraph's first sentence could not possibly arise unless believers first become aware that the brand exists, learn about the brand's intended position, and eventually come to understand and believe in the brand's unique values.

"Yet how are they to hear about him without someone preaching the good news?" "He," again, is the brand and ideas associated with the brand that create and drive brand's unique value. Meanwhile, preaching, evangelizing, or teaching any idea requires that communicators disseminate and broadcast the values associated with the idea, and usually doing so in a customized fashion targeted toward specific types of message recipients.

"As it is written, how beautiful are the feet of those who preach the good news!" These beautiful feet, why yes, they belong to marketers generally and to marketing communicators specifically.

Or so wrote the Apostle *Paul* in four quoted passages from the *New Testament* book called *Romans*, as he was held and writing inside a *Roman* prison.

The preceding text underscores the degree to which marketing organizations or individual marketers who create and communicate about truly great, new, and useful ideas of the sort that lead to innovative products or services—and the solutions generated by those innovation products and services—should end up blessed and profitable as they execute their promotional efforts. Such positive outcomes are especially likely to arise when marketers believe strongly in the value of the brand they are marketing. The beliefs of individual marketers will be made manifest and whole based on the subsequent trust that they earn and eventually receive from prospective/actual customers.

But the question of whether any of these desirable outcomes actually happens at all at some point will pivot in part based effective on marketing communications. Someone, some marketer acting as a messenger, must spread the word in ways designed from the start to initially attract and thereafter sustain attention from the "right sort of people." Marketers, of course, call these people targeted segments.

Marketing communications are also known as marketing promotions. Promotions are one of the traditional 4Ps or more recently coined 7Ps. Or the marketing mixes for products or for services, respectively. Promotional activities represent and function as another weapon marketers can extract from their value-creation arsenal in order to create and leverage sustainably differentiated value.

Promotions have often proven to be a most effective tool in any marketing organization's marketing mix toolbox. If you don't believe us just ask *GEICO Insurance, Progressive Insurance*, or *Southwest Airlines*.

PROMOTIONAL POINTS TO PONDER AND MASTER

Tricks of the Trade

Communicating marketers should account for and accommodate the fact that the ease with which humans recall messages and information is largely shaped by the impact that messages and their information make as each enters human minds.

Evolution has wired human brains to allocate more attention to threatening stimuli or to stimuli that merely appear threatening. In the past a much higher proportion of humanity genuinely had to worry genuine threats such as snakebites or tiger claws. Today, more people merely imagine how terrible it would be to wear the wrong brand of clothing or to not choose the proper deodorant. While the nature and gravity of these threats confronting humanity have changed, our human responses to those threats fundamentally have not.

For example, what else other than try to scare potential and actual voters do most political stories do? But why? First, to incentivize potential voters enough to convert them into likely voters—this threat emanating from the other side be stopped! Second, to motivate message recipients to vote for the political product that the marketing communicator deems best-suited to eliminate or alleviate the threat.

Negative information is more contagious and stickier than positive information. Contagious, here, means that the information, once received, will more likely be spread by initial recipients to others. Stickier, unsurprisingly, implies received information will more likely stick around, be remembered, inside the individual or collective minds of consumers or segments that receive it.

Information that is negative, scary, aggravating, or simply new spreads more quickly than information that features none of these characteristics. Information that spreads more quickly is also more contagious. Contagious information, in turn, is stickier and more difficult to dislodge once it takes hold. Three of these four information types—negative, scary, or aggravating—are notably negative. The sort of information that creates mild to extreme levels of tension inside consumers' minds and/or bodies. New information could be positive or negative. But since human brains instinctively push back against change, intrinsic human tendencies to view the new as bad also exist.

Good news doesn't fit readily into such narratives. Consequently, journalistic or reporter marketers usually don't report much of it. And if they did, many intended receivers probably would not attend to or even believe the good news today. Yes, this is why CNN or other media outlets rarely have anything good-newsy to say. This is also why media often manufacture and then market crises.

574 Section III Managing Key Marketing Activities

Crises drive ears and eyeballs toward the media's targeted stories as the human holders of those ears or eyeballs seek more information to understand more about or be titillated by the story. Which is exactly why *CNN* or *MSNBA*, being nothing more or less than marketers, strategically sought to secure and sustain consumer attention by leveraging *Trump Derangement Syndrome* during his presidency. *TDS* existed as both uncontrollable environmental factor and consumer stimuli. Or why *Fox News* ominously proclaims *FoxNewsAlerts* as crisis-warnings! complete with sound effects, even when the manufactured crises entailed nothing more substantive than the latest banal utterance offered by *Stormy Daniels' Creepy Porn Lawyer*—a clever brand name but not clever enough to keep him out of prison.

Traditional marketers of goods and services are not all that different. The makers and marketers of electronic devices, jeans, automobiles, pharmaceuticals, automotive insurance, legal services, or beefy burgers all also trade in and succeed based on ability to create or point toward real or imagined customer problems and to offer their presumable solutions to those problems. Naturally, those solutions arrive in the form of those marketers' well-branded products or services.

But *Big Media*[1] itself is one of the few professional marketing sectors that always does better itself when its customers are not doing well themselves. (Two other professional marketers' sectors—the vast medical industrial complex and its supply chain partner health-care insurance—also uniformly do better when their customers [patients or clients] are doing worse.) The phrase "does better itself" means that *Big Media* makes more money by emphasizing the negative and real or imagined things or events to fear as *Big Media's* spokespeople and writers develop and deliver their messages. Please note that their messages are the *Big Media's* products. The creation of more fear, stress, agitation, and anger draws more readers, viewers, and listeners to the media source, and the presence of more readers, viewers, and listeners draws more advertisers and advertising dollars to the media source.

Another major and possibly irresolvable problem with the contemporary news media is that its brands have to sell consumers supposedly-new news twenty-four hours a day. Meanwhile, the media only has about thirty minutes of genuinely-new news to report during most days. So, personalities, pretty or handsome faces, and biased opinions come into play, big-time, to the detriment of the entire purportedly journalistic—as in actual news-reporting—process.

Making Messages More Persuasive

When developing their brand's stories (each brand should have one), marketing communicators should be informed and directed by four keys to communication persuasiveness. The presence of these four keys will enhance the prospects that marketer's storytelling efforts will succeed. Relatedly, if one of more these keys is missing, the absence materially degrades the prospects that marketers' communications efforts will succeed.

The first key to communicating persuasively is comprehension. To persuade, branding messages must instantly communicate key points in understandable fashions to targeted receivers. If receivers

---

1. A representative sample of *Big Media* brands could include *CBS, The New York Times, Fox News* or *CNN, Twitter,* or *The Wall Street Journal.*

understand the message, marketers win. If recipients don't understand the message, marketers lose. To improve the prospects for comprehension, marketers must understand their target markets. Every generation has its own language and culture. Each new generation wants the contemporary language to submit entirely to its awesomeness.

The second key is connection. To persuade, branding messages must resonate favorably and trigger desired emotional or intellectual responses from targeted recipients. This notion that stories ideally should resonate favorably does not necessarily infer that receivers must always like or agree with the message, although these communication outcomes are usually useful. Instead, resonating favorably suggests that recipients, again ideally, pay attention to the branding message and can recall its basic its content. These two outcomes alone would represent a huge communication win for most marketers who have no choice but to brand-message inside a media market that is as noisy[2] as the current one.

The third key is credibility. To persuade, targeted segments must believe and trust what the marketing stories or messengers say. Otherwise, recipients won't buy—which often might include accept what marketers are selling.

The fourth key to brand-messaging success is message contagiousness. To persuade to their full potential, initial message recipients must spread the messages to other people.

These four keys are called the 4Cs of Persuasion. The absence of one or more of these four keys does not mean that a "failure to communicate"—a phrase made famous by the movie *Cool Hand Luke*—is pre-ordained. But the absence of one or more of these keys surely elevates the prospect that the communicated branding story will fail.

Mastering Marketing Communication Processes

Before communication actually successfully occurs, intended marketing messages must be received and understood by intended message targets in the manner in which the originating or initiating marketing communicator intended. This principle applies universally. This principle also relates to message comprehension. Intended message targets are typically customers or prospective customers.

Messaging is depicted as a bilateral, two-way, process inside traditional communication models. Senders, here the communicating marketers, develop messages. Messages are conveyed through communications media (channels). In turn, on the opposite end of these communication processes, receivers respond to receipt of messages. Communications media or channels include but are not limited to television, social networking, face-to-face, voice phone-to-voice phone, or text-to-text messaging.

---

2. Noise has earned negative connotations inside marketing communication contexts. Inside today's media environment there is so much promotional clutter, and so many other distracting environmental stimuli, that consumers grow weary of and frustrated by the noise. The net effect is that many consumers either don't pay attention to and/or remember specific content inside marketing messages even when they do attend to messages. Everyone intimately knows about "noise," even if they didn't know about "noise," because such distractions proliferate throughout everybody's noise life.

Successful marketing communicators must package or encode messages, along with the central ideas of those messages, in ways that can be understood by targeted audiences.

Receivers decode messages. The decoding process occurs exactly at the instant messages are received. During decoding processes receivers interpret, perceive, or make sense of and assign meanings to and ultimately respond or do not respond favorably or unfavorably to the story.

Successful communication never occurs unless receivers understand, or decode, the message in the manner that was intended by senders as they encoded the key idea or ideas of the message.

Noise is one among many impediments that frequently preclude the successful completion of marketing communication processes. Noise, however, is perhaps the most pressing obstacle that marketing communicators must work around or eliminate in order to promote successfully in contemporary markets. Noise entails physical/psychological barriers, distractions, or sources of interference that degrade recipients' willingness or ability to successfully decode messages.

The noise levels confronted by message recipients today are louder than at any point in history. A corollary applies. The noise levels that marketers must manage and mitigate are higher today than at any point in history.

Communicating Quickly

Successful marketers understand that they must quickly explain their brands' promised values as they communicate with targeted prospects or customers. Otherwise, "failures to communicate" will likely arise. In brief, marketers should be clear, concise, compelling, and quick as they message about and promote their brands.

Thirty or so seconds once was the average attention span of American consumers. Today, this information is way-dated. How long is the average consumers' attention span today? Three to five seconds? Less? The difference between attention spans "then and now" is like comparing the life cycles of fruit flies and Methuselah.

Almost everything that can be thought can be thought more clearly, concisely, and quickly. Almost everything that can be said can be said more clearly, concisely, quickly. Almost everything that can be written can be written more clearly, concisely, quickly. It's a shame when otherwise appealing and persuasive marketing stories are ruined not so much by bad endings but by endings that take too long to arrive.

What's missing in the previous paragraph? That's right, "compelling" is missing. But when messengers message more clearly, concisely, and quickly their messages and communicators themselves usually become more compelling, essentially by default.

MAKING MESSAGES MATTER

Before developing their promotional strategies, marketers should acknowledge that if they have nothing meaningful, material, and/or determinant to tell customers, it won't matter whether they have seemingly endless venues through which to transmit a message. Think about the internet and the tens of thousands of electronic media outlets through which marketers could convey promotional information. Now you understand what "seemingly endless" venues—or communication media or channels—means.

Messages matter. But few marketing stories will matter enough that firms can win minds and wallets by being all-pitch-and-no-product. Inside *Texas* cultural lore, "all-pitch-and-no-product" would be equivalent to being derisively branded as "all-hat; no-cattle"—or "all-talk; no action." Regardless of how clever their messaging may be, successful marketers also have to bring the value.

All clever promotion and little delivery of actual value is destined to fail, long-term. The other three or six elements that comprise any firm's product- or service-related marketing mix matter too. Particularly given that the good or bad things happening with respect to marketers' product development, distribution, pricing, and branding/positioning strategies would typically elevate or degrade the theme and content of their messages.

Incentivizing through Incentives

Successful marketing messengers understand, appreciate, and leverage the fact that B2B and B2C customers always respond to incentives. When doing/buying something becomes more costly or beneficial than doing/buying something else, which something will businesspeople and consumers decide to do/buy—if they are rational? This is why marketing promotions often deliver or promise existing incentives, create new incentives, and continuously emphasize value-enhancing incentives—generally in the form of solutions that the messages promise the brand will deliver.

Incentives may be defined as anything that moves decision-makers to act. The incentivizing-anything in question could involve money, savings, the promise of a new value, the opportunity to win something or visit somewhere, and so forth. Incentives typically work best in the short-term.

Showing . . . and Telling

Steve Jobs said, "It is not customers' job to know what they should want." One implication is that it is marketers' job to show, tell or inform, persuade, and ultimately remind customers what they should want. A second implication is that successful marketers usually understand that if they do not communicate key values to customers, customers are unlikely to appreciate or often even be aware those values exist.

What should customers want? Ideally, from the perspective of messaging marketers, customers should want what marketers tell them what they should want. At least inside an electronically virtual world created entirely by marketeering.

Is the sentence conveyed immediately above tongue-in-cheek? Hardly. The sentence and its message are each serious. When marketers are confident in the value and ethicality of what they're doing, saying, and selling, marketers absolutely should tell consumers what they should want. After all, the telling will help customers solve their problems. What could be more righteous, ethical, and logical than that?

KEY COMMUNICATION GOALS (OUTCOMES SOUGHT)

All promotional stories should effectively deliver one or more of the following five communication outcomes.

In no particular order, promotional messages should remind customers about brands they should love now, or again.

Or, promotional messages should inform customers about brands they should love, or at minimum consider, right now.

Relatedly, marketing messages should seek to persuade, to influence customers to love the brand being promoted and positioned in and through the marketing message. Attempts at persuasion should always follow the delivery of information, although persuading marketers may discover that their interests are better served by allowing the information to slowly seep into customers' minds for a while.

Marketing stories should likewise incentivize and thereby motivate targeted recipients to love promoted brands now, or again.

Finally, especially over the longer run, marketing messages should encourage customers to love more or draw closer in the relationship they already enjoy or could enjoy with brands being promoted. Greater customer intimacy, as a core competency, is always worth pursuing, again.

All marketing messages are promotional messages.

Emphasizing the Right (as in "Determinant") Values

When communicating with prospective or actual customers marketers should emphasize the aspects of their brands that are most valuable to the most customers. While reading the phrase "most valuable," think about what factors or solutions would prove "most important" to most targeted customers as they are making decisions about which brand to choose. When possible, as they message marketers also should emphasize aspects/dimensions of their brands that are different from and better than the brands offered by competitors.

The preceding paragraph describes the basic nature of both differentiation and the type of differentiation that could be designated as "determinant." The key word here is "determinant."

Framing Marketing Stories and Promises Powerfully: Negative Frames

How human beings shape—or "frame," inside their minds—the probability that certain positive or negative outcomes will actually happen matters greatly. For example, the way in which people phrase—or frame—their New Year's resolutions materially increases or decreases the likelihood that those individuals will honor these promises to themselves. Re-phrasing New Year's resolutions as "I will start to" do something as opposed to "I will avoid" doing something increases our chances of keeping the resolutions. In brief, framing, or phrasing, our resolutions in a positive rather than a negative manner elevates the likelihood that we will succeed.

However, when marketers are seeking to increase their message's persuasiveness the exact opposite framing approach works better. (Note that the flip was just flipped.) The most persuasive marketing stories are those that frame choices inside the context of potential losses rather than potential gains. Potential losses, that is, if decision-makers fail to make the right decision. What is the right decision for choosers to make? The one that marketers recommend, naturally.

What's described above is a negative frame. Negative, as opposed to positive. Negative framing processes entail presenting choices as situations in which something will be lost by decision-makers (customers) as opposed to something will be gained by those same decision-makers (customers) if they fail to make the right choice. The something to be gained or lost might include money, prestige, a more attractive appearance, or a good time. Clearly, this list of lost or gained things could grow dependent on messaging marketers' creative bend.

This discussion coalesces with the naturally arising human fear of losing something of value or about taking risks inside situations when the prospect of loss looms. Prospect theory is thus reintroduced as an explanatory factor. The underlying premise driving prospect theory is that consumers, along with everyone else, usually hate losing more than they love winning. This is why targeted consumers who have just been messaged will generally go to great lengths to avoid the pain or anguish of a loss.

Marketing messages, or stories, that use negative framing generally attempt to create feelings of stress/anxiety, fear, or anger. Fear, anger, and their cousin anxiety are each highly motivating. The primary reason why messages about terrorists and terrorism are so influential and powerful is not due to the damage that terrorists actually render but the fear that terrorists create.

Anxiety is preceded or followed by a single question that appears inside deciders' brains. The question is "what if?" Knowing this, marketers can and do lead customers off into directions that lean toward negative frames, particularly when messaging marketers insert genuine or merely perceived answers to "what if?" questions inside their branding stories. Feelings of stress, fear, or anger, in turn, can be manipulated in ways that incentivize (motivate) decision-makers to make choices consistent with the responses that persuasive marketers seek from customers.

Framing Marketing Stories and Promises Powerfully: Fear Works Too

As readers presumably have long since surmised, fear can function as a mechanism and as a tool through which all sorts of marketers can impose their influence on targeted others. Fear is the most powerful human emotion, presumably because fear is so primal, so basic, and let's admit, experienced in one form/time or another by everyone. The presence of fear often makes those who are afraid begin to feel anxious and/or irrational and consequently more susceptible to marketers' promotional efforts. Either fear-induced sensation (induced anxiety or irrationality), or any combination of the two, therefore plays right into marketers' hands. Sophisticated marketers are even able to sell based on the subtle or not so subtle fear that customers experience if they don't own and use their particular brands.

Fear is how most marketing politicians attempt to control and to motivate their base. This makes consumers miserable and occasionally probably induces post-traumatic-stress syndrome, better known by the branding acronym *PTST*. Fear is never free; feeling afraid imposes negative emotional, physical, and psychological side effects. Fear of the other—the liberal fearing the conservative, or vice versa—foments divisions too. Thus, the arrival of fear creates unnatural market segments who are unified only by their mutual fear(s). Just look around and see what is happening right now inside the US and its cultures. Divisions now abound and continue to widen, all due to marketing!

Managing Word-of-Mouth

Successful marketing communicators similarly understand that word-of-mouth (WOM) processes give legs to marketing stories. This is due to WOM's potentially contagious effects. How do these contagion processes work? Let's assume that a group of consumers were exposed to and then actually focused on a message. Some group members loved the message; others hated it. These lovers and haters subsequently talked up the story on *Facebook* or through texts, tweets, breakroom conversations, and the like. And through this process they influenced the thinking of additional actual or prospective customers—which is more likely than one might expect because WOM influencers are generally known, liked, and trusted recipients of their WOM messages. A second level of "other people" is thus produced who in turn might influence still additional others at a third level by leveraging the viral potential of e-communcation. That's how contagion works.

Notably, the first set of other people who receive the message have no dog in the fight. Meaning, they generally don't gain or lose anything as they pass along stories to others. Instead, they say what they say because they believe what they say. These unpaid and unbiased endorsers must be telling the truth, or so goes the logical reasoning of message recipients. The folks spreading WOM are, on average, perceived by message recipients as far more believable, trustworthy, likable, and persuasive than marketers themselves.

Meanwhile, what makes messages themselves contagious? The answer is simple. The typical reason why anyone who receives a message turns around and conveys—pushes—the communication forward to someone else is either because they believe the message speaks to or resonates with them, or speaks about them. These are the core reasons why consumers sometimes want to share messages with others, typically through WOM process. This same essence also drives, as in motivates, viral marketing.

People, in effect, evangelize for or against brands. These people function as well-known, well-respected and trusted human faces of those brands. Evangelical is another ancient Greek word. The E-word was used in the distant past to describe anyone who spread good news.

Bad news, however, fit more easily into the modern marketing narrative. Evangelicals, using the modern marketing parlance, are individuals or organizations who spread WOM or e-WOM. Unfortunately for marketers, bad news, the sort that delivers not just negative but often vicious information, is far more likely conveyed to and spread among others.

Public shaming of anyone or anything used to occur in the public square. By the 1800s shaming had migrated to the newspaper. During the 1990s and early 2000s—not so long ago—the primary forum was television.

These brands—in human-, product- or service-form—are more likely to be praised or scorned online. Such brands, of course, are more likely to be criticized than complemented. The internet is a product and a communication medium that gifts anonymity to users. The internet also features a general absence of gatekeepers. Finally, the internet is characterized by a remarkable ability to magnify the power and reach of real or imagined complaints and grievances.

Even worse, the now-seemingly-so-last-year blog, which had previously primarily functioned as a venue for self-reflection and self-expression, has long since mostly yielded to much briefer social media posts. By contrast tweets and texts favor and tend to facilitate vicious and impulsive attacks and piling on; otherwise known as negative viral effects.

Why Bad, Negative, Even Nasty Messages Are So Powerful

There are at least five reasons why bad rather than good news usually dominates. For starters, bad news is more likely than good news to attract attention from others (who may themselves feel threatened). And not surprisingly, many evangelical types are themselves dedicated attention-seekers. This trait does not make WOM mavens good or bad people; it makes them more or less likely to evangelize. Likely because attention they garner often operates like powerful drugs—to them.

Second, bad news usually arrives more suddenly while good news generally emerges more slowly, again making bad news more exciting and/or interesting.

Third, as noted, human beings are wired genetically and through their personal experience to more easily envision situations where things might quickly get worse than get better.

Fourth, bad news usually matters more to humanity; yes, good news actually matters less! The reason why can be expressed simply. In the past bad news—that plague, a drought creating a famine, a snake or lion on a trail—truly was more likely to kill people. So naturally modern, more highly evolved humans also react viscerally to bad news. The human predisposition to react in this manner is deeply embedded inside the genetic codes of human consumers.

Fifth, consumers usually think in relative, not absolute terms. As the world improves consumers have unsurprisingly expanded their definitions of what constitutes bad news. What matters most, most of the time, in contemporary settings is not how well you are doing, but rather how well you feel you doing in comparison to other consumers sharing your social circle. That's because these sorts of comparative advantages are what determines success in the ongoing struggle for additional resources, status, and attention.

Positive WOM is hugely beneficial to the brands or marketing firms that are being endorsed. The primary reason is because customers who receive WOM or e-WOM messages know, and generally trust and like the message-sender.

Negative WOM about brands or their marketing organizations is hugely detrimental to marketers. This is primarily because recipients of WOM or e-WOM stories know, and generally trust and like the message-sender.

Yes, the same explanation was just given twice.

WOM, e-WOM, or Gossip: Do Material Differences Exist?

The answer to the question embedded inside the header is no. No material differences distinguish the three concepts—WOM, e-WOM, and/or gossip—save the mode, or the communication channel, through which a message is transmitted.

E-WOM is traditional word-of-mouth transmitted potentially across the globe in viral fashions through electronic and typically socially-networked means. When used in marketing communication contexts the term viral implies that an original marketing message has the potential to spread rapidly (i.e., similar to how contagious viruses have the potential to spread quickly). This is another reason why WOM was previously described either as marketers' best friend or worst foe.

Likely to no one's surprise, negative WOM or e-WOM arises more frequently and diffuses more easily.[3] These diffusion processes often unfold unchecked through ways and means that damage the reputations of marketers and their brands. As negative information diffuses throughout consumers' social systems and social networks it rolls out and expands more like fog than fire. Diffused negative information is harder to discern and easier to dismiss. But like fire, negative information, once diffused, is incredibly powerful.

People love to dish; humans long for gossip, each trait makes negative stories more appealing, to write the least. Gossip allures. Gossip is difficult to resist. Gossip is like receiving stolen goods. Gossip puts one in immediate collusion with the one conveying the gossip. Gossip is fascinating speculation, it is unedited information.

Gossip, described, entails two or more people telling things about a third person or entity like a brand that the third party would prefer not be known or said. Gossip is probably the human activity most responsible for the comparatively fast evolution of human speech. Rather than discussing important matters such as wheels or transporting fire, two, three occupants of one cave likely sat around the fire at night talking about who was getting or not getting with whom two cave holes down.

For better or worse, marketers should accept that WOM or e-WOM is often the most powerful communication vehicle they have at their disposal. Largely because individuals who convey WOM are free from an original sin from which marketers themselves can never receive full absolution or forgiveness. Unfortunately for them, marketers cannot help but commit this sin, as discussed earlier. Furthermore, consumers who engage in word-of-mouth clearly do so while operating as opinion leaders.

By contrast, friends, family, or coworkers who offer positive or negative WOM advice—often in the form of gossip—about brands to us typically say what they say because they really believe their message, as noted. They do not do so because they have financial stakes in saying what they say. In this communication scenario, who will customers trust?

Yes, the factor that makes the successful management of these naturally-arising processes so important today is that all sorts of supercharged internet-enabled media exist through which positive or negative e-WOM can be spread virally to others in ways that prove highly sticky.

---

3. Diffusion is a natural process whereby molecules, atoms, and bad or good news moves from regions of higher concentration to areas of lower concentration. In its original *Latin* form diffusion meant "to spread way out fast"—not a joke or misprint.

WHAT DISTINGUISHES CELEBRITIES, INFLUENCERS, AND INTERNET INFLUENCERS?

Internet influencers are people who have built social media-based reputations for their knowledge and expertise on specific topics—or products. They make regular posts about that topic on their preferred social media channels and generate large followings of enthusiastic, engaged people who pay close attention to their views.

Similar to the words troll or blockchain, the term "influencer" is a word whose ubiquity has rendered it nearly meaningless. The designation as internet influencer can be simultaneously wielded as an insult or an aspiration. The practice has proven a scourge for many small business owners and may represent the future of marketing. Influencer is even a term that's used to describe middle-schoolers with middling sized followings and mega-celebrities alike. The *Catholic Pope* recently described the Virgin Mary as "an influencer." The label has been affixed to computer-generated teenaged DJs. Some elected officials are influencers, as are many annoyingly well-dressed pets. The latter group is widely perceived as more likable and trustworthy than the former cohort.

So, what are influencers? Ostensibly, an influencer is anyone who exercises influence. But this description doesn't fully align with the word's current marketing usage. Influencer culture is inextricably tied to consumerism and the rise of technology. Internet influencer, in turn, is shorthand for someone who possesses the power to affect consumers' buying habits by uploading some form of original—often sponsored—content to social media platforms like *Instagram, YouTube, Snapchat*, or *LinkedIn*. Be it moody photos, cheeky video reviews, meandering blogs, or blurry soon-to-disappear stories, the value of the direct or indirect endorsement in question follows directly from the perceived authority and authenticity of the messenger.

Not all popular social media users are influencers—some are simply online celebrities, entertainers, comedians, or cute animals—nor are all celebrities influencers. *Evan Rachel Wood*, for example, has an *Instagram* following. But she is not currently an internet influencer. On the other side of the spectrum are remarkable marketing figures like *Kim Kardashian*. She launched her internet position as prototypical celebrity for reasons that dare not speak their name here. But thereafter she quickly made a strategic transition to mega-successful influencer-hood.

That their perceived expertise and authenticity contribute most prominently to influencer power is ironic because the term internet influencer is increasingly synonymous with the more manipulative side of marketing. What once seemed corrupting and disqualifying is now often more the norm, and given the dismal state of truth online, it's unlikely the lines will ever be clarified

The history of influencer hood parallels the history of the modern web. The 1991 introduction of the new product now known as the *World Wide Web* ushered in a new era of unfettered marketer-customer connectivity and interactivity. Users around the world suddenly secured the means to build and maintain communication-based relationships with people they had never met in person. The world instantly shrunk. And the shrinkage made it remarkably easier for consumers and other decision-makers to access information and media content that was produced by non-mainstream sources.

The early web forums and bulletin board sites of the 1990s and early 2000s allowed people to publicly post and reply to messages from other users, paving the way for the development of niche virtual communities and some of the first instances of digital influence as we understand the term today. Some users who frequented these forums—which were usually organized around a hyper-specific topic or interest—would become proto-influencers themselves after earning reputations as authentic sources of WOM recommendations and valuable expertise among their posting peers. Hiking enthusiasts who visited the online forums of *Backpacker* magazine and *GORP.com* in the late 1990s found themselves engaged by the boards' camaraderie and the depth of users' expertise on subjects like gear to food to trail locations.

As consumers from all sorts of segments linked into virtual communities, marketers and brands began to understand their potential to shape public understanding. Consumers who interact with other product users inside forums or on internet message boards become radically more interested in the tangible or intangible product than those who read online promotions about the product that was issued by marketers themselves. Unlike traditional media advertisements or promotional copy embedded on marketer websites, posts from internet strangers are often relatable, funny, highly emotive (moving) and yes, influential. Since then, nothing has fundamentally changed other than the vast expansion of the numbers of consumers who routinely and increasingly exclusively engage with marketing promotional materials inside socially networked communication settings.

HOW DOES E-VIRAL HAPPEN?

When Twitter introduced a retweet button in 2009, one click could suddenly send a post careening throughout any social network. Both *Twitter* and *Facebook* rely on the human propensity to want to share—especially when information that titillates, amuses, scares, or makes others angry, jealous, or covetous is being shared. *Twitter* and *Facebook* each use complex algorithms to organize and rank the content that their consumers actually see. Both marketing sites base these rankings in part on how many others are in the original visitors' social networks and in part on how many others who are similar to the original visitors "liked," shared, or otherwise interacted with the initial post. The more people "like" the posts the further the messages travel.

An equation from epidemiology can be used to explain the reproduction rate of tweets, posts, and other internet-enabled and social networked messages. That's largely because science of epidemiology studies how germs and viruses spread from their original hosts to others, who in turn further spread the original viruses or germs, and so forth. In the equation $R = Bz$, "B" measures how many people were initially exposed to a message; z assesses how likely recipients are to share messages. The metric essentially measures how viral the original post is.

Leading the Opinions of Others

Opinion leadership, as both a concept and a reality, derives much of its power from the fact that consumers often want to change but also want to wait to change until others have changed. Many consumers are waiting for someone to lead them, so to speak. Think about this tendency and trend—does this description apply to you?

Perhaps this tendency explains why many supposedly non-conforming consumers end up all looking pretty much the same (i.e., conforming to a norm). Take the hipster, or is it the *Goth*, look. Dudes representing while attired in ski caps, little beards, and loose flannel-oriented clothes. Often the same folks who most studiously seek to set themselves apart by seeming different end up looking like other ironically "conformist" followers who end up supposedly setting themselves apart by all looking exactly the same!

The same sort of thing is seemingly happening with the once cutting edge but now standard notion of getting tatts to stand out. True story: Late fifty-something friend of an author recently began dating a late forty-something-year-old woman and told the author that she had no tatts, anywhere. What a non-comforming freak that woman must be? Funny how consumers want to follow the in-thing, but only after some other group of opinion leaders or an individual opinion leader stands up to lead them where they already want to go. Such is the power, inside consumer decision-making settings, of social influences.

Opinion leadership processes, which by their core nature are WOM-driven, mostly play out online these days. Throughout most of 2019, various members of the *World Cup*-winning *U.S. Women's Soccer Team*, emerged as big-time and highly-paid *Instagram* influencers. Consumers should always be carefully, however, to avoid blindly following leaders. These players, similar to all *Instagram* influencers, are paid to say what they say to as many people as possible. This is why the then-current world champs were guilty of marketing's original sin.

Each level of the digital-media economy has been configured to produce inherently sharable stories in the form of posts. The professionals who create advertising message logically understand from the jump that they must generate high B. Nearly all twenty-first-century social media marketers are optimized to generate viral content. On the consumer side, popular social media users gain and hang onto followers because they are sensitive to the mysterious element of B.

Over time this emphasis on share-ability has created huge changes in what everyone, not just social media users, experiences on their screens. Television news producers strive to create viral segments. Even benchwarmer *NBA* players, who spend game-time picking splinters from their basketball shorts, have learned how to scheme out sharable celebrations and generate tens of thousands of followers themselves. *Fortune 500* marketers spend millions on advertising that is purposefully weird enough to spur viral messaging. *Arby*'s (the place where they've "got the meat" for sandwiches) VP of Communications gifted a bag of sandwiches and a puppy—now that's an incentive—to the creator of the spoof *Twitter* account @nihilist_arbys. The reason? This account was high-B. Then the popular print and online publication *Business Week* did a story about the story. The BW story proved shareable too, generating more than a million additional page views.

But what happens when content that is most viral-like is not the best message? Experts have found that anger tops the list of shareable emotions inside the social media domain. Rage (i.e., extreme anger) spreads faster than joy, sadness, or disgust. Small ball stories, many that absolutely should not register as important or determinant, can dominate *Twitter* for days. Stories, for example, about doctors being dragged screaming off passenger planes; dentists shooting friendly lions; or something that is putatively offense that (insert your vilified celebrity here) said. *Twitter*, as noted elsewhere, can destroy perspective.

Social media giants such as *Facebook, Instagram,* or *Twitter,* being absolutely strategic about how their services are increasingly being reviewed, perceived, and criticized, understand that the systems they have created are not working well. Not working well, at least if their intentions were to act ethically by doing no harm and create beneficial social outcomes. *Facebook,* for example recently acknowledged that its service can prove detrimental to the well-being of people who use it to excess. A former *Facebook* executive confessed feeling guilty because his firm had helped create processes that was ripping-apart social fabric that formerly had held the culture together. *Twitter* executives surely must be aware of the degree to which users revel in self-loathing due to their use of the service. Many *Silicon Valley* titans have gone so far as to build e-walls, impenetrable electric-blocks, between their children and the devices their moms and dads have created. Wonder why? Presumably because they love their children and don't want them emotionally or psychologically damaged by using the products that their firms are marketing.

Not all social media platforms are organized around share-ability. *Instagram* doesn't even allow links, except for a single one in each user's profile. This dampens instances of self-promotion or broadcasted hatred and slows the spread of information from the internet on the platform. Instagram does not feature native reposting functionality either. *Instagram* is, by all accounts, a nicer place to visit and hang around on, while online.

Or take *Snapchat,* another still dominant social network. The dominant modes of interaction on *Snapchat* have little to do with viral-ability. Consumers use the brand and its service solution to post messages or create posts that disappear. The private or semiprivate and ephemeral nature of most Snapchats reduces share-ability. Yet the youngest social media users have migrated to it. Less share-ability, creating lower viral-ability; is this a harbinger of marketers' promotional future? Check out the next edition, and we'll tell you what happened. Because right now, we do not know ourselves. What was that chat about change and dynamic marketplaces?

Viral Marketing and e-WOM: They Had to Begin Somewhere

Breakout episodes of viral marketing—emerging as either accidental or intended forms—have been a thing for longer than most people likely realize. People old enough to have had an email account during 1997 probably remember those "dark and scary" pre-*Facebook*, pre-*Twitter,* and pre-*Instagram* days; a time, for example, when lots of people still read books, spoke face-to-face or directly on the phone with each other. Heck, those were even pre-*Google* days. Back then the only way to send odd or entertaining or infuriating messages to your friends or foes was to convey it as an email attachment. If you are this older person there's a reasonable chance that someone emailed you a video called "*badday.mpg*" as an attachment. Back during these more innocent internet times you likely comfortably opened the message too.

The video was twenty-six seconds long. The images suggested the file contained security camera videotape from an office filled with cubicles. A thick man boasting a mustache sat typing on his desktop computer inside the cubicle close to the camera. He suddenly and violently slaps the side of his computer with his hand. A woman in the adjoining cubicle peeks over the divider to see what's happening, then sits back down. Seconds later the man begins repeatedly pounding on his keyboard with his fists. He then gets up, grabs his keyboard like a baseball bat, and swings it at the monitor, knocking it off the desk and onto the floor outside the cube. Then, as his neighbor peeks up again, the man walks over to the monitor and begins kicking. That's the whole show.

This was all rather tame by today's standards. And small, megabyte-wise, by today's standards. Only five bytes. But back in 1997, five megabytes was a lot. The file could take more than twenty minutes to download on dial-up computer modems that prevailed then; this being a pre-cloud era. But when people received the video as an email attachment from their friends or coworkers most took the time to download it. Then, post-view, they were so entertained that they sent the file to other friends or family, who sent *Badday.mpg* to other friends or family members, in one of the original viral internet moments.

"*Badday*" was one of the first videos to spread virally across literally the entire world. Viewers must have wondered who the man was, where and when the footage was shot, and perhaps whether the video was real. But no one questioned why the man was so outraged. Who hasn't wanted to destroy their computer every now and then? Especially their work device. Our man actually went exactly where so many of us have wanted to go during their worktimes. The world could relate because the message resonated. The message probably delivered a sense of catharsis to many if not most recipients. And perhaps most importantly the video was funny.

Fans of the video ended up building websites dedicated to it; others studied the piece frame by frame seeking to draw out implications and flaws. Some characteristics that were suspect—fishy—about the video came to light. One thing that came to light—the computer the man hit, batted, and kicked was not wired into the wall. Wireless did not exist during this late stage wired age. Another issue, the hero or villain, dealers' choice, appeared to look right at the security camera located right behind him and smile. Would this have happened had the presumed technology-hater actually been outraged? Hmm.

Untold numbers of people had questions, nobody had answers, for about one year. In 1998, someone emailed the attached video to a friend who worked at *Loronix Information Systems*, a firm that was based in *Durango, Colorado. Loronix* had answers, because the firm had created the video.

At the time *Loronix* manufactured and marketed video surveillance systems and their software brains. When developing promotional materials during 1996, the marketer produced a few short videos demonstrating the detection benefits and solutions that the surveillance systems could deliver. Rather than hiring professional actors, the firm used its own employees to produce, shoot, and act in the video. The video was never intended for public consumption. The video was instead placed on a promotional CD that *Loronix* gave out at various trade conventions. Some potential or actual customer must have viewed the CD, liked this particular portion, pulled the video chunk off the CD, shared it electronically with a friend, and the rest is accidental, but genuine, viral marketing history. *Badday.mpg* can still be viewed on *Facebook, Twitter,* or *Google*, probably because so many people can relate to the message.

MODULE 14.1

The Last "P"

DESIRABLE COMMUNICATION (PROMOTIONAL) OUTCOMES

Promotion is a communication weapon that plays a prominent role and that often should be used aggressively inside marketers' value-creation arsenals. Marketers can manage promotional activities in ways designed to create many desirable communication outcomes.

These communication outcomes include generating greater awareness of the brand among targeted segments. Awareness might entail knowing that new brands exist or old brands continue to exist; that brands' determinant differences exist; or that other people, including non-customers, ascribe socially-prestigious values to particular brands. That one or more of these or similar communication outcomes be accomplished is crucial to marketing success. Unless they are aware of brands and their potentially greater comparative values no one would buy them.

Another prized marketing communication outcome that may be generated through promotions entails delivering additional knowledge about new or existing brands, deals, or other incentivizing opportunities to customers. Especially when new product decisions are involved, consumers must receive, assemble, and evaluate substantial amounts of new knowledge before deciding to purchase the new product, service, or idea.

A third highly coveted marketing communication outcome entails developing greater liking and preference for the brands being promoted.

The fourth communication outcome is especially important. The reason why is because customers might want to purchase a well-branded (which generally means effectively-promoted) product, but make no effort to acquire the brands until after those customers have actually encountered the types of problems for which known-brands from known-product categories are known to solve. Bottom line: If a brand has been effectively promoted, customers will become aware that the brand exists (achieving the first communication outcome), fundamentally know or understand the key values promised by the brand (achieving the second communication outcome), and like and prefer the brand (achieving the third communication outcome).

Sometimes consumers desperately want to buy a specific branded product now. Just because ... The object of consumers' acute affection might entail an esteemed, essentially lusted-after, luxury (positional) shoe or handbag brand. The branded object may be a *Porsche* or *Mercedes* convertible that customers have coveted for years. Or a long-coveted spring-season month spent eating, drinking, and loving in *Tuscany*. But many consumers, being a combination of frugal, patient, and responsible, make no effort to actually acquire the branded accessory automotive, or vacation solution until after they can actually afford it. Afford the solution either financially-, time-, or life cycle stage-wise. Marketers, through their ongoing promotional efforts, may plant trees now that don't cast shade for twenty years. But even this represents a big strategic win.

Properly managed marketing promotions can create customers' desires or preferences for particular branded solutions long before the sort of problems that would demand that particular branded solution as a remedy arrive. Or, as inferred, properly managed promotions can create consumers' desires or preferences for particular brands years before consumers possess the financial or temporal means to purchase the brand option in question.

Marketers should view themselves as problem-solvers. All the time. Successful marketers also understand that they should insert—position—their brands as high up as possible inside consumers' evoked sets. That way, when the sort of "problem" arises that can best be solved by a product from a known product category, the well-promoted brand will "come-to-mind-first" because it is positioned at or near the top-of-the-decision-maker's-mind. Again, all the time. And finally, successful marketers should understand how to develop promotions designed to stimulate, inside message recipients' minds, a sense that those recipients are currently experiencing or one day could experience the exact sort of problem that this particular brand was created to solve. Always.

Marketers are relatively capable of creating customer wants, or bringing customer wants to the surface. Here, the word "surface" refers to the point in their minds where customers become aware or cognizant of a want—a sense that something is lacking in or absent from their lives. But marketers cannot create customer needs. Human needs instead exist independent of anything marketers could do to create them. Human needs arrive naturally and routinely inside people's lives, and do so absent any marketing intervention.

Other Desirable Communication Outcomes

Other desirable communication outcomes exist. These outcomes can also be created by properly managing marketing promotions. Communication outcomes, of course, that are desirable from that perspective of marketers. These desirable communication outcomes include:

- ▶ Reminders made to customers (remember how much you once loved our brand, dear customer, well, we're still here and you can love us again);
- ▶ Calls to action issued to customers (please remove your fanny off the couch and into our *Outdoor World* store, and get there this weekend!);

- The creation of greater brand equity, brand loyalty, and pricing power, each of which play out inside individual consumers' and targeted segments collective minds; and . . .
- The creation of perceptions, again arising within the collective mind of targeted market segments, that determinant sorts of differentiation exists for the brand being promoted.

ANOTHER MIX IS IN PLAY . . .

The promotional mix, as part of the marketing mix, primarily consists of four promotional elements through which marketers can and do communicate with targeted audiences, or segments. In no special order the four primary promotional mix elements are:

- Advertising. Advertising includes any form of one-way; paid, which means the sponsor is identified; impersonal communication aimed at targeted customers; that is delivered en masse through electronic, print, or INET-based communication media; in order to persuade, inform, remind, or build new/strengthen existing relationships with targeted B2B or B2C customers about the value/differences associated with given brands. (This same definition is used again below.)
- Personal Selling. Personal selling includes any sort of interaction(s) initiated by one or a small team of marketers who engage directly—face-to-face, by phone, or through any other internet-mediated connection—with individual or small groups of prospective or actual customers. The interactions are scheduled and executed with one direct or indirect purpose in mind. That purpose entails creating and/or strengthening seller-buyer relationships that ultimately result in the buying and selling of products. Professional sorts of personal selling are far more likely to arise inside B2B as opposed to B2C buyer-seller relationships.
- Public Relations. Public relations entail communication efforts aimed at satisfying the need to build or sustain good relationships with various targeted publics that individual marketers or marketing organizations deem critical to their current and future success. When public relations are being used the emphasis is likely on sustaining rather than building good relationships, because public relations efforts are more likely to be initiated when something bad, generally something bad enough to damage someone's or some firm's brand, has happened.
- Sales Promotions. Sales promotions entail marketing communications and messages that are structured to deliver short-term incentives aimed at encouraging near-term customer purchases of products or services.

Various sorts of marketing stories can be conveyed through each of the four promotional mix elements that are listed just above. Each promotional mix element can be executed—delivered, if you prefer—through internet-mediated communication channels. Naturally each of these four promotional elements can be executed—again, delivered—through traditional communication channels such as face-to-face exchanges and various advertising or promotional media. Each promotion mix element is characterized by its own unique set of relative advantages or disadvantages. These advantages and disadvantages are discussed below.

Advertising: Advantages/Disadvantages

Advertising is effective at informing or reminding customers. However, advertising messages are relatively poor at persuading customers or closing out sales. Yet advertising offers marketers great potential opportunities to reach large numbers of targeted consumers, across time, relatively inexpensively. That is, on an eyeball- or ear-reached basis. Other communication outcomes that advertising strategies regularly pursue and often achieve include both the development and the maintenance of powerful and naturally desirable brand positions. These determinant brand positions are often build-out slowly, over time, through advertising. But at times, a just-right-for-the-moment advertising message can create powerful brands seemingly overnight. How do you spell gecko?

This is one major advertising downside. These days, who is actually still paying attention? The typical answer is not many, and especially not at given points in time. This is one major reason why advertisements must be repeated over and over again. This fact, in turn, is why we get sick of advertising—and often ignore it.

Another significant downside associated with the use of advertising is that if receivers don't like or understand ad messages no short-term opportunities exist for quick do-overs. Unlike a round of golf among friends the advertising game features no mullets. Advertising, after all, entails one-way, impersonal communication. No opportunities for instantaneous give and take between marketers and customers are in play.

Personal Selling: Advantages/Disadvantages

Personal selling is not just good but great at informing and reminding prospects and customers. Yet its capacity for persuasion, for converting prospects into customers and moving on-the-fence customers into loyal camps, are the primary reasons why personal selling is repeatedly used as marketers' go-to promotional device—especially inside B2B supply chains.

Personal selling is more persuasive in part because the process entails one-on-one, one-on-small group, or small sales-team on small buying-team interactions. Intimate buyer-seller interactions generate opportunities for salespeople to ask questions to customers; to listen to their responses; and to then customize their stories about "should-be-valued" solutions in response. Opportunities to build, strengthen, and/or sustain customers' relationships abound. On the other hand, listening too little while speaking too much often converts salespeople's tongues into weapons of mass dysfunction and destructive disruption—destroying present and future prospects of growing or maintaining a relationship.

Personal selling features one downside. The disadvantage is comparatively minor in nature. Personal selling is extremely expensive, because only one or a small group of industrial customers inside B2B supply chain or any sort of B2C contexts can be targeted and sold to at a time. But the extra pay-off is generally well worth the extra costs. However, the upside of personal selling kicks this downside to the curb.

Nothing happens inside any organization until someone sells something. The fundamental importance of this fact cannot be overemphasized.

At some level inside any supply chain setting, salespeople and the selling function will prove crucial. Personal selling is indispensable. The selling function cannot be separated from long-term marketing success. After all, in marketing, business, or in life, nobody gets "paid" until someone sells something, either.

Public Relations: Advantages/Disadvantages

Public relations is effective at spreading good news, such as the introduction of great new products. *Popeye's*, a well-known purveyor of spicy chicken dishes, famously introduced a spicy chicken sandwich during 2019. The new product, new for *Popeye's*, was a huge hit from the start—apparently because it tasted really good. *Popeye's* adroit management of its public relations function also generated a huge amount of free publicity for the sandwich.

Reliable estimates are that the new product's brand earned the equivalent of 26 million dollars in unpaid advertising value on various *ESPN* channels alone. Every host on every show that appeared on the network's various television, radio, internet, or print channels during one August day either led with a discussion of the new chicken sandwich story or prominently featured the new product story during their broadcast.

Usually, however, public relations is used to pick up and restore the pieces after disaster has struck and things, brand-wise, are falling apart. Examples of such disasters follow.

The downside of public relations is that marketers cannot control what is being said because public relations stories are not paid for by marketers. The targeted market segment's responses to the message are not controllable either.

P&G boasts dozens of well-known personal care brands. *Secret* deodorant, part of *P&G's* brand portfolio, is targeted primarily at females. Shortly after the *U.S. Women's Soccer Team* won the 2019 *World Cup* tournament, *Secret* donated $529,000 to the organization that pays the players—purportedly to close the wage gap between the male and female national teams. The amount nets out to just under $20,000 for each of the twenty-three players on the national team. Hardly a life-changing amount, but nearly everyone would gladly take it.

But how much value—public relations, branding, and visibility value—did *Secret* score from this smooth move? No, we don't know either. But to assume that tens of millions of dollars of said value resulted likely represents no exaggeration. And inferring that *Secret's* national visibility, which had hung around gravity-like levels for years (gravity is invisible), temporarily soared to stellar heights would again be on-goal. Public relations pass, kick, and goal! for *Secret*.

Public relations is potentially effective at arresting the spread of bad news, which is, as noted elsewhere, much more likely than good news to rear its ugly head. Of course, that's exactly how trashy publicity—be it well-deserved or un-deserved—works. Seems like the less you want the more you get is less a cliché than an iron rule of business, marketing, and branding management. By the way, lest anyone remain in doubt, there definitely is such a thing as bad publicity (i.e., not all publicity is good publicity).

Sales Promotions: Advantages/Disadvantages

Sales promotions are effective at incentivizing targeted customers to get off their butts and into stores or onto websites in the near term or even right now! Sales promotions work effectively because they are infused with incentives that encourage recipients to engage in a "marketer-directed" behavior in order to obtain this reward. Sales promotions also work effectively because pretty much all people turn into "hos for the money," at least every now and then—and especially when the monetary incentives involved are sufficiently high.

Sales promotions can also be successfully managed in ways that motivate targeted marketing personnel to do things the sales-promoting marketer wants them to do. These targeted personnel, generally sales or marketing employees, may work either inside the firm issuing the sales promotions or for supply chain partners to the promoting firm.

Sales promotions generally prove much more effective in the short-run than in the long-run. In particular, sales promotions fail to stimulate brand loyalty. Customers, in fact, often become more loyal to sales promotion deals themselves rather than to brands being promoted, as discussed more fully below.

OTHER PROMOTIONAL (COMMUNICATION) TOOLS

Other useful marketing promotional tools are available for marketers to use. These communication "tools" also exist as part of the promotional mix—particularly inside firms that sell tangible products. These tools can similarly be employed strategically to communicate crafted messages about brands' value to buyers. Such communication (promotional) tools include:

- Product design. The best designed products feature as near-perfect-as possible-blends of form and function in ways that suggest desirable meaning to customers exposed to them. This lofty design perch embodies the "communication outcome" toward which all promoting firms should aspire. Such an idealized outcome is easier to describe than to achieve, however.

- Products' prices, shapes, or the color/design of their packaging. *Jaguar* or *Porsche* automotive brands used to feature distinctively attractive shapes. Or consider *Hershey*'s *Chocolate Bars* where the packaging outside looks like the product inside. Cool. Or think, *pink*, and notice how either the *NFL* or *Susan B. Komen Race for the Cure* brands, each supporting the cause for additional breast cancer research funding, come to mind.

- The nature of retail stores' merchandising efforts and branded products. To illustrate the nature of this communication tool, take a minute and compare *Nordstrom*'s typical merchandising efforts to *Walmart*'s typical merchandising efforts; or the brands that *Neiman*'s carries to the brands that *Target* typically carries inside your mind. There is nothing wrong with *Walmart*'s merchandising efforts (or brands) or for that matter with *Target*'s branded product lines (or merchandising efforts). But are either discount retailers' merchandising efforts or brands truly comparable to *Nordstrom's* more prestigious merchandising efforts[4] or to *Neiman's* typically far more luxurious array of brands? The answer is no, because more prestigious retailers seek to signal different sets of values to their targeted customer segment than the signals being projected toward their targeted segments by the less prestigious retailers. Which retailers are less prestigious? Which retailers' brands are perceived as, and actually are, pricier? What does the fact that the *Neiman* brand as opposed to the *Target* brand distributes your brand say about your apparel firm's brand? What sort of customer profile generally shops inside the respective retailers or on their websites? In which retailer establishment is customer service likely to prove superior? The answers to these questions don't matter. What matters is that each answer communicates messages about each branded item sold by *Neiman, Nordstrom, Target,* or *Walmart.*

---

4. Retailers typically merchandise finished goods (brands) that they receive from supply partners. Merchandising entails promoting the sales of goods at the retail level. Merchandising activities include in-store or on-site display techniques, shelf-talking, spot demonstrations, personal selling in general, and other point-of-sale methods, as well as advertising messages conveyed to targeted audiences by stories about themselves.

MODULE 14.2

Advertising

DEFINITION; DESCRIPTION

Advertising includes any form of one-way; paid, which means the sponsor is identified; and impersonal communication aimed at targeted customers; and is delivered en masse through electronic, print, or INET-based communication media; in order to persuade, inform, remind, or build new or strengthen existing relationships with targeted B2B or B2C customers about the value/differences associated with given brands.[5] Advertising is routinely employed to create differentiation; to establish or sustain perceptions of differentiation; and to produce or strengthen brand loyalty and brand equity and ultimately, brand power.

There is more than meets the eye to this already-long definition. Advertising's one-way quality means that mistakes, oversights, or misstatements cannot be easily detected or corrected by marketers in the short run. Best to get advertising story right before the branding story is launched.

The paid, sponsor-identified dimension that characterizes advertising creates situations where marketers that over exaggerate their values or their competitors' deficiencies cannot long escape punishment for their lies. Except for political advertising. This form of advertising is regulated differently—who, after all, regulates advertising but politicians themselves? And the results of this non-regulated "regulation" have long been evident. As far back as the 1960s domestic political advertising was called out by advertising guru *David Ogilvy* as the only form of advertising where lying is routinely tolerated.

Advertising's impersonal communicative property creates situations where when situations arise in which intended recipients don't attend to, understand, or reject core messages (as often happens),

---

5. Yes, this same definition of advertising was provided earlier. But such repetition is a good thing, because people should "repeat, to remember" important things or ideas. Or should people "remember to repeat" important things or ideas? Actually, "remembering to repeat" or "repeating to remember" each represent useful approaches to improve our "recall." Especially when trying to remember people's names.

marketers receive no second chances to make better impressions on them. No second chances, that is, to make better impressions by, say, immediately delivering additional or clearer explanations, answering customer questions, or addressing customer concerns.

ADVERTISING: THEN, AND NOW

Mirroring the title of *Linda Ronstadt's* hit song, advertising's been around for a *Long, Long Time.* The known origins of advertising are ancient. Take the movie *Gladiator*, for example, which itself has by this point been around for a while. Why *Gladiator?* Because advertising goes at least as far back as advertising being painted on walls promoting gladiatorial upcoming contests in various arenas throughout the *Roman Empire.*

Since this time, the breadth, depth, or scope of advertising has expanded to breath-taking levels. And therein lies many, though not all, of the underlying causes of advertising's problems inside the developed world. These related problems are that too much advertising exists and that too few prospects/customers are paying attention to it.

As a group, contemporary marketers often encounter trouble as they risk offending viewers or hearers by issuing too many advertising messages. In a desperate attempt to grab the attention of consumers or businesspeople, marketers have long since created what is known as advertising clutter[6] and excessive noise.[7] Everyone knows what is being described here even if they have never heard the terms "noise" or "clutter" used inside an advertising context. There is, simply, a continuous blitz of advertising messages. Individual consumers, and the entire marketplace, is saturated with advertising messages begging for their and its attention. The results are not just annoying. At times they seem painful.

Domestic consumers have gone from being exposed to an average of about 500 advertisements a day during the 1970s to as many as 5,000 a day today. Many marketers apparently aspire to cover every blank space with some kind of brand logo, promotion, or advertisement. Marketers now use grocery carts, parking stripes, postage stamps, buses, and buildings like universal-advertising platforms that engulf consumers. Consumers are in near equal parts reeling from, while actively rejecting, the messages.

And naturally, most consumers are annoyed by the intrusions. Meanwhile, most marketers are responding with shrug-like "advertisers got to do what advertisers got to do" to get someone's attention. Indeed, some advertising messages and managers go further than that by making their ads purposefully annoying. And have been doing this for a surprisingly long time. Another advertising legend, *Reed Reeves*, once reportedly said, "I don't care if they hate my ad, I just need them to remember the brand when they need the product."

---

6. Advertising clutter refers to the inundating glut of ad messages to which domestic consumers are exposed to every day. Phrases such as "need to break-through-the-clutter" are commonly expressed by marketers, and with good cause. Advertisers often seek to break-through by shocking, provoking, or even annoying or outright pissing off the targets of their advertising messages.

7. Advertising noise refers to other stimuli in recipient's environments that undermine targeted audiences' willingness and ability to pay attention to advertising messages. Noise was also defined earlier.

Anacin aspirin ads from the 1950s and 1960s that were created by Mr. Reeves exemplified this "aggravate people so that they will remember" tactic. *Anacin* ads were universally reviled at time. But the brand sold trainloads of headache medicines. The *Don Draper* character, made famous as the lead character in the iconic television show *Madmen*, supposedly was modeled on Mr. Reeves.

A quick but purposeful peek at the domestic beer marketing sector underscores many of these same points. *Budweiser, Miller*, and *Coors* are the three leading American brewers and beer brands. Actually, more recently, the trio has merged into America's two leading brewers since *Miller-Coors* merged.

Even so, most adult consumers know that *Budweiser*, in terms of its position, stands for *Clydesdales* and old-time brewing tradition. These same consumers also broadly understand that *Miller* differentiates its well-positioned light beer brand as the one choice that *Tastes Great* and is *Less Filling. Coors*, yes, that brand is widely recognized as being brewed with *Rocky Mountain* streams' water, notwithstanding the fact that until recently *Coors'* second-largest brewery was located in *Eden, North Carolina*, as was discussed earlier.

Collectively, this three-headed set of beer brewers and marketers annually spends more than $1.6 billion on advertising inside America. The domestic total spent on advertising these three beer brands alone exceeds the individual Gross National Products of more than forty countries around the world. Yes, you read this number right.

To gain perspective think about how many other brands of beer are advertised inside the beer product category inside the US. Now envision all those thousands of other product category sectors that have nothing to do with beer but that are also competing equally vigorously inside domestic marketers and similarly are using advertising to promote and differentiate the values of their individually branded products as they target consumer segments. Yet there's no point in forgetting or ignoring organizations advertising to other organizations inside supply chains; the total numbers of advertisements and advertising expenditures laid out there are remarkable there, as well.

Now we're getting to the true scope of advertising, and to the core nature of advertising's primary problem. There is too much advertising. There is too much advertising-induced clutter and noise. As a result there are too many distracted, non-attentive, and/or annoyed advertising recipients or non-recipients, most of who are merely seeking some relief. That's advertising, writ large and small but still accurately described, inside both the internet-mediated and traditional dimensions of the contemporary marketplace.

THE THINGS ADVERTISERS DO . . . NOT FOR OUR LOVE, BUT FOR OUR ATTENTION

Change arrives on its own accord based on its own schedule. Change never asks for permission, either. True change doesn't need to be coaxed by an advertisement, masquerading as a public service announcement. Many but not all consumers would agree that one of the last things the *United States* needs right now is more *Hollywood* or *Madison Avenue* advertising executive using fully awakened celebrities and messages to tell them what they should think, how they should behave, or imposing another "teachable moment" on them.

And then there is *Gillette*—a previously rather straitlaced razor marketer that recently decided to teach *America* a lesson while advertising its razor brand. More specifically, there were a series of advertisements issued by *Gillette* that primarily focused on attacking toxic masculinity—a term of non-endearment that some critics argue is being leveraged to punish an entire gender category for the sins of a few. No more boys will be boys in the future, one must assume. Almost as if the marketers that make products for men will also hate on men to score a few virtue points.

But exactly how socially enlightened is *Gillette*? Well, for starters, the marketer is still marketing blue razors for males, pink razors for females, with pink costing far more—talk about clichéd gender stereotypes and gender-based price discrimination. To suggest behaviors associated with toxic masculinity are the norm is plain wrong. Most men simply want products that work.

Virtue-signaling now often functions as a communication-based insurance policy that many woke organizations use to fend off, often preemptively, social networking mobs. No need exists to paint a whole crew as bad because of the sins of a few. Inside this new, for *Gillette*, advertising messaging theme an implied assumption clearly existed. The assumption appeared to suggest or refused to recognize that men also have mothers, sisters, daughters, granddaughters, and wives in their lives. Is it possible that *Gillette* developed this campaign to appeal to women who purchase most razors, sometimes for men in their lives, in this country? The answer clearly is yes.

Outing the truth, however, what this tactic is about is increasing sales revenue by drawing attention to the Gillette brand. Nothing more, nothing less. When you hold 70 percent of the market, as *Gillette* does, $3 million over three years is but a drop in the advertising bucket. But alas, *Gillette* got what it wanted. Your attention.

Nothing New Under the Advertising Sun

On the other hand, *Madison Avenue* and *Hollywood* have long told American consumers what to think, how to behave, or has tried to deliver some teachable moments to us. Most prior lessons, however, were far more subtle than this. As for the commercial, marketers are trying to capitalize on a current hot button topic.

These are the sorts of things that marketers sometimes do—for purposes of getting or keeping customer attention. Marketers should be creative in getting their name out there and selling more product. The successful ones, such as *Gillette* are. *Gillette* simultaneously used and created editorial content driven by the goal of launching a conversation about contemporary social issues . . . and hoped to generate greater market share, sales, and profits from said editorial content. Particularly over the longer term.

Marketers as successful and as strategic as *Gillette* would never do something as controversial as this without first having conducted extensive market research and developing deep understanding of how the ad will affect company sales/value. *Gillette* would rarely if ever promote any ideas in their advertising stories merely as feel-good exercises. *Gillette* creates and distributes advertising for one core, and unchanging, reason: to sell more razors.

Few corporations know or have done marketing better than *Gillette*. The marketer knew perfectly well that this decision would cause it to lose some sales to white nationalists or elderly sorts who watch *Fox News* all day along. But apparently these niche market segments were not large parts of the razor-buying public and were also demographic segments that grow smaller every year. *Gillette* expected to sell more razors to men who want to be identified with doing the right thing and who understand that the rules for dealing successfully with women are changing. The giant marketer must have assumed there were many more of those men than the other sort. Or that older generations who might have been offended by this campaign don't buy many razors anymore and are less prone to changing their brand loyalties, anyway. *Gillette* used this virtual-signaling advertising campaign to target male millennials and male generations younger than that who were making their initial razor choices. *Gillette*, more so than most marketers, apparently remained mindful of the fact that these first-love brand relationships often transform into the sort of brand loyalty that lasts for lifetimes.

Know what? The getting attention tactic instituted by *Gillette* sort of worked, for a while. Got us talking didn't it? Until the new advertising and positioning strategy failed to work. Gillette ended up losing billions—eight billion dollars, more or less—in sales during 2019 as millions of mostly conservative customers silently boycotted the brand.

Yet virtues are good. Not supporting moral or virtuous decisions and behaviors is akin to not supporting motherhood, as was discussed during Module 8. But virtue-signaling, especially of the promotional sort that is motivated more by the notion of signaling false morality rather than the possession of any true distinguishing moral underpinnings, count us out.

And count out the many message recipients—targeted customers and prospective customers—who are perceptive enough to see through the game. However, as *P.T. Barnum* proclaimed, a new sucker is born every minute. Which explains why less than perfect virtue-signaling marketing organizations keep signaling their phony morality to millions of message recipients who are not perceptive, engaged, or knowledgeable enough to detect the ruse. But one indisputable fact remains: Marketers should only signal their virtues when they actually have something virtuous to signal.

GETTING-MAD; BUT NOT GOING CRAZY

The average nearly four-hour-long *NFL* football broadcast features about one hundred minutes of advertising and only about eleven minutes of actual play. Even fervent fans are increasingly zipping through games, after having DVR-ing them, or watching highlights on their phones, after rapidly clicking through advertising breaks. They do so to no small degree to escape advertising.

So why is there so much advertising, especially when so many people clearly are no longer paying attention? The answer relates to *MAD*.[8] *MAD* is the infamous branding acronym signifying Mutually Assured Destruction. *MAD* was and remains a global military strategy and national security doctrine in which it is mutually acknowledged that the full-scale use of nuclear weaponry by two or more opposing sides would end in the annihilation of both attacker and defender.

---

8. *MAD* should not be confused with *MADD*, or *Mothers Against Drunk Driving*, which operates as a well-positioned and effectively branded marketing organization.

MAD is based on deterrence theory.[9] Deterrence theory maintains that the threat of using overwhelmingly destructive weapons against an enemy prevents the enemy's use of those same weapons. The strategy is also an offshoot of the *Nash Equilibrium*[10] that argues that neither side in any warlike competition has much rational incentive either to initiate conflict or to disarm once each potential adversary perceives it is suitably armed.

The *Good, The Bad, and the Ugly* is an iconic *Clint Eastwood* spaghetti western, so-called because the movie was financed and filmed in *Italy*, and was directed by *Sergio Leone*, a famous *Italian* director. The movie features a famous ending (spoiler alert) that plays out as a riff on MAD as a riff on the *Nash Equilibrium*. There is a three-way showdown and anticipated shootout at the end of the movie involving the *Clint Eastwood, Eli Wallach,* and *Lee Van Clef* characters all holding and pointing equal-sized guns from equal distances toward each other. But the shootout never occurs, not in the expected form at least, because no one wanted to die by putting down his gun first. No one was willing to disarm.

There's an analogy in here somewhere, and here it is. No reason exists in real-life advertising contexts to halt an advertising campaign, either. No, not even inside promotional settings where everyone being targeted already knew your brand name.

Hello, not to the character *Norm* from the television program *Cheers* (where everyone knew your name), but to the even more famous brands that are named *Budweiser, Miller,* and *Coors*. Everyone knows their brand names, as well, at least for now. But no one among these three iconic brands can stand down, holstering the advertising weapon inside their promotional arsenal, because soon after anyone of the three beer brands stopped advertising the other two competitors who continued advertising would quickly step and grab its market share.

The *MAD* military doctrine, or strategy, has worked—so far. The presence of *MAD* may have kept the old *Soviet Union* and the *United States* from destroying one another at any point during an approximately forty-five-year-long so-called *Cold War*.

Everyone should understand the primary reason why there continues to be so much advertising. Advertising history has conclusively demonstrated that the first company, say, *Bud*, that stops advertising while competitors such as *Miller-Coors* continue to advertise quickly loses top-of-mind-awareness inside customer minds, falling further down in or completely existing those customers' evoked sets, and along the way losing any positioning and branding advantages that once were theirs. The brand equity and branding power of the first firm that stops advertising will thereafter die slowly or quickly die.

The final takeaway is that marketers must continue to advertise as they compete against each other, despite the fact that few customers are really paying attention at any particular point in time, because not one of those marketing competitors can afford to stop. After all, some consumers, some of the time, actually are paying attention.

---

9. "The Hopes of Mankind," *Wall Street Journal* (March 20, 2003): A18.

10. Ironically, lead *Gladiator* actor *Russell Crowe* starred in another movie as Professor Nash, father of the *Nash Equilibrium*. The film was branded *A Beautiful Mind*.

Attempting to Break through the Advertising Noise and Clutter

Marketers perpetually seek and occasionally find workarounds that actually alleviate maddening situations in which too few customers are watching their expensive, often highly creative advertising messages. For example, marketers have long outfitted professional golfers as if they were *NASCAR* stock cars and drivers as if both parties as well as the cars were walking/talking/swinging/driving billboards. Except here, the walking or speeding billboards simultaneously sport the brands of multiple sponsors. More recently marketers are festooning live television sporting programming with split screens featuring silent clips of live action on one half-screen and volume turned high videos of advertising on the other.

Or, if you watch golf tournaments on television, you're currently experiencing "let's play through" promotional breaks. "Playing through" is a golfing term of politeness where faster golfing twosomes or foursomes are invited to play through on this hole by slower playing groups. Television screens split inside these "let's play through" breaks while viewers strain to see live golf played on one side and hear and see advertising on the other side of the screen. No, that's not annoying. But a larger point is that contemporary marketers have apparently decided it is worth annoying some of the target audience to secure greater attention from the same target audience, especially inside DVR world.

More recently still, have any golf fans noticed really popular golfers like *Dustin Johnson (DJ)*, *Rory*, or *Jordan (Thomas or Spieth)* are frequently shown putting or teeing off during these non-break advertising breaks? *Tiger* too when he was still actively playing. (Notice how these golfer's first names function as brand signifiers themselves.) This tactic makes sense, because viewers want to see these particular golfers actually play and consequently won't reflexively zoom through the ads.

Hey, whatever works? Furthermore, any fans complaining about these turns of events should consider, if advertisers and their billions in expenditures did not exist, how much they would pay to watch *The World Cup, The Super Bowl, The Masters,* or *The World Series* live. Well, maybe not the *World Series*, because that's baseball, and baseball is a product category (and sport and brand) so far along in its Product Life Cycle that even if it has not actually entered its Decline Stage has still passed its sell-by date. Unless, and this trait is unique to baseball as a product, your hometown team is in this trait year's *World Series*.

ADVERTISING: STRENGTHS/WEAKNESSES, EXPANDED

Advertising Upside

Advertising was described earlier as being effective at reminding and informing consumers. The fact that advertising is also effective at conveying emotions and eliciting emotional responses from customers was also mentioned, but only briefly.

Think *Sara McLachlan,* her song *In the Eyes of the Angels,* the *Society for the Prevention of Cruelty to Animals (The S.P.C.A.),* and big-eyed kittens. Now triple-up, as in combine, all three marketing stimuli. The combined advertising music, imagery, and messaging is sufficiently evocative, emotionally speaking, to make even cat-haters cry. And more importantly, given the ad's communication goal, the brand's messaging is sufficiently evocative to make viewers at least consider ponying-up for (donating to) the not-for-profit marketing cause.

Few reasons could ever exist to discount the potential value of advertising messages that are able to finesse the emotions of consumers who are exposed to them. Potential value, that is, for the brands, products, and marketing organizations featured inside those emotion-laden advertisements. That's because the more consumers feel (emotionally) the less they think (logically). At that point consumers can be more easily manipulated by marketers. Good, bad, or indifferent, these are the facts.

This principle would rarely not apply.

In a 1957 book called *The Hidden Persuaders,* author *Vance Packard* outed the entire advertising sector for "treating American consumers like six-year-olds." Less than one decade later, a *Coca-Cola* commercial featured attractive people of all colors and nationalities grouped closely together on a *California* hilltop looking down upon the beautiful *Pacific Ocean* while harmonizing, "I'd like to teach the world to sing in perfect harmony." Uh huh, sure; us too. This historically effective marketing message finessed the entire world's emotions, an outcome that the advertising sector has long since mastered. The compelling advertisement essentially entranced gullible consumers while providing zero information about the qualities—such as they were—associated with *Coke,* the brand being advertised.

Excuse the cynicism, or don't. But does anyone actually believe *Coca-Cola,* the marketing organization, cared about anything beyond getting more people around the world to do anything besides drink more *Coke* products? No, *Coca-Cola* did not care who sang or not. Nor should have the marketer cared. *Coca-Cola*'s job was not to teach the world to sing in perfect harmony. The communication outcomes produced by the advertising message, however, aligned perfectly with *Coca-Cola*'s global strategy. You see, the firm's mission statement at the time stated the firm's purpose was "Putting a *Coke* within arm's reach of everyone in the world." A mission statement that *Coca-Cola* has since executed to a T.

That was then. This is now. Consumers are surely no longer quite so gullible. Not during an all-knowing, all-cynical-all-the-time internet age. You know, as in the times we are living out right now, wherein never before in history so many purposeless lives have been so relentlessly chronicled.

A photoshopped *Time* magazine cover once depicted a looming then-*President Trump* dispassionately looking down upon a two-year-old *Hispanic* child. The child was crying. She was (apparently) alone—falsely so, we must hasten to add, this image was photo-shopped after all. Many Americans, including the small numbers of people who actually read *Time,* quickly became outraged. Those numbers were expanded exponentially by the left- and right-leaning consumers who forwarded their *Time* magazine cover coverage to all their loyal readers, followers, hearers, or viewer in a classic WOM-inspired diffusion process. A communication outcome that was, beyond question, the primary outcome sought all along by the initiating marketing messenger, *Time.*

This purposefully emotionally-evocative magazine cover, an ad itself, quickly became more infamous because the facts revealed that the child was not separated from her illegal immigrant mother. The child's mother instead was standing by her side when the actual photo was taken and had left other children behind in her nation of origin. *Time* magazine eventually admitted this was true.

Yet this is not the point to be made or understood here. The point instead is that the photoshopped cover, this narrative, was designed to deliver two marketing outcomes. First, to rouse fierce emotional responses from viewers/readers in order to drive them toward purchasing [by ultimately voting for] the marketed idea that southern US borders should open or become more open. Second, to drive issues of the struggling *Time* magazine as both a product and brand off newsstands or its website. Despite a magazine-issued disclaimer that quickly followed, the initial message achieved each communication goal.

Advertising Downside

For starters, advertising is not as persuasive as other available marketing communication forms. Specifically, personal selling and sales promotion are more persuasive.

Beyond this, the question of whether many are really paying attention should never be ignored. Back in a day that was not so long ago, back when modern advertising was first being perfected, there were sixteen or so waking hours in a day in which you could reach targets. That timeline baseline has not much changed. But the number of marketing and non-marketing stimuli competing for our attention at any given moment has increased exponentially.

Effective advertising can also prove difficult and costly to create. But this potential downside risk should always be weighed against what happens when success stories and ad slogans such as *Can You Hear Me Now (T-Mobile)*; the New *Old Spice Man*; *15 Minutes Can Save You 15 Percent or More (GEICO)*; *Have It Your Way (Burger King)*; *The Best Part of Waking Up (Maxwell House Coffee)*; *Fair, Balanced and Unafraid (Fox News)*; *When It Absolutely Positively . . . (FedEx)*, and so forth are told. And readers know well how long this list could have been extended. For example, *No Pollen Shall Prevail Against Thee: Claritin 3:16*, to our knowledge, is still available.

Finally, as noted, advertising is one-way and impersonal in nature. If advertisements are misunderstood or misconstrued, or if recipients don't agree with or are offended by the advertising story, no quick correction mechanism in in place to assuage the potential hurt for marketers. Messages cannot be easily changed or explained. This is a genuine problem and downside for advertising.

THREE KEY ADVERTISING MANAGEMENT DECISIONS

Three key sets of advertising management decisions exist. Marketers must manage effectively each decision set when deciding whether and how to advertise. None of these decision sets should be ignored or skipped. The broad decisions also should be executed in the order presented below.

Advertising Management Decision 1: Establish Communication Objectives

Five primary advertising communication objectives exist. One or more of the communication objectives can be simultaneously pursued. But inside most individual advertisements or advertising campaigns one objective usually takes precedence.

One typical advertising communication objective entails informing customers. Hopefully making customers aware that a new product now exists to at least create a possibility that they will now try it out! Clearly, no one has bought anything until they first know that the thing existed. Or, informing the world that new features are now available on long-established products, and there's no reason not to take a renewed look, dear customer. Sometimes advertising might be used to inform target markets that new promotional opportunities, for example, an annual season closeout automotive pricing deal is about to be launched, and that consumers should take advantage of the opportunity now because the special promotion ends this Sunday. Such an advertisement issues both a reminder and a call to action.

A second typical advertising objective entails persuading customers that for one or more reasons the brand being advertised represents the highest value—the best possible—choice. Most of the time, however, advertising marketers would emphasize only one major value proposition[11] when developing persuasive advertising messages. Value propositions are usually based on a so-called big idea.

A third advertising objective, one that is frequently pursued, involves issuing reminders to customers. Targeted customer, we're still here, is what the advertising message says. Remember how much you once loved us. There's absolutely no reason why you could not love us again, or why you should not continue to love us. Here's a little incentive to remind you what you once had, or could have again.

Think about the 1986 movie *The Breakfast Club*. Despite the movie's age, you've probably seen the *Molly Ringwald, Judd Nelson, Emilio Estevez, Ally Sheedy* (i.e., the *Brat Pack*) vehicle. (Only *Rob Lowe* was missing.) Remember how it ends. That's right, with bad boy Judd smooching good girl Molly right in front of her aghast parents. And the song rolling over this final scene and the closing credits was *The Simple Minds* classic, *Don't Forget about Me*. The song title puts into words the outcome that reminder advertising is designed and was born to generate.

A fourth typical advertising objective entails communication efforts aimed at building new or strengthening old relationships with new or existing customers. Some experts on human aging suggest social aptitude, not intellectual brilliance or economic security, leads to successful aging; that the outcome mattering most inside elders' lives is their relationships with other people. Who knows, such experts may or may not be right.

But what's known for certain is that relationships, those initially developed and those eventually strengthened and sustained between customers and brands, contribute the most to marketing success. That's why surprisingly high percentages of, say, *Nissan* or *Honda* automotive advertisements are targeted at existing customers. These advertisements seek to reinforce the great decision these individuals have already made and inspire them toward greater brand loyalty and a continued relationship with the advertised brand.

---

11. The value proposition for any given brand summarizes all the reasons (the underlying values) regarding why customers should purchase this specific brand rather than alternative brands that are available in the same product and are being promoted/positioned by other marketing competitors. Value propositions are created through the marketing mix. Value propositions are expressed through market positions and are reflected in and communicated by the brand images and brand identifiers that marketers create as they manage their marketing mixes.

Brand loyalty functions as an ongoing expression of the close relationship that customers feel with the brand in question. There's more, however. Who knows how many more future *Honda* or *Nissan* brand disciples might be generated through these evangelists' positive-WOM transmissions.

Over time advertising messages can also be used to build, support, or sustain more desirable images and positions for brands, a fifth possible objective.

The choice of which objective or combination of objectives are most worth pursuing as advertising communication outcomes should be based on what is happening elsewhere with respect to the:

- Other three elements of the marketing organization's marketing mix;
- Organization's general positioning/differentiation strategy;
- Nature of the firm's targeted audience, meaning, primarily, the demographic, attitudinal, and lifestyle or psychographic tendencies that characterize the segment or segments being targeted; and
- Product life cycle stage currently occupied by the brand being advertised.

Advertising Management Decision 2: Establish Budgets

Once advertising communication objectives are put in place, advertising budgets should be established. Four possible budgeting approaches exist. However, one clearly superior alternative exists when marketers commit to being or remaining strategic. Even so, the other three alternatives are presented below because having any budget is better than having no budget at all.

One budgeting approach is called the affordable method. This budgeting approach entails going from your gut and spending the amount on advertising that you believe your firm can afford. While better than nothing, this method is deficient. No strategic considerations related to what marketers seek to accomplish through advertising is in play. This is highly problematic.

The percentage of sales method represents another budgeting approach. This method entails identifying a percentage (say, 3 percent) of revenues that the marketing organization will spend on advertising. If marketers generate $1,000,000 in revenue during the previous year, they will spend $30,000 on advertising during this year. If total sales continue to rise, firms advertise more next year. So far so okay. But if revenues decline—as often happens due to factors having nothing to do with advertising[12]—marketers spend less next year. Does anyone believe, *ceteris paribus*, that spending less on advertising is a good idea when sales are dropping? This approach is deficit. Because the percentage of sales method assumes advertising expenditures are the only factor driving revenues and market share. This is rarely if ever the case.

---

12. Imagine, in this scenario, that the marketing organization is a diner. The diner only serves breakfast and lunch and is located three-quarters of a mile down the road from a factory that employed 1,275 people, mostly men. Boom, the factory suddenly closes. Diner revenues are virtually assured to drop. But the decline likely had nothing to do with any advertising expenditures that did or did not happen.

A third alternative advertising budgeting approach is called the competitive parity method. The parity approach involves following suit, in terms of how much money is spent on advertising, with what competitors are doing. The budgeting tactic is tantamount to playing follow-the-leader games (i.e., what typically happens inside oligopoly-like markets where follower-firms price at essentially the same level as the leader-firm). This is a less-than-ideal budgeting strategy, for two reasons. First, follower-firms assume the leader-firm knows what it is doing. Second, follower-marketers are consigning themselves to being average. Satisfied with being average?

The fourth and only strategic approach is called the objective and task budgeting method. This approach entails first establishing the primary communication goals, and then conducting analytics to determine what's required, advertising-expenditure wise, to achieve those goals. Objective and task is far and away the best budgeting approach, given that it's strategic in nature.

Advertising Management Decision 3: Establish an Advertising Strategy

When establishing an advertising strategy, the first stage entails selecting the proper advertising media. The second stage entails creating and then selecting the proper advertising message.

Stage 1: Media Selection

Rising media costs and increasingly fragmented consumer markets have made media selection choices more important than ever. More alternative media communication channels through which marketers could deliver their advertising messages also exist today than at any point in history. All in all, media selection processes are more complicated than ever, as well.

Media channels should be chosen to ensure that the demographic, psychographic, attitudinal, lifestyle, and so forth characteristics of the media channel's viewers, listeners, readers, users, or visitors align as closely as possible with the customer profiles that are present inside the specific market segment that the advertising marketer seeks to reach and inform or remind or persuade—and with whom the advertiser seeks to create or strengthen relationships. The specific segment that is being targeted, of course, is the intended audience for the advertising message. *Dollar Shave Club*, a marketer that targets men who shave and covet bargains, used to advertise regularly on *ESPN's* now-canceled *Golic & Wingo* morning sports talk show. Which itself was formerly called the *Mike & Mike Show*. This media choice makes strategic sense given that each shows' core audience skewed male and younger male and aired during the morning, when men are more likely to shave or to consider shaving. There's more, however. Younger male viewers are also generally a less wealthy demographic that is thus more interested in securing pricing deals, such as the special price discounts that *Dollar Shave Club's* advertising messages always heralded—and emphasized.

Sirius Radio, as noted, is an organization that offers users the chance to listen to music sans advertising or to listen to talk/opinion radio services with less or no advertising. *Sirius Channel 94* delivers humor from a series of comedians who are collectively branded as *Comedy Greats*. The station features generally outrageous and offensive humor, traits that characterize most contemporary humor.[13] But programming on this station also provides an appropriate media vehicle on which messages about *Adam and Eve's* sex tools can be targeted toward listeners. This pairing of raucously sexy humor with people who want to listen to it with obviously sexual products absolutely makes strategic sense. The media choice allows *Adam and Eve*, a branded retailer that promotes sex toys, to reach listeners who are already inured to talking "dirty" or are proactive about sex and sexual practices.

Or assume a marketing organization has developed a new product. The new product is positioned on the promise it will enhance females' health and fitness, especially among younger women. Assume further that the innovating firm has identified and created the consumer segment it plans to target based on five segmentation criteria. First, age: people aged 18–25 years. Second, gender: segment membership, as noted, is female or identifies as such. Third, education: targets have completed high school, and preferably are either enrolled in or have graduated from college. Fourth, lifestyle preferences: segment constituents are outdoorsy, nature-loving, and physically active types. And five, attitudinally: segment members are typically already physically fit, committed to remaining so, and hope to get fitter still.

What communication channels or media should this marketer select? Select, that is, in order to effectively deliver advertising messages intended to inform this segment's membership about the fact that this appealing new promised solution is now available. What advertising medium should this firm, one that is essentially marketing a fitness and/or health solution, use to reach this specific sort of woman with its ad messages? Each question is best answered through marketing research. However, myriad advertising agencies exist as prospective supply chain partners who, for the right price, would happily also perform the media selection supply chain function for our hypothetical marketer.[14] Typical advertising media include television, *Facebook*, magazines and/or newspapers, billboards, radio, *Amazon*, tweets, social networking sites, dudes walking around wearing sandwich boards, and so forth.

Google and *Facebook* captured 99 percent of every new dollar spent on online advertising during 2019, according to the *Wall Street Journal*. Meanwhile, *Google* and *Facebook* already account for 84 percent of all digital advertising outside of *China*, and 94 percent of its growth. While *Facebook* boasted approximately 1.5 billion global customers during 2019, the 242 million American and *Canadian* users of *Facebook* were most valuable to the firm. *Facebook* earned $34.90 in advertising revenue for each of those customers, totally more than $200 billion. Each of the approximately 1.1 billion *Asian-Pacific* region users, by contrast, generated only $3.00 per person.[15]

---

13. Humor often plays powerful roles inside successful advertising efforts. Perhaps because, as *Francis Bacon* wrote: "Imagination was given to humanity to compensate for what we are not; a sense of humor was given to console us for what we are." Humor generally arises from the incongruity—the unexpected nature and/or arrival—of a subject just introduced. Humor is like a jack-in-the-box, in that the joke is only funny the first time Jack pops up. Jokes depend upon surprise. Absent surprise, there is no humor.

14. Of course, one should not excessively write or speak about the hypothetical or the abstract because no hypothetical or abstract marketing organizations or customers actually exist.

15. Axios.com.

Not all media-selection activities are esoteric or socially networked in nature, or mysterious and overly difficult to make. Imagine for a moment that you own a *Burger King* franchise located just north of I-40 as you turn onto the exit for *Forest City, Arkansas*. You have also invested ten years of hard-earned dollars to pay the fee to acquire the franchising rights too. This franchised business is both your life and source of your livelihood.

Forest City is located about forty miles east of *Memphis, Tennessee,* and about 110 miles east of *Little Rock, Arkansas,* but feels like the town is about 500 miles from anywhere important. Thousands of interstate drivers—cars, buses, or trucks holding one or more potential burger eaters—blow by the burg daily. And if you are that franchisee (the *Burger King* franchise owner) who seeks to inspire within passing vehicles a hankering to quickly exit and consume a traditional *Whopper* or *Impossible Burger King* anything the media channel that you are most likely to select to deliver your "advertising come-on-in" are two old-fashioned highway billboards. And logically so. One billboard would be located on the north side of the interstate about ten miles to the east of the *Forest City* I-40 exit; the other located on the south side of the interstate about ten miles west of *Forest City*.

As previously written, no mystique is in play here. Firms should choose the promotional media that are most likely to allow their brand's message to reach the highest number of customers that the advertising marketing organization is targeting and seeking to satisfy. And returning to the *Burger King* franchise scenario, the targeted customer is more likely driving a truck or American-made SUV than a *Mercedes* or *Volvo*, for what that's worth.

Stage 2: Message Creation

Finally, we're getting down to the real inside skinny of advertising. The part that laypeople think about when they think about advertising at all.

The advertising message itself should embody and should capture the key parts of the most important story that marketers should be most interested in telling to their various target audiences. Various questions should be considered—yet not necessarily completely, utterly, or absolutely answered—as precursors to the ability to successfully create advertising messages. For example, what should the marketer say in the advertising message? What underlying core idea or ideas should drive the advertising story that the marketing organization is seeking to tell and sell? How should the marketer frame its message? Should the advertising story be framed positively or negatively? Should the advertising story employ images, words, or images and words designed to stimulate humor or fear or anger or anxiety or disgust or merely stimulate stimulation, as in getting targeted folks to pay attention? Should the advertising message contain music and if so what type? Should the advertising story told through the message feature a spokesperson whose name or voice or both is known or unknown? Or should the message feature a spokes-dog; spokes-gecko, or spokes-tiger? Should the message primarily feature words or imagery? Should the advertising message inform, persuade, remind, stimulate recall, or strengthen existing relationships or pave the way for future creation of new relationships? How about the prospect that our message invoke some combination of all of these desirable communication outcomes? Talk about a *Denny's* restaurant-like *Grand Slam Breakfast*.

As a reminder please note that questions should have already been asked and successfully answered about where the story will be told; along with questions about to whom and through which communication channels the advertising message will be conveyed. The media that will be used to transmit or channel the intended story toward intended recipients should have already been identified.

Four steps are involved in creating an effective advertising message. These steps should be executed in the order shown below.

During the first step marketers should identify the most important benefits, values, and solutions delivered by the branded product or service that they plan to advertise. One or two, but likely only one of these benefits should then be identified as the key point of difference marketers subsequently seek to associate with their brand as marketing stories are developed to position key brand values. This key customer benefit should always be reflected in advertising message appeals.

Ideally, big ideas[16] are created that bring advertising messages to life and allow benefits and solutions offered by brands to be conveyed to targeted audiences in clear, distinctive, memorable, and persuasive ways. Big ideas are compellingly creative concepts. Successful big ideas can function as "sturdy hooks" on which branding marketers can hang advertising stories across a period of years if not decades. *De Beers*, for example, has used the *Diamonds are Forever* brand story for more than five decades. *Nike* will likely always be about *Just Doing It* for many shoe-buying consumers for the rest of their lives. Talk about owning words inside minds, or here, stories inside the collective minds of targeted markets.

Another classic big idea includes *MasterCard's* advertising/positioning tagline "*Priceless*." The core element of this big idea signals, to *MasterCard* customers, was that they should buy whatever and everything they want; damn the price; because they and their families are worth it. Responding affirmatively to such messages actually turns out poorly for many loyal customers, but never to marketers themselves. *MasterCard*, for example, recoups fees automatically when customers purchase, and secures punishingly high interest payments from customers answering the charge by buying whatever they want to the point where they cannot pay off monthly debts.

Other classic examples of big ideas include *Miller Lite—Tastes Great, Less Filling* (have more fun, consume fewer calories); *Intel—Intel Inside* (a compelling promise of performance); *Walmart*—EDLP (savings so large they genuinely improve customers' lives); and, believe it or not, the seemingly humble *KFC*. Inside a marketplace where many consumers finally realized that loading up on fried foods was not the best idea, the idea to remove the "fried" from *Kentucky Fried Chicken* was big indeed.

Or take *Dos Equis* beer, and its well-executed use of "the most interesting man in the world" messaging strategy as the brand's big idea. Well, yes, most consumers would surely prefer to self-identify as "the-most-interesting" beer drinker, and if drinking a specific brand of beer helps them secure that end, all the better. Worth noting, *Dos Equis* recently replaced the original most-interesting-man actor after his highly successful nine-year-run. The new guy and his campaign lasted less than one year. One marketing and universal lesson follows; no need exists to fix what's not broken.

If *Burger King,* the brand and firm, ever understood this lesson, it surely ignored the moral for more than a moment. About twenty years ago *Burger King* was nipping at *McDonald's* and almost

---

16. The phrase "big idea" is used to identify the core element of any advertising message. The "big idea" is the point or value that is intended to meaningfully differentiate the advertised brand because the big solution described in the message resonates with the problems or emotions of targeted segments.

earned as much market share as Mickey D. The question of whether *McDonald's* could sustain its first-in-mind fast-food market position inside the US fast-food market sector was much in doubt. *Burger King* was blowing up and going hard based on the taste and appeal of *The Whopper; Burger King* fries, which kicked *McDonald*'s old recipe for fries to the curb; and the compelling/appealing big idea hook on which *Burger King* had successfully hung its positioning/differentiating value for essentially the previous twenty years. The big idea in question was *Have It Your Way.*

Then *Burger King* inexplicably dropped *Have It Your Way* as a positioning and differentiating branding identifier. Actually, the reason why the big idea was dropped is well-known: *Burger King* hired a new advertising agency as part of its supply chain—and naturally the new guys could not continue to use the old guys' idea.

Burger King quickly lost its branding way and has never fully recovered, despite the fact that burgers and fries at *Burger King* have always rocked. Sometimes, apparently, consumers still won't eat the human food unless the right story has invited them to the table.

John Deere, by contrast, offers a classic illustration of a brand that did not attempt to fix something that was not broken. The something-that-was-not-broken was the iconic farm and lawn tractor brand's positioning statement and big (advertising) idea that *nothing runs like a Deere*. The brand slogan was first used in 1971. Meanwhile, *John Deere* green, as a differentiating advertising color, has remained unchanged for six decades longer than that.

During the second step marketers should identify the primary type of advertising message appeal that they plan to use.

The best advertising appeals are memorable. Advertising appeals that make consumers laugh, cry, laugh, get scared, or feel pissed-off—or generate some combination of these responses for the recipients of advertising messages—are likely to prove memorable.

The best advertising appeals are based on distinctive ideas. Distinctive, in this context, means that advertising appeals resulting from the creation and application of distinctive ideas are different from and more appealing than the advertising appeals executed by competitors. Two useful ideas about the sort of ideas that should drive appeals inside advertising messages follow. First, once they are executed, ideas always generate consequences. Second, if and when bad ideas are executed inside advertising messages, they will always claim victims. Marketers should carefully develop ideas for messages and then screen out "lacking" ideas using culling processes similar to those introduced inside the New Product Development Module.

The best advertising appeals are based on a determinant value that is uniquely associated with the brand being promoted. For any branded feature, function, or benefit that delivers value to prove determinant, it must be perceived by customers as different-from-and-better-than what competitors offer. However, the feature, function, or benefit also must be important to customers as they decide to buy or not buy the supposedly determinant brand option from a product category that features multiple brand choices. Remember the *Bags Fly Free* advertising promise made by *Southwest Airlines*? Perhaps the most determinant advertising benefit insofar as the other major domestic airlines do not provide this benefit, so real differentiation existed; and the fact that most people really would prefer to save more money and bring more stuff with them as they fly on airplanes.

The positioning slogans embedded inside advertising appeals matter greatly. In fact, the best of these appeals have at times convinced many recipients of advertising messages that determinant values are uniquely associated with the brand when this is not necessarily the case. For example, where would *Nike* be without its historically successful advertising messages and positioning slogans such as *Just Do It, Gotta be the Shoes, Chicks Dig the Long Ball, You Don't Win Silver, You Lose Gold, There is no Finish Line, I am Not a Role Model, My Better is Better Than Your Better, Believe in Something Even If It Means Sacrificing Everything,* or *Winning Takes Care of Everything.* (The list could on like the road. *Forever.*) Brief aside, *Nike* has simply owned the room since it selected *Just Do It* as an overarching branding slogan. And why not? The only way to do anything, including succeeding, involves just doing it. Or is success just about the performance of the shoes? The answer is no. *Nike's* now-lengthy record of success has not been driven entirely by just the shoes. The quality and the winning ways of *Nike's* advertising appeals have traditionally raced far ahead of their athletic show and gear competitors.

The best advertising appeals are also generally believable—Advertising appeals should be perceived as trustworthy. Recipients should view advertising appeals as stories making promises that ultimately will be kept.

But do all advertising appeals actually need to be believable? The answer is no; not in a world where puffery exists. Puffery entails advertising appeals that contain material featuring clearly overembellished or extraordinarily boastful claims about brands that are subjective rather than objective or measurable and which no reasonable person would presume is literally true. Puffery abounds inside modern advertising. And that's usually okay. Does anyone really think *Doing-the-Dew* allows *Mountain Dew* devotees to skitter across the surface of water and leap safely over waterfalls? Does anyone actually assume that *Snickers* solves all those problems that arise *When You Are Not Yourself*? Does *Red Bull* really give [anyone] wings? The answer to each question is an obvious no, and that's why the use of puffery inside advertising messages is generally okay. But when politicians, marketers who are always hell-bent on selling the value of their ideas, use puffery, the usage often does not turn out okay. Seriously, comparing *ICE* detention along the border to *Nazi* concentration camps is like comparing "eating hot soup and saying it's burning you alive" to actually "being burned alive while eating hot soup." But, unfortunately, many low-information consumers who slurp up this information don't know enough about what is actually happening to understand that puffery, purposeful exaggeration, is in play.

During step three of the message creation process marketers develop and select effective advertising message execution strategies. Advertising messages can generally be delivered by using some combination of:

- *Slice of life or death portrayals and story appeals*—This is an advertising execution style in which real-life problems are shown in dramatic presentations while the advertised brands are positioned as solutions to the problems. Show the problem; show the benefit or solution; then sell both the problem, this could happen to you! and the solution, basically at the same time.
- *Lifestyle-based portrayals and story appeals*—This advertising execution style focusing on selling branding images or identities, more so than products themselves. The basic communication goal is to convince consumers that brands are associated with specific lifestyles, presumably lifestyles targeted customers would find desirable. Lifestyle appeals generally emphasize the consumer type who would buy the brand, again more so than the brand itself. *De Beers* advertising might portray shadowy silhouetted and sleekly sexy people wearing diamond engagement rings and diamond necklaces, all the while portraying passion and intimacy and extolling how, yes, *diamonds are forever.*

- *Fantasy-based portrayals and story appeals*—Communication goals here entail creating desirable fantasies built around brand use. More than that, however, desirable fantasies are created into which consumers could easily insert themselves if they're smart enough to acquire the brand. Imagine how hot it would feel to blow around corners or down long country roads in this cool new ride.

- *Mood or emotionally-based portrayals and story appeals*—These appeals seek to associate attractive moods or emotions with brands and their images/identities. Moods might include feelings of peace, love, beauty, charity, or gratefulness, which might facilitate a willingness to give, on the upside. Consumers' moods, their emotions, are hardly always positive. In fact, the opposite mood condition often prevails. Consequently, marketing appeals are often negatively framed as in, buy-or-do-this-now in order to-avoid-this-horrible-fate-later. First, insert the "horrible fate" inside the advertising message. Then, insert the advertised brand as the "should-be-welcomed" hero or savior solution.

- *Musical portrayals and story appeals*—These appeals convey or frame the advertising message's key benefits through song. *Nike* has released advertising depicting a marathoner's tortured feet, professional skier *Pikabo Street's* surgically-scarred knee, and a surfer's thigh reformed by a shark attack while strains of *Joe Cocker's* poignant soft rock song *You Are So Beautiful* wafted in the background.

- *Personality symbol-based portrayals and story appeals*—Messaging appeals might be issued by *The Energizer Bunny*; *Star-Kist's Charlie the Tuna*; or *General Mills'* longtime branding icon, *Betty Crocker*, whose face, hairstyle, and wardrobe have been re-designed, re-positioned, and re-introduced as new products at least eight times since she was born as a full-grown woman in 1955.

- *Technical expertise/scientific evidence-based portrayals and story appeals*—These appeals use research-based assertions and other scientific evidence to advocate and support one's brand's brand superiority over competitors inside the same product category. Pain relievers like *Advil, Bayer,* and *Excedrin* use scientific evidence in their advertising campaigns.

- *Testimonial evidence/endorsement (celebrity/otherwise) portrayals and appeals*—Testimonial appeals might be issued by real celebrities such as *Sarah Michelle Gellar*, star of *Buffy the Vampire Slayer,* who endorses *Maybelline* cosmetics or by country singer *Shania Twain*, who introduced *Revlon's ColorStay Liquid Lip*. Or marketer-contrived celebrities such as Flo (and *Progressive Insurance*) or the *Cool Apple Guy* (and *Apple*).

- *Demonstration-based portrayals and story appeals*—This appeal is often used by laundry detergent stories that demonstrate how their brand cleans clothes whiter and brighter. *Fort James Corporation* recently demonstrated in a television advertisement how its *Dixie Rinse & ReUse* disposable stoneware brand can withstand a blow torch's heat and survive capture inside a rotating washing machine.

Think about some advertising story appeals to which you were recently exposed, and as importantly, advertising stories to which you paid attention. Now consider how many of these advertisements used one, two, or more of these message execution styles. The percentages likely will impress you.

During the fourth and final step involved in advertising message creation marketers should evaluate the effectiveness of their advertising stories. This step can only be executed after those messages have been created and actually conveyed through advertisements that were targeted toward predesignated market segments.

Two evaluation metrics are crucial. The names of the metrics are reach and frequency. Each is an important metric for marketers who are performing/making advertising functions themselves or who are outsourcing/buying advertising functions from supply chain partners.

Reach represents and captures the percentage of consumers within targeted segments who are exposed to a message during a pre-specified period of time. Reach measures how many?

Frequency represents and captures the number of times targeted consumers within targeted segments are exposed to an advertising message during a pre-specified time frame. Frequency measures how often?

Reach and frequency are critical success metrics for most marketers as they advertise because a factor called the Three-Hit-Rule exists and applies. The Three-Hit-Rule itself relates to the learning that results or fails to result when consumer or business recipients are exposed to advertising messages, or to other forms of communication. The Three-Hit-Rule suggests the recipients of advertising stories must be exposed at least three times to an opportunity to learn something before they can be expected to recall or understand new content, and subsequently retrieve, respond to, or apply the new content. Repeat, repeat, repeat; the message—until all targeted audiences who need to know, know and understand.

Whether its role is acknowledged or not, the Three-Hits Rule is why preachers, priests, or professors, marketing communicators all, routinely repeat key ideas or principles three times. Essentially rolling over messages; revealing new insights about old issues at every turn; illustrating key ideas or principle takeaways by introducing new and old examples. French author and 1947 *Nobel Prize Winner Andre Gide* never wrote directly about the Three-Hit Rule. Gide did suggest, however, that "everything that needs to be said has been said. But since no one was listening, everything must be said again." To which we add, and again, said one more time, or at least three times in total inside most advertising contexts.

SIX UNWRITTEN ADVERTISING RULES ABOUT ADVERTISING AND ADVERTISING MESSAGES

The following rules were unwritten, until now. But this rule set is so powerful and pervasive in its fit that it should inform any marketers' attempts to develop more effective advertising messages.

Advertising Rule 1

Marketers should treat advertisement messages as if their embedded stories also boasted entertainment and/or educational value that consumers can voluntarily and happily/gratefully consume.

Advertising Rule 2

Marketers should treat all their advertising stories as free-value value-adds, available at ridiculously low prices. The only thing that message recipients have to do to get the value is pay attention. (Of course, that's asking a lot these days, is it not?)

Advertising Rule 3

Marketers should embed messages inside these value-laden advertising spots. To envision how this rule might work one only must imagine how *GEICO* advertising campaigns have unfolded across two-plus decades. The entertainment and educational value for viewers or hearers emanates from humorous appeals or informative implications; there's value in being or getting smarter than other folks. There is near-universal value associated with understanding that *15 Minutes Can Save You . . .* what was the rest of that message?

Advertising Rule 4

Marketers should develop advertising messages that always feature presentations of pressing problems and the advertised brand as the logically-best or emotionally-best solution.

Advertising Rule 5

Through whatever ethical and resource-plausible means necessary, marketers should use advertising messages to pre-persuade consumers that all they have to do in order to grab the bargain is to pay attention to the message. This is clearly the most difficult challenge that most advertisers face. After all, their attention is surely a finite and highly-valued resource to consumers. But successful marketers never conflate the word difficult with the word impossible.

Advertising Rule 6

If an organization's balance sheet is sufficiently strong and its brand is already well-known, the decision to play the long game, as it relates to advertising, often makes strategic sense.

Marketers should uniformly realize that sometimes prospective customers' answer to all manner of promotional overtures, but particularly advertising, is not a "no" but rather a "not now." Those marketers selling expensively prestigious items such as *Mercedes* automobiles or *Gucci* "whatever" may win the current day, branding preference-wise, inside prospective customers minds even though the one-day customer may be months or even years away from actually being able to consummate the purchase. But you know? Often, marketers such as *Mercedes* or *Gucci* are willing to wait.

WHY TOO MUCH ADVERTISING MAY OR MAY NOT BE TOO MUCH

Thanksgiving ends, and an ongoing advertising tradition begins, again. While details vary the basic story remains constant. As depicted in a string of lovingly produced advertising messages, one family member surprises another family member with the *Christmas* gift of a bow-wrapped luxury car. The lucky beneficiary, usually a spousal partner, never displays a trace of consternation over the untold tens of thousands of dollars that have been spent. These prestigious brands often easily cost more than the medium income of an American family ($58,937 during 2021).

Naturally, most people who are exposed to the advertising message cannot afford the vehicle. But the envy produced by these advertisements serves an economic purpose, so long as the jealousy leaves majorities of consumers feeling bad about themselves—which, yes, creates great opportunities for advertisers who are forward-looking and sufficiently well-endowed, resource-wise, to play strategic long games of the sort referenced immediately above.

Advertising and other forms of marketing promotion always serve certain straightforward and highly useful marketing and economic purposes. Organizations that market goods and/or services have no alternative but to inform customers about the availability and desirability of favorable differences that are associated with their branded offerings. Marketers primarily use advertising, sales promotions, and personal selling to achieve these righteous ends. By telling prospective and current customers about the relative merits and thereby uniquely positioning the value of brands, the obese body of advertising enhances the quality of customer decision-making and, in theory, leaves customers and marketers alike better off than they would be in a promotions-free world.

But . . . and likely to no one's surprise—advertising practice itself often falls short of these ideal results. Marketing advertisers confront few moral or legal obligations to be completely honest and fully representative of the full range of availability options, all the time. You read the preceding sentence right. Some marketers target highly impressionable but rarely discerning children in ways that undermine their long-term physical and emotional health. Honest or not, ready or not, powerful advertising induces sometimes wasteful desires to spend, often on products that targeted segments neither need nor can afford. The informative, reminding, or persuasive content of advertising messages that promote expensive *European River Cruises*, high-end automobiles, or diamond-laced *Tiffany's* bling does not matter much for the vast numbers of message recipients who cannot afford them. But masses of consumers do experience distressful feelings of envy, regret, or outright anger, wrapped up inside indisputable facts, that other consumers are getting to enjoy products and experiences they will never possess or enjoy.

If advertising mostly prompts people to want things that they cannot afford, rather than steering people toward products or services that represent good matches for their needs, tastes, and pocketbooks, then more and more spending on advertising may degrade overall consumer satisfaction and happiness. Recent studies have confirmed that this latter undesirable outcome is actually happening. An inverse relationship between advertising expenditures and overall consumer satisfaction has been detected throughout the domestic marketplace.[17] The inverse relationship is simple: More spending, on advertising, apparently promotes less satisfaction among targeted customers. Is anyone surprised? Thinking back to when the idea that successful marketers are also effective "dissatisfaction creators" was introduced, it appears that advertising marketers may be performing better than many experts who criticize advertising's effectiveness are suggesting.

Thorsten Veblen published a book called *The Theory of the Leisure Class* in 1899. The book introduced and explained the nature of a concept called conspicuous consumption. Conspicuous consumption very definitely ties into positional goods. *Professor Veblen* argued that consumption is not just about satisfying needs but can also be wielded to signal status and prestige—and, therefore, well-branded positional products are well-positioned to solve those sorts of higher order needs, as *Professor Maslow* would have suggested (remember Module 6?). No need exists to write the more things change the more they . . . so we won't complete the sentence!

---

17. "Enough is Never Enough," *The Economist* (June 8, 2019): 70.

Pricey cars such as (insert your favorite brand here) surely offer niftier and with more features than *Chevrolets, Christmas* gift or not. But the vast difference in *Chevy* versus high-end *Benz* prices does not really relate to such functional differences. Instead, consumers paying extra for *Benz* buzz are often shelling out beaucoup bucks in exchange for the branded car's value as a status symbol. The status associated with the inverted peace sign symbol (i.e., the *Mercedes* brand branding identifier welded onto the cars' hood or pasted onto their grill) derives from the fact that most consumers cannot afford the vehicle.

Contemporary economists, though not most marketers, use the term "*Veblen Good*" to designate the sorts of prestigiously branded goods or services for which demand rises when their prices rise. Although, as discussed earlier, it is not the higher prices but rather the allure of exclusivity and greater status that elevates demand despite higher and higher prices. Normal economic logic is thereby kicked to the curb. Among typical shopping or convenience goods, the types of products that are routinely advertised to mass markets, the presence of opportunities to generate productivity-enhancing economics of scale allow marketers to promote superior products at lower prices as a path to success. Yet such cost-cutting, when coupled with lowered product prices, would prove an abomination to luxury marketers because lowered prices would not ensure sales growth but destroy the entire market.

The idea that consumers would knowingly pay exorbitant prices when lower priced but completely serviceable alternatives are available to elevate themselves above the less well-off might appear absurd, except for the observable fact that examples of exactly this happening abound. Advertising facilitates this process, and more advertising feeds and fuels more still. The kicker to this story is that in order for certain branded products to confer high status to those who use or own them, legions of consumers must exist who want the brands, because they have been made aware of their existence, but who have no means to pay for them. Advertising campaigns featuring sleek and sexy cars bedecked with oversized *Christmas*-like bows inform or remind the masses of how enviable—and how inaccessible—certain brands are.

The times, they do change. In 1899, when the *Theory of the Leisure Class* was first published, most rich people either did not work or did not work especially hard. Hence, use of the word "leisure" in the title of the book. Not so, today. In recent decades, most of the richest Americans also reside among the hardest working Americans. The *United States* yet again proves that for better or worse it has righteously earned its self-branded designation as an exceptional nation, because the global norm is that time spent working declines in lockstep with increases in income.

Who knows the status-envy production complex that is the advertising sector (complemented nicely by the mighty social networking sector) may be largely responsible for this particular type of marketing exceptionalism. In rich countries, most citizen consumers' basic needs have long since been made. US poverty lines begin at a level thirty-one times higher than global poverty lines, in adjusted 2020 dollar rates. To keep higher earning professionals striving for more, more desirable consumer goods and services must exist, out there, often slightly out of reach even for them! The sorts of perpetual dissatisfaction created implicitly and explicitly by advertising may actually juice economic growth by keeping productive workers who might otherwise enjoy more leisure time with their families bound to their desks.

Just enough, or is it really too much advertising, generates an ironic type of prosperity. A prosperity that rises and falls with how satisfied consumers are with their lives.

MODULE 14.3

Sales Promotion

Sales promotions deliver short-term incentives aimed at encouraging near-term customer purchases of products or services. Near-time, here, would usually involves forty-eight to seventy-two hours but may entail two to three minutes.

Hootchie's is a cooler than average *Denton, Texas,* restaurant located surprisingly near busy *Union Pacific Railroad* tracks. *Hootchie's* offers $1 beers whenever a train goes by because (according to local marketing lore) no one audibly talks due to the combination of roaring engines and screaming whistles as the train approaches and passes four or five nearby street-rail track intersections. (Trains are legally required to blow their whistles multiple times as they approach and pass through street or highway intersections.) This unusual, but not unique, marketing ploy illustrates a sales promotion that delivers incentives in the form of price discounts.

Sales promotions might also deliver short-term incentives intended to motivate more intense or more focused sales or marketing partnering efforts, typically either from marketers' supply chain partners or internal sales forces. Short term, here, references by the end of this week, month, or reporting quarter.

Sales promotions are often quite effective at achieving each outcome. Their effectiveness, in turn, is the primary reason why domestic marketers annually spend more money on sales promotions than is annually spent on advertising—shocking though this statement may initially appear.

Pfizer is the *Big Pharma* Corporation that created and markets *Viagra,* as previously stated. *Pfizer* still uses sales promotions to promote *Viagra.* In doing so *Pfizer* is following suit with other pharmaceutical firms that also employ sales promotions market solutions specifically designed to solve erectile dysfunction problems (branded, of course, as *ED)* that prospective or actual consumer users are experiencing. When using sales promotion, *Pfizer* strategically targets and seeks to incentivize various target audiences. Targeted audiences include:

- ▶ Final buyers, usually middle-aged or older male consumers; retailers, pharmacies such as *CVS*; various intermediaries or wholesalers, such as *McKesson*; various business customers, such as physicians and medical offices; and/or various sales force memberships, such as *Pfizer*'s own sales force of pharmaceutical sales representatives.

Each target audience referenced just above participates in and collectively constitutes the supply chain for *Pfizer*. Each supply chain partner engages in either the creation, distribution, marketing, promotion, or consumption of *Viagra* as a well-branded product and a promised marketing solution. Each supply chain partner, to greater or lesser degrees, buys from and sells to the other, and these exchange processes continue all the way to the end-user customer. The presumably male consumer only engages as a final purchaser/literal consumer/customer.

WHY ALL THE GROWTH IN SALES PROMOTIONS?

There are four reasons why the use of sales promotions has grown rapidly during recent decades.

The initial reason for this rapid growth follows from the intense short-term pressures to earn material marketing returns that are placed on marketing managers. Marketing managers, to greater degrees than many professionals, are subject to what-have-you-done-for-me-lately sorts of performance evaluations. "Lately" might include "what have you done for me" this week, month, or quarter but not much longer than that. Love it or leave it, the truth resonates. In marketing, you're often only as good as what you did, or sold, last week, month, or quarter. Meanwhile, the use of sales promotions typically produces results now, and the reality of this immediacy drives sales promotions' appeal.

The second reason driving sales promotions' mounting popularly ensues from increases in competitive pressures, particularly from global sources. Given this, refer back to reason one.

A third reason follows from the fact that most advertising does not work all that well anymore. Yet customers and prospects still need to reached, informed, reminded, and persuaded. And in the contemporary marketing world, sales promotions are often fit to do the trick. Most marketing managers logically put their money where their best results are most likely to be found. So they invest their limited promotional resources in sales promotions.

The fourth reason that explains the proliferation of sales promotion is that customers and their attitudes have themselves changed. The world—and the marketplace—is a more price-conscious place than it was a few years ago. Sales promotions work extremely effectively with price-conscious consumers. Results matter. Sales promotion usually generates agreeable short-term results in exchange for short-term investments.

TYPICAL SALES PROMOTION OBJECTIVES

Contemporary promotion objectives typically include the pursuit of one or more of the following marketing- or communication-related outcomes.

- ▶ *Sales- and market share-related objectives*—The related marketing goals in play here are straightforward. Marketers can either increase or sustain their current revenues or the market share percentages that they currently hold.
- ▶ *Retailer-related objectives*—The typical goal here is to encourage, promote, a greater emphasis on the sales efforts associated with certain brands—naturally, those associated with these exact sales promotions—more than other brands. This extra emphasis would prevail even in

situations where retailers being targeted by sales-promoting marketers merchandise two or more competing brands.

▶ *Sales force-related (motivational) objectives*—The sales force in question may work exclusively for the sales-promoting marketer, or the sales force may work for downstream supply chain partners. Either way, however, the sales promotion goal is to motivate the sales force to focus more attention on selling the brand that is "being promoted" though "the sales promotion."

Best Buy is a downstream supply chain retailer that markets both *Apple* and *Samsung* phones, among many other brands of electronic products. But, in this example, we assume *Best Buy* only markets *Samsung* or *Apple* brands. *Samsung*, as an upstream supply chain partner with *Best Buy*, absolutely would prefer that *Best Buy's* sales force spend more time selling its (as opposed to *Apple's*) electronic gear. To achieve this strategically-logical sales promotion objective, *Samsung* literally pays *Best Buy*, at a corporate level. That payment is the sales promotion. *Samsung* pays *Best Buy* based on the understanding, premise, and the promise that *Best Buy* will reward its top three to five in-store employees in each store who sells the most Samsung products during the next calendar month. Note our reference to the short term; a defined end time for the sales promotion is in place. *Samsung* dispenses monetary rewards for purposes of incentivizing *Best Buy's* salespeople. These payoffs, or incentives, are commonly described as either push money or spiffs.

Other, more general types of sales promotional communications that are also routinely used inside contemporary supply chains include:

▶ Reinforcing the visibility and position of new or existing brands.

▶ Building longer-term relationships with new or existing customers. This outcome might be pursued by getting new or current customers to try or retry—either way, by sampling—new or existing products. These new or existing customers subsequently may like the results enough to purchase the new or old thing again and again, even without the original incentivizing sales promotion.

▶ Motivating targeted recipients to do something right now.

TYPICAL SALES PROMOTION TOOLS

Samples and Sampling

Samples are akin to free giveaways. Free sampling is designed to encourage trial of brands themselves based on the premise that *"Mikey [might] like it"*[18] and ask mom to get the cereal, or whatever, for him

---

18. Once there was a little fictional media boy named Mikey. An advertising giant named *Rob McEnany*, who hailed from Chicago, inserted him inside an advertisement. The iconic commercial features three brothers eating breakfast. A heaping bowl of *Life* cereal, at the time a newly introduced product, sits uneaten before them. Two brothers question each other about the cereal; prodding the other to try it; noting, yuck, *Life* is supposed to be healthy. Neither submits ("I'm not gonna try it—*you* try it!"), so they con their little brother Mikey into sampling ("Let's get Mikey") to try the new product, while exclaiming, "He hates everything." Mikey briefly stares at the bowl. Post-contemplation, he takes one tentative bite and then begins to ravenously consume the cereal before him, resulting in his brothers excitedly exclaiming, "He likes it! Hey, Mikey!"

again, once he has ate the cereal one time. Of course, next time, "the-getting" (the purchasing act of acquisition) involves an actual full-blooded purchase. Samples are often used inside in grocery stores, experienced in perfume kiosks inside stores, or received in the mail or online.

Many readers are familiar with pop culture generally, and with military culture specifically. That's the reason why some readers are familiar with the phrase "*Smoke 'Em If You Got 'Em.*" But now all of you are. Here's why the phrase is important inside a marketing context.

Beginning with America's participation in *World War I* (1917–18), the phrase remained ubiquitous for generations—though not so much today. The use of product sampling—as practiced by the entire American cigarette industry—proved a key factor that contributed to a steady growth across decades in the per capita consumption of cigarettes. The growth culminated shortly after *World War II* ended. During 1946, substantially more than half of American males were smokers. The sampling process was simple; *Big Tobacco* (i.e., the entire domestic tobacco marketing sector) gave away millions of free packs to millions of active duty soldiers, sailors, airmen, and Marines.

This sampling ploy worked spectacularly well for an unusually simple reason. The sales promotional activity used by *Big Tobacco* motivated and incentivized legions of targeted users to try a smoke. The ability to generate product trial among consumers often proves half the persuasive battle; hence, all the free stuff. The ability to generate trial also always represents the first step toward getting targeted consumers to actually purchase the sampled product on their own accord at some future point. Naturally, this "get 'em to try 'em out" tactic and ultimately end up buying materially more for years to come, often until the customer dies, works so much better when the product is actually addictive.

While costly, free to the customer giveaways—sampling—often works far better than uninitiated marketers might otherwise assume. Especially within those industries where marketers are inclined to engage in the long game. The long game, as in do whatever is necessary—no matter the cost—to get folks to try the thing out, and then hook them forever. Imagine the lifetime value of a loyal customer to say, *R.J. Reynolds*, of a customer who begins sucking on their brand of cigarettes at age eighteen and puffs away until unfortunately he prematurely dies at age sixty-eight. But hey, that represented a great fifty-year-run for the marketer, didn't it?

Coupons

Coupons are still routinely used to incentivize customers. Coupons are dollars/cents/percentages-off price guarantees that encourage recipients to visit stores, restaurants, or websites—or to purchase specific branded products.

The first verified use of coupons inside the US occurred inside *Atlanta* during 1887 when *Asa Candler* gave away paper tickets that customers could redeem to exchange for a free glass of a new "soft drink" called *Coca-Cola*. Think this makes coupons *The Real Thing*? When it comes to effective sales promotions, we do. Today, most coupons are issued and applied through smart devices although the paper versions are still very much around.

Rebates

Rebates are a form of sales promotions that have been around a while. Rebates should not be confused with refunds. Rebates are amounts paid back by way of returned dollars out of prices that have already been paid by customers when they purchase products or services. Usually, the purchases involve large ticket items such as automobiles or refrigerators.

Rebates, or the opportunity to receive them, are designed to attract customers and motivate them to purchase now. Rebates can be offered by either manufacturers or retailers. The onus—or burden—is on customers to actually redeem, or return, them. This, in turn, is a factor that rebounds favorably toward marketers' bottom lines—insofar as more than half of customers fail to redeem their rebates—again, we see low involvement customers. Consequently, marketers retain dollars they otherwise owed the customer.

Special Price Deals

Special price deals are frequently wielded as sales promotion tools. Ah, let's see. When was the last time any male reader bought two blue or white dress shirts based on the fact that the store, say *Macy's*, was promoting a two-for-one pricing-deal? Well, for one author, that would be the last time he bought two or more new dress shirts as a way of prepping for the new semester.[19] (With the exception of the COVID-19 semesters when little to no motivation to buy new dress shirts to impress students existed.)

Therein resides a primary downside associated with the overuse of sales promotions, by the way. Some consumers get "trained" to not buy anything—such as new dress shirts—unless special deals are attached.

Or going back in time a couple decades to make a present-day point, *Northwest Airlines* (no, not *Southwest*) offered a stealth sales promotional special pricing deal. The now-merged airline offered two-way or round trip mystery tickets to anywhere for only $59.00 for the upcoming weekend; this Friday through Sunday. The hedge as well as the positioning hook was that no one or no couple knew where they were going until they arrived at the airport. The sales promotion gimmick worked. Flyership on *Northwest Airlines* surged. So did loyalty to and consumer buzz in the form of positive WOM about the brand. These desirable marketing outcomes blew-up, as well.

Special Sales Promotion Giveaways

Giveaways are pretty much what readers would suspect based on the name itself. Special promotion giveaways operate something like this:

▶ Dear Customer: We, a minor league baseball team, promise that you will receive "X" as you enter the ballpark. In exchange for your paid ticket, naturally. Marketers should tread carefully

---

19. Professors, like real humans, only get one chance to make a good first impression. So, professors, like pretty much everyone else, often wear their best new clothes on the first day of school.

here. Free Steak Knife giveaways, especially when coupled with special price deals such as Dollar Beer Nights at the old ball park, have not always worked out well during minor league baseball games. Especially that time when teams having fans from closely-located rival cities (*Greenville* and *Spartanburg,* both in *South Carolina*) were involved.

Yes, we're kidding. The alleged drunken brawl where steak knives were wielded to win the day never happened. Still, marketers should judiciously balance action and thought before engaging in giveaways or special price sales promotional offerings. Because what marketers do, as they give away crap, may say more than anticipated about their brands.

Contests, sweepstakes, games—targeted either at employees or customers who can play/participate in these events where the marketer seeks to motivate individuals by incentivizing them with promised rewards if they play—and win. The prior story, which could have been real, the one that involved *Apple, Samsung,* and *Best Buy* may well have also included *Best Buy's* managerial use of contests and games.

Sponsorships are yet another form of sales promotion and can be larger scale than one might suppose. *GEICO,* for example, "sponsors" all the "*GEICO-safe*" rest stops along all the interstate highways throughout *North Carolina.* Why, you might wonder, would GEICO do this? That is, until you have thought about the values that sponsoring rest stops actually deliver to the national insurer. To begin with, every driver and passenger who stops at any interstate rest stop throughout the entire state sees and consequently thinks about the brand, forcing or sustaining the GEICO brand name higher up in these perceivers' minds. And to end with, what consumer stopping at an interstate rest stop, particularly during particular times of the day (night!), doesn't want to feel safe?

Point-of-Purchase (POP) Displays

POP displays are signs placed at or near the point-of-purchase. POP display signs are designed to attract the attention of and then motivate, inspire, and inform customers regarding why—perhaps the inventive involves special price deals or limited-time offers—they should buy, now! What makes a POP display a POP display, however, is the fact that the sign was designed, purchased, and installed by one or more hosting retailer's upstream supply chain partners.

Patronage Awards

Patronage awards are widely used in certain marketing sectors and are generally to reward and further motivate customer loyalty. The airline, rental car, and hospitality service industries often employ these loyalty perks to motivate and reward customers.

Spiffs, Push Money, Slotting Allowances—Three Different Names, One Powerful Sales Promotion

Circling around to a sales promotion tool already mentioned, let's take a deeper dive. The tool is called spiffs but is also known as push money or slotting allowances. Spiff is a slang word for the dollar amount paid by manufacturers or distributors to retailers/retailers' sales forces in order to incentivize retailers and their sales forces to do something that sales-promoting manufacturers or distributors seek to have done. Spiffs may arrive in the form of immediate bonuses paid for successful sales. Spiff money is typically used to push demand for targeted brands downstream inside supply chains toward ultimate, or end-use, customers. This why spiffs are also called push money. These end-user customers are usually consumers.

Presumably you've heard about a big gentleman—and brand—named the *Green Giant*. Among other sets of values, the man specializes in making and marketing canned vegetables, including green beans. Assume, please, that Mr. Giant has recently developed a new, improved type of canned green beans.

Presumably you've similarly heard about this fine lady named Mrs. Kroger. Yep, the one who owns and manages all those *Kroger* grocery stores. Turns out, she happens to live downstream from Mr. Giant inside the grocery supply chain that each "partner" "shares." Among her managerial duties is the responsibility for purchasing the goods that are slotted on her stores' shelves or in her stores' freezers.

One fine day the Giant stoops through the front door of Mrs. Kroger's favorite store. He's there to see her; fine marketing gentleman that the Giant is, he had called and made an appointment. Getting right to the point, Mr. Giant asked Mrs. Kroger whether she has an open slot, on her shelves, on which to house and market his new green beans. Walking side-by-side the lady and gentleman stroll down her vegetable aisle, as she pointedly asks, in response to his question, "Dude, see any open slots [on my shelves]?" To his chagrin, the Giant admits, "no." "Well sorry, old friend (and supply chain partner), can't carry your new beans," she responds, in turn.

Undaunted, and being the flexible salesperson that he is, Mr. G. quickly asks Mrs. K: "Do you still run those special flyer ads in the Sunday and Wednesday issues of the newspaper? Heard those papers have really jacked up their prices?" Being the open-minded and flexible supply chain partner to the Giant that she is, Mrs. K responds, "Yes, I do, and YES, newspaper advertising prices have gone up." To which Mr. G., who knew the answers to his questions all along, intones: "Well, could I help you out by underwriting some of the costs associated with securing space in those papers? All I would ask in exchange is that you allow me to slide a few cans of my new beans onto a couple of slots on your shelves." Sales promotion deal offered; deal accepted; deal done.

This is what spiffs, push money, or ultimately, slotting allowances are all about. And that's generally how this particular sales promotion tool works.

Given all the different sales promotion tools that are available, as well as the various ways in which sales promotions can be strategically exploited, the fact that more money is spent on sales promotions than on advertising likely now appears more plausible. Of course, the fact that sales promotions work much better than advertising currently works, at least in the short-term, shouldn't be sold short as a causal factor, either.

TROUBLE IN PARADISE

Throughout history the use of bribes has effectively motivated bribed individuals to do what the bribing agent wanted them to do. In the short term, at least. History also reveals that the act of bribing tends to make bribed individuals want to come back for seconds, thirds, and so forth. Sales promotions, riven as they are with incentives (a form of bribes), operate in much the same fashion as do bribes. Any loyalty, such as it may develop, generally accrues to the bribe—or the incentive—and not to the brand.

The net result of this process is that sales promotions are not effective at building or sustaining lasting customer relationships. This is because customers who purchase products or visit retail locations usually do so because due to their receipt of the sales promotion rather than any values they view as inherent to branded products, services, or experiences (*Six Flags* is a branded experience). It remains possible that after consumers visit retailers or use specific brands whose use is being promoted through sales promotions, they may love either or both. But the facts are clear. Sales promotions usually do not encourage loyalty.

To the contrary, the excessive use of sales promotions is more likely to undermine customer loyalty. The reason is that deal-seeking consumers are often effectively trained (classically conditioned) to become loyal to the discount or incentive (the sales promotion) rather than becoming loyal to the value, prestige, or other benefits that emerge from being a loyal customer of the brand. Consequently, if and when other better deals stroll along, at least inside the minds of the sales promotion-sensitive customers, off they'll run toward another brand choice—effectively chasing the new and presumably more attractive deal.

MODULE 14.4

Managing Interpersonal Marketing Communication

Playacting, literally pretending, is a role that most successful marketers must learn to execute. These highly "strategic" communication behaviors are clearly self-aggrandizing and self-promoting. Neither condition, however, detracts from the fact that successful playacting—for example, the ability to fake sincerity, but only for moral reasons—is absolutely essential for professional salespeople and other marketers. Meanwhile, salespeople and other marketers generally should emphasize "showing" rather than "telling" inside all interpersonal interactions where doing so is possible and reasonable. Showing the values and solutions associated with the products or services they are selling as opposed to the telling of these same tales, when and where doing so is possible. As the old marketing cliche suggests: Demonstrate rather than explicate.

The skills and traits that successful salespeople and other marketers need to possess are similar to the skills required to perform as a successful actor. These skills and traits include the display of empathy, the actuation of imagination, a willingness and an ability to charm others without being overtly ingratiating or transparent, and the perceptive nuance necessary to willingly but ethically adjust one's message and offer reasonable accommodations as exigencies arise inside contexts in which they find themselves marketing. Another trait that successful marketers and actors share is a high tolerance for rejection. Successful actors and salespeople must manage personal doubts (beat them down) and rejection (pick yourself back up). Professionals performing inside marketing and/or acting roles must persist, which comes either relatively easily or results from hard work and focus, because the marketers or actors believe in the value of what they are pursuing. Successful salespeople and actors, in brief, reject rejection and keep slogging ahead toward their goals.

Most successful salespeople and marketers are also either taught or innately already understood that "me, me, me" is "dull, dull, dull" to any targeted or un-targeted audiences that are consigned to hearing it against their will. That's not all, however. Excessive amounts of self-interested dialogue—too much me, me, me—often proves extremely off-putting to customers and prospective customers. An excessive or perpetual "me-focus" always also eliminates opportunities for actual and potential buyers to talk about themselves and their personal or corporate problems. When they communicate, salespeople and marketers should routinely focus far more attention on the needs and interests of the party/parties sitting on the other side of the exchange relationship than their own. Salespeople and marketers should share details about their own lives only to the extent that the reciprocal nature of "give & take-like" conversations open up informational spigots and keep the valves stuck on full-on. Or, to the extent that sharing personal details helps salespeople or marketers establish common ground—building connective bridges rather than separating walls—between them and the targets of their persuasive efforts.

THE ART, THE SIMPLICITY, THE IMPORTANCE OF LISTENING

Two remarkably simple tactics can be employed to powerfully positive personal effect when anyone, including salespeople, are seeking to listen better. Relatedly, learning how to listen better is remarkably important for any marketer who aspires to achieve sustainable personal success. Learn better how to listen, that is, after having asked the right questions that simultaneously inspire and lead prospective or actual customers to reveal their real feelings, thoughts, and pain points (their problems) so as, upon their hearing, salespeople can adjust or readjust their subsequent presentation such that the communication that follows precisely aligns more closely with customers' thoughts and needs.

Now, to those two simple tactics. First, consciously choose to use the vertical pronoun as little as possible. Every time a salesperson makes reference to themselves through use of the I-word they are by default not listening to the other, to prospective or actual customers and their issues, concerns or desires. Few are the customers or prospects who are anxious to have to wade through salespeople's ego to get to the point where those buyers can share their own or actually receive salespeople's info. Avoid the "I."

Second, consciously choose to breathe before you speak. Almost immediately more patience, new and broader perspectives of the other person's points of view, and as a side benefit, more gratitude and respect from others should follow. The tactic is ridiculously simple to execute. The activity involves nothing more than pausing—breathing—after the person to whom you've been listening stops talking. The time gap between audible voices may seem like an eternity. But it's not; only a fraction of one second transpires. You will quickly get used to, appreciate, and actively benefit from the power this simple act of breathing confers to you. The trick, which is no trick at all, will draw you closely to nearly everyone with whom you interact, as you earn their respect by giving them their props. You soon will learn how much you benefit from giving others one of the rarest and most treasured gifts you can offer them. That's right, your attention.

Take a few minutes a couple of times a day when you're around crowds and observe conversations being shared among people around you. You'll probably quickly notice how often many people are anxiously waiting for their "turn" to speak. So often people are not really listening to the other, but simply waiting anxiously to pounce on any opening to express their views. People often complete the other party's sentences, or very rapidly respond with words or phrases such as "yeah, yeah," and "I know," effectively urging the conversation "partner" to hurry up so they can take their turn at the mic. Too many less than optimally successful marketers treat talking with others as a back-and-forth sparring session, as verbal ping-pong, as opposed to learning from the conversation—which frankly ought to be marketers' primary communication objective much of the time.

These hurried and harried conversational styles encourage each side to these communication exchanges to overreact, reject, or critize others' points of views, impute erroneous meanings, attribute false motives, and form opinions before the fellow speaker is done talking. While this malaise of misconstrual may represent business as usual for everyday conversationalists, it won't suffice as a baseline communication standard for successful marketers. Talk about an easy marketing tactic for standing out favorably as opposed to fitting in like everyone else. No wonder people today are so often irritated, out of sorts, and annoyed with one another. Sometimes, given our poor listening skills, it's a miracle that some people have any friends at all. And, of course, some people don't.

Most people have spent most of their lives to date waiting for their turn to speak. However, were they to try breathe before . . ., most people would be pleasantly surprised at the softer responses that emanate from those whom they allow to completely express their thoughts before they begin expressing theirs. Often, salespeople might be allowing customers or prospective customers to be listened to for the first times in their lives. Salespeople will experience a feeling of relief from their communication exchange partners—and a much calmer, more enlightening, and less rushed conversation can ensue. Salespeople, don't worry that you will not get your turn to speak—this will happen. And your turn to speak may bear more fruit because the person with who you are speaking will pick up on and honor your respect and patience and may begin to respond in a similar fashion.

One Biblical proverb recounts: . . . "He that keeps his mouth keeps his life. But he who open wide his mouth shall have destruction." Speak less than necessary, wherever and whenever speaking economically is possible and reasonable. Wisdom for those marketers who speak too much but still somehow foolishly assume that people will continue to listen carefully to what they say. Their ranks are filled with failed marketers.

SHOULD PROFESSIONAL SALESPEOPLE COMMUNICATE AS HUNTERS OR FARMERS?

Professional salespeople can, do, and should function as both hunters and farmers. Professional salespeople should role-switch (i.e., in hunt or farm) at various times for various reasons.

Hunters kill or capture prey. They do so for various reasons. Unless consumers/customers are vegan, they need hunters in their lives. Marketing organizations also need salespeople who are able to "hunt" effectively.

Farmers plant, cultivate, and harvest. They manage crops. Everybody needs farmers—in the full sense of the word, "need." Without farmers and the solutions they produce—let's brand it as food—everyone has problems. Marketing organizations likewise need professional salespeople who are willing and able to be farmers.

Successful salespeople combine elements of both the hunter and the farmer inside their professional activities. Salespeople, as expected, would typically prove better at performing one or the other function. But someone, presumably salespeople, must act as a hunter and capture a fair share of customers' attention, time, and wallet. This is true every bit to the degree that someone, possibly the same salesperson, should continue to function as a farmer who cultivates, plants, tills, and harvests value from salesperson-customer relationships after those associations have been established.

MODULE 14.5

Personal Selling, Sales Promotions, Push Money: Pulling Promotions Together

The history is clear. Opiate painkillers are good and bad; both a blessing and a curse. Opiate painkillers genuinely split the difference between pain and pleasure. Opiate painkillers exist as a paradox; their use creates dilemmas. Marketing sits right in the middle of this paradox and is partially responsible for creating this dilemma. The medical establishment occupies exactly the same spot and creates more than its fair share of opiate-based dilemmas, as well.

During the 1980s, a new cadre of highly trained medical pain specialists began to argue that narcotic pain pills, derived from opium poppies, should be used more aggressively. To them, not using opioid painkillers was inhumane. These specialists argued that opioid pills were non-addictive when used to treat pain. Opioids, these marketers (medical pain specialists, like everyone, are marketers) contended, could be prescribed in large quantities for long periods—not just to terminal cancer patients or the like but to almost anyone experiencing pain. This idea driving this solution had no scientific support, but it proved incredibly profitable. One influential academic article later acknowledged that the literature pain relief advocates relied upon the good intention of eradicating pain to make their points their actual case lacked real evidence. The paper plainly stated that "because the primary goal was to destigmatize, we often left evidence behind."[20]

These specialists, who defined their mission broadly as "delivering pain relief," quickly formed an alliance with various *Big Pharma* firms that made and marketed opioids. During the 1990s, when medical schools taught about pain relief at all, they focused on using non-opiate narcotics as solutions. But by the early 2000s, doctors were being educated and encouraged to prescribe opiate drugs after routine surgeries, be they appendectomy, ACL repair, or wisdom tooth extraction. Opiates were also prescribed for arthritis and back pain. Chronic pain had once been treated with a combination of therapeutic and holistic treatment strategies that only occasionally involved narcotics. By the early 2000s essentially all varieties of pain were treated almost exclusively through the use of opioids, as insurance marketers cut back on reimbursements for patients whose long-term pain therapies did not

---
20. Sam Quinones, "The Penance of Doc O," *The New Yorker* (May 2019): 59–69.

include opiate drugs. Marketers, by skillfully wielding communication and promotion processes, had won the day and taken ownership of the pain relief field.

The following discussion summarizes what happened next. The following content also illustrates how persuasively powerful marketing communication efforts can be when they are done right—or does the following exemplify what can happen when highly persuasive marketing communication is done wrong? During the mid-1990s the American drug industry began investing heavily in sales promotions and hired legions of young, unusually attractive female sales representatives to persuade doctors of their drugs' various miracles. Attractive females were generally employed because most doctors at the time were male. Nationally, the number of drug reps blew up from 38,000 in 1995 to 100,000 in 2005. Old-style drug reps, who previously had functioned as genuine experts in medicine or pharmacology, largely left the scene—replaced by sexy (in male physicians' perceptions) giveaway, or sales promotion, artists.

"It went from a dozen calls a week to a dozen calls a day," recalls one West Virginia-based doctor. "If you wrote a lot of scrips, you were high on their call list. You would be marketed to several times a day by the same company using different reps."[21]

Most domestic drug companies quickly adopted a new selling approach. Call it all sales promotions all the time. Foremost among these firms was the now infamous *Perdue Pharma*, which had developed a new timed-release opioid painkiller branded as *OxyContin* in 1996. *Perdue Pharma* paid legendarily large bonuses to members of their sales force—up to $100,000 per quarter, eight times the average that competitors were paying. To improve sales numbers, drug reps offered doctors mugs, fishing hats, baggage tags, and hundreds of all-expense-paid trips to desirable destinations for purportedly professional reasons—implicitly obligating docs to their brand in return. Drug reps purchased lunches for doctors' staffs, knowing that with staffs on their sides doctors became more malleable and easier to influence. Once they gained medicine's ear, reps leaned on specious and misrepresented data created by company-funded medical researchers to sell their product—these efforts entailed nothing more than other forms of sales promotions. *Perdue* promoted the mythical claim that *OxyContin* was effectively non-addictive because it gradually released an opioid, oxycodone, into patient bodies and thus did not create the intense highs and lows that facilitate addiction.

These opiate salespeople, in general, were marketing more than pills. They were also selling time-savings solutions to harried doctors who had been told an epidemic of pain was afoot but who possessed little time or professional training to address it. The patients themselves? Generally, all too happy to not be told to lose weight or increase exercise or eat healthier, not when magical little pills could be prescribed that promised to cure all ailments that pained them. A perfect marketing storm ensued. You may or may not know that average life expectancy inside America declined during 2017 and 2018 and then again during 2019 (this was all happening prior to COVID-19), for the first time during the nation's history. The first time in history, excluding the periods encompassing the *Civil War* or America's participation in *World Wars* I and II. A primary reason for domestic consumers' earlier demise, was opiate overdose-based deaths and suicides.

---

21. Sam Quinones, "The Penance of Doc O," *The New Yorker* (May 2019): 59–69.

Not to mention the damages wrought by so much lost ambition and prospective productivity among the growing population of pain pill poppers. The only way that swallowing oxy, or for that matter smoking pot or shooting heroin, won't rob users' ambition is if their only ambition is to get high and over-watch *YouTube*. This quip entails a riff on a line of dialogue written by *Quintin Tarantino* and uttered by *Samuel L. Jackson* in the movie *Jackie Brown*. Or, not coincidentally, dialogue created by a marketer, product and brand (*Tarantino*); expressed by a second marketer, product and brand (*Samuel L.*); and finally conveyed through another product and brand, the movie and the communication medium itself. Each of whom—save the movie itself, which after all is but an inanimate object—were seeking to get their new product development creativity buzz on and make big bucks in the process.

Marketing-induced addictions are cunning, baffling, and powerful. The nature of their source and the means through which addictions are created as a result of directed marketing efforts does not matter; the preceding statement remains true. Marketer-induced addiction is a war that will never be won on anything other than an individual consumer basis. Many addictions begin as the best party you could possibly imagine attending but end up being unimaginably worse than the worst, most boring and degrading job you have ever had. Rarely if ever is it worth anyone's while to consume any product that ultimately may control—as in "consume"—us. Ask yourself whether you have ever scrolled-around with your phone under the covers so as to not keep your bed partner awake late at night—oh yes, there's another marketer-induced addiction.

Once consumers get deeply addicted to any marketed thing, they no longer get high off of consuming the product in their original quantities but instead need to consume more of the product just to feel normal. Such marketed entities might include illicit (heroin or meth) or licit drugs (alcohol or tobacco), pornography, betting, *Facebook*, fast-food, or *Manolo Blahnik* shoes—the list is not endless but is too long to list here. Addictions rarely if ever represent good situations for consumers. But addictive habits—demonstrably intense episode of brand loyalty—deliver "wonderful" outcomes for marketers. Talk about what began merely as consumer wants turning into drop-dead must-have regardless-of-the-costs-I-must-satisfy consumer needs.

MODULE 14.6

A Special Form of Marketing Communication: Public Relations

Public relations communication efforts address the need to build or sustain good relationships with various targeted publics that marketers or marketing organizations deem critical to their current and future success. A list of likely publics for most sizable marketing organizations could include employees, investors, governmental agencies, the media, various public interest groups, along with customers and prospective customers.

The implicit goal of public relations communications is to create, sustain, or restore positive perceptions and predispositions about marketing organizations' positions and brands inside the collective mind of the aforementioned targeted publics. Perhaps, for example, when otherwise well-regarded brands such as *Toyota* or *Nissan* confront the need to publicly issue and explain the reasoning behind product recalls.

The success or failure of public relations communication efforts is measured through expressed public opinions/attitudes and other evidence of waxing or waning public support.

Public relations and the public relations communication function are each subsets of marketing and marketing promotion functions. By no means, however, are all marketing activities related to public relations.

Public relations communications can and should be used to build or protect existing brand equity. Public relations professionals operate more than a little like cosmetologists. Their mission and their reason to exist is to make their clients or organizations look better.

The fact remains, however, that even when brands enjoy strong publics relations support, as *Boeing* certainly did, the public relations equity can rudely crash back to earth on pretty much an overnight basis. The equity of the *Boeing* brand, generally, and its 737 passenger plane, specifically, failed hard and fast during 2019 after *Boeing's* 737 brand of airplane was involved in two consecutive highly publicized crashes.

Public relations communications can and should be used to announce great new breakthroughs or products.

The primary reason, however, why public relations is used is to clean up messes by issuing marketing apologies and carefully curated explanations after screw-ups have occurred; after the "stuff" has hit the fan for whatever reason.

Marketing apologies include all manner of verbal and/or written attempts to restore, rehabilitate, or reposition brand images that have been wounded. Getting personal; imagine if your personal brand was now suddenly being re-defined by the worst decision you had ever made or behavior you had displayed in your entire life. Well, imagine no more. This is basically what happens every day inside business settings when individual brands rightly or wrongly become associated with, and often blamed for, some sort of disaster or horrible deed.

Public relations experts are often pejoratively labeled as spin doctors.[22]

This label works given that public relations gurus are now routinely accused, often with good reason, of spreading fake news. When they function as spin doctors, public relations professionals often (but surely not always) seek to disorient the people they have targeted and sought to influence by engaging in a public-relations version of mushroom management. Mushroom managerial practices, lest you be unfamiliar, entail keeping the people one is managing and whose perceptions one is seeking to manipulate in the dark while feeding them full of crap.

Is this all that public relations professionals do? Of course not. But when presumably self-inflicted crises arise inside the lives of professional, corporate, or political brands the activities described just above do in fact encompass a material portion of the duties and responsibilities assigned to public relations experts. Right now, if you're thinking and feeling the spokespeople for politicians or for political candidates promoting themselves as purported solutions while on the campaign trail—well, no surprise to follow, so are we.

As an antidote, or using the current parlance, as a vacillation, the world needs more effective and thus more sincere apologies. Seriously, it does. Given this, it's worth considering why humans ascribe such high values to apologies. For starters, the public issuance of "I'm sorry(s)" initially signals that marketers and targeted recipients of apologies presumably share core values about right and wrong. Makes sense, insofar as if the usually apology-offering marketer and offended and/or injured customer don't share such common sentiments and values, why apologize? The very issuance of these "my-bads" further signals that professionals or their organizations surely can agree as exchange partners on what the one side, either buyers or sellers, can reasonably expect from the other side, again either customers or marketers, inside exchange relationships that previously unified them, and that hopefully will unify them again. These two reasons alone provide a sufficient case regarding why value of a good apology should be appreciated.

But who are we kidding? Public relations-type apologies in the early twenty-first century have become almost entirely self-interested affairs. Which means, in the end, apologies are often

---

22. Spin doctors attempt to forestall, overturn, explain-away, or justify (after the fact of disaster or scandal) negative publicity. These so-called "spinmeisters" make positive and/or diversionary pronouncements on behalf of marketing wayward, creepy, or malicious organizations, politicians, famous people, or whoever is willing and able to pay for the values their public relations experts' communication services can generate.

not authentic. Which seems fair enough, because inside overly politically correct or woke market environments apologies are often demanded for offenses that themselves are inauthentic.

Bottom-lining all this, whether the apology is sincere or not usually does not matter. What matters is whether the apology works. Cynical? Surely. But sometimes marketing is cynical. And before jumping too quickly into knee-jerk criticisms, how long is the list of high-end professionals or professional activities that are not also sometimes cynical themselves? That's right, the roll call inside that classroom would not take long to complete.

It remains true that public relations-sorts of apologies are frequently stage-managed in ways intended to signal brand virtues. In turn, this fact is responsible for much of the derision that's routinely targeted toward public relations.[23] Apologies are not easy conversations for regular people or even for experienced public relations professionals representing the interests of firms to have. But if firms don't determine how best to initiate and manage contrite (sincere!) conversations by managing public relations and subsequently establish/reestablish which behaviors are acceptable/out of bounds—and represent grounds for shame if not restitution, everybody who once shared a now diminished relationship with a damaged brand will also be sorry soon. Especially if apologists could eliminate some of their own virtue-signaling in the process.

HOW DO PUBLIC RELATIONS PROCESSES GENERALLY WORK?

Public relations experts handle and manage public relations on behalf of brands they represent by developing or executing:

- News releases—designed and intended to counter the negative or accentuate the positive.
- Speeches, either writing or actually delivering them.
- News conferences, grand openings, or fun promotional events such as *General Motors* displaying new cars and trucks targeted at younger demographics on university or college campuses.
- Website management, including blogs, tweets, and texts.

Ideally, marketing organization's public relations efforts are blended smoothly with other promotional activities within the firm's integrated marketing communications efforts (the IMC topic is discussed more fully below), wherein all messages, regardless of their source, are delivered clearly, consistently, and compellingly.

Marketing organizations generally do not pay for public relations press releases and news stories. Instead, public relations staffers develop and circulate information and attempt to manage the flow and favorable public perceptions about ongoing events and news cycles. Thus, in many cases, well-managed public relations efforts generate greater buzz much more quickly and less expensively than advertising. However, the fact remains that various types of marketers typically do not pay for public

---

23. In defense of public relationships, various other marketer-initiated communication conversations also purposefully signal marketers' virtues, often at the expense of their competitors (who by contrast are portrayed as less than virtuous).

relations efforts. The net result here is public relations experts have less control over what content is actually messaged or how it is said.

WHEN AND WHERE ARE PUBLIC RELATIONS INITIATIVES USUALLY DEPLOYED?

Myriad historical and current examples exist related to when and where natural, unintended, and often unfair or self-inflicted disasters occur. Brand-related disasters that in turn were handled poorly or well by public relations experts. This list is hardly exhaustive but is generally historical in nature. The list could be updated on almost a monthly basis so why not go with but a few classic examples.

- *British Petroleum*, the *Gulf of Mexico* oil spill; *Hurricane Katrina*, *New Orleans*, and President Bush the Younger's Administration's response; the U.S. *Secret Service*, drunken cavorting with prostitutes and strippers, while protecting the President on an international mission; *Bill Cosby, Anthony Weiner, Matt Lauer, Harvey Weinstein, Jeffrey Epstein,* and *Prince Andrew, Harry and Meghan* (and *Queen Elizabeth*); *Toyota*, brakes-*Volkswagen*, emissions; the *FBI* or *ICE, James Comey*, and can-everyone-agree-for-one-moment *inefficiently-managed investigations* and dissembling about *Russia, Hillary,* and the *Donald*; *Lance Armstrong*, doping; *Donald Sterling*, former *NBA* owner and his racist rants; the *NFL*, player (brain damage/partner abuse, ex-player dementia due to brain damage); player protests against flag, leadership mismanagement; *Affordable Health Care Act,* exploiting the "stupidity of the American voter" according to *Obamacare Architect* and *Harvard* Professor *Jonathan Gruber*; *Donald Trump* and *Stormy Daniels,* or *Bill Clinton* and *Monica*; *United Airlines*, the passenger carrier that beat up a customer on a plane during 2017; *JAY-Z, Taylor Swift,* and the myriad ex-boyfriends she kept writing about; *Boeing* and the 737 brand of airliner; and whatever happens anew next week. Because you know something will.

ALL-TIMERS, WORST AND BEST

Worst—*McDonald's*, typically a masterful marketer, was involved in an all-timer-PR screw-up. A few decades back, the fast-food giant actually said three things, in response to negative rumors about the wormy origins of their genuine U.S.D.A. inspected and approved hamburger meat. First, that eating red worm meat is healthier than eating red meat, beef. Second, that eating red worm meat is certainly better for Mother Earth than raising beef, which is true but hardly an appealing defense. Three, that read worm meat, at least at the time, cost more than hamburger meat on a per-pound basis. These three statements featured the upside of all being true. Sadly, the PR responses featured the downside of being uniformly-stupid-things-to-say in response to a false accusation. It's a wonder that *Ronald* has survived to this day.

Best—Nearly forty years ago a prominent consumer products marketer's worst nightmare became tragic reality for *Johnson & Johnson*. During a four-day stretch in the fall of 1982, seven Chicago area residents died after taking cyanide-laced capsules of Extra-Strength *Tylenol,* a painkiller that was and remains *Johnson & Johnson's* top-selling brand. The marketer immediately recalled all *Tylenol* products, which was the first major recall in US history.

Experts predicted that *Tylenol,* a brand accounting for 17 percent of the company's net income in 1981, would never recover from the act of terror. Yet just more than five months later Tylenol was headed back to store shelves, this time as a new product shielded in tamper-proof packaging (this new product innovation was the first of its kind, as well) and bolstered by an extensive public relations campaign. A year later, *Tylenol's* share of the $1.2 billion analgesic market, which plunged to 7 percent from 37 percent following the tragedy, had climbed back to 30 percent.

What set apart Johnson & Johnson's handling of the crisis from others? It took charge, responded quickly, assumed ownership—and blame, even though the tragedy was clearly not *Johnson & Johnson's* fault. The firm put consumer needs first by recalling 31 million bottles of Tylenol capsules from store shelves and offering free replacement products in the safer tablet form. Marketers too often fiddle while Rome burns. By contrast, *Johnson & Johnson,* in defending and restoring its lost brand equity, got after it and stayed after it.

A MORE RECENT PUBLIC RELATIONS HIT

Goya Foods markets authentic *Latino* foods and recipes and positions its brand as the largest *Hispanic*-owned food company in the *United States. Goya Foods,* in a burst of public relations brilliance, recently named U.S. House of Representatives member *Alexandria Ocasio-Cortez* (D., N.Y.) its marketer of the month. Representative Ocasio-Cortez is famous for many things including her constant internet posts. In one such post she very publicly supported the boycott of *Goya Foods* during 2020 after CEO Robert Unanue visited the Trump White House as a part of a *Hispanic Prosperity* initiative.

The *Goya Foods* CEO broke the news about *Ocasio-Cortez's* award while being interviewed on "*The Michael Berry Show*." Said he, "When she boycotted us, our sales actually increased more than 1000 percent. So we gave her an honorary," because she did not attend the ceremony, and conferred the award due to the "attention she had brought to *Goya* and its adobo."[24] Point in fact: *Goya* likely hit the double-double, here. First, when the representative, who is branded as *AOC* (and getting some free publicity here herself) publicly boycotted the Goya brand. And second, when Goya's CEO pulled off the public relations coup.

Oh yes, remember the branding and promotional and in this public relations value that follows simply from garnering the attention of consumers, yes, almost any form of attention.

---

24. "AOC's Latest Achievement," *The Wall Street Journal* (December 11, 2020): A14.

MODULE 14.7

Integrated Marketing Communication (IMC)

The concept called Integrated Marketing Communication has existed for about thirty years. Integrated Marketing Communications (IMC) suggests that marketers should mix or blend their various communication tools into an integrated whole for purposes of achieving one or more communication goals at any point in time. The communication exists as the entire set of promotional mix elements. While each communication goal may prove crucial to the success of all marketing organizations the importance of particular communication goals at various points in time is context-dependent.

As readers now know, typical communication goals for marketers and their branded products include:

- Informing targeted customers . . . Core message—Hey! We're here and here's why we're good!
- Reminding targeted customers . . . Core message—Hey! We're still here and here's why we're still good.
- Persuading targeted customers . . . Core message—Hey! Buy-me, not-them, because . . . .
- Executing never-ending efforts to create new/strengthen old customer relationships . . . by making . . . new-things-known and seemingly-more-valuable; or by making . . . old-things-appear-new and still-valuable.

PRECISE TARGETING INSIDE DIVERSE MARKETS

Innovative information management technologies have radically changed how marketing firms and customers communicate with each other. These innovations have radically altered how and how effectively marketers target customers.

For example, when today's readers purchase zombie or historical romance genre books online, they suddenly magically receive other stories promoting similar books that they *might* also like. And those precisely targeted promotional messages are usually right; the message recipients really are quite likely to like the new books that have been suggested to them.

Or, when prospective flyers page through *Cheap Flights* seeking to determine how much it'll cost to fly from the *DFW* to the *Charlotte, N.C.,* airports, other related ticketing deals suddenly pop up—and pop up and up for days—often arriving in the form of special sales promotions deals that bundle special car rental or hotel rates. That's precise segmentation and targeting—and all brought to your electronic door by the advent of new technology.

Metaphorically speaking, precisely aimed "rifles" featuring laser-like sights and degrees of accuracy are typically being used by marketers as they target segments today. Recall *Google* and its remarkable ability to track users as discussed during Module 6. Whereas in the not too distant past, marketers essentially just blasted away as if they were using shotguns to randomly "hit" customers with their promotional stories. When they are fired shotguns unleash broad patterns of shot or pellets; when they are fired rifles unleash precisely-targeted ordinance. Shotgunning marketers were essentially splattering their messages against walls, hoping against hope that sufficient proportions of messages would stick. Little targeting was used. These days and such non-targeting targeting practices have largely ended, particularly among successful marketing organizations.

The same sorts of innovative technologies that have been discussed throughout this book have simultaneously created incredibly heterogeneous, fragmented, and seemingly-irrevocably-splintered consumer markets segments. In effect, millions of markets comprised of mini-me's currently exist, or so things appear. These innovative technologies include the by-now usual sets of suspects: social networking sites, *Netflix, Amazon Prime*, 999+ satellite-enabled television stations, thousands of actual and internet-only magazines, dozens of new personal communication media and apps, and so forth.

These two technology-driven changes—one, more precise targeting opportunities; two, higher numbers of smaller but more heterogeneous market segments—represent either opportunities or threats (manageable challenges, each) to marketing organizations as they target prospects or customers and manage their promotional mixes. These environmental changes have necessarily changed how strategic marketing organizations execute their promotional efforts. Almost every contemporary marketing organization now engages in far less broad-casting and far more narrow-casting. Mass marketing communication efforts once were more effective and consequently were more widely used than they are now. Mass marketing (a "non-targeting" targeting tactic), entails undifferentiated targeting approaches where entire markets are pursued with little to no differentiation. This communication approach is now basically dead.

No need exists, however, to assume that all environmental changes are driven by technological innovations. Consumers' tastes, their preferred fashions, and their broad cultural or sub-cultural assessments of what's appropriate or inappropriate change naturally for their own reasons and at their own pace. A 1914 *Grape-Nuts* cereal newspaper and magazine advertisement (yes, more than one hundred years ago), written at the beginning of *World War I*, extolled the cereal's capacity for equipping children to prevail in fights: "Husky bodies and stout bodies and the ability to win fights depend—more often than we think—on the food eaten."[25]

---

25. Erik Larson, *Dead Wake* (New York: Broadway Books, 2015).

Note two factors that typically would not fly inside today's advertisements. First, the length of the brand message and positioning statement. Such length would neither abide nor succeed in today's three-to-five word, four-to-five-second-long sloganeering-based micro-advertising messages. Second, note the fact that the message would not pass muster with today's "woker than thou" (me more awakened than thee?) cultural sentinels. Today, *Post Cereal Co.*, the maker and marketer of *GrapeNuts,* would be doxed and boycotted inside a few seconds. Of course, *Post Cereal Co.*, or rather a third-party advertising agency functioning as a supply chain partner to *Post* Cereal, would never have created such an aggressive message today.

INTEGRATED MARKETING COMMUNICATION (IMC)

IMC as a promotional strategy, seeks to unify and integrate all modes of marketing communications. The purpose of these "integration" (unification) processes is to create unifying brand messages and positioning stories that are told clearly, compellingly, and CONSISTENTLY across all communication media channels that are used to convey any marketing message about whatever brand is being promoted. Using fewer words to say the same thing, IMC ensures that every message, regardless of its source, says the same thing. Those communication sources would include advertising, personal selling, sales promotion, social media management, and/or public relations—among other modes of communication such as design; product shapes; internet influencers; and other spokespeople who stand ready to be used as endorsers, confessors, explainers, informers, reminders, or apologists as the need for either or all might arise inside marketing organizations' promotional mix arsenals. The preceding is a beastly-long sentence. But then again, the average marketing organization's promotional mix is beastly in its diversity. There are, after all, lots of different ways to say the same thing.

The Need for Integrated Marketing Communications

Apart from the technological forces and more-splintered market segments that were discussed above, another primary reason why marketers increasingly need to use IMC approaches is because most customers don't make distinctions between the various communication sources that marketers use to convey messages. Most consumers do not care about the source of their marketing information. Of course, why should they? Customers and prospects have zero obligation to even pay attention much less to think intensely—in a highly-involved manner—about marketing communications. And as far as where they go to find the right or most accurate information about brands information, most B2B customers or B2C consumers could give a rip about this issue, as well. (Yes, sometimes this is not true. Sometimes customers are highly concerned about the sources of their brand information.)

Marketers' first job, then, is to create more branding stories that are deemed attention-worthy by customers. Fact is, most marketers today are happy if customers pay any attention at all to their messages. Marketers' second job is then to deliver these refined, attention-worthy brand messages in a unified (integrated) fashion through as many different communication channels as is reasonably possible.

Because these conditions prevail today, different media and different promotional messages are increasingly structured and "integrated" together such that the packaged communication sources meld into and deliver single, crisp, and ultimately unifying stories about the promoting firm's brand or brands. The word "integrated," when used inside an IMC context, means packaged- or bundled-together. Most marketers today face a practical imperative to integrate all their targeted promotions messages into single, crisp, unified communication packages. Because if and when conflicting or contradictory messages emerge from different marketing sources about the same brand, brand images and market positions get muddled. Marketing opportunities to secure favorable differentiation would subsequently be degraded or completely lost.

Consequently, three additional Cs emerge as key success factors for marketers as they communicate. The three new "C's" are Clear, Consistent, and Compelling. Clear, as in the meaning of the communicated message should be clear. Consistent, as in the meaning of the communicated message should be communicated in a consistent manner. Compelling, as in the communicated message should prove appealing, attractive, and "sticky" either to targeted consumer eyes, to targeted consumer ears, or to both the eyes and ears of message recipients.

The net takeaway inside this passage is that when marketers develop and communicate or convey promotional stories, the associated messages should be uniformly clear, consistent, and compelling—regardless of the communication selected to convey the message. Each of the three new "C's" represents an important trait, or characteristic, that should be built into branding stories as they are told and communicated.

MODULE 14.8

Pushing or Pulling Product Demand

Two extremely broad promotional strategies exist. The first is called push. The second is called pull. Push and pull promotional strategies are different from but complementary to each other. Each promotional strategy is routinely used inside supply chains. Which makes perfect sense, because as you have read before, the supply chain is exactly where most marketing activities occur.

PUSHING

Push generally entails the use of promotional strategies where firms attempt to take their products downstream throughout their supply chain to the final use B2B or B2C customers. Push, the word, stems from the idea that marketers are attempting to push their products downstream through supply chains on a partner-firm by partner-firm basis toward end-use consumers. Frequently used push promotional tactics include trying to sell products directly to customers via company-owned stores and by negotiating/partnering with retailers to sell their products for them, or by setting up point-of-sale displays. Often, targeted retailers receive special sales incentives, or sales promotions, in exchange for giving the pushing marketer's brand increased salesperson attention and visibility.

Push marketing promotions can be experienced inside department stores that sell perfume lines. The manufacturing brand of the fragrance often offers sales incentives to, say, *Dillard's* in exchange for the department store agreeing that its employees will push, say, the *Clive Christian No. 1* brand toward customers. Push promotional tactics work well for new brands that aren't well-established or for new products within established brand families that require additional promotion. For most consumers being introduced to the fragrance at the store would prove their first experience with the product. As noted, customers would not know to ask for the brand if they first did not know it existed.

PULLING

Pull follows an opposing path. The goal of pull promotions is to persuade or incentivize customers to come toward the marketer and brand. Hence, the term pull is used; insofar as marketers seek to pull demand (and desires) from customers upstream through the supply chain toward the sourcing point where their brand is produced (originates). Mass media promotions such as advertising, precisely targeted word-of-mouth referrals, and advertised sales promotions are often used to execute pull promotion strategies. Pull marketing campaigns are often recognizable by the amount of advertising being used in them. Pull marketing requires that substantial amounts of advertising dollars be spent on making brands household names among the segments toward which the push promotion messages are targeted.

To illustrate, consider toy marketing. In the first stage, *Mattel* targets its advertising about a new branded toy that it has developed toward end-users, customers (kids and their parents) who exist at the end of their toy supply chain. Second, children and their parents see the advertisements, hopefully develop a desire (or want) to purchase the toy, and acting based on their desires begin visiting either physical or online retailer sites that sell toys generally and this toy brand specifically. Third, as demand increases, retailers scramble trying to stock the product in their stores. At that point, *Mattel* has successfully pulled-in customers toward the *Mattel* toy brand.

PLAIN FACTS

Integrated promotional tactics can and should be used to achieve either push or pull promotional effects inside B2B or B2C supply chains. Each promotional approach is useful. Yet push and pull promotions each feature times and places where one or the other promotional tactic will likely prove more effective.

Pull promotions, for example, generally seek to create brand loyalty and keep customers coming back. Push promotions, by contrast, are more concerned with generating short-term sales.

Push and pull promotions are widely used as guiding promotional strategies. In fact, many marketers, including most large manufacturers, use both simultaneously in strategically integrated fashions. The question of which approach to use consequently is more one of proportionality as opposed to being all in or all out on either push or pull.

Typically, when marketing organizations employ personal selling, they are pushing. Typically, when marketers use advertising, sales promotions, or direct marketing, they are pulling.

MODULE 14.9

Communicating during Pandemics: Contingency Planning, Contingent Communication Responses

Progressive Insurance's communications team meet during June 2020, to plan an upcoming advertisement that shows the brand's mega pitchwoman, *Flo,* running out of a bowling alley to help a client whose car had been wrecked by a falling basketball hoop. The planning session, naturally conducted on *Zoom,* broke down into a debate over a sensitive environmental issue: Should the characters in the ad wear masks? Likely, not an unusual "argument" for *Madison Avenue* mavens to have during this particularly peculiar season.

Marketing is about telling a brand's story. And those stories are told through marketers' communication arm, or the promotional mix. During most of 2020 and 2021 marketing organizations wrestled over strategic questions related to what story to tell and the tone—or mood—to feature in the narrative. Genuine "what-to-leave-in" and "what-to-leave-out" dilemmas arose inside the head-sheds of legions of better and lesser known marketing organizations. Companies also struggled to determine how much to spend, on even the best new big ideas, as the normal and expected media through their messages would be conveyed either faltered or left town completely (albeit temporarily).

Madison Avenue has always and will ever remain highly cognizant of the nation's current mood keeping its finger on both the zeitgeist and consumer pulse through their ongoing execution of marketing research. There are pronounced tendencies, for example, to emphasize patriotic advertising messages during wartime or nostalgic ads during recessions to remind consumers that they have experienced and prevailed against hard times before and will again. (This patriotic fall-back makes sense. Because people who are acutely concerned about their futures generally don't desire or need much more than the necessities in their presence.) The year 2020 was, all things considered, at best a challenging and at worst a brutal year. There were persistent uncertainties and unknown unknowns about COVID-19, year-long anxieties and outrage about the November Presidential Election, and societal upheaval related to perceived or actual racial inequality and movements such as racial inequality, *Black Lives Matter,* or *Back-the-Blue.* (Small wonder that this book kept hammering about the importance of environmental trends.) To suggest that marketing communicators generally and advertisers specifically had to navigate a perfect storm of trend-lines is not hyperbole.

Some major corporations emphasized inspirational advertising spots during the pandemic's early days. In one advertisement *GM* showed a man loading bales of hay into a truck; another message showed a man turning on the lights at a previously dark *GM* dealership. *Apple* advertising spots portrayed a montage of satisfied customers using its technology to maintain their creativity, including actor *John Krascinski* crafting an episode for his *YouTube* show. *McDonald's* laid out a montage of *Golden Arches* signs. Collectively, the thematic Big Ideas that unified each message were a combination of emotions and sweetness so sticky they would have made *Hallmark Cards* or even its television network blush.

Other marketers more aggressively exploited COVID-19 as an environmental trend in an effort to drive. *Domino's Pizza* cribbed from *Tom Cruise's* breakout movie, 1983's *Risky Business* to promote a no human contact service delivery process—a new service value one must suppose. The advertising and service delivery target were customers who did not want to interact with delivery people. *Starbucks* aired a bubbly advertising message that promoted its new app and proclaimed "we are ready to welcome you back."

BEER

Other well-known firms strategized about whether to refocus or cut their advertising expenditures, especially when live sports events temporarily died. *Anheuser-Busch-InBev* (mothership for *Budweiser's* beer brands) temporarily decreased its advertising spend by double-digit percentages. Television advertising budgets were decreased with most cuts being reallocated toward purely digital media. Chief Marketing Officer Marcel Marcondes reported to the *Wall Street Journal* that, "We were freaking out about the business, no sports, no bars, no restaurants."

The macro-brewer leaned heavily into marketing research data to strategize about how best to reach consumers in this new world order. *Anheuser-Busch-InBev's* online daily poll of about 7,000 consumers revealed that many people were drinking while playing video games. In response, the brewing marketer created a gaming tournament that featured professional athletes, who were fundamentally functioning as celebrity endorsers, playing *Call of Duty* and narrow-casted the event on *Amazon.com's* *Twitch*. During this sales promotion play, ads promoted *Bud Light Seltzer* and informed viewers that the brand was available on *Drizly.com*, an *Anheuser-Busch-InBev's* supply chain partner that specializes in delivering beer. Sales of the product rose by more than 400 percent during the three-week-long sales promotion event (the gaming tournament).

SPICES

Other well-known consumer brands kept spending full-tilt on advertising during the depths of this environmental crisis while modifying key elements of their advertising messages. *McCormick & Co.*, the leading domestic spice marketer, modified existing advertising messages as consumers increasingly cooked and baked and of course ate at home. Again, we see how an uncontrollable event (the arrival of COVID-19) contributed directly to environmental trends that played out as threats to many restaurants and bars were treated as opportunities to producers of specialty and non-so-special foods and ingredients that could be prepared and consumed at home. As market researchers detected spikes in online searches for phrases such as "easy quarantine recipes" or "gourmet meals at home" *McCormick* spun out sales promotion cooking videos and posted them on media sites like *Instagram*. Sales of formerly near-dormant items such as vanilla extra—hey, the product does appear to last forever—skyrocketed. As did the usual spicy suspects such as pepper, salt, and garlic powder.

INSURANCE

Let's retreat in order to progress, or, stated differently, step back to *Progressive* (Insurance). During April 2020, *Progressive* constructed a marketing research-based roadmap to guide the corporation's marketing strategies throughout the balance of the COVID-19 pandemic—and its consequences. The core marketing research goal that ended up driving the strategy entailed tracking American consumers' collective mood as the consequences have ebbed and flowed, and have otherwise evolved. The roadmap suggested that domestic consumers, collectively, would pass through three predictable stages. The three phrases were:

- Relief—During the relief stage domestic consumers sought comfort and testimony about what companies were doing for the country and for their employees.
- Release—During the release stage domestic consumers were seeking breaks—relief—from thinking constantly about the pandemic.
- Recovery—During recovery restrictions began to loosen as people wanted to return to their normal lives.

As those stages were constructed, *Progressive* researchers gazed back into by tapping into secondary data in order to discern how consumers and marketers weathered past crises such as 9/11. Marketing researchers also collected/analyzed primary (and present-day) data on consumer sentiments, economic activity, and consumers' collective shopping behaviors as they responded to the crisis. Some of what *Progressive* discovered was actually predictable, especially given what you know after having almost completed this book. First, the insurance marketer discovered that determining what stage the nation is in at any point in time is extremely difficult (think the *Product Portfolio Planning Matrix*; or the *Product Life Cycle Concept*). Second, the insurer learned that *America's* mood varied radically across different geographic regions *(segmentation-fundamentals* fundamentally matter). And third, the marketer learned that deep levels of uncertainly about the nature of the consequences that the pandemic would generate prevailed, and that most consumer decision-makers preferred to postpone making whatever major decisions they could delay. As readers now know "risk" is generally manageable. But "uncertainty," that dreaded condition in which unknown-unknowns predominate, is anything but easily manageable among consumers and marketing strategists alike.

Predictably, these high levels of environmental uncertainty colored *Progressive* advertising decisions the most. *Progressive* sketched out more than half a dozen ideas for advertising campaigns that would be ran using the *National Football League* as a baseline media platform as the company deliberated over whether there would be a season (remember this was back in April/May 2020). The marketer eventually agreed upon one advertising idea that used *Cleveland Browns* quarterback *Baker Mayfield*. A debate arose within *Progressive* regarding how much to spend on advertising during 2020. Some brain-trusts argued that advertising expenditures represented an unwise investment during a period when customers or prospects were not driving much and were much less inclined to shop for car insurance. Fortunately, having read about MAD, *Progressive* wisely opted to not cut advertising expenditures. The insurance giant's Chief Marketing Officer told the *Wall Street Journal:* "You want to stay top-of-mind. You don't want people to see an ad from your rival and give them a shot."

PUTTING A RIBBON ON THINGS

The preceding text is interesting, likely a bit too busily clever, and at times even alliterative. But as always, readers should ponder and answer the so-what? Question before listening to anything that anyone is telling and selling. Anyone, like your authors. The so-what answer was that *Progressive* used marketing analytic-based predictive(s) about what stage the country was experiencing or entering and exiting to guide the big ideas (or idea, singular) embedded inside its advertising messages as well as to direct the messaging style through which those big ideas would be introduced to the world.

The insurance industry's marketing wars are brutal. Some $8.2 billion was spent on US ads alone during 2020, according to an ad-tracker organization named *Kantar*. *Flo*, the wacky character who wanders into homes and yards in an all-white gear to pitch *Progressive's* plans, complete fiercely for customers' mind-space against the likes of *GEICO's* smart-alecky *Gecko* and *Liberty Mutual's Emu*, a tall and unusual bird named *LiMu*. *Progressive* is among the top property-casualty insurers.

Progressive spent $1.8 billion during 2020 on expenditures and as such resides among the top ten advertising users in the country. The marketer was expected to spend close to $2 billion on ad efforts during 2021, despite the crisis, according to an executive familiar with the company's marketing plans.

Progressive bet that the declines in shopping for car insurance were temporary. The marketer also benefited from fewer drivers being on the road meaning that it had to pay out fewer claims. "*Progressive* were largely successful" in increasing market share, *Piper Sandler & Co* analyst Paul Newsome said of *Progressive*.

Many marketers treaded lightly during the pandemic's early stages. They presumably were wary about looking as if they were exploiting the crisis for their own gain. Moreover, research showed that consumers wanted brands to do more to help people and employees affected by the pandemic. *Anheuser-Busch* included a charity component in most of its ad campaigns. The professional athletes who participated in the video game tournament on *Twitch* won a donation to a charity of their choice. An online workout video series, which it created and aired on sites such as YouTube, promoted its *Michelob Ultra* beer and raised money for trainers and gym owners who were hurt by the pandemic.

As part of its "Relief" stage campaign, *Progressive* ran an advertisement called *Apron*. The message featured a montage of people putting on aprons. "What does an apron have to do with insurance?

An apron offers protection, an apron is not quitting until you've helped make something better," the voice-over intoned. The spot announced a program that provided credits on car insurance premiums, since people were driving less. *Progressive* CEO Tricia Griffith narrated the advertisement itself.

By mid-April, Mr. Charney felt the nation was ready to move beyond the "Relief" phase. A self-described news junkie, he has studied patterns in how people respond to traumatic historical events. He recalled the first sporting event to take place in *New York* after the September 11, 2001, terrorist attacks. On September 21, 2001, the *New York Mets* defeated the *Atlanta Braves* with a game-winning home run by Mike Piazza. "People were ready for sports, they needed a release," said Mr. Charney.

Similarly, as the pandemic stretched on, Mr. Charney noticed the heavy media buzz around *Tiger King*, the *Netflix* documentary series about zookeeper Joe Exotic. He took it as a sign that people were ready to escape pandemic life. Polling data, gathered by *Progressive's* advertising agency *Arnold*, revealed that 63 percent of domestic consumers believed brands could bring some much-needed humor to people during a tough time.

"Not only was the science telling us it was time for a change, but our gut was telling us too," Mr. Charney said. *Progressive* shifted to its "Release" stage, reintroducing funnier ads, including TV spots featuring *Flo* and her co-workers working from home and struggling to partake in company *Zoom* video calls. In one of the ads *Flo* struggles to connect to Wi-Fi and find the camera on her computer. Chaos ensues. One team member is using a vacuum during the call and a co-worker complains: "Whoever is doing that, can you go on mute."

Mr. Charney was worried about news reports that there could be a resurgence of coronavirus cases as American cities and states reopened following lockdowns. In late May, he added the "Relapse" stage to the road map after he visited a local *Mexican* restaurant in *Cleveland* and saw about one hundred people not wearing masks. "Everybody was trying to look in the rearview mirror" and act as though the pandemic was over, he said.

Progressive still sought to avoid overly optimistic or glib displays in its ads. Uplifting music that might convey the end of the crisis is in sight was pointedly eliminated. The company even created an advertising campaign that would air if a full-on second wave of the pandemic that came to fruition later this year. The company declined to share what the "Relapse" ads will look like but said the phase will focus on the psychological aspects of stopping, starting, and then stopping all over again.

Mr. Charney has resisted putting masks on his characters in ads, saying that would remind people too much of the crisis at hand. *Progressive* hasn't received any formal complaints, though some social media users have questioned the company's approach.

Progressive debated cutting the end of an ad in which *Flo* high-fived a coworker after they exited their vehicle, but decided it wasn't an issue since they were wearing driving gloves.

Brands were forced to navigate yet another new crisis in June. The upheaval over racial injustice that was sweeping the country following the killing of *George Floyd* caused marketers to scramble once again to make sure their ads didn't strike the wrong tone. Many firms simply stopped advertising and advertising spending for a brief time until things began to sort themselves out.

On a video call, *Progressive's* marketing executives reviewed ads the company had in its pipeline, including a radio spot featuring two men talking about switching to *Progressive*. The narrator says: "These days, nothing is normal and everything is weird. But you could still save big when you switch to *Progressive*." One executive said the word "weird" could be interpreted as a critique of the racial justice movement. "I don't want to characterize what is happening with racial injustice with being weird," one of the *Progressive* executives said. Other executives said the word was intended to describe the climate during the pandemic.[26]

The advertisement aired after the initial wave of protests died down. Such is a sample of how complex the lives of promotional managers have become during an era where change arrives in remarkably dynamic and unpredictable ways. These promotional managers, and indeed most modern marketers, are probably feeling something similar to the lyrics *Jacob Dylan* of *The Wallflowers* wrote in the band's song, *One Headlight*: "I know I ain't changed but I know I'm not the same."

What about you? How are you feeling after finishing this last marketing story? Surely Relieved? As if you need a Release to apply what you've learned? Or as if you need a period of Recovery?

EXHIBIT 14.1
The Communications Process

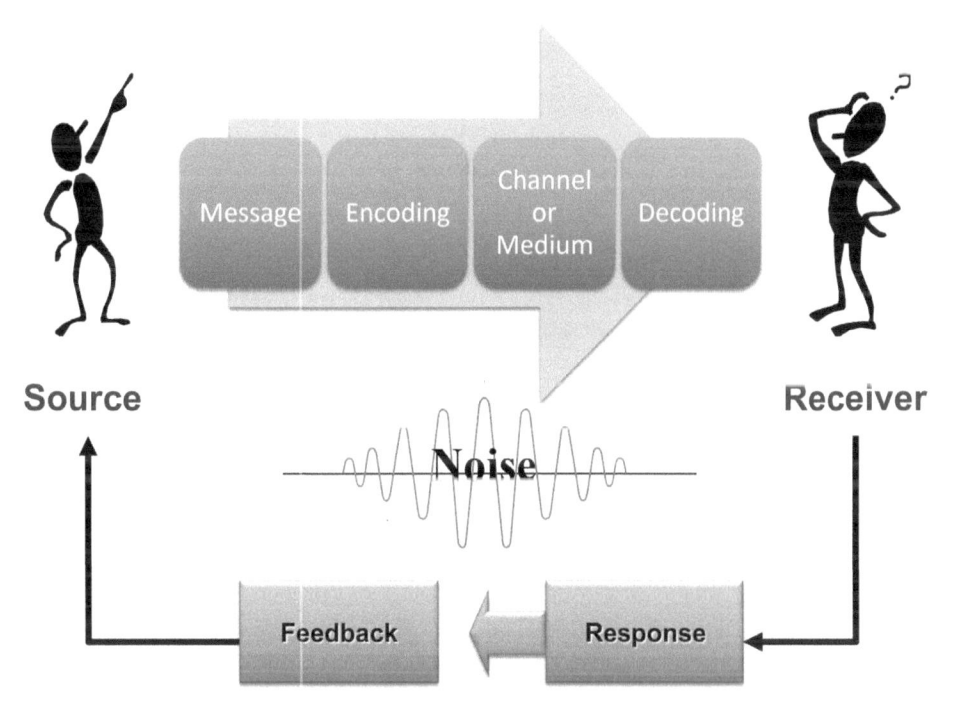

---

26. Suzane Vranica, "Pitching a Pandemic," *The Wall Street Journal* (October 3–4, 2020): C1-2.

EXHIBIT 14.2
The Advertising Process

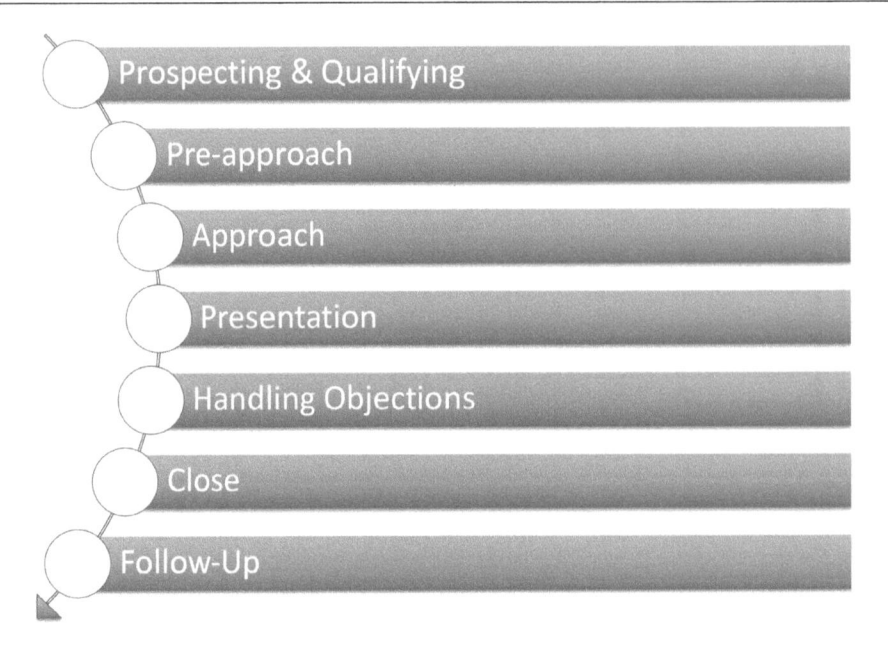

Establish Advertising Objectives → Identify Target Audience → Determine the Budget
- Affordable
- Percent of Sales
- Competitive Parity
- Objective and Task

→ Develop and Execute Advertising Strategy

Create the Message
Select and Schedule Media

→ Advertising Evaluation

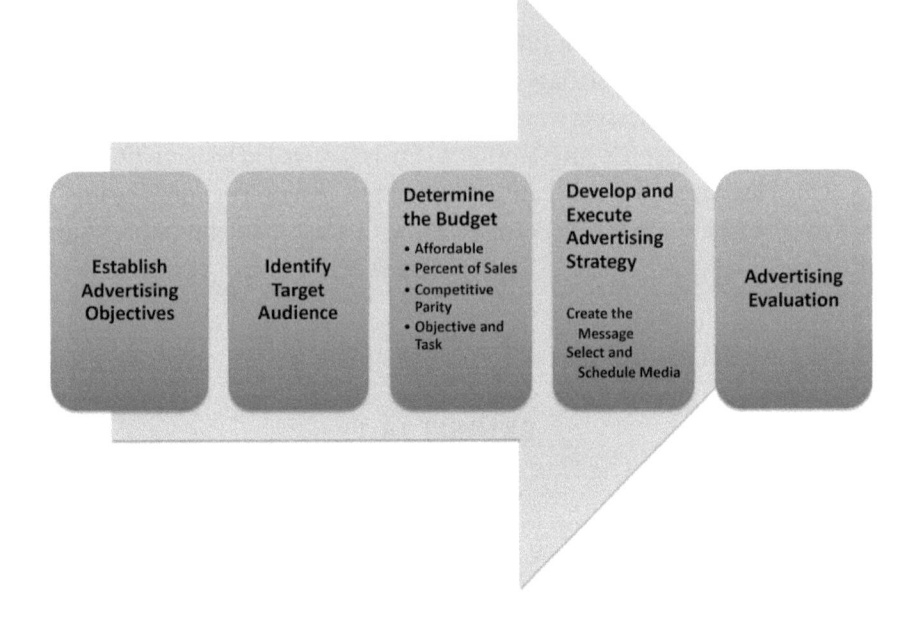

EXHIBIT 14.3
The Personal Selling Process

- Prospecting & Qualifying
- Pre-approach
- Approach
- Presentation
- Handling Objections
- Close
- Follow-Up

TABLE 14.1
Some Common Advertising Objectives

Lead Generation	Advertising to generate sales leads for follow-up by sales personnel.
Customer Engagement	Using various media to engage existing and potential customers by providing information, entertainment, and opportunities to participate with the brand. Using social media, for example, to encourage existing and potential customers to visit with the brand and talk about the brand with others. Engaging with existing customers can improve brand loyalty rates and boost *customer lifetime value*.
Engaging Influencers	Engaging with a group that can influence existing and potential customers to adopt the brand. For example, Olay is a P&G brand that makes extensive use of data analytics to identify and target the most influential opinion leaders for their brand. P&G then attempts to start conversations with these opinion leaders' social-media followers.[27]
Encourage Brand Switching	The objective is to advertise and provide supporting sales promotions to entice customers away from competitors' brands. Sprint, for example, advertises its "Unlimited Plus" for five lines at $24 per line. The plan includes unlimited text, talk, and data. Consumers are encouraged to "switch now."
Enhance Company Image/Reputation	The objective is to employ institutional advertising to improve or reinforce corporate image, rather than build product demand. BP, subsequent to the Gulf oil spill launched an "Olympic-themed" campaign it hoped would improve perceptions of the company. Ads, developed by Ogilvy & Mather, focused on six Olympic and Paralympic athletes from Team Great Britain.[28]
Brand Differentiation	The objective is to differentiate the brand from those of competitors on key *determinant attributes*—advertise superior value compared to that offered by competitors' brands on attributes important for choosing between brand alternatives.
Societal Engagement	The objective is to communicate the firm's stance on some important societal issue and, potentially sway the target audience's opinions in the direction advocated in the message. This objective is appropriate for *advocacy advertising* which is used to promote a particular message or cause. Advocacy advertising is intended to support the interests of a group or the public in general. It is not intended to promote any specific product or service.
Brand Positioning & Repositioning	The objective is to create the desired image for a new product, reinforce current brand image with target audiences, or attempt to change a brand's image to achieve a better fit with an alternative target audience. Old Spice effectively repositioned its brand with advertising employing Isaiah Mustafa in which the brand was portrayed as "sexy, surprising, fun, and youthful." A far different position from its prior image of a brand targeted toward older generations.[29]

---

27. Theodore Levitt, "Marketing Myopia," *Harvard Business Review* (July–August, 1960): 45–56.
28. Derek F. Abell, *Defining the Business: The Starting Point of Strategic Planning* (Englewood Cliffs, NJ: Prentice Hall, 1980), 1-6.
29. Kathleen Deveny, "Bally Is On a Winning Streak," *Business Week* (December 2, 1985): 30–31.

TABLE 14.2
Major Advertising Appeals

Fear appeals are employed to scare people into buying or not buying and using certain products. Michelin's ads emphasizing keeping one's family safe by selecting the correct tires and American Cancer Society ads aimed at de-marketing cigarettes and other tobacco products are among the better examples.
Sex appeals are intended to either make one feel more attractive by using a product ("Ultrabrite gives your mouth sex appeal"), attach sexual imagery to the product (the Oui ad for perfume linking the brand to an attractive woman in a provocative setting), or employ a "sexy" celebrity to endorse the product (Paris Hilton for Carl's Jr.).
Humor appeals are employed to gain attention and, hopefully, create a positive "affective" response to the ad that can rub off on the product. The idea is "like the ad, like the brand." Humor can be quite effective with both as long as the humor does not dominate the message to the point that viewers cannot recall the brand or its values.
Slice of life appeals show the product being used by the "typical consumer" in a normal setting. Personal care and home maintenance products are often advertised using this form of appeal. A Tide commercial, for example, may show the average homemaker enjoying brighter, cleaner laundry as a result of using Tide's latest formula.
Lifestyle appeals show the product being used within the context of someone enjoying a specific lifestyle orientation or experience. Think of the typical Mountain Dew ad showing young adults enjoying the refreshing coolness of a mountain lake while swimming and partying.
Demonstration ads show the product actually being used. The objective is to specifically highlight key benefits or features. Bounty paper towels employs demonstration ads in which the brand is demonstrated in a way that emphasizes absorbency and strength.
Testimonial ads attempt to use endorsers who appear likeable and believable to attest to the product's utility and value. The endorsers can be real people or paid celebrities. Weight loss products often use testimonials from real people who have successfully used the product to lose weight. Celebrities experiencing successful weight loss also have been employed. Jenny Craig for example has used both types of endorsers. Most recently Nutrasystem used Marie Osmond as a celebrity spokesperson.
Personality symbols are essentially trade characters (recall our discussion of trade characters from Chapter 9) that have been created to represent the brand. Examples include the Pillsbury Dough Boy, the GEICO Gecko, Betty Crocker, Progressive's Flo, Speedy Alka-Seltzer, and the Michelin Man.
Image appeals build a mood or image surrounding the product and its use. Usually there is no attempt to link the brand to any specific benefits or features. The objective is to create an emotional response or mood to the ad that may "rub off" on the brand. Common products advertised using image appeals include perfumes, jewelry, and designer clothing. Such ads attempt to link brands to romantic images or self-concept images. Imagery is the essential element for success.

EXHIBIT 14.4
Push and Pull Promotional Strategies

Push Strategy: Promotion directed at intermediaries pushes product from one supply chain level to the next.

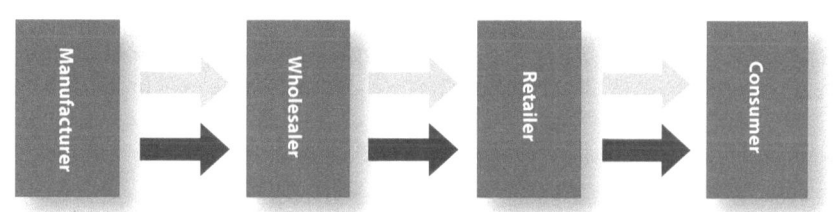

Manufacturer → Wholesaler → Retailer → Consumer

Pull Strategy: Product is pulled through supply chains due to promotion directly targeted at consumers.

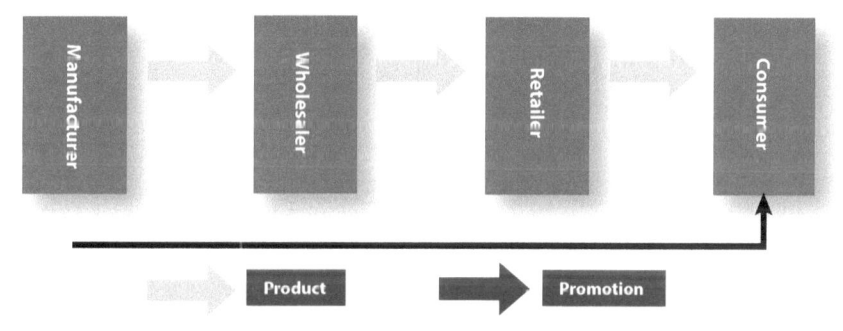

Manufacturer → Wholesaler → Retailer → Consumer

→ Product   → Promotion

TABLE 14.3
The Scope of the Promotion Decision

Promotion Element	Promotion Element

Promotion Objectives:
Specific promotion objectives are set that identify what we want promotion to accomplish for us.
Objectives determine what promotional elements will be employed.
	Sales Promotion Considerations:
	• Determining sales promotion objectives
	• Selecting the types of sales promotion activities to use:
	   • P-O-P devices;
	   • Samples;
	   • Specialty advertising;
	   • Premiums and trading stamps;
	   • Coupons;
	   • Trade shows and exhibits.
	• Evaluating the effectiveness of sales promotions.

Advertising Considerations: • Identifying the target audience; • Defining advertising objectives; • Selecting the advertising platform or theme; • Selecting the advertising budget; • Developing a media plan; • Creating the advertising message including copy and artwork; • Executing the advertising program; • Measuring advertising effectiveness; • Define advertising objectives.	**Public Relations and Publicity Considerations:** • Establish public relations and publicity objectives; • Select messages and vehicles; • Assess the effectiveness of public relations and publicity efforts.
Personal Selling Considerations: • Determining the number and types of sales people required; • Establishing sales force objectives; • Recruiting sales personnel; • Training sales personnel; • Compensating sales personnel; • Motivating sales personnel; • Identifying and managing sales territories; • Controlling and evaluating sales force efforts.	

GLOSSARY

Advertising—includes any form of one-way; paid, which means the sponsor is identified; and impersonal communication aimed at targeted customers; and is delivered en masse through electronic, print, or INET-based communication media; in order to persuade, inform, remind, or build new or strengthen existing relationships with targeted B2B or B2C customers about the value/differences associated with given brands.

AIOs (Activities, Interests, Opinions)—indirect measurements of consumers' behaviors and attitudes that is often used to effectively segment them. AIOs essentially measure what consumers prefer to do or contemplate (think about) during their free time. AIOs consequently capture portions of consumers' beliefs, attitudes, and opinions.

Art, What Is—anything that creates more energy than it consumes inside whatever setting it resides. (Art is contrasted with science below.)

Associative Barriers—function like chains holding down professionals, restraining them from thinking more creatively when facing the sorts of complicated business and customer problems that need to be solved today. The presence of associative barriers increases professionals' sense of certainty, even in situations where individual professionals' known solutions are wrong and their current perspectives are not up to the task.

Attitude—learned and enduring predispositions to respond positively or negatively toward certain stimuli.

Attractive Market Segments—should be measurable, accessible, substantial, differentiable, and actionable.

Attribute—features or functions associated with products or services that create value and benefit customers.

Attributes, Products (Brand Characteristics)—distinguish one brand from other brands competing inside the same product category. Any product's size, shape, color, features, design, style, quality, functionality, durability, reputation, quality, or price; these and possible product characteristics might exist as product attributes, or brand characteristics. Product attributes affect the appeal, levels of acceptability, and/or levels of desirability of individual brands.

B2B Marketing—when one or more organizations are involved in marketing and an organization is involved as a customer, the process is called B2B marketing. The success of B2B marketers is generally driven by their ability to satisfy customer needs.

B2C Marketing—when consumers are involved in marketing activities as customers and organizations are involved as marketers, the process is described as B2C marketing. The success of B2C marketers is generally driven by their ability to satisfy wants.

Bait & Switch—an illegal promotional practice wherein an extremely low-priced product is promoted as bait to lure customers into stores whereupon salespeople attempt to switch customers over to higher priced alternatives.

BCG Product Portfolio Matrix—a portfolio analysis model used to assess the probability that products will generate sufficient cash or market share. Marketing then uses this information to determine whether and how much to invest in the products going forward.

Behavioral Segmentation—a process that entails dividing prospective or actual consumers based on how they act toward or actually use a branded product.

Belief—descriptive thoughts that consumers develop, have, and hold about something. The "something" might include people, ideas, or products; but then again we just said the same thing three times. Whatever the something is, it has, by definition, functioned as a stimuli in that consumer's formulated perceptions about it.

Benefit—provides values and solutions that motivate or otherwise inspire customers to purchase or to continue to purchase particular products and brands.

Benefit-Based Segmentation—the process of dividing larger, more diverse marketers into smaller, more uniform segments based on the primary benefit that individual prospects or customers seek from purchasing and/or consuming a given brand.

Big Idea—the phrase "big idea" is used to identify the core element of any advertising message. The big idea is the point or value that is intended to meaningfully differentiate the advertised brand because the big solution described in the message resonates with the problems or emotions of targeted segments.

Brand Equity—reflects the extent to which customers willingly pay more for particular branded products as opposed to other branded products from the same product category. Brand equity functions as a proxy for the level of pricing power built into and is associated with powerful brands.

Brand Loyalty—the term used to describe strongly-held customer preferences for particular brands. The presence of brand loyalty provides marketers with an opportunity to raise prices without losing excessive market share.

Brands 1—defined as names, signs, symbols, designs, colors, or some combination of these and other dimensions that identify and distinguish or differentiate the marketer of a product/service from other organizations marketing the same product inside the same product category.

Brands 2—defined as psychological constructs that capture all meanings, images, sensations, and experiences that targeted customers or prospective customers associate with products offered by specific for-profit and not-for-profit marketing organizations.

Breaking Bulk—breaking bulk happens inside supply chains and entails dividing larger quantities of diverse sets of products into small quantities of more uniform sets products.

Cash Cows—high share, low growth products, as designated inside the BCG Product Portfolio Matrix.

Ceteris paribus—this Latin phrase and frequently used economic concept means "other things equal," "all other things being equal," "other things held constant," or "all else unchanged."

Clutter, as in Advertising Clutter—refers to the inundating glut of ad messages to which domestic consumers are exposed to every day. Phrases such as "need to break-through-the-clutter" are commonly expressed by marketers, and with good cause. Advertisers often break through by shocking, provoking, or even annoying or outright pissing off the targets of their advertising messages.

Commercialism—the final step, or go-to-market planning and steps, through which new products are introduced to the marketplace.

Competencies, often described as Core Competencies—resources that marketing organizations possess or marketing activities they can perform particularly well. Core competencies generally exist as resources and activities upon which lasting brand differentiation and successful brand positions can be established. The sources of core competencies might include branding advantages; design advantages; more efficient supply chain management processes leading to lower costs and/or higher product performance; technological advantages; or closer relationships, which lead to greater intimacy with and greater loyalty from customers.

Competitive Advantage—a condition, asset, circumstance, or core competency that places marketing organizations and their brands in favorable market positions. One core purpose of any marketing strategy is to create competitive advantages, hopefully advantages that prove sustainable.

Conflict, Inside Supply Chains—seemingly arises naturally from disagreements related to incompatible goals and responsibilities as well as poor communications.

Consumerism—a movement and set of laws and regulations whose collective goal is to improve the rights and power of buyers in relation to the rights and power of sellers.

Convenience Goods—goods purchased without much effort but with routine or even high frequency. Convenience goods are widely available.

Conventional Marketing Systems—multi-level supply chains in which each partnering organization operates independently from one another.

Cost-Based Advantages (a Core Marketing Competency)—to achieve cost-based advantages, firms must possess resource-based advantages, technological-based advantages (sometimes the sources of technological advantages are patent protected), supply chain partnership-based advantages, or economy of scale based-advantages (EOS) that allow those firms to lower their associated costs of doing business.

Creative Destruction—an economic concept that describes what happens as new ideas, products, organizations, or technologies emerge inside markets. What happens, fundamentally, is that new product entities and their solutions are created while old product entities and solutions are destroyed or displaced. Hence, continuous needs arise to engage in new product development as a prerequisite for sustainable organizational success.

Creativity—entails the ability to see or think about the same things, as stimuli, that everyone else is seeing or thinking about and yet deriving or creating "something" that is new, different, better, and most importantly, able to deliver greater value. Inside creative marketing settings, the sort that are typically involved with new product development, the "something" would typically begin as an idea and culminate as a product and/or solution.

Culture—the collective customs, attitudes and beliefs, arts, social institutions, norms, values, and acknowledged achievements that characterize particular social groups, regions, or nations.

Customer-Intimacy Based Advantages (A Marketing Core Competency)—to achieve customer-intimacy marketing organizations must know more about their prospects and customers than their competitors know about their prospects and customers.

Data—raw, unorganized facts that must be organized and processed into information and hopefully eventually into actionable knowledge.

Demand—customer desires for products or services combined with their possession of the resources necessary to acquire them.

De-marketing—entails using advertising or other promotional efforts in an attempt to lower demand for products that are in short supply or for products, such as cigarettes or alcohol, that often injure users.

Demographics—the **Greek** origins of the **English** word demographics indicate that "**demos**" meant "people" and that "graphics" meant "arithmetic measurement." People-measurements, in brief. One reason why demographics are used so frequently as a segmentation base (criterion) follows from its ease of measure.

Derived Demand—demand for B2B products is derived from demand that occurs further downstream for consumer goods and services.

Desirable Products—provide both immediate satisfaction and long-run benefits to customers.

Determinant—benefits or values that are meaningful, important, and decisive to consumers as they make decisions.

Determinant (Expanded Description)—for determinant branding differences to exist, two things must happen. First, actual or perceptual differences must exist between brands. Second, these brand differences must be important to customers as they are deciding—determining—which brand to purchase. The need to create and sustain determinant differences is important now and will never not be important.

Differentiation, Acts or Processes of—entails strategic attempts to create the perception or the reality that one brand is different from and better than alternative branded solutions that compete against one another inside the same marketplace and product category.

Diffusion—a natural process whereby molecules, atoms, and bad- or good-news moves from regions of higher concentration to areas of lower concentration. In its original **Latin** form diffusion meant "to spread way out fast"—not a joke. Marketing and WOM messages, for better or for worse, diffuse throughout markets and market segments.

Direct Marketing—direct communications to B2C or B2B customers or prospects that are intended to produce responses in the form of purchases, site or store visits, requests for additional information, or some sort of positive endorsement.

Discontinuous Innovation—radically new and useful goods or services that require customers to change their current behaviors as the new products are consumed.

Dogs—low share, low growth products, as designated inside the BCG Product Portfolio Matrix.

Dumping—a form of predatory pricing in which typically foreign-made products are priced at extremely low levels in comparison to the prices of the product that are normally present inside the product's country of origin.

Dynamic Pricing—takes ethical discriminatory pricing processes to new levels. Marketers use dynamic prices to change prices by the minute based on what is understood about the income, location, and spending history of individual buyers.

Economies-of-Scale—the term refers to the reduced costs **per unit** that would arise from the opportunity to produce, promote, or deliver larger **total** quantities of products.

Economy, as part of an organization's relevant external environment—entails the wealth and resources of a country or region, pertaining particularly to the marketing systems (supply chains) through production and consumption of products and services occurs.

Empirical—is used inside this textbook to describe situations in which marketing researchers or NPD decision-makers collect samples of information to factually answer questions in order to solve problems and identify opportunities or threats to determine which idea or stage in the NPD process (see immediately above) should or should not be pursued next. The results of empirical tests are used to support or invalidate certain hypothesized relationships.

Enlightened Self-Interests (Ethical Theory of)—suggests that marketing or other decision-makers who consciously act to further the interests of others, including the interests of the group to which they belong or customers they seek to serve, are ultimately serving their self-interest.

Entropy—as lack of order or predictability; a gradual decline into disorder. Entropy typically reigns supreme inside organizations, markets, and indeed inside all manner of environments unless someone manages the processes appropriately. The term originates from the study of physics.

Environmental Dimensions—examples of relevant environment trends for most marketing organizations include changes in the economy, society, culture, demographics, technological, governmental/regularity factors, and so forth.

Environmental Opportunities—are environmental trends that are breaking favorably for marketers because they enhance the success prospects of their current strategic marketing plans or future strategic marketing plans that they could develop.

Environmental-Scanning—technically entails observing, researching, and interpreting various, almost inevitably uncontrollable environment trends that might impact an organization. Explained more practically, environmental-scanning is a strategic process that entails continuously monitoring the relevant external and internal environments of firms in order to identify trends that pose opportunities or threats for strategic organizations and consequently either enhance or degrade marketers' prospects for survival and future success.

Environmental Trends—patterns of gradual or more rapid change unfolding along an environmental dimension. Environmental dimensions—examples of relevant environment trends for most marketing organizations include changes in the economy, society, culture, demographics, technological, governmental/regularity factors, and so forth.

Environmental Threats—are trends that are breaking-badly for marketers. Breaking-badly because the existence of the trend degrades the success prospects of marketer's current strategic marketing plans or future strategic marketing plans that marketers could develop.

Environments—the surroundings in which people, animals, plants, or organization live or operate—and in which those persons, animals, plants, or organizations strive to survive or hopefully thrive. Organizations possess and must address external and internal environments.

Essentialism—planners focusing intensely on only the utterly necessary and completely dispensing the trivial and thereby ensuring that only the right things get done right.

Ethics—moral principles that govern the decision-making and behaviors of individuals or organizations.

Evangelize (Evangelical)—in its original **Greek** usage the word "evangelize" meant "to spread good or bad news." This meant, further, that an evangelical was a person who spread good or bad news about any topic or idea. Marketers fervently seek to create loyal customers who evangelize about their brands through WOM or e-WOM processes.

Evoked Set—the limited, usually three to five, group or set of brands that comes to mind first when problems that brands from known product categories can solve arise inside customers' lives. Marketers need their brands to be in the evoked sets of segments they target. Also known as the "consideration set."

Exchange—the process entails a giving up and getting back of value. Simply stated, a get and a get is involved inside exchange. This premise holds true during all exchange processes. Exchange is the core concept in marketing and the activity around which all marketing activity revolves.

Experiments—a core marketing research technique that tests predicted (hypothesized) relationships between variables inside controlled settings (conditions are held constant) and ceteris paribus prevails.

Family-Life-Cycle Stage—the most basic family-life-cycle stages are single; married; never-married or divorced; never married with children; married with children; married with no children living at home; and widowed. At what stage is a family most likely to buy a refrigerator, or the new home to go with it?

Fear Appeals—advertisements that emphasize the negative consequences with not making the right choice (i.e., the choice being recommended to message recipients by advertisers!).

Flows—the successful execution of logistical or supply chain processes between partnering organizations is primarily driven by the presence and reciprocal flows of information. Numerous other entities also flow between and within supply chain partners. This includes but are not limited to finished goods, raw materials, and money. There are, by turns, physical flows, ownership flows, promotional flows, payment flows and, of course, information flows.

Focus Groups—small groups (9–12) of deliberately-selected people who participate in planned question-prompted discussions. Focus group discussions are designed and executed to secure consumer perceptions about particular topics or areas of interest in non-threatening and receptive environments.

Franchising—a supply chain form in which one organization or individual pays for and receives the right to adapt and use an entire system of conducting marketers and selling products.

Frequency—the average number of times that a target is exposed to a message; typically an advertising message, during a designated period of time.

Generalizability—is defined as a measure of how applicable the results of a market research study are to the entire population that is being investigated—or researched.

Geographic Segmentation—a segmentation process in which marketers tailor and target their marketing mix values based on where customers or prospective customers live.

Gossip—entails two or more people telling things about a third person or entity like a brand that the third party would prefer not be known or said. Gossip is probably the human activity most responsible for the comparatively fast evolution of human speech. Gossip is discussed inside this textbook because gossip plays such a powerful role inside WOM or e-WOM processes.

Greenwashing—this unethical practice arises when marketers report or infer that their branded products or organizations themselves are green—as in beneficial to the environment—when they are not.

Hedonic, or Hedonism—relates to human's natural pursuit of pleasurable sensations, or feelings.

Heterogeneous (Homogeneous)—if heterogeneous means "diverse, or different," and it does, then yes, homogeneous means "similar or the same."

Humor—often plays powerful roles inside successful marketing efforts. Humor generally arises from the incongruity—the unexpected nature and/or arrival—of a subject just introduced. Humor is like a jack-in-the-box, in that the joke is only funny the first time Jack pops up. Jokes depend upon surprise. No surprise, no humor.

Hypotheses—research questions that are typically subjected to empirical analysis.

Incentive(s)—something, truly anything, that motivates targeted individuals or organizations to make decisions and/or to perform actions that the incentivizing agent desires to have them perform. Inside this setting the incentivizing agent would typically be a marketer. The need to strategically design effectively incentivizing marketing mixes is a critical marketing activity. Incentives are usually developed as parts of products or services themselves; communicated and therefore delivered from promotions; or reflected, as in manifested, inside prices and pricing strategies.

Influencers, Internet or Otherwise—anyone who exercises influence. But this description doesn't fully align with the word's current usage. Influencer culture is inextricably tied to consumerism and the rise of technology. Internet influencer, in turn, is shorthand for someone who possesses the power to affect consumers' buying habits by uploading some form of original—often sponsored—content to social media platforms like **Instagram, YouTube, Snapchat**, or **LinkedIn**.

Innovation—exists as a process or a product. Innovation, as process, produces something new and useful. This description means that the word innovation functions as a verb. Innovation, as product, is something new and useful. This description means that the word innovation functions as a noun.

Inseparability—a characteristic associated with services that makes it impossible to separate the creation and delivery of services from the consumption of those services.

Intangibility—a characteristic associated with services that makes it impossible to see, touch, or smell services, or to store inventory or produce them before they are actually required for consumption purposes.

Integrated Marketing Communication—IMC, as a promotional strategy, seeks to unify and integrate all modes of marketing communications in order to create unifying brand messages and positioning stories told consistently across all communication channels used to convey marketing messages.

Intermediaries (Middlemen)—generally operate inside supply chains between manufacturers and retailers. Intermediaries perform shipping, inventory management, order processing, selling, merchandising, and many other roles or functions inside supply chains.

Intermediary Organizations, Take 2: for-profit or not-for-profit organizations, including individuals such as agents or manufacturers' representatives, that play fundamental roles in facilitating, promoting, or encouraging B2B relationships between marketing organizations or B2C relationships between marketing organizations and end-use consumers.

Involvement, Consumers' Level of—a measurement of the relative importance of any specific decision to the decision-makers (i.e., these decision-makers are usually consumers and their decision usually relates to products).

Just Noticeable Difference (JND)—strategic marketers should increase prices to barely below the point where the price difference is noticed. Consumers typically don't notice price increases until they bump up at least 10%. When decreasing prices, marketers usually should cut them to just below the point where customers begin to notice the price cuts.

Law of Category, The—suggests that if you or your organization, product, idea, and solution cannot be first-to-market or first-to-mind, then you or your organization, product, idea, or solution should strive to be first-in-a-category.

Law of Focus, The—grounded in the extreme differentiating and positioning value that results from owning something, typically well-positioned words or phrases inside customers' or segments' collective minds.

Law of Leadership, The—suggests marketers should be first to market, in order to have a chance to remain first in the mind.

Law of the Mind, The—suggests that if your organization and its brands cannot be first to market or first to a category, then you and your organization should do whatever is ethical and possible to become first and remain on top in the collective mind of whatever market segment your organization is targeting.

Law of Perception, The—is grounded in the fact that marketing competitions are often waged and won or lost based on perceptions.

Learning—relatively enduring changes in behaviors resulting from experiences or exposure to stimuli.

Lifestyle Measures—when used as segmentation criteria, are also commonly described as "psychographics."

Market or Marketing Segmentation—a process through which broader, larger, more heterogeneous markets are divided into narrower, smaller, more homogeneous market segments.

Market Segments—relatively homogeneous, smaller submarkets existing inside much larger and more heterogeneous markets. Homogeneous, here, means that the people, organizations, or institutions who comprise market segments share certain key characteristics in common.

Market Share—the ratio between the firm's sales volume and the entire industry sales volume (i.e., an organization's share of products sold throughout the market in which the marketing firm competes).

Marketing—a social and managerial process through which individuals and groups obtain what they need or want by creating and exchanging value with others.

Marketing Concept—a business philosophy that puts customers, and identifying and satisfying their wants and needs, first; as long as the marketing professionals or organizations also profit from the processes executed to solve those customer problems. The philosophy is grounded in an understanding that most strategic-level organizational goals are best achieved by correctly identifying and defining customers' problems and then solving those problems by delivering values and solutions perceived as superior to the values and solutions offered by competitors.

Marketing Information Systems—systematic processes through which determinations are first made regarding the data, types of information, and analytics that are necessary to produce the right sorts of marketing insights and knowledge as would prove necessary to solve the most pressing problems or to exploit the most appealing opportunities that are facing any given marketing organization.

Marketing Manager—the person responsible for developing and implementing marketing strategies for products sold to targeted groups.

Marketing Mix—a tool that firms manage with the intent of creating hopefully differentiating value for the branded products they make and market. AKA the 4Ps or the 7Ps.

Marketing Mix (for Products)—when products are marketed, organizations typically have four ingredients to "mix." The four ingredients are the product, price, promotion, and place. Place is the term used within the 4Ps to designate and capture the various distribution or supply chain activities that successful marketers must execute successfully.

Marketing Mix (for Services)—when services are marketed organizations or professionals must mix and manage seven ingredients. The seven ingredients, or 7Ps are again, Product; Price; Promotion; and Place, comprised of distribution or supply chain management processes. Plus, anew, People; Processes; and Physical Surroundings.

Marketing Research—Processes through which data about customers, market condition, competitors, and so forth is collected, analyzed, and interpreted in order to develop new or improve existing marketing strategies.

Marketing Research Insights—link customers/prospects to marketers through information that has been collected and analyzed.

Marketing Research Process, The—involves collecting and analyzing information relevant to a specific marketing problem or opportunity/threat facing the marketer that is conducting the research.

Markets—consist of all actual or potential customers for products or services. Markets are heterogeneous in nature.

Mass Markets—a large but relatively homogenous group of potential/actual customers for given products.

Mean, The Statistical—the average. To generate a mean all relevant numbers are added up and divided by the number of numbers to create a mean.

Media—communication platforms or channels through which various types of marketing communications are conveyed toward targeted marketing segments.

Median, The Statistical—the middle value in the list of numbers

Merchandising—activities that entail promoting the sales of goods at the retail level. Merchandising activities include in-store or on-site display techniques, shelf-talking, spot demonstrations, personal selling in general, and other point-of-sale methods.

Metrics—also called measurements or benchmarks, including timelines, should be established for both goals and objectives. The use of metrics permits and facilitates measurement of marketers' progress or lack of progress toward their strategically designated goals and objectives.

Mission Statements—marketing organizations' current vision equals that organizations' future directions and designates opportunities that marketing organizations can or cannot pursue, as well as opportunities that marketers should or should not pursue.

Mode, The Statistical—the number or response that occurs most frequently. If no number in the list is repeated, then no mode exists in the list.

Needs—exist inside human minds and bodies as states of felt deprivation. Needs reside inside the gap between where humans believe, feel, or perceive they currently exist, and where they want to be.

Needs, The Hierarchy of—the five basic types of human needs are described as physiological, safety, social, personal (self-esteem), and self-actualization, in that order, ranging up from the bottom to the top. Also known as Maslow's Hierarchy of Needs.

Negative Frames, The Use of: negative framing processes entail presenting choices as situations in which something will be lost by decision-makers (customers) as opposed to something that will be gained by those same decision-makers (customers) if they fail to make the right choice. The something to be gained or lost typically includes money, prestige, a more attractive appearance, or a good time. The use of negative frames is extremely persuasive.

New Product Development (NPD)—the process by which new products or services are developed. The process would almost always begin with ideas and end with commercialization efforts, or the execution of strategies designed to successfully introduce the new product or service to targeted markets.

New Products (services)—can be classified in various ways with the classifications ranging from truly new-to-the-world products to substantial improvements to existing products to simple additions to or deletions from existing products.

Niche/Niches—exist as highly customized and tightly defined market segment(s).

Noise, Advertising—noise has rightfully earned its negative connotations inside marketing communication contexts. Inside today's media environment there is so much promotional clutter, and so many other distracting environmental stimuli, that consumers grow weary of and frustrated by the noise. The net effect is that many consumers either don't pay attention to and/or remember specific content inside marketing messages even when they do attend to messages. Everyone intimately knows about "noise," even if they didn't know about "noise," because such distractions proliferate throughout everybody's noise life.

Occam's Razor—suggests the best solution to any pressing problem, when planners are analyzing and drawing inferences from data, is always the simplest explanation that accounts for all the data.

Operant—means effective, functional, or tending to produce useful results.

Opinion-Leaders—often exercise extreme effects on consumers as these potential customers seek, and sometimes struggle, to find "advice and counsel or recommendations" about how to make the best possible consumption decisions. Opinion-leaders are generally well-known individuals who are recognized as experts about particular product categories.

Opportunism, Acting Opportunistically—in this context, means identifying opportunities before anyone else does, but also being willing and able to strike first by delivering differentiating value after opportunities have been discovered. Opportunism can be viewed negatively in other non-marketing contexts.

Paradoxes—exist whenever two opposing arguments hold an equal claim on truth. One paradox: Most American consumers have less than they want. Yet nearly all Americans have more than they need.

Pavlovian Responses—refer to the pairing of conditioned and unconditioned stimuli and to the creation of learned responses through processes described as classical conditioning.

Perceptions 1—the "imagined realities" of human beings. Perceptions develop inevitably as individuals experience and attempt to make sense of stimuli that continuously surrounds them or flashes in and out of their worlds.

Perceptions 2—capture processes by which people select, organize, and then interpret or attempt to make sense of stimuli. Stimuli can consist of old or new information. Consumers create perceptions in an effort to develop meaningful and useful pictures of the world around them.

Personal Selling—includes any sort of interaction(s) initiated by one or a small team of marketers who engage directly—face-to-face, by phone, or through any other internet-mediated connection—with individual or small groups of prospective or actual customers.

Personality—people's habitual ways of thinking, feeling, and relating to others. ("Habitual ways," in this context, means how people regularly or routinely behave.) Individuals differ along certain personal characteristics and tendencies such as their propensities to display higher or lower levels of introversion or extroversion; fondness for details or attention to detail; tolerance for boredom; propensities for helping others; determination or grit; and a host of other personal qualities. Significantly, brands can develop personalities as well.

Planned Obsolescence—a strategic marketing practice wherein marketers design or market products with artificially limited useful lives so they become prematurely outdated in terms of function, formulation, or fashion.

Positional Goods—products or intangible services that consumers perceive as valuable largely because other consumers occupying their same broad social sphere (social class membership and social status) cannot have or enjoy them.

Positioning, the act or process of—entails executing the necessary strategic steps to ensure that marketing organization's market mix offering generates and delivers clear, distinct, and desirable images inside targeted segments' collective minds relative to the images that competitors have sought to create.

Positions, as in Market Positions 1—an image and set of benefits, or problem-solving values, that presumably is associated with branded products. Positions are created and reside inside the collective mind of targeted customers relative to the positioning image that competing organizations and their branded products have created for themselves.

Positions 2—collective sets of perceptions that targeted market segments develop and retain about brands' abilities to satisfy their needs or solve their problems.

Positions 3: the ways in which particular brands measure up against—are perceived as more or less desirable—than competing branded products from the same product category.

Price—captures what customers are willing to pay to acquire products. Alternatively stated, price is the amount of money marketers charge for their products or services. More broadly described, price represents the sum of ALL values customers must give up in order to get benefits or values associated with having or using products or services.

Price-Discrimination—arises when marketers sell the same product in the same quantities at different prices to different customers or groups of customers.

Price Elasticity—a measurement of the degree to which changes in price stimulate changes in demand for the brand or product being priced. If demand for brands hardly changes, either up or down, when their prices change, again either up or down, then demand for those brands is deemed inelastic. Gasoline prices have historically featured inelastic demand—up to a point.

Price-Fixing—occurs when two or more firms get together and agree mutually that each organization will set prices at some predetermined level. Price-fixing is illegal and unethical.

Primary (Marketing Research) Information—new or original information. Primary information never existed before the research processes used to generate it were conducted.

Product Life Cycle—every product category experiences—passes through—a life cycle. The Product Life Cycle concept is similar to the biological life cycle which informs us that all living entities on earth—trees, fish, humans—are born; hopefully grow rapidly; eventually level off in their growth while entering, often through a combination of strategy and good fortune, an extended maturity stage; and then, inevitably, experience decline and death.

Product Portfolios—consist of the entire set of products that any organization markets. The product portfolios inside any organization may feature different product categories or different product lines, and definitely will feature different products.

Products—broadly and appropriately defined as anything that can be offered to individuals, market segments' or entire markets for customers' attention, acquisition, use, or consumption that might also satisfy individuals', segments', or entire markets' wants/needs—or solve their problems. Products might also be appropriately described as anything that can solve customer problems and profit marketers/marketing organizations in the process.

Professional, as in Professional Positions—professional jobs differ from regular jobs in that for better or worse professionals' inner mental and emotional lives are tightly connected to their work. When people perform inside professional positions they are rarely not working, again for better or worse, because "the job" and its challenges and opportunities are typically rattling around inside their minds.

Promotions—collectively, promotions are the communication arm—or weapon/tool—that marketers or marketing organizations can wield to deliver their particular stories to targeted subsets of broader markets. Promotion is also the communication dimension—element or ingredient—inside any marketing mix.

Psychographic Segmentation—activities that involve dividing consumers into segments based on their social class status, preferred lifestyle choices as measured through a combination of their AIOs and personality characteristics.

Psychographics—as a measure entails a combination of consumers' preferred AIOs and their dominant personality traits. Also called lifestyles, psychographics capture individual consumers' patterns of acting and interacting with other people and various stimuli, including marketing stimuli, within the world.

Public Relations—entail communication efforts aimed at satisfying the need to build or sustain good relationships with various targeted publics that individual marketers or marketing organizations deem critical to their current and future success.

Puffery—entails advertising appeals that contain material featuring clearly over-embellished or extraordinarily boastful claims about brands that are subjective rather than objective or measurable and which no reasonable person would presume to be literally true.

Push Versus Pull Promotional Strategies—push entails the use of promotional strategies where firms attempt to take their products downstream throughout their supply chain to the final use B2B or B2C customers. The word push stems from the idea that marketers are attempting to push their products downstream through supply chains on a partner-firm by partner-firm basis toward end-use consumers. Pull follows an opposing path. Pull promotions seek to persuade or incentivize customers to come toward the marketer and brand. Hence, the term pull is used; insofar as marketers seek to pull in customers upstream through the supply chain toward their brand.

Quality—freedom from, or the absence of, defects.

Question Marks?—low share, high growth products, as designated inside the BCG Product Portfolio Matrix.

Reach—the percentage of a targeted audience that is exposed to a message, typically advertising, during a prescribed period of time.

Reference Groups—groups toward which consumers look to secure insights and implicit recommendations regarding what they should or should not consume and/or how they should or should not behave.

Regulations and Laws, as part of an Environment—entail rules that particular governmental institutions impose and that others are supposed to recognize as regulators or governors of their subsequent behaviors. Those others include marketing organizations and consumers.

Reliability—a statistical assessment (measurement) of the extent to which the results generated by marketing research efforts are free from systematic errors.

Retailers—typically merchandise finished goods (brands) that they receive from supply partners.

Sales Promotions—marketing communications and messages that are structured to deliver short-term incentives aimed at encouraging near-term customer purchases of products or services.

Salutary Products—are characterized by low immediate appeal (failing to deliver much short-term satisfaction) while featuring high potential for benefitting customers longer-run.

Science based on the results produced by empirical tests. Science is also based on already established concepts, principles, or laws, and existing theoretical relationships between the concepts and principles.

Secondary (Marketing Research) Information—already exists because it was previously collected for other purposes. Perhaps the secondary data was gathered through accounting or sales-tracking metrics.

Segment, Market—relatively homogeneous and smaller submarkets, or segments, existing inside more heterogeneous and much larger markets. The constituents of segments are quite likely to respond in similar fashions (negative or positive) when exposed to the values conveyed through unique marketing mixes.

Self-Concept(s)—how consumers feel about themselves, can be defined as mental images consumers hold deeply inside their minds about their own personal strengths, weaknesses, "coolness quotients," abilities to influence or exercise power over others, or social status and end up having to enjoy or endure about themselves. The self-concepts of consumers are essentially their self-identities.

Shopping Goods—when deliberating whether to purchase shopping goods consumers expend considerable effort in an attempt to make the best possible choice, make substantial brand versus brand comparison, and purchase them. Shopping goods themselves are widely available.

SMART Goals—the acronym SMART implies that any organization's marketing goals and objectives should be: Specific; Measurable; Actionable; Realistic, but motivating; and Time-Sensitive.

Social Media Influencers (Internet Influencers)—contemporary opinion leaders are often also called and/or aspire to be known as "social media influencers." Major difference, they do their influencing online.

Society (as part of an organization's external environment)—any group of people living together in a more or less ordered community; generally ordered divisions also exist inside societies.

Specialization, the need for—is the primary reason supply chains exist. This need is also the primary reason why firms enter supply chain relationships in the first place. Supply chains specialize in specialization. Supply chain member organizations should be allowed to concentrate on doing what they do best.

Specialty Goods—ironically, when purchasing specialty goods consumers generally don't expend much effort or engage in much if any brand comparison because they have already decided what is special to them. Specialty goods are not widely available in terms of distribution or affordability. But then again, if they were, specialty goods would not be special.

Spiffs, Push Money, Slotting Allowances—three terms that describe the same sales promotion practice, which entails the dollar amount paid by manufacturers or distributors to retailers/retailers' sales forces in order to motivate and incentivize retailers and their sales forces to do something sales-promoting manufacturers or distributors seek to have done. Spiff money is typically used to push demand for targeted brands downstream inside supply chains toward ultimate, or end-use, customers. This is why spiffs are also called push money. These end-user customers are usually consumers.

Stakeholder Capitalism (Sustainable Capitalism)—sustainable capitalism promotes the belief that an individual or organization can or should ultimately thrive unless wider society also flourishes. Stakeholder capitalism further holds that sometimes enough wealth, gathered inside one person's or small group's hands, is enough. These are two beliefs or principles that nearly everyone can get behind, unless you're the one or part of the few ones who are thriving or hoarding the wealth. That's where bad old-fashioned human greed and self-interestedness kicks in.

Staple Goods—inventoried items that are core to one's business or are core to the performance or conduct of consumers' or customers' normal activities. For example, hooks and fishing line are staple goods for any tackle shop. Meanwhile, hooks and fishing line also represent staple goods for any consumer who enjoys fishing—unless s/he exclusively uses nets or traps.

Stars—high share, high growth products, as designated inside the BCG Product Portfolio Matrix.

Stimulus, and Response Processes—entail actions or choices that are performed or made as responses to stimuli with or without conscious thought. A "stimulus" entails anything that incites, rouses, or provokes and consequently motivates consumers to take an action, think, experience emotions, or respond in any other way. A "response" is, well, you know what a response is.

Strategic Business Unit (SBU)—the smallest business units inside any organization for which independent planning can be done and for which sets of independent resources exist.

Strategic Planning—managerial decision-making processes wherein organization's 3Ts and capabilities are aligned with the pursuit of identified environmental opportunities in pursuit of sustainable long-term growth.

Subtraction—as in lowering costs, can also similarly facilitate marketing success. Marketing organizations that manage their supply chain relationships more efficiently routinely lower their costs.

Supply Chain Management, or **Place**, activities—entail the processes and relationships by which products, including services, move from their source points to whatever venues [either brick-and-mortar retailers or e-tailers (i.e., online retailers)] customers use to obtain products and services.

Sustainable Competitive Advantages (SCAs)—three ways exist to achieve advantages versus competitors that are likely to prove sustainable. These three core competencies include achieving greater customer intimacy; achieving cost/price leadership; or achieving technological leadership.

SWOT—is an acronym wherein the "S" and the "W" stand for Strengths and Weaknesses and the "O" and the "T" indicate Opportunities and Threats.

Target-Broadly—marketers market as if no segments exist. This targeting tactic is also called undifferentiated or mass marketing.

Target-Differentiated (Differentiated Targeting)—differentiated targeting, as a marketing strategy, entails pursuing multiple segments at the same time. This is called differentiated **or** segmented target marketing. Uniquely designed and consequently differentiated market mixes are then targeted at each segment the marketer elects to pursue.

Target-Extremely-Narrowly—this targeting approach is better known as micro-targeting. Again, only one segment is targeted. But this once merely niched segment is now extremely narrowly defined. The difference between niche-targeting and micro-targeting is a matter of degree.

Target Market—groups or a group of customers or prospective customers that marketing organizations are best prepared to pursue, serve, and satisfy. Marketers should select (target) the segment or segments whose needs (problems) they are best able to satisfy (solve).

Target Marketing—entails first identifying and thereafter attempting to satisfy the needs or solve the problems of a targeted segment of prospective or actual customers. Target marketing entails evaluating the various segments that have been identified in order to determine which ones are more or less attractive and then deciding which segments to pursue.

Target-Narrowly—this tactic is better known as concentrated or niche market targeting. When concentrated targeting is used marketing organizations target large shares of narrowly defined segments. Success requires fine-tuning of the marketing mix.

Targeting, Market Targeting—entails strategically identifying—selecting—the precise segment or segments that marketers target through their marketing mixes. Marketing organizations should strategically develop unique-and-uniquely-desirable marketing mixes for each segment they choose to target.

Technological Leadership-Based Advantage (a Core Marketing Competency)—to earn technological advantages firms should know more about what customers want or need in the technological realm, and then, once armed with this knowledge, actually develop the capability to deliver exactly what customers want or need, technologically-speaking.

Technology—entails applying practical knowledge to solve human and other sorts of problems (not as complicated as one might think, is it?).

Three (3) Hit Rule—is why effective preachers, priests, professors, salespeople, or advertisers—marketing communicators all—routinely repeat key ideas or principles at least three times. Essentially rolling over messages; revealing new insights about old issues at every turn; illustrating key ideas or principle takeaways by introducing new and old examples.

Top of the Mind—coming to mind first is also known as top-of-the-mind-awareness. Marketers engage in all manner of marketing mix activities in the hopes of earning or sustaining top-of-the-mind-awareness for their brands. Brands that are positioned near the top of the mind are also highly positioned inside consumers' evoked sets.

Trends, Environmental—see Environmental Trends as Opportunities or Threats.

Unique—"(the) one and only," or "nothing else like it exists." As such, **English** speakers or writers routinely misuse the word. Unique cannot be qualified. An idea, product, or message is either unique or not unique. An item or idea cannot be somewhat, extremely, or a little unique—there's no middle ground.

Unique Selling Propositions (USPs)—entail the development and promotion of dominant value propositions that are strategically associated with the brand because the USP holds great appeal to targeted consumer segments.

Validity—a statistical assessment (measurement) of the extent to which the results generated by marketing research efforts measure what they are purposed (supposed) to measure.

Value—as the difference, hopefully positive, between the benefits that are gotten and the costs that must be given up by customers before they can own and possibly use a product. Value could also be described as the problem-solving ability of any particular branded product.

Value Propositions—value propositions capture and reflect the sum of potential and actual values that positioned products offer to prospects or customers. The total value-proposition associated with wedding dresses, automobiles, homes, or vacation destinations, for example, are extremely complex in nature.

Variance or Range, the Statistical—a sample of responses is determined by the difference between the largest and smallest values present inside the entire data set.

Vertical Integration—combining some combination (all or part) of manufacturing, intermediary, and retailing organizations into a unified whole inside marketing supply chains.

Vertical Marketing System—supply chains in which formal agreements or actual ownership and operative control over how various functions and flows exist. The net is that one supply chain member exercises a disproportionate influence over the operations and performance of other supply chain members.

Viral Marketing—marketing activities intended to increase brand awareness or brand sales by inspiring consumers to pass along messages to other consumers through traditional or electric means.

Virtue Signaling—entails conspicuous publicly-issued expressions or demonstrations of one's superior moral values. The wealthy might signal their charity; the religious might signal their piety; the environmentally-conscious might signal their green bona fides. An irony is often associated with virtue-signaling: "Virtuous" citizens routinely signal their virtues by boldly proclaiming how much they hate something or someone.

Wants—the form into which needs transform as naturally-arising human needs are shaped by individual personality and culture. Please note that marketing and their efforts and stimuli are part of everyone's cultural experience.

Waterline Principle, the—suggests marketing planners generally should avoid making bets big enough to blow holes below waterlines, if things were to go wrong. All or nothing sorts of less than well-calculated strategic thinking, betting practices, more often lead to nothing than something.

Wicked Problems—are "wicked" to the point where no one best solution to the challenge or difficulty could ever truly exist.

Word-of-Mouth (WOM)—a marketing communication process that marketers can influence but not control; involves oral or written recommendations made by satisfied or unsatisfied customers to prospective or actual customers of branded marketing products. Electronic word-of-mouth (e-WOM) includes the exact same communicative processes as they are conducted through electronic means.

Zeitgeist—a German word that literally means spirit of the times in "spirit (geist) of the times (zeit)" in the English language. The word zeitgeist is also frequently used in the contemporary English language.

4Ps of Marketing—Product, Place, Price, and Promotion.

4Ps of Stakeholder Capitalism—the Principle of Governance, the Principle of Planet, the Principle of People, and the Principle of Prosperity.

7Ps of Services Marketing—Product, Place, Price, Promotion, People, Physical surroundings, and Processes.